AWS Certified Data Engineer Associate Study Guide
In-Depth Guidance and Practice

Sakti Mishra, Dylan Qu, and Anusha Challa

O'REILLY®

AWS Certified Data Engineer Associate Study Guide

by Sakti Mishra, Dylan Qu, and Anusha Challa

Published by O'Reilly Media, Inc., 141 Stony Circle, Suite 195, Santa Rosa, CA 95401.

O'Reilly books may be purchased for educational, business, or sales promotional use. Online editions are also available for most titles (*http://oreilly.com*). For more information, contact our corporate/institutional sales department: 800-998-9938 or *corporate@oreilly.com*.

Acquisitions Editor: Megan Laddusaw	**Indexer:** Potomac Indexing, LLC
Development Editor: Shira Evans	**Cover Designer:** Susan Brown
Production Editor: Gregory Hyman	**Interior Designer:** David Futato
Copyeditor: Charles Roumeliotis	**Cover Illustrator:** José Marzan, Jr.
Proofreader: Vanessa Moore	**Interior Illustrator:** Kate Dullea

September 2025:   First Edition

Revision History for the First Edition

2025-08-22:   First Release

See *http://oreilly.com/catalog/errata.csp?isbn=9781098170073* for release details.

978-1-098-17007-3

[LSI]

Table of Contents

Preface

As Data Analytics Specialist Architects at Amazon Web Services (AWS), we—Sakti, Dylan, and Anusha—spent more than five years collaborating to solve some of the most challenging and innovative data problems for diverse clients. Our collective experience spans a wide range of industries and use cases: helping Chief Data Officers shape organizational data strategies, architecting petabyte-scale lakehouses, and building operationally excellent data platforms through proven best practices in performance, cost optimization, security, and comprehensive data governance. In today's landscape, the demand for skilled data professionals has become more critical than ever, with the rise of generative AI compelling companies to leverage their data as a key business differentiator.

Throughout our tenure at AWS, we were constantly asked by colleagues from diverse backgrounds how they could break into the dynamic field of data engineering. Our consistent recommendation was to use the AWS Certified Data Engineer Associate (DEA-C01) certification as a starting point. Our rationale is not simply about acquiring another credential but about leveraging the certification's curriculum as a structured framework to gain a fundamental understanding of data engineering principles, both in general and specifically on the AWS Cloud. This book is the result of that shared experience and our passion for teaching, created to provide the clear, comprehensive, and practical guide we wished we had.

What This Book Isn't

Before we detail what this book covers, it's important to clarify what it isn't. This book is not an exhaustive deep dive into a single AWS service, nor is it a comprehensive manual for hands-on implementation. While many excellent books approach data engineering from a specific technology perspective, their focus can be narrow. Instead, our goal is to provide comprehensive coverage of the fundamental concepts and architectural patterns for data engineering on AWS.

What This Book Is About

This book is designed to be your comprehensive guide to mastering the skills for the AWS Certified Data Engineer Associate (DEA-C01) certification. Our goal is to provide a clear path from foundational concepts to advanced, practical application.

By the end of this book, you will understand:

- The format of the DEA-C01 exam, how to prepare effectively, and strategies for success on test day
- The key responsibilities and mindset of an AWS Certified Data Engineer
- How core AWS database, analytics, and auxiliary services function and how to apply them to solve real-world data challenges
- The art of selecting the right services to architect solutions that are optimized for cost, performance, security, and high availability

Who Should Read This Book

Our primary audience is any technical practitioner who wants to prepare for the DEA-C01 certification. This guide is crafted to serve a diverse group of professionals, and you will find this book especially valuable if you are:

- A software engineer, data scientist, or data analyst interested in transitioning into data engineering. We provide the foundational knowledge and practical AWS skills needed to make a successful career pivot.
- A current data engineer focused on specific technologies who wants to broaden their perspective across the entire AWS data ecosystem. This book will help you connect the dots and build a more comprehensive skill set.

How This Book Is Organized

The book is organized into four parts, each building upon the last to create a complete learning journey:

Chapters 1 to 3
  This part lays the essential groundwork. We begin by defining the data engineer's role and breaking down the AWS Certified Data Engineer Associate exam itself—what it covers, how to register, and a recommended study plan. We then cover the prerequisite knowledge every data engineer needs, including foundational concepts in databases, data lakes, distributed processing frameworks like Spark and Flink, and the fundamentals of the AWS Cloud. This part ensures you have the solid base needed to tackle the core technical content.

Chapters 4 to 7

This is the heart of the book, diving deep into the four technical domains of the certification. This part is meticulously structured to align with the official exam guide, helping you build a solid understanding of the required knowledge. You will learn to design and implement pipelines for data ingestion and transformation (Chapter 4), select and manage the right data stores for any use case (Chapter 5), maintain and optimize data pipelines for operational excellence (Chapter 6), and secure your data with robust governance and security controls (Chapter 7).

Chapters 8 and 9

Here we transition from theory to practical application and exam readiness. In Chapter 8, we provide a hands-on implementation guide for building both batch and real-time streaming data pipelines, allowing you to apply the concepts learned in previous chapters. To solidify your knowledge and build confidence for the exam, Chapter 9 provides an extensive practice exam with over 40 certification-style questions, complete with detailed explanations and rationales that guide you on how to approach and solve them.

Chapter 10

Finally, we look to the future, covering the latest services and features in the AWS data landscape. While some of these newer capabilities may not yet be on the current exam, understanding them is vital for any forward-looking data engineer. We are committed to keeping this guide relevant and will update this section in future editions as the certification scope and AWS services evolve.

Accessing the Book's Images Online

Readers of the printed book can access large-format versions of the book's images at *https://oreil.ly/aws-certified-data-engineer-images*.

Conventions Used in This Book

The following typographical conventions are used in this book:

Italic

Indicates new terms, URLs, email addresses, filenames, and file extensions.

`Constant width`

Used for program listings, as well as within paragraphs to refer to program elements such as variable or function names, databases, data types, environment variables, statements, and keywords.

Constant width bold

> Used to highlight snippets of special interest in program listings.

This element signifies a tip or suggestion.

This element signifies a general note.

O'Reilly Online Learning

O'REILLY® For more than 40 years, *O'Reilly Media* has provided technology and business training, knowledge, and insight to help companies succeed.

Our unique network of experts and innovators share their knowledge and expertise through books, articles, and our online learning platform. O'Reilly's online learning platform gives you on-demand access to live training courses, in-depth learning paths, interactive coding environments, and a vast collection of text and video from O'Reilly and 200+ other publishers. For more information, visit *https://oreilly.com*.

How to Contact Us

Please address comments and questions concerning this book to the publisher:

> O'Reilly Media, Inc.
> 141 Stony Circle, Suite 195
> Santa Rosa, CA 95401
> 800-889-8969 (in the United States or Canada)
> 707-827-7019 (international or local)
> 707-829-0104 (fax)
> *support@oreilly.com*
> *https://oreilly.com/about/contact.html*

We have a web page for this book, where we list errata and any additional information. You can access this page at *https://oreil.ly/aws-certified-data-engineer*.

For news and information about our books and courses, visit *https://oreilly.com*.

Find us on LinkedIn: *https://linkedin.com/company/oreilly-media*.

Watch us on YouTube: *https://youtube.com/oreillymedia*.

Acknowledgments

We would like to extend our deep appreciation to our technical reviewers, Julian Setiawan, Pooja Chitrakar, and Sam Warner, for their invaluable feedback that helped enhance the quality of this work.

Working with the O'Reilly team has been a true pleasure. We extend special thanks to Shira Evans for her excellent organization and assistance; Greg Hyman, our diligent production editor; Kate Dullea, our wonderful technical illustrator; and Megan Laddusaw, our content acquisition editor.

On a personal note:

Sakti extends his heartfelt gratitude to his coauthors, Dylan and Anusha, whose invaluable collaboration and insights were instrumental in bringing this work to fruition. He is deeply thankful to his wife, Soumya Mishra, for her unwavering support and patience throughout this journey. He is deeply grateful to his parents, Asoka and Bijayalaxmi Mishra, and his sister, Sabujima Mishra, who have been constant pillars of strength in his life and instilled in him the value of continuous learning and perseverance.

Dylan would like to express his sincere gratitude to his coauthor Sakti, who first proposed this book and assembled such a dream team to bring it to life. He is also immensely thankful for his coauthor Anusha, whose dedication and deep technical insights were essential to the quality of this guide. A special thanks to his wife, Surui Qu, for her constant support and encouragement throughout this entire process. He is also deeply grateful to his mother, Xin Li, and father, Anjing Qu, for surrounding him with love and inspiring him to strive for excellence from a young age.

Anusha is grateful to her coauthors, Dylan, and Sakti, whose collaboration transcended into meaningful personal connections. Anusha owes gratitude to her husband Saravana, whose understated support made the long hours manageable. She is blessed to have her mother, Padmavati, father, Buddha Bhagavan, and sister, Praveena, who take immense pride in her smallest achievements. Each of these individuals played a vital part in the completion of this work, and their contributions were truly irreplaceable.

## CHAPTER 1

Certification Essentials

Welcome to your journey toward becoming an AWS Certified Data Engineer Associate! This comprehensive study guide is designed to equip you with the essential skills and knowledge to excel as a proficient AWS data engineer and assist you in passing the certification.

In today's data-driven landscape, organizations are grappling with an avalanche of data, seeking ways to unlock its potential and gain valuable insights. As a data engineer, you hold the power to transform raw data into actionable intelligence, driving innovation and business growth.

In this chapter, you will learn the following:

- Understand the role and responsibilities of a data engineer.
- Gain a comprehensive overview of the AWS Certified Data Engineer Associate certification, establishing a foundational understanding of the domains covered in the exam.
- Learn the significance of obtaining this certification, the topics covered in the exam, and the exam format.
- Gain insights into the registration process for the exam and a recommended study plan to prepare effectively.

By the end of this chapter, you will have a clear grasp of the certification's importance, the exam structure, and other key information required for successful preparation.

Who Is a Data Engineer?

Data engineers are the architects behind the scenes, building the critical infrastructure that powers all data solutions, from real-time analytics to artificial intelligence.

These professionals design and implement sophisticated systems that transform vast amounts of raw data into valuable business insights.

At its core, data engineering involves creating high-performance data workflows that handle petabytes of information with low latency while providing high reliability. This includes developing robust ETL (extract, transform, load) processes as well as data warehouses and lakes, implementing real-time streaming solutions, and ensuring data quality at scale. Data engineers serve as the bridge between raw data and actionable insights, enabling data scientists to build machine learning models, analysts to generate business intelligence, and applications to access data seamlessly.

AWS offers a comprehensive set of capabilities that data engineers can leverage to build data pipelines. From data processing and SQL analytics to streaming, search, and business intelligence, AWS delivers unmatched price performance and scalability with governance built in. In this book, we'll explore AWS's powerful suite of data engineering services, diving deep into how industry leaders architect solutions for massive-scale data processing. You'll master services like Amazon EMR, AWS Glue, Amazon Redshift, and Amazon Kinesis, understanding not just how to use them individually but how to orchestrate them into comprehensive data platforms that drive business value.

Whether you're preparing for the AWS Certified Data Engineer Associate certification or advancing your technical expertise, this guide will equip you with the skills required for success. Through real-world scenarios and hands-on examples, you'll learn to design and implement data architectures that scale effortlessly, handle complex transformations efficiently, and deliver insights reliably in the AWS ecosystem.

Becoming an AWS Data Engineer Associate

Amazon Web Services (AWS) holds a leading position in cloud computing and offers an extensive suite of data analytics services. Many organizations of varying sizes use AWS to store, process, and analyze their data. As data continues to proliferate and organizations increasingly rely on cloud-based solutions for their data analytics needs, there are several compelling reasons to obtain your AWS Certified Data Engineer Associate certification. The five major benefits are as follows:

Gain comprehensive and applicable knowledge
> The AWS Certified Data Engineer Associate certification and accompanying study resources provide a thorough and practical understanding of AWS data engineering principles, best practices, and services. You'll acquire knowledge and skills applicable to roles such as data engineer, data architect, and other AWS data-related positions.

Enhance career opportunities
AWS Data Engineer is an in-demand role with a limited supply of skilled professionals. Organizations across industries are actively seeking professionals with proven expertise in cloud-based data analytics solutions. Holding the AWS Certified Data Engineer Associate certification can open doors to new career opportunities or career progression within your current organization.

Stay current with best practices and industry standards
The certification process requires you to demonstrate a deep understanding of AWS best practices for data analytics, including data governance, security, operational excellence, and compliance. By achieving this certification, you demonstrate your ability to design analytics solutions that meet industry standards, best practices, and regulatory requirements.

Join a thriving community of innovators
Earning your AWS Certified Data Engineer Associate credential connects you with a global network of professionals who share your passion for data and innovation. From meetups and conferences to online forums, you'll have countless opportunities to network, share insights, and collaborate with industry leaders and peers.

Future-proofing your skills in an AI era
Here's the secret no one tells you: AI is only as good as its data. Behind every ChatGPT, DeepSeek, or self-driving car are armies of data engineers who cleaned, structured, and delivered the training data. By earning this certification, you position yourself at the heart of the AI revolution.

Exam Topics

AWS Certified Data Engineer Associate certification (*https://oreil.ly/6qdmH*) validates skills and knowledge in core data-related AWS services, including the ability to ingest and transform data, orchestrate data pipelines while applying programming concepts, design data models, manage data lifecycles, and ensure data quality.

The exam has the following content domains and weightings:

Domain 1: Data Ingestion and Transformation (34% of scored content)
This domain assesses your understanding of how to perform data ingestion, transform and process data, orchestrate data pipelines, and apply programming concepts to your pipelines and queries.

Domain 2: Data Store Management (26% of scored content)
This domain focuses on evaluating your understanding of choosing the right data store, comprehending data catalog systems, managing the data lifecycle, designing data models, and handling schema evolution.

Domain 3: Data Operations and Support (22% of scored content)
> For this domain, the focus is on analyzing data with AWS services, automating data processing, maintaining and monitoring data pipelines, and ensuring data quality.

Domain 4: Data Security and Governance (18% of scored content)
> For this domain, the focus is on evaluating your knowledge of applying authentication and authorization mechanisms, ensuring data encryption and masking, preparing logs for auditing, and understanding data privacy and governance.

Exam Format

The exam contains two styles of questions:

Multiple choice
> These have exactly one right answer and three wrong ones (distractors). The distractors are designed to seem reasonable, especially to someone with partial knowledge of the topic.

Multiple response
> These questions may have several correct answers.

For multiple-choice questions, while several answers might technically work, pay close attention to specific requirements in the question, such as "lowest cost" or "least operational overhead." The correct answer must satisfy these specific criteria.

Multiple-response questions, on the other hand, have two or more correct responses out of five or more response options. You'll need to select all the correct responses to answer these questions successfully.

Unanswered questions are scored as incorrect, and there is no penalty for guessing, encouraging you to attempt every question.

Exam details are as follows:

- *Type*: Associate-level certification
- *Delivery method*: Available at Pearson VUE testing centers or through online proctored exams
- *Number of questions*: 65 (50 scored, 15 unscored)
- *Time*: 130 minutes
- *Cost*: $150 USD. Refer to the exam pricing page (*https://oreil.ly/4Np6C*) for prices in local currency for other countries (look for the Associate row in the pricing table).
- *Language*: English, Japanese, Korean, and Simplified Chinese

The 15 unscored questions are used by AWS to evaluate their suitability for future exams and do not contribute to your final score. These questions are not identified on the exam. For more information about the exam, visit the AWS Certified Data Engineer Associate page (*https://oreil.ly/dxrPK*).

Registering for the Exam

To register for an exam, navigate to *aws.training* (*https://oreil.ly/j78c6*). Next, click Certification in the top menu and sign in using your AWS Builder ID (or create one if you don't already have one). Then, choose Exam Registration in the left navigation pane and click on "Schedule an exam." Find the exam using the title "AWS Certified Data Engineer – Associate" or the code "DEA-C01" and click the Schedule button. You will then be redirected to the test delivery provider's scheduling page, where you will complete your exam registration.

Exam-Style Questions

In *skillbuilder.aws*, AWS has provided a free Exam Prep Official Practice Question Set for AWS Certified Data Engineer Associate (*https://oreil.ly/IU4Ji*), which features 20 questions developed by AWS experts, designed to simulate the style and format of the certification exam. These exam-style questions come with detailed feedback and recommended resources, aiding your preparation efforts for the actual exam.

Furthermore, each domain chapter within this book presents additional exam-style questions, allowing you to hone your skills. The final chapter provides an extensive collection of exam-style queries, enabling you to further explore and solidify your understanding.

Think Like an AWS Solutions Architect: Translating a Real-World Problem-Solving Framework into Certification

AWS certification exams do more than just test your memory—they validate your ability to think systematically and solve practical business and technical problems effectively. The questions you encounter in these exams are deliberately designed to mimic the real-world challenges faced by AWS Solutions Architects and Data Engineers. By adopting a structured approach to interpreting and responding to these questions, you not only boost your chances of certification success but also sharpen the same skills you'll need daily in your role as an AWS professional.

In this section, we'll explore how the structured thought process used by AWS Solutions Architects to solve real-world problems translates directly into successfully navigating certification scenarios. You will see how applying a clear, repeatable framework can help you quickly detect question intent, eliminate distractors, and pinpoint the best answers efficiently.

The Solutions Architect's Problem-Solving Framework

Whether addressing a complex customer requirement or deciphering an intricate certification scenario, a successful solutions architect follows a structured, repeatable thought process. This approach ensures that solutions align closely with customer needs, constraints, and business goals. Here's a practical framework that solutions architects commonly follow:

1. *Understand the use case.*
    First, get a clear picture of what problem needs to be solved. This means actively listening to the customer's description of their challenge or goal. For example, is the customer trying to process streaming data in real time, migrate a database with minimal downtime, or ensure their data lake is secure? Knowing the core use case sets the target for the solution.

2. *Gather current solutions and pain points.*
    In many cases, the customer already has some legacy solution that might not fit their forward-looking use cases. The architect's job here is twofold: to understand what currently exists and to identify where it falls short. Are there performance bottlenecks during peak usage? Is the current solution too costly to maintain? Does it require excessive manual effort or lack the flexibility to support new data formats or sources? By surfacing both the strengths and limitations of the current state, the architect builds a strong foundation for designing a solution that delivers measurable improvements and aligns with the customer's evolving goals.

3. *Determine and rank success criteria.*
    It's crucial to know what a successful solution looks like for your customer. This might be defined by key performance indicators (KPIs) or outcomes (e.g., reducing latency by 50%, cutting costs by 30%, achieving 99.9% availability, etc.). Success criteria help prioritize trade-offs. For instance, if the top success metric is cost reduction, the architect will favor a simpler, cost-efficient design over a feature-rich but expensive one.

4. *Consider customer specificity and context.*
    Every customer has a context—their industry, their existing architecture, the skill set of their team, and so on. Are they a startup all-in on serverless, or an enterprise with legacy systems? Do they have a strong preference for open source technologies, or do they prefer managed proprietary solutions for simplicity? Context helps tailor the solution. Great architects frame the problem within the bigger picture of the customer's environment. They carefully consider these

specifics to ensure that solutions are not only technically viable but also practical and culturally aligned.

5. *Explore possible solutions.*

Only after understanding the preceding points do architects start brainstorming solutions. They will typically consider multiple approaches—for example, if the use case is "real-time analytics on streaming data," possible solutions might include Amazon Kinesis Data Streams, Amazon MSK (Managed Kafka), or even nonstreaming options if near real time is acceptable.

6. *Evaluate trade-offs and choose the best fit.*

Finally, solutions architects evaluate each potential solution against the previously defined success criteria and customer context. They explicitly address trade-offs—such as cost versus performance or feature richness versus operational simplicity. This step results in selecting the optimal solution that aligns closely with customer objectives while respecting their constraints and specific circumstances.

Following this structured approach ensures the solutions architect delivers effective, practical, and customer-aligned recommendations. In essence, they act as the customer's trusted advisor, balancing what's ideal with what's practical.

Real-World Example: Designing a Serverless Stream Analytics Platform to Detect Fraud

Let's apply this framework to a real-world use case from a leading fintech company focused on delivering fast and reliable banking services. The customer needed to detect fraudulent activity on their platform in near real time, requiring a scalable and low-latency analytics pipeline capable of handling millions of events per day:

1. *Understand the use case.*

The core challenge was to analyze incoming transaction data in near real time and identify suspicious behavior patterns, allowing them to act swiftly against potential fraud.

2. *Gather current solutions and pain points.*

The customer had legacy detection mechanisms that were batch-oriented, leading to several minutes of delay between event ingestion and fraud detection. These systems also lacked scalability and required heavy operational management.

3. *Determine and rank success criteria.*

The primary goals were low-latency detection (subsecond), high scalability to support business growth, and a reduction in operational overhead.

4. Consider customer specificity and context.

As a fintech startup, the customer was cloud-native with a preference for managed, serverless technologies to minimize undifferentiated heavy lifting. Their engineering team was small but skilled in event-driven architectures.

5. Explore possible solutions.

For the streaming layer, the customer had two main options: Amazon Kinesis Data Streams or Amazon MSK (Managed Kafka). On the data processing side, they considered Spark Structured Streaming hosted on AWS Glue or Amazon EMR, and Apache Flink hosted on Amazon Managed Service for Apache Flink. Each option came with trade-offs in terms of operational complexity, performance tuning, and developer familiarity.

6. Evaluate trade-offs and choose the best fit.

Given the need for simplicity and tight AWS integration, Kinesis was favored over MSK. While MSK offered more flexibility and control, it required more operational overhead. On the processing side, the customer team had stronger technical experience with Spark Structured Streaming than with Flink. As a result, Spark hosted on AWS Glue was chosen as the best fit. This combination provided the necessary scalability and low latency while minimizing operational complexity and aligning with the team's existing expertise. Figure 1-1 illustrates the design fitting these needs.

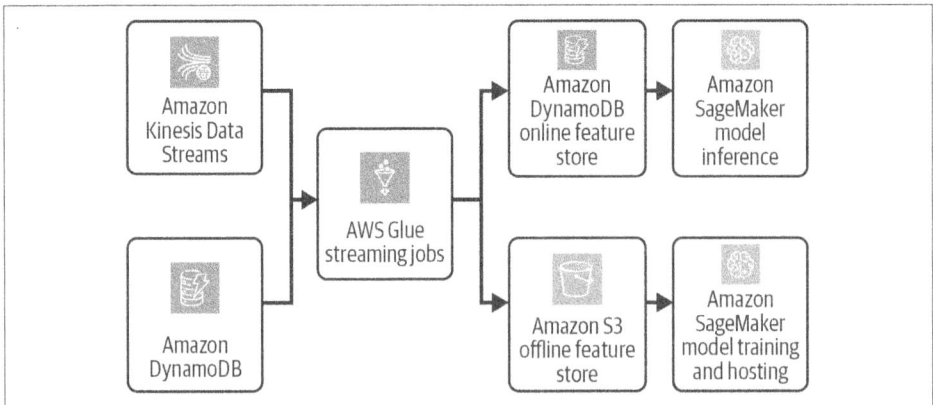

Figure 1-1. Stream-based fraud detection system

How This Thought Process Applies to Certification Questions

I hope you've realized by this time that AWS certification questions are, in many ways, simplified customer case studies. The exam presents you with condensed versions of real-world problems—focused on a specific requirement, constraint, or outcome. What these questions are really testing is your ability to think like a solutions architect under time constraints.

Let's walk through the same reference customer example we discussed earlier but in a certification question format, to see how the six-step problem-solving framework maps to a certification-style scenario.

Here's our sample question:

A data engineering team is building a new analytics pipeline to process real-time clickstream data from their mobile app. The solution must support rapid ingestion and low-latency processing. The team has limited operational capacity and prefers managed services. They already use Apache Spark for batch jobs and are familiar with its APIs. Which solution will meet the requirement with the least operational overhead?

A. Amazon MSK with Apache Flink on Amazon Managed Service for Apache Flink

B. Amazon Kinesis Data Streams with AWS Lambda

C. Amazon MSK with Spark Streaming on Amazon EMR

D. Amazon Kinesis Data Streams with Spark Structured Streaming on AWS Glue

Let's apply the framework:

1. *Understand the use case.*
   The question is about processing real-time clickstream data, so it's a streaming analytics use case with low-latency requirements.

2. *Gather current solutions and pain points.*
   The team currently uses Spark for batch jobs—indicating they are familiar with Spark's ecosystem. Their stated pain point is limited operational capacity, so self-managed or complex services may not be a good fit.

3. *Determine and rank success criteria.*
   The key phrase here is "least operational overhead." This is the dominant decision factor, more important than flexibility or advanced capabilities.

4. *Consider customer specificity and context.*
   They prefer managed services and have Spark experience. That suggests a solution combining managed infrastructure and Spark would align best with their context.

5. *Explore possible solutions.*
   Here we consider each of the possible solutions:

   - A (MSK + Flink): Managed Flink is good, but the team lacks Flink familiarity. MSK requires cluster management.

   - B (Kinesis + Lambda): Operationally light but limited for complex analytics.

- C (MSK + EMR + Spark): More operational burden with EMR and MSK.
- D (Kinesis + Glue + Spark): Fully managed, Spark-friendly, and minimal overhead.

6. Evaluate trade-offs and choose the best fit.

Option D stands out as the best combination of managed services and Spark compatibility, with minimal operational overhead. Others either require more setup/management or are mismatched with the team's expertise.

Correct answer: D. Amazon Kinesis Data Streams with Spark Structured Streaming on AWS Glue

This approach mirrors how you'd think through real customer problems. Certification questions just compress the story and require you to apply this structured mindset quickly and confidently.

A Word on the AWS Certified Data Engineer Associate Exam

This particular certification targets the data engineering persona. While many questions follow the data architecting patterns we've discussed so far, expect some to test hands-on familiarity with data engineering workflows and tools. These questions may evaluate your experience working directly with services like AWS Glue, Amazon Redshift, or Lake Formation, including configurations, CLI usage, performance tuning, and troubleshooting. They're designed to reflect real-life experience using the technology, beyond architectural knowledge. We will cover many such examples in the sample questions later in this book.

Study Plan

Preparing for the AWS Certified Data Engineer Associate exam requires a structured approach. Here is a sample study plan that you can follow while tailoring it to your specific studying style:

1. Get to know the exam-style questions as described in the preceding section.
2. Refresh your AWS knowledge and skills by reading this study guide. Complete the practice questions at the end of each chapter and in Chapter 9 to assess your understanding and readiness.

3. Get hands-on experience using:

AWS Builder Labs (https://oreil.ly/vLAKN)
> These AWS Skill Builder self-paced labs provide hands-on cloud skills practice in the AWS Management Console. They are available with an AWS Skill Builder individual subscription (*https://oreil.ly/SEHiz*) and team subscription (*https://oreil.ly/TyVLC*).

AWS Cloud Quest (https://oreil.ly/ZZd0J) (Choose Data Analytics domain)
> AWS Cloud Quest is the only 3D role-playing game to help you build practical AWS Cloud skills. Choose your role—Data Analytics Specialist—then learn and apply your cloud skills to help the citizens of your virtual city.

AWS Jam (https://oreil.ly/JUgqF)
> AWS Jam is an immersive gamified training that helps you apply your AWS Cloud skills to solve real-world, open-ended problems using AWS services.

4. Assess your exam readiness by taking the AWS Certification Official Practice Exam. You will get access to this exam after you register for the exam.

Conclusion

In this chapter, we explored the fundamental role of data engineers and their critical responsibilities in modern organizations. We delved into why the AWS Certified Data Engineer Associate certification is valuable for your career growth and professional development. You've gained a clear understanding of the exam's structure and registration process as well as familiarity with the exam question formats and key content domains that you'll need to master.

## CHAPTER 2

Prerequisite Knowledge for Aspiring Data Engineers

Before being introduced to AWS services, you need to have some prerequisite knowledge on data engineering concepts. This chapter briefly covers the foundational knowledge related to databases, data lakes, data ingestion, data processing, data consumption, working with code repositories, and AWS Cloud that you're going to need before you begin preparing for AWS Certified Data Engineer Associate certification.

Databases and Types of Databases

Most applications require persistent storage of their data and an efficient way to query it. The data can be stored in different formats depending on use case, but for most use cases, storing in databases is one of the best solutions for persistent storage (if the data is available in structured or semi-structured format). Let's understand what a database is, and the different types of databases that you can consider while designing your application.

What Is a Database?

A database is a collection of data that can help represent an entity as a table or view having a fixed or flexible set of attributes stored electronically for easier access and management. It provides better performance compared to storing data in files and reading from them.

What Is a Database Management System?

The software system that integrates database features such as create, insert, update, and delete is called a database management system (DBMS). It acts as an interface between the database and the end user. Apart from the end user operations, a DBMS also provides support for administrative tasks such as managing performance, in-memory cache, storing indexes, export/import, and many more. DBMS systems store data in a proprietary format that is efficient for data ingestion and queries. Some examples of DBMSs are MySQL, PostgreSQL, Oracle, MSSQL Server, and Amazon Aurora.

Types of Databases

There are several types of databases such as hierarchical, relational, and NoSQL. Each one of them excels in performance for different use cases. Let's learn a bit more about these databases.

Hierarchical Databases

Hierarchical databases became popular around 1970. They store data in a tree kind of structure that maps parent records to child records and each one of them is treated as a node of the tree. For example, if you need to design a hierarchical database for a university, you can define a department as a parent with employees and courses as child records. Similarly, you can also map students as parents and courses as child records. In hierarchical databases, you can maintain a one-to-many relationship by mapping multiple children to one parent with a constraint that a child can have only one parent.

Over time, adoption of these kinds of databases has reduced because of their complexity and inability to scale with data size and number of entities.

Relational Databases

Around the 1980s, relational databases became very popular because of their simple tabular storage structure where each entity type is treated as a table or view, entities within the tables and views are treated as records, and attributes of the entity are treated as columns of the table or view. It is very simple for end users to visually understand the data and represent it as records and columns. If you consider the same university example, then the department can be treated as a table within which each department will be treated as a record and the attributes of the department such as department name and department ID will be treated as columns.

Even today, after so many years, relational databases are the most popular database type and are a great fit for a lot of use cases. Next, let's understand what SQL is and how it relates to relational databases.

Structured Query Language (SQL) is a programming language that interacts with databases. You can leverage SQL client tools or programming SDKs to submit SQL queries to the database engine for the operations the database engine supports.

The database operations may include create table, select/insert/update/delete records, execute stored procedures, and many more.

Relational databases provide SQL interfaces to insert, update, and query data. They also provide PL/SQL (Procedural Language for SQL), which is a procedural language that combines more than one SQL statement to achieve a common task or return a set of values.

SQL commands are categorized as follows:

Data Definition Language (DDL)
    DDL helps manage objects and their structures, such as CREATE tables, views, indexes, and more.

Data Manipulation Language (DML)
    DML helps modify the data using INSERT, UPDATE, and DELETE statements.

Data Query Language (DQL)
    DQL helps retrieve data from the database using SELECT statements.

Data Control Language (DCL)
    DCL helps database administrators manage authorization on database objects and data in tables using GRANT statements.

Transaction Control Language (TCL)
    TCL helps the database engine make automatic changes to the database, for example reverting erroneous transactions using ROLLBACK statements.

Next, let's learn about NoSQL databases.

NoSQL Databases

Relational databases are great when you have a fixed schema and the values across columns are well populated or expected to be populated. When you have a use case that will have variable schema, which means each record may have a different set of attributes, then NoSQL databases are a great fit. You can still leverage relational databases in this case, by adding more columns with ALTER statements, but that will create a sparse table, which has a lot of NULL values and is inefficient. In addition, NoSQL databases do not provide referential integrity between multiple tables and you cannot perform table JOINs to retrieve data.

There are other use cases that may require you to choose a NoSQL database as well, as there may be a specific query pattern for which a specific type of NoSQL database may give better performance. Some of the popular NoSQL database types are key value store, document store, graph database, in-memory database, and search database. We will dive deep into each of these NoSQL database types in future chapters.

Now let's understand the difference between two data processing systems, OLTP and OLAP.

OLTP Versus OLAP

Online transaction processing (OLTP) and online analytical processing (OLAP) are two different data processing systems designed for two different purposes. OLTP systems primarily perform record-level processing and serve frontend applications that require request responses in a few seconds. Conversely, OLAP systems primarily perform column-level operation and serve analytics and business intelligence (BI) reporting use cases.

OLAP system response time varies depending on the data volume it scans, data distribution, query complexity, and the architecture of the compute system. But the response time of queries and concurrency for queries are generally lower than OLTP systems. In general, OLTP databases are more suited for record-level operations that require high concurrency (e.g., insert product or order record as it is placed by the user through frontend applications), whereas OLAP systems are more suited for analyzing larger volumes of records to find insights (e.g., find month over month sales growth for the last five years).

In terms of storage, data lake and data warehousing systems are primarily leveraged for OLAP use cases. Next, let's learn about the big data and distributed processing frameworks that are popular in the OLAP world.

Overview of Big Data

Traditional database technologies are not able to scale to process petabyte-scale data volume. This triggered the next stage of innovation for distributed processing frameworks that can scale horizontally by adding more nodes to an existing cluster. Let's understand what big data represents, and from a technology standpoint, what options are available today.

In simple terms, big data represents terabyte- to petabyte-scale data, collected from various sources through different frequencies, that is complex to process. These datasets are large enough that traditional data processing software can't efficiently process or manage their storage and retrieval. But these massive volume datasets add a lot of value. Organizations can derive insights using analytics, provide forecasts for the future using machine learning, or generate new content using generative AI.

Oftentimes big data is referred to as the five Vs. It started with three Vs, including *Volume*, *Velocity*, and *Variety*, but as it evolved, *Veracity* and *Value* also became major aspects of big data. The following provides an explanation of each of the five Vs:

Volume

This represents the amount of data you have or receive for analytics, which depends on your organization and the use case. It can range from terabyte to petabyte scale. Depending on the volume of data, you can design your data processing pipeline and align the compute capacity needed.

Velocity

This represents the speed or the frequency at which data is being collected or processed for analysis. This can be a daily data feed you receive from your vendor or it can be a real-time streaming use case, where you receive data every few seconds.

Variety

This refers to the different forms or types of data you receive for processing or analysis. In general, there are three types of data:

Structured

This refers to data that has a fixed schema or is readable by distributed processing frameworks such as MapReduce, Apache Spark, or Apache Flink. We commonly treat data from relational databases, CSVs, and delimited datasets as structured.

Semi-structured

Data where some parts of fields are structured and other parts are unstructured, are treated as semi-structured. JSON, XML, and emails are good examples of semi-structured datasets.

Unstructured

Datasets on which a schema cannot be applied are treated as unstructured. Media files such as audio, video, and PDF documents are good examples of unstructured data.

Veracity

This represents how reliable or truthful your data is. The accuracy or quality of the data is critical to deriving the correct insights. For example, you may expect one data source to send a 5 GB file every day with 100 attributes, and the attributes or columns in the structured dataset should be at least 70% populated.

Value

This is often referred to as the worth of the data you have collected, as it is meant to give insights that can help a business drive growth.

The primary challenge from big data is to efficiently process it, as single-server-based processing frameworks cannot scale to process such a large volume of data. Big data needs a distributed processing framework that can process data in parallel with a cluster of servers. After understanding what big data represents, let's learn about Hadoop, Spark, and a few other data processing frameworks that have become popular to process big data.

Distributed Processing Frameworks for Big Data

In simple terms, distributed processing means that the processing happens in a multinode cluster instead of a single virtual or physical machine. In the past 10 to 15 years, the Apache Hadoop framework (*https://oreil.ly/QcpQ7*) has become popular because of its massive parallel processing capability on top of commodity hardware and its fault-tolerant nature, which has made it more reliable. It has been extended with additional tools and applications to form an ecosystem that can help to collect, store, process, analyze, and manage big data.

Hadoop clusters consist of a master node and several data nodes that can scale horizontally as the data or processing volume increases. The common storage layer built on top of all the data node disks is called Hadoop Distributed File System (HDFS).

There were several distributed processing frameworks or applications during the evolution of the Hadoop framework; let's learn about some of the popular ones.

MapReduce

MapReduce (*https://oreil.ly/IjVYm*) is a distributed processing framework, originally designed to process data concurrently from HDFS by splitting data into 64 MB or 128 MB chunks. It primarily consists of the following processes:

A map process
    This process takes input as key-value pairs then processes and transforms them and writes another key-value pair as intermediate output.

A reduce process
    This takes key-value pairs as input, aggregates them, and writes output as another key-value pair.

A combiner process
    The combiner process is an optional stage that acts as a mini-reducer. It aggregates records available in a single data node before it reaches the reducer stage.

With the growing popularity of Hadoop and MapReduce, continued innovations have resulted in several other frameworks built on top of Hadoop that provide better performance and address different use cases. Let's look at a few other frameworks.

Spark

Apache Spark (*https://oreil.ly/sgMJJ*) is an open source framework that provides optimized query execution compared to MapReduce and does most of its processing in-memory to boost performance. Similar to MapReduce, it provides batch processing capability but also provides real-time streaming, machine learning, and graph processing capabilities. Another reason for its wide adoption is that Spark provides, as shown in Figure 2-1, its APIs in the Java, Scala, Python, and R programming languages.

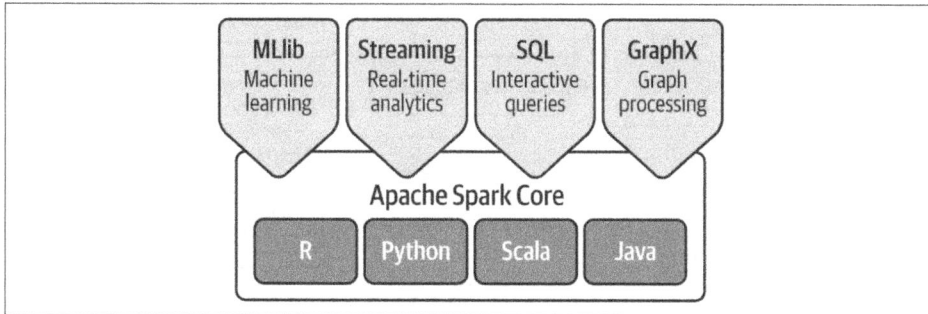

Figure 2-1. Apache Spark languages and library support

Spark represents the data it reads or writes as Resilient Distributed Datasets (RDDs), DataFrames, or Datasets and it provides the following two operations:

Transformations
> Transformations are operations in which you create a new RDD, DataFrame, or Dataset from an existing one after applying transformation rules such as map, filter, join, and more. It is executed in a lazy manner, which means transformations are only executed when Spark invokes an action operation.

Actions
> Actions are operations that trigger transformations and write the final output to an external location or return the output to the Spark driver program.

Figure 2-2 shows the high-level Spark architecture, where:

- Spark provides the option to execute in a standalone mode or in a cluster mode. In cluster mode, you have a cluster manager and the driver program submits a job to the cluster. The job gets split into multiple tasks that get executed in different worker nodes.

- Each worker node may have more than one executor, with each executor having a fixed amount of memory and CPU cores for execution. The executor may execute a map transformation task, or an action that writes to the output location.

- Each worker node has its own cache memory to which you can write small datasets that may be repeatedly used by multiple tasks; the tasks will get performance boost as the requested dataset will be available in memory. A great example of this is caching reference lookup data that transformation tasks may use.

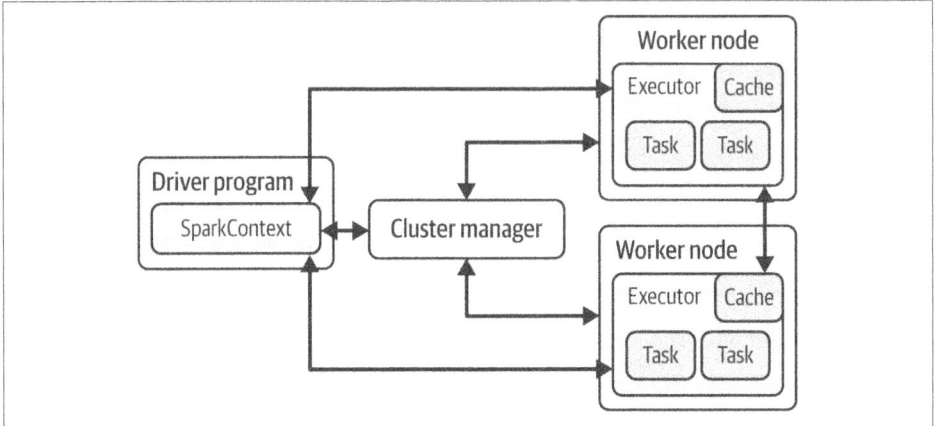

Figure 2-2. Apache Spark architecture in cluster mode

Next, let's learn about Apache Flink.

Flink

Apache Flink (*https://flink.apache.org*) is an open source distributed processing framework primarily designed for real-time stream processing of high throughput workloads. Similar to Spark, Flink also does most of its processing in-memory and is stateful while processing both unbounded streaming data or bounded data as a batch. It provides advanced capabilities such as out-of-order event processing, exactly-once semantics, and backpressure control.

Figure 2-3 shows the high-level Flink architecture and its two primary components—JobManager and TaskManager:

JobManager
JobManager has three subcomponents (ResourceManager, Dispatcher, and Job-Master) that help to schedule new tasks, coordinate checkpoints, react to task failures or completion, and more. You can increase the reliability of a cluster by having more JobManagers where one becomes the leader and the other stays on standby to provide high availability.

TaskManager

TaskManagers or workers execute the tasks of a dataflow that includes multiple task slots. For a job, you will have at least one TaskManager and one task slot that scale horizontally for concurrent execution.

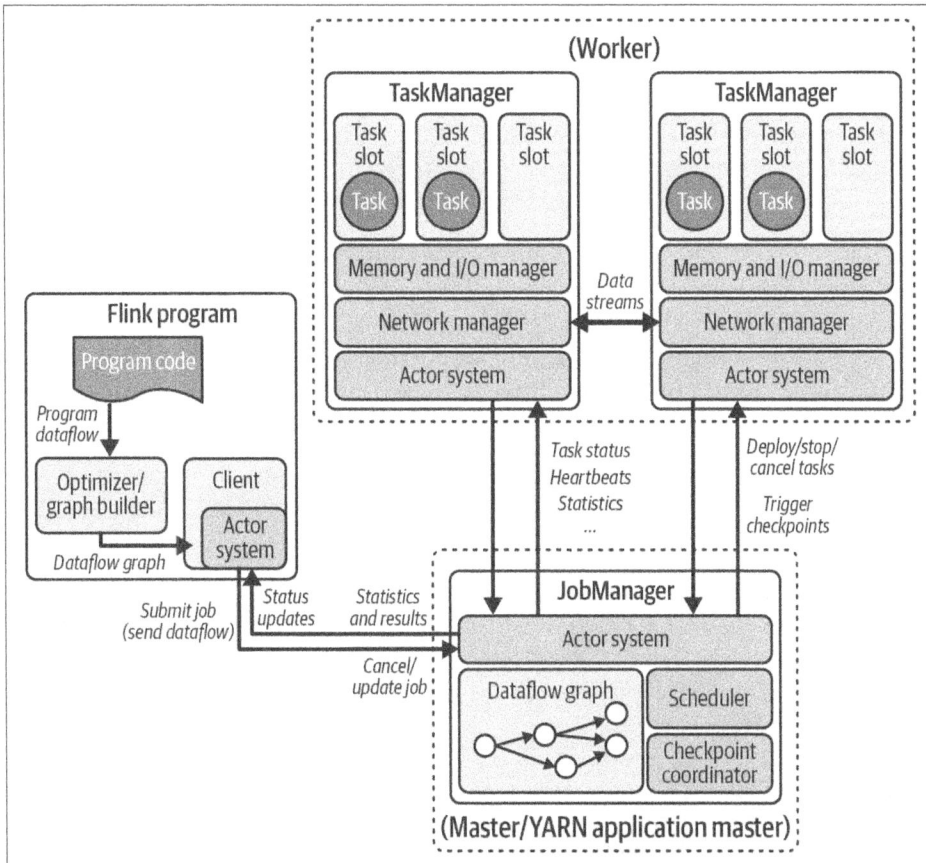

Figure 2-3. Apache Flink high-level architecture

Client applications or programs submit a job to the JobManager and may stay active to receive the result; they can also close the session to let the job run in background. Next, let's learn about Hive, Presto, and Trino, all of which provide SQL interfaces to end users to analyze big data.

Hive

Apache Hive (*https://oreil.ly/lON99*) is a popular open source application that data analysts and data scientists use to query or prepare data for analytics. You need not write complex Java or Scala programs using MapReduce or Spark APIs to analyze the data and you can write your transformation logic using SQL. It was originally created at Facebook (now Meta) around 2008 to simplify data processing on Hadoop clusters.

Hive is positioned as the data warehouse in the Hadoop ecosystem and users can configure it to leverage MapReduce, Tez, or Spark as its backend processing engine. It provides a SQL-like query interface called Hive Query Language (HiveQL).

Hive keeps all its schema metadata in a relational database, maintained by the Hive Metastore Server (HMS). HMS enables you to define a virtual table schema on top of the data available in HDFS (or other object stores), so that end users can query them using SQL standards.

Presto

Similar to Hive, Presto (*https://oreil.ly/2r4BW*) (or PrestoDB) is also an open source, distributed SQL query engine that is optimized for low-latency data access from the distributed file system. It's used for complex queries, aggregations, joins, and window functions. It is capable of querying from the schema defined in HMS or other object stores.

The Presto engine complies the end user SQL queries, executes them through multiple stages in-memory, and takes the compute capacity of the Hadoop clusters. You can scale the parallelism of Presto queries with additional nodes.

Presto has become a popular alternative to Hive because of its higher performance and in-memory processing capability. It was also open sourced by Facebook around 2013. Presto provides a lot of connectors to query data from additional sources such as object stores, relational databases, and NoSQL databases such as Cassandra, MongoDB, and HBase.

Trino

In January 2019, a few engineers of the original Presto project left Meta (formerly known as Facebook) and forked the open source Presto to better serve the open source community. They named it PrestoSQL, which got rebranded as Trino (*https://trino.io*) in December 2020.

Today, Spark for batch processing, Spark Structured Streaming, and Flink for real-time streaming are very popular among data engineers. Similarly Hive, Presto, and Trino are very popular among data analysts and data scientists to analyze or prepare data using SQL-like queries.

Next, let's understand what a data lake is and how it helps optimize data analytics.

What Is a Data Lake?

A data lake is treated as a centralized repository that can store structured, semi-structured, and unstructured datasets at any scale. Data lakes store the raw data as it is, on top of which you can integrate distributed processing frameworks to process and query the petabyte-scale datasets.

Data lakes became popular with the growing popularity of Hadoop clusters. HDFS storage was treated as a data lake that can scale horizontally with the addition of more nodes to the cluster. Later, cloud object stores such as Amazon S3 got widely adopted for data lake storage compared to disc-based block storage, because of its higher reliability, scalability, cheaper cost, and operational efficiency.

A data lake can bring in all data together to build one source of truth and make it available for analytics. Data lakes enable data science teams to leverage historical data for machine learning, transforming a subset of data for downstream systems, and many more use cases. While managing a data lake, it is important to make sure the data lake does not end up as a data swamp. A data swamp represents a repository of data that has become unmanageable over time and lacks structure, metadata, and governance around it.

What Is a Data Warehouse?

Data warehouses (DW) are also meant to act as a centralized repository to enable data analysis and BI reporting, but they are primarily built to support structured and semi-structured relational datasets, and the compute architecture supports low-latency queries. DW systems store data in a proprietary format designed to analyze larger volumes of data efficiently.

Most data warehouses support tiered storage and different data distribution techniques that you can integrate based on your use cases. Different data warehousing systems may have different options, but at a minimum they support storing some of the frequently accessed data in-memory (less frequently accessed data is in SSD storage). DW systems support distributing the data through different mechanisms for efficient querying based on the use cases. The mechanism may include distributing the data across all nodes evenly, or by the unique key of the records to facilitate faster joins, or storing all the data in every node if the data is smaller and needs to be cached in each node.

In addition to centralized data warehousing systems, certain organizations integrate data marts that may hold subsets of data for a specific business unit or department such as finance, marketing, or human resources. Data marts are smaller in data size compared to data warehouse and may have aggregated data for a specific use case.

Data Warehouse Versus Data Lake

Ideally you need to have both data lakes and data warehouses in your organization as both serve different use cases. Data warehouses are not meant to store all historical data and are best utilized to store the last few years of data needed for analytics with lower latency. Compared to that, data lakes are generally meant to store both structured and unstructured datasets and store historical data to support analytics as well as time series or machine learning use cases.

Data warehouses support SQL for data analysis, as the data is generally structured, and are built on top of database engines. Similar to databases, data warehouses follow a "schema on write" approach where the schema of the tables are defined first and then the data is ingested. But data lakes follow a "schema on read" approach, which means the data is stored in a storage layer and a virtual schema is applied on top of it while reading or querying the data to represent the datasets as a table or view.

While data warehouses support SQL-focused interfaces, data lakes primarily support programming interfaces with Python or distributed processing frameworks like Spark, Flink, Hive, or Tez. Irrespective of use case requirements, sometimes customers choose commercial licensed data warehouses that have better technical support to meet service-level agreements (SLAs) defined for their production applications as compared to open source technologies.

ETL Versus ELT

When you plan to ingest data to your data lake or data warehouse and make it available for consumption, depending on the usage pattern you may choose between extract, transform, and load (ETL) or extract, load, and transform (ELT):

Extract
> Extract represents fetching the data from a data source such as databases, third-party APIs, FTP systems, or object stores. The extraction process may involve fetching all datasets or incremental datasets based on the use case.

Transform
> Transform represents modifying the data based on consumption pattern. The transformation process can be done using SQL or a distributed processing framework, such as Spark, or any single-threaded programming language, such as Python.

Load
> Load represents saving the data in a storage layer from which end users intend to query the data. The storage layer can be a database, data lake, or data warehouse.

ETL and ELT vary based on what stage the data transformation occurs. If the data gets transformed first before getting loaded into the target, then it is ETL; if the extracted data gets loaded first and then gets transformed, then it is ELT.

Let's assume the data is completely structured and the data analysts would like to access the raw data first (because the data freshness latency requirements are low), then write their own SQL-based transformation for consumption. In that case, ELT is a great approach. Compared to that, let's assume the data is semi-structured or in a format that cannot be consumed directly and needs to be transformed first. In that case, ETL is better. There are other factors that customers consider while choosing between ELT and ETL. For example, if the data is structured and the data analysts are not comfortable with data processing frameworks like Spark, then they choose ELT.

There is no clear winner between ETL and ELT; you need to choose the approach that provides better efficiency for your use case. Next, let's understand the different ways to ingest and process the data.

Different Ways to Process Data

The frequency of data extraction and processing varies depending on use case and different factors such as processing the data in a scheduled manner, triggering the processing when the data arrives, or processing the data on a continuous basis if the data source is a streaming data. Let's understand how batch and stream processing methods vary and what factors to consider.

Batch Processing Pipeline

If you have datasets that need to be processed in a regular interval by combining data collected over time, then it's treated as a batch execution. The size of data in every batch may vary depending on the amount of change that happens in the source system and whether the business has a need to process it in real time.

Here are a few example scenarios that we can treat as a batch execution:

- The source system sends files every few hours that need to be processed nightly.
- Process all the files that arrive every hour (for example, application logs).
- Pull all the data from the source database or SaaS system and process them at once.

In general, batch jobs process a higher volume of data, and they may take more time to process.

Real-Time Stream Processing

Batch jobs are best suited for bounded datasets, but you may have data sources that are unbounded, such as streaming data, which need to be processed on a continuous basis and therefore require real-time stream processing.

Here are a few examples of real-time stream processing:

- Ingesting or processing user clicks from a website or mobile app as soon as they are received
- Processing events coming from IoT devices
- Ingesting database changes (e.g., inserts, updates, deletes) to a data warehouse system as they happen through the change data capture (CDC) mechanism
- Processing incremental data from SaaS sources

In general, the data volume for real-time stream processing systems are smaller compared to batch jobs and involve additional complexities such as processing out-of-order records, late arriving records, checkpointing, and retries for failed processing.

Event-Driven Processing

Event-driven processing is somewhat similar to batch processing but is triggered on a particular event. You may have a requirement to process the data as soon as it arrives, but you cannot keep a real-time streaming infrastructure active as the data does not flow continuously or the source system does not send it in regular intervals. In such scenarios, to reduce cost you may prefer event-driven processing. The volume of data may be small or big depending on the source system. The compute infrastructure generally scales to accommodate the variable data volumes.

High-Level Architecture Overview of Data Processing Pipelines

Figure 2-4 shows a high-level architecture for a data pipeline irrespective of the technologies you choose to integrate. This architecture can evolve based on specific use case requirements.

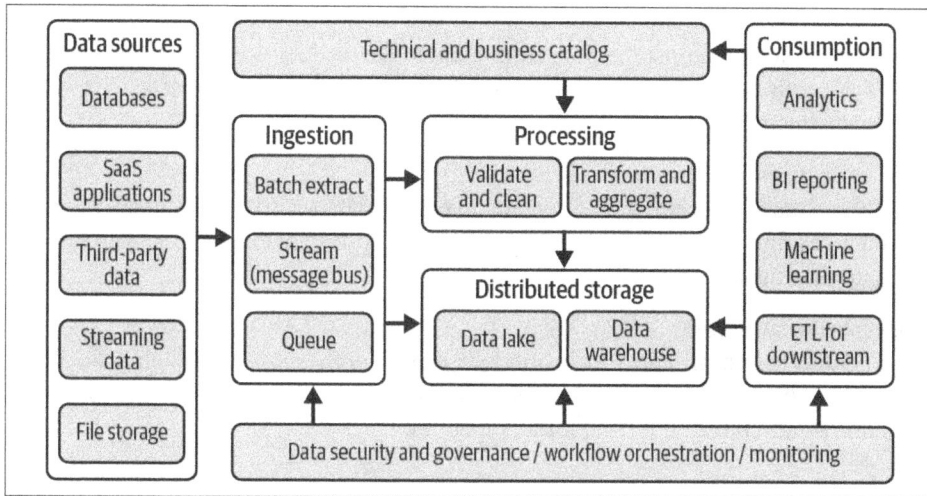

Figure 2-4. High-level architecture for data pipeline

Let's understand each block of the architecture diagram:

Data sources

This component of the architecture highlights different data sources that you may plan to integrate in your data pipeline.

Ingestion

You need to extract the full or incremental data from the data sources through the ingestion layer. It may include scheduled batch jobs to extract data from a source, a message bus such as Kafka to which the data source pushes incremental data, or a queue that keeps the filepaths or messages that need to be processed sequentially.

Distributed storage

The ingestion layer pushes raw input data to the distributed storage layer, which may include a data lake, data warehouse, or database for further processing.

Processing

The raw input data gets validated against data quality, then enriched, transformed, and pushed to the final distributed storage layer.

Technical and business catalog

Once the data is in the storage layer, you can integrate a metadata catalog (which may include databases, table, and column-level information) for data discovery.

Consumption
> Data consumers consume data from a data lake or data warehouse for analytics, BI reporting, machine learning, or to further transform the data to push to downstream systems.

Data security and governance
> This spans all preceding components to enable data security and governance that includes fine-grained access control, data encryption, data masking, data lineage, data sharing, and more.

Workflow orchestration
> The data ingestion and processing jobs can be orchestrated through a workflow service that may help monitor job execution status, enable retry in case of job failures, and build reporting for all pipelines.

Monitoring
> This component helps monitor compute infrastructure health, analyze logs for troubleshooting, audit access logs, and build alerting for failures.

Next let's get an overview of code repositories and what value add they provide during software development.

Working with Code Repositories

Code repositories are basic core components of application development. They improve developer productivity and provide an efficient way to release and deploy approved code.

What Is a Code Repository?

Code repositories provide centralized storage and management of application codes where multiple developers can collaborate. They provide:

Collaboration
> Multiple developers can push code or pull code from a single repository and modify a single file.

Version control
> Any change to the repository and code files are tracked incrementally with an ability to revert back to any previous version.

Security
> An organization or team can define access control to define who from the team can read, write, or merge code in the repository.

Productivity

When a team of developers work on a single project and can efficiently collaborate to read and write code, maintenance time is reduced and accuracy improves.

Code review and release

Repositories facilitate team members' ability to review code, test it, and merge the changes with production branches for smoother release.

How to Work with Code Repositories

There are several popular code repositories such as GitHub, BitBucket, Gitlab, and more. Let's use GitHub as an example to learn a few ways to manage your code and interact with repositories.

You can interact with GitHub using its web interface or command-line utility, or via third-party source control tools such as Sourcetree. The following are some example commands that show how you can interact with the repository.

The following command shows how you can clone a repository from GitHub to your local system:

```
$ git clone https://github.com/<YOUR-USERNAME>/<YOUR-REPOSITORY>
```

If you already have a local codebase directory that is linked to a specific GitHub repository, then you can execute the following command to fetch all the new changes pushed by others to your local directory to keep it up to date. Please note, this command points to the "origin/main" branch of the remote repository:

```
$ git fetch <REMOTE-NAME>
```

There might be a different branch of the Git repository to which your other members pushed code and if you would like to merge those changes, then you can execute the following command:

```
$ git merge <REMOTE-NAME>/<BRANCH-NAME>
```

You may also consider using the `rebash` command, which is a process of combining a sequence of commits to a new base:

```
$ git rebash <REMOTE-NAME>/<BRANCH-NAME>
```

Alternatively, you can also use the `git pull` command, which is a combination of `git merge` and `git fetch`:

```
$ git pull <REMOTE-NAME> <BRANCH-NAME>
```

The following command shows how you can push code from your local system to the GitHub repository:

```
$ git push <REMOTE-NAME> <BRANCH-NAME>
```

If someone else from your team modified the same file and same line number that you modified, then the above push command will fail by highlighting a conflict in merging the file. In such cases, you take the following steps:

1. From the command-line terminal, navigate to your local directory: `$ cd <REPOSITORY-DIRECTORY>`.

2. Execute the following command to list all the files that have a conflict: `$ git status`.

3. Using a code editor such as Visual Studio, navigate to the specific file that has a merge conflict.

4. You will notice the following structure in the line where you have conflict. The `<<<<<<< HEAD` represents the beginning of the line from the base branch. The `=======` represents a separator between the base branch code and the other branch code that has a conflict, and `>>>>>>> branch-a` represents the end of the conflict and the branch name:

   ```
   If you have questions, please
   <<<<<<< HEAD
   open an issue
   =======
   ask your question in IRC.
   >>>>>>> branch-a
   ```

5. You should manually modify the preceding block of code to keep the correct one for your application logic and delete the rest. Then to add or stage your changes, use the following command: `$ git add`.

6. Finally, execute `git commit` with a comment on the file merging action: `$ git commit -m "Resolved merge conflict by incorporating the correct code"`.

To learn more about GitHub commands, please visit the GitHub documentation (*https://oreil.ly/bmBCE*). Next, let's understand what CI/CD is and what value it brings while releasing or deploying applications.

CI/CD

CI/CD are the core components of DevOps that allow you to integrate and validate code merged by developers and then create a build that can be released for deployment. It makes software development and deployment easier by automating most of the processes:

Continuous integration
   Continuous integration (CI) integrates code from multiple developers in a repository and creates an automated build that has gone through test case validations.

Continuous delivery
> Continuous delivery (CD) delivers the code to a preproduction environment for quality assurance and validates the build in an equivalent runtime environment.

Continuous deployment
> Continuous deployment (CD) automatically deploys the build to a production environment.

You can leverage different tools to implement the CI/CD pipeline such as Jenkins (*https://www.jenkins.io*), GitHub Actions (*https://oreil.ly/x7-0p*), and AWS Code-Pipeline (*https://oreil.ly/Z1DER*).

Cloud Computing and AWS

Traditionally if an organization needs a set of servers for their applications, they need to pay in advance to preprovision the servers, configure them with necessary software libraries, and then make them available for application teams. Preprovisioning servers and maintaining one's own data center has several challenges, such as:

- Longer time for procurement
- Additional cost
- Inability to scale capacity when needed
- Complexity of managing infrastructure spread across different geographies

Even if the application servers are needed for a short period of time, customers need to go through the complete procurement cycle, which delays projects. Let's understand what a cloud is and how it addresses all these challenges.

What Is Cloud Computing?

Cloud computing refers to a vast amount of remote computing resources that may include physical servers, virtual machines, networking components, managed services (related to storage, database, analytics), machine learning, and many more that are available in various locations throughout the world.

You can access these computing resources on demand with a pay-as-you-go model or reserve them for a longer duration with a discounted price. The availability of computing resources in specific parts of the world and their capabilities depends on the cloud provider. The following are the key benefits of cloud computing:

Agility
> Amazon Web Services (AWS) offers multiple services that solve different business problems and map to different technology domains such as data, AI, IoT,

AppDev, storage, and more. You get the flexibility to choose, experiment, and deploy quickly to validate your business idea.

Elasticity

This enables you to scale up server capacity or increase the number of servers when needed and scale down when you have reduced application load. In addition, with serverless services you can avoid thinking about infrastructure scalability. Depending on business demand, you can scale your capacity up and down, instead of provisioning for the highest capacity you need.

Cost savings

You can access a pay-as-you-go pricing model, which means you pay for what you use. Compared to traditional on-premises server procurement processes, where you pay in advance and get resources for the highest potential capacity you need, AWS gives you cost savings as you can provision resources for a few minutes or few hours and then terminate to save cost.

Deploy globally in minutes

Avoiding the server provisioning delay, you can make servers available in any AWS region in minutes with a few clicks. You don't need to go through creating a data center in different regions of the globe, which takes months to years of time and involves a huge investment as well.

There are many popular cloud providers such as AWS, Microsoft Azure, Google Cloud Platform, Oracle Cloud, and a few others. Each of these cloud providers offer computing resources through infrastructure as a service (IaaS), platform as a service (PaaS), and software as a service (SaaS).

Let's learn more about AWS.

An Overview of Amazon Web Services

AWS is a cloud computing platform that provides computing resources (i.e., servers) plus many managed services to reduce the operational burden of customers. The following are some key benefits of AWS:

- It provides agility and the flexibility to choose from 200+ services based on the use case.
- It offers cost-saving measures with a pay-as-you-go model, reserved instances, savings plans, and more.
- It enables developers to choose from many purpose-built services and exposes automation using AWS CDK, SDK, and CloudFormation services.

- Its services and compute/storage resources are available across the globe through its Regions and Availability Zones, which allows users to provision resources within minutes.

Let's learn how AWS makes computing resources available across the globe using Regions and Availability Zones.

The AWS global infrastructure consists of Regions and Availability Zones (AZs). AWS Regions are geographically separated areas that consist of two or more Availability Zones, which are separated from each other but are connected through low latency, high throughput, and a redundant network. Figure 2-5 shows an AWS Region with three Availability Zones that are connected through the network.

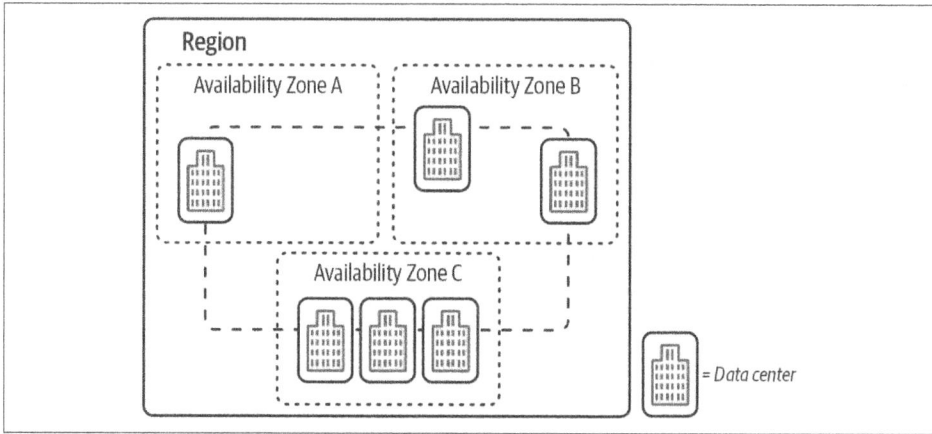

Figure 2-5. AWS Region and Availability Zone example

In AWS, most of the services are regional, which means you need to first choose an AWS Region based on your business and customer presence, then choose the AWS services in that Region. But there are few services that are global in nature, such as AWS Identity and Access Management (IAM).

Some of the regional managed services of AWS leverage multiple AZs for reliability and scalability, and there are some services that are AZ dependent, meaning that you will have to choose an AZ where you plan to deploy the resources.

> If a managed service has multiple AZs built into it, then there is no additional cost for data transfer between AZs, whereas applications you deploy across multiple AZs will incur AZ data transfer charges. Similarly, data getting transferred between AWS Regions also incurs data transfer charges.

Please refer to the AWS documentation (*https://oreil.ly/gVLJn*) to identify the list of Regions and Availability Zones available across the world.

Getting Started with AWS

AWS outlines a sequence of steps (*https://oreil.ly/RlX19*) to onboard someone new to it. At a high level, here are the steps you will need to take to get started with AWS:

1. Set up an AWS account.
2. Configure access with AWS IAM.
3. Choose the primary AWS Region for your account.
4. Provision compute and storage services as per your needs.

As you continue to operate, there are a few best practices you can follow for operational efficiency, such as:

- Defining a budget in AWS Budget and monitoring cost using AWS Cost Explorer
- Having a tagging strategy to tag resources by team, application, and other criteria for cost reporting
- Implementing logging with Amazon CloudWatch and audit reporting with AWS CloudTrail
- Having a disaster recovery strategy for your application data and workloads so you can recover within a defined recovery point objective (RPO) and recovery time objective (RTO)
- Implementing security controls by leveraging AWS security best practices and integrating AWS security services
- Optimizing cost by monitoring your usage and integrating serverless services, utilizing capacity reservations, integrating autoscaling, and optimizing storage costs

Next, let's look at how you can set up an AWS account.

How to Set Up an AWS Account

An AWS account is a formal business relationship with AWS. To set up an account, you will need to provide the following details:

- Root user email address
- AWS account name
- Address
- Phone number

Navigate to the Amazon Web Services home page (*https://aws.amazon.com*) and click "Create account" to get started. You need to specify the root email address and verify the email address to proceed. You can follow the detailed steps outlined in the AWS documentation (*https://oreil.ly/nwVb9*) to create an account.

> Please note AWS offers a Free Tier for more than 100 AWS products. Please refer to the AWS website (*https://oreil.ly/ycBZd*) to identify which AWS services are eligible for the Free Tier and how much free credit they offer.

The following are a few of the best practices you can follow while setting up your AWS account:

- If the AWS account is for a business, then it is important that you use a corporate email address that is managed by a group and a corporate phone number instead of any individual employee's details, so that you can retain the account even if the employee leaves the organization.

- To keep your account secure, turn on multifactor authentication (MFA) for the root user after signing in to the AWS console. It provides additional security in case your password gets compromised.

- If you have multiple business units or workloads that need to be isolated through multiple AWS accounts, then it is recommended to leverage AWS Organizations (*https://oreil.ly/tbRLx*), which enables you to link accounts with parent–child relationships for better structure and governance. In addition, leverage AWS Control Tower (*https://oreil.ly/DGC5S*) to set up a multiaccount environment quickly.

- Understand the AWS Shared Responsibility Model (*https://oreil.ly/GMt3G*) to be clear on what part of cloud security is owned by AWS and how you can follow security best practices to secure your AWS account and deployed resources.

Next, let's learn how you can configure access using AWS IAM.

Configure Access with AWS IAM

AWS Identity and Access Management is a global AWS service that helps to define and manage access to AWS resources using IAM users, groups, policies, and roles. To define permissions, you need to create an IAM policy that includes the AWS service, the service action you plan to allow, and the specific resource ID with any optional permission boundaries. The root user of the AWS account ideally has all permissions to all the AWS services.

You can leverage AWS IAM features at no additional cost and most AWS services support authorization with AWS IAM. For a complete list of services that support AWS IAM, please refer to the AWS documentation (*https://oreil.ly/gY9vy*).

Create an IAM User for Authentication

You can create an AWS IAM user using AWS console, AWS CLI, or AWS APIs and then attach policies to it or to the role the user is going to assume to manage access. It is recommended to follow the least-privilege access principle and provide AWS console access or access keys to users based on need. Users should change their password after first login and enable MFA for better security.

You can also integrate your existing Active Directory with AWS Identity Center, which allows your existing corporate users to sign in to AWS using the same corporate credentials.

Add Permissions to Authorize the User

Before you add permissions, you need to first come up with a strategy on how many policies, roles, and groups you need to create to be able to manage permissions efficiently. Lack of planning may lead to duplicate policies and too many permissions to maintain and will create operational overhead and security risk in the future. Let's understand how IAM policies and roles help define permissions.

What Is an IAM Policy?

An IAM policy is an IAM entity that enables combining multiple permissions to create an object, which can be assigned to an IAM user, role, or group. This improves operational efficiency as you do not need to attach individual permissions to users or roles, rather you can group permissions that serve the need of a specific function. Most policies are stored as JSON documents in AWS.

AWS IAM supports three types of policies:

AWS-managed policies
> You can attach these policies to your IAM user or role directly, but you cannot modify them.

Customer-managed policies
> You can create these policies to meet your specific requirements.

Inline policies
> You can add these policies to an IAM user or role directly. They are not available for attachment to other users or roles.

What Is an IAM Role?

An IAM role is an IAM entity that you can attach multiple IAM policies or permissions to, so that different end users can assume the IAM roles to interact with AWS services.

IAM roles provide several benefits, such as:

- Providing efficiency, as you can avoid attaching the same set of permissions to all users, reducing operational overhead
- Improving security posture, as you can avoid providing long-term credentials as users can use temporary credentials when they assume the role
- Enabling you to delegate access to users, applications, or services that do not have access to AWS resources

Next, let's learn some of the best practices you can follow while integrating AWS IAM.

Best Practices to Follow with AWS IAM

The following are a few of the best practices you can follow while configuring access to AWS IAM:

- Enable MFA for IAM users to achieve tighter security for authentication.
- Instead of attaching permissions or policies directly to the user, it is recommended to create IAM roles and let the user assume roles for different actions.
- Implement least-privilege permission, meaning that you should grant only the required specific permissions, instead of providing broader permissions. For example, a user who needs read-only access to a specific Amazon S3 bucket should not get full S3 permission for that bucket, or an IAM user needing AWS console access should not create access keys.
- Let human users use federation with an identity provider to access AWS using temporary credentials instead of using IAM users with long-term credentials. You should use IAM users only for specific use cases (*https://oreil.ly/MQPWB*) that are not supported by federated users.
- Leverage IAM Identity Center as a centralized way to manage users across multiple AWS accounts or to easily connect to your existing SAML 2.0 identity provider.
- Add metadata to IAM users, so that you can do user-based audit reporting.

You can read more about AWS IAM in the AWS IAM documentation (*https://oreil.ly/8_AFY*).

Conclusion

In this chapter, we have explained some of the prerequisite knowledge that you should have before diving deep into AWS. We provided an overview of the different types of databases and discussed how big data and distributed processing frameworks help with OLAP. We also showed different ways to ingest data, and how to work with code repositories. Then we explained what benefits cloud computing provides over self-managed on-premises infrastructure. We also provided an overview of AWS and how to get started with it.

This chapter will help refresh your fundamentals and provide a stepping stone before you learn about different AWS services in Chapter 3.

Resources

The following are a few additional resources that will help you dive deeper and gain more knowledge on the fundamentals of databases, data lakes, data warehouses, and more:

- NoSQL databases (*https://oreil.ly/S5zdf*)
- Key-value stores (*https://oreil.ly/bnl6P*)
- Document databases (*https://oreil.ly/45Jg2*)
- Graph databases (*https://oreil.ly/K1YgQ*)
- In-memory databases (*https://oreil.ly/tuNcm*)
- Search databases (*https://oreil.ly/y7hka*)
- OLAP versus OLTP (*https://oreil.ly/HLtKq*)
- Data lakes (*https://oreil.ly/_dd2A*)
- Data warehouses (*https://oreil.ly/MS9_f*)
- "Getting Started with an AWS Account" (*https://oreil.ly/PRqKM*)
- AWS Identity and Access Management (*https://oreil.ly/Ewqx8*)

## CHAPTER 3

Overview of AWS Analytics and Auxiliary Services

This chapter aims to equip you with foundational knowledge of the primary AWS services in scope for the AWS Certified Data Engineer Associate certification. We will explore key analytics services, including Amazon Redshift, Amazon Athena, Amazon EMR, and AWS Glue, among others, highlighting their core functionalities and roles within a modern data architecture. By understanding these services, you will gain insights into how AWS enables scalable, flexible, and cost-effective data analysis solutions.

Additionally, we will dive into auxiliary services that enhance and support analytics workloads, such as Amazon S3 for data storage, AWS Lambda for serverless processing, and AWS IAM for security and access management. This comprehensive overview will include reference architectures to illustrate how users can integrate these services to build robust and efficient analytics solutions.

By the end of this chapter, you will be well versed in the AWS analytics landscape, prepared to design and implement data engineering solutions that leverage the full power of AWS, thus laying a strong foundation for your certification journey.

AWS Analytics Services

AWS provides a comprehensive set of analytics services (*https://oreil.ly/bZpuG*) designed to meet all your data analytics needs, enabling organizations of all sizes and industries to reinvent their business with data. With the broadest selection of analytics services, AWS empowers users to process, analyze, and visualize vast amounts of data efficiently and effectively. These managed services are not only cost-effective but also simplify data management across various data stores and data lakes, ensuring seamless integration and accessibility. Moreover, AWS analytics services offer extension points to machine learning and generative AI services, allowing businesses to derive deeper insights and drive innovation. This section will dive into the key AWS analytics services, exploring their features, benefits, and use cases to help you harness the full potential of your data.

Amazon Kinesis Data Streams

Amazon Kinesis Data Streams (*https://oreil.ly/_obJz*) is a real-time, fully managed, and scalable data streaming service that allows you to collect, process, and analyze data continuously. It enables organizations to ingest and analyze data streams from a wide variety of sources, such as website clickstreams, database event logs, financial transactions, social media feeds, and IoT devices. With its ability to handle large volumes of data in real time, Kinesis Data Streams allows businesses to gain timely insights and react to new information almost instantaneously.

Feature highlights include:

Easy administration
> Amazon Kinesis Data Streams simplifies the administration of real-time data streaming. The service is fully managed, meaning you do not need to worry about provisioning, managing, or maintaining the infrastructure. You can focus on building and deploying your applications. This ease of administration reduces operational overhead and allows you to rapidly develop and iterate on your streaming applications.

Native AWS services integration
> Amazon Kinesis Data Streams integrates natively with a range of other AWS services, creating a seamless and cohesive ecosystem for your data streaming needs. You can ingest data from AWS IoT Core, Amazon CloudWatch Logs, or Amazon Database Migration Service, and process it with AWS Lambda, Amazon Firehose, or Amazon Managed Service for Apache Flink. These native integrations enable you to leverage the full power of the AWS ecosystem to build comprehensive, end-to-end data processing and analytics solutions.

Autoscaling with on-demand mode
> Amazon Kinesis Data streams in the on-demand mode (*https://oreil.ly/nioTs*) require no capacity planning and automatically scale to handle gigabytes of write and read throughput per minute. This means that your data streams can handle spikes in traffic without any manual intervention. The on-demand capacity mode is ideal for workloads with unpredictable traffic patterns, ensuring that you always have the capacity you need without overprovisioning resources.

Flexible retention options

Amazon Kinesis Data Streams provides flexible data retention options, allowing you to retain data in your streams from 24 hours up to 7 days by default, and up to 365 days with extended retention. This flexibility enables you to revisit and reprocess data as needed, supporting use cases like troubleshooting, historical analysis, and replays of data streams for machine learning model training.

Reduced latency with enhanced fan-out

The enhanced fan-out feature (*https://oreil.ly/xTL_a*) in Amazon Kinesis Data Streams significantly reduces latency by providing dedicated throughput per consumer. Each consumer can receive up to 2 MB/second per shard, ensuring that multiple consuming applications can process the data stream concurrently without being throttled. This feature is particularly beneficial for high-throughput, low-latency applications, such as real-time analytics and complex event processing.

Some common use cases for this service include:

Streaming log and event data

Ingest and collect terabytes of data per day from application and service logs, clickstream data, sensor data, and in-app user events to power live dashboards, generate metrics, and deliver data into data lakes.

Powering event-driven applications

Build applications that process and react to data in real time, such as monitoring systems, fraud detection, and customer experience personalization.

Evolving from batch to real-time analytics

Transition from traditional batch processing to real-time data analytics, enabling faster decision making and more timely insights.

Amazon Data Firehose

Amazon Data Firehose (*https://oreil.ly/jPVO6*), previously known as Amazon Kinesis Data Firehose, is a fully managed near-real-time streaming ETL (extract, transform, and load) service. It simplifies the process of capturing, transforming, and loading vast volumes of streaming data from various sources into data lakes, data warehouses, and analytics services. Amazon Data Firehose continuously processes data streams, automatically scales based on the data volume, and delivers data within seconds.

Feature highlights for this service include:

Native integration with AWS services

Amazon Data Firehose natively integrates with various AWS services, facilitating seamless data flow and processing. It can ingest data from sources like Amazon MSK and Amazon Kinesis Data Streams, apply lightweight transformations using AWS Lambda, and deliver data to destinations such as Amazon S3, Amazon Redshift, and Amazon OpenSearch Service. This tight integration within the AWS ecosystem streamlines the process of building comprehensive data pipelines.

Integration with popular third-party destinations

Besides AWS services, Amazon Data Firehose integrates with popular third-party services (*https://oreil.ly/D-nUA*), enabling versatile data streaming solutions. You can configure Data Firehose to deliver data to third-party destinations such as Splunk, Datadog, Snowflake, MongoDB, and New Relic. This integration extends the utility of Data Firehose, allowing you to leverage various tools for data analysis, monitoring, and visualization.

Easy to set up

Amazon Data Firehose is designed to be straightforward and user-friendly, requiring no custom code to set up data streams. You can configure data producers to send data to Data Firehose, and it automatically handles data capture, transformation, and delivery. This ease of use allows you to quickly start loading stream data without extensive development efforts.

Serverless

As a fully managed, serverless service, Amazon Data Firehose removes the complexity of managing the underlying infrastructure. It automatically scales to match the throughput of your data streams and adjusts capacity based on the incoming data volume.

Enable lightweight transformation

Amazon Data Firehose allows for lightweight data transformations before loading the data into the final destination. You can use AWS Lambda functions to perform operations like data formatting, filtering, and enrichment. Additionally, Data Firehose buffers incoming data to optimize data delivery based on the destination's requirements, ensuring efficient and reliable data processing.

Some common use cases for this service include:

Streaming into data lakes and warehouses

Seamlessly load streaming data into Amazon S3 and Amazon Redshift for long-term storage, analytics, and reporting.

Streaming log data into SIEM tools

Deliver log data from applications and infrastructure to security information and event management (SIEM) tools like Splunk for real-time security monitoring and analysis.

Amazon Managed Service for Apache Flink

Amazon Managed Service for Apache Flink (*https://oreil.ly/mOM4H*), previously known as Amazon Kinesis Data Analytics, is a fully managed service that simplifies building and running real-time streaming applications with Apache Flink. Amazon Managed Service for Apache Flink provides the underlying infrastructure for your Apache Flink applications. By leveraging Amazon Managed Service for Apache Flink, you can process gigabytes of data per second with subsecond latencies and respond to events in real time, enabling you to make real-time decisions and insights.

Feature highlights include:

Fully compatible with Apache Flink
Apache Flink (*https://flink.apache.org*) is an open source distributed processing engine, offering powerful programming interfaces for both stream and batch processing. It supports complex event processing, data enrichment, and machine learning on streaming data. A standout feature of Flink is its support for *stateful computing*, which allows applications to maintain and manage state information over time, enabling critical tasks such as session management, anomaly detection, and complex event processing. Additionally, Apache Flink ensures *exactly-once processing*, which guarantees that each event is processed precisely once, even in the case of failures or retries. This ensures data consistency and reliability, making Flink an ideal choice for building fault-tolerant, real-time data processing applications that require high accuracy and precision.

Interactive development experience with Studio notebook
The Studio notebook feature (*https://oreil.ly/TTUYq*) in Amazon Managed Service for Apache Flink provides an interactive development environment that allows customers to build, test, and deploy real-time streaming applications with ease. Powered by Apache Zeppelin, the Studio notebook supports SQL, Python, and Scala, enabling users to write and run code in a serverless environment without worrying about infrastructure management. This feature is particularly beneficial for data scientists and developers who need to iterate quickly, visualize results, and experiment with different data transformations in real time.

Flexible APIs with multilanguage support
Amazon Managed Service for Apache Flink offers flexible APIs in Java, Scala, Python, and SQL specialized for different use cases including stateful event processing, streaming ETL, and real-time analytics. This feature significantly reduces development time and fosters collaboration among teams with diverse skill sets.

AWS service integrations with connectors
Amazon Managed Service for Apache Flink offers seamless integration with various AWS services through a rich set of built-in connectors. These connectors enable you to easily ingest and process streaming data from sources like Amazon

Kinesis Data Streams and Amazon Managed Streaming for Apache Kafka and deliver the processed data to destinations such as Amazon S3, Amazon Redshift, and Amazon OpenSearch Service. By leveraging these connectors, customers can quickly deploy scalable, real-time analytics and processing solutions that are deeply integrated with their existing AWS infrastructure, ensuring consistency, reliability, and ease of use across their data workflows.

Some common use cases for this service include:

Real-time analytics
Amazon Managed Service for Apache Flink is commonly used for real-time analytics, where it processes continuous data streams to generate immediate insights. This is crucial for applications such as monitoring user activity on websites, tracking financial transactions, or analyzing sensor data from IoT devices. Flink's ability to handle high-throughput data with low latency ensures that businesses can react quickly to changing conditions and make data-driven decisions in real time.

Fraud detection
Flink's stateful processing capabilities make it ideal for detecting fraudulent activities in real time. By continuously analyzing patterns across multiple data streams, such as transactions or login attempts, Flink can identify anomalies and trigger alerts when suspicious behavior is detected.

Event-driven applications
Amazon Managed Service for Apache Flink is often used to power event-driven architectures where applications need to respond to specific events or triggers in real time. This is especially useful in scenarios such as dynamic pricing, personalized recommendations, or automated responses in customer service. By processing events as they happen, Flink enables businesses to offer highly responsive and personalized user experiences, enhancing customer satisfaction and engagement.

Amazon Managed Streaming for Apache Kafka

Amazon Managed Streaming for Apache Kafka (Amazon MSK) (*https://oreil.ly/ yd2Mz*) is a fully managed service that simplifies the process of building and running applications that use Apache Kafka to process real-time streaming data. Amazon MSK provides high availability, security, and seamless integration with other AWS services, making it an ideal choice for enterprises looking to implement event-driven architectures and real-time data processing pipelines.

Feature highlights include:

Fully compatible with Apache Kafka
Apache Kafka (*https://oreil.ly/203_E*) is a distributed, open source event streaming platform used by organizations to build real-time data pipelines and streaming applications. It is highly scalable, fault-tolerant, and designed to handle high-throughput, low-latency data streaming.

Amazon MSK runs native versions of Apache Kafka, ensuring complete compatibility with existing Kafka applications and tools. This means you can migrate your Kafka workloads to AWS without any code changes and continue using familiar custom and community-built tools such as MirrorMaker. Additionally, MSK integrates with AWS security features like VPC isolation, encryption, and IAM-based access control, making it easier to secure your Kafka workloads while focusing on innovation and real-time data processing.

Managed scaling with Amazon MSK Serverless
Amazon MSK Serverless is an option within Amazon MSK that automatically scales your Kafka workloads based on demand, eliminating the need to manually manage cluster capacity. This feature allows you to handle variable workloads efficiently, optimizing costs and performance.

Extended data retention with tiered storage
Amazon MSK offers tiered storage (*https://oreil.ly/bB2Hh*), which enables you to retain data for extended periods cost-effectively. With tiered storage, older data is automatically moved to a lower-cost storage tier. This feature is particularly useful for applications that require long-term storage of streaming data, such as for compliance or historical analysis.

Amazon MSK Connect
Amazon MSK Connect (*https://oreil.ly/M7_x8*) is a managed feature of Amazon MSK that streamlines streaming data between Apache Kafka and various sources or destinations. It simplifies deployment and management of Kafka connectors without handling infrastructure, allowing seamless integration with AWS services. MSK Connect offers scalability, security, and reliability, making it ideal for real-time data movement across diverse applications and platforms.

Automated data replication with Amazon MSK Replicator
Amazon MSK Replicator provides a fully managed solution for replicating data across Amazon MSK clusters, even across different AWS Regions. This feature ensures data consistency and availability across multiple locations, enabling disaster recovery scenarios and global data distribution. It also simplifies the migration process for your Kafka workloads.

Some common use cases for this service include:

Real-time data analytics and processing
Amazon MSK enables organizations to ingest, process, and analyze large volumes of data in real time, providing valuable insights for business intelligence and decision making. This capability is particularly valuable in industries such as ecommerce and fintech for real-time analysis of user behavior, driving personalized recommendations and fraud detection.

Building event-driven architectures and microservices
Amazon MSK provides a robust foundation for implementing event-driven architectures and microservices. By using MSK as an event hub, developers can decouple different components of their applications, allowing for independent scaling and easier maintenance. This architecture style is particularly beneficial for large-scale, distributed systems where loose coupling between services is essential for agility and scalability.

Implementing change data capture (CDC)
Amazon MSK facilitates efficient CDC processes, enabling real-time database replication and synchronization across different systems. By streaming database changes through MSK, organizations can maintain consistent data across multiple data stores, power real-time analytics on operational data, and implement robust disaster recovery solutions.

Powering IoT data streaming solutions
Amazon MSK serves as a scalable and reliable platform for ingesting and processing data from IoT devices, enabling real-time device monitoring and management. Organizations can build sophisticated IoT applications that provide real-time insights, predictive maintenance capabilities, and automated responses to device events by using MSK to handle high-volume, high-velocity data streams generated by IoT sensors and devices.

Reference Architecture: Streaming Analytics Pattern with Apache Flink and MSK

The following reference architecture illustrates a streaming analytics pipeline employing Amazon MSK and Amazon Managed Service for Apache Flink for real-time fraud detection. As you'll see in Figure 3-1, events are ingested through an API Gateway and then streamed into Amazon MSK. Subsequently, Apache Flink applications perform real-time computations, such as anomaly detection or data enrichment, utilizing reference data from Amazon S3.

The processed output supports three primary use cases: (1) delivering fraud detection notifications via Lambda and Amazon SNS; (2) enabling real-time search and reporting with Amazon OpenSearch Service; and (3) facilitating long-term log storage in Amazon S3. This architecture is well suited for event-driven applications, fraud monitoring, and the processing of high-velocity logs.

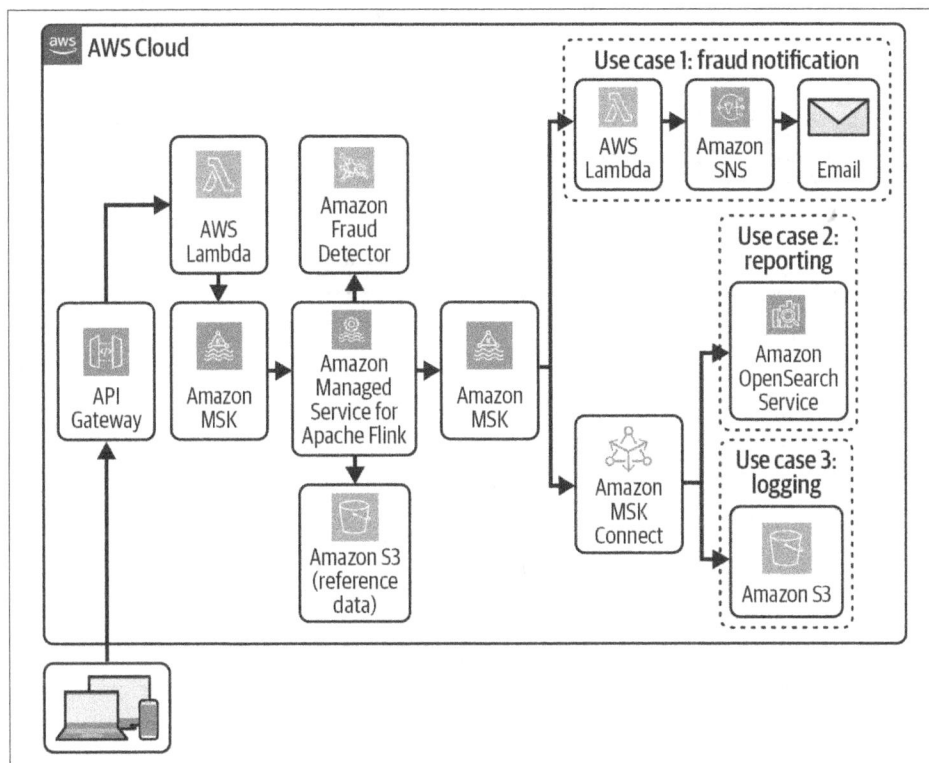

Figure 3-1. Real-time fraud detection system

AWS Glue

AWS Glue (*https://oreil.ly/sS3Cl*) is a fully managed, serverless data integration service that simplifies the process of discovering, preparing, and loading data for analytics. As you'll see in Figure 3-2, AWS Glue provides a comprehensive suite of tools, including a data catalog, ETL capabilities, and support for event-driven workflows, enabling data engineers to quickly and easily build scalable and cost-effective data pipelines. Glue reduces the time and effort required to prepare data, allowing teams to focus more on deriving insights and less on managing infrastructure.

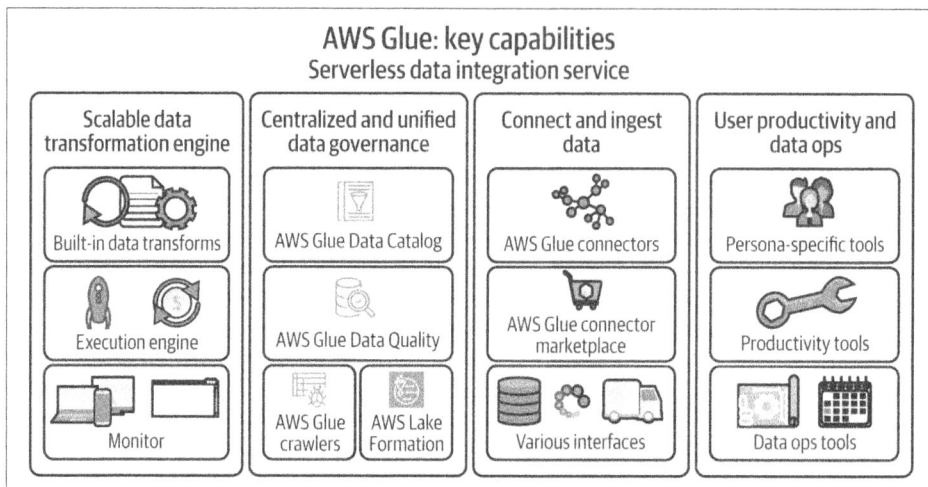

AWS Glue: key capabilities
Serverless data integration service

Scalable data transformation engine	Centralized and unified data governance	Connect and ingest data	User productivity and data ops
Built-in data transforms	AWS Glue Data Catalog	AWS Glue connectors	Persona-specific tools
Execution engine	AWS Glue Data Quality	AWS Glue connector marketplace	Productivity tools
Monitor	AWS Glue crawlers / AWS Lake Formation	Various interfaces	Data ops tools

Figure 3-2. AWS Glue key capabilities

Feature highlights include:

Scalable data transformation engine
AWS Glue features a robust, serverless ETL engine that supports various deployment options to match different workload requirements. For batch processing, Glue provides Apache Spark–based ETL jobs that can efficiently handle large-scale data transformations. For real-time data processing, Glue Streaming ETL uses Apache Spark Structured Streaming to manage continuous data flows. Additionally, Glue offers lightweight Python shell jobs for simpler transformations. This versatility allows organizations to select the most appropriate processing model for their specific needs.

Centralized technical catalog and unified data quality control
AWS Glue provides a centralized platform for managing and governing your data assets. The AWS Glue Data Catalog serves as a centralized technical metadata repository. Glue Crawlers automatically discover, catalog, and classify data from various sources, populating the Glue Data Catalog with schema definitions and metadata. This catalog integrates seamlessly with AWS Lake Formation and Amazon DataZone, providing fine-grained access control and enabling data sharing. Glue Data Quality features allow you to define, run, and monitor data quality rules, ensuring the integrity and reliability of your data assets. This unified approach enhances data discovery, compliance, and consistent management practices across the organization.

Tailored ETL interfaces

AWS Glue enhances user productivity by providing a variety of interfaces tailored to different personas, including data engineers, data scientists, and data analysts. AWS Glue Studio offers a visual drag-and-drop interface for designing ETL workflows, while notebooks and interactive sessions cater to those who prefer a code-centric approach. Additionally, AWS Glue includes robust monitoring and logging capabilities, allowing users to track job performance, troubleshoot issues, and ensure that data operations run smoothly and efficiently.

Connect and ingest data with ease

AWS Glue simplifies the process of connecting to and ingesting data from a wide array of sources through its extensive library of built-in connectors. These connectors support a broad range of data stores, including relational databases, NoSQL databases, data warehouses, and SaaS applications. Glue's ability to connect effortlessly to diverse data sources and ingest data in various formats reduces the complexity of data integration projects and accelerates time-to-insight for analytics initiatives.

Some common use cases for this service include:

Building and managing data lakes

AWS Glue is often used to build and manage data lakes on AWS. By automating the discovery, cataloging, and transformation of data, AWS Glue simplifies the creation of a data lake, allowing organizations to quickly ingest, store, and analyze large volumes of data from various sources. Glue's integration with services like Amazon Athena and Amazon Redshift enables efficient querying of the data lake, supporting a wide range of analytics use cases from ad-hoc queries to complex data science projects.

Data warehouse ETL

AWS Glue simplifies the process of loading and transforming data for data warehousing solutions like Amazon Redshift and Snowflake. It efficiently extracts data from various sources, performs necessary transformations such as data cleansing and format conversion, and loads the processed data into data warehouse tables. Glue's ability to automate ETL code generation and support incremental data loading is particularly valuable for maintaining up-to-date data warehouses.

Real-time data processing

AWS Glue supports real-time data processing scenarios where data needs to be ingested, transformed, and analyzed on the fly. For example, Glue can process streaming data from sources like Amazon Kinesis or Amazon MSK, perform transformations with Apache Spark Structured Streaming, and load the results into analytics-ready destinations.

Data preparation for machine learning

Data preparation is a crucial step in the machine learning (ML) process. AWS Glue's ability to clean, normalize, and transform large datasets makes it an excellent tool for feature engineering and data preprocessing. Glue's integration with Amazon SageMaker streamlines the process of moving prepared data to ML training environments, accelerating the development and deployment of machine learning models.

Data integration from multiple sources

AWS Glue allows organizations to easily extract, transform, and load (ETL) data from a wide range of sources, such as on-premises databases, cloud data stores, and third-party applications. It enables automated schema discovery and provides prebuilt transformations to streamline data integration. This use case is essential for businesses looking to consolidate data into a unified format for analytics or reporting.

AWS Glue DataBrew

AWS Glue DataBrew (*https://oreil.ly/oeu7H*) is a visual data preparation tool that allows users to clean, normalize, and transform data without writing any code. With over 250 prebuilt transformations, DataBrew empowers users of all skill levels to prepare data quickly and efficiently for analytics, machine learning, and other data-driven projects. While AWS Glue (as introduced in the preceding section) is tailored for developers, engineers, and analysts building scalable ETL pipelines, DataBrew is designed for those who prefer a no-code, visual interface for interactive data preparation.

Feature highlights include:

Visual data exploration and profiling

AWS Glue DataBrew offers robust data profiling capabilities. Users can quickly understand data distributions, identify outliers, and detect data quality issues through its interactive visualizations. The service generates detailed profile reports that include column-level statistics, data type suggestions, and correlation analysis. These features enable users to gain a comprehensive understanding of their data's characteristics, facilitating informed decisions about necessary data transformations and cleansing steps.

No-code data transformation

AWS Glue DataBrew enables users to perform complex data transformations without writing code. Its drag-and-drop interface allows users to apply a wide range of transformations—such as filtering, grouping, joining, and pivoting data—using a library of over 250 prebuilt functions. This feature empowers users, regardless of their technical expertise, to execute advanced data preparation tasks efficiently.

Automated data quality and validation

AWS Glue DataBrew includes automated data quality checks and validation rules that can be applied to datasets. Users can define custom data quality rules based on their specific requirements, such as value ranges, data formats, or business logic. This feature ensures that the resulting datasets meet predefined quality standards, enhancing the reliability of downstream analytics and machine learning processes.

Reproducible and auditable workflows

AWS Glue DataBrew enables the creation of reusable recipes, which are sequences of data transformation steps that can be applied to multiple datasets or rerun on updated data. This automation reduces manual intervention and ensures consistency in data preparation. The service also maintains detailed logs of all data preparation activities, supporting audit requirements and enabling users to track changes over time.

Some common use cases for this service include:

Ad-hoc data exploration and analysis

Data analysts frequently use AWS Glue DataBrew for ad-hoc data exploration and analysis. The ability to quickly profile and transform datasets allows analysts to gain insights into data patterns, identify trends, and prepare data for more in-depth analysis.

Data preparation for business intelligence (BI) reporting

AWS Glue DataBrew transforms raw data into structured formats that can be easily ingested by BI tools. By applying transformations such as aggregations, calculations, and data enrichment, users ensure that the data used in dashboards and reports is accurate, consistent, and up-to-date, leading to more reliable business insights.

Data cleaning and preprocessing for machine learning
> AWS Glue DataBrew is often used to clean and normalize data before feeding it into machine learning models. By applying transformations like handling missing values, standardizing formats, and normalizing distributions, DataBrew ensures that the dataset is in optimal condition for training accurate and reliable models.

Amazon Athena

Amazon Athena (*https://oreil.ly/ZxJNV*) is a serverless, interactive analytics service built on open source frameworks, supporting open table and file formats. It enables users to analyze petabytes of data in Amazon S3 and 30 other data sources, including on-premises and cloud systems, using SQL or Python. Built on Trino, Presto, and Apache Spark, Athena requires no infrastructure management, offering a simplified way to query data where it resides. Its pay-per-query pricing model and support for various data formats provide a cost-effective and flexible solution for ad-hoc analysis, log processing, and building data-driven applications.

Feature highlights include:

Serverless SQL query engine
> Athena's core functionality is its serverless SQL query engine, which allows users to analyze data using ANSI SQL. It supports a wide range of data formats, including CSV, JSON, ORC, Avro, and Parquet. The service automatically scales to handle query workloads, ensuring high availability and performance. This design, coupled with a pay-per-query pricing model where users are charged only for the amount of data scanned by each query, makes Athena highly cost-effective for ad-hoc analysis and intermittent workloads.

Amazon Athena for Apache Spark
> Amazon Athena offers the ability to run Apache Spark workloads alongside SQL queries. This feature allows data engineers and data scientists to leverage the in-memory processing capabilities of Apache Spark for faster, more complex data transformations and analyses. Athena for Spark provides a simplified notebook experience in the Athena console, with instant-on resources that start in seconds.

Native support for open table formats
> Athena provides native support for open table formats, most notably Apache Iceberg. Iceberg tables offer advanced features like schema evolution, hidden partitioning, and time travel queries. This feature allows users to perform read, time travel, write, and use DDL operations on Iceberg tables directly through Athena.

Federated query and prebuilt data source connectors
Athena's federated query capability, coupled with its wide array of prebuilt data source connectors, enables querying data from various sources beyond Amazon S3 without data movement. With connectors for popular systems like Amazon DynamoDB, Amazon Redshift, MySQL, and PostgreSQL, Athena allows joining data from multiple origins in a single query. This feature provides a unified interface for querying distributed data ecosystems. It simplifies complex data analysis by eliminating the need for data movement or ETL processes, making Athena a powerful tool for organizations with heterogeneous data environments.

Some common use cases for this service include:

Data lake exploration and analytics
Athena excels in supporting interactive, ad-hoc querying of large datasets stored in S3. Data analysts and business users can quickly explore data, test hypotheses, and answer business questions without the need for complex ETL processes or data warehousing solutions. The ability to run SQL queries directly on data in S3 enables rapid insight generation, supporting agile decision-making processes across various business functions.

Business intelligence reporting
Users can easily integrate Athena with BI tools like Amazon QuickSight to power dashboards and reports. The ability to query data directly in S3, coupled with Athena's support for various data formats and open table standards, ensures that your BI tools are always accessing up-to-date data.

Log analysis and operational intelligence
Organizations frequently use Athena to analyze log and event data stored in Amazon S3. Whether it's analyzing application logs, security events, or user activity logs, Athena provides the ability to query and filter large volumes of log data quickly. This enables teams to troubleshoot issues, monitor systems, and generate reports without setting up complex data pipelines. However, for scenarios that require keyword search, Amazon OpenSearch may be a more efficient choice due to its optimized search engine.

Amazon EMR

As shown in Figure 3-3, Amazon EMR (Elastic MapReduce) (*https://oreil.ly/9VhJC*) is a cloud-native big data platform that simplifies the processing and analysis of vast amounts of data. It manages the complexities of running popular open source frameworks like Apache Hadoop, Apache Spark, and Presto on dynamically scalable clusters. By abstracting cluster management tasks, EMR allows users to focus on extracting insights from their data efficiently and cost-effectively.

Amazon EMR
Easily run Spark, Hive, Presto, Flink, and more open source framework applications

Latest versions	Best performance at lowest cost	Flexible and versatile	Unified data access with governance
Updated with latest open source frameworks within 90 days Support for popular open table formats like Iceberg, Hudi, and Delta Lake	Spark workloads run 5.5x faster compared to OSS 50-80% reduction in costs with EC2 Spot and Reserved Instances Per-second billing	Run batch, streaming, interactive notebooks, and SQL workloads Choice of deployment options: serverless, EC2, and EKS	Fine-grained access control, using AWS Lake Formation Across frameworks: Spark, Trino

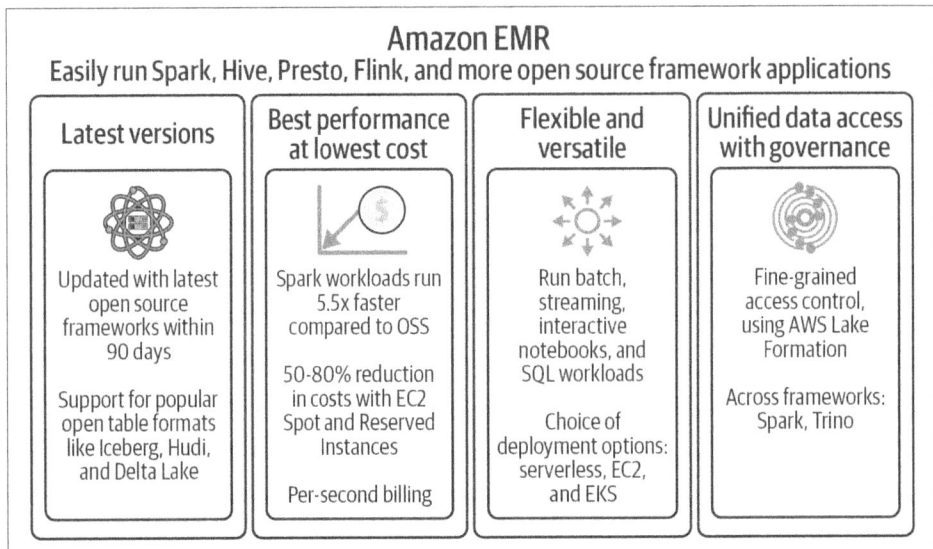

Figure 3-3. Amazon EMR value proposition

Feature highlights include:

Support for multiple big data frameworks
> Amazon EMR natively supports a comprehensive range of open source big data frameworks, including Apache Hadoop, Apache Spark, Apache HBase, Apache Flink, and Presto. It also supports open table formats like Apache Iceberg, Apache Hudi, and Delta Lake, enabling advanced data management features such as time travel and schema evolution. This broad support allows users to efficiently process and analyze large datasets using the most suitable tools for their specific needs.

Versatile workload and user interfaces
> Amazon EMR is designed to handle various workloads, including batch processing, real-time streaming, interactive querying, and machine learning. Users can interact with EMR through multiple interfaces, such as command-line tools, APIs, or interactive notebooks. For SQL-based analytics, EMR integrates with tools like Hive and Presto, allowing users to run interactive queries on massive datasets.

Flexible deployment options
> Amazon EMR offers flexible deployment options to meet different operational needs. You can run EMR on EC2 instances for traditional cluster-based processing, providing full control over the infrastructure. For containerized

environments, EMR on EKS integrates seamlessly with Kubernetes, enabling consistent deployment and management across hybrid environments. Additionally, EMR Serverless provides a fully managed, autoscaling environment, eliminating the need for cluster management. EMR also supports EC2 Spot Instances, offering significant cost savings for fault-tolerant workloads. Amazon EMR on AWS Outposts enables you to run big data applications in on-premises facilities.

Some common use cases for this service include:

Large-scale batch data processing
Amazon EMR is widely used for batch ETL processes, transforming large volumes of raw data into structured formats suitable for analysis. With robust support for Apache Spark and Apache Hadoop, EMR efficiently processes data stored in Amazon S3, enabling companies to extract valuable insights and make data-driven decisions. Its distributed computing capabilities make it ideal for handling large-scale data transformation tasks.

Real-time data processing
Amazon EMR is an excellent choice for real-time data processing, leveraging frameworks like Apache Flink and Apache Spark Streaming. Organizations use EMR to process and analyze streaming data from sources such as IoT devices, clickstreams, and social media feeds.

Big data analytics and machine learning
With its ability to run machine learning frameworks like Apache Spark MLlib, Amazon EMR is often used for big data analytics and machine learning workloads. Data scientists can process large datasets, train models, and perform predictive analytics directly within EMR. Integration with AWS services like Amazon SageMaker enhances EMR's capabilities, enabling end-to-end machine learning workflows from data preparation to model deployment.

Amazon Redshift

Amazon Redshift (*https://oreil.ly/5hvYC*) is a managed, petabyte-scale data warehouse service that enables users to store and analyze large volumes of data using standard SQL. It is designed to handle datasets ranging from a few hundred gigabytes to several petabytes, offering fast query performance through its Massively Parallel Processing (MPP) architecture. As you'll see in Figure 3-4, it integrates seamlessly with other AWS services, making it an ideal solution for businesses looking to leverage cloud-based data warehousing for analytics, reporting, and machine learning needs.

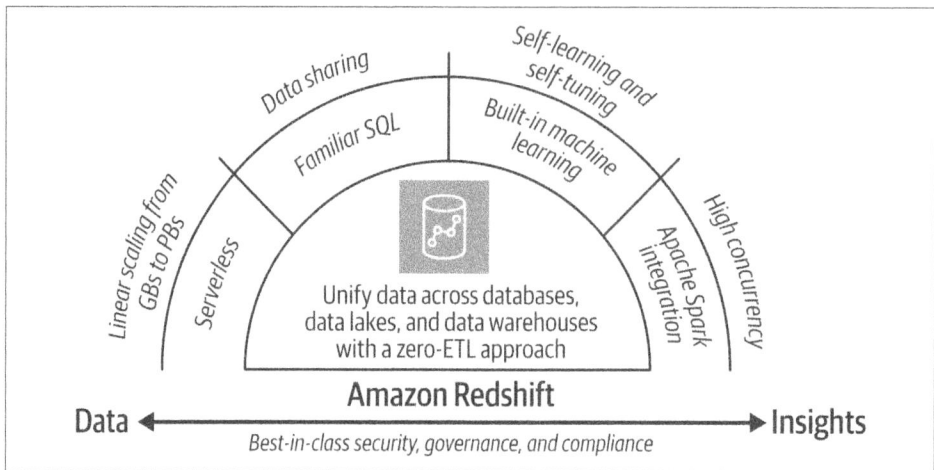

Figure 3-4. Amazon Redshift feature highlights

Feature highlights include:

Scalability and elasticity
> Amazon Redshift offers exceptional scalability and elasticity to meet evolving data warehousing demands. With RA3 instances, Redshift decouples storage and compute, allowing independent scaling for cost efficiency. Redshift Serverless further enhances the storage-compute decoupling by automatically adjusting the compute capacity for analytics workloads without infrastructure management.

Seamless integration with the AWS ecosystem
> Amazon Redshift integrates deeply with the AWS analytics ecosystem. It works cohesively with services like AWS Lake Formation for data governance and Amazon QuickSight for business intelligence. Redshift Spectrum enables you to query and analyze data directly in Amazon S3 without the need to load it into your Redshift cluster. Redshift also supports zero-ETL data ingestion from various data sources like Aurora and DynamoDB, simplifying data collection and loading. This tight integration accelerates analytics workflows and streamlines data management across your AWS environment.

Secured data collaboration
> With Amazon Redshift data sharing (*https://oreil.ly/F4rv8*), you can seamlessly share live data across Redshift clusters, workgroups, AWS accounts, and regions without duplicating or moving the data. This enables database administrators and data engineers to provide secure, real-time access to data for analytics. Data sharing supports both read and write permissions across different clusters, allowing users to access the most up-to-date information immediately after it's committed.

Maximize value with machine learning

Amazon Redshift empowers organizations to maximize the value of their data by integrating machine learning capabilities directly within the data warehouse. With Amazon Redshift ML, you can create, train, and deploy machine learning models using familiar SQL commands. This feature leverages Amazon SageMaker's power without requiring data movement, enabling advanced analytics and predictive insights.

Some common use cases for this service include:

Empowering business intelligence and reporting

Amazon Redshift enhances business intelligence by enabling efficient processing and analysis of large datasets. Its fast query performance and integration with tools like Amazon QuickSight facilitate the creation of detailed dashboards and reports.

Enabling big data analytics

Companies leverage Amazon Redshift for big data analytics on massive datasets. With parallel processing and columnar storage, organizations perform complex queries faster, uncovering patterns and deriving insights from extensive data assets.

Accelerating machine learning with SQL

Amazon Redshift integrates machine learning into SQL workflows, allowing users to build and deploy ML models directly within the data warehouse. Using familiar SQL commands with Redshift ML, they can predict customer behavior or detect anomalies without moving data to separate ML platforms, streamlining predictive analytics.

Monetizing data assets

Redshift facilitates data monetization through secure sharing and collaboration. Integration with AWS Data Exchange allows businesses to license datasets to third parties, creating new revenue streams. By combining internal and external data, organizations can offer enriched products and expand market opportunities.

Amazon QuickSight

Amazon QuickSight (*https://oreil.ly/1JSDc*) empowers organizations with unified business intelligence (BI) at scale. Designed to provide fast, easy-to-understand insights from data, it helps businesses make informed decisions. QuickSight is both scalable and serverless, enabling it to support thousands of users without requiring infrastructure management. With Amazon QuickSight Q, business analysts can use natural language to discover, build, and share insights in seconds.

Feature highlights include:

Serverless and scalable architecture
Amazon QuickSight's serverless architecture allows it to seamlessly accommodate varying numbers of users without requiring manual infrastructure management. This scalability ensures consistent performance, whether you have a handful of users or tens of thousands. In addition to traditional per-user licensing, Quick-Sight offers a cost-effective, pay-per-session pricing model, where organizations are billed only when users access dashboards or reports. This approach reduces costs, especially for organizations with large or fluctuating user bases.

Super-fast, Parallel, In-memory Calculation Engine (SPICE)
QuickSight's SPICE engine delivers rapid data retrieval and analysis at scale. By storing data in-memory, SPICE reduces data load times and accelerates query performance. It automatically replicates data for high availability, allowing thousands of users to simultaneously perform fast, interactive analyses without compromising performance.

Embedded analytics
QuickSight enables organizations to embed interactive dashboards and analytics into their own applications, portals, or websites. This feature allows developers to integrate rich data visualizations directly into their user experience, enhancing engagement and providing immediate insights to end users without the need to switch contexts.

Generative BI
Generative BI, powered by Amazon QuickSight Q, allows users to interact with their data through natural language queries. Users can ask questions in plain English and receive accurate answers in the form of visualizations or narratives, democratizing access to data insights across the organization.

Pixel-perfect reports
Amazon QuickSight allows users to create and deliver pixel-perfect reports tailored to specific formatting and layout requirements. This capability is crucial for organizations needing high-quality reports for regulatory compliance, financial reporting, or executive presentations. QuickSight's comprehensive reporting tools offer detailed customization options to ensure alignment with organizational standards and branding needs.

Some common use cases for this service include:

Business reporting
Organizations use Amazon QuickSight for business reporting by connecting it to operational data warehouses or data lakes on AWS. It provides an efficient way

to generate reports and dashboards that help track performance metrics, visualize trends, and make informed decisions based on real-time data.

Embedded analytics in customer applications
Independent software vendors (ISVs) and enterprises embed QuickSight dashboards into their customer-facing applications to enhance value propositions. By providing users with interactive analytics within the application context, companies improve user engagement and satisfaction.

Reference Architecture: Lakehouse with Glue, Redshift, and Athena

Figure 3-5 illustrates a modern lakehouse setup, combining a centralized Amazon S3 data lake with Amazon Redshift as the data warehouse. Data is initially ingested into the Amazon S3 data lake. Subsequently, an AWS Lambda function triggers AWS Glue jobs to transform the raw data into structured formats, storing the processed data back in Amazon S3 for downstream analytics. Amazon Redshift then consumes this curated data for high-performance SQL analytics. Simultaneously, Amazon Athena enables interactive, serverless querying of raw and semi-structured data directly within Amazon S3.

Amazon QuickSight provides business users and analysts with visualization dashboards, while another AWS Lambda function triggers SPICE refreshes for near-real-time reporting. This architecture supports ad-hoc queries, batch reporting, and BI use cases across large datasets.

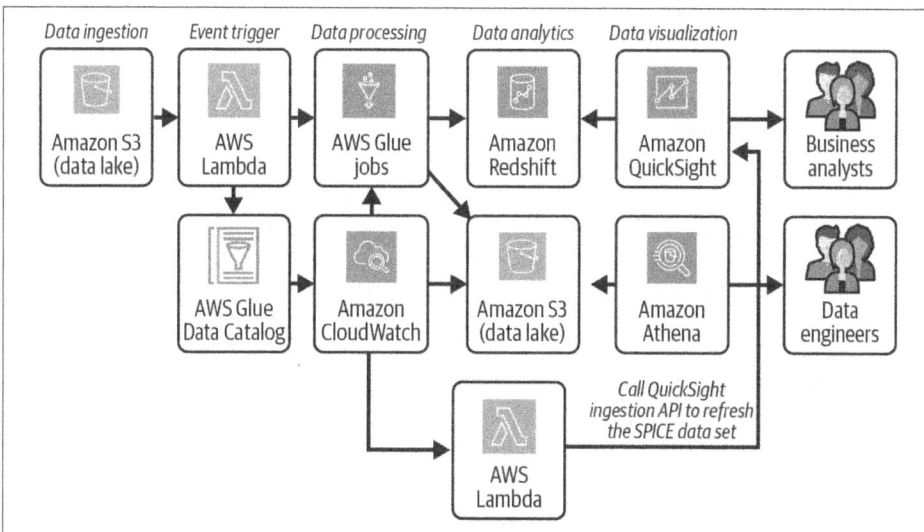

Figure 3-5. Lakehouse pattern with AWS Glue, Amazon Redshift, and Amazon Athena

Amazon OpenSearch Service

Amazon OpenSearch Service (*https://oreil.ly/S_NHG*) is a managed solution that simplifies deploying, operating, and scaling OpenSearch workloads in the cloud. As illustrated in Figure 3-6, OpenSearch, an open source search and observability suite, empowers users to derive insights from large volumes of unstructured data. With built-in visualization tools like OpenSearch Dashboards, users can search, analyze, and explore their data without worrying about infrastructure management complexities.

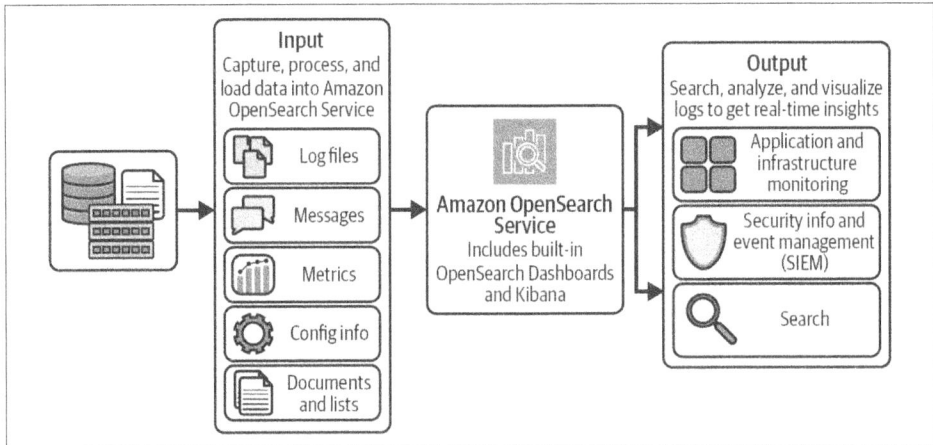

Figure 3-6. Amazon OpenSearch reference use cases

Feature highlights include:

Managed OpenSearch solutions
Amazon OpenSearch Service provides both provisioned OpenSearch clusters and OpenSearch Serverless options, offering flexibility for different workloads. Provisioned clusters suit predictable workloads, while serverless configurations are ideal for dynamic, on-demand scaling, reducing the need for infrastructure management and improving operational efficiency.

Price-performant features
Amazon OpenSearch Service offers multiple features designed to optimize performance and cost. It supports Graviton instances for enhanced performance and cost savings, as well as the OpenSearch-optimized OR1 instance type, designed specifically to deliver superior performance for heavy operational analytics workloads. Additionally, tiered storage allows users to store infrequently accessed data cost-effectively while ensuring fast access to frequently queried data, helping optimize costs for different data patterns.

Managed data ingestion and transformation

Amazon OpenSearch Service streamlines data ingestion through OpenSearch Ingestion, powered by Data Prepper. This fully managed service automates the process of ingesting, filtering, enriching, transforming, and routing data to OpenSearch domains or serverless collections. It scales automatically to accommodate changing data volumes, eliminating the need for managing complex, multinode ingestion pipelines.

Comprehensive security governance

Amazon OpenSearch Service provides comprehensive security governance, including fine-grained access control, encryption at rest and in transit, and integration with AWS Identity and Access Management (IAM). These features ensure that your data remains secure and compliant with industry standards.

Integration with open source tools

OpenSearch Service integrates natively with popular open source tools such as OpenSearch Dashboards for data visualization, and log ingestion solutions like Logstash, Fluent Bit, and Fluentd. This allows users to maintain familiar workflows while leveraging the benefits of a fully managed service.

Some common use cases for this service include:

Log analytics and observability

Amazon OpenSearch Service is ideal for real-time log analytics and system observability. It enables users to monitor application performance, detect security issues, and respond to incidents efficiently by aggregating and analyzing logs from multiple sources in real time. This proactive insight facilitates quick issue resolution, ensuring system health and an improved customer experience.

Lexical search

Amazon OpenSearch Service delivers fast and precise lexical search for applications like ecommerce, content discovery, and document repositories. It supports key search features such as keyword search, fuzzy matching, and auto-completion, allowing users to quickly locate relevant information and improving the overall search experience.

Semantic search and retrieval-augmented generation (RAG)

Amazon OpenSearch's advanced vector search capabilities improve the accuracy of natural language queries. This feature is crucial for applications requiring semantic understanding and context-aware responses, such as personalized recommendations and AI-driven chatbots. It plays a key role in RAG workflows, enhancing the relevance of AI-generated results in knowledge-driven applications.

Amazon DataZone

Amazon DataZone (*https://oreil.ly/vBEWM*) is a data management service designed to streamline cataloging, discovering, governing, and consuming data across various sources, including AWS, on-premises, and third-party platforms. It provides a unified portal for efficient data management, enabling collaboration among data engineers, scientists, analysts, and business users while ensuring appropriate data access and governance.

Feature highlights include:

Managed business data catalog
Amazon DataZone's core feature is its managed business catalog, which provides a centralized repository of data assets enriched with business context. It automatically extracts metadata from sources like data lakes and data warehouses, ensuring that the catalog is always comprehensive and up-to-date. Additionally, Amazon DataZone leverages large language models (LLMs) to recommend accurate metadata, generating consistent business descriptions and names for data assets.

Personalized data portal
The personalized data portal offers a unified interface for data producers and consumers. This web-based application allows users to access, analyze, and collaborate on data assets without logging into the AWS Management Console. Users can search the catalog, request access to data, and perform analyses using tools such as Amazon Redshift or Amazon Athena, all within a single, streamlined environment.

Governed data sharing
Amazon DataZone simplifies data sharing across teams, departments, or business units with fine-grained access control and approval workflows for data subscriptions. Additionally, Amazon DataZone offers the ability to group data assets into predefined data products, simplifying cataloging and discovery for specific business use cases.

Automated data quality and data lineage management
Amazon DataZone provides automated tools for managing both data quality and lineage. Organizations can define rules to assess dataset accuracy, completeness, and consistency. The data lineage capabilities offer an end-to-end view of data movement over time, helping users understand data provenance, trace changes, and conduct root cause analysis.

Some common use cases for this service include:

Enterprise data cataloging
Large enterprises often struggle to maintain visibility into their scattered datasets. Amazon DataZone helps build a unified, searchable data catalog across multiple AWS services. It significantly enhances data discoverability across an organization.

Cross-business unit or cross-account data sharing
Amazon DataZone facilitates secure and governed data sharing across organizational boundaries, enabling self-service access for distributed teams.

Streamlined analytics workflows
Amazon DataZone integrates with AWS analytics services and third-party tools, allowing seamless transitions between different stages of the data lifecycle—from discovery to analysis—without switching contexts.

AWS Lake Formation

AWS Lake Formation (*https://oreil.ly/iyZ7c*) simplifies centralized data governance, security, and global data sharing for analytics and machine learning workloads. It integrates with the AWS Glue Data Catalog, providing a unified platform for managing data permissions with fine-grained access controls. The service facilitates both internal and external data sharing while offering comprehensive auditing by tracking user- and role-based data interactions.

Feature highlights include:

Centralized data permission management
AWS Lake Formation provides a centralized interface to manage permissions for data lakes and data warehouses in AWS. Users can define and manage access controls using database-like grants. This security model applies not only to AWS services such as Amazon Redshift, Amazon Athena, and Amazon EMR, but also extends to third-party platforms like Starburst and Dremio, ensuring a unified security framework for all data consumers.

Advanced data governance at scale
Lake Formation helps organizations implement fine-grained access controls (FGAC) and tag-based access controls (TBAC) for more scalable data governance. With FGAC, users can control access at multiple levels, including database, table, and column levels, allowing for a granular approach to data security. With TBAC, users can label data resources with tags and manage data access based on tags. This feature enables organizations to enforce policies and track compliance effectively across a large number of users and services.

External data sharing

> Lake Formation integrates with AWS Data Exchange to facilitate external data sharing without requiring data movement. This allows organizations to license structured tables to external parties such as partners, vendors, or clients. Data consumers can query and analyze this shared data using Lake Formation–compatible engines like Amazon Athena, reducing ETL overhead and accelerating insights from third-party data.

AWS Lake Formation plays a crucial role in simplifying data governance within and beyond organizational boundaries. Internally, it allows administrators to enforce fine-grained and tag-based access controls across teams and accounts, ensuring users have appropriate access while maintaining compliance. Externally, the integration with AWS Data Exchange enables secure data sharing with partners and clients. This unified approach ensures secure collaboration while meeting both regulatory and organizational requirements.

Auxiliary Services for Analytics

In the previous section, we covered the core AWS analytics services that are in scope for the AWS Certified Data Engineer Associate (DEA-C01) exam. These services provide a comprehensive set of tools for data ingestion, processing, storage, and analysis. However, to build complete and efficient analytics solutions on AWS, it's essential to understand the auxiliary services that work in conjunction with these core analytics offerings.

In this section, we will explore the key auxiliary AWS services that support and enhance analytics workloads. These services span various categories, such as application integration, compute, containers, databases, and more. By leveraging these auxiliary services, you can create robust, scalable, and secure analytics architectures that meet your specific requirements. For a comprehensive list of in-scope AWS services and features for the DEA-C01 exam, refer to the official exam guide (*https://oreil.ly/jUCwO*).

Application Integration

Application integration services enable communication and coordination between applications, microservices, and distributed systems. These services facilitate event-driven architectures, workflow orchestration, and decoupling of components, allowing developers to build scalable, resilient, and modular applications that can respond quickly to changing business needs.

In analytics workloads, application integration services play a crucial role in enabling real-time data ingestion, triggering analytical processes, and orchestrating data pipelines. For example, an organization might use Amazon EventBridge to trigger real-time analytics workflows when new data arrives in an Amazon S3 bucket. Additionally, AWS Step Functions can be used to orchestrate an ETL pipeline that processes data as it becomes available.

The application integration services covered in this certification include:

Amazon EventBridge (https://oreil.ly/MIhU1)
A serverless event bus that enables you to build event-driven architectures by routing events from various sources to target services for processing and analysis. The service makes it easy to connect applications using data from your own applications, integrated SaaS, and AWS services.

Amazon Simple Queue Service (Amazon SQS) (https://oreil.ly/CrCAJ)
A managed message queuing service that enables decoupling and scaling of microservices, distributed systems, and serverless applications. It allows you to send, store, and receive messages between microservices at scale.

Amazon Simple Notification Service (Amazon SNS) (https://oreil.ly/rYlFY)
A managed pub/sub messaging service for application-to-application and application-to-person communication. It enables message fan-out from one producer to multiple subscribers.

Amazon Managed Workflows for Apache Airflow (Amazon MWAA) (https://oreil.ly/8T7ce)
A managed service for Apache Airflow that allows you to orchestrate data pipelines and workflows. With Amazon MWAA, you can design directed acyclic graphs (DAGs) that define and orchestrate your workflows without the operational burden of managing the infrastructure.

AWS Step Functions (https://oreil.ly/XzZ4x)
Acts as a serverless orchestration service that provides tight integration with over 220 AWS services, enabling you to define and execute workflows that automate processes, handle errors, and ensure the proper sequence of steps in your data pipelines.

Amazon AppFlow (https://oreil.ly/OPwD7)
A managed integration service that enables secure and automated data transfer between SaaS applications and AWS services.

Compute and Containers

Compute and container services in AWS form the backbone of cloud-based applications. These services encompass virtual servers, serverless computing, and container orchestration platforms, enabling you to choose the optimal compute model for your workloads. They allow you to run code, manage applications, and process large-scale data efficiently without the overhead of managing physical hardware.

In analytics workloads, these compute services are essential for processing, transforming, and analyzing vast amounts of data, particularly for customers who are self-managing their analytics workloads in the cloud. For example, you can self-manage Amazon EC2 or Amazon EKS clusters to run Spark or Hadoop workloads for distributed data processing. AWS Batch allows you to efficiently orchestrate batch computing jobs, such as data preprocessing or model training. AWS Lambda enables you to run code in response to events, making it ideal for event-level data processing and lightweight transformations.

The key compute and container services include:

Amazon EC2 (https://oreil.ly/pQUXS)
> Provides scalable virtual servers in the cloud, allowing you to launch virtual servers with a wide range of instance types and configurations.

Amazon Elastic Container Service (Amazon ECS) (https://oreil.ly/ANkj9)
> A fully managed container orchestration service that simplifies running and managing Docker containers. It deeply integrates with the AWS environment and provides an easy-to-use solution for running container workloads on AWS.

Amazon Elastic Kubernetes Service (Amazon EKS) (https://oreil.ly/Hy5Mb)
> A managed Kubernetes service that makes it easy for you to run Kubernetes on AWS and on-premises. Amazon EKS manages the availability and scalability of the Kubernetes control plane, making it easy to deploy, manage, and scale containerized workloads.

Amazon Elastic Container Registry (Amazon ECR) (https://oreil.ly/AL_2d)
> A fully managed container registry that makes it easy to store, manage, and deploy container images securely and at scale.

AWS Lambda (https://oreil.ly/IylSZ)
> A serverless compute service that lets you run code without provisioning or managing compute resources. It allows you to take actions in response to events, ideal for event-driven or real-time data processing tasks.

AWS Serverless Application Model (AWS SAM) (https://oreil.ly/oR0UE)
> An open source framework that streamlines the development and deployment of serverless applications, offering a simplified syntax to define functions, APIs, and databases.

AWS Batch (https://oreil.ly/IjWoJ)
> A fully managed batch processing service that dynamically provisions the optimal compute resources based on the volume and specific requirements of the batch jobs you submit. It can provision workloads on ECS clusters, EKS clusters and EC2 instances.

By leveraging these compute and container services, you can build scalable and efficient analytics solutions on AWS, whether you prefer the flexibility of virtual machines, the simplicity of serverless, or the portability of containers.

Database

AWS offers a wide range of database services designed to support diverse data models and workload requirements. These include relational databases, key-value stores, document databases, in-memory data stores, graph databases, and more—providing the flexibility to choose the right tool for each job. By managing the underlying database infrastructure, AWS enables organizations to focus on application development and innovation rather than database administration.

AWS database services are integral to analytics workflows, serving as the original data store for structured and unstructured data. They act as data sources for analytics workloads, enabling real-time analytics, data warehousing, operational analytics, and more. For example, Amazon Aurora powers high-performance transactional workloads for ecommerce or financial applications, while Amazon DynamoDB is ideal for ingesting high-velocity data from web applications, gaming, ad tech, and IoT devices. By integrating these databases with analytics services like Amazon Redshift or AWS Glue, organizations can perform comprehensive data analyzes to support decision making and strategic planning.

Key database services include:

Amazon Relational Database Service (Amazon RDS) (https://oreil.ly/VR5cf)
Simplifies the setup, operation, and scaling of relational databases in the cloud. It supports multiple database engines like MySQL, PostgreSQL, Oracle, and SQL Server.

Amazon Aurora (https://oreil.ly/VSefE)
A high-performance, fully managed relational database compatible with MySQL and PostgreSQL. It offers enhanced speed and availability by separating compute and storage layers, allowing for automatic scaling and replication across multiple Availability Zones.

Amazon DynamoDB (https://oreil.ly/uSkpM)
A fast and flexible key-value database providing single-digit millisecond latency at any scale. It's ideal for applications requiring consistent, low-latency performance.

Amazon DocumentDB (https://oreil.ly/nTsT-)
A fully managed NoSQL database service compatible with MongoDB, optimized for JSON documents and scalable performance.

Amazon Keyspaces (for Apache Cassandra) (https://oreil.ly/_oGb7)
> A scalable, highly available, and managed Apache Cassandra–compatible database service. Apache Cassandra is an open source, distributed NoSQL database engine ideal for handling large volumes of data across many servers without a single point of failure.

Amazon MemoryDB (https://oreil.ly/hxXXt)
> A durable, in-memory database service that delivers ultra-fast performance for modern applications, compatible with Redis data structures and APIs.

Amazon Neptune (https://oreil.ly/eoudF)
> A managed graph database service for building and running applications that work with highly connected datasets, optimized for storing and navigating graph structures.

We will dive into when to use each database in more detail in Chapter 5.

Storage

AWS offers a comprehensive suite of storage services designed to cater to various data types and access patterns. From block-level storage for EC2 instances to object storage for massive amounts of unstructured data, these services provide the flexibility and reliability needed to meet the diverse requirements of modern applications.

In analytics workloads, these storage services are foundational for storing, managing, and archiving data. For example, Amazon S3 is commonly used as the storage layer for data lakes, enabling easy access for analytics services like Amazon Athena. Additionally, Amazon EBS can serve as the underlying storage for Hadoop workloads, allowing for distributed processing of large datasets.

Key storage services include:

Amazon Elastic Block Store (Amazon EBS) (https://oreil.ly/QWzR_)
> Provides easy-to-use, scalable, and high-performance block-storage volumes for Amazon EC2 instances. EBS volumes deliver consistent, low-latency performance, making them suitable for applications that require rapid access to data.

Amazon Elastic File System (Amazon EFS) (https://oreil.ly/mmHJX)
> A scalable, elastic file storage service that lets you share file data across Amazon EC2 instances. It supports the Network File System (NFS) protocol, enabling concurrent access and file sharing among instances.

Amazon S3 (https://oreil.ly/V6kRP)
> An object storage service that allows organizations to store and retrieve any amount of data from anywhere. It offers industry-leading scalability, data

availability, security, and performance, making it ideal as the storage layer for data lakes.

Amazon S3 Glacier (https://oreil.ly/n2g9M)
A secure, durable, and low-cost storage class within Amazon S3 designed for data archiving and backup use cases. It provides a cost-effective solution for infrequently accessed data, with retrieval times ranging from milliseconds to hours.

AWS Backup (https://oreil.ly/XdmtV)
A fully managed backup service that simplifies the creation, management, and restoration of backups across multiple AWS services, including Amazon EBS, Amazon EFS, and Amazon S3. It helps ensure data protection and enables quick recovery in case of disasters.

Machine Learning

Machine learning (ML) is a field of study within artificial intelligence that focuses on developing algorithms using mathematical and statistical models, with an objective to imitate human intelligence. Machine learning models are trained with a huge volume of historical data and are expected to predict future patterns, derive insights, or generate new data. For example, an organization's data science team can train an ML model with the last 10 years of sales data to help them predict the sales growth in the next quarter. The accuracy of ML models depends on various factors such as the quality of data, volume and veracity of the data, training process, and model evaluation process.

There are multiple ways to integrate ML models such as developing your own custom model by training it with your own data, fine-tuning an existing ML model with data that is already trained with historical data, or integrating a purpose-built ML model that is already trained with similar data as your use case.

AWS offers a few services to serve different use cases of customers with different integration options. Let's learn about some of the popular services AWS offers under the machine learning domain:

Amazon SageMaker (https://oreil.ly/8mVIx)
A fully managed machine learning service that enables data scientists and ML engineers to build, train, and deploy ML models into a production-ready environment. It provides features and workflows that can help developer productivity and fast-track your model development and deployment. SageMaker natively integrates with other AWS services that enables data science teams to query data from their data lake or data warehouse, store model artifacts in an object store, integrate security with AWS IAM, enable model inference with an API service layer, and provide end-to-end monitoring capability for operational efficiency.

Amazon Bedrock (https://oreil.ly/wAAi3)
> A fully managed service that enables you to choose from high-performing foundation models (FMs) available in Bedrock or import your own custom model to fast-track your generative AI application development. Some of the popular model providers available in Bedrock are Anthropic, Meta, Cohere, Mistral AI, Stability AI, AI21 Labs, and Amazon's own Titan models. In addition to a managed environment to host foundation models, Bedrock also provides knowledge bases to support RAG architecture, agents to perform complex tasks, and Guardrails to filter harmful content and safeguard from prompt attacks.

Amazon Q (https://oreil.ly/tc29o)
> A generative AI–powered assistant built on Amazon Bedrock that includes several capabilities. It includes Amazon Q Business, which can help answer questions, provide summaries, and generate content. Amazon Q Developer helps improve developer productivity by transforming code or generating new code. In addition, Amazon Q is also integrated into multiple AWS services such as Amazon QuickSight to generate visualizations with natural language, AWS Glue to generate code, Amazon Redshift to generate SQL, Amazon Connect for better customer service, and AWS Supply Chain to help inventory managers with supply demand planning.

We have highlighted a few of the popular ML services here but you can learn about other ML/AI services from the AWS documentation (*https://oreil.ly/PfQnZ*).

Migration and Transfer

With the popularity of cloud services and AWS, a lot of customers are looking to migrate their workloads to AWS, which requires a large amount of historical data transfer. To help such customers, AWS offers multiple services that can help with one-time or continuous data transfers from on-premises or other cloud providers to AWS. The data being transferred may involve files or databases and the varying size may require a different approach for the data transfer. Let's learn about some of the popular AWS services that help with data migration and transfer:

AWS Database Migration Service (DMS) (https://oreil.ly/mbScC)
> A managed service that helps move data between data stores such as between AWS cloud services and from on-premises or other cloud providers to AWS. You can migrate data from relational or NoSQL databases to AWS databases or object stores by defining the data movement as a one-time full load activity or by loading incremental data on a continuous basis.

AWS Schema Conversion Tool (SCT) (https://oreil.ly/hsiNs)
> Integrated as part of AWS DMS to help modify the schema and provide schema compatibility reports between the source and target database during

data movement. Please read the documentation (*https://oreil.ly/HjH15*) to check which data stores are supported as source and target for SCT.

AWS DataSync (https://oreil.ly/6LIYk)
An online data transfer and discovery service that enables the secure transfer of files or objects from, to, and between AWS services. If you have a large volume of NFS or HDFS files and plan to migrate to an AWS object store then DataSync might be a good option.

AWS Data Exchange (https://oreil.ly/9da3h)
An AWS service that provides a data marketplace with data from AWS and other third parties with a subscription pricing model. It helps streamline data consumption and also enables you to sell your data to external customers through the marketplace. It makes the data available in a secured manner that can be accessed through files, APIs, or Amazon Redshift queries.

AWS Snow Family (https://oreil.ly/39UkO)
Enables processing of data at the edge or moving petabyte-scale data from and to AWS. It includes the AWS Snowball and Snowcone services. Snowball is popular for moving petabyte-scale data and is available with compute or storage optimized options. Snowcone is the most compact service and specifically designed to be used outside of traditional data centers.

AWS Transfer Family (https://oreil.ly/qx9X2)
Enables secure transfer of data from and to AWS over the SFTP, AS2, FTPS, FTP protocols. You can move data from and to the Amazon S3 object store or Amazon EFS. It is a fully managed service that provides workflow to easily configure, run, and monitor files being transferred.

You can learn more about all of the migration and transfer services from the AWS documentation.

Networking and Content Delivery

As AWS is a public cloud that is being used by millions of customers, network isolation, low-latency access, and domain routing are some of the key components for security and efficiency. AWS offers multiple services to address these needs that customers can take advantage of. Let's review some of these services:

Amazon Virtual Private Cloud (VPC) (https://oreil.ly/kEfzI)
Provides virtual network isolation, which you can integrate to deploy workloads that need to be logically isolated from other workloads. An AWS VPC includes the option to create a public subnet or a private subnet. A public subnet will have a route to the internet, which means applications deployed in a public subnet can

be configured to be accessible from the internet. Private subnets are meant to be accessible within VPC only and are not accessible over the internet.

AWS PrivateLink (https://oreil.ly/odtoR)
Enables applications hosted within a VPC to access other AWS services through the AWS network, without getting routed through the internet. For example, if an application running within a VPC needs to access objects available in an Amazon S3 object store, then AWS PrivateLink will help establish that connection in a secured manner. This helps improve efficiency as the request gets routed through the Amazon internal network.

Amazon Route 53 (https://oreil.ly/fLO-3)
Provides a highly scalable and available Domain Name System (DNS) with which domains such as *example.com* can get routed to a designated IP address of a server, which serves the response for the HTTP/HTTPS request. It provides several features to configure domain routing such as latency-based routing, IP-based routing, geo-based routing, DNS failover, health-check monitoring, and many more.

Amazon CloudFront (https://oreil.ly/NHiY4)
A content delivery network (CDN) service from which you can serve geospecific requests from CloudFront's nearby edge locations in a secure manner, which reduces network latency and improves performance. It also provides computing at the edge through the CloudFront Functions and Lambda@Edge features. It natively integrates with the Amazon S3 object store and supports continuous deployment with real-time metrics and logging capabilities.

AWS offers several other networking services that you can dive into from the AWS documentation (*https://oreil.ly/8hAvD*).

Security, Identity, and Compliance

AWS defines security as its top priority and makes sure all of its services are built with security at their core. It provides several products to address different security needs including identity management, user authentication, authorization, data encryption at rest and in transit, securing applications from external security attacks, and features that can enable you to monitor and audit access requests. AWS provides compliance certifications (*https://oreil.ly/-e8IE*) for its services to help customers who follow specific industry regulations.

Key security, identity, and compliance services include:

AWS Identity and Access Management (IAM) (https://oreil.ly/BFm0X)
A fully managed global service that enables authentication of users and authorized access to AWS resources. You can integrate external identity services to

enable single sign on, implement fine-grained access control on AWS actions, enable just-in-time temporary credential vending, and much more.

AWS Key Management Service (KMS) (https://oreil.ly/e8eLz)
A managed service that helps you create and manage encryption keys in AWS. It is able to encrypt data at rest that is stored in object stores, databases, or filesystems. You can take advantage of certain advanced features of AWS KMS such as multiregion KMS keys (replica of KMS keys in each region), creating KMS keys in an external key store (protect AWS resources using cryptographic keys outside of AWS), and connecting to KMS keys using private VPC endpoints.

Amazon Macie (https://oreil.ly/VIc6b)
A managed service that enables detecting sensitive data from storage layers such as Amazon S3 and sends notifications to respective stakeholders. It leverages machine learning and pattern matching to automatically detect sensitive data (e.g., names, address, phone number, credit card numbers, and more) in a cost-effective way.

AWS Secrets Manager (https://oreil.ly/asurm)
Enables storing and managing sensitive data elements such as database credentials, so that developers can avoid hardcoding them in scripts. You can control access to the secrets using IAM roles and let your application code refer to the Secrets Manager keys to get the credentials.

AWS Shield (https://oreil.ly/Gxm0t)
Provides protection against distributed denial of service (DDoS) attacks for applications deployed in AWS. Additionally, AWS Shield Advanced managed threat protection service helps improve security by providing DDoS detection, mitigation, and response capabilities.

AWS WAF (https://oreil.ly/jfQBq)
An AWS service that acts as a firewall for web applications hosted on AWS by protecting HTTP or HTTPS requests. You can control access to your web content using WAF as it supports integration with multiple AWS resources such as CloudFront distribution, the REST APIs of API Gateway, application load balancers, AppSync GraphQL APIs, Cognito user pool, and many more.

You can learn about additional security services in the AWS documentation (*https://oreil.ly/eSWmg*).

Management Governance

To be operationally efficient, AWS offers several services that you can integrate in your data analytics workloads to automate resource creation using infrastructure as code (IaC), enable observability through logging and monitoring, and improve management and auditability of resources. In this section, we will highlight a few of the services that are commonly integrated:

AWS CloudFormation (https://oreil.ly/eFGWj)
 A managed service that enables you to automate the creation and deployment of AWS services using an IaC approach. It reduces your effort compared to manually deploying, tracking failure, and rolling back failed deployments.

AWS CloudTrail (https://oreil.ly/nNyu7)
 A managed service that keeps track of all the events or API actions taken by any user, role, group, or a service, which enables auditing actions and meeting compliance needs. It keeps track of activities including actions taken through SDKs, the console, and the CLI. CloudTrail is active by default when you create an AWS account.

Amazon CloudWatch (https://oreil.ly/DpQBt)
 An AWS service that enables logging and monitoring of AWS resources and applications you are running in AWS. You can monitor metrics, define alarms, build dashboards, and analyze logs to improve system performance.

AWS Config (https://oreil.ly/iub4o)
 An AWS service that helps audit configuration changes in AWS resources and also provides a detailed view of how resources are related to each other. The AWS resources are entities such as EBS volume, VPC, security groups, VPC endpoints, and more. You can leverage AWS Config to identify how configuration values have changed for a resource over time and also build alerting for configuration changes.

Amazon Managed Service for Prometheus (https://oreil.ly/_zLg4)
 A managed offering for the open source Prometheus solution, which is popular for metrics monitoring and alerting. It has native integration for container-based applications and also can be integrated into an organization-wide metrics monitoring solution. The managed offering from AWS helps integrate autoscaling capability and reduce operational overhead compared to a self-managed setup.

Amazon Managed Grafana (https://oreil.ly/GIdQl)
 A managed offering for the open source Grafana solution, which is popular for building visualizations on top of metrics, traces, and logs. It is a great solution for observability and can be easily integrated on top of Prometheus, Elastic, and many third-party products. The managed offering from AWS helps reduce operational overhead and integrate security standards.

AWS Systems Manager (https://oreil.ly/bgXJL)
 An AWS service that provides visibility and control of your infrastructure on AWS. You can leverage Systems Manager for application management, node

management, change management, and operations management. It provides a visual interface that offers a common view across your infrastructures and also enables you to automate a lot of operational tasks. For example, you can automate patch upgrades and common library installations across multiple services in a few easy steps.

Developer Tools

AWS offers a comprehensive set of tools and services that empower developers to efficiently develop, build, test, and deploy applications on the AWS platform. By automating tasks, enhancing collaboration, and seamlessly integrating with other AWS services, these tools streamline the software development lifecycle and accelerate innovation.

In the context of analytics workloads, AWS Developer Tools play a crucial role in the rapid development and deployment of data processing pipelines and applications. For example, developers can use AWS CodeCommit to store and version-control their ETL scripts, ensuring a single source of truth for data processing logic.

Key developer tools and services include:

AWS Command Line Interface (AWS CLI) (https://oreil.ly/P0LDl)
A unified command-line tool that enables developers to manage AWS services directly from the terminal, facilitating automation through scripts and commands.

AWS CloudShell (https://oreil.ly/aqmWf)
A browser-based, preauthenticated shell that provides command-line access to AWS resources directly from the AWS Management Console, simplifying access without the need for local installation or configuration.

AWS Cloud Development Kit (AWS CDK) (https://oreil.ly/NQ-ef)
An open source software development framework that allows developers to define cloud infrastructure using familiar programming languages such as TypeScript, Python, Java, .NET, and Go. Infrastructure is then provisioned through AWS CloudFormation, ensuring infrastructure-as-code practices.

AWS Code Services (https://oreil.ly/Fm-Xr)
Includes AWS CodeCommit, AWS CodeBuild, AWS CodeDeploy, and AWS CodePipeline. This suite of managed services facilitates continuous integration and continuous delivery (CI/CD) workflows. AWS Code Services enable developers to store and version-control their code (CodeCommit), build and test their applications (CodeBuild), automate the deployment of their applications to various compute services (CodeDeploy), and orchestrate the entire release process (CodePipeline).

Cloud Financial Management

Effective cost management is essential when working with cloud services, especially in data-intensive analytics workloads. AWS provides Cloud Financial Management tools that empower organizations to monitor, manage, and optimize their cloud spending. These services offer visibility into cost drivers, enable budget setting, and facilitate forecasting. By leveraging these tools, organizations can ensure that their analytics workloads remain within financial constraints while maximizing resource efficiency.

Key Cloud Financial Management tools include:

AWS Cost Explorer (https://oreil.ly/X7439)
A tool that helps you visualize, understand, and manage your AWS costs and usage over time. It provides a set of default reports and the ability to create custom reports, allowing you to analyze your cost and usage data, forecast spending, identify trends, and uncover areas for potential savings.

AWS Budgets (https://oreil.ly/m3nyl)
Allows you to set custom cost and usage budgets for your AWS services. You can configure alerts to notify you via email or Amazon SNS when your actual or forecasted costs exceed your defined thresholds. This proactive approach helps you stay within budget and avoid unexpected expenses.

AWS Well-Architected Tool

The AWS Well-Architected Tool (*https://oreil.ly/E9wao*) is a service in AWS that provides a trusted framework that you can utilize to apply design best practices from AWS, implement improvements, and monitor progress. The WA tool integrates with AWS Trusted Advisor (*https://oreil.ly/nfZpn*) and AWS Service Catalog App-Registry (*https://oreil.ly/288hX*), which help review and answer Well-Architected Tool questions.

The Well-Architected Framework (*https://oreil.ly/MGIcu*) explains key concepts of design principles and architectural best practices that can be applied for your workloads deployed in the AWS Cloud. The best practice guidelines are categorized into six pillars: Security, Reliability, Sustainability, Operational Excellence, Performance Efficiency, and Cost Optimization.

Additionally, Well-Architected Lenses extend the best practices of Well-Architected Tools to specific technology domains such as machine learning, IoT, SAP, and industries such as financial services, healthcare life science, sports, and more. Please read more about Well-Architected Lenses in the AWS documentation (*https://oreil.ly/tyIM9*).

Conclusion

In this chapter, we have explored the core AWS analytics services and auxiliary services that are essential for certification. By understanding the features, use cases, and integration capabilities of services like Amazon Kinesis, AWS Glue, Amazon Redshift, and Amazon QuickSight, you are now well equipped to design robust, scalable, and cost-effective data analytics solutions on AWS.

Additionally, we have highlighted the importance of auxiliary services spanning application integration, compute, databases, storage, machine learning, security, governance, and cloud financial management. These services work in conjunction with the core analytics offerings to create comprehensive, end-to-end analytics architectures.

As you progress through this book, you will dive deeper into each service, learn best practices for their implementation, and gain hands-on experience through practical exercises. By mastering the concepts and services covered in this chapter, you will be well on your way to becoming an AWS Certified Data Engineer, ready to tackle real-world data challenges and drive innovation in your organization.

Additional Resources

The following are a few additional resources that will help you dive deeper and gain more knowledge:

- "Overview of Amazon Web Services" (*https://oreil.ly/033me*)
- "Analytics on AWS" (*https://oreil.ly/bZpuG*)
- "What Is Data Strategy?" (*https://oreil.ly/mAQHB*)
- "Choosing an AWS Analytics Service" (*https://oreil.ly/nFppL*)
- "Amazon SageMaker" (*https://oreil.ly/qG_Jk*)

## CHAPTER 4

Data Ingestion and Transformation

The ability to efficiently collect, ingest, and transform data from diverse sources is crucial for driving valuable insights and well-informed decisions. Organizations constantly strive to unlock insights from their data by analyzing their data assets and making better business decisions through data analytics.

For data engineers, optimizing this end-to-end data ingestion and transformation process is a core responsibility. They are often tasked with building reliable pipelines that power an organization's data-driven initiatives. However, selecting the appropriate data ingestion and transformation solutions is critical, as different varieties of data sources with varying volumes, velocities, and transformation needs may necessitate the use of various AWS services and approaches.

In this chapter, you will learn how to do the following:

- Design and implement efficient data ingestion pipelines using appropriate AWS services
- Choose the right AWS services for real-time/near-real-time and batch data processing
- Build reliable data pipelines for both batch and real-time scenarios
- Implement efficient data transformation strategies
- Apply best practices for data ingestion and transformation
- Orchestrate complex data workflows

By the end of this chapter, you will have a comprehensive understanding of how to build data pipelines with data ingestion and transformation capabilities in AWS, and how to orchestrate them. You will learn how to carefully evaluate the trade-offs, implementation complexity, performance implications, and cost factors, and you will also answer a set of practice questions similar to the kind of questions you can expect in the Data Engineer Associate certification exam.

Data Ingestion

Data ingestion is the process of importing data from various sources into AWS storage and processing systems. Organizations typically deal with the following three ingestion patterns:

Real-time streaming
> This is high-velocity data requiring immediate ingestion and/or processing. Examples include IoT sensor readings, clickstream data, and social media feeds. Streaming data is characterized by a continuous flow of small data records.

Batch
> Ingesting batch data means periodic data loads at scheduled intervals. Examples include daily database dumps and weekly report files. Larger volumes of data are processed together and the focus is on throughput over latency.

Near real time
> Near real time is data with semi-frequent updates with slight delay tolerance. Examples include inventory updates, price changes, and the like. While ingesting it, it is important to balance between timeliness and efficiency. Typically CDC (change data capture) mechanisms are used for ingestion.

Modern organizations typically need to ingest data from multiple sources such as streaming sources that generate events and messages, databases, files, and third parties. Let's now take a look at various patterns on how to ingest all your data into an analytics data store for reporting and analytics.

Real-Time Streaming Data Ingestion

Organizations have thousands of data sources that typically simultaneously emit messages, events ranging in size from a few bytes to several megabytes (MB). These sources span across user interactions (e.g., website clickstreams, mobile app activities, gaming events), IoT and equipment data (e.g., sensor readings, connected vehicle data, industrial equipment notifications, security system alerts), and business transactions (e.g., financial trades, payment processing, order updates).

A streaming data pipeline for data analytics typically consists of five primary components, as shown in Figure 4-1.

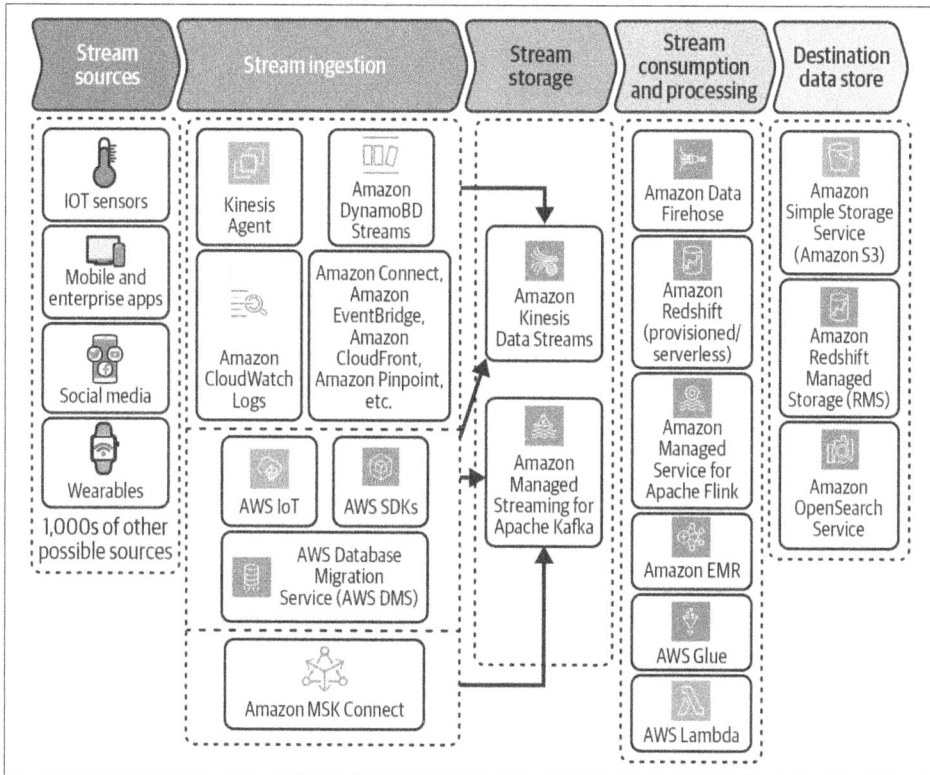

Figure 4-1. Streaming data pipeline for data analytics on AWS

This pipeline ingests and optionally transforms streaming data in real time. It then loads into target analytics data stores for further processing, reporting, and analytics:

Stream sources

Streaming data sources can be application logs, clickstream logs, mobile apps (e.g., user actions, location data, sensor data, social media interactions), etc.

Stream ingestion

The stream ingestion layer is responsible for ingesting data into the stream storage layer. It provides the ability to collect data from tens of thousands of data sources and ingest in near real time. After collecting data, the data is sent to stream storage containing a stream name, data value, and sequence number:

- Kinesis Agent (*https://oreil.ly/qfPdU*) is a standalone Java application that can be used to monitor files (e.g., logs) and ingest new data continuously into Kinesis Data Streams. It can be installed on Linux-based server environments such as web servers, log servers, and database servers. By default, it considers each newline (\n) as a record. However, you can configure it to parse multiline records (see the Amazon Kinesis documentation (*https://oreil.ly/mgrF_*)).

- DynamoDB Streams (*https://oreil.ly/Um4Jq*) captures and produces a stream of time-ordered sequences of item-level modifications in any DynamoDB table. This data can be streamed through Kinesis Data Streams using a direct integration.

- Data produced from many AWS services such as Amazon CloudWatch, Amazon Connect, Amazon EventBridge, Amazon CloudFront, Amazon Pin-Point, etc. can stream data directly into Kinesis Data Streams.

- AWS IoT Core (*https://oreil.ly/u07vn*) can connect to IoT devices and stream data into Kinesis Data Streams and Amazon MSK. IoT devices can send public data to AWS IoT Core using MQTT messages. AWS IoT Core can then route the data into Kinesis Data Streams or Amazon MSK.

- AWS DMS (*https://oreil.ly/mbScC*) can connect to transactional databases, perform change data capture, and load the data into both Kinesis Data Streams and Amazon MSK.

- Amazon MSK Connect (*https://oreil.ly/M7_x8*) can continuously ingest data from files, perform change data capture from databases, and load streaming data into Amazon MSK.

- If these out-of-the-box stream producers don't work for your use case, you can build custom stream producers using AWS SDK (*https://oreil.ly/DgoWQ*) and Kinesis Producers Library (KPL) (*https://oreil.ly/wOVUL*). This option has high implementation complexity and high operational overhead; carefully evaluate your needs before choosing this option.

Stream storage

This is the central layer for streaming data pipelines. They can collect data from stream producers, store it for a set duration of time (typically a few hours to days), and distribute the stored data to consumers. Stream data collectors store streaming data in the order it was received for a set duration of time, and can replay it indefinitely during that time. They decouple the stream producers from stream consumers. In AWS, there are two stream data collectors. In the next section, you will learn how to choose between these two services:

- Amazon Managed Streaming for Apache Kafka (Amazon MSK)

- Amazon Kinesis Data Streams (KDS)

Stream consumption and processing

Stream consumers read data from stream storage and load it into the target data store. They can either load the data as is into the target data store or apply transformations before loading the data into the target data store for analytics. The following are the relevant stream consumption and processing services:

- Amazon Data Firehose
- Amazon Redshift (Provisioned/Serverless) compute
- Amazon Managed Streaming for Apache Flink (MSF)
- AWS Glue streaming jobs
- Apache Spark Streaming or Apache Flink in Amazon EMR
- AWS Lambda
- A custom application with Kinesis Consumer Library (KCL)

These processing services will be discussed in detail later in this chapter.

Destination data store

The storage layer used for analytics streaming data pipelines needs fast, inexpensive, and repeatable reads and writes of large data streams. You should be able to load large volumes of continuously streaming data with low latency. The most common target data stores for streaming data in the context of data and analytics are typically the following:

- Data lakes: Amazon S3
- Data warehouses: Amazon Redshift
- Search and log analytics solutions: Amazon OpenSearch

Kinesis Data Streams Versus Amazon MSK

When choosing between the AWS streaming services KDS and Amazon MSK for your streaming data ingestion needs, it's important to carefully assess your specific requirements and use case.

Check if your data sources and targets have direct integration with the streaming service. A direct integration significantly simplifies your solution and will be the one with least operational overhead. Amazon Kinesis Data Streams offers direct integrations with many AWS services, as shown in Figure 4-2.

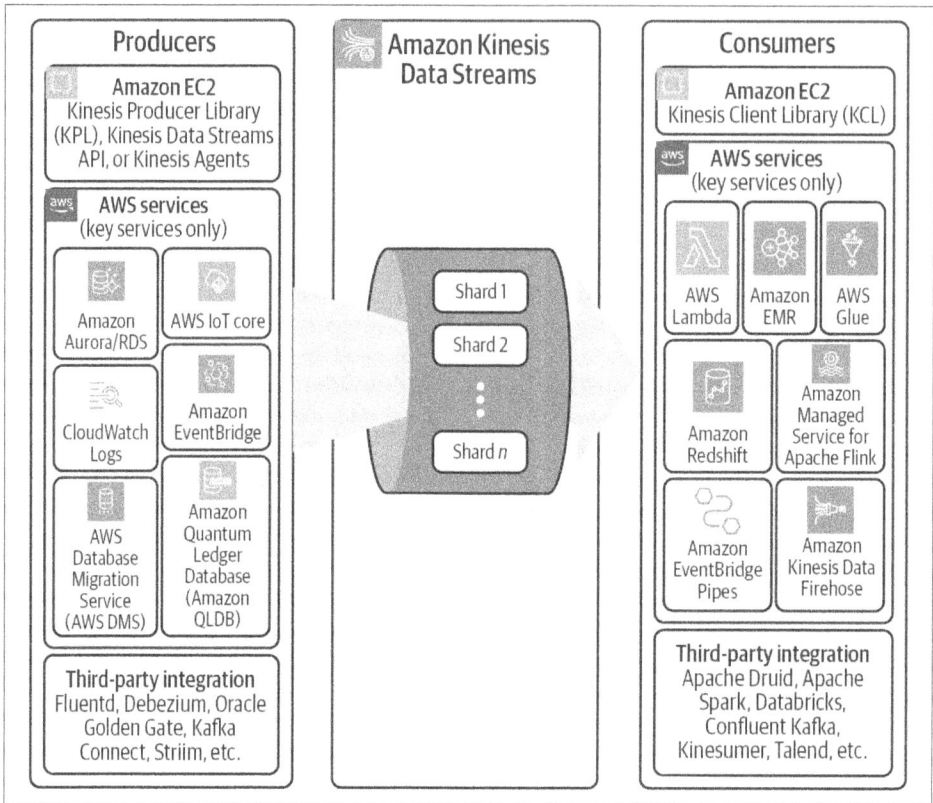

Figure 4-2. Integration for Amazon Kinesis Data Streams

Figure 4-2 describes the integrations available for Amazon Kinesis Data Streams for producers and consumers at the time of writing. Kinesis offers AWS-focused integrations and simplicity in operational management. On the other hand, Amazon MSK is an open source ecosystem with richer connectors and a higher level of flexibility. If you prefer open source ecosystem support (e.g., if you use DuckDB or ClickHouse), you will find MSK easier to use. In addition to integrations, consider the options in Table 4-1.

Table 4-1. Comparison between Kinesis Data Streams and Amazon MSK

Attribute	Kinesis Data Streams	Amazon MSK
Management overhead	Low	Low (Amazon MSK Serverless) to medium (Amazon MSK Provisioned)
Scalability	Scale in seconds with one click	Scale in minutes with one click
Throughput	On-demand scaling is available, but scaled within certain limits	Highest throughput of two options
Open source	No	Yes

Attribute	Kinesis Data Streams	Amazon MSK
Data retention	You can retain data for up to 365 days.	You can retain data for a longer duration and it is configurable. With the tiered storage feature of Amazon MSK, you can cost-efficiently store vast amounts of data in Amazon S3.
Latency	70 milliseconds when using enhanced fan-out consumers, 200–500 milliseconds without the enhanced fan-out	Lowest

Sample Streaming Ingestion Use Cases

Let's now take a look at some common streaming data ingestion use cases and how to solve them.

Ingesting streaming data from IoT devices into a data lake

The first use case is to ingest data from thousands of IoT devices into an Amazon S3 data lake for further transformation and analytics with the least operational overhead, implementation complexity, and lowest latency. To achieve this, you can use the ELT architecture described in Figure 4-3.

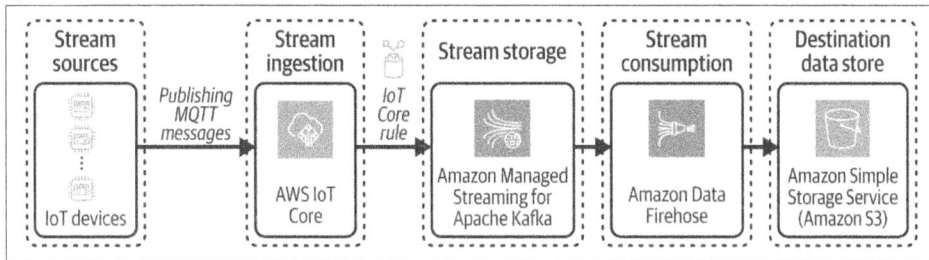

Figure 4-3. Streaming ingestion architecture for IoT data into an Amazon S3 data lake

In this architecture, the IoT devices publish MQTT messages to AWS IoT Core. An IoT Core rule will then load these streaming messages into Amazon MSK. MSK is chosen over KDS because it provides the lowest latency. Once the data is read into Amazon MSK, you'll need a consumer to load it into the Amazon S3 data lake. This is where Amazon Data Firehose (ADF) comes into play. It is a fully managed consumer service that can read from both Amazon KDS and Amazon MSK and load the data reliably into Amazon S3. You will learn more about this later in this chapter.

Often, the incoming data is not in a format that is optimized for data lake consumption. It is produced in formats like JSON. ADF has built-in transformations to support converting JSON to optimized Apache Parquet and Apache ORC formats. These columnar data formats save space and enable faster queries on the Amazon S3 data lake. If your input is in non-JSON data format (like CSV, XML, structured text, etc.), ADF can invoke an AWS Lambda function that first transforms these files into JSON, before converting it to Apache Parquet or ORC. Additionally, ADF can compress the data using GZIP, ZIP, or SNAPPY before delivering it to the Amazon S3 data lake.

Ingesting click streams into a data warehouse for real-time reporting

The second use case is to ingest clickstream data into columnar storage in Amazon Redshift within 10 seconds of data generation with the lowest operational overhead and lowest implementation complexity. Data warehouses like Amazon Redshift are high-performance hubs. Ingesting streaming data into a data warehouse opens up new opportunities for high-performance, real-time analytics with minimal query response latency, enabling faster decision making.

Figure 4-4 presents an architecture diagram for ingesting clickstream data into an Amazon Redshift data warehouse using the streaming ingestion feature (*https://oreil.ly/VPJ-D*).

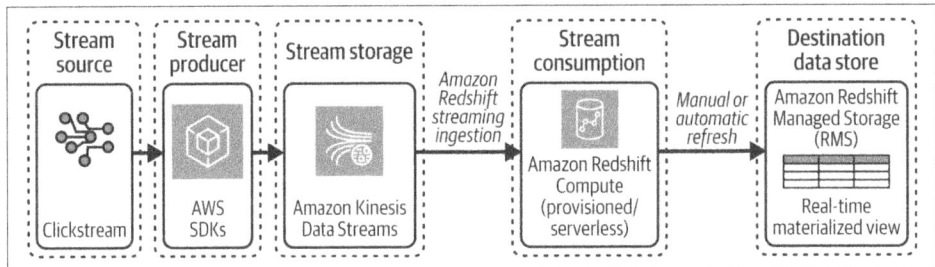

Figure 4-4. Streaming ingestion for Amazon Redshift data warehouse

Using this feature, you can directly ingest streaming data from KDS, Amazon MSK, or self-managed Apache Kafka into Amazon Redshift in real time with minimal operational overhead and implementation complexity.

With streaming ingestion, the data read from the stream is seamlessly loaded into a materialized view (MV) within the Amazon Redshift database. Streaming sources typically stream data in semi-structured formats like JSON. You have the flexibility to either load the semi-structured format data as is into the semi-structured data type in Amazon Redshift (called SUPER (*https://oreil.ly/NDUvS*)), or you can shred the data into individual columns. You can define transformations in the MV definition to apply business logic on incoming data.

As the MV is refreshed, Amazon Redshift automatically and incrementally consumes the new data from the stream and loads it into it. This incremental refresh ensures that only the newest records (e.g., 100 new records since the last refresh) are loaded, rather than reloading the entire dataset.

The MV refresh can be set to run manually or automatically. With automatic refresh, Amazon Redshift automatically updates the MV as soon as possible, as new data becomes available in the streaming source. Amazon Redshift prioritizes your workloads over auto-refresh and might stop auto-refresh to preserve the performance of your workload. This approach might delay refresh of some materialized views. In some cases, you might need more deterministic refresh behavior for your materialized views. If so, consider using manual refresh as described in the AWS documentation (*https://oreil.ly/e64o2*).

Streaming Amazon DynamoDB data into a centralized data lake

The third use case is to ingest financial data from a DynamoDB database into an Amazon S3 data lake for real analytics. DynamoDB has a feature called DynamoDB Streams that captures and streams changes made to DynamoDB in real time. The changes can be loaded into KDS using a direct integration between DynamoDB Streams and KDS. This data can then be delivered through any consumer that KDS supports.

For this use case, the data is delivered into Amazon S3 using Amazon Data Firehose for analytics as shown in Figure 4-5. For more details on this solution refer to the blog "Streaming Amazon DynamoDB Data into a Centralized Data Lake" (*https://oreil.ly/DCMBy*).

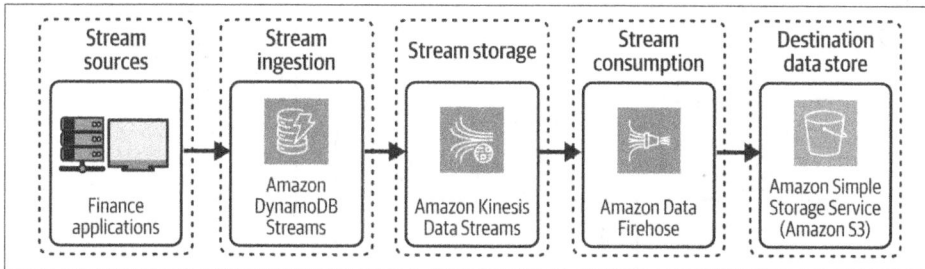

Figure 4-5. Streaming finance data from DynamoDB into S3

Ingesting AWS logs into log analytics solutions

The fourth use case is to ingest logs from AWS services into Amazon OpenSearch for real-time monitoring and analysis. This allows organizations to detect and respond to issues, security threats, or anomalies in near real time, facilitating timely incident response and enhancing overall operational efficiency. You can use subscription filters in Amazon CloudWatch log groups to ingest data directly to ADF, as shown in Figure 4-6. The data can be delivered to the Amazon OpenSearch service or third-party log analytics solutions like Splunk.

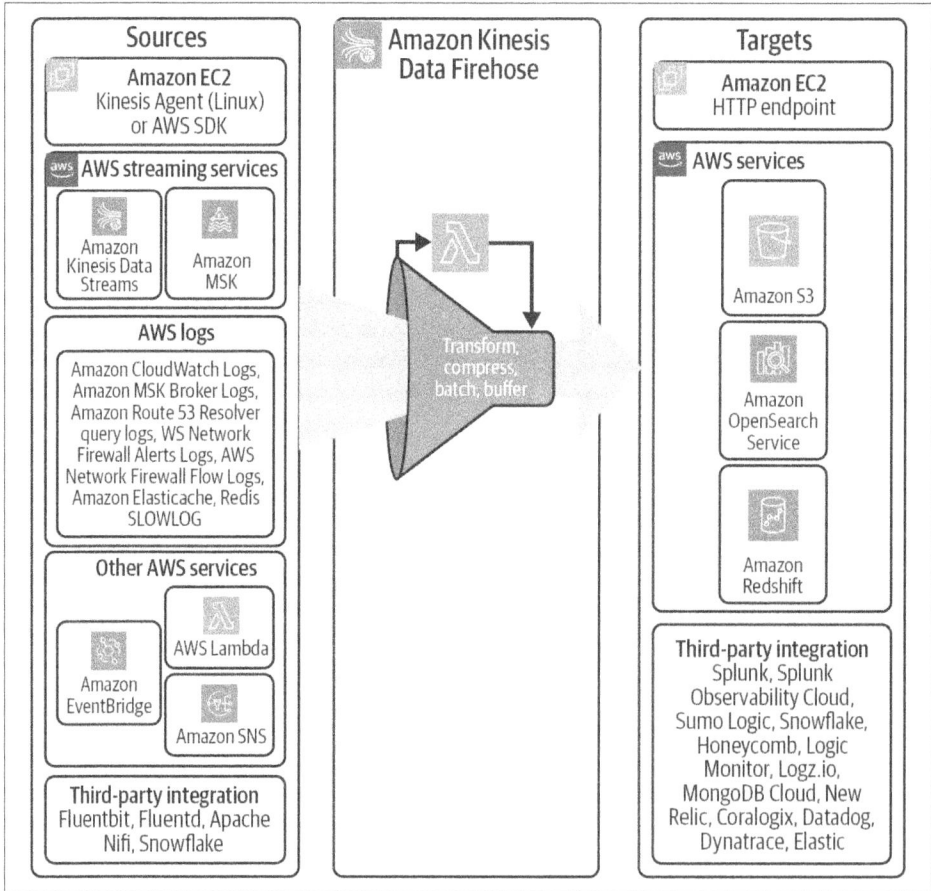

Figure 4-6. Integrations for Amazon Data Firehose

ADF is designed for batch-oriented, higher-latency data processing, making it suitable for applications that can tolerate higher latency. It automatically delivers data to the selected destination in batches, with typical latencies of a few minutes to an hour. It has native integration with the following targets, making it an operationally efficient and low implementation complexity solution to load data into these supported targets:

- Multiple third-party solutions like Splunk, Dynatrace, etc.
- Amazon Redshift and Amazon OpenSearch
- Amazon S3 to Iceberg format tables or plain Parquet

ADF is a good choice for use cases that require streaming ingestion to Iceberg tables or S3 data lakes for data lake ingestion, log data collection, and data backup.

ADF has the capability of taking an optional backup of the raw incoming data into an Amazon S3 bucket. While applying transformations, if any records have errors, they are routed into a separate S3 location.

Ingesting Data Using Zero-ETL Integrations

Zero-ETL (*https://oreil.ly/m2OKt*) is a set of integrations that minimizes the need to build complex ETL data pipelines to extract data. Traditional ETL processes are time-consuming and complex to develop, maintain, and scale. Instead, zero-ETL integrations facilitate continuous, point-to-point data movement without the need to create ETL data pipelines.

AWS offers zero-ETL integrations into Amazon S3 data lakes, Amazon Redshift data warehouses, and Amazon OpenSearch from a variety of sources, including the following:

- AWS relational databases: Amazon Aurora, Amazon RDS
- AWS NoSQL databases: Amazon DynamoDB, Amazon DocumentDB
- SaaS applications: Salesforce, ServiceNow, Zendesk, SAP, etc.
- Files from Amazon S3

Even though zero-ETL integrations are not available for all source and target combinations, when a zero ETL integration is available, it is the easiest, most cost-effective and reliable solution with the lowest operational complexity. Note that the zero-ETL integrations offer *near-real-time latency*.

If you have real-time sub second latency requirements for ingestion, consider the options that we discussed in "Real-Time Streaming Data Ingestion" on page 80. Table 4-2 shows the zero-ETL integrations available in AWS at the time of writing. Please refer to the links provided to learn further about these integrations.

Table 4-2. AWS zero-ETL integrations

	Amazon S3 (data lake)	Amazon Redshift (data warehouse)	Amazon OpenSearch (search and log analytics)
Amazon DynamoDB	Amazon DynamoDB zero-ETL integration with Amazon S3 (*https://oreil.ly/FvNFy*) enables integration of DynamoDB data with Iceberg format tables is Amazon S3	Amazon DynamoDB zero-ETL integration with Amazon Redshift (*https://oreil.ly/Bun4c*) enables high-performance analytics on DynamoDB data in Amazon Redshift	Amazon DynamoDB zero-ETL integration with Amazon OpenSearch Service (*https://oreil.ly/UfIc_*) provides advanced search capabilities, such as full-text and vector search, on Amazon DynamoDB data
Amazon DocumentDB			Amazon DocumentDB zero-ETL integration with Amazon OpenSearch Service (*https://oreil.ly/O7ViD*) provides advanced search capabilities, such as fuzzy search, cross-collection search, and multilingual search, on Amazon DocumentDB documents
Amazon Aurora MySQL		Amazon Aurora zero-ETL integration with Amazon Redshift (*https://oreil.ly/OkmKq*) makes transactional data from Aurora available in Amazon Redshift for analytics	
Amazon Aurora Postgres			
Amazon RDS MySQL		Amazon RDS MySQL zero-ETL integration with Amazon Redshift (*https://oreil.ly/47qgb*) makes transactional data from RDS MySQL available in Amazon Redshift for analytics	
Amazon S3		Simplifies data ingestion from Amazon S3 to Amazon Redshift using auto-copy (*https://oreil.ly/Yu4zJ*)	Amazon OpenSearch Service zero-ETL integration with Amazon S3 (*https://oreil.ly/bDKLI*), an efficient way to query operational logs in Amazon S3 data lakes, removing the need to switch between tools to analyze data
SaaS applications	Zero-ETL integration is available	Amazon Redshift and support for zero-ETL integrations from SaaS applications (*https://oreil.ly/UU2eZ*) including Facebook Ads, Instagram Ads, Salesforce, Salesforce Marketing Cloud Account Engagement, SAP OData, ServiceNow, Zendesk, Zoho CRM	

	Amazon S3 (data lake)	Amazon Redshift (data warehouse)	Amazon OpenSearch (search and log analytics)
Amazon CloudWatch Logs			Amazon OpenSearch Service zero-ETL integration with Amazon CloudWatch Logs (*https://oreil.ly/bfr3b*) enables direct querying and visualization of log data in near real time
Amazon Security Lake			Amazon OpenSearch Service zero-ETL integration with Amazon Security Lake (*https://oreil.ly/03Ooe*) enables direct searching and analysis of security data

Ingesting Data from Databases with CDC Using AWS Data Migration Service

When zero-ETL integrations are not available and/or when you want to load data into a data lake, you can use the AWS Data Migration Service (DMS), an AWS service that leverages change data capture (CDC) capabilities to enable near-real-time data ingestion from databases into AWS services like Amazon S3, Amazon Redshift, Amazon RDS, and others.

This technique monitors and captures insert, update, and delete operations performed on a database in near real time. It provides a stream of change events reflecting the actual data modifications occurring, including details like operation type, data values before and after the change, timestamp, and contextual information. CDC enables capturing data source changes with low impact, without directly querying the transactional systems.

As illustrated in Figure 4-7, DMS uses a replication instance to connect to the source database, capture changes using transaction logs, and stream those data changes to the target in near real time.

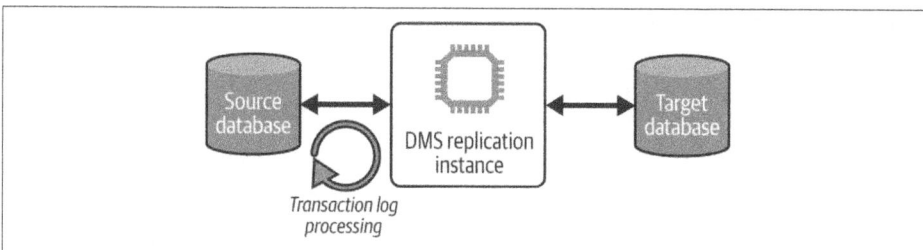

Figure 4-7. Change data capture (CDC) using AWS DMS

This CDC approach reduces the impact on source databases during data migration compared to bulk extraction methods. DMS supports homogeneous and heterogeneous database migrations while providing features like multi-AZ deployment for high availability.

DMS can perform one-time migration of data in addition to performing CDC. Review the following supported sources and targets to understand if it is a good fit for your use case.

Supported Sources for AWS DMS

AWS DMS publishes a list of supported sources for data migration (*https://oreil.ly/ 8JeXR*) in their documentation. Refer to it to see if your database and its version are supported as a source. At the time of writing, the key sources supported are as follows:

- On-premises databases such as Oracle, Microsoft SQL Server, MySQL, MariaDB, PostgreSQL, MongoDB, SAP Adaptive Server Enterprise (ASE), IBM Db2
- Third-party managed database services such as Microsoft Azure SQL Database, Microsoft Azure PostgreSQL, Microsoft Azure MySQL, Google Cloud for MySQL, Google Cloud for PostgreSQL, OCI MySQL Heatwave
- Amazon RDS database instances including Amazon RDS Oracle, Amazon RDS Microsoft SQL server, Amazon RDS MySQL, Amazon RDS MariaDB, Amazon RDS PostgreSQL, Amazon Aurora MySQL, Amazon Aurora PostgreSQL, Amazon RDS for IBM Db2 LUW
- Amazon S3 data lakes
- Amazon DocumentDB

Supported Targets for AWS DMS

AWS DMS also publishes a list of supported targets for data migration (*https:// oreil.ly/aktds*) in their documentation. Refer to it to see if your database and its version are supported as a target. At the time of writing, the key supported targets are as follows:

- Amazon RDS database instances (Oracle, SQL Server, MySQL, MariaDB, PostgreSQL, Aurora)
- Amazon Redshift data warehouses
- Amazon S3 data lakes
- Amazon DynamoDB NoSQL databases
- Amazon OpenSearch clusters
- Apache Kafka clusters
- Kinesis Data Streams for real-time data streaming

- Amazon DocumentDB document databases
- Amazon Neptune graph databases
- Databases like Oracle, SQL Server, PostgreSQL hosted on EC2 or on premises

Sample Use Cases

Following are some sample use cases for AWS DMS.

Ingesting data into an Amazon S3 data lake using DMS

As you have seen in the supported targets list, AWS DMS allows you to ingest data in near real time into an Amazon S3 data lake from any of the supported database sources. Figure 4-8 presents the architecture diagram for loading data from source databases into an Amazon S3 data lake in near real time using AWS DMS.

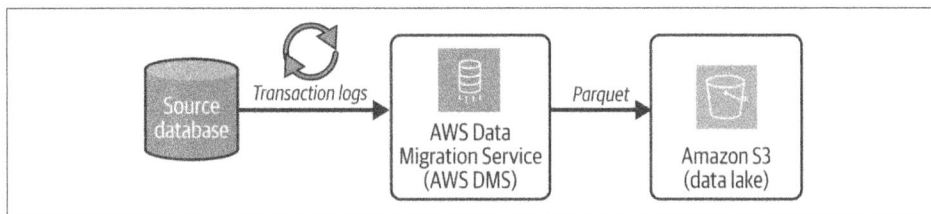

Figure 4-8. Change data capture (CDC) into Amazon S3

When loading data into S3, DMS doesn't preserve the transaction order by default. In order to preserve transaction order for CDC data, configure the target S3 endpoint settings to specify a folder path for storing CDC transaction files.

DMS allows you to control the frequency at which CDC files are written to the S3 target during a data replication task. This is done by setting the following extra connection attributes. Choose these values in such a way as to avoid files that are too small or too large (more than 1 GB):

cdcMaxBatchInterval
This attribute specifies the maximum time (in seconds) to accumulate CDC data before writing it to the S3 target as a file. A higher value means less frequent file writes, but larger file sizes.

cdcMinFileSize
This attribute sets the minimum file size (in KB) before AWS DMS will write a CDC file to the S3 target. A higher value means fewer, larger files.

To enable faster queries on the loaded data, set the target file format as Apache Parquet instead of the default CSV. Parquet is a columnar format and has efficient compression and encoding for improved query performance and lower storage costs.

Ingesting data into Amazon Redshift using DMS

For those source databases that don't have a zero-ETL integration with Amazon Redshift, you can use AWS DMS to ingest data using CDC techniques. Before setting up ongoing replication from a source database to Amazon Redshift, it is often common to perform a one-time schema conversion from the source database format to the Redshift format, and a one-time data migration. For schema conversion, you can use the AWS Schema Conversion Tool (SCT), and for the one-time data migration and ongoing replication, you can use AWS DMS. DMS also supports creating schemas; however, for good performance, it is recommended to use AWS SCT instead of DMS for schema conversion.

Figure 4-9 presents the architecture diagram for both one-time schema conversion and ongoing CDC from supported source databases and Amazon Redshift.

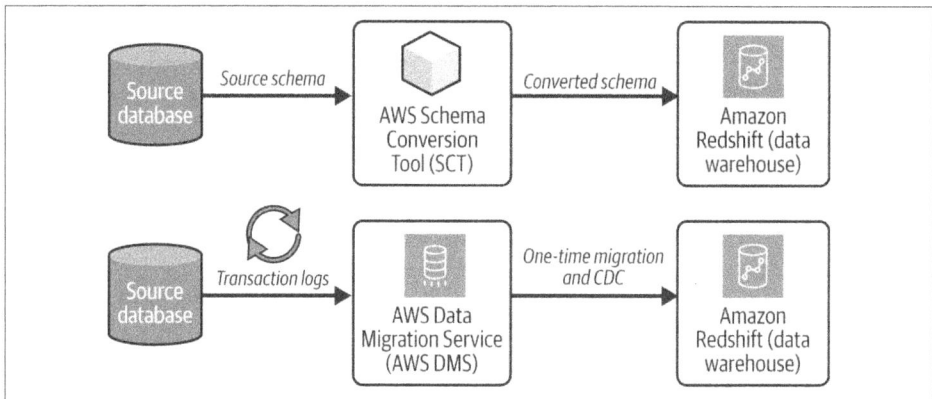

Figure 4-9. Change data capture (CDC) into Amazon Redshift using AWS DMS

Converting schema using DMS Schema Conversion

DMS Schema Conversion (*https://oreil.ly/EZfnu*) facilitates database migrations between different types. Using DMS Schema Conversion you can first create a report to assess the complexity of your migration. Then you can convert database schemas and code objects and apply the converted code to your target database.

DMS Schema Conversion automatically converts your source database schemas and most of the database code objects to a format compatible with the target database. This conversion includes tables, views, stored procedures, functions, data types, synonyms, and so on. Any objects that DMS Schema Conversion can't convert automatically are clearly marked. To complete the migration, you can convert these objects manually.

Ingesting files from on premises

Most enterprises have a mix of cloud and on-premises applications/data sources. Ingesting on-premises file data into the cloud allows combining it with cloud data for a unified analytical view across the hybrid landscape. AWS DataSync (*https://oreil.ly/ 6LIYk*) is a managed data transfer service that makes it simple and fast to move large amounts of file data online between on-premises storage systems and AWS storage services. DataSync uses proprietary technology to accelerate transfers by moving data in parallel, minimizing network overhead, and automating encryption and data integrity validation.

With DataSync, you can schedule one-time or recurring data transfers to keep data updated between your on-premises servers, NAS, and AWS storage like S3 and EFS. DataSync copies only changed files/objects after the initial data seeding, minimizing transfer times for subsequent syncs. It handles a wide variety of storage formats natively without needing to convert data, while preserving metadata and permissions. With pay-as-you-go pricing based on data volume transferred, DataSync provides a reliable, secure, cost-efficient, and operationally efficient way to move large file datasets to AWS.

Ingesting third-party datasets

Third-party data sources like demographic, geographic, economic, weather, etc., can enrich and add context to an organization's internal data, enabling more comprehensive and insightful analytics. AWS Data Exchange (*https://oreil.ly/9da3h*) is a service that simplifies the process of accessing and integrating third-party data. It serves as a comprehensive marketplace where data providers can publish and sell their datasets, and data consumers can easily discover, subscribe to, and integrate the data they need. It offers a wide range of datasets across various industries, such as S&P Global Ratings data, weather decision data, FINRA regulation data, etc., which can be easily found, subscribed to, and integrated using the AWS Data Exchange API.

Once subscribed, data consumers can access the datasets through a user-friendly console or API. The Data Exchange service supports a variety of data formats, making it easy to integrate the data into existing analytics and machine learning pipelines. With its robust data governance features and seamless integration with other AWS services, AWS Data Exchange simplifies the process of accessing and leveraging third-party data to drive business insights and innovation.

Best Practices for Data Ingestion

When there is a zero-ETL integration available to ingest data, it is almost always the best option to choose for data ingestion. Zero-ETL integrations are the most cost-effective and operationally simple options. In all other cases, a number of best practices should be followed.

Best Practices for Streaming Ingestion

Kinesis Data Streams (KDS), Amazon MSK, and Amazon Data Firehose (ADF) form an integral part of streaming ingestion pipelines. By following some best practices you can get the most value from using these services.

It is important to understand the architecture of KDS to grasp the best practices when using it. Figure 4-10 represents the high-level architecture.

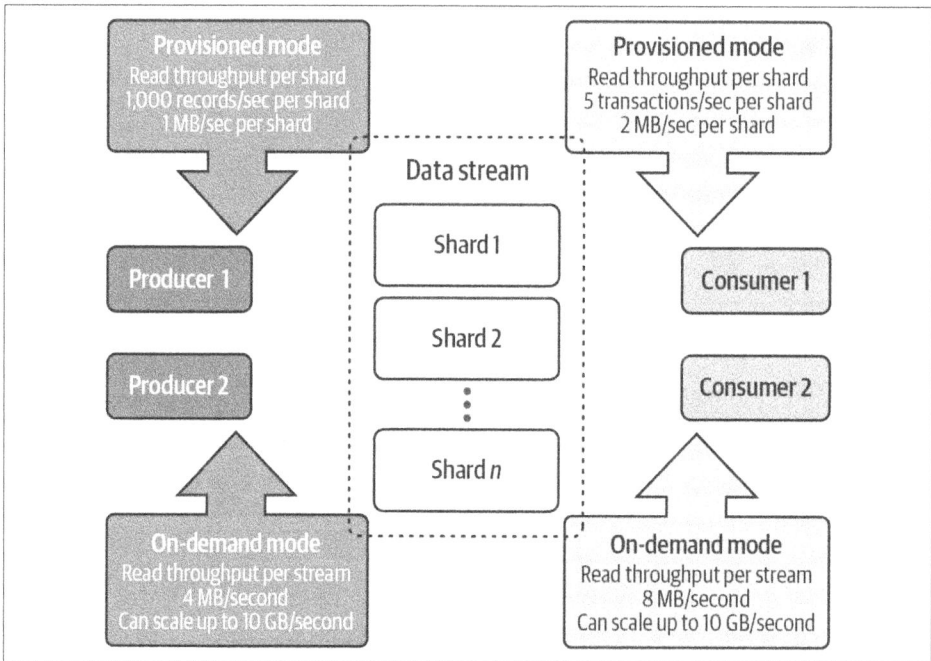

Figure 4-10. Kinesis Data Stream architecture

The fundamental resource that you will create when using KDS is a data stream. Each data stream is a set of shards and each shard has a sequence of data records. Each data record can be up to 1 MB in size. The sources that push data into the data stream are called *producers*, and the *consumers* process the data in real time.

You can choose a capacity mode for each data stream which determines how the capacity of a data stream is managed and how you are charged for the usage of your data stream. There are two capacity modes: *on-demand* mode and a *provisioned* mode.

Each shard has write throughput and read throughput. Write throughput is the rate at which data can be written into a shard and read throughput is the rate at which data can be read from the shard:

Provisioned mode

In provisioned mode, each shard has the following:

- A write throughput of 1,000 records per second for writes, for up to a maximum total data write rate of 1 MB per second (including partition keys).

- A read throughput of 5 transactions per second, for up to a maximum total data read rate of 2 MB per second.

The data capacity of your stream is the sum of the capacities of its shards. If your data rate increases or decreases, you can reshard a stream (*https://oreil.ly/k5oW-*) to increase or decrease the number of shards allocated to your stream.

On-demand mode

In on-demand mode, Kinesis Data Streams automatically manages the shards to ramp them up and down and provide the necessary throughput. You are charged only for the actual throughput that you use. You need not determine the number of shards, the service determines it for you. In on-demand mode:

- Each stream has a base write throughput of 4 MB per second, which can automatically scale up to 10 GB per second.

- Each stream has a base read throughput of 8 MB per second, which can automatically scale up to 20 GB per second.

Leveraging Amazon KDS for real-time data streaming requires careful consideration of several factors to optimize performance, scalability, and cost-effectiveness.

Best Practices for Choosing Data Stream Capacity Mode

Use on-demand capacity mode when you have unpredictable data volume or traffic spikes and prefer AWS to automatically manage capacity. Use provisioned capacity mode for predictable data volumes where you want fine-grained control over shard allocation and can forecast your capacity needs precisely:

On-demand

- Ideal for applications with fluctuating traffic or unknown data volume.

- Automatically scales the number of shards based on data throughput.

- Pay-per-use model, billed based on actual data processed.

- Less management overhead, as you don't need to manually adjust shard count.

Provisioned

- Best for predictable data flow where you can accurately estimate required capacity.

- You explicitly define the number of shards needed for your application.

- Offers more control over data distribution across shards.

Best Practices for Sharding

Data records in Kinesis are partitioned across shards based on their partition key. The partition key is a unique identifier associated with each data record that determines which shard the record will be stored in. Each data record in a shard is assigned a unique sequence number. Sequence numbers are used to track the order of records within a shard and enable ordering guarantees. In provisioned mode, increasing the number of shards increases the overall read and write throughput of the stream. In on-demand mode, KDS does it automatically for you. The following are the best practices for sharding when using provisioned mode:

Determine the optimal number of shards
> Analyze the expected data throughput and adjust the number of shards accordingly. Start with the minimum number of shards and scale up as needed.

Distribute data evenly across shards
> Use a well-distributed partition key to ensure that data is evenly distributed across shards. Avoid using predictable or sequential partition keys, as this can lead to partition skewing. Consider hashing or using a random prefix in the partition key to achieve better distribution.

Handle shard splits and merges
> Monitor shard utilization and be prepared to split or merge shards as the workload changes. Splitting a shard increases the overall stream capacity, while merging shards can help reduce costs. Use the UpdateShardCount API to adjust the number of shards programmatically.

Ensure data ordering within shards
> Maintain ordering guarantees within a shard by processing records in the order of their sequence numbers. If the order of records is important, design your application to process data within a shard in sequence.

Implement shard-level checkpointing
> Maintain checkpoints or offsets for each shard to enable reliable processing and reprocessing of data. This allows your application to resume from the last processed record in case of failures or restarts.

Best Practices for Consuming Data from KDS

Parallelism and read throughput are crucial for consuming applications. Multiple consumer applications can read from a stream in parallel. Consumers can use the following two modes of operations:

Shared throughput consumers

This is the default mode for consumers. As we saw earlier, the read throughput for each shard in a Kinesis Data Stream is 2 MB/sec. In shared throughput mode, this 2 MB/sec is shared across all consumers reading from that shard. If you add more consumers, each consumer will get a fraction of the 2 MB/sec.

Enhanced fan-out consumers

With enhanced fan-out, each consumer gets its own dedicated 2 MB/sec read throughput, regardless of how many other consumers are reading from the same stream. This means that multiple consumers can read data from the same stream in parallel, without contending for read throughput with each other. With enhanced fan-out you get data latencies as low as 70 milliseconds.

Table 4-3 compares the key differences between shared throughput and enhanced fan-out.

Table 4-3. Shared throughput versus enhanced fan-out consumers

Feature	Shared throughput	Enhanced fan-out
Read throughput	2 MB/sec per shard, shared across all consumers	2 MB/sec per shard, per consumer
Scaling consumers	Limited by shared throughput	Can scale consumers linearly without contention

Therefore, in order to improve the performance of the consuming application, use enhanced fan-out consumers.

Best Practices for Amazon MSK

Let's start by learning some Amazon MSK concepts. When using Amazon MSK, the main resource you provision is an Amazon MSK cluster. As shown in Figure 4-11, logically, data in a cluster is organized into topics. Each topic has multiple partitions. Data records are routed into partitions based on the partition key. All records with the same partition key will go to the same partition. From a hardware resources standpoint, a cluster is made up of multiple brokers; there are different kinds of Amazon MSK clusters.

Amazon MSK provisioned cluster versus serverless

The provisioned cluster has three brokers by default across 3 AZs by default. Each of the three brokers is a replica of each other. You can add more brokers as needed. For each new broker you add, two replicas will be created. The default maximum number of brokers per cluster is 30 for ZooKeeper-based clusters and 60 for KRaft-based clusters. You can request a limit increase if you need more.

As shown in Figure 4-11, there are two kinds of brokers—standard and express:

Standard brokers

They provide flexibility to configure a cluster's performance. You can choose from a wide range of broker sizes (*https://oreil.ly/M8cnb*). Each broker has a fixed storage attached to it. Amazon MSK handles the hardware maintenance of standard brokers and attached storage resources, automatically repairing hardware issues that may arise. Follow the best practices listed in the AWS documentation (*https://oreil.ly/3TVSk*) for standard broker sizing.

Express brokers

Express brokers for MSK are simpler to manage, more cost-effective to run at scale, and more elastic with the low latency you expect. Express brokers all use a common elastic Amazon MSK managed storage with pay-as-you-go pricing. It requires no sizing, provisioning, or proactive monitoring. Depending on the broker size (*https://oreil.ly/M8cnb*) selected, each broker node can provide up to 3 times more throughput per broker, scale up to 20 times faster, and recover 90% quicker compared to standard brokers. Express brokers come preconfigured with Amazon MSK's best practice defaults and enforce client throughput quotas to minimize resource contention between clients and Kafka's background operations. Follow the best practices listed in the AWS documentation (*https://oreil.ly/gXxps*) for express broker sizing.

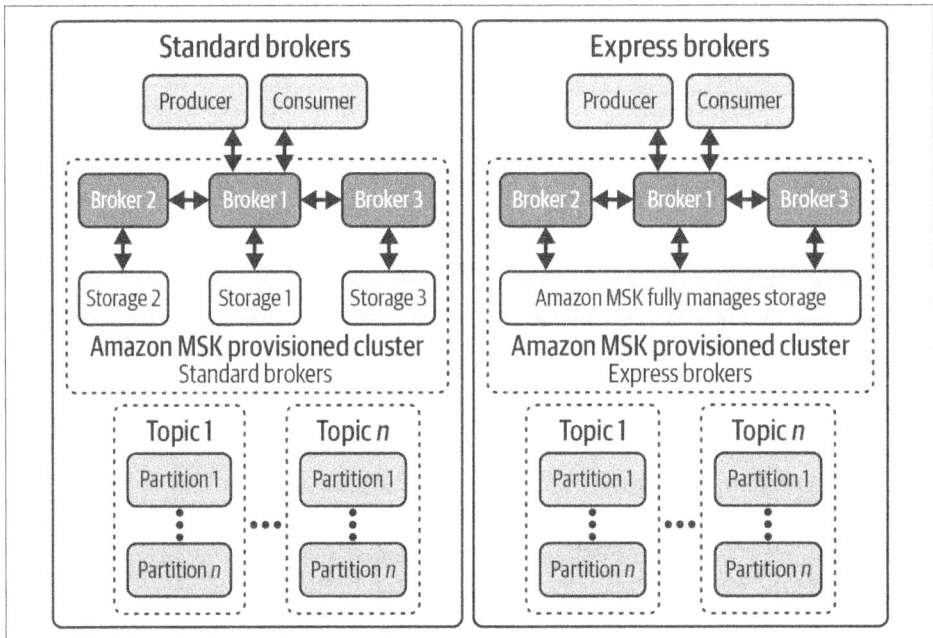

Figure 4-11. Amazon MSK provisioned cluster architecture with different broker types

Amazon MSK serverless cluster

With MSK serverless, you can easily run Apache Kafka clusters without needing to rightsize the cluster. It automatically and instantly scales I/O without you needing to worry about scaling up and down. It has a maximum write throughput of 200 MiB/second, maximum read throughput of 400 MiB/second, maximum number of partitions of 2400, and unlimited storage.

Use the chart in Figure 4-12 to determine whether a provisioned MSK cluster or serverless MSK cluster is better for your use case and if you are choosing provisioned, whether you need standard or express brokers. Using a provisioned cluster with express brokers is a good place to start.

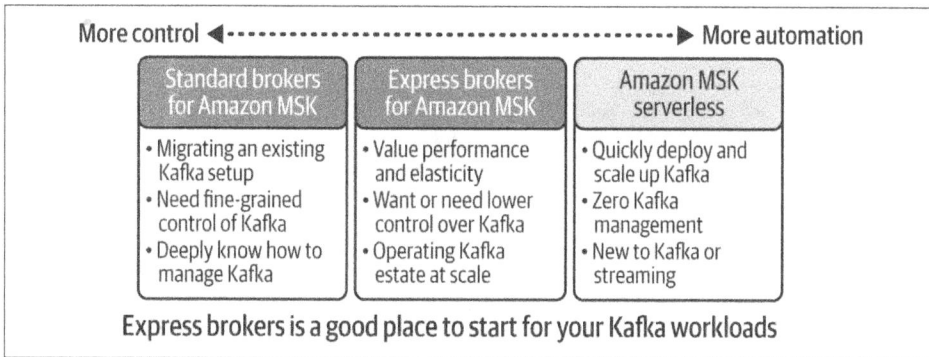

Figure 4-12. Choose the cluster type and broker type

General practices when using Amazon MSK

Here are some recommended general practices when using Amazon MSK:

- When selecting a partition key, carefully consider the distribution of your data to prevent partition skewing. Your chosen key should enable an even spread of data across partitions. A common mistake is selecting a key that results in disproportionate data distribution. For instance, if your dataset contains multiple resource IDs but one particular resource accounts for 90% of the total data, using a resource ID as your partition key would create a heavily imbalanced system with one overloaded partition. The ideal partition key should distribute data uniformly across partitions, ensuring balanced storage and efficient query performance across your entire dataset.

- Rightsize your Amazon MSK cluster by ensuring the best practices for standard brokers (*https://oreil.ly/3TVSk*) and best practices for express brokers (*https://oreil.ly/gXxps*).

- Use Amazon MSK Connect (*https://oreil.ly/M7_x8*) for easy integration between Amazon MSK and external data sources/targets. It is a fully managed service that provides connectors that stream data into Amazon MSK clusters from external systems like databases, storage engines, etc., as shown in Figure 4-13, with the least operational overhead. It can also act as a consumer that reads data from Amazon MSK clusters and writes into various targets. There are different connector categories:

Source connectors

These pull data from an external data source (like a database, queue, API, etc.) and push this data into the Amazon MSK cluster.

Sink connectors

These pull data from the Kafka cluster and push it into an external data sink (like Amazon S3, search engine, analytics system, etc.).

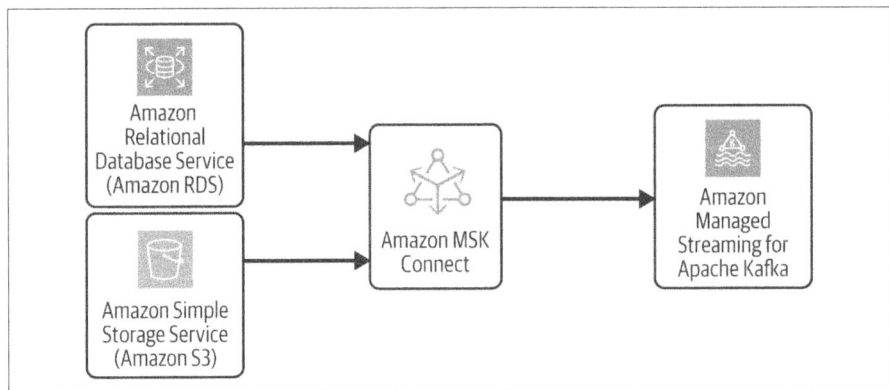

Figure 4-13. MSK source connectors example

Connectors can perform lightweight transformations, format conversions, or data filtering before delivering the data. Each connector consists of workers (JVM processes) that run the connector logic. The workers create parallelized tasks that do the actual work of copying data in a resilient and scalable manner.

- Use Amazon MSK Replicator (*https://oreil.ly/CJjic*) to build highly available and regionally resilient streaming applications across AWS Regions. It is a feature of Amazon MSK that enables replicating data between MSK clusters in different AWS Regions or within the same region. It provides automatic and reliable asynchronous replication without requiring custom coding or cross-region networking setup. Follow these best practices when using MSK Replicator:

  — Since Replicator acts as a consumer, high replication throughput can throttle other consumers on the source cluster. To avoid this, apply a network bandwidth quota (bytes per second rate) on the Replicator's service execution role at the broker level. This controls how much cluster capacity the Replicator can consume. Verify that the `ReplicatorThroughput` metric stays within the set quota.

— Set the log retention period to 7 days for source and target MSK clusters to ensure periodic clearing of older data to free up disk space, while still providing sufficient data history based on requirements.

- Optimize cluster throughput for larger instance types (e.g., m5.4xl, m7g.4xl, or larger) by tuning `num.io.threads` and `num.network.threads` configurations.

- Build highly available clusters by using 3 Availability Zones, a replication factor of at least 3, a proper `min.insync.replicas` setting, and client connection strings with brokers from each AZ.

- Monitor and maintain CPU usage under 60% to allow headroom for operations like broker replacement.

- Monitor disk space usage and adjust data retention parameters or scale storage when usage exceeds 85%.

- Monitor Kafka memory usage via the `HeapMemoryAfterGC` metric and take corrective actions when it exceeds 60%.

- Don't add non-MSK brokers to avoid incorrect cluster information.

- Enable in-transit encryption.

- Use the partition reassignment tool to rebalance clusters after scaling operations.

Best Practices for Amazon Data Firehose

Amazon Data Firehose can reliably deliver data streams into Amazon S3, Amazon OpenSearch, and Amazon Redshift. It has the ability to do some lightweight operations like:

- Converting data from JSON to Parquet format
- Compressing and decompressing output
- Adding delimiters
- Batching data for optimal file size
- Creating dynamic partitions for Amazon S3 buckets

It can also optionally invoke a Lambda function to perform transformations like data format conversion from CSV/XML to JSON and eventually to Parquet. Since Kinesis Data Streams and Amazon MSK don't have the ability to directly connect to target data stores in Amazon S3 and Amazon OpenSearch, Amazon Data Firehose acts as a delivery solution for these targets.

Utilize the following best practices when using Amazon Data Firehose:

- Optimize buffering hints for delivery requirements. Amazon Data Firehose buffers incoming data to a certain size and for a certain period before delivering it to the destinations. You can configure the buffering size (in MB) and buffering interval (in seconds) to control batching and delivery behavior:
  - For real-time, low-latency use cases, setting a 0 second buffering interval triggers immediate delivery for minimum lag.
  - For high-throughput destinations like S3, increase buffer size and interval to allow bigger batches for better performance.
- Leverage dynamic partitioning when you expect significant variance or spikes in your data ingestion rates over time. This allows Firehose to automatically scale up the number of shards to handle increased throughput during peak periods and scale back down when traffic subsides, saving costs. Dynamic partitioning is also useful when you have very high sustained data rates that could overwhelm the capacity of a single shard. Dynamically distributing the load across more shards enables achieving higher overall parallelism and throughput to destinations like Amazon S3 or Redshift.
- Amazon Data Firehose supports various data destinations, such as Amazon S3, Amazon Redshift, Amazon Elasticsearch Service, and Amazon Splunk as shown in Figure 4-6. Carefully evaluate your data storage and processing requirements and select the most suitable destination(s) for your use case.
- If Amazon Data Firehose has a direct integration with your desired target, using it will most likely provide you the least operational overhead.
- Configure delivery stream settings, such as buffer size, buffer interval, compression, and file type to optimize the delivery of data to your chosen destination. This can help reduce costs and improve overall performance.
- Utilize Firehose's batching and partitioning capabilities to group multiple records into a single delivery and partition data based on time or other relevant attributes.

Best Practices for AWS DMS Replication Instances and Tasks

Ensuring optimal performance is crucial when executing database migrations with AWS DMS, especially for large datasets or mission-critical workloads. AWS provides a range of configuration options and best practices to boost migration speeds and throughput while minimizing downtime and impact on source and target databases. Key performance considerations include:

- Provision a proper replication instance:
  - Use larger instance types like C4 or R4 for CPU-intensive heterogeneous migrations.

- Ensure sufficient memory (R4 instances provide more memory per vCPU).
- Increase storage if needed for logs/cached data.
- Use multi-AZ instances for better availability.
- Load multiple tables in parallel:
  - By default, DMS loads eight tables at a time.
  - Increase this number slightly for larger replication instances.
  - Reduce for smaller instances.
- Use parallel full load:
  - For partitioned/subpartitioned tables from certain sources.
  - Split large tables into segments and load in parallel.
- Manage indexes/constraints during migration:
  - Drop secondary indexes, constraints, and triggers before full load.
  - Add indexes before the CDC phase.
  - Enable triggers before cutover.
- Turn off backups/logging on target during migration:
  - Use multiple tasks for different table sets.
  - Use batch optimized apply mode (violates referential integrity).
- Tune LOB (large binary objects) settings:
  - Use Limited LOB mode (32 KB default limit).
  - Increase LOB limit if needed.
  - Use per-table LOB settings.
  - Use Inline LOB mode for mixed LOB sizes.
- Improve performance for large tables:
  - Use row filtering to break into multiple tasks.
  - Use parallel load by ranges/partitions.
  - Identify and eliminate bottlenecks on source and target databases.

Best Practices for AWS DMS Tasks with Amazon Redshift Target

Use the following best practices when using AWS DMS to ingest data into Amazon Redshift:

- Enable the `BatchApplyEnabled` task setting and configure `BatchApplyTimeout` `Min/Max` based on how frequently you need data refreshed. Redshift is optimized for analytical workloads, not transactional changes. Enabling

`BatchApplyEnabled` allows DMS to efficiently handle changes to Redshift tables during change data capture (CDC) by batching transactions, as applying transactional changes one-by-one can impact Redshift performance.

- Set `BatchSplitSize=0` to allow unlimited batch sizes, and increase `BatchApply MemoryLimit` to a higher value (e.g., 1024 MB) to process more records per commit batch. Large batch sizes can improve CDC performance to Redshift by maximizing the number of records processed in each commit batch. This reduces the overhead of committing transactions and takes advantage of Redshift's strengths in handling analytical workloads.

- For large data migrations, increase the `maxFileSize` (e.g., 250,000 KB) and `file TransferUploadStreams` (e.g., 20) connection attributes. DMS transfers data to Redshift via CSV files in S3, so increasing the file size and number of parallel upload streams can improve full load performance by reducing the overhead of transferring data, particularly for large data volumes.

- Use primary keys on both source and target tables to improve CDC performance to Redshift. Without primary keys, updates and deletes are applied one-by-one, which can impact performance.

- Avoid `VARCHAR` data types larger than 64 KB, as Redshift doesn't support them. DMS will convert `BLOB/CLOB` to `VARCHAR`. Redshift has limitations on certain data types, so avoiding unsupported data types ensures data compatibility between the source and Redshift target, preventing errors or data loss during migration.

- Use `ParallelApplyThreads` for multithreaded CDC and `ParallelApplyBuffer Size` for buffers to improve performance. Parallelizing CDC operations can improve throughput by leveraging multiple threads for applying changes and buffering data during CDC, which can significantly improve performance, especially for high-volume transactional workloads.

- For full loads, use `ParallelLoadThreads` along with `MaxFullLoadSubTasks` to leverage parallel loading into Redshift. Allocate sufficient replication instance memory. Redshift can benefit from parallel loading for large data volumes, speeding up the full load process by parallelizing the data transfer and loading, reducing the overall migration time by utilizing multiple threads and the resources of the replication instance.

- Create target Redshift tables with appropriate distribution and sort keys for optimized data storage and querying. Redshift's performance is heavily influenced by its data distribution and sort strategies, so properly defining distribution and sort keys can significantly improve query performance and reduce the need for resource-intensive data redistribution, ensuring efficient data storage and retrieval in Redshift.

- Monitor Redshift metrics like WLM queue disk spill. Use AutoWLM or customize WLM queues if workloads impact performance. Redshift's Workload Management (WLM) system manages memory allocation and concurrency. By monitoring WLM metrics and adjusting queue configurations, you can prevent the DMS workload from impacting other workloads on the Redshift cluster and ensure optimal performance.

- Ensure there are no locks or blocking sessions in Redshift that can impact performance. Redshift can experience performance issues due to locks or blocked queries. Identifying and resolving any potential locking or blocking issues in Redshift prevents reduced throughput and increased latency, ensuring DMS migration performance is not negatively affected.

Data Transformation

Data integration and transformation are essential steps in modern data analytics pipelines. As organizations collect data from diverse sources, there is a critical need to integrate this data into a consistent format, clean it, and transform it into a structure suitable for analysis. Depending on the use case, data transformation can be applied in either batch mode or streaming mode.

Batch Data Transformation

In batch mode, the data is processed in large, discrete chunks, allowing for more complex transformations and validations. This approach is well suited for scenarios where the data is accumulated over time and needs to be processed periodically, such as hourly, daily, or weekly data aggregations. Batch transformations can be performed using Apache Spark jobs or SQL-based transformation. In AWS you can author Spark batch jobs using the fully managed Spark service AWS Glue or Amazon EMR. For SQL-based data transformation, you can use Amazon Redshift.

Streaming Data Transformation

Streaming data transformations involve processing continuous flows of data in real time as events occur. Think of it like a flowing river of data where you need to analyze, modify, or aggregate information as it passes by. Spark Structured Streaming and Apache Flink provide ways to handle these transformations but approach them differently.

Spark Structured Streaming treats streaming data as an unbounded table that continuously grows as new data arrives. You can apply SQL-like operations (such as filtering, grouping, or joining) to this "table," making it familiar to anyone who has worked with batch data processing. For example, you might compute real-time averages of sensor readings or filter out unwanted events as they arrive. In AWS you can run

Spark Structured Streaming jobs with either the fully managed service AWS Glue or using Spark Structured Streaming jobs in Amazon EMR.

Flink, on the other hand, processes each event individually as it flows through the system. It can do both stateless and stateful transformations. Stateless transformations don't need to retain state information across event records. These are operations like filtering, routing, data enrichment by performing lookups to external databases, etc. Stateful transformations include maintaining state between events and providing capabilities like event aggregation, windowing operations, event correlation, streaming joins, etc., to group and process related events together. This makes it particularly good at tasks like detecting patterns in real time (such as potential fraud in financial transactions) or maintaining up-to-the-second aggregations. In AWS you can run Flink jobs either with the fully managed service Amazon Managed Streaming for Flink (MSF) or using Flink jobs with Amazon EMR.

By leveraging the appropriate data transformation service, you can ensure that the data is cleansed, formatted, and enriched, enabling you to derive meaningful insights and make informed decisions. In Chapter 3, you learned that AWS Glue, Amazon EMR, Amazon Managed Streaming for Flink (MSF), AWS Lambda, and Glue Data-Brew all have data transformation capabilities. Let's take a deeper look at them.

Data Transformation Using AWS Glue

AWS Glue is a serverless data transformation service with which you can perform both batch and streaming data transformation. Glue uses Spark for batch processing and Spark Structured Streaming for stream processing. In addition for lightweight data processing, Glue provides the ability to author Python shell jobs.

To perform the data transformation, you create AWS Glue jobs. Jobs consist of scripts that contain the programming logic that connects to sources, performs the transformation, and writes the transformed data to the target. Let's understand some AWS Glue concepts and terminology.

Glue Connectors

Glue connectors enable you to access and read data from various data sources, including databases, data lakes, and SaaS applications. These prebuilt, configurable components allow you to easily ingest data from different sources, without having to write custom code to handle all the specifics. This makes it much simpler to set up and maintain batch data ingestion pipelines, as you can leverage the out-of-the-box connectors to quickly and reliably ingest data. Examples of Glue connectors include connectors for Amazon S3, Amazon RDS, Amazon Redshift, and popular SaaS applications like Salesforce and ServiceNow. For a complete list, refer to the available connectors (*https://oreil.ly/dhcwD*).

Glue Bookmarks

Job bookmarks in AWS Glue enable incremental batch data processing over constantly changing data sources like S3 and databases. They help with CDC. They store information about previously processed data in previous job runs, like processed filepaths for S3 sources and primary key ranges for JDBC sources. The Glue ETL jobs that use bookmarks can pick up where they left off and process only new or modified data instead of redundantly reprocessing the entire dataset on each scheduled run.

By leveraging Glue connectors and bookmarks, you can simplify the process of batch data ingestion, making it easier to set up, maintain, and scale your data integration pipelines. This can be especially beneficial for use cases where you need to regularly ingest data from a variety of sources into your data lake or data warehouse.

Data Processing Units

The compute power in AWS Glue is provided by data processing units (DPUs); you are charged for the number of DPUs and duration of your job. A DPU consists of 4 vCPUs of compute capacity and 16 GB of memory, operating as a combination of compute and memory resources that process your ETL jobs. AWS charges for Glue usage per second based on the number of DPUs used, making it important to balance performance needs with cost considerations.

Worker Type

Glue job workers are the compute resources in AWS Glue that execute your jobs. Workers determine the amount of computing power for the job. They are responsible for running the actual job tasks and processing the data, whether it's batch processing with Spark jobs, real-time data streaming with streaming ETL jobs, or executing Python scripts with Python shell jobs. AWS Glue automatically scales the number of Glue job workers up or down based on the job requirements, ensuring efficient resource utilization and optimizing performance.

The worker types available are G.1X. G.2X, G.4X, G.8X, and G.025X:

- Use the G.025X worker for low volume streaming jobs. It is only available for AWS Glue version 3.0 streaming jobs.

- Use the G.4X and G.8X workers for the jobs that contain your most demanding transforms, aggregations, joins, and queries and require more compute power.

- Use the G.2X worker to perform lightweight data transforms, joins, and queries. It offers a scalable and cost-effective way to run most jobs.

Glue Jobs

AWS Glue offers distinct job types to cater to various data processing needs:

Spark jobs

AWS Spark jobs are executed within an Apache Spark environment that is fully managed by AWS Glue. These jobs excel at batch processing of large datasets, leveraging the power of Apache Spark's distributed computing capabilities. The minimum DPUs required for Spark jobs is 2, ensuring sufficient resources for efficient batch data processing.

Streaming ETL jobs

Streaming ETL utilizes the Apache Spark Structured Streaming framework to seamlessly perform ETL operations on continuous data streams. The jobs process and write data in configurable time windows, with a default of 100 seconds. This allows efficient processing and permits aggregations on late data. Supported compression formats like GZIP, Snappy, and Bzip2 are automatically decompressed. You can supply custom ETL scripts or use AWS Glue's built-in transforms as well as Apache Spark Structured Streaming operations to transform the data. Supported streaming sources require creating a Glue Data Catalog table, which can optionally use schema detection on the data. These jobs require a minimum of 2 DPUs. AWS Glue can transform data from streaming data sources including Amazon Kinesis Data Streams and Apache Kafka.

Python shell jobs

Python shell jobs offer a flexible environment for running Python scripts and are ideal for lightweight ETL jobs that don't require a lot of compute power. Because the minimum required DPUs for Python scripts is only 1/16, they are a cost-efficient option for lightweight data transformations.

Jobs contain scripts that connect to sources, perform transformations, and load data into targets. Let's take the example of Glue Spark jobs and look at the various components of a job. For other job types, please refer to the AWS Glue documentation (*https://oreil.ly/uE0_q*).

Data Sources and Destinations

AWS Glue offers a wide selection of *connectors* for multiple applications and databases. You can use a native connector, a connector from AWS Marketplace, or create your own custom connectors. After you choose a connector, you can create a connection based on that connector.

The AWS documentation has a list of available connectors (*https://oreil.ly/dhcwD*) for AWS Glue. You will notice the following:

- There are connectors available for databases such as Amazon Aurora, Amazon DocumentDB, Amazon Redshift, MongoDB, MongoDB Atlas, MySQL, Oracle database, PostgreSQL, Salesforce, SAP HANA, Snowflake, Teradata Vantage, Vertica, etc.
- There are connectors for applications like Instagram Ads, LinkedIn, Facebook Ads, Asana, Salesforce, Zendesk, SAP, etc.
- When creating a connection on AWS Glue, you can choose the source you are trying to connect to in the "Choose data source" section, as shown in Figure 4-14.

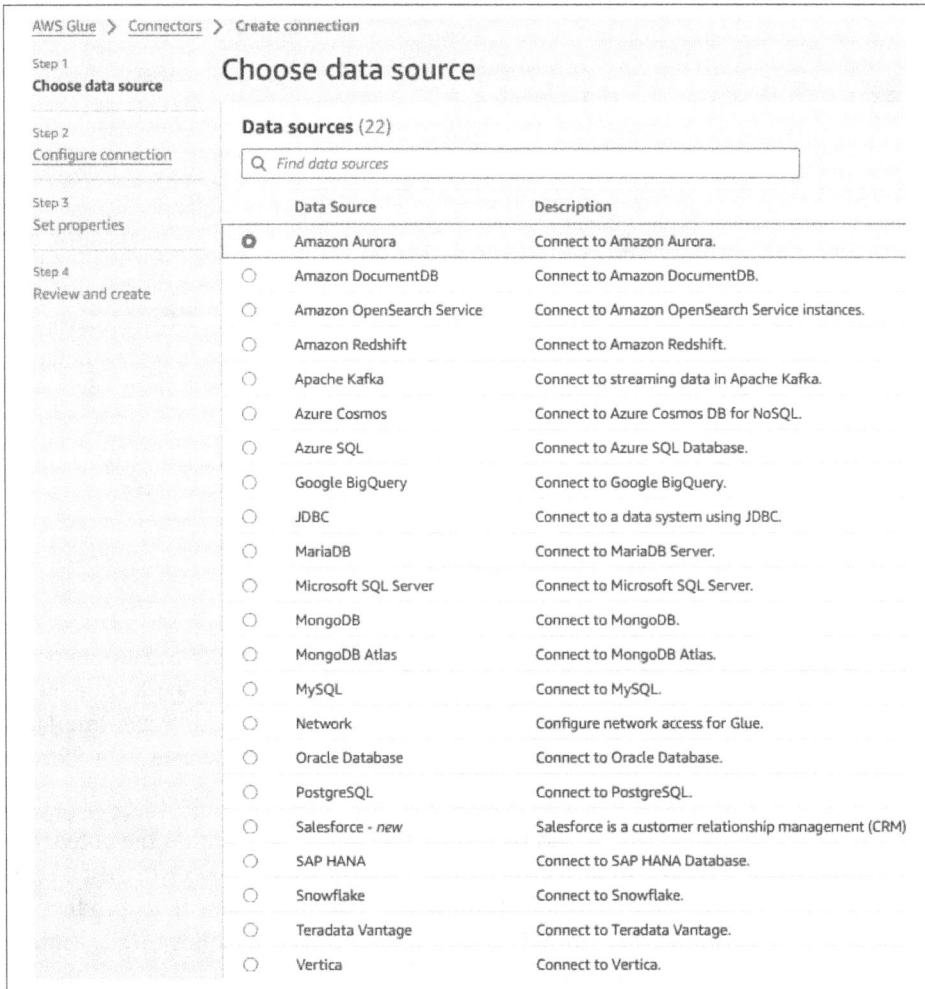

AWS Glue > Connectors > Create connection

Step 1
Choose data source

Step 2
Configure connection

Step 3
Set properties

Step 4
Review and create

Choose data source

Data sources (22)

Q Find data sources

	Data Source	Description
●	Amazon Aurora	Connect to Amazon Aurora.
○	Amazon DocumentDB	Connect to Amazon DocumentDB.
○	Amazon OpenSearch Service	Connect to Amazon OpenSearch Service instances.
○	Amazon Redshift	Connect to Amazon Redshift.
○	Apache Kafka	Connect to streaming data in Apache Kafka.
○	Azure Cosmos	Connect to Azure Cosmos DB for NoSQL.
○	Azure SQL	Connect to Azure SQL Database.
○	Google BigQuery	Connect to Google BigQuery.
○	JDBC	Connect to a data system using JDBC.
○	MariaDB	Connect to MariaDB Server.
○	Microsoft SQL Server	Connect to Microsoft SQL Server.
○	MongoDB	Connect to MongoDB.
○	MongoDB Atlas	Connect to MongoDB Atlas.
○	MySQL	Connect to MySQL.
○	Network	Configure network access for Glue.
○	Oracle Database	Connect to Oracle Database.
○	PostgreSQL	Connect to PostgreSQL.
○	Salesforce - *new*	Salesforce is a customer relationship management (CRM)
○	SAP HANA	Connect to SAP HANA Database.
○	Snowflake	Connect to Snowflake.
○	Teradata Vantage	Connect to Teradata Vantage.
○	Vertica	Connect to Vertica.

Figure 4-14. Data sources page in AWS Glue

AWS Glue accommodates different user preferences and expertise levels through three distinct job authoring interfaces.

Glue Studio

Glue Studio offers a drag-and-drop environment for building ETL workflows with minimal coding. After you design a job in the graphical interface, it generates Apache Spark code for you. When the job is ready, you can run it and monitor the job status using the integrated UI. Figure 4-15 shows a sample ETL job authored using Glue Studio, which has two source tables from Amazon S3, which are joined, aggregated, and eventually written into Amazon S3 after transformations.

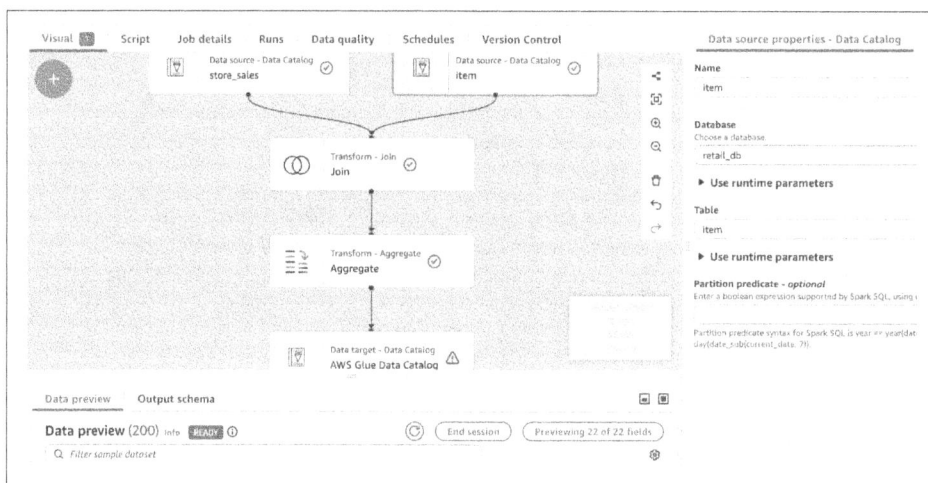

Figure 4-15. Sample ETL job authored using AWS Glue Studio

Glue Studio notebooks

For those who favor a notebook-based development experience, AWS Glue supports Jupyter notebooks. These notebooks allow you to write and test PySpark code interactively, combining code, visualizations, and documentation in a single interface. This approach suits data scientists and engineers who are comfortable with Python and want to develop complex transformations.

Once you have developed and tested your data integration logic within the notebook, AWS Glue Studio seamlessly converts your notebook into a Glue job with just a click of a button. This seamless transition from interactive development to production job execution streamlines the entire data integration process, enabling you to rapidly iterate and deploy your ETL workflows.

AWS Glue interactive sessions

Interactive sessions enable real-time development and debugging of Glue ETL scripts. They provide a development environment where you can test your code against live data, examine results immediately, and iterate quickly. This interface is ideal for developers who need to fine-tune their ETL logic or troubleshoot complex transformations.

Best Practices for AWS Glue

Here are some of the best practices to follow when using AWS Glue:

Use appropriate worker types
> Choose the worker type that best fits your workload requirements. For compute-intensive jobs, consider using G.4X or G.8X workers, which have more CPU and memory resources.

Optimize data partitioning
> Partitioning your data can significantly improve the performance of Glue jobs by reducing the amount of data that needs to be scanned. Partition your data based on frequently used filters or predicates in your queries.

Use the right file format
> Different file formats have varying performance characteristics. For example, Apache Parquet and ORC formats are generally more efficient for analytical workloads compared to CSV or JSON formats.

Leverage Glue Data Catalog partitions
> AWS Glue Data Catalog supports partitioning, which can improve query performance by pruning unnecessary data. When creating or updating tables in the Data Catalog, make sure to partition your data appropriately.

Enable job bookmarks for incremental data processing
> AWS Glue supports job bookmarks, which allow you to resume failed jobs from the last successful checkpoint, reducing the need to reprocess the entire dataset.

Use Glue job monitoring
> AWS Glue provides job monitoring capabilities that can help you identify performance bottlenecks and optimize your jobs accordingly. Analyze the job metrics and logs to identify potential areas for improvement.

Use Glue Spark UI
> For Apache Spark–based Glue jobs, you can use the Glue Spark UI to analyze the performance of your Spark jobs, including identifying slow stages, data skew, and other potential issues.

Use AWS Glue autoscaling
Automatically scale your jobs based on processing needs:

- When transforming data from or data into a data lake, ensure you have the optimal file size. Avoid too many small files as both source and target. Also avoid files larger than 1 GB.
- Use the Flex execution class for non-sensitive jobs to save cost.

Data Transformation Using Amazon EMR

Enterprises often deal with large volumes of data originating from diverse sources, requiring robust and scalable solutions for data integration and processing. While AWS Glue provides a serverless and managed solution to run ETL workloads using Apache Spark or Python shell scripts, there are scenarios where more big data frameworks and customizations are needed. This is where Amazon Elastic MapReduce (EMR) comes into play, offering a powerful and flexible platform for processing and analyzing vast amounts of data using open source frameworks like Apache Hadoop, Apache Spark, Apache Hive, Apache HBase, Apache Flink, and Apache Presto.

With EMR, organizations can do batch processing, real-time stream processing, or interactive analytics. Batch processing can be done using Spark, Hive, Presto, Trino, etc. Stream data processing can be done using Apache Spark Structured Streaming or Apache Flink frameworks.

Storage

When running long-running workloads on Amazon EMR, organizations need to consider the persistent data storage options available. Amazon EMR supports two primary options for persistent data storage:

Hadoop Distributed File System (HDFS)
HDFS is a distributed file system designed for storing and processing large datasets across multiple nodes in a Hadoop cluster. It provides fault tolerance and high throughput access to data. However, managing an HDFS cluster can add operational complexity and costs.

Amazon S3
Amazon S3 is a highly durable, scalable, and cost-effective object storage service provided by AWS. Using Amazon S3 as a persistent data store eliminates the need for separate HDFS storage, reducing operational overhead and costs. Data stored in Amazon S3 persists even after the Amazon EMR cluster terminates, allowing for efficient data reuse and long-running workloads. We recommend using Amazon S3 as storage instead of HDFS.

Deployment Options

Amazon EMR supports multiple deployment options for various business needs:

EMR on EC2

The EMR on EC2 deployment option is the classic approach to running Amazon EMR. This option provides maximum control over your big data infrastructure. With this option, you can run multiple big data frameworks (Spark, Hive, Pig, Presto, Trino, and others) concurrently within a single cluster.

This option offers extensive customization options. You can select specific EC2 instance types for your workloads or use instance fleets to combine different instance types within node groups. Bootstrap actions—shell scripts that execute during startup—allow you to configure the software environment to your exact specifications.

EMR on EC2 also enables strategic cost optimization. For predictable workloads, you can reduce costs using Reserved Instances or Savings Plans, while Spot Instances can significantly lower expenses for interrupt-tolerant jobs.

EMR Serverless

In contrast, the EMR Serverless deployment option provides the most managed and simplified approach to running Amazon EMR. With EMR Serverless, you don't have to worry about provisioning or managing the underlying infrastructure—it's all handled by AWS. This option currently supports the Spark and Hive frameworks. You can choose between x86 and Graviton instances, and you only pay for the runtime of your jobs, without the need to manage clusters. EMR Serverless automatically applies updates, further reducing the management overhead. This deployment option is well suited for users who have intermittent or unpredictable workloads, as the automatic scaling and pay-per-use pricing model can be more cost-effective than managing a constantly running cluster.

EMR on EKS

The EMR on EKS deployment option allows you to run Amazon EMR on top of Amazon Elastic Kubernetes Service (EKS), a managed Kubernetes service. This approach simplifies infrastructure management, as EKS handles the underlying compute resources and scaling of the worker nodes. By deploying EMR components on top of EKS, you can benefit from the flexibility and portability offered by Kubernetes. This option is particularly suitable for users who are already familiar with EKS and Kubernetes, as it consolidates the management of multiple versions of Spark on the same EKS cluster and simplifies Spark application upgrades. Additionally, by leveraging EKS, you can take advantage of multi-AZ resiliency, with worker nodes distributed across multiple Availability Zones. The EMR on EKS deployment option provides a balance between infrastructure management and the customization capabilities required for more complex or hybrid cloud deployments.

Instance Types

Amazon EMR supports various instance types for its core nodes (which manage the cluster) and task nodes (which execute the jobs). Organizations can choose from different instance families based on their workload requirements and cost considerations. Some of the instance types available for Amazon EMR include:

x86-based instances
These are the traditional instances based on x86 architecture, such as the M5, R5, and C5 instance families. They offer a balance of compute, memory, and storage resources for a wide range of workloads.

Graviton instances
These instances are based on AWS's own ARM-based Graviton processors, which provide better performance and cost savings compared to x86-based instances for certain workloads. For Apache Spark workloads, Graviton instances can offer up to 30% better price-performance compared to x86-based instances.

Spot Instances
Amazon EMR supports the use of Spot Instances, which are spare Amazon EC2 compute capacity offered at a significant discount compared to on-demand instances. However, Spot Instances can be interrupted by AWS when capacity is needed, making them less suitable for long-running workloads that require high reliability.

Best Practices for Amazon EMR

Here are some best practices to get the most out of Amazon EMR:

- Use Amazon S3 as your persistent data store instead of HDFS, as S3 is cheaper and more reliable for storage.
- Compress, compact, and convert your data to optimized file formats like Parquet and ORC to reduce storage and improve performance.
- Partition and bucket your data in S3 to reduce the amount that needs to be scanned.
- Choose the right EC2 instance types for your workloads (e.g., compute-optimized for CPU-heavy, memory-optimized for memory-intensive).
- Use Spot Instances, which can provide up to 90% discount compared to on-demand pricing.

- Mix Spot and on-demand instances to lower costs while still meeting SLAs. Use on-demand for core nodes and Spot for task.
- Enable EMR-managed scaling to automatically adjust cluster size based on workload.
- Rightsize your application containers and resources to fully utilize instances.
- Use the latest EMR version, which includes performance optimizations and cost savings.
- Use EMR Serverless for sporadic workloads.

AWS Glue Versus Amazon EMR Options

In this section let's learn how to choose between the data processing options we have discussed so far by considering various factors such as serverless options, framework support, startup time for jobs, solution scaling, etc. (Table 4-4).

Table 4-4. Comparison of AWS Glue and Amazon EMR options

	AWS Glue	Amazon EMR Serverless	Amazon EMR on EC2	Amazon EMR on EKS
Serverless solution	Yes	Yes	No	No (unless Fargate is used)
Supported frameworks	Spark, Python	Spark, Hive	Spark, Hive, Trino, HBase, Flink, and more	Spark
Data processing job startup time	~10 seconds	~2 minutes or few seconds if preinitialized capacity	Cluster creation time is ~5 minutes. If the cluster is precreated then job submission is immediate	~10 seconds if instances are available (~2 minutes if Fargate)
Scaling	Fully managed scaling	Fully managed scaling	Autoscaling with custom policies based on CloudWatch metrics	EKS autoscaler/ Karpenter or serverless if Fargate is used
Interactive analytics	Yes Glue interactive sessions, Glue Studio, Glue notebooks	Yes, EMR Studio	Yes, EMR Studio JupyterHub, Zeppelin, Hue	Yes, EMR Studio
Multi-AZ (high reliability and resilience)	No	Yes	No	Yes
Cost optimization options	Flex execution	Not applicable	Spot Instances, reserved instances, Graviton instances, and managed scaling	Spot Instances, reserved instances, Graviton
Management overhead	Low	Low	Medium	Medium (Kubernetes expertise is needed)

SQL-Based Data Transformation Using Amazon Redshift

Amazon Redshift is a fully managed, petabyte-scale data warehouse service that uses SQL and PL/SQL for data transformation and analysis. Think of it as a massive, high-performance database optimized for analyzing large datasets using familiar SQL commands. Amazon Redshift has a cluster architecture with compute and storage separation.

Amazon Redshift Compute

Amazon Redshift has massively parallel compute. It is available in both provisioned and serverless modes. Serverless compute provides better ease of use. Provisioned compute nodes are called RA3 and are available in four different sizes—large, xlarge, 4xlarge, and 16xlarge. The documentation has compute specifications (*https://oreil.ly/VUj7w*). Provisioned compute has on-demand and reserved pricing. With on-demand you are charged for each second of usage. You can pause the on-demand cluster when the cluster is not in use. To get 30%–60% cost savings you can use reserved instances. You can reserve for 1 year or 3 years. A 3-year reservation will give you the lowest price.

Amazon Redshift Serverless measures data warehouse capacity in Redshift Processing Units (RPUs). RPUs are resources used to handle workloads. One RPU provides 16 GB of memory. Unlike provisioned, serverless doesn't charge for idleness. There is a charge only when an active query or load is running. Serverless compute gives you better ease of use compared to provisioned compute.

Amazon Redshift Storage

Amazon Redshift has high-performant, proprietary columnar storage that is optimized for analytics on large datasets. RMS is a combination of local SSDs on compute and Amazon S3. SSDs are used to cache the most frequently accessed data.

Figure 4-16 showcases various aspects of the Amazon Redshift architecture. Amazon Redshift's compute is capable of accessing both data in proprietary format from RMS and data in open source formats (like Iceberg, Hudi, Delta Lake, JSON, CSV, Parquet, etc.) from an Amazon S3 data lake.

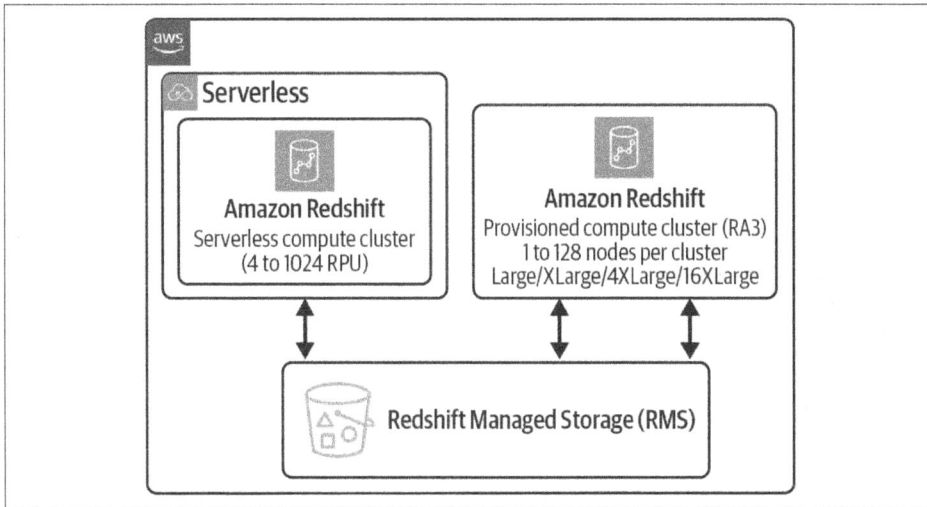

Figure 4-16. Amazon Redshift architecture

Using Amazon Redshift, you can design your data warehouse as a distributed data mesh, instead of a single monolith. Monoliths pose resource contention and scalability concerns. On the other hand, a distributed architecture can isolate workloads, thereby improving scalability and performance. There are two common types of multicluster architectures:

Hub and spoke

In this architecture pattern, there is a separate Redshift cluster for each workload. Typically, data warehouses have workloads such as ETL, reporting, data science, etc. By using a separate cluster for each and isolating these workloads completely from one another, you can reduce workload interference (i.e., while ETL is running, your reporting jobs are not impacted and vice versa). You can onboard new workloads rapidly.

Data mesh

In this architecture pattern, there is a separate Redshift cluster for each business unit. Each business unit gets complete control of their data assets. They choose which ones to share with other units and which ones not to share to achieve their compliance and governance requirements.

Figure 4-17 shows the hub-and-spoke architecture and data mesh architecture. In the hub-and-spoke architecture, notice two Redshift clusters performing transformations and populating data assets and three Redshift clusters consuming those data assets. In the data mesh architecture notice how each business unit (finance, HR, operations, etc.) gets their own compute endpoint.

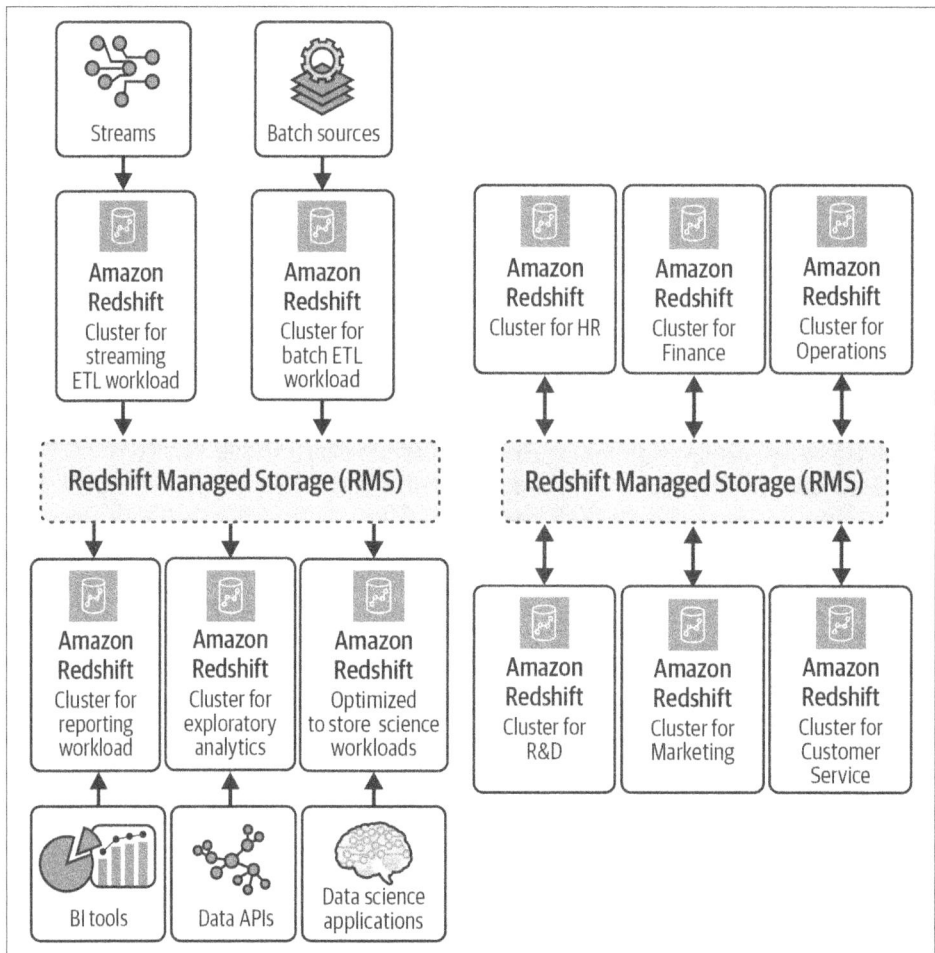

Figure 4-17. Hub-and-spoke and data mesh architectures

These multicluster architectures are powered by an Amazon Redshift feature called data sharing. Data sharing (*https://oreil.ly/F4rv8*) allows for reading live data assets populated by other endpoints in place, without making data copies, with transactional consistency. Using data sharing you can also write into common data assets (like tables) using multiple endpoints thereby scaling the write workload horizontally.

SQL Data Transformations

Amazon Redshift has the following data transformation and orchestration capabilities:

- Provides materialized views for stored transformations for batch data and streaming data
- Supports stored procedures for complex logic

Amazon Redshift materialized views

Materialized views store precomputed query results, acting like a cache for complex queries. Think of them as snapshots of your query results that get periodically refreshed to maintain data freshness. The most common use case for materialized views is to improve performance of dashboard queries. If your dashboard query has complexity including multiple table joins, aggregations, complex calculations, etc., consider creating a materialized view to prepopulate the required dataset so that it need not be generated at runtime. This helps in achieving latency in seconds for your analytics dashboard:

```
-- Example: Creating a materialized view for daily sales analytics
CREATE MATERIALIZED VIEW daily_sales_summary AS
    SELECT
        date_trunc('day', sale_timestamp) as sale_date,
        product_category,
        region,
        COUNT(*) as transaction_count,
        SUM(amount) as total_sales,
        AVG(amount) as avg_sale_amount
    FROM sales_transactions
    GROUP BY 1, 2, 3;
```

Amazon Redshift's materialized views have some notable features:

Automatic query rewriting
> If you think that your queries will benefit from converting them into a materialized view, you can just go ahead and create the materialized view and don't need to change your existing queries to use this MV. Redshift has the capability to automatically use materialized views when applicable.

Incremental and automatic refresh
> Incremental refresh is an optimization technique where Redshift updates only the changed data in a materialized view instead of recomputing the entire view. Incremental refresh is possible when the base tables are RMS tables created by the cluster, RMS tables shared by another cluster, or external tables where data resides in Amazon S3 in open formats. If you use certain operations in

your materialized view query, the view will not be able to incrementally refresh. Please refer to the limitations for incremental refresh (*https://oreil.ly/8PiFP*) to understand more.

Amazon Redshift also supports automatic refresh. It can detect changes in the base tables and automatically trigger a refresh when the load on the cluster is low so that it doesn't impact a user's processes. Automatic refresh is supported on views whose base tables are RMS tables created by the same cluster or shared from another cluster. Automatic refresh doesn't happen if the base tables are external tables.

Amazon Redshift stored procedures

Stored procedures in Amazon Redshift can be used to encapsulate logic for data transformation, data validation, and business-specific logic. They combine multiple SQL steps that can all be executed in a single stored procedure call.

In Redshift, the stored procedures are typically used to populate the tables in Amazon Redshift Managed Storage (RMS). You can define an industry standard data model like a star schema and use stored procedures to periodically refresh the data model tables with new incoming data from the source. The typical steps include:

1. Extracting data from sources (such as S3) and loading into staging tables
2. Merging the data from staging into the target dimension or fact table

You can define an Amazon Redshift stored procedure using the PostgreSQL procedural language PL/pgSQL. You can control the flow of statement execution using procedural language constructs such as looping and conditional expressions. You can also use stored procedures for delegated access control. For example, you can create stored procedures to perform functions without giving a user access to the underlying tables.

Following is a sample stored procedure that loads sales data into a staging table and finally merges into the sales fact table:

```
CREATE OR REPLACE PROCEDURE sp_merge_sales_data()
LANGUAGE plpgsql
AS $$
BEGIN
    -- Create staging table if it doesn't exist
    DROP TABLE IF EXISTS staging.sales_staging;

    CREATE TABLE staging.sales_staging
    (
        salesid INTEGER NOT NULL, listid INTEGER NOT NULL,
        sellerid INTEGER, buyerid INTEGER, event id INTEGER,
        dateid INTEGER, qtysold INTEGER, pricepaid DECIMAL(8,2),
        commission DECIMAL(8,2), saletime TIMESTAMP
```

```
    );

    -- Load data into staging table. This example copies from S3
    COPY staging.sales_staging
    FROM 's3://your-bucket/sales_data/'
    IAM_ROLE 'arn:aws:iam::your-account-id:role/your-role'
    FORMAT CSV
    DELIMITER ','
    IGNOREHEADER 1;

    -- Perform the merge operation
    MERGE INTO dwh.fact_sales
    USING staging.sales_staging source
    ON ( salesid = source.salesid AND listid = source.listid )
    WHEN MATCHED THEN
        UPDATE SET
            qtysold = source.qtysold,
            pricepaid = source.pricepaid,
            commission = source.commission,
            last_updated = GETDATE()
    WHEN NOT MATCHED THEN
        INSERT (salesid,listid,sellerid,buyerid,eventid,dateid,qtysold,
            pricepaid,commission,saletime,created_date)
        VALUES (source.salesid,source.listid,source.sellerid,
            source.buyerid,source.eventid,source.dateid,source.qtysold,
            source.pricepaid,source.commission,source.saletime,
            GETDATE());

    -- Clean up staging table
    DROP TABLE IF EXISTS staging.sales_staging;

END;
$$;
```

Amazon Managed Service for Apache Flink

Amazon Managed Service for Apache Flink (MSF) is a fully managed service that allows you to query and analyze streaming data using the Apache Flink framework. To perform real-time transformations, aggregations, windowing operations, and stateful computations on streaming data from Amazon Kinesis Data Streams or Amazon MSK, you can use Amazon MSF. It is the solution that offers the lowest latency and highest throughput for streaming data transformations and has the least operational overhead. When MSF is consuming data from Kinesis as a consumer, it can use enhanced fan-out mode (which was described earlier in the chapter when discussing Kinesis Data Streams) to get dedicated read throughput. The transformed data can be written to Amazon S3 data lakes. It can also be written back to Amazon Kinesis Data Streams or Amazon MSK for further delivery to a target such as an Amazon Redshift data warehouse, as shown in Figure 4-18.

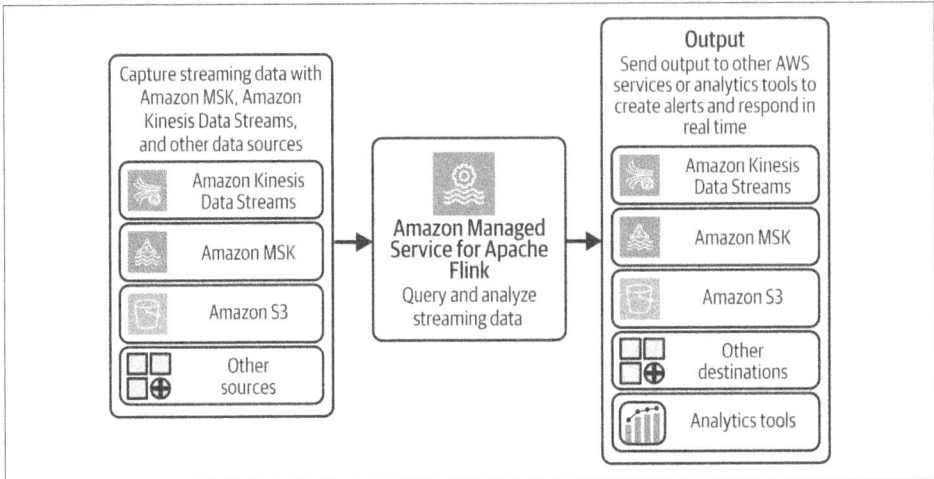

Figure 4-18. Integrations for Amazon Managed Service for Apache Flink

When using MSF, follow these best practices:

- Understand the cost model. Costs are determined by the number of Kinesis Processing Units (KPUs), which are based on the parallelism and parallelism per KPU settings.

- Monitor for overprovisioning. Look for low CPU and memory utilization metrics over time, or if the application is purely I/O bound, which may indicate too many KPUs allocated.

- Increase parallelism per KPU. For I/O bound workloads, increasing parallelism per KPU can allow for running more tasks per KPU to densify workloads.

- Rightsize KPUs during load testing. Start with 1 KPU per 1 MB/s throughput and adjust parallelism up/down based on performance testing.

- Use autoscaling. Enable metric-based or scheduled autoscaling to automatically adjust KPUs based on load.

- Optimize code. Use higher-level APIs, eliminate data skew, and use async I/O to improve efficiency.

- Evaluate whether Flink is indeed needed. For stateless, high-latency workloads, consider alternatives like AWS Lambda.

Amazon Data Firehose for Transformation

As discussed earlier in the chapter when reviewing streaming ingestion, Amazon Data Firehose's main function is data stream delivery to various AWS analytics services including Amazon S3, OpenSearch, and Redshift. Given that Kinesis Data Streams and Amazon MSK lack direct connectivity to Amazon S3 and OpenSearch, Firehose plays a crucial role as an intermediary delivery solution.

While delivering data, it can perform lightweight operations, such as converting data from JSON to Parquet format, handling output compression and decompression, adding delimiters, optimizing data through batching, and creating dynamic partitions for Amazon S3 buckets. Firehose can also leverage AWS Lambda functions for slightly more complex transformations, such as converting data formats from CSV/XML to JSON and subsequently to Parquet.

AWS Lambda for Transformation

When you have simple, event-driven data transformation tasks that can be handled by short-running (less than 15 minutes), stateless functions you can use AWS Lambda. It can perform lightweight data transformation needs, such as data format conversions, basic filtering, or small-scale aggregations in a cost-efficient manner as you can take advantage of the scalability, fault tolerance, and pay-per-use pricing model of AWS Lambda.

Choosing the Right Streaming Transformation Service

There are multiple options for running streaming jobs on AWS, with trade-offs between operational simplicity and control (Table 4-5).

You can run Spark Structured Streaming jobs on either:

- AWS Glue (fully managed, serverless)
- Amazon EMR (either provisioned clusters or serverless)

For Flink applications, your choices are:

- Amazon MSF (fully managed)
- Amazon EMR (either provisioned clusters or serverless)

Table 4-5. Choosing between Spark Streaming jobs and Flink applications

Criteria	Amazon Data Firehose + AWS Lambda	Spark Streaming jobs *(Glue Streaming or Spark Structured Streaming jobs on Amazon EMR)*	Flink jobs *(Amazon MSF / Flink jobs on Amazon EMR)*
Data transformation	If you want to use AWS Lambda for transformation Simple stateless transformations or limited windowing (15 min. windows)	Stateless/stateful transformations Use if you want to use Spark Structured Streaming specifically	Rich stateless/stateful transformations Use for complex transformations
Schema evolution	Limited (new column addition/changes)	Yes	No
Schema registry support	No	Yes	Yes
Write operations	Can do insert/update/delete	Appends rows of microbatch to the table or completely replaces the table content at each microbatch or merge using foreachbatch	Append, upsert, overwrite
Low-latency requirements	Flink generally has lower latencies	Flink generally has lower latencies	Offers the lowest latency of the options
High-throughput requirements	Flink often outperforms for high throughput	Flink often outperforms for high throughput	Flink is optimized for high throughput
Large batch workloads	Small batches	Spark Streaming is efficient for large batch processing	Flink is more geared toward stream processing
Exactly-once processing	No	With additional configuration, but some limitations	Provides exactly-once processing guarantees natively
Handling out-of-order events	Limited capabilities	Limited capabilities	Efficiently handles out-of-order events within windows
Integration with Spark ecosystem	No	Yes, integrates well with other Spark libraries	No
Ease of use for existing Spark users	Yes, leverages familiar Python/Java code	Yes, leverages familiarity with Spark APIs	No, has a steeper learning curve

AWS Glue and Amazon MSF are fully managed solutions that handle infrastructure management, scaling, and maintenance tasks. This significantly reduces operational overhead and is ideal for teams that want to focus on application logic rather than infrastructure. Amazon EMR, while offering both provisioned and serverless options, requires more operational expertise. However, it provides granular control over job parameters, cluster configurations, and runtime environments.

Choosing the Right Batch Transformation Service

When it comes to batch data transformation in AWS, you have four main options: AWS Glue, Amazon EMR, Amazon Redshift, and AWS Lambda.

The choice depends on factors such as the complexity of your transformation requirements, the need for customization and control, the scale and performance demands of your workload, and the expertise of your development team. Let's take a closer look at when to use each service in Table 4-6.

Table 4-6. Choosing the right batch transformation service

Criteria	AWS Glue	Amazon EMR	AWS Lambda	Amazon Redshift
Suitable use cases	• Spark-based data processing • Batch-oriented ETL pipelines • Data format conversions • Ease of use and serverless operational simplicity desired	• Data processing with any of Spark (*https://oreil.ly/AvcV3*), Hadoop (*https://oreil.ly/VJdo9*), HBase (*https://oreil.ly/eVjlR*), Hive (*https://oreil.ly/ryqzt*), Hudi (*https://oreil.ly/ZbkQ4*), Presto (*https://oreil.ly/4_7iv*) • Complex, large-scale data transformations • High performance, low latency • Highly customized ETL workflows	• Data processing using NodeJS, Python, Java, .NET, Ruby • Event-driven, lightweight data transformations • Small-scale aggregations and filtering	• SQL-based data processing • Data warehouse workloads • Use cases that require seconds or subsecond latency for reports • High-performance analytics
Complexity of transformation	For large-scale data transformations using Apache Spark jobs; also suited for lightweight transformations using Python shell scripts that run for more than 15 minutes	Suitable for complex, large-scale data transformations that require the full capabilities of frameworks like Spark or Flink	Suitable for lightweight, event-driven data transformations that can be encapsulated in short-running (less than 15 minutes) functions	Suitable for complex, large-scale data transformations using SQL. Especially good for aggregations on massive structured datasets
Customization and control	Provides a managed, abstracted layer with limited customization options	Offers a high degree of customization and control over the data transformation pipeline, including the ability to use custom libraries and integrate with other AWS services	Provides a serverless, event-driven approach with limited customization options beyond the function code	Offers both serverless and provisioned modes. Provisioned mode offers more customization and control

Criteria	AWS Glue	Amazon EMR	AWS Lambda	Amazon Redshift
Infrastructure management	Fully managed service, eliminating the need to provision or manage servers	Requires some management of the underlying EMR cluster infrastructure, but provides a managed service on top of EC2. EMR Serverless offers fully managed solution for Apache Spark, Hive, and Presto	Fully managed, serverless service with no infrastructure provisioning or management required	Fully managed service. In provisioned mode, you choose node types and number. In serverless, you only choose RPUs
Expertise required	Relatively lower barrier to entry, suitable for data engineers with general ETL experience	Requires expertise in using and managing open source big data frameworks like Spark or Flink	Suitable for developers with experience in writing and deploying serverless functions, but may have a lower barrier to entry compared to the other options	Relatively lower barrier to entry, suitable for data engineers with general SQL skills

Data Preparation for Nontechnical Personas

Data transformation capabilities empower nontechnical individuals to independently manipulate and restructure raw data into insightful formats, democratizing data exploration and analysis across various roles. AWS Glue DataBrew (*https://oreil.ly/oeu7H*) is an AWS service designed to assist nontechnical personas with data cleaning and preparation tasks. As a fully managed, low-code, visual interface solution, it offers a comprehensive set of over 250 built-in transformation and cleaning functions to address a wide range of data quality issues. DataBrew caters specifically to data analysts, data scientists, and business users who may not possess extensive coding skills, enabling them to leverage its powerful data transformation and enrichment capabilities effortlessly. The AWS Certified Data Engineer Associate certification exam may include questions related to specific function names and their roles within DataBrew, reflecting the importance of understanding this service for effective data preparation and transformation.

The following are Glue transformations for some of the common data cleansing and data transformation scenarios.

Fill Missing Values

Missing data is predominant in all datasets and can have a significant impact on the analytics or ML models using the data. Missing values in datasets can skew or bias the data and result in invalid conclusions. In a DataBrew project, you can get a quick view of the missing values in your sample data under the Data Quality section in the Schema view and within the Column Statistics. This provides valuable insights into the extent and distribution of missing data in your dataset. DataBrew offers several built-in functions to handle missing values, including:

Fill missing values
> This allows you to replace missing values with a constant value, the mean/median/mode of the column, or the previous/next nonmissing value.

Drop rows with missing values
> This transformation removes any rows that contain one or more missing values.

Impute missing values
> DataBrew provides advanced imputation methods, such as k-nearest neighbors (KNN) and decision tree imputation, to estimate missing values based on the patterns in the data.

These missing value handling transformations can be easily incorporated into your DataBrew recipes using a visual interface as shown in Figure 4-19.

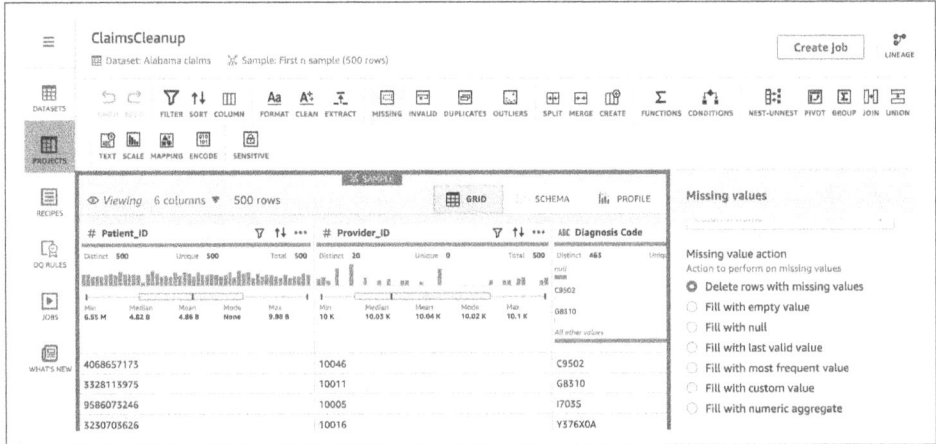

Figure 4-19. Handling missing values using DataBrew

For any data column, you can choose to either remove the missing rows or fill them with an empty string, null, last valid value, most frequent value, or custom value. For numerical data columns, you can also fill missing values with numerical aggregates of values like average, mode, sum, or median. Figure 4-19 shows a menu of all the options that DataBrew provides to handle missing values. It also shows an example of how rows with missing values will be deleted.

Identify Duplicate Records

Using the FLAG_DUPLICATE_ROWS functions, DataBrew can return a new column with a specified value in each row that indicates whether that row is an exact match of an earlier row in the dataset. When matches are found, they are flagged as duplicates. The initial occurrence is not flagged, because it doesn't match an earlier row.

Formatting Functions

AWS DataBrew provides a comprehensive suite of text manipulation functions categorized into formatting, extraction, and replacement capabilities. The formatting functions include various case modifications (CAPITAL_CASE, LOWER_CASE, UPPER_CASE, SENTENCE_CASE), quote additions, and date formatting options. The extraction functions enable pulling text between delimiters, from specific positions, using regular expression patterns, and from nested data structures.

For data cleaning and standardization, DataBrew offers robust replacement functions that include removing specific character combinations (REMOVE _COMBINED), replacing text between delimiters or positions (REPLACE_BETWEEN _DELIMITERS, REPLACE_BETWEEN_POSITIONS), and performing simple text substitutions (REPLACE_TEXT). These functions collectively provide a powerful toolkit for transforming and standardizing data within your AWS DataBrew workflows.

Integrating Data from Multiple Sources

In data analysis, it's common to need information from multiple datasets to arrive at useful insights. DataBrew provides two powerful transformations to combine data from different sources—union and join.

Nesting and Unnesting Data Structures

As you work with data from various sources, you may encounter complex data structures, such as nested fields, arrays, and maps. Effectively handling and transforming these data structures is a critical part of the data preparation process. AWS Glue DataBrew offers a set of powerful data structure recipe steps (*https://oreil.ly/z5Gr4*) that allow you to work with these complex data formats, simplifying the task of preparing your data for analysis and downstream applications.

The nesting and unnesting functions in DataBrew provide a flexible way to work with complex data structures:

Nesting functions
> The nesting functions allow you to consolidate related data elements into a more compact and structured format:

NEST_TO_ARRAY
> Combines multiple columns into a single array column

NEST_TO_MAP
> Combines multiple columns into a single JSON-formatted map column

NEST_TO_STRUCT
> Combines multiple columns into a single structured column

These nesting functions are useful when you need to consolidate related data elements into a more compact and structured format, which can simplify downstream processing and analysis.

Unnesting functions
> Unnesting functions enable you to "flatten" these complex structures into a tabular format that is more easily consumable by analytics tools and applications:

UNNEST_ARRAY
> Extracts values from an array column into individual rows

UNNEST_MAP
> Extracts key-value pairs from a map column into individual rows

UNNEST_STRUCT
> Extracts fields from a structured column into individual columns

UNNEST_STRUCT_N
> Extracts a specific field from a structured column

The unnesting functions allow you to "flatten" complex data structures, breaking them down into more easily consumable tabular formats. This can be particularly useful when integrating data from different sources with varying schemas or when preparing data for analysis tools that work better with flat, tabular data.

By leveraging these nesting and unnesting transformations in your DataBrew recipes, you can efficiently handle and reshape complex data structures, making it easier to prepare your data for downstream analytics and reporting.

Protecting Sensitive Data

When working with real-world data, you may encounter sensitive or personally identifiable information (PII) that requires special handling to ensure data privacy and compliance. AWS Glue DataBrew provides a set of functions specifically designed to help you protect and obfuscate sensitive data elements within your datasets.

At the time of this writing, the PII data handling functions available in DataBrew include:

CRYPTOGRAPHIC_HASH
> Applies a cryptographic hash function to a text value, such as SHA-256 or MD5, to create a one-way, irreversible transformation of the data.

DECRYPT
> Decrypts a value that has been encrypted using a specified key.

DETERMINISTIC_DECRYPT
> Decrypts a value that has been encrypted using a deterministic encryption algorithm, which produces the same ciphertext for the same plaintext and key.

DETERMINISTIC_ENCRYPT
> Encrypts a value using a deterministic encryption algorithm, which produces the same ciphertext for the same plaintext and key.

ENCRYPT
> Encrypts a value using a specified key.

MASK_CUSTOM
> Masks a value using a custom masking pattern.

MASK_DATE
> Masks a date value by replacing it with a randomly generated date within a specified range.

MASK_DELIMITER
> Masks a value by replacing characters between delimiters with a specified character.

MASK_RANGE
> Masks a numeric value by replacing it with a random value within a specified range.

REPLACE_WITH_RANDOM_BETWEEN
> Replaces a value with a randomly generated value within a specified range.

REPLACE_WITH_RANDOM_DATE_BETWEEN
> Replaces a date value with a randomly generated date within a specified range.

SHUFFLE_ROWS
> Shuffles the order of rows in a dataset, to help obfuscate any potential correlation between rows.

Refer to the AWS documentation (*https://oreil.ly/oPzLt*) to get the current list of functions to handle PII. These PII data handling functions allow you to protect sensitive information while still maintaining the overall structure and integrity of your data. By incorporating these transformations into your DataBrew recipes, you can ensure that your data preparation process aligns with data privacy regulations and best practices.

Other Data Preparation Transformations

AWS Glue DataBrew extends beyond basic data cleaning to offer a comprehensive suite of advanced transformation capabilities. These include sophisticated outlier detection and handling mechanisms, robust column structure manipulations (merging, splitting, and flagging), formatting functions for numeric and phone data, and specialized data science transformations like binarization and one-hot encoding. The service further enhances its utility with mathematical operations, text manipulations, date calculations, window-based transformations, and web-specific functions for handling IP addresses and URL parameters, making it a powerful all-in-one solution for complex data preparation needs in modern analytics and machine learning workflows.

Orchestrating Data Pipelines

Orchestration refers to the coordinated execution and management of the various components and steps involved in a data processing pipeline or workflow. Effective orchestration is crucial for building robust data systems, as it ensures that the different stages of data ingestion, transformation, analysis, and delivery are seamlessly integrated and executed in the correct sequence. In AWS services, users can orchestrate with AWS Step Functions, Amazon Managed Workflows for Apache Airflow (MWAA), AWS Glue workflows, Amazon Redshift query scheduler, or Amazon EventBridge. Let's learn about each of them and understand how to choose the right solution for your use case.

AWS Step Functions

AWS Step Functions is a serverless orchestration service that allows data engineers to build and run serverless applications and workflows using AWS services. It provides a way to visualize and coordinate event-driven architectures using a graphical console to arrange and visualize the components of your application as a series of steps. Step Functions enables you to easily create and update serverless workflows that combine various AWS services. Key use cases for Step Functions include automating ETL processes, orchestrating large-scale parallel workloads, coordinating microservices, and automating IT/security workflows with approval steps. Depending on your use case, you can have Step Functions call AWS services, such as Lambda, to perform tasks. You can create workflows that process and publish machine learning models.

Step Functions is based on *state machines* and *tasks*. In Step Functions, state machines are called *workflows*, which are a series of event-driven steps. Each step in a workflow is called a *state*. For example, a Task state (*https://oreil.ly/FPBcK*) represents a unit of work that another AWS service performs, such as calling another AWS service or API. Figure 4-20 shows a sample Step Functions state machine.

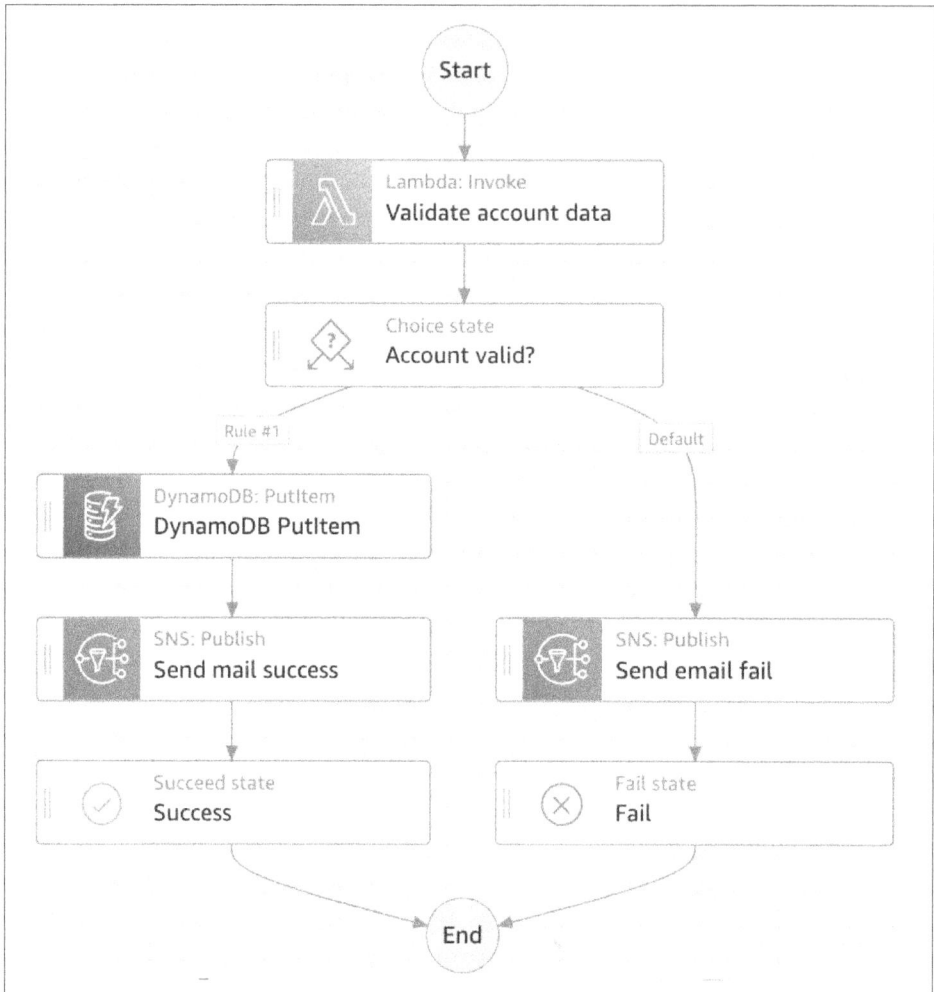

Figure 4-20. Sample Step Functions state machine

Managed Workflows for Apache Airflow

Amazon Managed Workflows for Apache Airflow (Amazon MWAA) is a fully managed orchestration service for the open source Apache Airflow platform. Amazon MWAA allows you to orchestrate workflows that span both AWS and non-AWS resources. With Amazon MWAA, you can programmatically author, schedule, and monitor workflows consisting of sequences of processes and tasks, known as directed acyclic graphs (DAGs). Figure 4-21 is a sample DAG for a data pipeline that checks for files in Amazon S3, creates tables for those files in Amazon Athena, joins them, and transfers the data to Amazon Redshift for reporting.

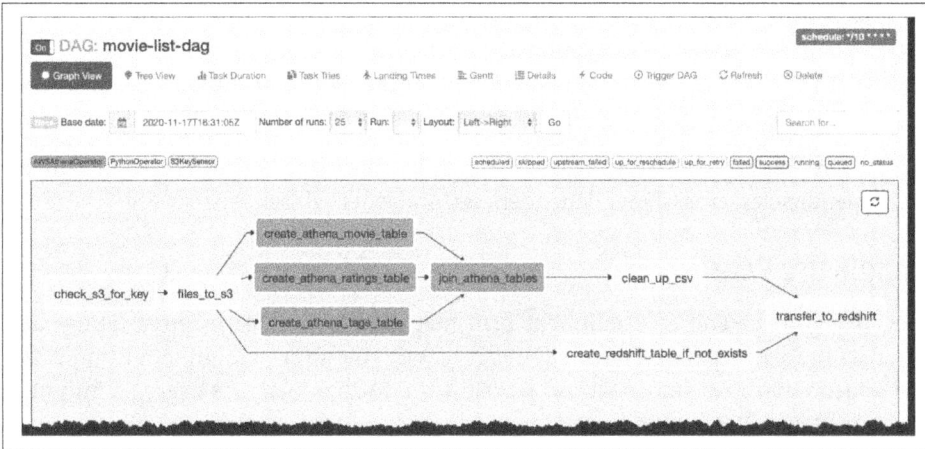

Figure 4-21. Sample MWAA DAG

Following are the key components in MWAA:

DAGs (directed acyclic graphs)
DAGs represent the workflows in Airflow, which are collections of tasks that need to be executed in a specific order. DAGs are written in Python scripts and define the tasks, their dependencies, and the overall flow of the workflow. Each DAG has a schedule that determines when it should be executed (e.g., hourly, daily, or based on specific conditions). DAGs in MWAA can be created using a visual interface as shown in Figure 4-21.

Tasks
Tasks are instances of operators within a DAG. Each task represents a specific unit of work that needs to be executed as part of the workflow. Tasks can have dependencies on other tasks, which determine the execution order within the DAG. Each task invokes an operator.

Operators
Operators define the actual work that needs to be performed, such as running a Python function, executing a Bash command, transferring data between systems, or interacting with various data sources.

Airflow provides a wide range of built-in operators for common operations, and you can also create custom operators for specific use cases. Examples of built-in operators include `PythonOperator`, `EmailOperator`, `BashOperator`, `MySqlOperator`, `S3FileTransferOperator`, `RedshiftDataOperator`, and many more.

Dependencies

Dependencies define the relationships between tasks in a DAG. They specify the order in which tasks should be executed, ensuring that tasks with dependencies are executed only after their upstream tasks have completed successfully.

Airflow supports different types of dependencies, such as upstream/downstream dependencies, cross-DAG dependencies, and external task sensors.

Sample Use Case

Consider a media and entertainment firm that gets movie data in three ratings and tags data in three separate files. As the files arrive, you want to join them using Amazon Athena and load into Amazon Redshift for further analytics every 10 minutes. The workflow that solves this use case and orchestrates the interactions is represented in Figure 4-21.

movie-list-dag is the MWAA DAG. Each box you see in the DAG is a task. Following is information on each task's function and the operators that it is invoking:

- The check_s3_for_key task uses the S3KeySensor operator to check if the required files are present in the S3 bucket.
- The create_athena_movie_table, create_athena_ratings_table, and create _athena_tags_table tasks use the AWSAthenaOperator to create external tables in Amazon Athena for the movie, ratings, and tags data, respectively.
- The join_athena_tables task uses the AWSAthenaOperator to perform a join operation on the Athena tables to retrieve the movie titles and ratings.
- The clean_up_csv task uses the PythonOperator to clean up the CSV data downloaded from Athena.
- The create_redshift_table_if_not_exists task uses the RedshiftData Operator to create a Redshift table if it doesn't already exist.
- The transfer_to_redshift task uses the S3ToRedshift operator to transfer the cleaned-up CSV data from S3 to the Redshift table.

The tasks are then connected using the right-shift >> operator, which defines the dependencies between the tasks. For example, check_s3_for_key >> files_to_s3 means that the files_to_s3 task can be executed only after the check_s3_for_key task is completed successfully. The complete dependencies code for the DAG is presented here:

```
check_s3_for_key >> files_to_s3 >> create_athena_movie_table \
    >> join_athena_tables >> clean_up_csv >> transfer_to_redshift

files_to_s3 >> create_athena_ratings_table >> join_athena_tables

files_to_s3 >> create_athena_tags_table >> join_athena_tables

files_to_s3 >> create_redshift_table_if_not_exists >> transfer_to_redshift
```

AWS Glue Workflows

AWS Glue workflows serve as a powerful orchestration tool, seamlessly coordinating the interactions between AWS Glue's core components—crawlers and jobs. You can get started in two primary ways: you can either use prebuilt AWS Glue blueprints for common scenarios or construct your workflow piece by piece using the visual user interface available in the AWS Management Console or AWS Glue API.

Within these workflows, triggers act as the connective tissue, initiating jobs and crawlers based on various conditions. These triggers can fire when previous components complete their execution, creating a chain of dependent tasks. The workflow itself begins with a start trigger, which you can configure to run on a schedule, on-demand, or in response to Amazon EventBridge events—including the ability to handle event batches.

One particularly useful feature is the workflow's ability to maintain state through run properties. These properties, defined as name/value pairs, are accessible to all jobs within the workflow, enabling them to share information. Jobs can both read and modify these properties through the API, affecting the behavior of subsequent jobs in the pipeline.

Sample Use Case

Let's explore a practical retail scenario where AWS Glue workflows offer an efficient solution. Imagine a retail company processing payments from two sources: ACH transactions and check payments. These payments land in separate S3 locations with different data formats, and the business needs to combine and analyze them daily. Figure 4-22 shows an AWS Glue workflow that solves this use case.

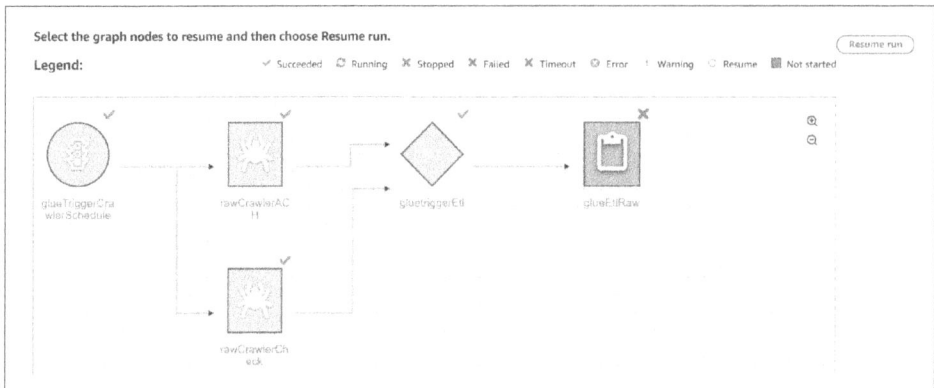

Figure 4-22. Sample AWS Glue workflow

First, two AWS Glue crawlers scan the S3 locations, one for ACH payments and another for check payments, and automatically detect and catalog the structure of the input files, regardless of their different formats. Once both the crawlers complete their schema inference, the workflow triggers an AWS Glue ETL job that performs the necessary transformations and aggregations on the combined dataset.

This entire process is orchestrated using AWS Glue workflows, which is particularly cost-effective since all components (crawlers and jobs) are native to AWS Glue. There's no need for additional orchestration tools or their associated costs—the workflow functionality comes built-in with AWS Glue. You can schedule this workflow to execute daily with minimal operational overhead, automatically managing dependencies between the crawlers and the transformation job. It ensures that the transformation job starts only after both crawlers have successfully updated their schemas, maintaining data consistency and reliability.

Amazon Redshift Scheduler

Amazon Redshift Query Editor v2 provides a straightforward solution for automating SQL queries through its built-in scheduler. This feature allows you to run Amazon Redshift SQL statements automatically at specified times or intervals without managing complex infrastructure or dependencies. It's particularly useful for standalone operations like refreshing materialized views, running recurring analytics, or performing regular maintenance tasks. For example, if you need to refresh a materialized view daily at 8:00 p.m. EST, you can simply schedule the refresh query once, and the scheduler will handle the execution automatically. This native scheduling capability offers the most operationally simple approach for basic query automation needs, though for more complex workflows with dependencies, you might want to consider other AWS orchestration services.

Amazon EventBridge

Amazon EventBridge is a serverless service that facilitates event-driven orchestration by acting as a serverless event bus, allowing you to connect applications and services, and route events to multiple targets for downstream processing, such as AWS Lambda, AWS Glue workflows, Amazon Redshift, Amazon KDS, Amazon API Gateway, Amazon Simple Notification Service (SNS), or Step Functions. EventBridge was formerly called Amazon CloudWatch Events; it uses the same CloudWatch Events API.

The primary resource in EventBridge is an event bus (Figure 4-23). An event bus is a router that receives events (*https://oreil.ly/udOxo*) and delivers them to zero or more destinations, or *targets*. Event buses are well suited for routing events from many sources to many targets, with optional transformation of events prior to delivery to a target.

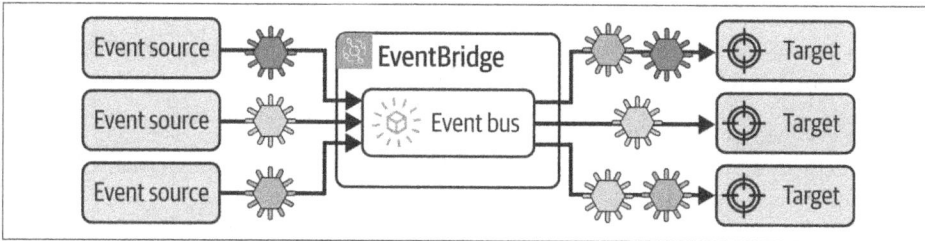

Figure 4-23. EventBridge architecture

Each event bus is associated to rules (*https://oreil.ly/_YU87*). There are two kinds of rules—event-driven rules that respond to changes (such as file arrival in S3), and schedule-based rules that execute at specified times (like 8:00 p.m. EST on weekdays).

The event routing process follows a straightforward flow. An event source, which can be an AWS service, custom application, or SaaS provider, sends an event to an EventBridge bus. EventBridge then evaluates the event against rules defined for that bus. For matching rules, EventBridge forwards the event to specified targets. During this process, optional event transformation can occur before delivery to targets. The target actions that EventBridge rules can perform are as follows:

- Send payloads of the events received to Amazon Data Firehose, Amazon Kinesis Data Streams, Amazon SNS topic, or Amazon SQS queue.

- Initiate AWS Lambda functions for further processing, such as initiating a Lambda function to resize images after they arrive.

- Initiate batch processing by triggering AWS Glue workflows or AWS Step Functions state machines.

- Initiate queries on an Amazon Redshift data warehouse using the Amazon Redshift data API.

- Initiate ML workflows using the Amazon SageMaker AI pipeline.

- Route event to API Gateway endpoints.

In schedule-driven scenarios, EventBridge initiates actions at configured times, commonly triggering data processing workflows, ETL jobs, or analytics queries. The service offers flexible configuration options: a single event can match multiple rules, each rule can specify up to five targets, and event transformation can be configured within rules. This architecture supports both real-time data processing and scheduled batch operations within the same service, all without requiring infrastructure management, making it effective for diverse data pipeline requirements.

Some use cases that can be solved using EventBridge are as follows:

Orchestrating workflows
You can use EventBridge to trigger complex workflows by routing events to Step Functions, AWS Glue workflows, Amazon MWAA, etc.

Building event-driven applications
EventBridge simplifies the process of building loosely coupled, scalable, and event-driven applications.

Integrating with SaaS applications
You can connect SaaS applications to your AWS services using EventBridge.

Connecting to private APIs
EventBridge allows you to securely integrate legacy systems with cloud-native applications using event-driven architectures and workflow orchestration.

Sample Use Case

Event-driven ingestion is a powerful data processing approach that leverages the power of Amazon S3 and AWS Lambda to ingest and transform files in near real time. The ingestion process begins when a user or application adds, modifies, or deletes a file in an Amazon S3 bucket. Amazon S3 is then configured to generate an event notification whenever a new object is created, modified, or deleted in the bucket. This event notification can be sent to Amazon EventBridge to trigger an AWS Lambda function, which can be designed to perform the necessary data ingestion and processing tasks.

Consider the following use case: you receive Parquet format files from a source into a raw data bucket in Amazon S3. Upon arrival, you need to validate that the files have the correct schema in near real time before loading them into the processed Amazon S3 bucket for reporting. The architecture shown in Figure 4-24 can solve this use case in an operationally efficient and cost-effective manner by using all serverless services.

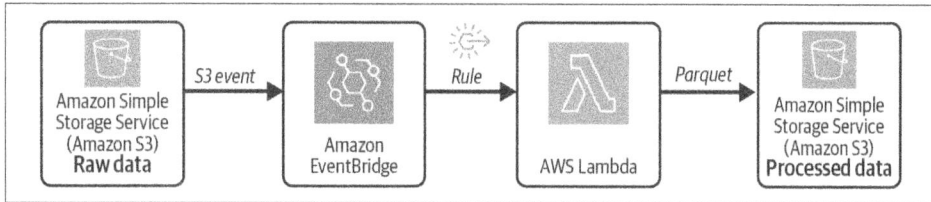

Figure 4-24. Event-driven architecture for S3 file format conversion

When a new Amazon S3 file arrives, it sends it to an Amazon EventBridge bus, and the EventBridge rule triggers a Lambda function that does schema validation and loads the file into the processed data layer in the data lake. By using this architecture, the schema validation can happen almost immediately after the file is uploaded, eliminating the need for periodic batch processing or manual intervention.

The benefits of this approach include the following:

Decoupling

Event-driven architecture promotes loose coupling between services, making your applications more flexible and scalable.

Scalability

EventBridge can handle a large volume of events, ensuring that your applications can scale to meet demand.

Simplified integration

EventBridge simplifies the process of integrating different services and applications.

Serverless

EventBridge is a serverless service, meaning you don't need to manage infrastructure.

Faster time to market

By eliminating the need to write and maintain custom networking or integration code, developers can build extensible systems and add new capabilities easily.

Choosing the Right Orchestration Service

When choosing the right orchestration service among AWS Step Functions, Amazon Managed Workflows for Apache Airflow (MWAA), AWS Glue workflows, Amazon Redshift scheduler, and Amazon EventBridge, it's important to consider the specific requirements of your use case. Here are some key considerations:

Interactions

Analyze the interactions that you need to orchestrate:

- If you only need to orchestrate interactions between AWS Glue crawlers and/or AWS Glue jobs, use AWS Glue workflows. It will be the most cost-efficient solution for this specific scenario.

- If you only need to schedule Amazon Redshift SQL statements without dependencies, such as running table maintenance on Amazon Redshift tables at a certain time every week/day, running a recurring data export from Amazon Redshift to Amazon S3, refreshing Amazon Redshift materialized views, etc., then use the Amazon Redshift query scheduler.

- If you need to orchestrate interactions between AWS services only and have no external dependencies, consider using AWS Step Functions. Step Functions is serverless and can help in building end-to-end serverless or event-driven applications.

- If your orchestration involves interaction with external services/dependencies, or if you prefer open source technology for orchestration, consider using MWAA.

- If you need event-based orchestration, then use Amazon EventBridge.

Coding

Understand which coding language each orchestration service uses:

- AWS Step Functions uses Amazon States Language (ASL) to define the workflow. It has a visual interface.

- MWAA jobs are written in Python code. For ease of use, MWAA has a visual interface that provides a visual representation of the DAGs written in Python.

- AWS Glue workflows can be built using a visual user interface or programmatically using JSON.

- The Amazon Redshift scheduler uses one-time (`at` format) or recurring (`cron` format) scheduled action. Schedule invocations must be separated by at least one hour. There is no visual interface.

- You create event buses and associate rules that either respond to an event or run at a schedule. Schedules are defined either using (1) cron-based schedules (a schedule set using a `cron` expression that runs at a specific time, such as 8:00 a.m. PST on the first Monday of every month) or (2) rate-based schedules (a schedule that runs at a regular rate, such as every 10 minutes).

Monitoring and debugging

MWAA provides detailed logging and monitoring capabilities through Apache Airflow's UI, making it easier to debug and troubleshoot workflows. Step Functions, Glue workflows, Amazon Redshift scheduler, and Amazon EventBridge also offer monitoring and logging features, but they may not be as comprehensive as MWAA.

Community and support

Apache Airflow, which MWAA is based on, has a large and active open source community, providing access to a wide range of resources, plug-ins, and community support. Step Functions, Glue workflows, Amazon Redshift scheduler and Amazon EventBridge are proprietary AWS services, so support and resources are primarily provided by AWS.

Cost

Utilizing Glue workflows does not incur additional charges beyond the costs associated with the individual components they orchestrate. The same applies to Amazon Redshift scheduler.

AWS Step Functions incurs additional cost; however, it is generally more cost-effective for simpler use cases, as the pricing has a pay-per-use model. MWAA has a higher up-front cost due to its managed service nature, but it may be more cost-effective for complex workflows with multiple dependencies and requirements.

Conclusion

This chapter has provided a comprehensive overview of the various approaches and best practices for ingesting and transforming data in AWS. We've explored how to effectively ingest streaming data, data from databases, SaaS applications, third-party datasets, and on-premises files using a variety of AWS services like Amazon Kinesis, MSK, DMS, and DataSync. We've also delved into the specifics of batch and real-time data transformation capabilities offered by services like AWS Glue, Amazon EMR, Amazon MSF, and AWS Lambda, highlighting the strengths and trade-offs of each approach. Additionally, we covered how to orchestrate these data pipelines using AWS Step Functions, Amazon Managed Workflows for Apache Airflow, and AWS Glue workflows.

By understanding the nuances of data ingestion and transformation in AWS, data engineers can build reliable, scalable, and cost-effective data pipelines that power an organization's data-driven initiatives. Mastering these techniques is essential for the AWS Certified Data Engineer Associate certification exam, as they form the foundation for building robust and efficient data processing solutions in the cloud.

Next, let's try to validate our knowledge with a few practice questions that may help you prepare for the AWS Certified Data Engineer Associate certification exam.

Practice Questions

These practice questions may help you understand what kind of questions to expect on the exam so you can prepare accordingly. The answers are listed in the Appendix.

1. A marketing team at a retail company needs to regularly ingest data from their Salesforce CRM into their Amazon Redshift data warehouse. The data includes customer information, sales transactions, and marketing campaign details. The team wants to ensure the data is ingested reliably, with minimal manual intervention, and in a cost-effective manner.

   Which AWS service would be the best choice to meet these requirements with the least operational overhead?

   A. AWS Glue ETL jobs

   B. AWS Data Migration Service (DMS)

   C. Zero-ETL integration between Salesforce and Redshift in AWS Glue

   D. Amazon Data Firehose

2. A marketing team at a retail company needs to automatically process customer survey data that is uploaded to an Amazon S3 bucket. The team wants to create an AWS Lambda function that will convert the customer survey data from *.txt* format to *.json* format whenever a new *.txt* file is added to the S3 bucket.

   Which solution will meet these requirements with the least operational overhead?

   A. Create an Amazon CloudWatch event rule that triggers the Lambda function when an S3 ObjectCreated event occurs. Use a filter to only trigger the event for files with the *.txt* extension.

   B. Create an Amazon EventBridge (Amazon CloudWatch Events) rule that triggers the Lambda function when an S3 ObjectCreated event occurs. Use a filter to only trigger the event for files with the *.txt* extension.

   C. Create an S3 event notification that triggers the Lambda function when an S3 ObjectCreated event occurs. Use a filter rule to only trigger the event for files with the *.txt* extension.

D. Create an S3 event notification that triggers an Amazon SNS topic when an S3 ObjectCreated event occurs. Subscribe the Lambda function to the SNS topic and use a filter rule to only trigger the event for files with the *.txt* extension.

3. The data engineering team at a large ecommerce company needs to clean, transform, and prepare customer data from various sources before loading it into their Amazon Redshift data warehouse. The data includes customer profiles, order history, and product reviews, stored in a mix of CSV, JSON, and Excel files in an Amazon S3 data lake.

   The team wants to implement a data preparation process that can handle missing values, inconsistent formatting, and other quality issues, while also allowing them to combine and enrich the data from multiple sources. The solution should require minimal coding, be easy to configure and maintain, and provide visibility into the data transformation steps.

   Which AWS service and approach would be the best choice to meet these requirements?

   A. Use AWS Glue to create custom ETL jobs that extract data from the S3 data lake, transform it using PySpark code, and load it into Redshift. Leverage AWS Glue's built-in data quality checks and error handling features.

   B. Implement a data preparation pipeline using Amazon EMR and Apache Spark, writing custom Scala or Python code to handle the data cleansing, transformation, and integration requirements.

   C. Use AWS Glue DataBrew to visually design and configure data preparation recipes that can address the various data quality issues, combine datasets, and output the transformed data directly to Redshift.

   D. Create an Amazon Athena query federation to integrate the disparate data sources, then use Amazon Athena's built-in data type conversion and transformation functions to prepare the data for loading into Redshift.

4. A marketing team at an ecommerce company needs to analyze customer activity data in near real time to identify trends and optimize their online campaigns. The data includes website clicks, product views, and shopping cart activities, which are currently being captured in various AWS services, including Amazon CloudWatch Logs, Amazon Kinesis Data Streams, and Amazon DynamoDB.

   The team wants to set up a data processing pipeline that can consolidate all this real-time data and send it to their Datadog instance for further analysis and reporting.

   Which solution will meet these requirements with the least operational overhead?

   A. Configure an Amazon Kinesis Data Streams data stream to use Datadog as the destination. Create separate CloudWatch Logs subscription filters, Kinesis

Data Streams, and DynamoDB Streams to send the data to the Kinesis Data Streams.

B. Create an Amazon Data Firehose delivery stream to use Datadog as the destination. Configure CloudWatch Logs, Kinesis Data Streams, and DynamoDB Streams to send the data to the Amazon Data Firehose delivery stream.

C. Create an Amazon Data Firehose delivery stream to use Datadog as the destination. Write an AWS Lambda function to pull the data from CloudWatch Logs, Kinesis Data Streams, and DynamoDB Streams, and send it to the Amazon Data Firehose delivery stream.

D. Configure an AWS Lambda function to pull the data from CloudWatch Logs, Kinesis Data Streams, and DynamoDB Streams, and send it directly to the Datadog instance, bypassing the need for an intermediate streaming service.

5. A data engineering team at a retail company needs to process customer purchase data stored in JSON files. The files contain the following structure:

```
{ "customer_id": "123", "purchase_date": "2023-04-15", "items":
[ { "item_id": "ABC123", "item_name": "T-Shirt", "quantity": 2, "price":
19.99 }, { "item_id": "XYZ456", "item_name": "Jeans", "quantity": 1,
"price": 49.99 } ], "total_amount": 89.97 }
```

The team wants to create a new column that calculates the total revenue generated from each customer's purchases, based on the item quantity and price.

Which AWS Glue DataBrew transformation would be the best solution to meet this requirement with the least coding effort?

A. Use the UNNEST_STRUCT transformation to extract the item data, then apply the SUM and MULTIPLY functions to calculate the total revenue.

B. Leverage the EXTRACT_VALUE transformation to access the nested item data, and then use the SUM function to calculate the total revenue.

C. Implement the CUSTOM_CODE transformation in AWS Glue DataBrew to write a Python script that processes the JSON data and calculates the total revenue.

D. Use the APPLY_MAPPING transformation to map the relevant fields from the JSON data and then apply a custom formula to calculate the total revenue.

6. A financial services company has several on-premises file servers that store customer account records, transaction history, and compliance documents. The company wants to regularly transfer this data to an Amazon S3 data lake for long-term storage and analytical processing.

The data is updated daily, and the company needs to ensure that only the changes are transferred to S3, minimizing the time and resources required for each data transfer. The solution should also provide the ability to monitor the data transfer process and troubleshoot any issues that may arise.

Which AWS service would be the best choice to meet these requirements with the least operational overhead?

A. Amazon S3 Batch Operations

B. AWS DataSync

C. Amazon S3 cross-region replication

D. AWS Storage Gateway

7. A data engineering team at a media company needs to build a data processing pipeline that ingests data from various sources, including real-time event streams, batch files, and third-party APIs. The pipeline includes several steps, such as data validation, transformation, and loading into a data warehouse and data lake that depend on external dependencies. The team wants to ensure the pipeline is reliable, scalable, and easy to monitor and manage.

Which orchestration service would be the best choice to meet these requirements, based on the best practices discussed in the content?

A. AWS Step Functions

B. Amazon Managed Workflows for Apache Airflow (MWAA)

C. AWS Glue workflows

D. A combination of AWS Step Functions and AWS Glue workflows

8. A marketing team at an ecommerce company needs to cleanse and deduplicate their customer database, which contains information such as customer name, email address, phone number, and address. The database has been built up over time from various sources, and it contains many duplicate records for the same customers.

The team wants to implement an automated solution to identify and merge these duplicate records, ensuring that the customer data is accurate and up-to-date. They want to minimize the manual effort required to maintain the customer database and ensure that the deduplication process is reliable and scalable as the data grows.

Which solution will meet these requirements with the least operational overhead?

A. Use the `FindMatches` transformation in AWS Glue DataBrew to identify and merge duplicate customer records.

B. Write a custom Python script using the Dedupe library and run it as an AWS Lambda function to deduplicate the customer data.

C. Leverage Amazon Comprehend to perform entity extraction and matching on the customer data, then use Amazon Redshift to consolidate the records.

D. Implement a custom ETL pipeline using AWS Glue to perform fuzzy matching and record linkage on the customer data.

9. A media company needs to build a real-time analytics pipeline to monitor user engagement data from their online streaming platform. The data, which includes video views, user interactions, and device information, is currently being captured in an Amazon Kinesis Data Streams stream.

   The company wants to set up a solution that can continuously ingest this real-time data, store it in an Amazon Redshift Serverless data warehouse, and enable near-real-time analytics on both the latest and historical data.

   Which AWS service and approach would be the best choice to meet these requirements with the least operational overhead?

   A. Configure an Amazon Data Firehose delivery stream to ingest the data from the Kinesis Data Streams and load it directly into the Amazon Redshift Serverless warehouse.

   B. Leverage the streaming ingestion feature of Amazon Redshift Serverless to directly consume the data from the Kinesis Data Streams.

   C. Create an AWS Lambda function to read the data from the Kinesis Data Streams, store it in an Amazon S3 data lake, and then use the COPY command to load the data into the Amazon Redshift Serverless warehouse.

   D. Utilize DMS to load data into Amazon Redshift Serverless.

10. A data engineering team at an ecommerce company has set up an Amazon Kinesis Data Streams stream to ingest real-time customer event data, such as website clicks, product views, and shopping cart activities. The team has configured several AWS services, including Amazon Data Firehose and AWS Lambda, to consume data from the Kinesis stream and process it for downstream analytics.

   However, the team has noticed that the stream's read throughput is lower than expected, and they are seeing increased latency in the data processing pipeline. The team suspects that there may be an issue with the partitioning or sharding of the Kinesis stream.

   Which steps should the data engineering team take to troubleshoot and resolve the performance issues with the Kinesis Data Streams stream? (Choose two)

   A. Monitor the shard-level metrics in Amazon CloudWatch and identify any hot shards or uneven data distribution across shards.

   B. Increase the number of shards in the Kinesis Data Streams stream to scale the overall read and write throughput.

   C. Modify the partition key used to distribute data across shards, ensuring a well-distributed and random partition key.

D. Increase the number of Amazon Data Firehose delivery stream instances to handle the increased read throughput from the Kinesis stream.

E. Configure the Amazon Kinesis Client Library (KCL) to use the enhanced fan-out feature to improve the read throughput for consumer applications.

Additional Resources

The following are a few additional resources that will help you dive deeper and gain more knowledge on data ingestion and transformation:

- "Data Ingestion Methods" (*https://oreil.ly/P0Qmd*) and "Transforming Data Assets" (*https://oreil.ly/yntAw*)
- "Data Ingestion and Preparation" (*https://oreil.ly/orsmV*)
- "Data Ingestion" (*https://oreil.ly/R8u-q*) and "Data Transformation" (*https://oreil.ly/M86lY*)
- "Solving Different Data Ingestion Use Cases with AWS" (*https://oreil.ly/LAxmJ*)
- "Ingestion Layer" (*https://oreil.ly/wcF16*)
- "Workflow Orchestration" (*https://oreil.ly/x4jQh*) and resources on building an operationally excellent data pipeline (*https://oreil.ly/he7Zn*)

## CHAPTER 5

Data Store Management

In this chapter, you'll gain essential skills for managing your data efficiently, regardless of whether you're working with structured, semi-structured, or unstructured data. Selecting the appropriate data store significantly affects your organization's capability to store, retrieve, and analyze data effectively.

In this chapter, you'll learn more about the following topics:

- How to choose the right data store based on your use case
- How to classify your data and build a data catalog for data discovery
- How to manage the lifecycle of data
- How to design data models and manage schema evolution

By the end of this chapter, you will have a solid understanding in data store management, supported by practice questions to reinforce your learning and prepare you for the certification exam and real-world scenarios. You will also answer a set of practice questions similar to the kind of questions you can expect in the AWS Certified Data Engineer Associate certification exam.

Let's dive deep into the specific topics.

Choosing a Data Store

We will begin by exploring how to choose the right data store based on your specific use case, considering factors such as data volume, variety, velocity, value, and veracity. A deep understanding of different data storage options will help you make informed decisions that align with your business requirements and technical constraints.

AWS offers a comprehensive suite of storage services, each tailored to meet diverse workload requirements. In this section, we focus on two primary categories: core storage services and managed databases.

AWS Core Storage Services

AWS core storage services include block, file, and object storage. Block storage, offered by Amazon Elastic Block Store (Amazon EBS), is ideal for enterprise applications such as databases and ERP systems that demand dedicated, low-latency storage. Similar to direct-attached storage (DAS) or a storage area network (SAN), block-based cloud storage provides ultra-low latency essential for high-performance workloads. Amazon EBS can be attached to Amazon Elastic Compute Cloud (Amazon EC2) instances and managed by the operating system or application, offering various options to suit different use case needs. With Amazon EBS Elastic Volumes, you can increase the volume size, change the volume type, or adjust the performance of your EBS volumes without detaching the volume. This feature offers better scalability and flexibility over DAS. Amazon EBS volumes are automatically replicated within their Availability Zone (AZ) to protect against hardware failures.

File storage is essential for applications that require shared file access through a file system, typically supported by network attached storage (NAS). AWS offers managed file storage through two primary services: Amazon Elastic File System (Amazon EFS) and Amazon FSx. Amazon EFS provides simple, scalable, multi-AZ file storage using the NFS protocol, suitable for general-purpose workloads. Amazon FSx, on the other hand, offers specialized file storage options, including Amazon FSx for Lustre for high-performance computing and machine learning workloads, Amazon FSx for Windows File Server optimized for Microsoft applications, and Amazon FSx for NetApp ONTAP, which supports both block and file storage. Amazon FSx also supports multi-AZ deployments, ensuring high availability and resilience for mission-critical applications.

Object storage, offered by Amazon Simple Storage Service (Amazon S3), provides vast scalability and flexibility, making it ideal for modern cloud-native applications, data analytics, backup, and archival purposes. Amazon S3 is most commonly used as the storage layer for data lakes in the data analytics world. Its security features ensure data is protected by default. It enables architectures that decouple storage from compute, allowing for more efficient resource management. Among the three core storage categories, Amazon S3 is the most cost-effective option, supporting virtually unlimited scale and accommodating structured, semi-structured, and unstructured data. It integrates seamlessly with AWS native analytics services and the vast majority of SaaS solutions. Furthermore, Amazon S3 offers multiple storage classes to meet different pricing, access, and availability requirements, which we will discuss in more detail in "Managing the Lifecycle of Data" on page 167. Amazon S3 is optimized primarily for throughput rather than low-latency, random-access workloads. As a result, it might not be the best fit for transactional database applications or workloads that require frequent, small-file updates and high IOPS. For such scenarios, block or file storage solutions like Amazon EBS or Amazon FSx may provide superior performance.

Data engineers commonly interact with Amazon S3 directly if they are managing data lakes on AWS. In many cases, Amazon EBS and Amazon EFS are either abstracted by a managed service such as Amazon Relational Database Service (Amazon RDS) or managed by a separated infrastructure team. Now let's look at different managed database and data warehouse services that can come up in the certification.

AWS Cloud Databases

In this section, we will dive into the diverse landscape of AWS cloud databases. AWS offers a broad array of database services, each designed to meet specific application requirements. Understanding the supported data structure of these services and their common use cases is essential for architects and developers aiming to build efficient, scalable, and robust data-driven applications on the AWS platform.

The AWS Certified Data Engineer Associate exam covers the following database types:

- Relational databases:
  - *Data type*: Structured data with predefined schemas and relationships between them.
  - *Characteristics*: These databases are designed to support ACID transactions and SQL-based queries and to maintain strong data consistency.
  - *Use cases*: Traditional applications, enterprise resource planning (ERP), customer relationship management (CRM), and business intelligence.
  - *AWS services*: Amazon Aurora, Amazon RDS, and Amazon Redshift.
- Key-value databases:
  - *Data type*: Key-value pairs.
  - *Characteristics*: These databases are designed for simple, fast, and highly efficient data retrieval. They excel at handling high concurrency and are specifically optimized for well-defined access patterns. Importantly, with key-value databases, you design your schema explicitly around your most common and important queries, making these queries as fast and cost-effective as possible.
  - *Use cases*: High-traffic web applications, gaming, IoT applications, real-time bidding, and session management.
  - *AWS services*: Amazon DynamoDB.

- Document databases:

  — *Data type*: Semi-structured data stored as documents, typically in JSON, BSON, or XML formats.

  — *Characteristics*: These databases enable developers to build and update applications quickly by accepting flexible and hierarchical data structures.

  — *Use cases*: Content management systems, user profiles, and mobile applications.

  — *AWS services*: Amazon DocumentDB (with MongoDB compatibility).

- In-memory databases:

  — *Data type*: Key-value pairs and semi-structured.

  — *Characteristics*: Data stored in-memory for faster read and write operations, typically providing submillisecond latency.

  — *Use cases*: Real-time analytics, caching, session storage, leaderboards, and high-frequency trading.

  — *AWS services*: Amazon ElastiCache and Amazon MemoryDB for Redis.

- Graph databases:

  — *Data type*: Nodes, edges, and properties.

  — *Characteristics*: Graph databases are for applications that need to navigate and query complex relationships and interconnections between highly connected graph datasets.

  — *Use cases*: Social networks, recommendation engines, fraud detection, knowledge graphs, and network analysis.

  — *AWS services*: Amazon Neptune.

- Search engine:

  — *Data type*: Semi-structured data stored as documents or unstructured free text (e.g., log files, metrics).

  — *Characteristics*: These databases are optimized for search functionalities, providing full-text search, indexing, and real-time search capabilities.

  — *Use cases*: Ecommerce search, enterprise search, and semantic search. It can also function as an analytics engine, facilitating interactive log analytics, real-time application monitoring, and security analytics.

  — *AWS services*: Amazon OpenSearch.

When choosing between different managed databases, start by considering the target use case and the nature of your data. This approach will help you narrow down your options to a specific database category and, in most cases, a particular AWS service. If there are multiple AWS services within the chosen category, focus on the differentiated features of each service to make your final decision.

Choosing between Amazon Aurora/RDS and Amazon Redshift in the relational database category is a common technology decision. It's important to understand that, while all three are relational databases, they serve different purposes. Amazon Aurora/RDS are designed for online transaction processing (OLTP) workloads, which mostly handle high-concurrency record-level transactions. In contrast, Amazon Redshift is optimized for online analytical processing (OLAP) workloads, which involve complex queries and data analysis.

The fundamental difference between OLTP and OLAP systems lies in their design and targeted use cases. OLTP systems prioritize transaction speed and data accuracy, with a physical data layout optimized for quick access and updates. They can process high-concurrency application transactions and require a highly normalized database structure to minimize data redundancy. Conversely, OLAP systems are built for query performance and data retrieval efficiency, often employing a denormalized schema to reduce the number of joins and facilitate faster query responses. These systems support complex querying of large datasets to facilitate business intelligence and analytical applications.

Data Storage Formats for Data Lakes

When designing a data lake, choosing the appropriate data storage format is critical for optimizing performance and efficiency. The two primary types of file formats are row based and column based, each suited to different use cases and access patterns.

Row-Based File Formats

Row-based file formats, such as CSV and JSON, store data in rows. All data associated with a specific record is stored adjacently. These formats are advantageous for transactional and operational workloads where entire records need to be accessed quickly. Row-based file formats are commonly used for smaller datasets or at the raw data layer when the new data first lands at the data lake. Common row-based formats include:

CSV (comma-separated values)
 Simple and widely used for data exchange and initial data ingestion. CSV files are in text format and therefore human readable.

JSON (JavaScript Object Notation)
 Flexible and suitable for semi-structured data, often used in web applications and APIs. JSON files are also in text format and human readable.

Avro
> A row-based binary format that supports schema evolution, often used in data serialization and stream processing.

Column-Based File Formats

Column-based file formats, such as Parquet and ORC, store data in columns. The values of each table column (field) are stored next to each other. This format is ideal for analytical workloads where specific columns need to be queried and aggregated. Columnar formats enable efficient data compression and faster query performance, particularly for read-heavy operations. They are suitable for large-scale data analytics use cases and processed data layers in a data lake. Common column-based formats include:

Parquet
> Optimized for complex nested data structures, widely used in big data processing and analytics.

ORC (Optimized Row Columnar)
> Designed for high-performance data processing, particularly in Hadoop ecosystems.

Table Formats

Table formats have emerged as a new trend, enabling more flexible and efficient data lake management (Figure 5-1). These formats offer a layer of abstraction over data files stored in data lakes and introduce database-like functionalities. They provide useful features such as ACID transactions, scalable metadata handling, schema evolution, and time-travel capabilities, making data lakes more robust and easier to manage. The three major open source table formats are as follows:

Apache Iceberg
> Apache Iceberg is a high-performance format for huge analytic tables. Iceberg brings the reliability and simplicity of SQL tables to big data, while making it possible for data readers and writers to safely work with the same tables, at the same time.

Apache Hudi

> Apache Hudi is a transactional data lake platform that brings database and data warehouse capabilities to the data lake. Hudi enhances traditional batch data processing with a powerful incremental processing framework for low-latency analytics.

Delta Lake

> Built on top of Apache Spark, Delta Lake enhances data lakes with ACID transactions and scalable metadata handling.

In summary, selecting the right data storage format and table format for your data lake is a crucial decision that impacts performance and efficiency. By understanding these formats and their appropriate use cases, you can optimize your data lake for both current and future data processing needs. We will dive into data lake storage best practices in the last section of this chapter.

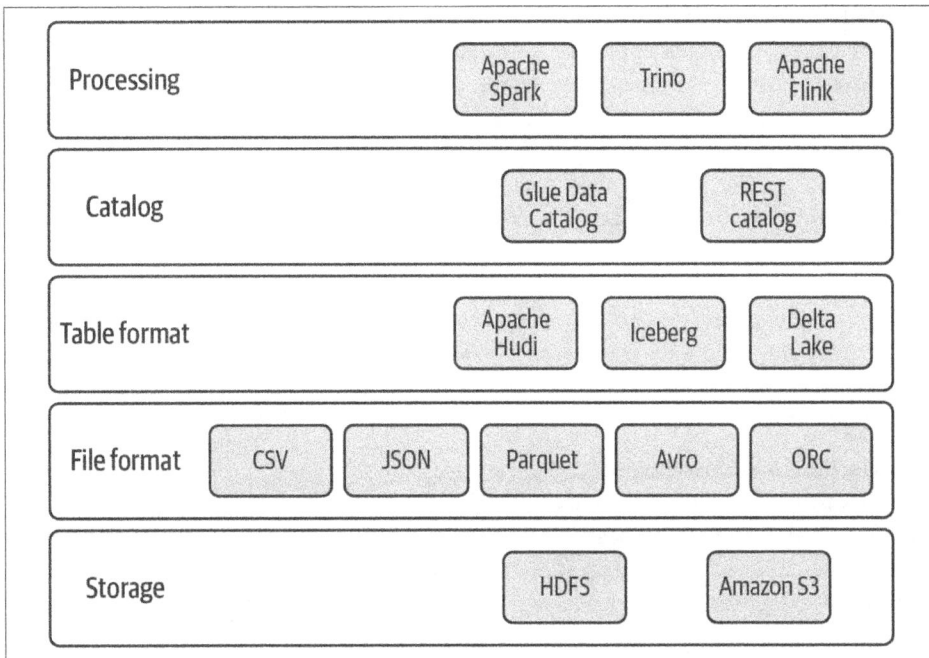

Figure 5-1. Table formats in the data lake file stack

Building a Data Strategy with Multiple Data Stores

Building a robust data strategy often involves leveraging multiple data stores to accommodate diverse data types and workloads. Organizations can gain deeper and richer insights by bringing together all their relevant data, regardless of structure or source, for comprehensive analysis. To achieve this, they are aggregating data from various silos into centralized locations, where they can perform analytics and machine learning directly on the centralized data. In parallel, they are also utilizing purpose-built data stores to optimize performance for specific use cases. This multifaceted approach ensures that organizations can harness the full potential of their data to drive better decision making and innovation. This section will explore the concepts of the lakehouse architecture and federated queries for creating a cohesive and effective data strategy.

The lakehouse architecture is a modern data strategy that combines the benefits of data lakes, data warehouses, and other purpose-built data consumption services. At the storage layer, this approach leverages the scalability and cost-effectiveness of data lakes to store and manage vast quantities of data, while also utilizing the performance and schema enforcement of data warehouses for structured data analysis. A modern lakehouse architecture goes beyond merely integrating data lakes with data warehouses. It relies on seamless data movement from sources into the lakehouse, cost-efficient data transformation, unified governance, and the use of purpose-built data consumption services. This comprehensive approach ensures efficient data management and maximizes the value extracted from diverse data sources. A lakehouse architecture shines for use cases such as business intelligence and reporting that require standard data transformation, large-scale centralized analytics, machine learning, and long-term storage with unified governance and security. You can stack a lakehouse architecture into five logical layers, as shown in Figure 5-2.

The lakehouse architecture on AWS leverages Amazon S3 as the object storage service for the data lake and Amazon Redshift as the data warehouse service. Amazon S3 offers industry-leading scalability, data availability, security, and performance. Additionally, S3's seamless integration with AWS and third-party ingestion, analytics, and machine learning services allows for comprehensive data management and analysis. Complementing Amazon S3 in the lakehouse architecture is Amazon Redshift. Amazon Redshift Spectrum (*https://oreil.ly/fieIM*) is one of the centerpieces of the natively integrated lake house storage layer. Redshift Spectrum enables Amazon Redshift to present a unified SQL interface where the same query can reference and combine datasets hosted in the data lake as well as data warehouse storage. Refer to the AWS document "The Lakehouse Architecture of Amazon SageMaker" (*https:// oreil.ly/MdFws*) for more information.

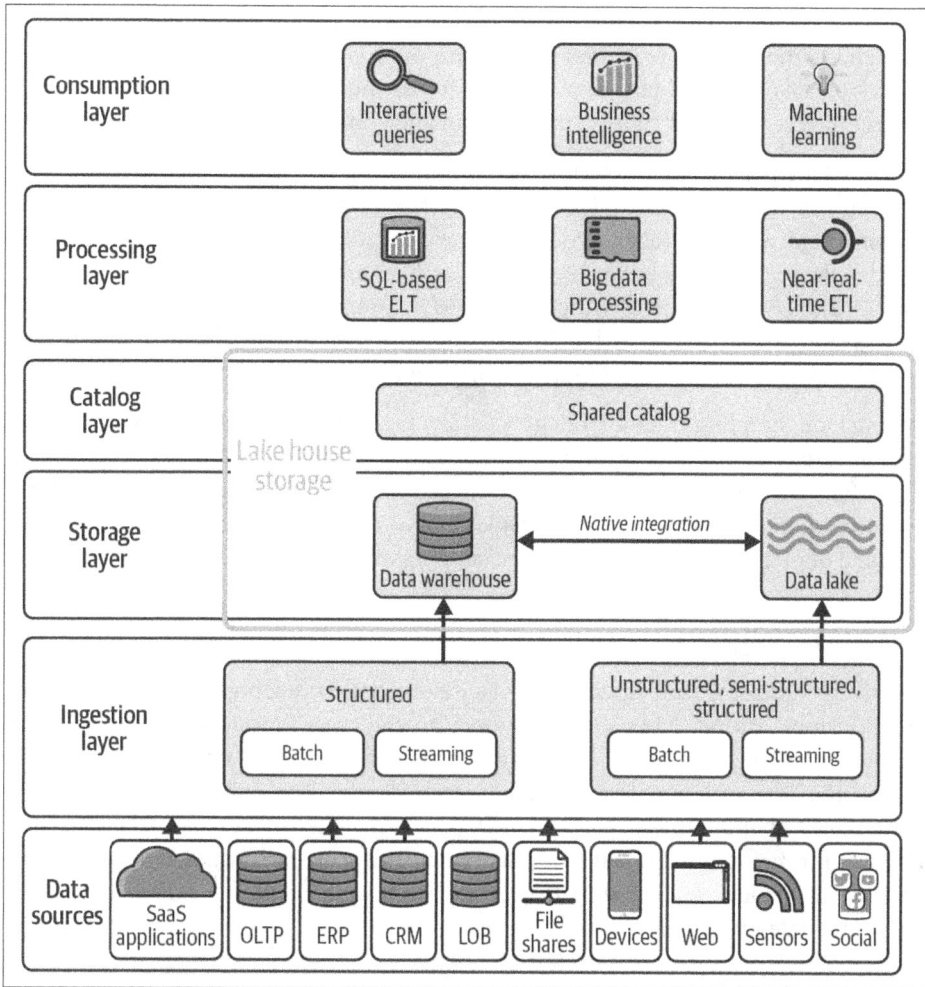

Figure 5-2. Lakehouse architecture on AWS

In addition to the lakehouse architecture, another powerful approach to managing and querying data across multiple stores is the use of federated queries. Unlike the lakehouse architecture, which often involves moving data into a centralized data lake, federated queries enable you to query data in place without moving or duplicating it. This in-place query pattern makes federated queries ideal for real-time analytics and ad-hoc analysis, as it reduces the operational overhead associated with data transfer, storage, and management. However, federated queries also come with limitations. Since the queries are executed directly on the data sources, they can cause compute overhead on those sources, potentially impacting their performance. Additionally, the scale and complexity of federated queries are often limited compared to centralized queries on lakehouses. Managing security across multiple data systems can also be more complex, requiring robust coordination and consistent security policies.

Amazon Athena Federated Query is a common example of federated query on AWS, allowing you to run SQL queries across a variety of data sources, both in the cloud and on premises. This means you can query not only data stored in Amazon S3 but also data residing in other AWS services like Amazon RDS, Amazon Redshift, and third-party data stores without the need to move the data into a centralized repository. Refer to the AWS blog "Extracting and joining data from multiple data sources with Athena Federated Query" (*https://oreil.ly/3I4ju*) for more information.

To conclude, building a data strategy that leverages multiple data stores is essential for managing diverse data types and workloads effectively. It is crucial for architects to carefully decide when to centralize data into a lakehouse versus when to perform federated queries. Together, these strategies empower organizations to harness the full potential of their data, driving better decision making and innovation.

Data Cataloging Systems

Effectively managing and discovering data is crucial for enabling efficient analytics and decision making. This section dives into the core aspects of data cataloging systems, focusing on their role in organizing and managing data stores. We will explore the key components of metadata and data catalogs and introduce different approaches to populating an AWS Glue Data Catalog. Additionally, we will cover best practices for maintaining an effective data catalog. By understanding and implementing these principles, you can enhance your organization's ability to manage, discover, and utilize data more effectively.

Components of Metadata and Data Catalogs

Metadata and data catalogs are the backbone of any data system, providing critical context and information about the data stored within an organization. Metadata can be broadly categorized into two types: technical metadata and business metadata.

Technical metadata includes details about the data's structure and format, such as table schemas, column data types, partition layout, table statistics, data lineage, and data source information. This type of metadata is essential for developers and data engineers to understand the technical aspects of data and how it flows through various systems.

Business metadata, on the other hand, provides context about the data from a business perspective. This includes definitions of business terms, data ownership, usage policies, and data quality information. Business metadata helps bridge the gap between technical teams and business users, ensuring that everyone has a common understanding of the data's meaning and relevance. It also aids in data governance and compliance by clearly defining data ownership, quality standards, and usage policies.

AWS offers managed catalog services for both types of metadata. The AWS Glue Data Catalog is a centralized repository that stores technical metadata about your organization's datasets. It integrates with various AWS services to provide a comprehensive view of your data landscape, making it easier to manage and query your data.

Amazon DataZone supports business data cataloging. This service, which became generally available in October 2023, provides a platform for managing business and technical metadata, helping organizations to catalog, discover, analyze, share, and govern data at scale. Although Amazon DataZone offers significant capabilities for data cataloging, the following sections of this book will primarily focus on AWS Glue, as Amazon DataZone is not yet included in the certification due to its relatively recent introduction.

A robust data catalog can significantly improve data discoverability and usability. A well-implemented data catalog not only drives better decision making and innovation but also enhances data governance and compliance by providing a single source of truth for metadata management. By ensuring that users can easily access and understand the data, organizations can unlock the full potential of their data assets.

Populating an AWS Glue Data Catalog

Populating the AWS Glue Data Catalog is a crucial step in building an organized and efficient data management system. There are four major approaches to populating an AWS Glue Data Catalog. This section will dive into each method, highlighting their benefits and appropriate use cases.

Using Glue crawlers

Glue crawlers are the most scalable and common approach to populating the AWS Glue Data Catalog. Crawlers automatically discover and catalog metadata from various data stores, including Amazon S3, Amazon DynamoDB, JDBC-based data sources (e.g., Amazon Redshift, Snowflake, and various RDBMS sources), and MongoDB client-based databases (e.g., Amazon DocumentDB and MongoDB). They can infer the schema and create or update tables in the Data Catalog, making them ideal for large-scale environments where automation and scalability are essential. Glue crawlers are particularly useful for handling dynamic and evolving data structures, as they can be scheduled to run at regular intervals, ensuring the catalog is always up-to-date. The general workflow of Glue crawlers is illustrated in Figure 5-3 and further described here:

1. *Crawler runs*

    The process begins with the crawler being initiated, either as a scheduled task or triggered via APIs. The crawler requires an IAM role with the appropriate permissions. This role should be able to access the necessary AWS resources, such as Amazon S3, AWS Glue, and optionally, AWS KMS if you're dealing with encrypted data.

2. *Classifiers*

    The crawler works with custom classifiers (*https://oreil.ly/HKJ0X*) that you choose to infer the format and schema of your data. You provide the code for custom classifiers (*https://oreil.ly/Z5sTC*) and they run in the order that you specify. If no custom classifier is provided or matches your data's schema, built-in classifiers attempt to recognize your data's schema.

3. *Connection*

    The crawler connects to the data store where the data resides. Some data stores require a preconfigured connector (*https://oreil.ly/3YZ3B*) that stores information such as login credentials, URI strings, and virtual private cloud (VPC) information.

4. *Schema inference*

    The crawler reads the data and infers the schema. This involves determining the structure, format, and partition layout of the data.

5. *Metadata writing*

    Finally, the crawler writes the inferred metadata into a database in the AWS Glue Data Catalog by creating/updating the necessary tables. You can configure Glue crawlers to log schema changes or update the table schemas directly. Glue supports schema versioning, meaning each schema change is versioned and stored. This allows you to track changes over time and revert to previous versions if necessary.

> For more information, refer to "Configuring a Crawler" (*https://oreil.ly/BgPGt*) in the AWS Glue User Guide.

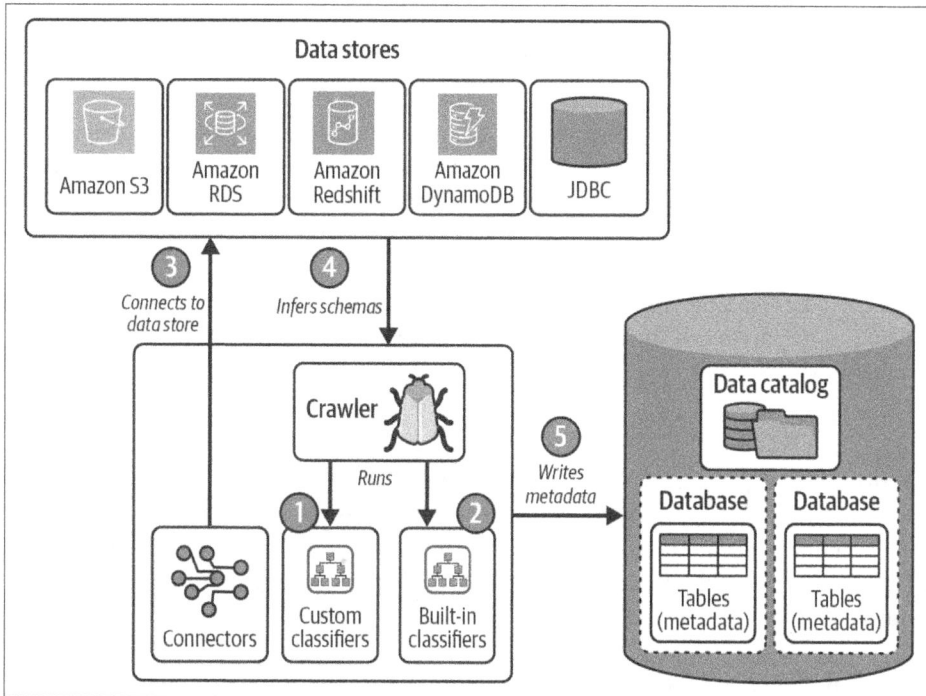

Figure 5-3. Glue crawler workflow

Defining metadata manually

Manually defining metadata is another approach to populating the Glue Data Catalog. This method is ideal when working with unsupported data formats, when you need full control over the schema, or during proof-of-concept (POC) projects at a small scale. By manually specifying the metadata, you can ensure full control over the metadata definitions. This approach requires more operational effort and expertise but provides the highest level of customization and precision.

Integrating with other AWS services

Integration with other AWS services, such as Amazon Athena, offers an alternative way to populate the Glue Data Catalog. This approach is less common but beneficial when you prefer to use ANSI SQL-based data definition language (DDL) statements to manage schemas. For example, you can create tables in Athena using `CREATE TABLE` statements, and the metadata will be stored in the Glue Data Catalog. You can also use the `MSCK REPAIR TABLE` command in Athena to load Apache Hive–style partitions into the Glue Data Catalog.

Migrating from an existing Hive catalog

Migrating from an existing Hive catalog is another approach to populate the Glue
Data Catalog. This method is useful for organizations that have an established Hive
metastore and wish to leverage the capabilities of AWS Glue without losing their
existing metadata. Hive Metastore to AWS Glue Data Catalog migration typically
requires Glue ETL jobs to extract metadata from the source database and load it into
Glue Data Catalog.

> For more information, refer to "Migration Between the Hive Meta-
> store and the AWS Glue Data Catalog" (*https://oreil.ly/Dd9n1*) on
> GitHub.

Choosing the right approach to populate the AWS Glue Data Catalog depends on
your specific use cases and the nature of your data environment. By understanding
and leveraging the methods described here, you can effectively populate your Glue
Data Catalog, ensuring accurate, organized, and accessible technical metadata for all
your data assets.

Data Catalog Best Practices

When implementing a data catalog, adhering to best practices ensures the catalog
is efficient, scalable, and secure. The following best practices focus on organizing
and managing AWS Glue Data Catalogs effectively, but these principles can also be
applied to other technical data catalogs.

Establish a consistent naming convention

A well-organized Data Catalog starts with clear and consistent naming conventions
for databases and tables. Use meaningful and descriptive names that reflect the data's
content and purpose. This makes it easier for users to find and understand the data
they need. Group related tables into logical databases and use prefixes or suffixes
to indicate different environments (e.g., dev, test, prod) or data types (e.g., raw,
processed).

Secure the Data Catalog

Security is paramount in managing the Data Catalog. Implement fine-grained access
control to ensure that only authorized users can view or modify the metadata. Use
AWS Identity and Access Management (IAM) policies to define who has access to
what resources. Encrypt sensitive data at rest and in transit to protect against unauthorized access. Regularly audit access logs to detect and respond to any suspicious
activity.

Manage schema changes effectively

Managing schema changes is crucial for maintaining data integrity and ensuring that downstream processes function correctly. Take advantage of the schema inference capabilities of AWS Glue crawlers to detect schema changes. Schedule regular crawls or use trigger-based crawls to automatically update the catalog when there are changes in the data schema. This proactive approach ensures that your metadata stays up-to-date and accurate. Use schema evolution features to handle schema changes gracefully.

Monitor schema changes

Review and update schema changes before applying them to avoid breaking downstream applications. Monitoring tools and notifications can alert you to schema changes, allowing you to take corrective actions promptly. For more details, refer to the AWS blog "Identifying Source Schema Changes Using AWS Glue" (*https://oreil.ly/R7N10*).

Use crawlers effectively

Incremental crawls (*https://oreil.ly/tftYW*) are particularly useful for frequently changing data sources. They add new partitions to existing tables when the schemas are compatible, without recrawling the entire dataset. This approach saves time and resources, ensuring that the catalog is updated promptly as new data becomes available. Please note that with incremental crawls, no schema changes are made to existing tables and no new tables will be added to the Data Catalog after the first crawl run.

Optimize performance with Glue Data Catalog

AWS Glue allows you to compute column-level statistics for AWS Glue Data Catalog tables in data formats such as Parquet, ORC, JSON, ION, CSV, and XML. Glue Data Catalog supports statistics for column values such as minimum value, maximum value, total null values, total distinct values, and average length of values. AWS analytical services such as Amazon Redshift and Amazon Athena can use these column statistics to generate optimized query execution plans that improves query performance. For more information, refer to "Optimizing Query Performance Using Column Statistics" (*https://oreil.ly/Z5bCE*) in the AWS Glue documentation.

Additionally, working with partition indexes in the AWS Glue Data Catalog can further enhance performance. Partition indexes allow for faster retrieval of partition (*https://oreil.ly/84W13*) information by maintaining indexes of the partitions, reducing query planning time. This feature is useful for tables with large amounts of partitions. More details can be found in "Creating Partition Indexes" (*https://oreil.ly/tQ5gU*) in the AWS Glue documentation.

Enriching Data Catalogs with Data Classification

Having explored the foundational aspects of technical metadata and the maintenance of technical catalogs on AWS, we now turn our attention to enriching these catalogs with data classification. Data classification enhances the utility of your Data Catalog by adding meaningful context and enabling more efficient data management practices.

Data classification is a crucial step in managing and utilizing data effectively. It involves organizing data into categories to streamline data discovery and control permissions. This classification not only aids in identifying and retrieving data more efficiently but also enhances security and compliance by ensuring that sensitive information is properly protected. By classifying data according to requirements, organizations can establish clear guidelines for how data should be handled, accessed, and used, aligning with regulatory requirements and internal policies.

One primary benefit of data classification is its ability to facilitate data discovery. When data is classified, users can easily search and locate the information they need based on predefined categories. This is particularly important in large organizations where data is distributed across various departments and systems. By classifying data by ownership, such as by business unit, organization, or project, it becomes easier to track and manage data assets. Additionally, classifying data by sensitivity levels ensures that sensitive information is flagged and handled appropriately, reducing the risk of data breaches and unauthorized access.

Another common classification is to categorize datasets in stages, such as raw, cleansed, and processed data, or sandbox and production data. This classification is particularly useful for tracking the data transformation process and managing different environments within the data pipeline. Raw data represents unprocessed information directly collected from sources, cleansed data has undergone preliminary processing to remove errors or inconsistencies, and processed data is fully transformed and ready for analysis or business use. Similarly, sandbox data is used for development and testing purposes, while production data is the final, operational data used in live applications. Categorizing data in these stages ensures that each dataset is used appropriately and maintains its integrity throughout its lifecycle.

Data classification also plays a vital role in permission control. By tagging data with specific classifications, organizations can enforce fine-grained access controls, ensuring that only authorized users can access certain types of data. AWS Lake Formation is a service that exemplifies the power of data classification in a data cataloging system. It allows users to tag data at the database, table, and column level, providing a high degree of granularity in data classification. This capability enables organizations to apply fine-grained classifications that align with their specific needs and use cases. We will expand on this topic in Chapter 7. The concept of data classification can be applied to other cataloging services as well, ensuring that data is organized, secured, and utilized effectively across different platforms.

In conclusion, enriching a Data Catalog with data classification is essential for effective data management. It enhances data discovery, improves permission control, and provides valuable insights into data usage patterns. By implementing robust data classification strategies, organizations can ensure that their data is secure, compliant, and easily accessible to those who need it.

Managing the Lifecycle of Data

Understanding the nuances of data lifecycle management is crucial for organizations to make informed decisions about storing, moving, and deleting data, ensuring both efficiency and regulatory compliance. In this and the following section, we will explore strategies and best practices for managing the data lifecycle, with a focus on the data storage layer. We will cover a range of topics, including selecting appropriate storage solutions, optimizing storage costs, and meeting business and legal compliance requirements. Additionally, we will provide practical insights into performing load and unload operations between Amazon S3 and Amazon Redshift, managing S3 lifecycle policies, and utilizing tools like DynamoDB TTL to automate data expiration. Through these discussions, you will gain the knowledge and skills needed to effectively manage your data throughout its lifecycle.

Selecting Storage Solutions for Hot and Cold Data

In the realm of data analytics, understanding the distinction between hot and cold data is fundamental for efficient data lifecycle management. Hot data refers to information that is frequently accessed and requires rapid retrieval times. This type of data is critical for real-time analytics, operational processes, and data analyses demanding immediate access to up-to-date information. Examples of hot data include transactional records, streaming data, and near-real-time analytical tables. These datasets are essential for driving real-time to near-real-time decision making and providing insights that support dynamic business operations. Conversely, cold data is accessed infrequently and can endure longer retrieval times. It is often used for archival purposes, historical analysis, and regulatory compliance. Examples of cold data include historical transaction logs, long-term sensor data, and compliance records. Recognizing the characteristics of hot and cold data is essential as it directly influences storage decisions, performance, and cost.

The spectrum of storage solutions ranges from high-performance, in-memory store to block storage to object storage. In-memory storage solutions, such as Amazon ElastiCache, offer extremely fast data retrieval suitable for hot data but come at a higher cost. Block storage solutions, like Amazon EBS, provide high performance and are ideal for applications requiring low-latency access to data. Object storage solutions, such as Amazon S3, offer scalable storage at lower costs and are suitable for both hot and cold data depending on the chosen storage class.

To choose the right storage solution, it is crucial to evaluate the data access patterns and performance requirements. Key criteria include the following:

Analytics technology and engine
Determine the analytics technology and compute engine based on your use case, query pattern, and data structure. This is the first decision to make and it helps you zoom in on the storage solutions you can select.

Latency requirements
Define the maximum acceptable delay for data updates and retrievals to ensure performance meets user expectations.

Query performance
Ensure the system can handle typical query loads within acceptable time frames to support business operations.

Cost
The unit data storage cost must be aligned with the budget while meeting performance needs.

Access frequency
Determine how often data needs to be accessed to select the most efficient storage tier.

Scalability
Ensure the storage solution can expand as data grows without compromising performance. Assess the amount of data being stored to choose a storage solution that can handle the scale efficiently.

Durability and availability
Consider the need for data protection and continuous availability to avoid data loss and downtime.

Evaluating these factors helps in aligning storage solutions with specific business needs, ensuring both efficiency and cost-effectiveness. Hot data storage solutions, which provide high-speed access and low latency, are typically more expensive. These solutions are designed to deliver rapid performance to support real-time to near-real-time analytics at scale. Conversely, cold data storage solutions offer significant cost savings by sacrificing data retrieval speed and decoupling compute from storage. These solutions are optimized for data that does not require immediate access, thus allowing organizations to store large volumes of data at a reduced cost.

By strategically balancing these trade-offs, organizations can optimize their storage expenditures while meeting their performance requirements. Additionally, some cold storage options also provide lower availability or durability. Consider the availability and durability of different solutions during the selection of technology to ensure that data remains accessible and protected as organizational needs evolve.

Example: Building a Petabyte-Scale Log Analytics Solution on AWS

Let's say you need to build a log analytics solution on AWS with 10 TB of raw application logs generated every day. The development teams send new logs to the analytics layer in an append-only fashion and most query the past 2 days of data. The development teams query the past 14 days of data 5 to 10 times per week and might perform historical data analytics that spans 6 months of data once per month. You need to store the logs in your S3 bucket for 2 years for compliance requirements.

The first decision to make is selecting the appropriate analytics technology and compute engine based on the use case, query pattern, and data structure. For this use case, Amazon OpenSearch Service is chosen as the analytics engine due to its robust capabilities in handling large-scale log data and providing powerful search, analytics, and visualization functionality.

Storage Tier Decisions for Different Access Patterns

After selecting Amazon OpenSearch Service, the next step is to decide the appropriate storage tiers for different query patterns and data lifecycle stages. As you see in Figure 5-4, Amazon OpenSearch offers three storage tiers: Hot, UltraWarm, and Cold, each optimized for specific data access requirements and cost efficiencies. Amazon OpenSearch also supports direct query with Amazon S3, which is a new way to query operational logs in Amazon S3 and S3 data lakes without needing to switch between services. This feature extends cold data from service-attached storage to object storage:

- Hot storage:
  - *Data*: Latest 2–7 days of logs.
  - *Characteristics*: Frequently accessed, requires rapid retrieval and updates.
  - *Benefits*: Provides the fastest access to data, supporting real-time analytics and indexing.
- UltraWarm storage:
  - *Data*: Logs between the past 1 week to 2 months.
  - *Characteristics*: Less frequently accessed, read-only.
  - *Benefits*: Offers a cost-effective solution for older data while still providing an interactive experience similar to Hot storage.

- Cold storage:
  - *Data*: Logs between the past 2 months and 1 year.
  - *Characteristics*: Infrequently accessed, long-term storage.
  - *Benefits*: Provides significant cost savings by storing data at near S3 prices, suitable for historical analysis.
- Zero-ETL direct query:
  - *Data*: An archive copy of the past 2 years of logs.
  - *Characteristics*: Ultra-infrequent access, mainly for archival usage.

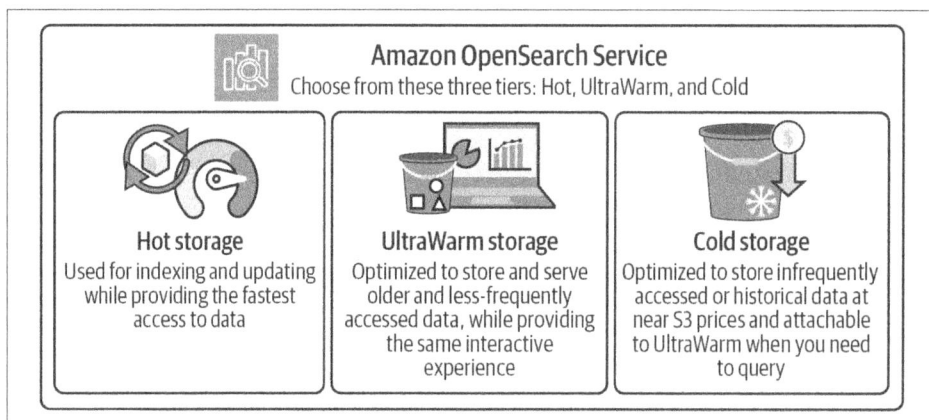

Figure 5-4. Three storage tiers for Amazon OpenSearch Service

Effectively managing the lifecycle of data requires selecting appropriate storage solutions that align with the specific access patterns and performance needs of the data. By understanding the characteristics of hot and cold data, evaluating cost considerations, and choosing the right storage options, organizations can ensure efficient and cost-effective data management. It's important to note that hot and cold data is a relative concept.

In the preceding example, UltraWarm storage is considered a colder tier compared to Hot storage in Amazon OpenSearch but a hotter tier compared to Cold storage in OpenSearch or archived data in S3. Keep this concept in mind when selecting different storage options in the certification and in architecting data solutions.

Defining Data Retention Policy and Archiving Strategies

Data retention policies dictate how long data should be kept and when it should be moved between different storage tiers to optimize efficiency and cost-effectiveness. In data lifecycle management, these policies ensure that data is stored appropriately based on its usage patterns and regulatory requirements. By systematically transitioning data from high-performance, expensive storage to more economical options as it ages, organizations can reduce storage costs while maintaining data accessibility and integrity. This approach not only enhances operational efficiency but also ensures compliance with legal and business mandates.

Data archiving strategies, on the other hand, focus on the long-term preservation of data that is no longer actively used but must be retained for compliance, historical reference, or other purposes. Archiving helps organizations meet regulatory requirements by ensuring that data is preserved in a secure, retrievable manner for specified periods. This strategy is crucial for maintaining the integrity of critical data over time, enabling businesses to reference historical data for audits, legal inquiries, or strategic analysis. Effective archiving ensures that cold data is stored cost-effectively while remaining accessible when necessary.

Implementing data retention and archiving strategies involves several best practices. First, it is essential to work backward from business and compliance needs to determine appropriate retention periods and archiving requirements for different data types. This alignment ensures policies meet organizational objectives and regulatory standards. Second, implementing automation is crucial to operationalize data movement. Tools such as AWS S3 Lifecycle policies and automated scripts can manage the transition of data between storage tiers, reducing manual intervention and minimizing errors. Finally, periodic review and validation of data lifecycle management practices are necessary to ensure retention and archiving strategies remain effective and compliant with evolving business needs and regulatory changes.

To effectively manage data retention and archiving, organizations should adopt a holistic approach that integrates these strategies into their broader data management framework. This includes defining data classification tiers, mapping data retention and archiving policies to data classes, leveraging automation for data movement, and regularly reviewing practices to ensure ongoing compliance and efficiency.

In the following sections, we will dive into detailed examples of how to operationalize these strategies. We will explore specific techniques such as unloading Redshift data to S3 in a lakehouse architecture and managing S3 lifecycle policies to automate data retention. These practical examples will provide a deeper understanding of how to implement effective data lifecycle management in your organization.

Performing COPY and UNLOAD Operations to Move Data Between Amazon S3 and Amazon Redshift

Organizations can gain deeper insights by aggregating data from various silos into a centralized location known as a data lake. In addition, they use purpose-built data stores like data warehouses to perform complex queries on structured data. To maximize insights from all their data, organizations need to facilitate easy data movement between data lakes and these specialized stores. To address this, AWS introduced the lakehouse architecture (*https://oreil.ly/MdFws*), which integrates a data lake, a data warehouse, and other purpose-built stores. This architecture is a common architecture pattern for large enterprises and a popular topic in the certification.

Amazon S3 and Amazon Redshift serve different purposes within this architecture, distinguished by the types of data they store. Amazon S3 is designed for durable and scalable storage of all types of data. It is a colder and more cost-efficient storage layer compared to Amazon Redshift. It commonly stores raw data from various sources before it gets cleaned, enriched, and ingested into Redshift. It also acts as an archive layer for less frequently accessed tables and older partitions. Redshift Spectrum allows users to query data that resides in S3 buckets from their Redshift clusters.

On the other hand, Amazon Redshift is optimized for structured data that requires complex queries and high-performance analytics. Data in Redshift is typically frequently accessed, transformed, and organized based on common query patterns, making it ideal for business intelligence applications, reporting, and data analysis tasks.

Amazon Redshift provides SQL commands for data loading and unloading:

COPY command
> The COPY command loads data from S3 into Amazon Redshift tables. It supports various data formats and applies transformations during the load process, making it highly flexible and efficient.

UNLOAD command
> The UNLOAD command exports data from Redshift tables to S3. It allows you to extract data in parallel, compress it, and specify various output formats.

Efficient data lifecycle management between Amazon S3 and Amazon Redshift is crucial for a lakehouse architecture. It ensures data is accessible and manageable throughout its lifecycle, optimizing both storage costs and query performance. Figure 5-5 shows different data flow patterns for a lakehouse architecture:

- You can perform ETL (extract, transform, and load) operations with Amazon EMR or AWS Glue to prepare the raw data into curated format and then use the COPY command to load the data into Amazon Redshift.

- You can directly load raw data into Amazon Redshift and then prepare the data with an ELT (extract, load, and transform) pattern.

- You can unload less-frequent data from Amazon Redshift into Amazon S3 with the UNLOAD command. The unloaded data can be further assessed via Amazon Athena or Amazon SageMaker for ad-hoc analytics and ML usage.

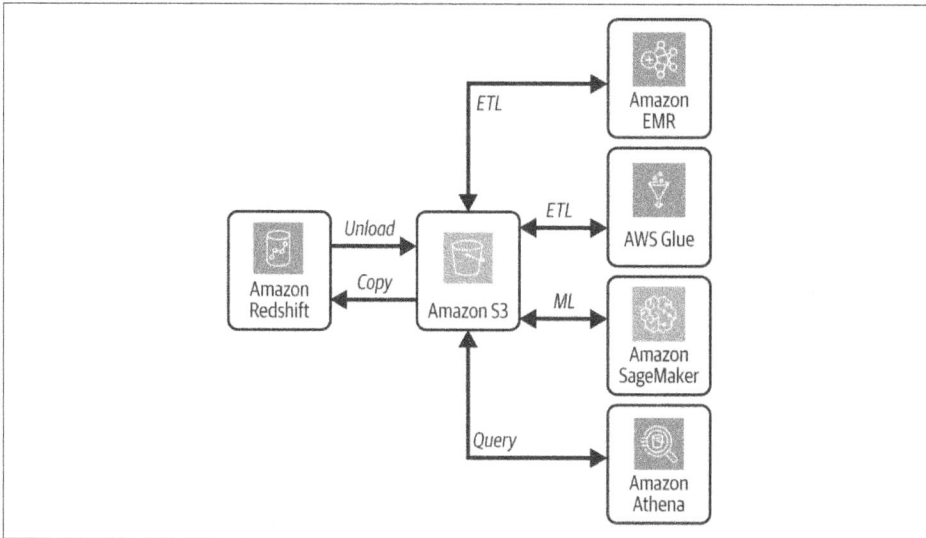

Figure 5-5. Data flow patterns for a lakehouse architecture on AWS

Optimizing Data Management with Amazon S3

As data volumes continue to grow exponentially, managing storage costs becomes crucial for businesses. Amazon S3 data lifecycle management offers a powerful solution to optimize storage costs by automating the movement of data between different storage classes based on its lifecycle. By implementing S3 lifecycle policies, organizations can efficiently handle data from creation to deletion, ensuring cost-effective storage management. This section explores the value of S3 lifecycle management, starting with an understanding of the various S3 storage classes.

Overview of S3 Storage Classes

Amazon S3 offers a range of storage classes designed to cater to different access patterns and cost requirements. By categorizing data based on access patterns, you can select the most suitable storage class to optimize costs and performance.

Frequently accessed storage classes

Frequently accessed storage classes include the following:

S3 Standard
> This is the default storage class, designed for frequently accessed data. It offers high durability, availability, and low-latency access, making it suitable for a wide range of use cases including cloud applications, dynamic websites, and content distribution:

- *Durability*: 99.999999999%
- *Availability*: 99.99%
- *Retrieval speed*: Milliseconds

S3 Express One Zone

Designed for latency-sensitive applications that require single-digit millisecond data access. S3 Express One Zone is the lowest-latency cloud object storage class available today, with data access speed up to 10x faster and request costs up to 80% lower than S3 Standard. However, it has a higher storage cost than S3 Standard and stores data in a single Availability Zone, making it suitable for workloads that prioritize performance and frequent access over storage costs and multi-AZ redundancy:

- *Durability*: 99.999999999%
- *Availability*: 99.5%
- *Retrieval speed*: Milliseconds

Infrequently accessed storage classes

Following are infrequently accessed storage classes:

S3 Standard-IA (Infrequent Access)

Ideal for data that is accessed less frequently (once a month) but requires rapid access when needed. It provides the same high durability and low latency as S3 Standard but at a lower cost for data that is not accessed often:

- *Durability*: 99.999999999%
- *Availability*: 99.9%
- *Retrieval speed*: Milliseconds

S3 One Zone-IA

Similar to S3 Standard-IA but stores data in a single Availability Zone, making it less resilient. It's suitable for infrequently accessed data that can be easily re-created if lost:

- *Durability*: 99.999999999%
- *Availability*: 99.5%
- *Retrieval speed*: Milliseconds

Rarely accessed storage classes

Rarely accessed storage classes comprise the following:

S3 Glacier Instant Retrieval
Designed for archival data that requires millisecond retrieval times. It is ideal for long-term data that is rarely accessed but needs to be retrieved quickly when required:

- *Durability*: 99.999999999%
- *Availability*: 99.99%
- *Retrieval speed*: Milliseconds

S3 Glacier Flexible Retrieval
Suitable for archival data that does not require immediate access. It offers a lower cost option with retrieval times ranging from minutes to hours:

- *Durability*: 99.999999999%
- *Availability*: 99.99%
- *Retrieval speed*: Minutes to hours

S3 Glacier Deep Archive
The lowest-cost storage class designed for long-term retention of data that is rarely accessed. Retrieval times can take up to 12 hours, making it suitable for data that is accessed very infrequently:

- *Durability*: 99.999999999%
- *Availability*: 99.99%
- *Retrieval speed*: Hours

Storage class for changing or unknown access patterns

Finally, S3 Intelligent-Tiering is a storage class suitable for changing or unknown access patterns:

S3 Intelligent-Tiering
Designed for data with unknown, changing, or unpredictable access patterns. It automatically moves data to the most cost-effective access tier, without performance impact or operational overhead:

- *Durability*: 99.999999999%
- *Availability*: 99.9%
- *Retrieval Speed*: Milliseconds to minutes

We will dive deeper into this class in the next section.

Choosing the Right Storage Class

When picking the storage class, it's essential to understand the type of data you have and its access pattern. This will help you categorize your data into frequently accessed, infrequently accessed, or rarely accessed classes. Once categorized, you can then choose the specific storage class based on additional factors such as:

Data retrieval speed
> Determine how quickly you need to access the data. For example, use S3 Glacier Instant Retrieval for millisecond access or S3 Glacier Flexible Retrieval for archival data that can tolerate longer retrieval times.

Data re-creation ability
> Consider if the data can be easily re-created. For example, use S3 One Zone-IA for data that can be regenerated if the Availability Zone fails, while using S3 Standard-IA for critical data that can't be re-created.

By aligning your data storage strategy with these considerations, you can optimize costs and performance effectively. For more detailed information on these storage classes, visit the AWS S3 Storage Classes documentation (*https://oreil.ly/RYdki*).

S3 Intelligent-Tiering

Amazon S3 Intelligent-Tiering is designed to optimize storage costs by automatically moving data to the most cost-effective access tier when access patterns change. This storage class is ideal for data with unpredictable access patterns, and therefore no predefined data retention policy. This storage class eliminates the need to manually move data between different storage classes, reducing operational overhead and ensuring cost optimization.

S3 Intelligent-Tiering works by monitoring object access patterns and moving objects that haven't been accessed for some consecutive days to a lower access tier. S3 Intelligent-Tiering includes three default access tiers and two optional archival tiers:

Frequent Access tier (automatic)
> This is the default access tier that any object created or transitioned to S3 Intelligent-Tiering begins its lifecycle in. An object remains in this tier as long as it is being accessed. The Frequent Access tier provides low latency and high-throughput performance.

Infrequent Access tier (automatic)
> Objects are moved to this tier after 30 consecutive days of inactivity, providing lower storage costs while maintaining low access latency.

Archive Instant Access tier (automatic)
> If an object is not accessed for 90 consecutive days, the object moves to the Archive Instant Access tier. The Archive Instant Access tier provides low latency and high-throughput performance.

Archive Access tier (optional)
> Suitable for archival data that can be retrieved within minutes to hours, offering lower storage costs but longer retrieval times. After activation, the Archive Access tier automatically archives objects that have not been accessed for a minimum of 90 consecutive days. You can extend the last access time for archiving to a maximum of 730 days.

Deep Archive Access tier (optional)
> Intended for long-term archival data that can tolerate retrieval times of up to 12 hours, providing the most cost-effective storage for rarely accessed data. After activation, the Deep Archive Access tier automatically archives objects that have not been accessed for a minimum of 180 consecutive days. You can extend the last access time for archiving to a maximum of 730 days.

To move data to S3 Intelligent-Tiering, specify this storage class when uploading objects to S3 using the AWS Management Console, AWS CLI, or SDKs. Additionally, you can configure lifecycle policies to transition objects from other storage classes to S3 Intelligent-Tiering based on specific criteria.

To enable archive tiers, you can activate one or both of the archive access tiers by creating a bucket, prefix, or object tag level configuration using the AWS Management Console, AWS CLI, or Amazon S3 API. Following is a code example to transition objects that have not been accessed under the prefix images to Archive Access after 90 days and Deep Archive Access after 180 days:

```
aws s3api put-bucket-intelligent-tiering-configuration \
    --bucket DOC-EXAMPLE-BUCKET \
    --id "ExampleConfig" \
    --intelligent-tiering-configuration \
      file://intelligent-tiering-configuration.json
```

Contents of *intelligent-tiering-configuration.json*:

```
{
    "Id": "ExampleConfig",
    "Status": "Enabled",
    "Filter": {
        "Prefix": "images"
        },
    "Tierings": [
        {
            "Days": 90,
            "AccessTier": "ARCHIVE_ACCESS"
        },
```

```
        {
            "Days": 180,
            "AccessTier": "DEEP_ARCHIVE_ACCESS"
        }
    ]
}
```

Managing the Data Lifecycle with Amazon S3 Lifecycle

Amazon S3 Lifecycle enables you to manage your objects so that they are stored cost-effectively throughout their lifecycle. A lifecycle configuration is a set of rules that define actions that Amazon S3 applies to a group of objects, such as transitioning them to another storage class or deleting them after a certain period. These rules help automate the process of managing the lifecycle of your data, ensuring that it is stored in the most cost-effective way over time.

Amazon S3 Lifecycle and S3 Intelligent-Tiering both help manage storage costs, but they are suited to different use cases:

Amazon S3 Lifecycle
> Best suited for data with a well-defined data retention policy and known access pattern. With that information, you can automate storage class transitions with corresponding lifecycle configurations. For example, you can create lifecycle configurations to transition logs to archival storage after a specific period or delete them after the compliance required period.

S3 Intelligent-Tiering
> This is ideal for data with unpredictable or changing access patterns. Intelligent-Tiering automatically moves objects between frequent and infrequent access tiers based on access patterns, without the need for manual intervention or predefined rules.

To create an Amazon S3 Lifecycle configuration, you define a set of rules in an XML file that specify the actions to be performed on objects during their lifetime. These actions can include transitioning objects to different storage classes or deleting them after a certain period. You can create and manage lifecycle configurations using the AWS Management Console, AWS CLI, AWS SDKs, or the REST API.

Here's an example configuration that transitions objects to progressively cheaper storage classes and then deletes them after a specified period. This example assumes you want to move objects to the Standard-IA storage class after 30 days, to Glacier Flexible Retrieval after 90 days, and then delete them after 365 days:

```
<LifecycleConfiguration>
  <Rule>
    <ID>example-id</ID>
    <Filter>
      <Prefix>logs/</Prefix>
```

```
      </Filter>
      <Status>Enabled</Status>
      <Transition>
        <Days>30</Days>
        <StorageClass>STANDARD_IA</StorageClass>
      </Transition>
      <Transition>
        <Days>90</Days>
        <StorageClass>GLACIER</StorageClass>
      </Transition>
      <Expiration>
        <Days>365</Days>
      </Expiration>
    </Rule>
</LifecycleConfiguration>
```

> For more examples, refer to "Examples of S3 Lifecycle Configura-
> tions" (*https://oreil.ly/Nc6Wq*) in the AWS documentation.

Monitoring the Amazon S3 Data Lifecycle

Effective monitoring and management of Amazon S3 data lifecycle configurations are
essential for ensuring cost optimization and data accessibility. AWS provides several
tools and features to help you monitor data usage patterns, identify objects that may
benefit from lifecycle policies, and ensure your S3 storage is cost-effective.

S3 Storage Lens

S3 Storage Lens offers a comprehensive view of object storage usage and activity
across hundreds, or even thousands, of accounts in an organization. S3 Storage
Lens delivers more than 60 metrics on Amazon S3 storage usage and activity to an
interactive dashboard in the Amazon S3 console. It helps you analyze storage usage,
identify cost-saving opportunities, and ensure compliance with lifecycle policies. At
no additional cost, all Amazon S3 users can access an interactive S3 Storage Lens
dashboard in the Amazon S3 console containing preconfigured views to visualize
storage trends. S3 Storage Lens provides the following key information when it comes
to S3 data lifecycle management:

Identify largest buckets
  With S3 Storage Lens, you get a centralized view of all the buckets in your
  account. You can rank your buckets by the total storage metric for a selected date
  range. S3 Storage Lens helps you visualize and sort your buckets by size, making
  it easier to identify the ones that require immediate attention. By pinpointing

your largest buckets, you can focus your cost-optimization efforts where they will have the most impact.

Uncover cold S3 buckets
S3 Storage Lens exposes activity metrics about how your storage is requested (for example, all requests, get requests, put requests), bytes uploaded or downloaded, and errors, which allows you to detect buckets or prefixes that have not been accessed frequently. "Cold" buckets may contain data that can be transitioned to lower-cost storage classes such as S3 Glacier or S3 Glacier Deep Archive.

Identify buckets without lifecycle rules
The tool helps you identify buckets that do not have lifecycle policies in place. By uncovering these buckets, you can add appropriate lifecycle rules to ensure that your data is transitioned to the correct storage classes over time, optimizing costs.

S3 Storage Lens provides automated recommendations to help you optimize your storage. You can also publish S3 Storage Lens metrics to Amazon CloudWatch to create a unified view of your operational health in CloudWatch dashboards (*https:// oreil.ly/rPyJc*).

Storage Class Analysis

Storage Class Analysis helps you analyze the access patterns of your data to determine the most appropriate storage class. It is particularly useful for identifying objects that are infrequently accessed and may benefit from transitioning to lower-cost storage classes, such as S3 Standard-IA or S3 Glacier. Run Storage Class Analysis periodically to keep track of changing access patterns and ensure that data is stored in the most cost-effective class.

AWS Cost Explorer

AWS Cost Explorer helps you visualize and analyze your AWS costs and usage over time. It provides detailed insights into your S3 storage costs, allowing you to track trends, identify anomalies, and discover opportunities for savings. AWS Cost Explorer offers the following capabilities when it comes to S3 data management:

Break down S3 charges by components
Use Cost Explorer to break down your S3 charges by different components such as storage, requests, and data transfer. This detailed view can help you identify specific areas where you can optimize costs.

Break down S3 charges by cost allocation tags
Use cost allocation tags to categorize and track costs by different projects or business units, making it easier to identify specific areas where cost optimization is needed.

Forecast and budget

Utilize Cost Explorer to forecast future costs and set budgets, helping you proactively manage and optimize your S3 storage expenses.

For more details, refer to the AWS blog "Analyzing Request and Data Retrieval Charges to Optimize Amazon S3 Cost" (*https://oreil.ly/3kPAo*).

By leveraging these monitoring tools, you can effectively manage your Amazon S3 data lifecycle configurations, ensuring that your storage costs are optimized and your data remains accessible as needed.

Expiring Snapshots from Open Table Formats

As part of managing the data lifecycle effectively on Amazon S3, it's crucial to optimize storage not only at the individual object level, as described in previous sections, but also when using advanced table management frameworks. Open table formats such as Apache Hudi (*https://hudi.apache.org*), Apache Iceberg (*https://oreil.ly/KgJJO*), and Delta Lake (*https://delta.io*) offer unique capabilities—like upsert operations, merges, schema evolution, and time travel—that extend beyond the basic object storage functionality of Amazon S3.

A key concept underlying these advanced formats is *snapshots*, which capture the state of a table at specific points in time. Snapshots enable powerful capabilities such as data versioning, historical queries, and consistent views. However, snapshot accumulation over time can significantly increase storage costs, counteracting your optimization efforts in data lifecycle management.

While traditional Amazon S3 lifecycle rules operate on individual objects without awareness of these snapshot relationships, open table formats manage snapshots as collections of interdependent files. Therefore, to effectively control storage growth and complement broader Amazon S3 cost-management practices, it's essential to use the native snapshot expiration capabilities provided by these open table formats (Iceberg Expire Snapshot (*https://oreil.ly/e-7R4*), Hudi Cleaning (*https://oreil.ly/oBWsj*), Delta Lake Remove Files (*https://oreil.ly/JRY3z*)). These functions understand the internal structure and dependencies of snapshot files, enabling expiration of outdated snapshots in a safe, performance-friendly, and cost-effective manner that integrates seamlessly with your overall data management and lifecycle optimization strategies on Amazon S3.

> For more information, refer to the AWS documentation on optimizing storage with Apache Iceberg (*https://oreil.ly/h_0zW*).

Archiving Data from Amazon DynamoDB to Amazon S3

Another common data lifecycle management pattern is to archive data from an application backend such as Amazon DynamoDB to Amazon S3. Customers frequently use DynamoDB to store time series data, such as webpage clickstream data or transaction events. Instead of deleting older, less frequently accessed items, many customers prefer to archive them to ensure compliance with various regulatory requirements and support further analytical needs.

Figure 5-6 shows a solution that uses DynamoDB Time to Live (TTL) to automatically delete expired items from DynamoDB tables and subsequently archive these expired items in Amazon S3 through the use of DynamoDB Streams.

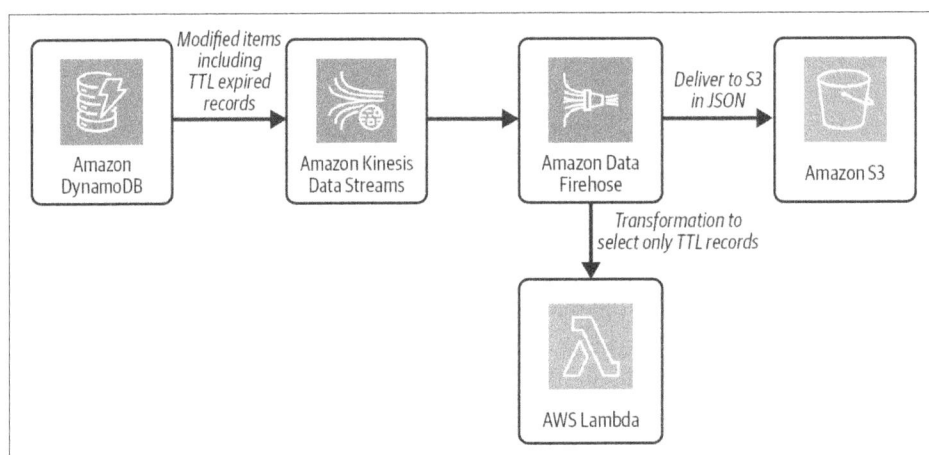

Figure 5-6. Archive data from Amazon DynamoDB to Amazon S3

Here is how the process works:

Enable DynamoDB TTL
> DynamoDB TTL is a feature that allows you to define a per-item expiration timestamp, after which the item is automatically deleted. This is particularly useful for managing the lifecycle of data that has a specific retention period. To set up TTL on a DynamoDB table, you need to enable TTL and specify the attribute that will store the expiration timestamp. Once enabled, DynamoDB will periodically scan the table for expired items and delete them.

Set up DynamoDB Streams with Kinesis Data Streams
> DynamoDB Streams capture a time-ordered sequence of item-level modifications in a DynamoDB table. The stream records the data modification, including deletions, which can then be processed further. When TTL deletes an item, this deletion is recorded in the DynamoDB Stream. In the architecture in Figure 5-6, the DynamoDB Stream sends these change logs to Amazon Kinesis Data

Streams, providing a reliable and scalable way to capture and process the deletion events.

Create a Lambda function to select TTL records
In this architecture, Amazon Data Firehose, formerly known as Amazon Kinesis Data Firehose, is configured to receive data from Kinesis Data Streams. You can attach an AWS Lambda function to Amazon Data Firehose to filter and transform the data. Specifically, the Lambda function filters out expired items that were deleted by the TTL process. Items deleted by TTL will have the attribute `userIdentity.principalId: "dynamodb.amazonaws.com"`, which can be used as a filter criterion.

Set up an Amazon Data Firehose to archive the records in Amazon S3
The transformed data, now filtered to include only TTL-deleted items, is delivered to Amazon S3 in JSON format. Storing the data in S3 provides a cost-effective and scalable solution for long-term retention. This archived data can then be used for compliance with data lifecycle policies. By storing the data in JSON format, it remains flexible and accessible for various data processing and analysis tools, enabling deeper insights and value extraction from the archived data.

This pattern not only optimizes storage costs by efficiently managing the data lifecycle but also ensures regulatory compliance and enhances the potential for data analytics. For more details, refer to "Archive data from Amazon DynamoDB to Amazon S3 using TTL and Amazon Kinesis integration" (*https://oreil.ly/V7j6t*) in the AWS documentation.

Ensuring S3 Data Resiliency with S3 Versioning

Versioning is another fundamental concept designed to enhance data resiliency and support compliance and governance requirements. Maintaining multiple versions of an object, throughout some timespan, allows organizations to preserve, retrieve, and restore data to previous states. This capability is essential for ensuring data integrity and availability, especially in environments where data accuracy and recoverability are critical.

Versioning helps protect against accidental deletions and unintended modifications, which are common risks in data management. In the context of compliance and governance, versioning is critical. Many regulations, such as the General Data Protection Regulation (GDPR) and Health Insurance Portability and Accountability Act (HIPAA), require strict data retention and protection policies. Versioning facilitates compliance by ensuring that historical data is preserved in its exact state, supporting audit trails and legal hold requirements. Organizations can demonstrate adherence to data retention policies and respond to regulatory inquiries more effectively when they can access every version of their data.

Moreover, versioning aids in implementing robust data governance practices. It allows for the tracking of data changes over time, providing a clear history of modifications. This transparency is crucial for maintaining accountability and traceability within an organization. In scenarios where data must be retained for specific periods due to legal or business requirements, versioning ensures that older versions of data are not inadvertently deleted or altered.

Amazon S3 Versioning is a feature that allows you to keep multiple versions of an object in the same bucket. Once versioning is enabled on a bucket, S3 automatically generates a unique version ID for each object stored, making it possible to preserve, retrieve, and restore every version of every object stored in the bucket. This capability is especially useful for protecting against accidental deletions or overwrites, as each change to an object creates a new version rather than replacing the existing data.

Enabling Versioning on an S3 Bucket

Enabling versioning on an S3 bucket is straightforward and can be done via the AWS Management Console, AWS CLI, or SDKs. To enable versioning using the AWS Management Console, navigate to the S3 service, select the desired bucket, go to the Properties tab, and under the Versioning section, click Edit and enable versioning. Using the AWS CLI, you can enable versioning with the following command:

```
aws s3api put-bucket-versioning \
  --bucket your-bucket-name --versioning-configuration Status=Enabled
```

Once versioning is enabled, S3 starts keeping track of all versions of the objects in the bucket. This means that any subsequent operations such as PUT, DELETE, or POST will create new versions instead of overwriting the existing ones. It is important to note that versioning cannot be disabled once it is enabled; it can only be suspended, which stops S3 from creating new versions but retains the existing versions in the bucket.

When working with S3 Versioning in Amazon S3 buckets, you can optionally add another layer of security by configuring a bucket to enable MFA (multifactor authentication) delete. When you do this, the bucket owner must include two forms of authentication in any request to delete a version or change the versioning state of the bucket.

S3 Versioning and Object Lifecycle Management

Integrating S3 Versioning with lifecycle policies is essential for managing storage costs and ensuring efficient data management. Lifecycle policies allow you to define actions to transition objects between different storage classes and to expire objects after a specified period. By combining versioning with lifecycle policies, you can automatically manage the lifecycle of both current and noncurrent object versions.

For instance, you can create a lifecycle policy that transitions noncurrent versions to colder storage classes such as S3 Glacier or S3 Glacier Deep Archive after a certain number of days. This helps in reducing storage costs while retaining the ability to restore previous versions if needed. Additionally, you can set policies to permanently delete noncurrent versions after a specified period, ensuring that obsolete data does not accumulate and consume storage space unnecessarily.

Here is an example of a lifecycle policy that transitions noncurrent versions to S3 Glacier after 30 days and permanently deletes them after 365 days:

```
<LifecycleConfiguration>
  <Rule>
    <ID>TransitionNonCurrentVersions</ID>
    <Status>Enabled</Status>
    <NoncurrentVersionTransition>
      <NoncurrentDays>30</NoncurrentDays>
      <StorageClass>GLACIER</StorageClass>
    </NoncurrentVersionTransition>
    <NoncurrentVersionExpiration>
      <NoncurrentDays>365</NoncurrentDays>
    </NoncurrentVersionExpiration>
  </Rule>
</LifecycleConfiguration>
```

By implementing such lifecycle policies, you can automate the management of versioned objects, ensuring data resiliency while optimizing storage costs.

For more detailed information, refer to the AWS documentation on S3 Versioning (*https://oreil.ly/zU6al*).

Designing Data Models and Schema

Effective data model design is essential for achieving efficient data storage, retrieval, and analysis. Proper data modeling not only enhances performance but also ensures scalability, maintainability, and data accuracy. This section explores the importance of this concept, highlighting best practices for different types of data stores. We will provide detailed examples of structured data models with Amazon Redshift, discuss data modeling strategies for Amazon DynamoDB, and examine data lake data modeling techniques.

Introduction to Data Modeling

Data modeling is a foundational concept in database management and data engineering. It involves creating a virtual representation of an entire information system or parts of it, illustrating the types of data, their relationships, and how they interact within the system. It ensures that data is organized systematically, enhancing understanding and communication among stakeholders. There are three main types of data models: conceptual, logical, and physical, each serving a distinct purpose and level of detail:

Conceptual data models

These models provide a high-level overview of the data structure, focusing on the entities and their relationships without diving into technical specifics. They are useful for communicating with business stakeholders, ensuring that all parties have a common understanding of the data requirements and share common terminologies.

Logical data models

These add more detail to the conceptual model by defining data attributes, primary and secondary keys, and the relationships between different data entities. These models are crucial for developers, database administrators, and data engineers as they provide a blueprint for the actual schema design without considering physical storage details.

Physical data models

Physical data models translate the logical models into technical specifications that can be implemented at the physical level. They include detailed configuration about data storage tiering, physical layouts, indexing, and performance optimization strategies specific to the data stores being used.

The benefits of well-designed data models and physical layouts are manifold. They ensure data accuracy and consistency, reduce data redundancy, and improve query performance. Well-structured data models make it easier for data consumers to extract insights, predict trends, and make informed business decisions. They also streamline the development process, making it faster and less error-prone, and provide a scalable foundation that can evolve with the organization's needs. In this book, we will mainly focus on the design of logical and physical data models.

A general best practice in data modeling is to work backward from data access patterns to derive the data models. This approach ensures that the data structures are optimized for the types of queries that will be performed, enhancing performance and efficiency. For instance, in a retail scenario, if the primary query pattern involves analyzing sales data by store and product, the data model should be designed to facilitate these queries with appropriate indexing and partitioning strategies.

Effective data modeling involves several key steps: engaging stakeholders, gathering requirements, creating initial designs, validating and refining these designs, and finally implementing them in a physical data store. Each step is iterative and involves feedback loops to ensure the model aligns with business objectives and technical requirements.

By following these practices, organizations can ensure their data models and physical layouts are well designed, scalable, and optimized for performance, thereby enabling efficient data management and robust analytics capabilities. Now let's look at data model best practices for different AWS data stores.

Data Modeling Strategies for Amazon Redshift

Structured data modeling is a critical component of modern data strategy, enabling organizations to efficiently store, manage, and analyze large volumes of relational data. Amazon Redshift, a fully managed data warehouse service in the AWS cloud, offers robust capabilities for handling structured data. This chapter dives into the methodologies and best practices for designing and implementing structured data models in Amazon Redshift. We will explore common schema design patterns and discuss trade-offs between them. Furthermore, we will discuss the benefits of denormalization in online analytical processing (OLAP) systems. The section also covers a dimensional modeling technique, the Kimball methodology, and provides insights into the intricacies of physical data modeling on Amazon Redshift.

Common schema design patterns

In relational database management systems (RDBMS), several schema design patterns are commonly used: star schema, snowflake schema, and third normal form (3NF) schema. Each has its advantages and trade-offs, particularly in terms of data normalization and performance:

Star schema
  The star schema is a type of denormalized schema used in data warehousing. It consists of a central fact table surrounded by dimension tables. The fact table stores the core data, usually numerical, such as sales figures, transaction amounts, or other quantitative metrics. Each dimension table contains descriptive attributes related to the facts (e.g., dates, products, customers). This schema is designed for efficient querying and is optimized for read-heavy operations. It minimizes the number of joins, thus speeding up query performance.

Snowflake schema
  The snowflake schema is an extension of the star schema, featuring a more complex and normalized design. In this design, dimension tables are further normalized into multiple related tables, forming a structure that resembles a snowflake. While this approach can save storage space and reduce data redundancy, it often results in more complex queries due to the increased number of joins needed to retrieve data.

Third normal form (3NF)

A 3NF schema is a highly normalized form where data is organized to eliminate redundancy and ensure data integrity. In 3NF, tables are structured so that each non-primary-key attribute is only dependent on the primary key. This design is beneficial for transactional systems where write operations are frequent, but it can be less efficient for read-heavy analytical queries due to the need for multiple joins to assemble data. Thus it is an anti-pattern for Amazon Redshift.

The primary distinction between star, snowflake, and 3NF schemas lies in their levels of data normalization. Data normalization is the process of organizing data to reduce redundancy and improve data integrity. This is typically achieved by dividing a large flat table that contains columns of various entities into smaller, related tables and defining relationships among them. The primary goal of normalization is to minimize data anomalies during operations such as updates, insertions, and deletions, thereby enhancing data consistency and integrity. However, while normalization reduces redundancy and improves data integrity, it can also lead to complex queries due to the need for multiple joins between tables.

In Online Analytical Processing (OLAP) systems, such as data warehouses, a certain level of denormalization is often beneficial. Denormalized schemas, such as the star schema, simplify query structures and enhance performance by reducing the need for multiple joins. This results in faster data retrieval and improved query efficiency, crucial for large-scale data analysis and reporting.

Amazon Redshift, with its columnar storage format, further amplifies the benefits of denormalization. In Redshift, data is stored column-wise, allowing it to efficiently scan only the necessary columns during query execution. This significantly reduces I/O operations and accelerates query performance, especially for denormalized tables where fact and dimension data are closely integrated. Additionally, Redshift's advanced compression techniques can effectively reduce storage requirements and speed up data retrieval processes, making denormalized schemas even more efficient.

Logical data modeling in Amazon Redshift

Logical data modeling is an essential phase in designing data warehouse schemas. It focuses on defining the structure and relationships of data without diving into technical implementation details. One widely used logical modeling approach specifically designed for analytical workloads is dimensional modeling. Dimensional modeling organizes data into dimensions and facts, simplifying complex business queries and improving analytical performance.

The Kimball methodology (*https://oreil.ly/w8H6Z*), developed by Ralph Kimball, is a widely adopted approach to dimensional modeling. It provides a systematic method for designing data models that are optimized for query performance and ease of use. While there are other dimensional modeling techniques, we use the Kimball methodology here to demonstrate the process.

The Kimball methodology emphasizes creating a data warehouse through a series of incremental steps, focusing on individual business processes. The workflow of the Kimball methodology can be broken down into the following steps:

1. *Identify the business process.*
   Determine the key business processes within the organization. These processes are the operational activities such as taking an order or processing an insurance claim. Each process is represented by a fact table.

2. *Declare the grain of your data.*
   Define the level of detail, or grain, of the data in the fact table. For example, in a sales process, the grain could be individual sales transactions.

3. *Identify and implement dimensions.*
   Develop dimension tables that describe the context of the business process. These tables typically include descriptive attributes like time, product, customer, and location.

4. *Identify and implement facts.*
   Develop fact tables with numerical measurements and foreign keys that link to dimension tables. For example, in a sales transaction fact table, numerical measurements can be sales amount, unit price, and commission.

The Kimball methodology ensures that data is organized in a way that aligns with business requirements, providing a robust foundation for data analysis and decision making. The AWS blog "Dimensional Modeling in Amazon Redshift" (*https://oreil.ly/XhTkR*) provides an example of implementing dimensional modeling using this approach.

Physical data modeling in Amazon Redshift: Choosing the best distribution style

Physical data models translate the logical table schemas into technical specifications that can be implemented at the data store level. Physical data modeling in Amazon Redshift heavily influences overall query performance. Key considerations include distribution styles, sort keys, compression encodings, and column sizes.

When you run a query, the query optimizer redistributes the data to the compute nodes as needed to perform any joins and aggregations. The goal in selecting a table's distribution style is to minimize the data redistributions. Amazon Redshift provides four primary distribution styles to manage how data is distributed across nodes in a cluster:

AUTO distribution

   With AUTO distribution, Amazon Redshift assigns an optimal distribution style based on the size of the table data. We recommend using AUTO distribution by default. Only choose a distribution key manually if you have a thorough understanding of the query patterns and wish to fine-tune the data distribution.

EVEN distribution

   Data is distributed evenly across all nodes using a round-robin approach, regardless of the values in any particular column. EVEN distribution is appropriate when a table doesn't participate in joins.

KEY distribution

   Data is distributed based on the values in one specified column (the distribution key). Rows with the same key are stored on the same node. A general best practice is to use KEY distribution for large tables that are frequently joined with other large tables. If both tables in a join are distributed using the same key, data with the same key is colocated, resulting in faster join operations. When choosing the distribution key, ensure that the column has high cardinality to minimize the likelihood of data skew.

ALL distribution

   A complete copy of the table is stored on every node. This style is ideal for small dimension tables that change seldomly, as it eliminates the need for data movement during joins.

> To view the distribution style of a table, query the PG_CLASS_INFO view or the SVV_TABLE_INFO view.

Physical data modeling in Amazon Redshift: Choosing the best sort key

Sort keys determine the order in which data is stored on disk, significantly impacting query performance. Properly chosen sort keys enable efficient data retrieval by allowing Amazon Redshift to skip large data blocks that do not match the query criteria. Some best practices to select the best sort keys are:

Let Amazon Redshift choose

   Let Amazon Redshift choose the appropriate sort order by specifying SORTKEY AUTO when you create your tables. Amazon Redshift will pick the appropriate sort key bases on your access pattern.

Analyze common query patterns

Analyze common query patterns if you prefer to configure the sort keys on your own. For example, if queries often filter by `order_date` and `customer_id`, consider making these columns part of your sort key.

Optimize for large tables first

For large tables, sort keys can significantly impact query performance by reducing the amount of data scanned. Prioritizing your effort on large tables provides you the best ROI on physical data modeling.

Use compound sort keys

Use compound sort keys when queries frequently filter on a consistent set of leading columns. A compound key is made up of all of the columns listed in the sort key definition. The data is then sorted based on the order of columns specified in the sort key. The performance benefits of compound sorting decrease when queries depend only on secondary sort columns, without referencing the primary columns. Therefore, it works best when most of your queries filter on a consistent set of leading columns.

Sort on commonly joined columns

Specify the join column as both the first column of the sort key and the distribution key for commonly joined tables. Doing this enables the query optimizer to choose a sort merge join instead of a slower hash join.

> For more information, see the AWS documentation on working with sort keys (*https://oreil.ly/sVeTc*).

Additional best practices for data modeling with Amazon Redshift

In the following we list some other key best practices to consider when data modeling with Amazon Redshift:

Optimize column size

Using the smallest possible column size reduces storage requirements and improves query performance by minimizing the amount of data read from disk. You can define precise data types and lengths (e.g., `VARCHAR(50)` instead of `VARCHAR(255)`) based on your data requirements.

Choose the appropriate compression encodings

Compression reduces storage requirements and enhances I/O performance by minimizing the amount of data read from disk. You can specify compression encodings when you create a table, but in most cases, automatic compression produces the best results. Create a table with `ENCODE AUTO` to let Amazon

Redshift manage compression encoding for all columns in the table. Additionally, it is a best practice to avoid compressing sort key columns.

For more information, see the AWS documentation on Amazon Redshift best practices for designing tables (*https://oreil.ly/5JS9R*).

In summary, designing and implementing structured data models in Amazon Redshift involves understanding and applying various schema design patterns, with careful consideration of the trade-offs between normalization and denormalization. Dimensional modeling, particularly using the Kimball methodology, provides a robust framework for organizing data in a way that aligns with business processes and analytical needs. Physical data modeling decisions, such as choosing the best distribution styles, sort keys, compression encodings, and data types, are crucial for optimizing query performance and storage efficiency. By leveraging the capabilities of Amazon Redshift, organizations can effectively manage and analyze large volumes of structured data, driving informed decision making and achieving business goals.

Data Modeling Strategies for Amazon DynamoDB

In this section, we will explore the data modeling strategies for Amazon DynamoDB. Understanding the differences between NoSQL and relational database design is crucial, as DynamoDB operates fundamentally differently from traditional relational databases. By the end of this section, you will have a comprehensive understanding of key DynamoDB concepts such as partition keys, sort keys, and global secondary indexes (GSIs). You will also learn how to strategically select and utilize these elements to meet your application's unique access patterns and performance requirements.

NoSQL versus relational data modeling

NoSQL databases, such as Amazon DynamoDB, and relational databases (RDBMS) have distinct advantages and challenges that influence their use. RDBMS utilize a highly structured format with tables, rows, and columns, enabling flexible data access patterns through table joins. However, this flexibility can hinder scalability and performance under high throughput. In contrast, NoSQL databases prioritize scalability and performance. In a NoSQL database like DynamoDB, data can be queried efficiently within specific access patterns, but outside of these patterns, queries can become expensive and slow.

Designing a schema for a NoSQL database like DynamoDB requires a shift from traditional relational database design. In RDBMS, data modeling often starts with normalization, organizing data into separate tables based on entities and relationships without initially considering access patterns. Data models can be adjusted and extended later as new query requirements arise. However, in NoSQL databases, it is crucial to understand data access patterns up front before designing the schema, as query performance and cost-efficiency rely heavily on how well the schema supports specific queries. It is typically hard, if not impossible, to perform table joins with NoSQL databases to accommodate unexpected query patterns. Additionally, unlike the large number of tables in a highly normalized RDBMS, maintaining as few tables as possible in a NoSQL database simplifies scalability, improves data locality, and reduces the complexity of permissions management, contributing to lower operational costs.

The first step in designing your NoSQL database application is to identify the specific query patterns that the system must satisfy. It is important to understand three fundamental properties of your application's access patterns: the list of entities to be stored (such as users, orders, or products), the list of access patterns (including entity reads and writes), and the approximate size of each entity, including cardinality (number of distinct values) and throughput. By carefully considering these factors, a robust and efficient table schema can be developed to meet the application's specific needs.

Example use case: Ecommerce website

To illustrate the data collection process, let's consider an example of data modeling for an ecommerce website. The list of entities to be stored includes the following:

1. Customers
2. Products
3. Shopping carts
4. Orders

The list of access patterns include the following:

1. Customer accesses the inventory info of a specific product
2. Customer adds products to their shopping cart
3. Customer checks out a shopping cart
4. Customer views the status of their most recent orders
5. Company wants to view all unfulfilled orders

Sample entity cardinality and query frequency analysis are as follows:

- Customer accesses the inventory info of a specific product:
  — *Entity*: Products
  — *Cardinality*: Medium to high (potentially millions of products)
  — *Query frequency*: Very high (frequent query by customers)

- Customer views the status of their most recent orders:
  - *Entity*: Orders
  - *Cardinality*: High
  - *Query frequency*: Medium (2-3 queries per customer per week)

We will use this use case in the following sections for DynamoDB data modeling. Working backward from the access patterns will ensure that the database schema is optimized for the most frequent and critical queries.

Core concepts of DynamoDB

Let's first level-set some core DynamoDB concepts. Understanding these core concepts is crucial for designing effective and scalable data models in DynamoDB:

Table, items, and attributes
   At the heart of Amazon DynamoDB lies the table, a collection of data organized into items, which are analogous to rows in traditional databases. Each item is a collection of attributes, where an attribute is a fundamental data element, similar to a column in relational databases. Attributes can be of various data types, including strings, numbers, binaries, and more complex structures like sets and maps. DynamoDB tables are schemaless, which means that neither the attributes nor their data types need to be defined beforehand. Each item can have its own distinct attributes.

Primary key, partition key, and sort key
   DynamoDB tables must have a primary key, which uniquely identifies each item. There are two types of primary keys: simple primary keys and composite primary keys. A simple primary key consists of a single attribute, known as the partition key. In contrast, a composite primary key comprises two attributes: the partition key and the sort key. The partition key determines the physical storage units where the item is stored, ensuring scalability by distributing data across multiple partitions. Items with the same partition key are bucketed into the same physical location. The sort key allows for sorting and querying of items within the same partition, facilitating complex data retrieval patterns and enhancing query performance.

Secondary indexes
   To enhance querying capabilities beyond the primary key, DynamoDB supports secondary indexes. A secondary index is a data structure that contains a subset of attributes from a table, with the physical data organized in a different way. There are two types: local secondary indexes (LSIs) and global secondary indexes (GSIs). An LSI uses the same partition key as the base table but allows for a different sort key, providing an additional query dimension within the same

partition. In contrast, a GSI permits the use of different partition and sort keys, enabling queries on attributes that are not part of the primary key. Secondary indexes consume additional storage space, as they maintain a copy of the indexed attributes. Every secondary index is automatically maintained by DynamoDB. When you add, modify, or delete items in the base table, any indexes on that table are also updated to reflect these changes.

Querying and scanning

DynamoDB provides two primary mechanisms for retrieving data: querying and scanning. The query operation is efficient and uses the primary key or secondary indexes to fetch specific items or a range of items that match given filters. This operation is preferred for its speed and cost-effectiveness. On the other hand, the scan operation examines every item in the table or index, filtering the results based on specified attributes. While flexible, scanning is resource-intensive and should be used judiciously, especially for large datasets. One key goal in DynamoDB data modeling is to make sure all critical data access patterns can be done via query operations.

Selecting the right partition key

Selecting the right partition key is critical for ensuring efficient data distribution and performance in DynamoDB. Here are some best practices to guide you through the process:

Starting with entities and access patterns

Start by identifying all the entities that will be stored in the table and the access patterns required by your application. Consider the queries your application will perform most frequently. For example, a customer can be identified by their name, email, or UUID. Those are all potential partition keys for the customer entity.

Ensuring high cardinality

Choosing a partition key with high cardinality helps distribute the workload evenly across multiple partitions. In the preceding customer example, among name, email, or UUID, UUID is the one with the highest cardinality. It is the best fit for the partition key because each customer generates distinct traffic patterns, reducing the risk of hot partitions and improving performance.

Leveraging owner entities for data bucketing

The partition key is an efficient way to bucket relevant data of different entities into the same physical partitions. For example, in a single-table design, where you store customers, shopping carts, and orders in the same DynamoDB table, most queries are initiated at the customer level. Thus, the customer UUID is the best partition key for all three entities. Entities of the same customer are further sorted by the sort key.

Avoiding hot partitions

Hot partitions occur when a disproportionate number of requests target a single partition, leading to throttling and performance issues. To avoid this, you can employ a sharding strategy, which involves adding a random suffix to the partition key. For example, if you expect a high volume of writes for a single partition key, you can add a suffix from a predetermined range (e.g., 0–9) to spread the load across multiple partitions. This technique is particularly useful for write-heavy workloads.

In the ecommerce example, the following are good mappings of partition key (PK) selections for all entities:

- Customer: Customer UUID
- Product: Product UUID
- Shopping cart: Customer UUID
- Order: Customer UUID

Selecting the right sort key

Designing an effective sort key in DynamoDB is essential for optimizing data retrieval and ensuring efficient querying. Here are some best practices to help guide your sort key design:

Grouping related data

The primary function of a sort key is to group related items together under the same partition key, enabling efficient queries. By using sort keys, you can retrieve sets of related items using range queries with operators like `begins_with`, `between`, `<`, `>`, etc. For example, assuming the Order entity has an incremental Order ID, a sort key of `ORDER#OrderID` sorts the order of a customer from the latest to the oldest.

Implementing hierarchical relationships

Sort keys are particularly useful for defining hierarchical relationships. By structuring the sort key in a hierarchical manner, you can effectively model one-to-many relationships. For instance, you might want to group items in shopping carts into different status like `ACTIVE` and `SAVED`, then a sort key of `CART#STATUS#ProductUUID` can be useful.

Using sort keys for time-ordered data

Sort keys are often used to store time-ordered data, such as logs, events, or messages. By using a timestamp as part of the sort key, you can efficiently retrieve data within a specific time range.

Maintaining version control

Sort keys can also be used to manage item versioning. A common pattern is to include a version number in the sort key, allowing you to store multiple versions of an item. This is particularly useful for applications that need to track changes or maintain audit logs.

In the ecommerce example, the following are good mappings of PK and sort key (SK) selections for all entities:

- Customer:
  - PK: Customer UUID
  - SK: VersionNumber
- Product:
  - PK: Product UUID
  - SK: VersionNumber
- Shopping cart:
  - PK: Customer UUID
  - SK: `CART#STATUS#ProductUUID`
- Order:
  - PK: Customer UUID
  - SK: `ORDER#OrderID`

Utilizing global secondary indexes and local secondary indexes

Amazon DynamoDB provides two types of secondary indexes to enhance query flexibility beyond the primary key structure: *global secondary indexes* (GSIs) and *local secondary indexes* (LSIs). Both index types allow you to query data efficiently based on attributes other than the primary key but differ in flexibility, performance characteristics, and constraints:

Global secondary indexes

GSIs allow you to define an entirely new partition key and an optional sort key, independent from your base table's primary key. They offer significant flexibility, as they can be created or modified at any time after table creation, making them particularly suitable for evolving application requirements. GSIs support queries against attributes not present in the table's primary key and enable you to define different projections (all attributes, keys-only, or selected attributes).

Local secondary indexes

LSIs share the same partition key as the base table but use an alternative sort key. They are more restrictive, as they must be created when you define your table and cannot be added or removed afterward. LSIs enable queries based on alternative sort keys within the same partition, which can help with queries requiring different sort orders or conditions within partitions.

Table 5-1 outlines how to decide when to use GSIs versus LSIs.

Table 5-1. When to use GSIs versus LSIs

Feature / Trade-off	Global secondary index (GSI)	Local secondary index (LSI)
Partition key flexibility	Can use any attribute independently	Must use the base table's partition key
Creation and modification	Can be created or modified any time after table creation	Must be created at table creation; cannot be modified later
Read/write costs	Consumes additional read/write capacity separately from the base table	Shares read/write capacity with the base table
Read consistency	Eventually consistent reads supported, newly written data may not appear immediately	Supports strongly consistent reads
Storage efficiency	Can be sparse; indexes only items with the indexed attribute	Includes all items sharing the base partition key, even if the indexed attribute is absent

Common use cases and considerations

Key considerations for GSIs and LSIs for your use case include the following:

GSIs
> GSIs are ideal when you need flexible queries across multiple partitions or when query requirements evolve over time. The trade-off is increased cost (in terms of provisioned capacity), eventual consistency and potentially higher storage usage if projecting many attributes.

LSIs
> LSIs are beneficial when you need alternative sorting or querying capabilities within the same partition. They are cost-effective because they share provisioned capacity with the base table. However, their fixed nature might limit your flexibility.

For example, if you frequently query products by a specific category and subcategory across many partitions, a GSI with `Category#Subcategory` as the partition key is appropriate. If you regularly query orders for a customer by different timestamps or statuses within the same customer partition, an LSI would be a good choice.

Data modeling in DynamoDB requires a deep understanding of your application's access patterns and entity relationships. By carefully selecting partition and sort keys and utilizing secondary indexes, you can optimize your database schema for performance, scalability, and cost-efficiency. The ecommerce example demonstrates how these concepts are applied in practice, ensuring that your DynamoDB tables are well suited to handle the demands of real-world applications.

Data Modeling Strategies for Data Lakes

Many AWS customers require a data storage and analytics solution that offers more agility and flexibility than traditional data management systems. A data lake has emerged as a powerful solution for storing and managing vast amounts of structured and unstructured data. A well-architected data lake not only facilitates efficient data storage but also enables robust data processing and analytics. This part of the chapter dives into the essential techniques for effective data lake management, focusing on the layered architecture known as the medallion architecture—comprising Bronze, Silver, and Gold layers—and best practices for data storage in Amazon S3. By understanding these foundational elements, data engineers can ensure their data lakes are optimized for performance, scalability, and data quality, setting the stage for advanced analytics and machine learning applications. We'll first look at the common data layers for data lakes.

Raw data layer: The landing zone for raw data

The raw data layer is the initial landing zone for all raw data flowing into the data lake from various sources such as databases, APIs, and files. This layer captures data in its most unprocessed form. General best practice is to retain a fully unprocessed raw data layer in a cost-efficient storage tier. This raw data can be used for reprocessing if needed, without having to re-ingest from the original sources.

Stage data layer: Cleansed and conformed data

The stage data layer contains intermediate, processed data that is optimized for consumption. The raw data is cleaned, conformed, and minimally transformed to provide a trusted, enterprise-wide view of key business entities and transactions. This layer is optimized for agility and speed, enabling self-service analytics for ad-hoc reporting, advanced analytics, and machine learning. Common transformations can be converting CSV files into Apache Parquet format, data quality checks, and merging change data capture logs to the latest view of tables.

Analytics data layer: Curated and aggregated data

The analytics data layer represents the final, consumption-ready state of the data, where complex business rules, aggregations, and cross-referencing are applied to produce highly refined and enriched datasets. These datasets power analytics, machine learning models, and production applications. The analytics data layer often employs denormalized, read-optimized data models, to ensure low latency and high performance for business intelligence tools and dashboards.

Amazon S3 Data Lake Best Practices

The following presents some best practices for Amazon S3 Data Lake.

Partition your data

Partitioning divides your table into parts and keeps the related data together based on column values such as date, country, and region. Partitioning your data is crucial for optimizing query performance in a data lake. By dividing data into partitions based on a specific key, you can significantly reduce the amount of data scanned during queries, leading to faster performance and lower costs.

When selecting partition keys for your data, it is crucial to work backward from your queries and find fields that are often used to filter the dataset. Effective partition keys should have a relatively low cardinality to avoid excessive metadata overhead and maintain optimal file sizes. Additionally, be mindful of data skew; if your data is heavily concentrated around a single partition value frequently used in queries, the performance benefits of partitioning might be diminished.

Bucket your data

Bucketing is another technique to enhance query efficiency by organizing data into a fixed number of buckets, each containing a subset of the data. This helps in evenly distributing data across the storage and can improve the performance of join operations by reducing data shuffling.

Bucketing is useful when you have a column with high cardinality and many of your queries look up specific values of the column. Good candidates for bucketing are columns such as IDs for users or devices.

Use compression

Applying compression to your data reduces storage costs and can improve query performance by decreasing the amount of data transferred between storage and compute resources. Various compression algorithms can be used depending on the data and query requirements. The SNAPPY format focuses on high compression and decompression speed rather than the maximum compression of data. The zstd (Zstandard) format (*https://oreil.ly/fKjbJ*) is a newer compression format with a good balance between performance and compression ratio.

Optimize file size

Queries run more efficiently when data can be read in parallel, and as much data as possible can be read in a single read request. Optimizing file sizes is essential for achieving a balance between reducing the number of files (to avoid excessive metadata overhead) and maintaining file sizes that are manageable for the storage system. Large files are preferred over numerous small files. A general guideline is to aim for files that are around or above 128 MB.

Use columnar file formats

Columnar file formats are designed to store data by columns rather than rows, enabling higher compression ratios and more efficient queries by only reading necessary columns. Apache Parquet (*https://oreil.ly/lbDa0*) and Apache ORC (*https://oreil.ly/3wx0L*) are popular file formats for analytics workloads. They both also store metadata such as the minimum and maximum value of a column each block of data, allowing query engines to skip irrelevant data blocks.

Another benefit of Parquet and ORC is that they are splittable. A splittable file format allows efficient parallel processing of large files. This means a large file can be divided into smaller chunks, and each chunk can be processed independently by multiple processors or nodes in a distributed system. This capability is crucial for large-scale data processing and analytics, as it enables faster data loading and querying by leveraging parallel computing. Parquet and ORC files are always splittable because these formats compress sections of the files separately and include metadata that contains the locations within the files for the different sections.

Use open table formats

Leveraging open table formats such as Apache Iceberg, Apache Hudi, and Delta Lake allows you to manage large-scale data lakes with transactional consistency and schema evolution capabilities. These formats support ACID transactions, time-travel queries, and other features that make it easier to maintain data quality and reliability.

Conclusion

In this chapter, we have explored the fundamental aspects of data store management. We began by discussing how to choose the appropriate data store based on specific use cases, ensuring that the storage solution aligns with performance, scalability, and cost considerations. We then dived into the importance of classifying your data and building a comprehensive data catalog to facilitate efficient data discovery and accessibility. Effective data lifecycle management was another critical topic, emphasizing strategies to maintain cost performance balance and compliance throughout the data's lifecycle. Lastly, we covered the principles of designing robust data models. Together, these topics form a cohesive framework for managing data stores that not only support but also enhance your organization's data-driven initiatives.

Next, let's try to validate our knowledge with a few practice questions that may help you prepare for the AWS Certified Data Engineer Associate certification exam.

Practice Questions

These practice questions may help you understand what kind of questions to expect on the exam so you can prepare accordingly. The answers are listed in the Appendix.

1. A company has been using HDFS for their on-premises data storage to handle large-scale data processing. They use Apache Spark as the analytics engine. They plan to migrate their data to AWS and are looking for a scalable and cost-efficient storage solution in the cloud.

   Which cloud storage option should the company choose for this migration?

   A. Migrate the data to Amazon S3 and use Spark on Amazon EMR clusters for data processing.

   B. Migrate the data to Amazon EBS volumes and attach them to EC2 instances for data processing.

   C. Migrate the data to Amazon EBS volumes and set up HDFS on Amazon EMR clusters.

   D. Migrate the data to Amazon Elastic File System (Amazon EFS) and configure Lambda functions to mount the file system.

2. A retail company uses Amazon OpenSearch Service to index and visualize its application logs. Over time, the index size has grown significantly, impacting performance and increasing costs. The company wants to implement a strategy to manage index lifecycle and reduce costs. The following are the log data access patterns:

   - The development team queries the past 3 days of logs frequently.

   - The development team performs historical data analytics that spans 6 months of data rarely.

   - You need to store the logs in the OpenSearch cluster for 2 years for compliance requirements.

   Which solution will meet these requirements with the least operational overhead?

   A. Land new logs on OpenSearch Hot storage. Use Amazon OpenSearch Service's Index State Management (ISM) policies to move logs older than 3 days to UltraWarm and further move logs older than 6 months to Cold storage.

   B. Land new logs on OpenSearch Hot storage. Use Amazon OpenSearch Service's Index State Management (ISM) policies to move logs older than 3 days to UltraWarm. Use Lambda to snapshot logs older than 6 months to Amazon S3.

   C. Land new logs on OpenSearch Hot storage. Schedule Lambda functions to automatically move indexes to UltraWarm and Cold storage.

D. Land new logs on OpenSearch Hot storage. Use Amazon OpenSearch Service's Index State Management (ISM) policies to move logs older than 3 days to Cold storage. Migrate them back to UltraWarm when you need to query the data.

3. A financial services company uses Amazon Redshift for its data warehouse and stores historical data in Amazon S3. The company wants to query both the current data in Redshift and the historical data in S3 without moving the data.

Which Amazon Redshift feature allows this capability?

A. Redshift RA3 Nodes

B. Redshift Data Sharing

C. Redshift Spectrum

D. Redshift Serverless

4. A development team noticed that their storage costs have increased greatly after they enabled versioning on their S3 bucket to safeguard against accidental deletions. How can the team manage their storage costs while retaining the benefits of versioning?

A. Enable S3 Intelligent-Tiering for the bucket.

B. Use S3 Lifecycle policies to delete older versions after a certain period.

C. Enable S3 Versioning and set a legal hold by using S3 Object Lock.

D. Transition older S3 objects to the S3 Glacier Deep Archive storage class.

5. An ecommerce company wants to ensure that their product catalog data stored in Amazon S3 is consistently organized and up-to-date. They need to automatically detect changes in the data schema and update the catalog accordingly.

Which solution will meet their requirements with the least operational overhead?

A. Create an AWS Glue crawler to scan the data in Amazon S3 and to populate table metadata in an AWS Glue Data Catalog. Schedule the crawler to run periodically to identify any changes in the schema and to generate new versions of the tables.

B. Schedule a Lambda function to scan and classify the data in Amazon S3. Configure the Lambda function to create tables and columns in an AWS Glue Data Catalog.

C. Use Amazon Redshift to query the data and manually manage the catalog updates.

D. Configure Amazon EMR to process the data and manually synchronize the schema changes with the AWS Glue Data Catalog.

6. A retail company uses Amazon RDS, Amazon S3, and Snowflake to store their sales and customer data. They want to catalog data from these sources in one place to enable unified data access and analysis.

   Which solutions will achieve this with minimal operational overhead? (Select two.)

   A. Use AWS Glue crawlers to connect to Amazon RDS and Snowflake, automatically cataloging the data into an AWS Glue Data Catalog.

   B. Create an AWS Glue crawler to scan the data in Amazon S3 and to populate table metadata in an AWS Glue Data Catalog.

   C. Manually export data from Amazon RDS and Snowflake to Amazon S3 and then use AWS Glue crawlers to catalog the data.

   D. Write custom scripts using AWS Lambda to extract data from Amazon RDS and Snowflake and populate the AWS Glue Data Catalog.

7. A media company stores large volumes of web server logs on Amazon S3 and intends to analyze this data with Amazon Athena. The majority of their queries are analytical, focusing on logs from a specific region or a specific period of time.

   To optimize query performance in Athena and reduce costs, which combination of techniques should they use? (Select two.)

   A. Partition the data by region, year, and month.

   B. Store the data in CSV format.

   C. Use SELECT * in queries.

   D. Use compressed file formats like gzip or Snappy.

   E. Keep logs in their original format.

8. An ecommerce company stores user order histories in an Amazon DynamoDB table. Each order contains a user ID, product ID, purchase timestamp, delivery timestamp, and delivery location.

   The primary access patterns are the following:

   • Retrieve all orders for a specific user sorted by the purchase time.

   • Retrieve the latest order for a specific user.

   Which schema design will meet these requirements most efficiently?

   A. Table Partition Key: 'UserID' Table Sort Key: 'PurchaseTimestamp'

   B. Table Partition Key: 'UserID' Table Sort Key: 'ProductID'

   C. Table Partition Key: 'ProductID' Table Sort Key: 'UserID'

   D. Table Partition Key: 'ProductID' Table Sort Key: 'UserID#'Purchase Timestamp'

9. A company uses Amazon Redshift as its data warehouse. The company stores the data in multiple tables and selects the EVEN distribution style for all tables. Some tables are hundreds of gigabytes in size. Others are less than 10 MB in size. You need to manually configure distribution styles to optimize query performance. At the same time, you must keep data storage as low as possible.

Which solution will meet these requirements?

A. Use a distribution style of ALL for large tables. Specify primary and foreign keys for all tables.

B. Use a distribution style of ALL for small and rarely updated tables. Specify primary and foreign keys for all tables.

C. Use a distribution style of KEY for all tables. Specify distribution, primary, and foreign keys for all tables.

D. Use a distribution style of EVEN for the all tables. Specify primary and foreign keys for all tables.

10. A healthcare company needs to store patient data in Amazon S3. The data is accessed frequently within the first year and must be available immediately. Due to regulatory requirements, the data must be retained for five years. Data older than one year must be securely stored and made available when needed for compliance evaluation within 48 hours. Data older than five years must be deleted.

Which solution will meet these requirements in the most cost-effective manner?

A. Store new data on the Amazon S3 Standard storage class. Create a lifecycle rule to transition the data to the S3 Glacier Flexible Retrieval storage class after one year. Configure the lifecycle rule to delete the data after five years.

B. Store new data on the Amazon S3 Infrequent Access storage class. Create a lifecycle rule to migrate the data to the S3 Glacier Flexible Retrieval storage class after one year. Configure the lifecycle rule to delete the data after five years.

C. Store new data on the Amazon S3 Standard storage class. Create a lifecycle rule to migrate the data to the S3 Glacier Deep Archive storage class after one year. Configure the lifecycle rule to delete the data after five years.

D. Store new data on the Amazon S3 Intelligent-Tiering storage class. Opt in to the deep archive access tier. Create a lifecycle rule to delete the data after five years.

Additional Resources

The following are a few additional resources that will help you dive deeper and gain more knowledge on data store management:

- "What Is Data Management?" (*https://oreil.ly/55-qP*)
- "What Is a Data Store?" (*https://oreil.ly/HXHQP*)
- "Storage Best Practices for Data and Analytics Applications" (*https://oreil.ly/wuWM-*)
- "Amazon Redshift Best Practices for Designing Tables" (*https://oreil.ly/5JS9R*)
- "Best Practices for Designing and Architecting with DynamoDB" (*https://oreil.ly/nosla*)

## CHAPTER 6

Data Operations and Support

In the evolving world of data-driven decision making, the ability to effectively manage, monitor, and optimize data processing pipelines is crucial for organizations seeking to unlock the full potential of their data assets. As data engineers, you play a pivotal role in ensuring the reliability, performance, and cost-effectiveness of these data pipelines, which power the critical analytics and business intelligence initiatives within your organization.

This chapter will explore the key aspects of data operations and support, equipping you with the knowledge and skills required to automate data processing, analyze data, maintain and monitor data pipelines, and ensure data quality. By mastering these techniques, you will become a valuable asset in your organization's data-driven journey, enabling seamless data operations and supporting the delivery of actionable insights.

This chapter will help you learn how to do the following:

- Analyze data using a variety of AWS services, including Amazon QuickSight, Amazon Athena, and Amazon Redshift.

- Monitor data pipelines by deploying comprehensive logging and monitoring solutions, leveraging tools like Amazon CloudWatch, AWS CloudTrail, Amazon Macie, and system tables for specific services.

- Apply best practices for performance tuning and troubleshooting data processing pipelines.

- Build robust data pipelines to achieve your recovery point objective (RPO) and recovery time objective (RTO) in case of unlikely outages.

By the end of this chapter, you will have a comprehensive understanding of the data operations and support capabilities within the AWS ecosystem, enabling you to design, implement, and maintain efficient and reliable data processing pipelines that support your organization's data-driven initiatives. You will also answer a set of practice questions similar to the kind of questions you can expect in the AWS Certified Data Engineer Associate certification exam.

As a data engineer, analyzing data is a crucial step in unlocking the value of your organization's data assets. By leveraging the powerful analytics capabilities within AWS, you can uncover meaningful insights, identify trends, and make informed, data-driven decisions to support your business initiatives.

In the first part of this chapter, you will learn about three key AWS services that can help you analyze data effectively: Amazon QuickSight, Amazon Athena, and Amazon Redshift. Each of these services offers unique features and capabilities. The guidance here will help you understand how to leverage them to meet your specific data analysis requirements.

Amazon QuickSight

Amazon QuickSight is a scalable, serverless, and fully managed business intelligence (BI) service that enables you to create and publish interactive dashboards and reports, enabling data visualization and analysis for various data sources. To get started with QuickSight, you'll first create a *dataset* from a *data source*. Using the dataset, you can create *visualizations*, group them into *analyses*, and publish them as *dashboards*. You can also build interactive *stories*. Let's understand each of these key concepts in further detail.

Data Sources

In Amazon QuickSight, you can use a variety of data sources such as AWS databases, AWS analytics services, third-party services, on-premises data sources, and more. At the time of this writing, the following is the list of supported data sources:

- Relational databases:
  - AWS databases: Amazon Aurora and Amazon RDS (MySQL, PostgreSQL, SQL Server, Oracle)
  - Third-party and open source databases. Some common ones are Snowflake, Starburst, Trino, Teradata, Microsoft SQL Server 2012 or later, MySQL 5.7 or later, MariaDB 10.0 or later, Oracle 12c or later, PostgreSQL 9.3.1 or later

- Big data and analytics services:
  - — Amazon Redshift
  - — Amazon S3 (including data in various file formats like CSV, TSV, JSON, XLSX)
  - — Amazon OpenSearch Service
  - — Amazon Athena
  - — AWS IoT Analytics
- SaaS applications and web services: Products such as Salesforce, ServiceNow, Jira, GitHub, Adobe Analytics (via OAuth), etc.
- Other sources: Sources such as on-premises databases accessible via Amazon VPC or Direct Connect

For a more up-to-date list, please refer to the supported data sources webpage (*https://oreil.ly/UFlhE*).

The flexibility to integrate data from such a diverse set of sources is a core strength of QuickSight. By bringing together information from across your organization and beyond, you can build dashboards and visualizations that provide a comprehensive, 360-degree view of your business. Figure 6-1 shows a screenshot of data sources available at the time of writing.

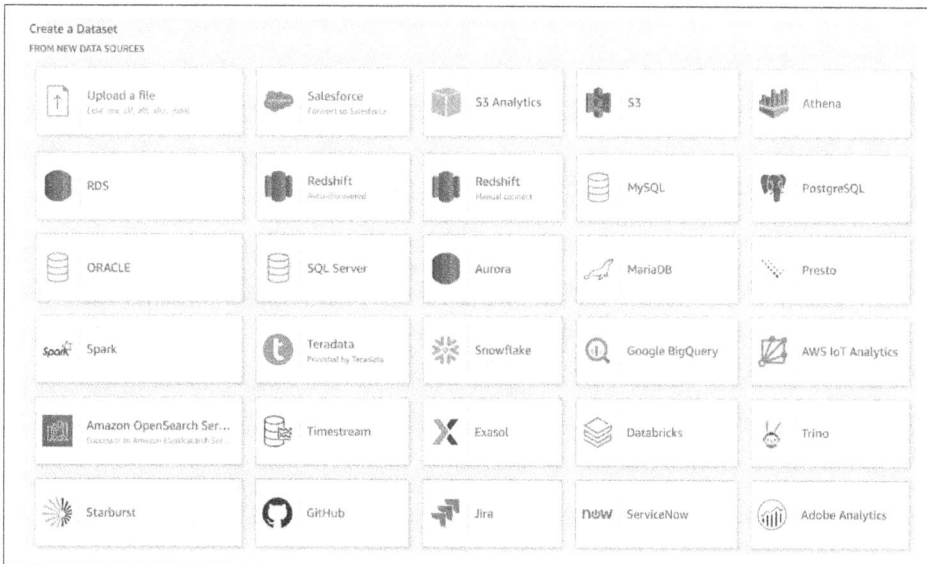

Figure 6-1. Data sources for use with QuickSight

Datasets

After you connect QuickSight to a data source, such as a database, data lake, or SaaS application, you create a dataset from that data source. The datasets can do one of the following two things:

- Directly query the live data from the data source.
- Import data from the data source source and store it in a highly optimized, in-memory cache called SPICE (Super-fast, Parallel, In-memory Calculation Engine).

SPICE is a highly optimized in-memory cache that significantly enhances analytical query performance compared to direct querying. Instead of waiting for time-consuming queries to process against the underlying data source, SPICE executes queries against preprocessed and cached data, resulting in faster response times and a more responsive analytical experience. Also, since data stored in SPICE can be reused multiple times without additional querying costs, it can lead to significant cost savings, especially when working with pay-per-query data sources like Amazon Athena. When using SPICE, you need to set up refreshes to periodically fetch data from data sources.

Refreshing SPICE Datasets

You have several options to refresh the data stored in SPICE:

Manual refresh
> You can manually trigger a refresh of a SPICE dataset from the QuickSight console or during data preparation. On the Datasets page, select the dataset and choose the *Refresh* option. During data preparation, you can refresh the dataset by clicking the *Refresh now* button.

Scheduled refresh
> You can schedule refreshes to ensure that your SPICE data is automatically updated at regular intervals, keeping your analyses aligned with the latest data from your sources. By default, the refreshes are full refreshes (i.e., the complete dataset is fetched from source and refreshed in SPICE). You can configure refresh schedules to run *Daily*, *Weekly*, or *Monthly*.

Incremental refresh
> In enterprise edition, for SQL-based data sources such as Amazon Redshift, Athena, Snowflake, etc. that can identify incremental data using a date column, you can schedule incremental refreshes. For incremental refresh, you will choose a column on which the lookback window is based on and a window size that determines how long back you are looking. For example, if your dataset contains a *transaction_date* field, which is the date on which the transaction is created,

you can schedule an incremental refresh to look back based on transaction_date for the last day and refresh the SPICE dataset. You can choose to incrementally refresh *Every 15 minutes*, *Every 30 minutes*, *Hourly*, *Daily*, *Weekly*, or *Monthly*.

API and automation

If you want to do a trigger-based refresh, for example, you want to refresh the SPICE dataset after a file arrives each day, you can use QuickSight APIs. They allow you to programmatically refresh SPICE datasets and manage refresh schedules. You can integrate QuickSight dataset refreshes into your existing data pipelines or automation workflows, enabling seamless data synchronization.

Manual refresh is ideal for test environments, allowing users to update datasets on-demand as needed. Scheduled refresh is best suited for scenarios where data updates occur at regular intervals and there are no upstream dependencies—this automated approach ensures your reports consistently reflect the latest data. For event-driven requirements, such as when a vendor uploads new files to Amazon S3, the API and automation approach is most appropriate. This method enables immediate dataset updates in response to specific triggers, ensuring your reports reflect new data as soon as it becomes available.

Visualizations

Once the datasets are ready, you can start visualizing data. A visualization is a graphical representation that can present complex data in an easily understandable and visually appealing fashion. QuickSight offers a wide range of visualization types to suit different various visualization needs. Some of the commonly used chart types include the following:

Bar charts (vertical, horizontal, stacked)

Bar charts are used to compare magnitudes of different categories, groups, or dimensions. They can be displayed vertically or horizontally. Stacked bar charts are used to show the composition of a total value across multiple categories. Figure 6-2 represents various kinds of bar charts.

Figure 6-2(a) shows the number of occurrences for each event. Figure 6-2(b) represents the number of website visits for each event with separate colored sets of bars for unique and total visits. Figure 6-2(c) shows the number of visits for each event by categorizing weekdays and nonweekdays in different colors. Figure 6-2(d) does the same as Figure 6-2(c) by normalizing using percentages instead of counts.

Line charts

Line charts are used to compare changes in one/multiple measures over a period of time, as in Figure 6-3.

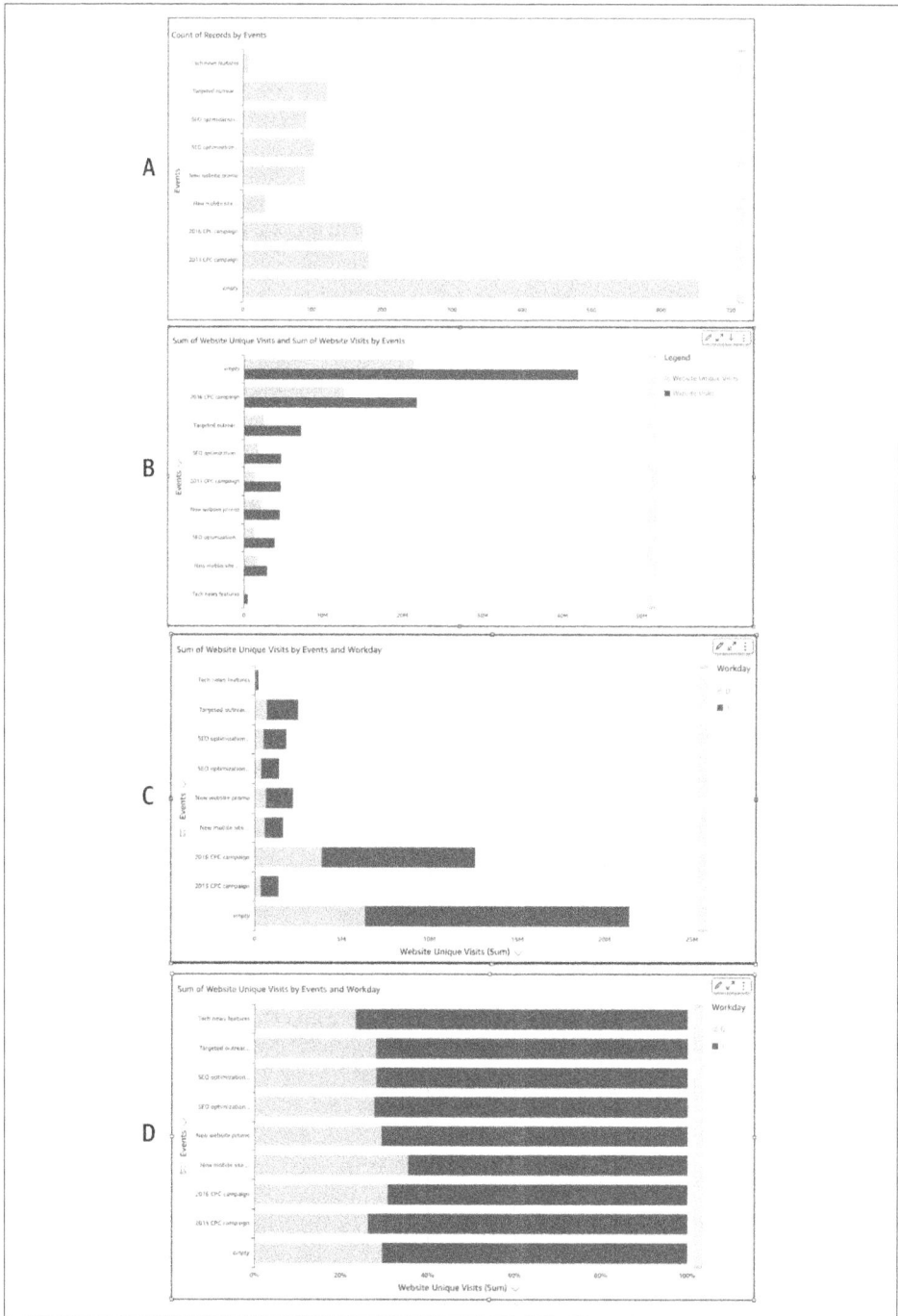

Figure 6-2. Types of bar charts: (a) single-measure, (b) multimeasure, (c) stacked, and (d) stacked 100%

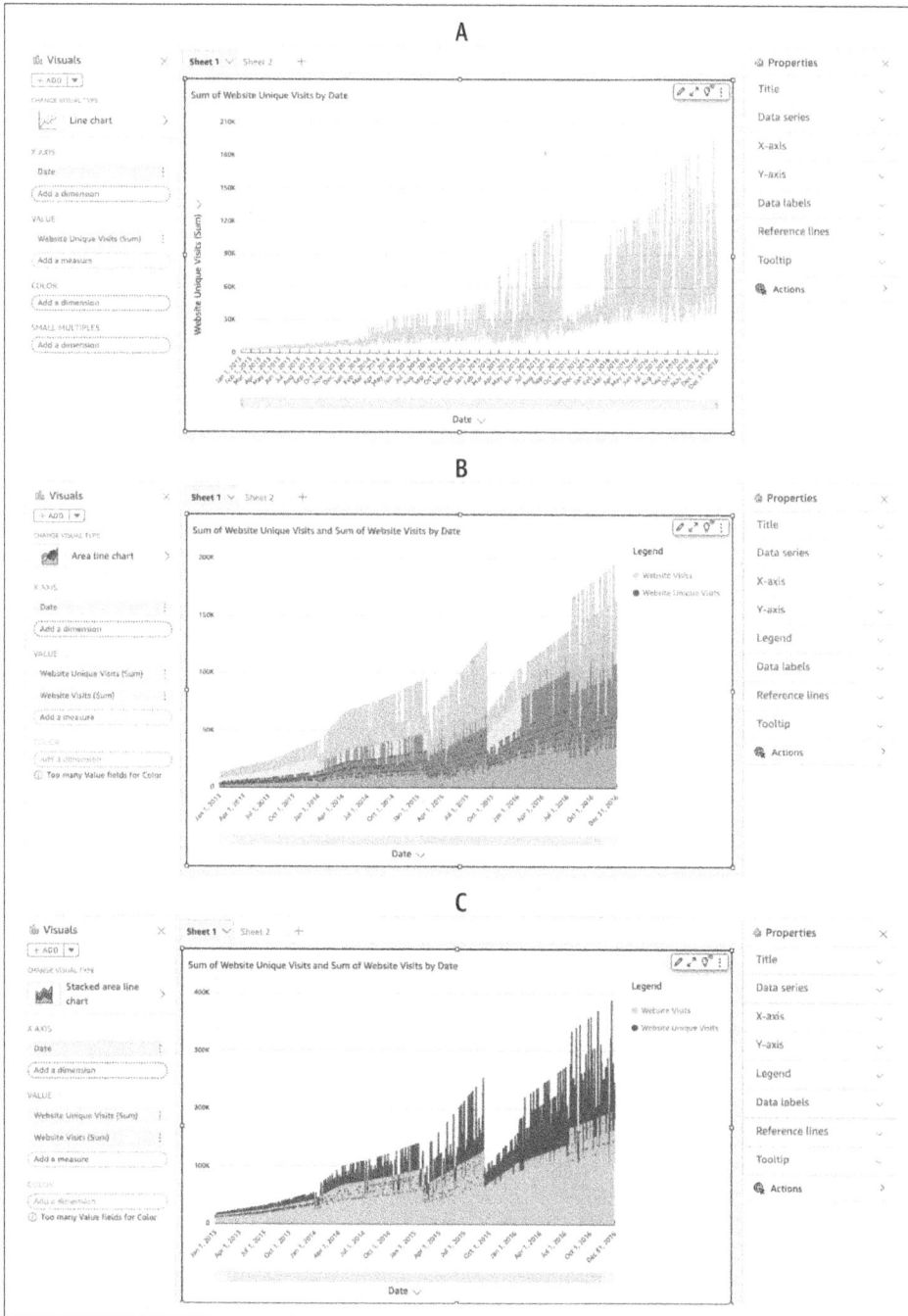

Figure 6-3. Types of line charts: (a) area line chart, (b) stacked, and (c) stacked area line chart

The first line chart in Figure 6-3 shows a trend of unique visits by date. The other two show trends for two metrics stacked with overlap and without overlap for comparison.

Pie charts/donut charts

Pie and donut charts show a proportion or percentage of a total. Figure 6-4 shows the proportion of the number of occurrences of an event.

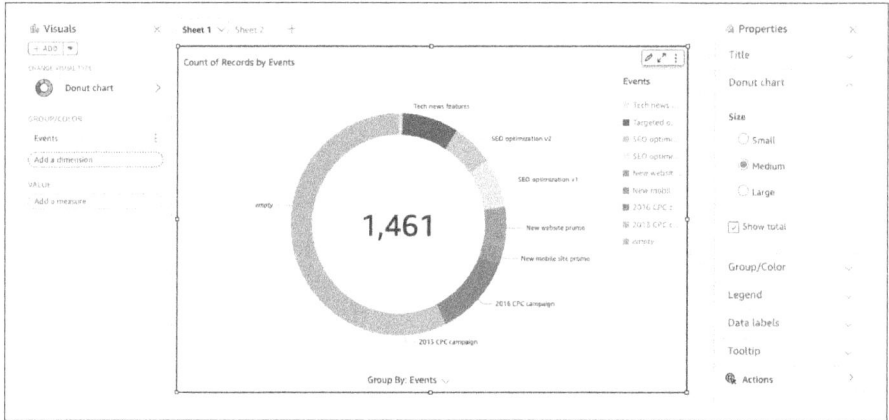

Figure 6-4. Donut chart for count of records by event

Scatter plots

Scatter plots are useful for identifying trends, clusters, and outliers in the data. Figure 6-5 presents a scatter plot that shows sales and profit correlation for various product categories.

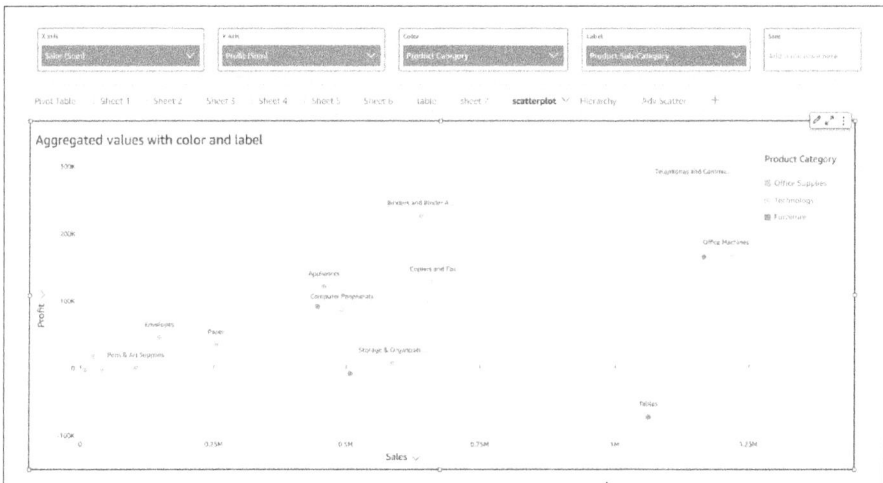

Figure 6-5. Scatter plot for sales across different categories

Histograms

Using histograms you can analyze distribution of a single measure, as they provide insights into the center, spread, and shape of data. Figure 6-6 shows a histogram of distribution of Twitter mentions.

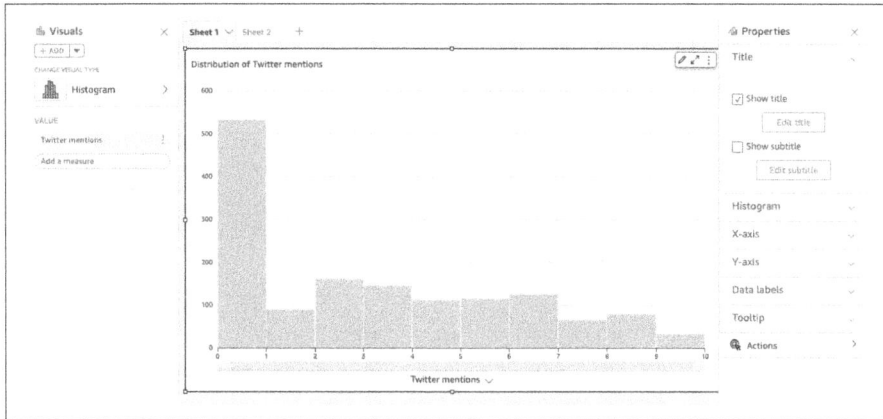

Figure 6-6. Histogram showing spread of Twitter mentions

Box plots

Box plots are used to compare distribution of data between different groups. They are a compact summary of the data, showing the median, the middle 50% of the data (the box), and the minimum and maximum values (the whiskers). The box plot in Figure 6-7 compares distribution of website visits between two workdays while showing min/max/median and mid 50% for both days.

Treemaps

Treemaps are used to display hierarchical data in a compact and easy-to-understand format. They are particularly useful when you need to visualize how a larger whole is composed of its parts. Figure 6-8 shows how each opportunity contributed to the whole.

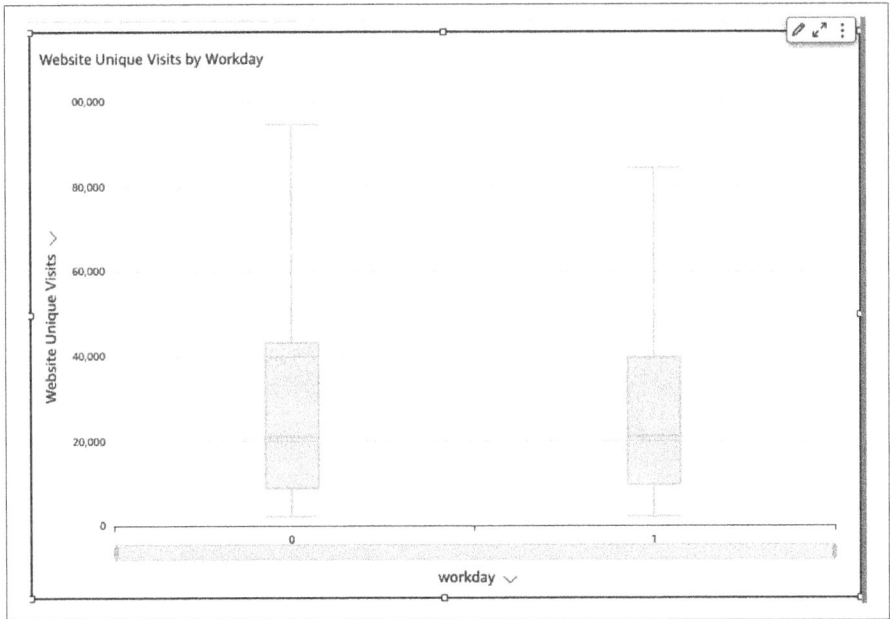

Figure 6-7. Box plot comparing website visits across two days

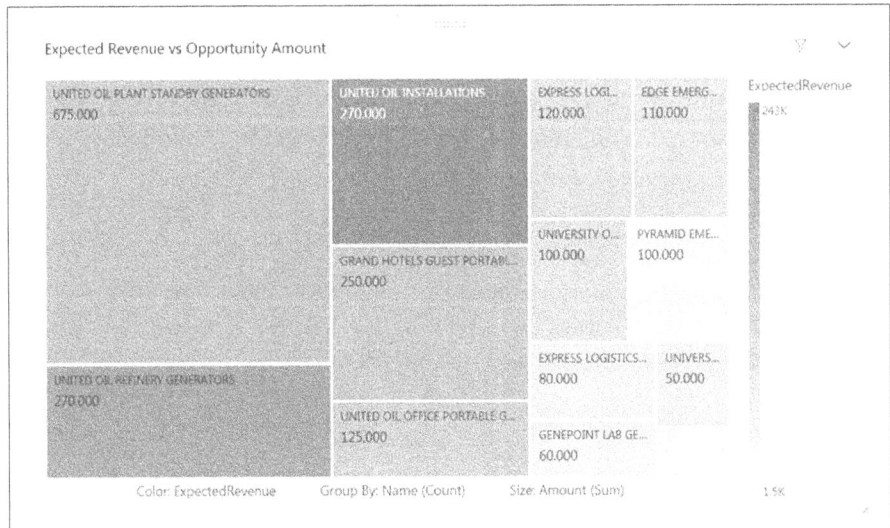

Figure 6-8. Treemap of Salesforce opportunities

Pivot tables

Pivot tables enable you to build interactive multidimensional reports where you can slice and dice data across any number of dimensions without needing to modify the underlying data structure. They are very similar to Excel pivot functions where you can drag dimensions and measures and show them in a tabular format. The pivot table in Figure 6-9 shows how the Billed Amount measure can be sliced and diced across four dimensions, with two dimensions (customer region, consumption channel) as rows and the other dimensions (customer segment, service line) as columns.

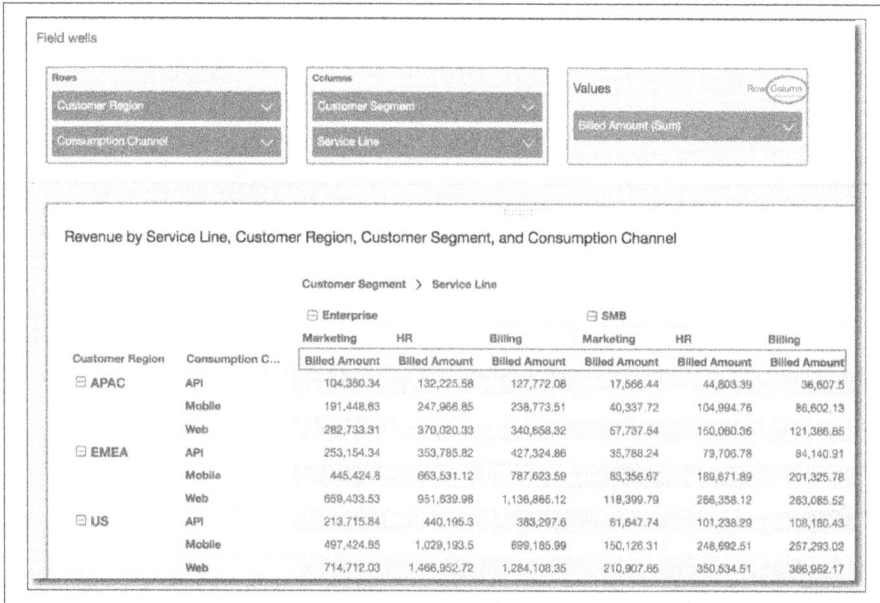

Figure 6-9. Pivot table for Billed Amount

KPIs (key performance indicators)

A KPI displays a value comparison, the two values being compared, and a visual that provides context to the data that's displayed. Figure 6-10 shows the number of customers KPI. It shows a 25.4% increase from November 2023 to October 2023.

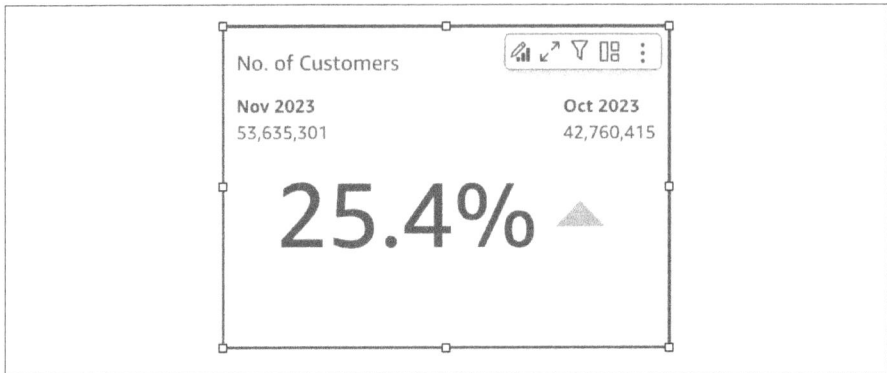

Figure 6-10. KPI: number of customers

In addition to these standard chart types, QuickSight also provides more advanced visualizations such as:

- Geospatial maps for location-based data
- Funnel charts for visualizing stages in a process
- Gauges and meters for displaying performance against targets
- Calendar heatmaps for identifying trends over time

QuickSight makes it easy for you to generate the visualizations using the AutoGraph feature. It intelligently suggests the most suitable visualization type based on the data fields you select.

Presentation Formats

You can present visualizations in various formats:

Analyses
> An analysis organizes multiple visualizations on different sheets or pages. It allows you to combine various charts, graphs, and tables to tell a comprehensive data story.

Sheets
> Within an analysis, you can have one or more sheets, which are individual pages or sections displaying a specific set of visualizations and insights. Sheets help organize and separate different aspects of your data story.

Dashboards
> A dashboard is the published, shareable version of an analysis. It presents the finalized visualizations in an interactive format that can be accessed by other users with specified permissions.

Data stories

You can create data stories, which are narrative-driven presentations that guide viewers through visualizations with descriptive text, commentary, and annotations. Stories are ideal for explaining insights and conveying a cohesive message using your data.

Figure 6-11 presents a sample QuickSight dashboard showing a business summary. It has KPI charts, sales trends, and order trends. It also has a donut chart showing sales by industry, a bar chart showing orders by state, heatmaps showing top customers by state, a profit segmentation map showing shipments by state, a profitability waterfall chart, and a box plot for scores by gender. The visuals are organized into multiple sheets in this dashboard for summary, details, metrics boards, etc.

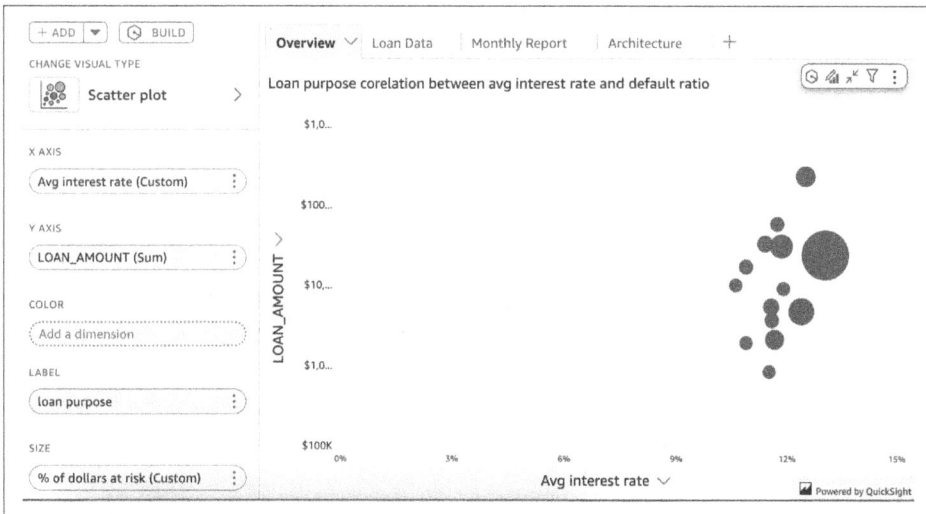

Figure 6-11. Sample QuickSight dashboard

QuickSight GenBI Capabilities (QuickSight Q)

To make building visualizations easy, QuickSight offers a GenAI-based feature called QuickSight Q that allows you to build visualizations and stories and generate executive summaries using natural language prompts. You ask questions about your data in plain English and get answers in the form of charts, graphs, and visualizations. The following subsections detail the various capabilities of QuickSight Q.

Generate stories

Amazon Q in QuickSight helps you jumpstart your data storytelling process. You simply enter a prompt and select your visuals, and Amazon Q will create an initial draft of your data story. While these AI-generated drafts aren't meant to replace your analysis or creative input, they provide a solid foundation that you can build upon.

The system intelligently combines your prompts with chosen visualizations to suggest relevant content, giving you a customizable framework for your final data narrative.

Figure 6-12 shows a sample prompt to QuickSight Q asking it to build a story on how to increase conversion for free trial customers and the generated story.

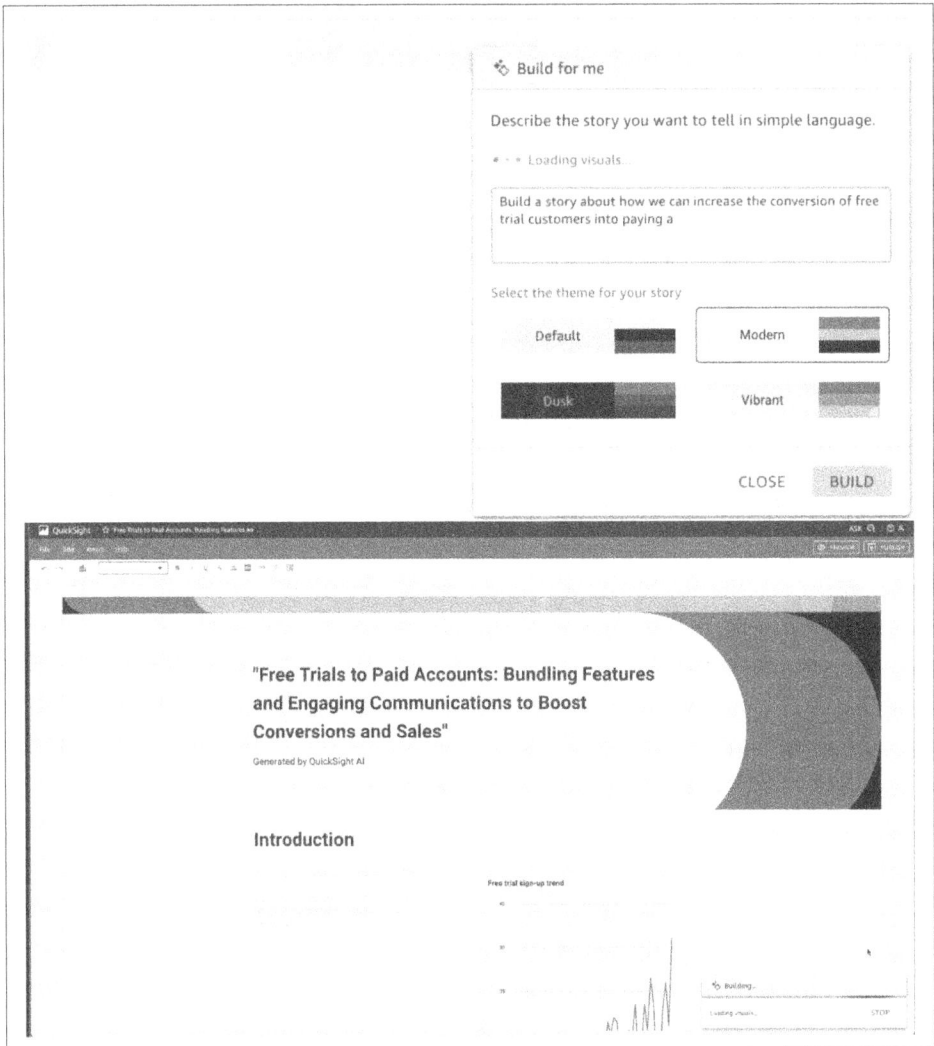

Figure 6-12. Ask QuickSight Q to build a story

Create executive summaries

You can use executive summaries to set the big picture from your dashboards. These summaries automatically highlight key insights from your dashboard's data, making it easy for readers to grasp important findings without diving into individual visualizations. Enabling executive summaries is simple—just select "Allow executive summary" when publishing your dashboard.

Enhanced dashboard Q&A

You can enable Q&A on your QuickSight dashboards. It's as simple as checking the "Allow data Q&A" box when publishing your dashboard. When activating dashboard Q&A, you can select which datasets to include, ensuring users have access to the most relevant information. This feature leverages the data displayed on your dashboard, allowing users to explore different angles of the same information they see.

For example, in Figure 6-13 you can see the answers QuickSight Q generated for the question, "Why did revenue go down in October 2022?"

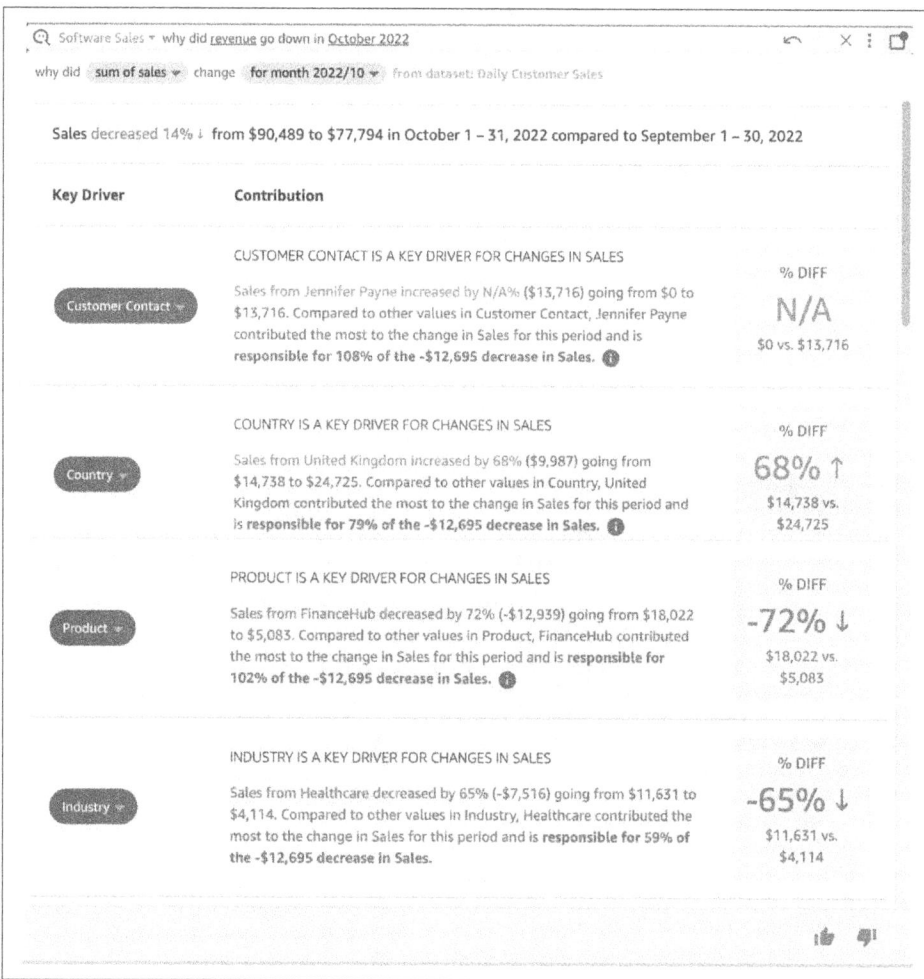

Figure 6-13. Q&A in QuickSight Q

SQL Analytics Using Amazon Athena

SQL (Structured Query Language) is a common and powerful tool for analyzing and modifying datasets. Using SELECT statements, you can choose the columns you want, filter and sort data using WHERE and ORDER BY clauses, and perform calculations and aggregations using functions like SUM, AVG, and COUNT. SQL provides capabilities for joining multiple tables, enabling you to combine data from different sources and gain a more comprehensive understanding of the relationships between different entities. Additionally, SQL offers advanced analytical functions, such as window functions and subqueries, which allow for complex data transformations and analysis. These features enable analysts to perform tasks like ranking, moving averages, and data partitioning, making SQL a versatile tool for exploring and uncovering patterns and trends within large datasets. In AWS, you can perform SQL data analytics using two services: Amazon Athena and Amazon Redshift (the subject of a later section).

Amazon Athena (*https://oreil.ly/ZxJNV*) is a serverless, interactive query service that makes it easy to analyze data stored in Amazon S3 and other federated sources using standard SQL. Athena is particularly well suited for ad-hoc, cost-effective, low-operational overhead data exploration and analysis, as it allows you to quickly run queries on your data without the need to set up and manage any infrastructure, on a pay-per-query basis.

Choice of Querying Engine

In Athena, you have a choice of leveraging Trino SQL using the Athena SQL engine or the PySpark engine to query data, as shown in Figure 6-14.

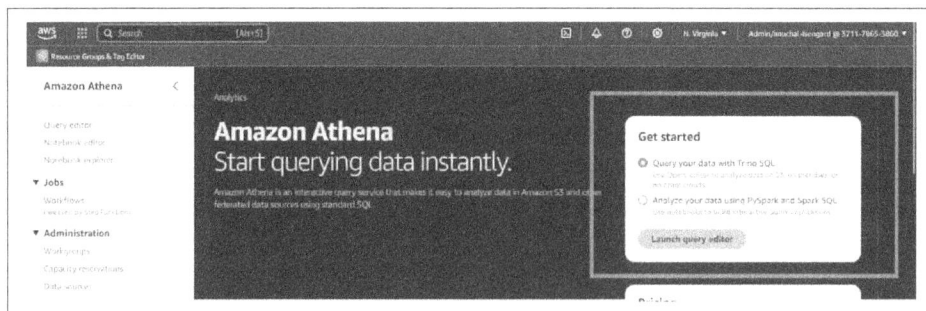

Figure 6-14. Amazon Athena console landing page

Trino SQL

To query your data with Trino SQL, you will use Athena's query editor, as shown in Figure 6-15, or use Athena APIs such as StartQueryExecution (*https://oreil.ly/YTP3R*).

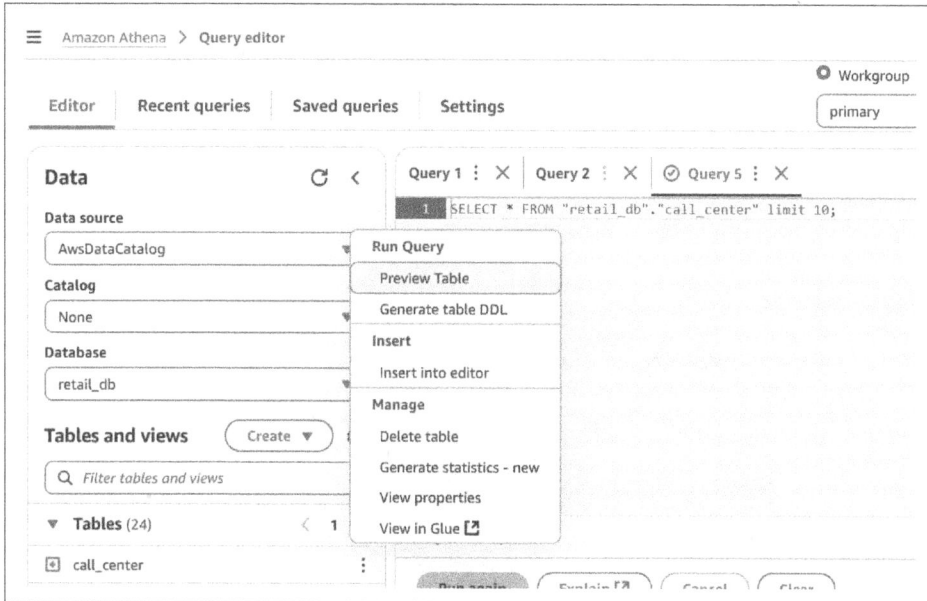

Figure 6-15. Amazon Athena query editor

When you log in to Amazon Athena query editor, you will see all the Data sources, databases, and tables that your IAM role has access to. You can query this data using simple SQL statements, as shown in Figure 6-15. Your queries are run in a workgroup named Primary by default.

Spark SQL/PySpark

To query your data using Apache Spark SQL, you will use the Amazon Athena notebook editor. These notebooks integrate with Spark's distributed processing engine and enable you to run Spark SQL, work with Spark DataFrames, and utilize Spark's advanced analytics functions to analyze data. Figure 6-16 shows a screenshot of the Athena notebook editor with which you can run Spark SQL queries.

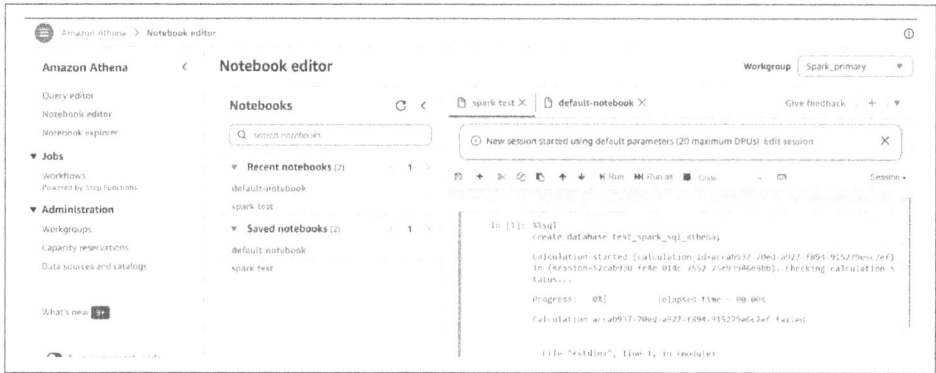

Figure 6-16. Amazon Athena notebook editor

Workgroups

Workgroups are resources within Amazon Athena that allow you to separate and control different query workloads and users. For each workgroup you can choose the Athena engine or PySpark engine, as shown in Figure 6-17.

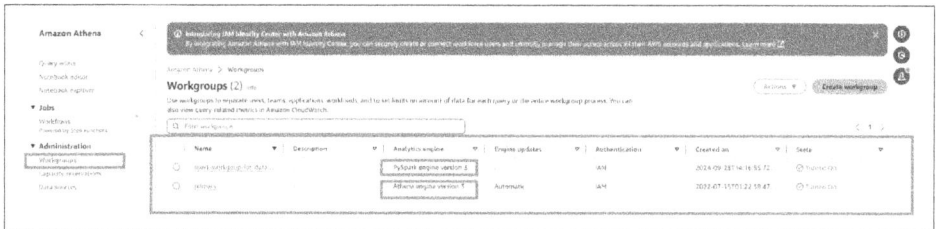

Figure 6-17. Amazon Athena workgroups

Athena workgroups can be used for the following purposes:

- You can create different workgroups for different types of workloads (e.g. one for automated scheduled applications like report generation, and another for ad-hoc queries by analysts).

- Control access by teams for each workgroup. Since workgroups act as IAM resources, you can use IAM policies to control which teams/users can access and run queries in each workgroup. This allows you to isolate queries for different teams.

- You can set workgroup-wide settings like query result location, encryption, etc. that all queries in that workgroup must follow.

- You can publish query metrics to CloudWatch, monitor usage metrics, and set data usage controls and cost allocation tags at the workgroup level to better track and control costs.

Capacity Reservations

By default, workgroups use on-demand pricing. However, with Athena's default on-demand pricing, there's no way to guarantee that your critical queries will have enough compute resources when you need them, especially during peak loads.

Capacity reservations solve this by allowing you to preallocate and reserve a specific amount of computing power exclusively for your use. This reserved capacity is measured in data processing units (DPUs), where 1 DPU = 4 vCPUs and 16 GB RAM. You can assign one or more workgroups (which logically group your queries) to this reserved capacity. Any queries submitted to these workgroups will run on the reserved capacity you purchased, while queries in other workgroups still use the on-demand capacity.

Athena Federated SQL

Amazon Athena Federated extends Athena's querying capabilities beyond S3, allowing you to query data stored in various AWS and non-AWS data sources using AWS Lambda–based data source connectors.

Figure 6-18 shows how Amazon Athena Federated Query works. When you execute a federated query, Athena uses data connectors to translate your SQL query into the appropriate format for the target data source, executes the query against that source, and then processes the results seamlessly. The connector, running as an AWS Lambda function, handles connecting to the external source (like RDS, DynamoDB, Snowflake, Google BigQuery, or other databases), managing authentication, optimizing the query for that specific data source, retrieving the data, and converting it into a format that Athena can process.

For example, if you query both S3 data and Snowflake data in a single SQL statement, Athena coordinates the execution across both sources, handles the data federation, and combines the results before presenting them to you. As a user, you simply write standard SQL queries regardless of where the underlying data resides, making it possible to analyze data across multiple sources without moving or copying the data. The following are some of the most common data sources:

Data source connectors for non-AWS services
> Snowflake, Google BigQuery, Azure Data Lake Storage, Azure Synapse, Cloudera Hive, Cloudera Impala

Data source connectors for AWS services
> Amazon DocumentDB, DynamoDB, Amazon OpenSearch, Amazon CloudWatch, Amazon Redshift, Amazon MSK (Apache Kafka)

Refer to the available list of Athena connectors (*https://oreil.ly/eNJh0*) for a full list of connectors.

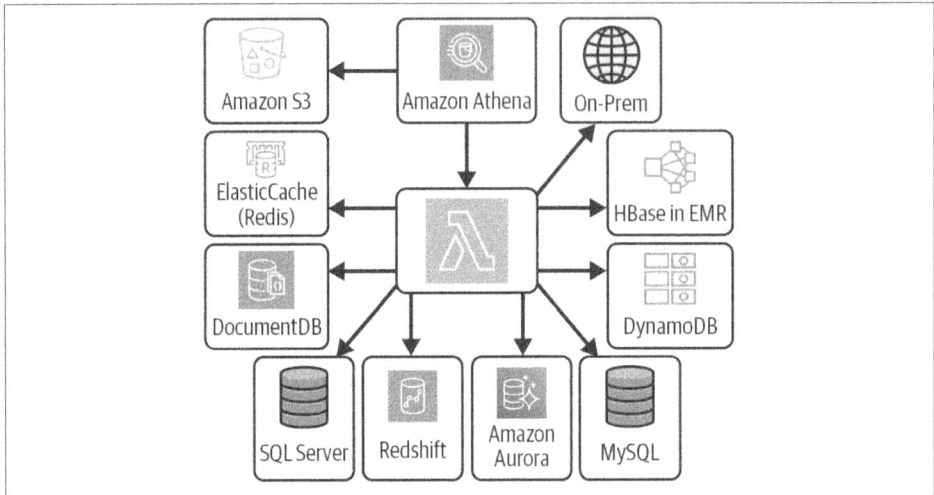

Figure 6-18. Amazon Athena Federated Query

Some common use cases for Athena's federated queries include the following:

Multicloud analytics
Leverage connectors for Azure Data Lake, Google BigQuery, etc., to analyze data across cloud platforms without data egress fees.

One-time analysis jobs across multiple data sources
The serverless and pay-per-use nature of Athena makes federated queries cost-effective for ad-hoc analysis jobs spanning multiple data sources like Amazon S3, Google BigQuery, Azure Data Lake Storage, Snowflake, etc.

Ad-hoc data exploration
Query data across various data sources without up-front data movement, enabling self-service exploration and analysis.

Use Cases

Using Athena's SQL Analytics, you can solve the following use cases:

- Query data stored in Amazon S3, such as AWS service logs stored in S3, or data lake tables in various open formats.

- Query data from various external data sources using Athena Federated Query.

- Query Apache Iceberg tables, including time-travel queries, and Apache Hudi datasets.

- Perform geospatial analytics using geospatial functions and datatypes (*https://oreil.ly/6j_wa*).

- Perform machine learning (ML) inference from Amazon SageMaker (*https://oreil.ly/KreSy*):

  — You can prebuild ML models in Amazon SageMaker and run inferences using them without complex programming and using familiar SQL.

  — To use this feature, define a function in Athena using the USING EXTERNAL FUNCTION clause. This function references a SageMaker model endpoint that you want to use and specifies the variable names and data types to pass to the model. Within the SQL query, you invoke this function, passing in data values as input to the ML model. The model processes the input data using its algorithms and returns the inference results to the query, as shown in Figure 6-19.

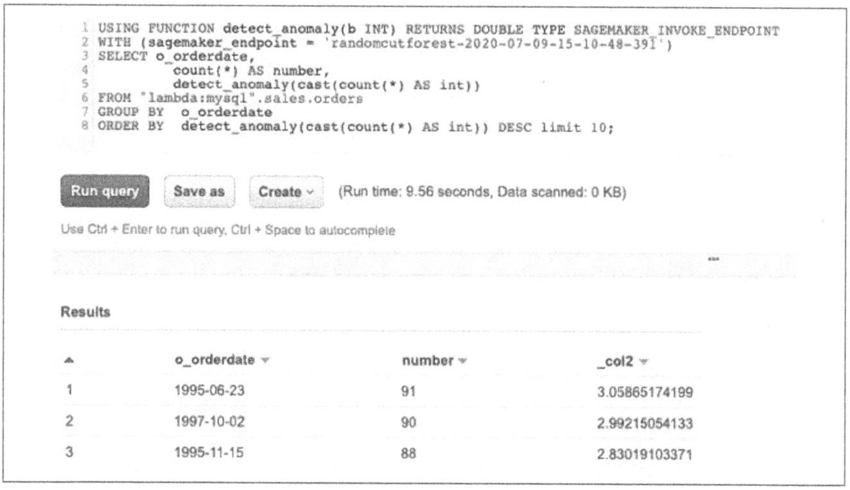

```
1 USING FUNCTION detect_anomaly(b INT) RETURNS DOUBLE TYPE SAGEMAKER_INVOKE_ENDPOINT
2 WITH (sagemaker_endpoint = 'randomcutforest-2020-07-09-15-10-48-391')
3 SELECT o_orderdate,
4         count(*) AS number,
5         detect_anomaly(cast(count(*) AS int))
6 FROM "lambda:mysql".sales.orders
7 GROUP BY  o_orderdate
8 ORDER BY  detect_anomaly(cast(count(*) AS int)) DESC limit 10;
```

| Run query | Save as | Create ˅ | (Run time: 9.56 seconds, Data scanned: 0 KB) |

Use Ctrl + Enter to run query, Ctrl + Space to autocomplete

Results

▲	o_orderdate ▼	number ▼	_col2 ▼
1	1995-06-23	91	3.05865174199
2	1997-10-02	90	2.99215054133
3	1995-11-15	88	2.83019103371

Figure 6-19. Machine learning inference with Amazon Athena and Amazon SageMaker

For example, you can integrate an anomaly detection ML model. The query passes data to the model, which analyzes it to identify and flag any anomalous values in the results.

- Query using your own user-defined functions defined in AWS Lambda (*https://oreil.ly/mMmaW*):

  — You can extend Athena's extending SQL capabilities through user-defined functions (UDFs) powered by AWS Lambda. You define a UDF in your Athena SQL query and specify the Lambda function containing its implementation. When the query calls the UDF, Athena invokes the corresponding Lambda function.

  — UDFs enable custom data transformations, integrations with AWS services, calling external APIs, and more—all within Athena SQL queries. For example, you can create UDFs for text translation, sentiment analysis, or custom data processing.

For example, the following SQL invokes a Lambda function to convert polygons to cells:

```
USING EXTERNAL FUNCTION polygon_to_cells(polygonWKT VARCHAR, res INT)
RETURNS ARRAY(BIGINT) LAMBDA '<MY-LAMBDA-ARN>'
SELECT polygon_to_cells('POLYGON (
    43.604652 1.444209,
    47.218371 -1.553621,
    50.62925 3.05726)');
```

DDL Capabilities

DDL (Data Definition Language) is a subset of SQL used to define and modify the structure of database objects. It includes commands that create, alter, and delete database structures like tables, views, etc. Common DDL commands include CREATE (to make new database objects), ALTER (to modify existing objects), and DROP (to remove objects).

Amazon Athena supports a range of DDL statements that allow you to create, modify, and manage databases, tables, and views directly in the Athena query engine. While not all Hive DDL statements are supported, the following DDLs are supported:

- CREATE DATABASE, TABLE, VIEW

- DROP DATABASE, TABLE, VIEW

- ALTER TABLE to add/drop partitions, rename partitions, replace columns

- DESCRIBE to get metadata on tables and views

  — This shows information about the columns in a table, including details on complex column types like structs and arrays.

- SHOW statements to list databases, tables, views, columns, etc.

- MSCK REPAIR TABLE to synchronize partition metadata:

  — Use this command to update the metadata in the AWS Glue Data Catalog after you've added new Hive-compatible partitions to your data files in Amazon S3. It scans the S3 filesystem for partitions that were added after the Athena table was created, compares them to the partitions recorded in the catalog metadata, and adds any new partitions found to the table's metadata in the Data Catalog.

  — Running this command reconciles this metadata discrepancy, allowing Athena to query the newly added partitions.

  — It's recommended to use MSCK REPAIR TABLE when initially creating a partitioned table from existing data, or when you are unsure if the partitions in the data match the metadata. However, for frequent metadata updates like daily partitions, `ALTER TABLE ADD PARTITION` may be more efficient to avoid query timeouts from excessive scanning.

Best Practices When Using Amazon Athena

Athena's query performance and cost depends on the volume of data scanned. Use the following best practices to improve performance and reduce cost:

- *Partition your data and pick partition keys that will support your queries.* Select partition keys that align with your most common query patterns. Good partition keys are those that you frequently use in `WHERE` clauses to filter your data. For instance, if you often query data by date, partitioning by date (e.g., year, month, day) can be highly effective.

- *Improve query performance on highly partitioned tables using partition projection (https://oreil.ly/gvvx1).* Partition projection is a feature in Amazon Athena that can speed up query processing for highly partitioned tables. The key benefit is that by avoiding the metadata lookup, partition projection can reduce query execution time, especially for queries constrained by partition metadata retrieval from the data catalog. In addition, it can also perform automated partition management.

- *Partition projection is useful in the following scenarios:*

  — When queries against a highly partitioned table are not completed quickly enough.

  — When you regularly add new date/time partitions to tables as new data arrives. With partition projection, you can configure relative date ranges that can accommodate new data.

  — When you have highly partitioned data in Amazon S3 that is impractical to fully model in the AWS Glue Data Catalog, and your queries read only small parts of the data.

  — When your partition structure follows a predictable pattern like a sequence of integers, dates, or enumerated values that can be defined in the partition projection configuration.

- *Optimize cost and performance using query result reuse.* Query result reuse is a performance and cost optimization that allows Athena to return cached results for identical queries, significantly reducing query execution time and costs, especially for recurring or parameterized queries with stable data sources. Use this feature when the query results are unlikely to change within a given timeframe:

  — *This is an opt-in feature*: You can enable or disable query result reuse on a per-query basis.

— *Maximum age setting*: You can specify a maximum age (in minutes, hours, or days) for the previous query results to be reused. The maximum is 7 days.

— *Matching criteria*: For Athena to reuse the previous results, the query string, database, catalog, and result configuration must exactly match the previous execution.

— *Supported table types*: Athena supports reusing results for queries that reference Apache Hive, Apache Hudi, Apache Iceberg, and Linux Foundation Delta Lake tables registered with AWS Glue Data Catalog.

— *Workgroup scoped*: The reused query results are specific to the Athena workgroup where the previous execution took place.

— *Limitations*: Certain query types like CTAS, INSERT INTO, MERGE, UNLOAD, and DDL are not supported for query result reuse. Tables with fine-grained access controls or that are governed by Lake Formation are also not supported.

- *Optimize cost and performance using columnar formats like Parquet and include only required columns in your select queries to limit the amount of data scanned.* When dealing with large datasets, the way you store and query your data significantly impacts both cost and performance. Columnar file formats like Parquet store data by columns rather than rows, allowing you to read only the specific columns you need instead of scanning entire rows. For example, if you have a table with 100 columns but only need data from three columns, a columnar format lets you read just those three columns, dramatically reducing the amount of data processed. This is particularly cost-effective with services like Amazon Athena, where you pay for the amount of data scanned per query. Additionally, when writing queries, following the practice of specifically listing needed columns (using SELECT column1, column2 instead of SELECT *) further reduces data scanning, leading to faster query execution and lower costs.

You can read through "Top 10 Performance Tuning Tips for Amazon Athena" (*https://oreil.ly/7reqL*) for more best practices.

SQL Analytics Using Amazon Redshift

You can use SQL to analyze data in a Amazon Redshift data warehouse as well. As you learned in Chapter 2, Amazon Redshift is a fully managed, petabyte-scale data warehouse service that enables you to efficiently store, query, and analyze large volumes of data. Amazon Redshift is designed to handle complex SQL queries and supports a wide range of analytical and business intelligence use cases. One of the key strengths of Amazon Redshift is its ability to process and analyze data at scale. Redshift uses a massively parallel processing (MPP) architecture, which allows it to distribute the computational workload across multiple nodes, resulting in fast query performance even on large datasets.

To run SQL queries, Amazon Redshift offers a web-based IDE called Redshift Query Editor v2, which is available from the AWS Management Console. You can also use a SQL IDE of your choice like DBeaver, SQLWorkbench, etc. to connect to Redshift using JDBC/ODBC drivers. For data analysis, you can connect to your Redshift cluster using standard SQL clients or business intelligence tools, such as Amazon QuickSight, Tableau, or Power BI. You can also query Amazon Redshift programmatically using Amazon Redshift Data API.

SQL Functions

Amazon Redshift is built on the foundation of PostgreSQL database software. However, Redshift has been extensively modified to excel at analyzing and reporting on massive datasets quickly. It provides advanced functions for aggregation, calculations, working with dates/times, text manipulation, JSON data, machine learning, and processing specialized data types like arrays and spatial data.

As an example, let's consider aggregation functions. Amazon Redshift provides standard SQL aggregate functions like AVG, COUNT, MAX, MIN, and SUM to combine values over groups of rows. It also supports advanced aggregate functions that go beyond traditional database capabilities. This includes approximations like APPROXIMATE PERCENTILE_DISC for estimating percentiles and LISTAGG for concatenating strings within groups. There are statistical aggregates like MEDIAN, STDDEV_SAMP, STDDEV_POP, VAR_SAMP, and VAR_POP. It provides specialized aggregates like ANY_VALUE to return any value from a group, and PERCENTILE_CONT for computing percentiles over numeric data. Amazon Redshift even has bit-wise, HyperLogLog, and array aggregation functions for advanced analysis of encoded, probabilistic, and array data types, respectively. For a full list of functions, please refer to the SQL functions reference documentation (*https://oreil.ly/p3EAm*).

Semi-Structured Data Analysis

Amazon Redshift allows you to query and analyze semi-structured data like JSON, Avro, or Ion alongside your structured data as is, without having to shred the JSON attributes into separate columns.

Semi-structured data doesn't have a fixed schema or format like tables with columns. Amazon Redshift provides a special data type called SUPER that can store semi-structured data natively without having to first define all the fields or structure. You can just insert entire JSON documents into a SUPER column. This makes it very flexible to ingest evolving, schemaless data without having to predefine a rigid structure. The data can have nested objects and arrays within it.

To query the semi-structured SUPER data, Redshift uses an extended SQL called PartiQL. PartiQL understands nested data structures and allows you to navigate into them using familiar SQL syntax. PartiQL is schema-flexible, so you can explore and query the semi-structured data dynamically without strict schema validation during querying.

Let's dive into semi-structured data analysis in Redshift using an example. The customer_orders_lineitem table has the following two records. The c_orders column has semi-structured data in JSON format in Redshift:

id	c_name	c_orders

100	Customer#1	```[
		    {
		        "o_orderkey": 1,
		        "o_orderdate": "1996-04-12",
		        "o_lineitems": [
		            {
		                "l_partkey": 1,
		                "l_extendedprice": 45.67
		            },
		            {
		                "l_partkey": 2,
		                "l_extendedprice": 89.34
		            }
		        ]
		    },
		    {
		        "o_orderkey": 2,
		        "o_orderdate": "1996-03-21",
		        "o_lineitems": [
		            {
		                "l_partkey": 3,
		                "l_extendedprice": 56.78
		            }
		        ]
		    }
		]```

101	Customer#2	```[
		    {
		        "o_orderkey": 3,
		        "o_orderdate": "1996-05-09",
		        "o_lineitems": [
		            {
		                "l_partkey": 10,
		                "l_saleprice": 56.78
		            }
		        ]
		    }
		]```

The first record shows that Customer#1 has two orders (o_orderkey = 1 and o_orderkey = 2) with two line items and one line item, respectively. The second record shows that Customer#2 has one order (o_orderkey = 3) with one line item. Now let's look at how to query for order information from this table for various use cases:

Navigating into JSON objects/arrays

In the first use case, you want to retrieve the order keys of the first orders for each customer. This is a simple use case. c_orders is an array that lists all the orders that the customer made. Each array element can be accessed using a subscript, c_orders[0] will be the first order and c_orders[1] will be second order for each customer. Each order is a structure that has various attributes. You can query those attributes using a simple dot (.) notation. To retrieve o_orderkey for the first order of each customer, you need to select c_orders.o_orderkey as shown in the following SELECT statement:

```
SELECT c_orders[0].o_orderkey FROM customer_orders_lineitem;
```

Result:

```
o_orderkey
------
1
2
```

Unnesting arrays

In this use case, you want to un-nest the orders array and print one row for each order that the customers made. That is, as Customer#1 made two orders, there should be two rows for Customer#1, and as Customer#2 made one order, there should be one row. In order to un-nest arrays, you need to include array(c_orders) in the FROM clause as shown in the following query. Each element inside the array can then be accessed using dot (.) notation:

```
SELECT c.c_name, o.o_orderkey, o.o_orderdate
FROM customer_orders_lineitem c, c.c_orders o;
```

Result:

```
c_name      | o_orderkey | o_orderdate
------------+------------+------------
Customer#1  | 1          | 1996-04-12
Customer#1  | 2          | 1996-03-21
Customer#2  | 3          | 1996-05-09
```

Unpivoting objects

This query unpivots the JSON object stored in c_orders[0]. It uses the UNPIVOT keyword to treat the object properties as individual rows, with the attr column containing the property name and the val column containing the property v:

```
SELECT attr, val
FROM customer_orders_lineitem c, UNPIVOT c.c_orders[0] AS val AT attr
WHERE c.c_custkey = 100;
```

Result:

```
attr          | val
--------------+----------------------------------------
o_orderkey    | 1
o_orderdate   | "1996-04-12"
o_lineitems   | [{"l_partkey":1 ,"l_extendedprice":45.67},    {"l_partkey":2,
                "l_extendedprice":89.34}]
```

The queries showcase how PartiQL in Amazon Redshift allows you to query and analyze semi-structured data.

Geospatial Data Analysis

As a data engineer, working with spatial data can be a powerful way to unlock additional insights and capabilities within your data processing pipelines. Amazon Redshift provides robust spatial data analytics features that you can leverage to support your geospatial use cases.

Redshift allows you to store and query geographic data types like points, polygons, and more using the GEOMETRY data type. It offers a suite of spatial SQL functions, such as ST_Distance, ST_Within, and ST_Intersects, that enable you to perform advanced spatial analysis and querying on your data. It also supports popular spatial data formats like Well-Known Text (WKT) and GeoJSON for importing and exporting geographic information. Additionally, you can utilize spatial predicates like the && operator to perform efficient spatial joins between your datasets.

To illustrate how you might apply these spatial capabilities, let's consider an example scenario. Suppose you have an "accommodations" table that stores Airbnb rental listings in Berlin, including a "shape" column that stores the geographic coordinates of each property as POINT data. You also have a "zipcode" table that contains polygon geometries representing the postal code boundaries in Berlin.

Here are some sample queries you could run to unlock valuable spatial insights:

- Counting accommodations within 500 m of a point (Brandenburg Gate):

```
SELECT count(*)
FROM accommodations
WHERE ST_DistanceSphere(
    shape,
    ST_GeomFromText('POINT(13.377704 52.516431)', 4326)
) < 500;
```

This query uses the `ST_DistanceSphere` function to calculate the distance between each accommodation's coordinates and the Brandenburg Gate point, returning the count of accommodations within 500 m radius.

- Finding accommodation within a ZIP code polygon:

```
SELECT a.price, a.name, z.spatial_name
FROM accommodations a, zipcode z
WHERE price = 9000 AND ST_Within(a.shape, z.wkb_geometry);
```

This query uses the `ST_Within` predicate to find the accommodation with the highest $9,000 price that falls within the polygon geometry of the corresponding ZIP code area.

Query Data from Data Lake

One of Redshift's key strengths is its ability to query and analyze data across both data lakes and data warehouses through its Redshift Spectrum feature. With Redshift Spectrum, you can directly query vast amounts of data stored in open data formats like Parquet, ORC, RCFile, TextFile, SequenceFile, RegexSerde, OpenCSV, and Avro in Amazon S3 data lakes, without having to load the data into Redshift tables first. You can also query tables in open table formats (OTFs) like Apache Iceberg, Delta Lake, and Hudi. To use Spectrum, you can follow these steps:

1. Define the structure of the files that are stored in S3. You can do this in more than one way. You can create external schemas and tables within Redshift using `CREATE EXTERNAL TABLE` and `CREATE EXTERNAL SCHEMA` statements. You can also use an external data catalog like AWS Glue or Apache Hive metastore.

2. You can partition the external tables for optimized query performance. Amazon Redshift can ignore unwanted partitions through partition pruning.

3. You can query and join the external S3 tables with tables in your Redshift cluster.

4. When S3 data files are updated, the data is immediately available for queries across all your Redshift endpoints.

Analyzing Data from Operational Data Stores Using Amazon Redshift

You can combine data from Amazon RDS and Amazon Aurora databases with data in your Amazon Redshift database. You do this using a special Amazon Redshift feature called federated queries. Federated queries let you directly query operational data stored in the source databases, without having to move the data first. After running the query, you can modify or transform the results, and then insert them into your Amazon Redshift tables.

When running these federated queries, some of the computational work is split between Amazon Redshift and the remote databases holding the source data. First,

Amazon Redshift connects to the remote database and gets information about the tables there. Then it runs queries on those tables and retrieves the rows of data matching the query. Finally, it sends those rows of data to Amazon Redshift's own computing systems for any additional processing.

In simple terms, federated queries allow you to integrate and analyze data from different databases all in one query. The work is shared across multiple systems, taking advantage of their combined computing power.

Redshift ML and Generative AI

Amazon Redshift ML makes it easy to leverage machine learning technology within Amazon Redshift, without requiring deep expertise. It provides direct integration with AWS ML services like Amazon SageMaker, Amazon Forecast, and Amazon SageMaker JumpStart. With Redshift ML, you can create models for prediction use cases by providing training data, and it automatically chooses the best model using Amazon SageMaker Autopilot under the hood. You can then make predictions on new data using familiar SQL commands. Redshift ML currently supports algorithms like XGBoost, neural networks, k-means clustering, linear regression, forecasting, and invoking generative AI models to augment datasets. This feature allows SQL users to solve machine learning use cases seamlessly within Amazon Redshift.

Amazon Redshift ML can solve various use cases such as customer churn prediction, fraud detection, sales forecasting, and product recommendation—all without having to move data out of Redshift or having deep machine learning expertise:

Prediction use cases
> You can use historical customer information from Amazon Redshift with Redshift ML to train models to predict the future. You can solve binary classification use cases such as churn prediction for customers and fraud prediction for financial transactions. You can solve multiclass classification problems such as classifying text documents into categories like news, sports, entertainment, politics, etc. You can also solve linear regression problems such as predicting the amount of original and counterfeit banknotes, finding the average observation for an original and a counterfeit banknote, etc.

Clustering use cases
> You can solve clustering problems such as grouping customers who have similar viewing habits on a streaming service, or grouping shows that have similar tones, actors, or locations, etc.

Generative AI use cases
> Use generative AI models using SQL statements in Redshift to solve use cases such as sentiment analysis for reviews, summarization of text, translating data from one language to another, etc.

User-Defined Functions

Amazon Redshift enables you to create custom scalar user-defined functions (UDFs). Three types of scalar UDFs are supported by Amazon Redshift:

SQL UDFs
> These are created using a SQL SELECT clause. SQL UDFs help with simple data transformations or calculations that can be expressed in SQL. This logic is then made reusable and can be applied across multiple queries.

Python UDFs
> These are created using a Python program. While you can use standard Python functionality, you can also import your own custom Python modules. Using Python UDFs you can perform data processing that requires Python's rich data manipulation capabilities. You can perform complex data transformations that are easier to implement in Python.

Lambda UDFs
> These allow you to use custom functions defined in AWS Lambda as part of your SQL queries. Lambda UDFs can be written in any language supported by Lambda like Java, Go, PowerShell, Node.js, C#, Python, Ruby, or a custom runtime. They provide more capabilities compared to Python and SQL UDFs. Using Lambda UDFs, you can integrate with third-party APIs, services, or data sources outside of Redshift for which Redshift doesn't already have an integration (for example, integration with third-party tokenization solutions).

Analyzing Data Using Notebooks

Notebooks give you an easy way to leverage open source Apache Spark in Amazon EMR (Elastic MapReduce) or AWS Glue for data science, interactive analytics, preparing and visualizing data, collaborating with peers, prototyping jobs before bringing them to production, etc.

AWS Glue Interactive Sessions

Glue interactive sessions is a feature within AWS Glue that provides a powerful way for data engineers and data scientists to interactively explore and analyze datasets. The key aspects of Glue interactive sessions are:

Notebooks
> Glue interactive sessions are based on Jupyter-compatible notebooks, which are interactive coding environments that allow you to write and execute code, visualize data, and document your work in a single interface.

On-demand Apache Spark

The backend compute for Glue interactive sessions is based on Apache Spark. You need not manage any underlying infrastructure to be able to process and analyze large datasets using Spark.

Visualization

Glue interactive sessions include native support for popular data visualization libraries like Matplotlib and Seaborn, using which you can create rich, interactive visualizations of your data directly within your notebook. If you want additional libraries, just upload them to Amazon S3 and specify the full path as a parameter value to the `additional_python_modules` magic command.

Let's walk through an example on how you can run a sample visualization on the Iris dataset (*https://oreil.ly/MPkCJ*). The following shows the notebook code:

```
import seaborn as sns ❶
import matplotlib.pyplot as plt ❶

# Load the Iris dataset
iris = sns.load_dataset("iris") ❷

# Create a pair plot
sns.pairplot(iris, hue="species") ❸
%matplot plt ❹
```

❶ These lines import two popular Python libraries for data visualization: Seaborn and Matplotlib. Seaborn is a high-level data visualization library that's built on top of Matplotlib, which is the core data visualization library.

❷ This line is loading a well-known dataset called "Iris" into a variable called `iris`. The Iris dataset contains measurements of different species of iris flowers, such as petal length, petal width, sepal length, and sepal width.

❸ This is where the visualization happens. The `pairplot()` function from the Seaborn library creates a grid of scatter plots, where each scatter plot shows the relationship between two of the variables in the Iris dataset. The `hue="species"` argument tells Seaborn to use different colors to represent the different species of iris flowers in the scatter plots.

❹ This line is a "magic command" in the Jupyter notebook environment that tells the notebook to display the visualization created by the previous line of code.

In summary, this code is taking the Iris dataset, creating a visual grid of scatter plots that show the relationships between all the different measurements in the dataset, and coloring the data points by the species of iris flower. This type of visualization can help you quickly identify patterns and relationships in the data, which can be very useful for exploratory data analysis and understanding the structure of a dataset.

Amazon EMR Notebooks

Amazon EMR Notebooks is a managed environment based on Jupyter notebooks. It enables users to interactively analyze and visualize data, collaborate with peers, and build applications using EMR clusters. EMR Notebooks is designed for Apache Spark. It supports Spark Magic kernels, which allows you to remotely run queries and code on your EMR cluster using languages like PySpark, Spark SQL, Spark R, and Scala.

With EMR Notebooks, there is no software or instances to manage. You can either attach the notebook to an existing cluster or provision a new cluster directly from the console. You can attach multiple notebooks to a single cluster, detach notebooks, and reattach them to new clusters. Here is a typical workflow for using EMR Notebooks:

1. Create an EMR cluster with the required components (e.g., Spark, Hive, Presto) for your data processing and analytics needs.

2. Create a new EMR Notebook instance and connect it to the EMR cluster.

3. Use the Jupyter notebook environment to read data from various sources (e.g., S3, Glue Data Catalog), perform exploratory data analysis, and visualize the results.

4. Share the notebook with other team members, allowing for collaboration and knowledge sharing.

5. Productionize the analytics workflows by creating scheduled jobs or integrating the notebooks into your data pipeline.

You can run analytics similar to what was shown in the AWS Glue interactive sessions using EMR notebooks.

Data Pipeline Resiliency

Building resilient data pipelines is crucial for ensuring continuous and reliable data flow despite potential disruptions. It involves implementing robust error handling, data validation, comprehensive monitoring and alerting, scalability and load management capabilities, data backup and recovery processes, rigorous testing frameworks, secure access controls, controlled change management, and robust operational practices such as incident response and disaster recovery plans. By prioritizing resiliency through these measures, organizations can maintain data integrity, ensure availability, minimize downtime, and enhance the overall reliability of their data-driven systems and applications.

Monitoring

Effective monitoring and observability are essential for ensuring the reliability, performance, and cost-effectiveness of your data processing pipelines. By continuously monitoring your data pipelines, you can quickly identify and address issues, optimize resource utilization, and maintain the overall health and integrity of your data infrastructure. In this section, we will explore the key AWS services and tools that you can leverage to monitor your data processing pipelines, including Amazon CloudWatch, AWS CloudTrail, and system tables within your data processing services.

Monitoring metrics using CloudWatch

Amazon CloudWatch is a comprehensive monitoring and observability service that provides you with visibility into your AWS resources, applications, and services. Each AWS service reports its metrics to CloudWatch. CloudWatch collects and tracks these metrics, logs, and events, and provides insights into the performance, health, and utilization of your data pipelines. You can also publish custom metrics to CloudWatch using the `put-metric-data` API and AWS CLI. Figure 6-20 shows a sample metric graph for CPU utilization.

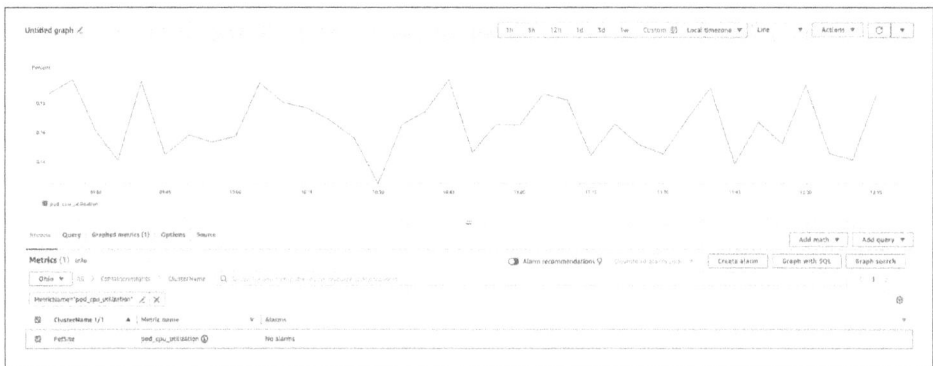

Figure 6-20. Amazon CloudWatch metric sample

CloudWatch dashboards

CloudWatch dashboards allow you to visualize and monitor data over time, in context with other related metrics and information. They provide a way to tell a "story" about the health and performance of your applications and infrastructure by combining visualizations, annotations, and context in a single view. Figure 6-21 is a sample CloudWatch dashboard.

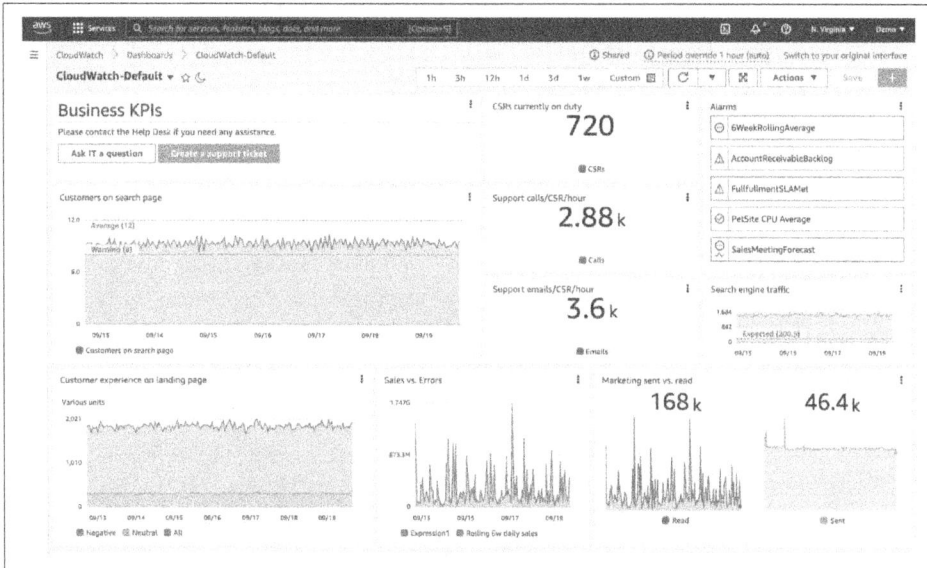

Figure 6-21. Amazon CloudWatch dashboard

Monitoring API calls with CloudTrail

In addition to monitoring the performance and utilization of your data processing resources, it's important to track the API calls and actions performed on your AWS services. This is where AWS CloudTrail comes into play.

CloudTrail is a service that records API calls and related events within your AWS environment, providing a comprehensive audit trail of the actions taken by users, roles, and services. When it comes to data processing pipelines, CloudTrail can help you track activities such as the creation, modification, or deletion of AWS Glue jobs, AWS Step Functions state machines, Amazon Redshift clusters, etc. among other data-related resources.

AWS CloudTrail will only show the results of the CloudTrail event history for the current region you are viewing for the last 90 days; it supports the AWS services found in the AWS CloudTrail documentation (*https://oreil.ly/kuyUR*). These events are limited to management events with create, modify, and delete API calls and account activity. For a complete record of account activity, including all management events, data events, and read-only activity, you'll need to configure a CloudTrail trail.

By analyzing the CloudTrail logs, you can identify any unauthorized or unexpected actions, monitor for potential security breaches or compliance issues, and investigate any changes or anomalies that may impact the operation of your data pipelines. This level of visibility and auditability is crucial for maintaining the overall security and governance of your data infrastructure. You can find CloudTrail log file examples in the documentation (*https://oreil.ly/TeVqG*).

Monitoring logs and traces

While CloudWatch and CloudTrail provide valuable insights into the performance and API usage of your AWS services, it's also important to analyze the application-level logs generated by your data processing workloads. These logs can contain detailed information about the execution of your data pipelines, such as job status, error messages, and any transformations or processing steps performed.

Depending on the data processing services you're using, you may have access to different types of application logs. For example, AWS Glue provides detailed logs for your ETL jobs, including the execution status, runtime metrics, and any errors or warnings encountered. Similarly, Amazon EMR generates logs that capture the execution and performance of your Spark, Hive, or other big data workloads.

To analyze these application logs, you can leverage AWS services like Amazon Cloud-Watch Logs, Amazon Athena, and Amazon OpenSearch Service. CloudWatch Logs allows you to centrally collect and store your application logs, while Athena can be used to run SQL queries on the log data, enabling you to identify issues, analyze trends, and troubleshoot problems. Additionally, you can use Amazon OpenSearch Service to provide advanced log analysis and visualization capabilities, allowing you to quickly identify and respond to anomalies or critical events within your data pipelines.

Monitoring using system tables

In addition to monitoring the performance, API usage, and application-level logs of your data processing services, you can also leverage built-in system tables and views to gain deeper insights into the operation of your data pipelines.

System tables are available on the data warehouse service Amazon Redshift. The following are some of the most commonly used system tables in Amazon Redshift:

STL_QUERY_METRICS
Tracks query execution metrics like rows processed, CPU usage, and disk I/O. Contains metrics for completed query segments. Useful for analyzing query performance.

STL_ALERT_EVENT_LOG
Records alerts and warnings during query execution. Helps identify potential issues like disk space and memory constraints. Useful for proactive monitoring.

STL_LOAD_ERRORS

Contains details about data load errors. Records specific rows that failed to load and why. Essential for troubleshooting COPY command failures.

STL_LOAD_INFO

Tracks information about data load operations. Contains statistics about files loaded and rows processed. Useful for monitoring load performance of COPY commands.

SYS_QUERY_HISTORY

Records user-submitted queries in original form. It has single row per query execution. Contains query metadata like user_id, transaction_id, and start/end times.

SYS_QUERY_DETAIL

Provides detailed metrics about query execution. Used for troubleshooting query performance bottlenecks.

STL_PLAN_INFO

Contains query execution plan details. Shows how queries are processed. Useful for query optimization.

STL_USAGE_CONTROL

Tracks resource usage and limits. Monitors concurrency scaling usage. Helps manage cluster resources.

For more, consult the complete list of Amazon Redshift system tables (*https://oreil.ly/P4OC0*) and the most used tables for troubleshooting in the SYS monitoring views documentation (*https://oreil.ly/jiwzK*).

Alerting

As your data processing pipelines grow in complexity and scale, manually monitoring and maintaining these systems can become increasingly challenging and time-consuming. To address this, you can leverage various AWS services to automate the monitoring and maintenance of your data pipelines, enabling you to proactively detect and respond to issues, as well as maintain the overall health and integrity of your data infrastructure.

CloudWatch Alarms

When monitoring data pipelines with CloudWatch, you can track metrics like CPU, memory, network utilization for compute resources (EC2, Redshift, Lambda), data throughput and latency for streaming services (Kinesis, MSK), query performance and execution times for analytical services (Athena, Redshift), and more. Cloud-Watch alarms proactively notify you before experiencing issues, such as Lambda errors, DynamoDB throttles, API Gateway 500 errors, high CPU utilization in Redshift, and others, enabling timely remediation and preventing pipeline disruptions.

There are two types of CloudWatch Alarms:

Metric alarms
> These are the basic types of alarms that watch a single metric, like CPU usage, network traffic, etc. You set a threshold, and the alarm goes into an ALARM state if the metric value goes above or below that threshold. When the alarm state changes, it can trigger actions like sending a notification or making an API call.

Composite alarms
> These are "alarms of alarms." Instead of watching a single metric, a composite alarm evaluates the states of other metric alarms or even other composite alarms based on a rule you define. For example, you could create a composite alarm that only goes into ALARM state if both a CPU metric alarm AND a memory metric alarm are in ALARM state. The benefit is that it allows you to combine and filter out noise from multiple underlying alarms.

There are two different ways you could set up metric alarms based on CloudWatch metrics:

Static threshold
> A static threshold represents a hard limit that the metric should not violate. You must define the range for the static threshold, which defines the behavior during normal operations. If the metric value falls below or above the static threshold, the alarm status will change to ALARM.

Anomaly detection
> CloudWatch anomaly detection analyzes past metric data and creates a model of expected values by taking into account the typical hourly, daily, and weekly patterns in the metric. You can apply the anomaly detection for each metric as required and CloudWatch applies a machine-learning algorithm to define the upper limit and lower limit for each of the enabled metrics. It generates an alarm only when the metrics fall out of the expected values.

Alarm state

Alarms have the following possible states:

OK
> The metric or expression is within the threshold. The alarm is not active, and all is well.

ALARM
> The metric or expression is outside of the threshold. The alarm is active.

INSUFFICIENT_DATA
> The alarm has just started, the metric is not available, or not enough data is available for the metric to determine the alarm state.

Notifications

CloudWatch allows you to set notifications to proactively detect and respond to issues or performance degradations within your data pipelines. CloudWatch uses the Simple Notification Service (SNS) under the hood, as shown in Figure 6-22. SNS is a notification service that can inform you in case of any errors. It sends notifications like emails, SMS, or in-app notifications. You can also attach an AWS Lambda function to the SNS topic to:

- Take automated actions to fix the issue (e.g., resize an Amazon Redshift cluster in response to an alarm).
- Send notifications to third-party tools like Slack, MS Teams, Discord, etc.

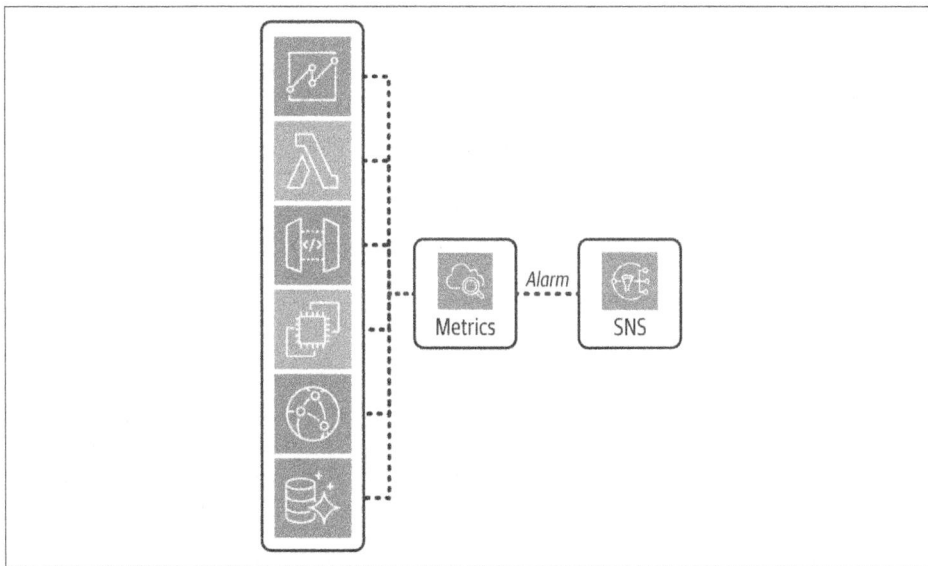

Figure 6-22. Amazon CloudWatch alarm

Event-Driven Pipeline Maintenance with EventBridge

Another powerful tool for automating the maintenance of your data processing pipelines is Amazon EventBridge. EventBridge is a serverless event bus service that allows you to connect your applications and services, enabling them to communicate and respond to events in near real time.

When it comes to data pipeline maintenance, you can use EventBridge to create rules that automatically trigger actions in response to specific events, such as the completion of an AWS Glue job, the addition of a new file to an Amazon S3 bucket, or the failure of an AWS Lambda function. You can create robust, self-healing data pipelines. For example, you can create a rule that automatically restarts an AWS Glue job if it fails to complete successfully. You can set up an EventBridge rule that triggers an AWS Lambda function to perform data quality checks whenever a new file is added to your data lake.

Ensuring Data Quality and Reliability: Deequ and DQDL

Maintaining high-quality, reliable data is essential for driving accurate and meaningful insights from your data processing pipelines. As data engineers, you play a crucial role in ensuring the integrity, completeness, and accuracy of the data that flows through your infrastructure, enabling your organization to make informed, data-driven decisions. The data quality solutions in AWS are based on the open source Deequ framework. Deequ is an open source library developed by Amazon for data quality validation in large-scale data processing pipelines. It is built on Apache Spark. It treats data quality checkers as testable assertions, similar to how unit tests work for code.

The Data Quality Definition Language (DQDL) is a declarative language used to define data quality rules in a structured and standardized way when using Deequ. Instead of writing data quality checks in code, DQDL lets you express them as simple configurations, enabling even nondevelopers to write and manage rules.

In this section, we will explore the various AWS analytics services that use Deequ and DQDL to provide data quality solutions.

AWS Glue Data Quality

AWS Glue Data Quality is a managed serverless service that allows you to measure and monitor the quality of your data to make informed business decisions. It is built on top of the DeeQu framework and uses DQDL to define data quality rules.

There are two main entry points for using AWS Glue Data Quality:

- AWS Glue Data Catalog:
  - You can generate data quality rule recommendations by analyzing tables in your Data Catalog.
  - AWS Glue automatically identifies and suggests rules based on your data.
  - You can edit the recommended rulesets or create custom rulesets using DQDL.

— Calculate a data quality score showing the percentage of rules that passed.

— View the score, passed/failed rule results, and run history in the AWS Glue console.

— Requires an IAM role with permissions for AWS Glue, Amazon S3, and CloudWatch.

— Set up scheduling, alerts, and save results to S3.

Figure 6-23 shows how you can create a data quality rule in AWS Glue Data Catalog. The UI provides a helper with a + button. You can click on it to add it to the ruleset to generate your roles, as shown in the figure. The rule in Figure 6-23 is checking that the correlation between columns A and B is less than 0.5, the average of both ratings is greater than or equal to 0.9, and the number of columns is 10.

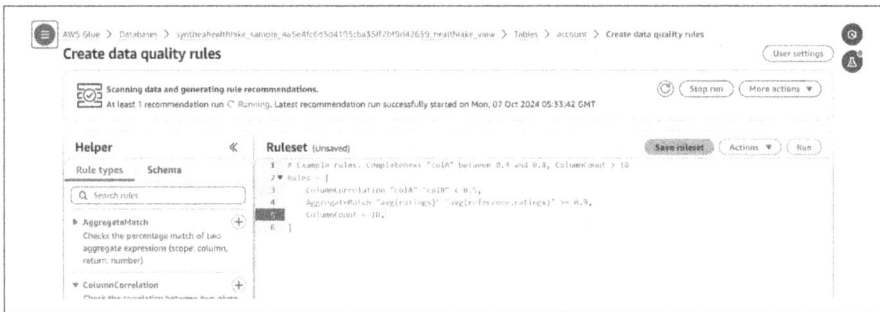

Figure 6-23. Creating a data quality rule in the Glue Data Catalog

- AWS Glue ETL jobs:

  — Perform proactive data quality tasks before loading data into your data lake.

  — Identify and filter out bad data before ETL processing.

  — Incorporate data quality tasks directly into your ETL job scripts and pipelines.

  — Write code to define data quality rules in ETL scripts using DQDL.

  — Manage data quality through AWS Glue Studio, Studio notebooks, and interactive sessions.

  — Use AWS Glue libraries and APIs for data quality in ETL scripting.

Figure 6-24 shows the Evaluate Data Quality transform available in AWS Glue Studio. The rule is validating that the values for the fare amount field are between 1 and 100.

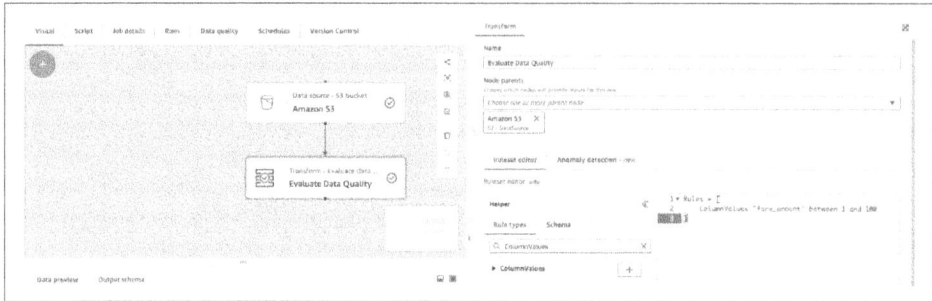

Figure 6-24. Data quality in AWS Glue jobs using Glue Studio

Let's learn more about DQDL.

AWS Glue Data Quality DQDL syntax

In AWS Glue, a DQDL document is case sensitive and contains a ruleset, which groups individual data quality rules together. To construct a ruleset, you must create a list named Rules (capitalized), delimited by a pair of square brackets. The list should contain one or more comma-separated DQDL rules like the following example:

```
Rules = [
    IsComplete "order-id",
    IsUnique "order-id"
]
```

The rules generally fit the following format:

```
<RuleType> <Parameter> <Parameter> <Expression>
```

RuleType is the case-sensitive name of the rule type that you want to configure. Some of the most common rule types are listed in Table 6-1.

Table 6-1. Common rule types in AWS Glue Data Quality

Rule type	Description
DistinctValuesCount	Checks for duplicate values.
ColumnCount	Checks if any columns are dropped.
ColumnDataType	Checks if a column is compliant with a data type.
ColumnExists	Checks if columns exist in a dataset. This allows customers building self-service data platforms to ensure certain columns are made available.
IsUnique	Checks if the column has all unique values, excluding NULLs.
IsPrimaryKey	Checks if a column is a primary key (not NULL and unique).
Sum	Checks if the sum matched a threshold.
AggregateMatch	Checks if two datasets match by comparing summary metrics like total sales amount. Useful for financial institutions to compare if all data is ingested from source systems.

Rule type	Description
ColumnCorrelation	Checks how well two columns are correlated.
ColumnLength	Checks if length of data is consistent.
ColumnNamesMatchPattern	Checks if column names match defined patterns. Useful for governance teams to enforce column name consistency.
ColumnValues	Checks if data is consistent per defined values. This rule supports regular expressions.
Completeness	Checks for any blank or NULLs in data.
DataFreshness	Checks if data is fresh by evaluating the difference between the current time and the values of a date column.
DatasetMatch	Compares two datasets and identifies if they are in sync.
Entropy	Checks for entropy of the data.
IsComplete	Checks if 100% of the data is complete.
Mean	Checks if the mean matches the set threshold.
ReferentialIntegrity	Checks if two datasets have referential integrity.
RowCount	Checks if record counts match a threshold.
RowCountMatch	Checks if record counts between two datasets match.
StandardDeviation	Checks if standard deviation matches the threshold.
SchemaMatch	Checks if schema between two datasets match.
Uniqueness	Checks if uniqueness of a dataset matches threshold.
UniqueValueRatio	Checks if the unique value ratio matches threshold.
FileFreshness	Checks if files in Amazon S3 are fresh.
FileMatch	Checks if contents of file match to a checksum or with another file. This rule uses checksums to validate if two files are the same.
FileSize	Checks if the size of a file matches with a specified condition.
FileUniqueness	Checks if files are unique using checksums.
CustomSQL	When the existing rule types don't satisfy your requirement, this allows you to define your own rule using a custom SQL statement.

Composite rules

You can combine multiple rules using and and or operators. For example:

```
(IsComplete "id") and (IsUnique "id")
```

Let's consider an example data quality pipeline where a data engineer ingests data from a raw zone and loads it into a curated zone in a data lake. The data engineer is tasked with not only extracting, transforming, and loading data, but also identifying anomalies compared against data quality statistics from historical runs. The dataset is the New York taxi dataset and the data engineer wants to validate the following:

- At least 90% of rides must have passengers (passenger count greater than 0).
- The average trip distance should be less than 1.5 times the highest average from the last 3 runs.

- The total amount of all fares should be above 80% of the lowest total from the last 3 runs and below 120% of the highest total from the last 3 runs.
- The number of unique pickup locations should be more than 80% of the average from the last 3 runs.
- The number of columns should exactly match the highest count from the last 2 runs.

The DQDL ruleset that can check these are as follows. Note that the first rule is custom SQL that checks if 90% of rides have passengers. Also the last() function can be used to check the values for the last *N* job runs:

```
CustomSql "select vendorid from primary where passenger_count > 0"
    with threshold > 0.9,
Mean "trip_distance" < max(last(3)) * 1.50,
Sum "total_amount" between min(last(3)) * 0.8 and max(last(3)) * 1.2,
RowCount between min(last(3)) * 0.9 and max(last(3)) * 1.2,
Completeness "fare_amount" >= avg(last(3)) * 0.9,
DistinctValuesCount "ratecodeid" between avg(last(3))-1 and avg(last(3))+2,
DistinctValuesCount "pulocationid" > avg(last(3)) * 0.8,
ColumnCount = max(last(2))
```

Using Deequ with Amazon EMR

Since Deequ is based on Apache Spark, you can use this library in Amazon EMR. Amazon EMR provides an ideal platform for leveraging the power of Deequ. By running Deequ on an Amazon EMR cluster, you can take advantage of the scalable and distributed processing capabilities of Apache Spark to verify the quality of your large-scale datasets. Whether your data lives in Amazon S3 or other distributed data sources you can easily access and analyze your data for quality assurance. Here are the steps:

1. Create an Amazon EMR cluster with Spark 2.2.0 or later. EMR takes care of the Spark configuration for you.
2. Download the Deequ JAR by connecting to the Amazon EMR master node using SSH and launch the Spark shell using Deequ:

    ```
    wget \
    http://repo1.maven.org/maven2/com/amazon/deequ/deequ/1.0.1/deequ-1.0.1.jar
    spark-shell --conf spark.jars=deequ-1.0.1.jar
    ```

3. Read data into a Spark DataFrame; in this example we will use sample Amazon reviews dataset:

    ```
    val dataset = spark.read.parquet(
        "s3://amazon-reviews-pds/parquet/product_category=Electronics/")
    ```

4. Use `AnalysisRunner` to define the metrics you want to compute:

```
from com.amazon.deequ.analyzers.runners import (
    AnalysisRunner,
    AnalyzerContext
)
from com.amazon.deequ.analyzers.runners.AnalyzerContext import (
    successMetricsAsDataFrame
)
from com.amazon.deequ.analyzers import *

val analysisResult: AnalyzerContext = {
  AnalysisRunner
    .onData(dataset)
    .addAnalyzer(Size())
    .addAnalyzer(Completeness("review_id"))
    .addAnalyzer(ApproxCountDistinct("review_id"))
    .addAnalyzer(Mean("star_rating"))
    .addAnalyzer(Compliance("top star_rating", "star_rating >= 4.0"))
    .addAnalyzer(Correlation("total_votes", "star_rating"))
    .addAnalyzer(Correlation("total_votes", "helpful_votes"))
    .run()
}

val metrics = successMetricsAsDataFrame(spark, analysisResult)
```

5. Use `VerificationSuite` to define data quality checks:

```
import com.amazon.deequ.{VerificationSuite, VerificationResult}
import com.amazon.deequ.VerificationResult.checkResultsAsDataFrame
import com.amazon.deequ.checks.{Check, CheckLevel}

val verificationResult: VerificationResult = {
  VerificationSuite()
    .onData(dataset)
    .addCheck(
      Check(CheckLevel.Error, "Review Check")
        .hasSize(_ >= 3000000)
        .hasMin("star_rating", _ == 1.0)
        .hasMax("star_rating", _ == 5.0)
        .isComplete("review_id")
        .isUnique("review_id")
        .isComplete("marketplace")
        .isContainedIn("marketplace", Array("US", "UK", "DE", "JP", "FR"))
        .isNonNegative("year")
    )
    .run()
}

val resultDataFrame = checkResultsAsDataFrame(spark, verificationResult)
```

6. Call `resultDataFrame.show(truncate=false)` to inspect the data quality check results. You can also look at the computed metrics using `VerificationRe sult.successMetricsAsDataFrame(spark, verificationResult).show(trun cate=False)`.

For more information, you can refer "Test Data Quality at Scale with Deequ" (*https://oreil.ly/MwxKP*) in the documentation.

Automated Data Quality Checks and Error Handling

In addition to automating the monitoring and maintenance of your data processing pipelines, you can also leverage AWS services to implement automated data quality checks and error handling mechanisms.

For example, you can use AWS Glue DataBrew to define and apply data validation rules, such as checking for missing values, detecting and handling sensitive information, or deduplicating records. These data quality checks can be integrated into your ETL workflows, ensuring that your data is consistently clean and reliable before it is processed or loaded into your data warehouse or data lake.

Furthermore, you can leverage the error handling capabilities of services like AWS Glue and AWS Step Functions to automatically retry failed tasks, route data to dead-letter queues for further investigation or trigger custom remediation actions in response to specific error conditions. This helps to ensure the overall resilience and fault tolerance of your data processing pipelines, minimizing the impact of temporary failures or issues.

Troubleshooting and Performance Tuning

As data processing pipelines grow in complexity and scale, identifying and resolving performance issues and bottlenecks becomes increasingly crucial. In this section, we will explore various techniques and best practices for troubleshooting and optimizing the performance of your data processing pipelines. We can use AWS CloudWatch Logs to review detailed error messages. From the error message, we can identify the kind of error. Some of the common errors are discussed in the following sections.

Connection timed out errors

This error means that a client or an AWS service is unable to establish a connection with the service/server that it is trying to connect to within a set period. This often indicates a problem with network connectivity. When it comes to networks, there are multiple layers you need to check:

VPC configuration

Most AWS resources like Amazon Redshift, OpenSearch, or EMR clusters are deployed within VPCs. For successful connections to them, both the client and server should either be in the same VPC or have proper connectivity between different VPCs. If services are in different VPCs, you'll need to either:

- Set up VPC peering to connect the VPCs.

- Create a VPC endpoint to enable service communication.

For example, when an AWS Glue job is attempting to connect to Amazon Redshift to perform data processing, you may see a connection timed out error. To fix this you need to ensure that the Glue connection is using a VPC, and the VPC that the connection is using is the same as the VPC in which the Redshift cluster is deployed.

Security group settings

Security groups act as virtual firewalls controlling traffic to and from resources. The security group attached to your target resource must explicitly allow incoming traffic from the client/service trying to connect. For example, if an AWS Glue job needs to access Redshift, the Redshift cluster's security group must permit incoming traffic from AWS Glue.

Access denied exceptions

These typically occur when an AWS service or user attempts to perform an action they don't have permission for. This is typically due to insufficient or incorrectly configured IAM policies. Do the following to fix these:

- Ensure the IAM role associated with your analytics service has the necessary permissions. For example, an Amazon Athena query might fail if its execution role lacks permissions to read from the S3 bucket containing the data.

- Some AWS resources have their own policies (e.g., S3 bucket policies, Amazon Redshift grants). Ensure that these policies are allowing the action you are intending to perform. For example, if Amazon QuickSight can't access an S3 bucket, check if the bucket policy allows QuickSight's access.

Example scenario: Consider an Amazon EMR cluster trying to read data from an S3 bucket:

- Verify the EMR cluster's IAM role has S3 read permissions.

- Check that the S3 bucket policy allows access from the EMR cluster's IAM role.

- If using KMS encryption, ensure the EMR role has permissions to use the KMS key.

Troubleshooting tips:

- Review CloudTrail logs to identify the exact permissions being denied.
- Use the IAM Policy Simulator to test and validate IAM policies.
- For S3 access issues, enable S3 access logs to see detailed access attempts.

Throttling errors

Throttling errors happen when too many API requests are made in a short time. For example, too many concurrent Glue job starts, excessive API calls to QuickSight, rapid S3 requests, or too many query requests through Redshift data API or Athena. The solution is to implement exponential backoff and request rate limiting. With exponential backoff, when an error occurs, you retry the request with progressively longer wait times between attempts (for example, waiting one second, then two seconds, then four seconds, and so on), helping to avoid overwhelming the service while still attempting to complete the operation. Rate limiting complements this by controlling how many requests you make within a specific time period—for instance, limiting to 100 requests per second.

In addition, consider partitioning your data more effectively to distribute requests. For S3, avoid having a large number of small files; instead, use AWS Glue ETL to periodically compact your files. Monitor your usage and adjust your service quotas if necessary. For Athena, consider using workgroups to manage query concurrency and execution.

Resource constraints

Resource constraints can occur when the service doesn't have necessary resources to complete the task, for example, a Lambda function doesn't have enough memory or processing power to handle the analytics task. To fix it, increase resource allocation, if it is fixed. For example, increase the memory allocation for your Lambda function, which also increases CPU power proportionally.

CI/CD Pipelines

Implementing a CI/CD (continuous integration/continuous deployment) pipeline for AWS analytics projects can streamline the process of developing, testing, and deploying analytics solutions. Here is an overview of how you can set up a CI/CD pipeline for an AWS analytics workflow involving services like Amazon Redshift, Glue, Athena, EMR, or other related data processing tools.

Continuous integration (CI)

Continuous integration is a software development practice where developers frequently integrate their code changes into a central repository, after which automated builds and tests are run. This helps catch issues quickly and ensures the mainline codebase is always in a deployable state. You can use AWS CodeBuild (*https://oreil.ly/MA8Ru*) for CI, which is a fully managed build service that compiles source code, runs tests, and produces deployment-ready artifacts without requiring you to manage build servers. It offers preconfigured environments for popular programming languages like Java, Node.js, Python, etc. It scales automatically and allows custom configurations while charging only for actual usage.

Continuous deployment (CD)

Continuous deployment is a software release process that automatically deploys every change that passes through the production pipeline to production environments. There is no human intervention, and deployments happen automatically and seamlessly. You can use AWS CodePipeline (*https://oreil.ly/Z1DER*) for CD. It is a continuous delivery service you can use to model, visualize, and automate the steps required to release your data pipeline.

Version Control and Collaboration

Store your data processing scripts, transformation code, and infrastructure as code using AWS CodeCommit. AWS CodeCommit is a version control service that enables you to privately store and manage Git repositories in the AWS Cloud. You can implement workflows that include code reviews and feedback by default, and control who can make changes to specific branches.

Infrastructure as Code

Infrastructure as code (IaC) is the practice of managing and provisioning cloud infrastructure resources through defining them using code and configuration files instead of manually clicking through consoles or running scripts. Just like application code is written in programming languages and version controlled, infrastructure definitions are also codified using AWS services like CloudFormation or the Cloud Development Kit. This allows infrastructure to be built in a repeatable, consistent manner across multiple environments through configuration files that are version controlled. Infrastructure deployments can then be automated and tracked just like deploying application code changes.

AWS CloudFormation

AWS CloudFormation allows you to define and provision your entire AWS infrastructure resources using simple text files. Instead of clicking around the AWS

Console to manually provision resources like Amazon Redshift data warehouses, AWS Glue jobs, Lambda functions, databases, load balancers, etc., you can specify all your required resources and their configurations in a CloudFormation template file in JSON or YAML format. This template acts like an executable blueprint for your infrastructure. You just provide this template to CloudFormation, and it provisions all the resources specified in the template in an automated, coordinated manner. It figures out dependencies and runs everything in the right order. A CloudFormation template has the following three main sections:

Parameters

Parameters allow you to pass in values to the template when you create a stack. These could be things like instance types, CIDR blocks, database passwords, etc., that may vary across environments. Parameters make your templates reusable.

Resources

This is the core section where you define all the AWS resources you want CloudFormation to create (e.g., EC2 instances, S3 buckets, RDS databases, etc.). You specify the resource type and configuration properties.

Outputs

Outputs are values that CloudFormation exposes after creating resources. For example, it could output the public IP of an EC2 instance or the endpoint for an Elastic Load Balancer (ELB). You can use these outputs for data that may be needed after provisioning.

For more information on CloudFormation, you can refer to the documentation (*https://oreil.ly/AUW1M*). Following is a sample CloudFormation template that deploys an AWS Glue database:

```
---
AWSTemplateFormatVersion: '2010-09-09'
# Sample template to create a glue database
# Input parameters
Parameters:
  CFNDatabaseName:
    Type: String
    Default: cfn-mysampledatabse
# Resources section defines resources that will be deploys
Resources:
# Create an AWS Glue database
  CFNDatabaseFlights:
    Type: AWS::Glue::Database
    Properties:
      CatalogId: !Ref AWS::AccountId
      DatabaseInput:
        Name: !Ref CFNDatabaseName
        Description: Database to hold tables for flights data
        LocationUri: s3://public-us-east-1/flight/2016/csv/
```

The great thing is that this template is reusable. You can use the same template to rebuild your infrastructure over and over in any region, ensuring consistency across environments. If you need to make changes, you just modify the template file and CloudFormation updates only what needs to be changed.

AWS Serverless Application Model

AWS Serverless Application Model (AWS SAM) is an open source framework that makes it easier to build serverless applications on AWS. Building CloudFormation templates for multiservice applications can be complex. AWS SAM, which is an extension of CloudFormation, helps simplify this for serverless services:

- It provides shorthand syntax to define serverless resources like AWS Lambda functions, Amazon API Gateway APIs, and Amazon DynamoDB tables in simple and clean CloudFormation templates.

- It handles all the CloudFormation syntax around Lambda functions, API Gateways, etc., so you can focus on just the application logic.

- It supports modern development workflows including local development, testing, and debugging of serverless apps before deploying to AWS.

- It extends and builds on top of AWS CloudFormation, so you get all the deployment capabilities of CloudFormation.

- It allows organizing related components and resources into versioned units that can be deployed together as one entity.

- It lets you define and share common configurations across resources like memory, timeouts, etc.

- It enables infrastructure-as-code best practices for serverless apps by defining them declaratively.

AWS Cloud Development Kit (AWS CDK)

AWS CDK is an open source framework that allows you to define and provision your cloud application resources using popular programming languages like TypeScript, Python, Java, and .NET. Instead of JSON or YAML configuration files, you write actual code to model your infrastructure. With the CDK, you can leverage their existing integrated development environments (IDEs) with benefits like autocompletion, inline documentation, and coding best practices.

Under the hood, the CDK uses AWS CloudFormation; however, you don't have to deal with raw CloudFormation syntax. The core building blocks are called "constructs," which represent components like Amazon Redshift data warehouses, AWS Glue jobs, EC2 instances, Lambda functions, databases, etc. The AWS CDK includes the AWS Construct Library (*https://oreil.ly/5Xw6i*), containing constructs representing many AWS services. By composing these constructs together using programming languages, you can programmatically define and provision even complex cloud architectures on AWS through code.

AWS also provides CDK extensions for Kubernetes (AWS Cloud Development Kit for Kubernetes (*https://oreil.ly/8D2Fp*)) and Terraform (AWS Cloud Development Kit for Terraform (*https://oreil.ly/OfiP4*)) to model infrastructure on those platforms using code as well. Refer to the AWS Samples GitHub repository for CDK examples (*https://oreil.ly/ijGQY*).

Choosing the right IaC solution

Consider the aspects discussed in Table 6-2 when choosing the right IaC solution for your use case.

Table 6-2. Choosing the right IaC solution

Aspect	SAM	CDK	CloudFormation
Best for	Simple serverless applications, Lambda-focused workloads	Complex infrastructure, full-stack applications	Traditional infrastructure, broad AWS resource management
Learning curve	Lower: simple YAML syntax	Higher: Requires programming knowledge (TypeScript/Python/Java/etc.)	Medium: YAML/JSON syntax with complex template structure
Infrastructure scope	Specialized for serverless (Lambda, API Gateway, DynamoDB)	All AWS services and resources	All AWS services and resources
Template format	YAML/JSON	Programming languages (TypeScript, Python, Java, C#, Go)	YAML/JSON
Development speed	Quick for serverless apps	More setup initially, but faster for complex systems	Slower: requires detailed template writing
Testing capabilities	Basic unit testing, local Lambda testing	Comprehensive testing options, unit/integration testing	Basic template validation
Team background	Better for teams familiar with CloudFormation	Better for teams with programming experience	Better for teams familiar with infrastructure-as-code concepts
Reusability	Limited to CloudFormation macros	High: can create custom constructs and libraries	Medium: using nested stacks and parameters

Disaster Recovery and High Availability

Disaster recovery (DR) and high availability (HA) refers to a system's ability to remain operational and accessible for extended periods, minimizing downtime through redundancy and fault tolerance. In the context of analytics systems, high availability ensures that data and analysis capabilities remain accessible even when components fail or during maintenance windows.

Recovery point objective (RPO) and recovery time objective (RTO) are crucial metrics in disaster recovery planning. RPO defines the maximum acceptable amount of data loss measured in time—essentially how far back in time you might need to go when recovering data. For example, an RPO of one hour means you could lose up to one hour of data in a disaster scenario. RTO, on the other hand, specifies how quickly you need to restore your service to operation after a disruption. An RTO of four hours means your system must be back online within four hours of an incident.

The first step in curating a DR plan is defining maximum acceptable data loss (RPO) and maximum acceptable service downtime (RTO) by working with your business stakeholders. For example, not all business reports are business critical so it's important that your DR plans are aligned with the severity of the outage.

With these concepts in mind, organizations typically choose between three main resilience architectures:

Active-active setup
Maintains multiple fully operational environments simultaneously, with data continuously synchronized between them. This approach offers the highest availability and lowest RTO, as traffic can immediately shift to the functioning environment if one fails. However, it's the most complex and expensive option, requiring careful management of data consistency and operational processes across environments.

Active-passive architecture
Maintains a primary environment that handles all workloads while keeping a standby environment ready for failover. This approach balances cost and resilience, offering good recovery times while avoiding the complexity of active-active setups. The standby environment remains ready but inactive, regularly receiving data updates from the primary system. While this means paying for resources that aren't actively used, it provides a reliable failover option when needed.

Backup-restore approach
Represents the most basic resilience strategy, regularly creating backup copies of data that can be restored when needed. While this is the most cost-effective option, it typically results in longer recovery times and more potential data loss, as you can only restore to the last backup point. This approach works well for systems with less stringent RPO and RTO requirements.

AWS analytics services protect against disruptions through various HA features. Serverless analytics solutions include built-in HA capabilities that work automatically without additional configuration. For provisioned services like Amazon EMR, Amazon MSK, Amazon OpenSearch, and Amazon Redshift, you can manually configure high-availability options to match your specific business continuity requirements.

These features ensure your analytics workloads remain operational even during potential outages or disasters. Let's understand how to configure high-availability options in these services.

HA for Amazon EMR clusters on EC2

When you launch an Amazon EMR cluster, you can choose to have either one or three primary nodes (master nodes). Having three primary nodes instead of one provides high availability, which means if one of the primary nodes fails, the other two can take over and keep the cluster running without interruption. This way, the primary node is not a single point of failure. Amazon EMR can automatically replace a failed primary node with a new one that has the same configuration and settings as the original.

To further improve cluster availability, you can use Amazon EC2 placement groups. This ensures that the primary nodes are placed on different underlying hardware, so if one hardware fails, the other primary nodes can still function.

HA for Amazon Redshift provisioned clusters

Amazon Redshift is a fully managed service that comes with built-in resiliency. It has an automatic fault detection system that swiftly identifies and replaces any failed nodes within your cluster. When a replacement is necessary, Redshift seamlessly integrates the new node into your existing infrastructure with minimal disruption. To expedite the recovery process, Redshift prioritizes the restoration of your most frequently accessed data, retrieving it first from Amazon S3. In addition to this, Redshift offers features that you can configure based on your RPO and RTO requirements.

Availability Zone (AZ) failure recovery

Two main approaches exist in case of an unlikely event that an entire AZ fails:

Active-passive (relocation)
> For single-AZ deployments, Redshift automatically relocates clusters to another AZ when needed. Recovery typically takes 10–60 minutes and requires cluster relocation to be enabled.

Active-active (multi-AZ)
> Provides simultaneous operation across multiple AZs with automatic failover in under 60 seconds. This offers the highest availability but is only available for provisioned clusters, not Redshift Serverless. This option has an RPO of 0 (i.e., your data remains up-to-date and current in the event of a failure). With multi-AZ, Amazon Redshift offers a 99.99% service-level agreement (SLA), compared to 99.9% for a single-AZ deployment.

Backup and restore

Amazon Redshift provisioned clusters provide two types of backups: automated snapshots and manual snapshots:

Automated snapshots

Redshift provisioned clusters take automated snapshots every 8 hours or after 5 GB of data changes per node, whichever comes first. While automated snapshots are enabled by default with a one-day retention period, you can configure them to be retained for up to 30 days without incurring additional charges. You can also create custom snapshot schedules with a minimum frequency of one hour. These automated snapshots are automatically deleted after their retention period expires, and they're also removed when the cluster is deleted.

Manual snapshots

Manual snapshots allow you to retain backups for any length of time. You can convert automated snapshots to manual snapshots or create new manual snapshots. They are retained indefinitely by default, though you can specify custom retention periods. These snapshots incur storage charges until deleted. Manual snapshots can be shared with other AWS accounts, enabling collaborative data access and querying.

In Amazon Redshift Serverless, there are also two types of backups—recovery points and manual snapshots:

Recovery points

Recovery points are automated backups created every 30 minutes and retained for 24 hours before automatic deletion. These recovery points can be converted to manual snapshots for extended retention and to enable point-in-time recovery capabilities.

Manual snapshots

Serverless manual snapshots work the same way as manual snapshots do in provisioned clusters. They are manual backups that users create explicitly for their serverless namespace. These snapshots can be restored to either a new serverless namespace or a provisioned cluster, with the flexibility to choose node types and quantities when restoring to a provisioned environment.

Both snapshots and recovery points represent the entire state of objects and data in your Redshift cluster or serverless namespace at that point in time. You can tag snapshots and recovery points with key-value metadata for better organization. All backups are stored encrypted on Amazon S3. You can restore an Amazon Redshift data warehouse from any snapshot. Tables can be excluded from snapshots to reduce backup time/space by specifying the BACKUP NO option on your tables.

Region failure recovery

While Redshift operates within a single region, cross-region disaster recovery is supported through cross-region snapshots. By enabling this feature, all snapshots (automated and manual) are automatically copied to a designated backup region, allowing cluster restoration in a new region if the primary region fails. Figure 6-25 shows an architecture diagram illustrating how cross-region snapshot copy works in Redshift.

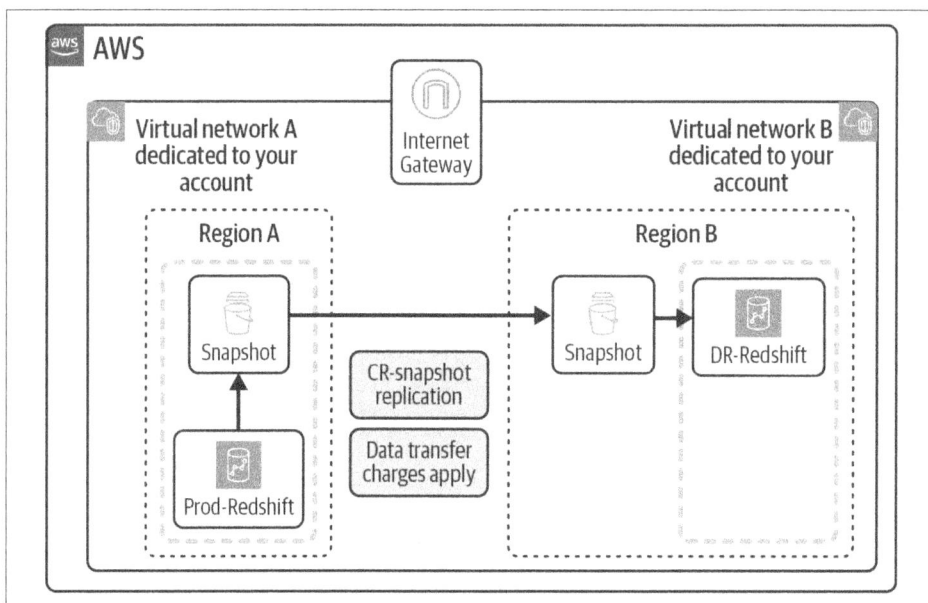

Figure 6-25. Cross-region snapshot recovery in Amazon Redshift

For more information about how to enable cross-region snapshots, refer to the following:

- Configuring cross-region snapshot copy for a non-encrypted cluster (*https://oreil.ly/VG-D7*)
- Configure cross-region snapshot copy for an AWS KMS-encrypted cluster (*https://oreil.ly/3JVYJ*)

HA for Amazon MSK

Amazon MSK is designed with high availability as a core feature. By default, clusters are distributed across multiple Availability Zones, and single-AZ deployments aren't permitted. For maximum resilience, you can deploy across three AZs. The service's tiered storage capability separates compute and storage resources, allowing you to configure both local and remote storage tiers, which enhances cluster availability and resilience. For protection against regional failures, Amazon MSK Replicator enables data replication between MSK clusters, whether they're in the same region or different regions. This multilayered approach ensures robust disaster recovery capabilities for your Kafka workloads.

HA for Amazon OpenSearch

Data nodes are responsible for processing indexing and search requests in the Amazon OpenSearch domain. You can deploy your data nodes across multiple Availability Zones to improve the availability of your domain. With a multi-AZ deployment, your domain can remain available even when a full AZ becomes unavailable.

You can use dedicated cluster manager (CM) nodes (*https://oreil.ly/FfDOn*) in your OpenSearch clusters to improve cluster stability. A CM node tracks the cluster's health, the state and location of its indexes and shards, the mapping for all the indexes, and the availability of its data nodes, and it maintains a list of cluster-level tasks in process. This offloading of cluster management tasks increases the stability of your domain.

OpenSearch organizes data through indexes, which are logical collections of documents. These indexes are divided into primary shards for parallel processing, with each shard serving as a physical storage and processing unit. The service supports both primary and replica shards, with replicas providing data durability and improved search performance. When a primary shard fails, OpenSearch Service automatically promotes a replica to primary status. The service strategically places primary and replica shards across different nodes and AZs to maximize reliability.

Cost Optimization for Data Pipelines

As data processing pipelines grow in scale and complexity, it's crucial to continuously optimize costs to ensure the long-term sustainability and profitability of your data-driven initiatives. By leveraging the right mix of AWS services and cost optimization strategies, you can maximize the value derived from your data processing investments while minimizing unnecessary expenses.

In this section, we'll explore various approaches to cost optimization for your data pipelines, including the use of serverless and on-demand services, optimizing resource utilization, monitoring and controlling data transfer costs, and leveraging caching and materialized views for Amazon Athena.

Leveraging Serverless Services

One of the key ways to optimize costs for your data processing pipelines is to take advantage of AWS's serverless services. These services, such as Amazon Athena,

AWS Glue, and AWS Lambda, allow you to scale resources up and down as needed, without the overhead of managing and provisioning underlying infrastructure.

By using serverless services, you can avoid the need to overprovision resources to handle peak loads, as these services will automatically scale to meet your processing requirements. Additionally, with a pay-as-you-go pricing model, you pay only for the resources you actually consume, reducing the risk of idle or underutilized capacity.

Similarly, for compute-intensive workloads, you can leverage Amazon EC2 Spot Instances, which provide access to spare Amazon EC2 capacity at significantly discounted rates. While Spot Instances can be interrupted, they can be a highly cost-effective option for certain types of data processing tasks, such as batch ETL jobs or exploratory data analysis.

Autoscaling

Autoscaling can scale resources up and down based on demand, optimizing costs by avoiding overprovisioning. Amazon EMR has Managed Scaling to automatically size the cluster based on workload metrics. AWS Glue provides autoscaling for ETL and streaming jobs to allocate only the required computing resources. Amazon Redshift offers AI-driven autoscaling to automatically scale based on your preferences. Application autoscaling can be used to dynamically scale resources for services like Amazon EMR, Amazon MSK, and EC2 instances.

Tiered Storage

Tiered storage enables you to balance cost and performance based on your data usage patterns. Several AWS analytics services and storage services offer tiered storage capabilities, including Amazon OpenSearch Service (with Hot, UltraWarm, and Cold storage), Amazon MSK (with tiered storage for brokers), and Amazon S3 (with Intelligent-Tiering, Glacier, and Glacier Deep Archive).

Columnar Formats

For optimal data analysis in Amazon S3, remember to compress your data files, partition them using columns that are frequently used in filter conditions, and utilize columnar file formats like Parquet. While these practices have been discussed in previous chapters, their importance warrants emphasis as they are fundamental to efficient data storage and retrieval.

Monitor and Control Data Transfer Costs

Another important aspect of cost optimization for data pipelines is the management and control of data transfer costs. AWS charges for data transferred between different

AWS services or regions, and these costs can quickly add up, especially if you have large volumes of data flowing through your pipelines.

To mitigate these data transfer costs, you should monitor your data transfer patterns and identify opportunities to optimize data ingestion, processing, and storage workflows. This may involve strategies like:

- Minimizing data transfers between AWS services and regions
- Leveraging AWS Direct Connect or VPC Peering to reduce data transfer costs between your VPCs
- Compressing or aggregating data before transferring it between services

Additionally, you can use AWS Cost Explorer and AWS Budgets to track and manage your data transfer expenses, setting alerts and budgets to proactively identify and address any cost overruns.

Follow Cost Optimization Best Practices

In previous chapters, we discussed cost optimization and performance optimization techniques for each major analytical service. For example, using Spot Instances for re-retryable jobs on EMR on EC2 clusters, using the Flex execution class in AWS Glue, using reserved instances in Amazon Redshift provisioned clusters, choosing columnar file formats to improve Athena query performance, using Athena capacity reservations to provide necessary compute capacity for queries, etc. Review and revise these best practices and ensure you follow them. Best practices are crucial for passing the exam.

Conclusion

Throughout this chapter, we have explored the key aspects of data operations and support, equipping you with the knowledge and skills required to automate data processing, analyze data, maintain and monitor data pipelines, and ensure data quality. By mastering these techniques, you have become a valuable asset in your organization's data-driven journey, enabling seamless data operations and supporting the delivery of actionable insights.

From orchestrating data pipelines using AWS Step Functions, Amazon Managed Workflows for Apache Airflow (MWAA), and AWS Glue workflows, to analyzing data with Amazon QuickSight, Amazon Athena, and Amazon Redshift, you have developed a comprehensive understanding of the data operations and support capabilities within the AWS ecosystem.

Moreover, you have learned how to effectively monitor and maintain your data processing pipelines, leveraging services like Amazon CloudWatch, AWS CloudTrail, and system-specific monitoring tools to ensure the overall health and reliability of your data infrastructure. You've also explored strategies for ensuring data quality and reliability, including the use of AWS Glue DataBrew for data validation and cleansing, and techniques for detecting and handling sensitive data.

To further optimize your data processing pipelines, you have discovered cost-saving approaches, such as leveraging serverless and on-demand services, optimizing resource utilization, and implementing caching and materialized views. Additionally, you have learned how to integrate various AWS services, including AWS Lambda, Amazon API Gateway, and Amazon Redshift, to enhance the automation, security, and flexibility of your data processing workflows.

As you continue to navigate the evolving landscape of data-driven decision making, the knowledge and skills gained from this chapter will empower you to design, implement, and maintain efficient and reliable data processing pipelines that support your organization's strategic objectives. By leveraging the comprehensive capabilities of the AWS ecosystem, you will become a key contributor in unlocking the full potential of your organization's data assets and driving impactful, data-driven initiatives.

Next, let's try to validate our knowledge with a few practice questions that may help you prepare for the AWS Certified Data Engineer Associate certification exam.

Practice Questions

These practice questions may help you understand what kind of questions to expect on the exam so you can prepare accordingly. The answers are listed in the Appendix.

1. A company's analytics team frequently queries partitioned data stored in Amazon S3 using Amazon Athena. The team reports that query planning is becoming increasingly slow as their dataset grows, particularly due to the high number of partitions. Which solutions would most effectively improve query planning performance while maintaining the existing architecture? (Select two.)

   A. Implement AWS Glue partition indexing with partition filtering enabled.

   B. Configure Athena partition projection based on partition patterns.

   C. Convert all data files to the Apache Parquet format with Snappy compression.

   D. Create a new partitioning scheme based on the most common WHERE clause columns.

   E. Use AWS Glue jobs to combine smaller partition files into larger files (over 128 MB).

2. A data engineer is using an Amazon Redshift data warehouse to load and analyze historical data in batches. The engineer faced a failure when running a COPY command to load data from Amazon S3 to the Redshift table. A data engineer

must choose a system table in Amazon Redshift that records the load failures. Which table views should the data engineer use to meet this requirement?

A. STL_LOAD_INFO

B. STL_LOAD_ERRORS

C. STL_ALERT_EVENT_LOAD

D. SYS_QUERY_HISTORY

3. A company has deployed a serverless ETL pipeline where AWS Lambda functions orchestrated by Step Functions process data from Amazon Kinesis and store results in Amazon DynamoDB. After deployment, the Step Functions executions consistently fail during the Lambda invocation steps. What troubleshooting approaches would be most effective in identifying the root cause? (Select two.)

A. Check IAM configuration and permissions by validating the Step Functions execution role, reviewing Lambda function permissions, verifying Kinesis read access, and confirming DynamoDB write permissions.

B. Examine network configuration details by verifying VPC endpoint configurations, checking Lambda function VPC settings, reviewing security group rules, and analyzing subnet routing tables.

C. Modify the state machine workflow by adding wait states between steps, implementing choice states, increasing timeout values, and adding parallel processing branches.

D. Update the deployment process to use AWS SAM for deployment, implement blue-green deployment, add CloudFormation drift detection, and enable automatic rollbacks.

E. Enhance error tracking setup by configuring x-ray tracing, setting up CloudWatch alarms, enabling detailed logging, and implementing custom metrics.

4. A data architect wants to ensure that their Amazon Redshift deployment is highly available with the least operational overhead. What options can they choose? (Select two.)

A. Choose the multi-AZ deployment option in Amazon Redshift.

B. Choose the multiregion deployment option in Amazon Redshift.

C. Copy snapshots to another region using cross-region snapshot copy.

D. Create two Amazon clusters in two AZs and perform parallel data loads into each of them.

5. The company must schedule an Amazon Redshift stored procedure that can run for more than 15 minutes at 8:00 p.m. every night. Which solution will meet this requirement with the least cost and effort?

A. Create an MWAA DAG to run the stored procedure at 8:00 p.m. each day.

B. Create a Step Functions state machine to call a Lambda that calls the Redshift data API to run the CALL stored procedure statement.

C. Use the scheduler in Query Editor v2 in Amazon Redshift to schedule the stored procedure run.

D. Use an AWS Glue workflow to call a Glue Python job that calls the Redshift data API to run the CALL stored procedure statement.

6. A data engineer must orchestrate a data pipeline that consists of two AWS Glue crawlers and one AWS Glue job. Which solution will meet these requirements with the least management overhead and most cost efficiency?

A. Use an AWS Step Functions workflow to run the three Lambda functions. Two of them will run crawlers and one will run the AWS Glue job.

B. Use an Apache Airflow workflow that is deployed on an Amazon EC2 instance. Define a directed acyclic graph (DAG) in which the first two tasks will call Lambda functions that will run the AWS Glue crawlers while the third task will call a Lambda function to run the AWS Glue job.

C. Use an AWS Glue workflow to orchestrate the AWS Glue crawlers and AWS Glue job.

D. Use an MWAA directed acyclic graph (DAG) with three tasks. The first two tasks will call Lambda functions that will run the AWS Glue crawlers and the third task will call Lambda to run the AWS Glue job.

7. A healthcare analytics company needs to analyze patient treatment data stored in Amazon S3 (several terabytes) using Amazon Athena. The data is updated daily through AWS Glue jobs that run overnight. Multiple departments run identical reports throughout the day, causing unnecessary query processing and increased costs. The reports need to reflect data no older than four hours to meet compliance requirements.

The analytics team needs to optimize Athena usage while maintaining data freshness requirements and minimizing additional infrastructure costs.

Which solution is most cost-effective with the least operational overhead?

A. Implement Athena workgroups with query result caching enabled, setting a cache duration of four hours for frequently run queries.

B. Convert all data files to Apache ORC format with Zlib compression and implement partitioning by date.

C. Deploy an Amazon RDS read replica to cache frequently accessed data from Athena queries.

D. Create materialized views in Athena for commonly used query patterns.

E. Implement an Amazon DynamoDB table to cache query results with a TTL of four hours.

8. A data analyst wants to create a visualization but is not well versed with Amazon QuickSight. How can the analyst develop visualizations with the least support?

   A. Using Amazon Q to generate visuals using natural language prompts.

   B. Read through the Amazon QuickSight documentation and master all visuals.

   C. Try different visualization options in Amazon QuickSight.

   D. Use the autograph feature in QuickSight.

9. A retail company deployed an application on Amazon EC2 instances inside a VPC. In order to detect suspicious traffic patterns or potential security threats the company wants to analyze VPC flow logs. Which solution will meet these requirements with the least operational overhead most cost-effectively?

   A. Publish flow logs to Amazon S3 in Parquet format. Use Amazon Redshift provisioned clusters for analytics.

   B. Publish flow logs to Amazon CloudWatch. Use Amazon Redshift provisioned clusters for analytics.

   C. Publish flow logs to Amazon CloudWatch. Use Amazon Athena for analytics.

   D. Publish flow logs to Amazon S3 in Parquet format. Use Amazon Athena for analytics.

10. A healthcare provider processes patient records using AWS Glue ETL jobs. The data team needs to implement strict data validation to ensure Patient IDs follow a specific format, date fields are within valid ranges, required fields are not null, and numeric values fall within acceptable medical ranges.

    What is the most efficient way to implement these data quality requirements in their ETL pipeline?

    A. Implement using AWS Glue Data Quality rules. Example:

    ```
    dq_rules = {
        'Patient_Validation': {
            'PatientID': 'Matches "[A-Z]{2}\\d{6}"',
            'DateOfBirth': 'Between "1900-01-01" AND current_date',
            'BloodPressure': 'Between 60 AND 200' }}
    ```

    B. Create custom PySpark validation functions.

    C. Use AWS Glue Data Catalog validation.

    D. Implement AWS Lake Formation tags.

Additional Resources

- SQL analytics using Amazon Athena (*https://oreil.ly/OIMHV*)
- Amazon Redshift SQL reference (*https://oreil.ly/j7Li8*)
- Data Quality Definition Language (DQDL) (*https://oreil.ly/92ddz*)
- AWS Glue notebooks (*https://oreil.ly/t1ZLq*) and Amazon EMR notebooks (*https://oreil.ly/t79DL*)
- "Amazon S3 Backups" (*https://oreil.ly/LKVEo*)
- "Amazon Redshift Backups and Snapshots" (*https://oreil.ly/H5LNF*)
- Cost optimization in AWS analytics services (*https://oreil.ly/9_3uW*)
- Performance efficiency in AWS analytics services (*https://oreil.ly/piuMn*)
- Reliability in AWS analytics services (*https://oreil.ly/xgH_U*)

## CHAPTER 7

Data Security and Governance

In today's internet world, the size of data is growing exponentially and is expected to grow even faster in the future. Irrespective of data size, you need to prioritize data security to avoid unauthorized data access and utilize governance to make sure your data meets the expected quality, has the required access controls in place to expose the data to your consumers, and has audit controls in place that can help you meet regulatory compliance needs.

In this chapter, we will dive deep into the following topics:

- How to secure your AWS workload with VPC and security groups
- How to integrate user authentication and authorization with AWS IAM
- How to enable data security and privacy by integrating different AWS services
- Understanding the different data governance pillars and which AWS services can be integrated to meet your requirements

At the end of this chapter, we will also provide a set of practice questions related to data security and governance that can help you understand the kind of questions you can expect and prepare for the role and certification exam accordingly. Let's dive deep into the specific topics.

Network Security

In this section, we will explain how you can secure the networking elements involved in your AWS data analytics workloads with Amazon VPC, security groups, VPC endpoints, and more.

Amazon VPC Overview

An Amazon VPC (Virtual Private Cloud) (*https://oreil.ly/kEfzI*) is a logical construct that enables you to define a network perimeter for a set of workloads that you plan to isolate from other workloads. VPC integration resembles a network in an on-premises data center.

When you create an AWS account, for every region, you will have a default VPC that allows you to create EC2 instances within the VPC. You can create additional VPCs as needed to isolate workloads. An Amazon VPC will have a subnet for every Availability Zone (AZ) in a specific region, and you can define the subnets as private or public by controlling the network traffic to them through the internet gateway.

Let's assume you have a web application, which has web servers for the application and a database for persistent storage. As a general practice, both components should be in a single VPC, with the web servers in the public subnet so that they are accessible by public users and the database in the private subnet.

Figure 7-1 represents a reference architecture for this setup. You can read more on this in the AWS documentation (*https://oreil.ly/T2T8G*).

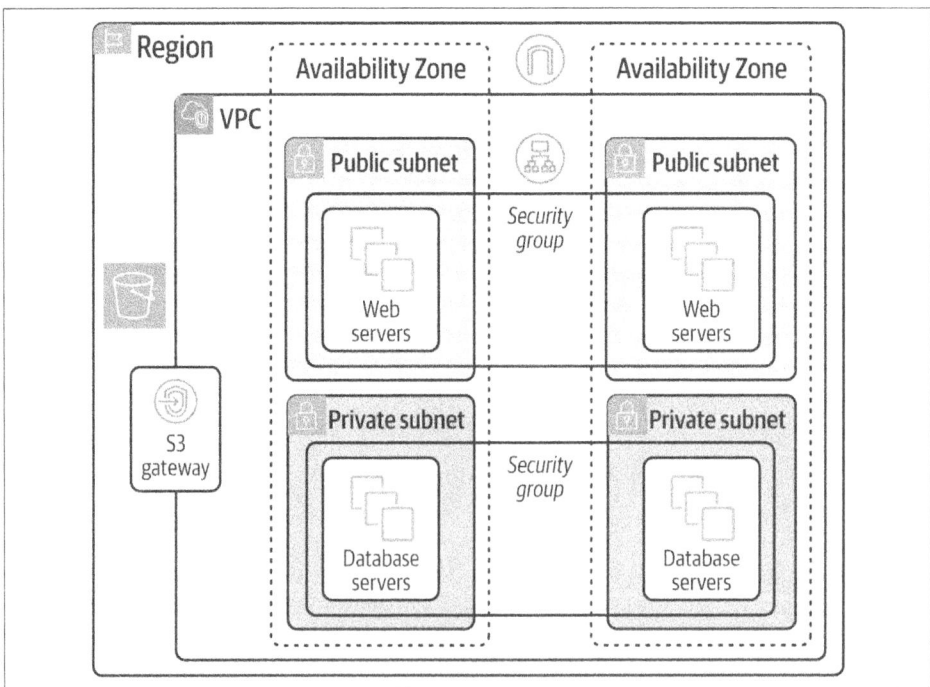

Figure 7-1. Web application with database deployed in a VPC with two Availability Zones

Security Groups Overview

A security group is similar to a virtual firewall, with which you can control traffic to a single instance or cluster. As shown in Figure 7-1, security groups provide restrictions so that only the web servers can access the database server, which is available in the private subnet so no other application inside or outside the VPC can access it. Let's learn some of the best practices you should follow while integrating security groups.

> Learn more from the AWS documentation (*https://oreil.ly/5Lb50*) on how you can control traffic using security groups.

Best Practices for Configuring Security Groups for Your Workloads

The following list provides some of the common best practices you should follow while configuring security groups for your workloads:

Don't configure 0.0.0.0/0 as the inbound access in security groups.
: To follow the least-privilege principle, you should never configure 0.0.0.0/0 as the source for the inbound connection in your security groups, which means anyone inside or outside of AWS can access it. Ideally you should control access by specifying specific IPs as the source or a specific security group as the source.

  You may configure 0.0.0.0/0 as the outbound connection, if you have a use case where your application needs to pull data or code from public repositories. For example, your EC2 instance might need to pull the latest code from a public GitHub repository or your Lambda function needs to connect to a few third-party APIs to fetch data.

Try to group security groups that are related for operational efficiency.
: Assume you have multiple Lambda functions that need to connect to a single RDS (Relational Database Service) database for different functionalities. You have the option to create a security group for each Lambda function and configure them in the RDS for inbound access, but it may not be operationally efficient to manage.

  The ideal way to implement this will be to create one single security group or a limited number of security groups by grouping related Lambda functions and including them for inbound access in the RDS security group.

Avoid using the default VPC or default security group for production workloads.
: When you create an AWS account, you will have a default VPC and security groups readily available to integrate in your workloads. The default VPC and security groups may not have least-privilege access integrated, which means

they are not recommended for production workloads that may require keeping resources within a private subnet or do not need access through the public internet.

So, it's best to create new VPCs and security groups and give them the specific permissions they need for your workload.

As an example, let's look at how you can configure a VPC and security group for one of the analytics services such as Amazon EMR.

Configuring a VPC and Security Group for an Amazon EMR Cluster

Amazon EMR provides multiple deployment options such as EMR on EC2, EMR on EKS, EMR Serverless, and EMR on AWS Outposts. Let's take the example of EMR on EC2 to understand how you can configure a VPC and security group for the cluster.

You can configure an EMR cluster in a public subset or private subnet depending on your use case. Figure 7-2 represents an EMR on EC2 cluster deployment in a private subnet of the VPC that connects to Amazon S3 using VPC endpoints. We will explain more about VPC endpoints later in the chapter.

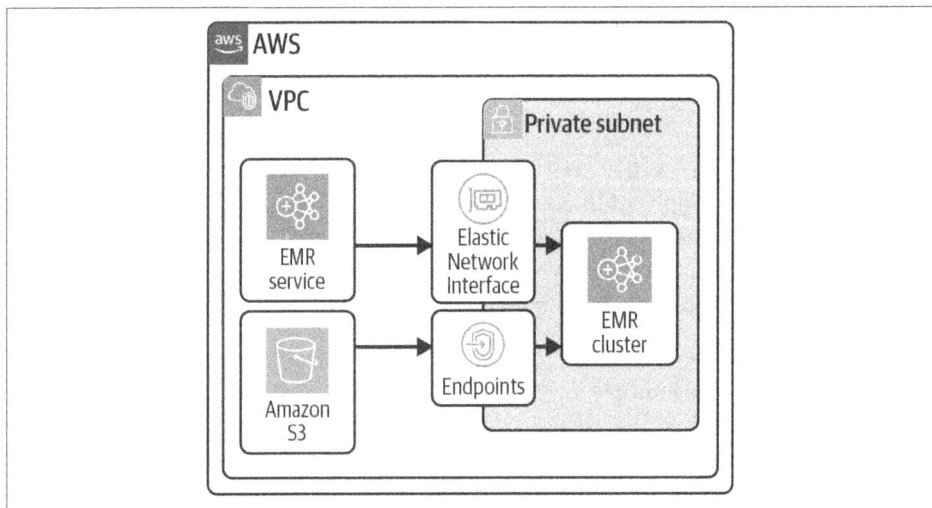

Figure 7-2. EMR cluster deployed in a private subnet

When you deploy an EMR cluster in a private subnet, the following some considerations you need to take note of:

- Once you have deployed an EMR cluster in a private subnet, you cannot modify the setup to take it to a public subnet or vice versa.

- Not all AWS services provide VPC endpoints; for services that do not have endpoints, plan to integrate a NAT instance/NAT Gateway or Internet Gateway.
- EMRFS (EMR File System) integrates Amazon DynamoDB under the hood, so if you have deployed an EMR cluster in a private subnet, then plan to configure the route from the private subnet to the DynamoDB service.

> Please read the EMR documentation (*https://oreil.ly/XnN9U*) to learn more about networking options available for Amazon EMR.

Managed Services Versus Unmanaged Services

Before discussing the difference between managed and unmanaged services, let's take a look at the shared responsibility model published by AWS (*https://oreil.ly/GMt3G*), which is represented in Figure 7-3.

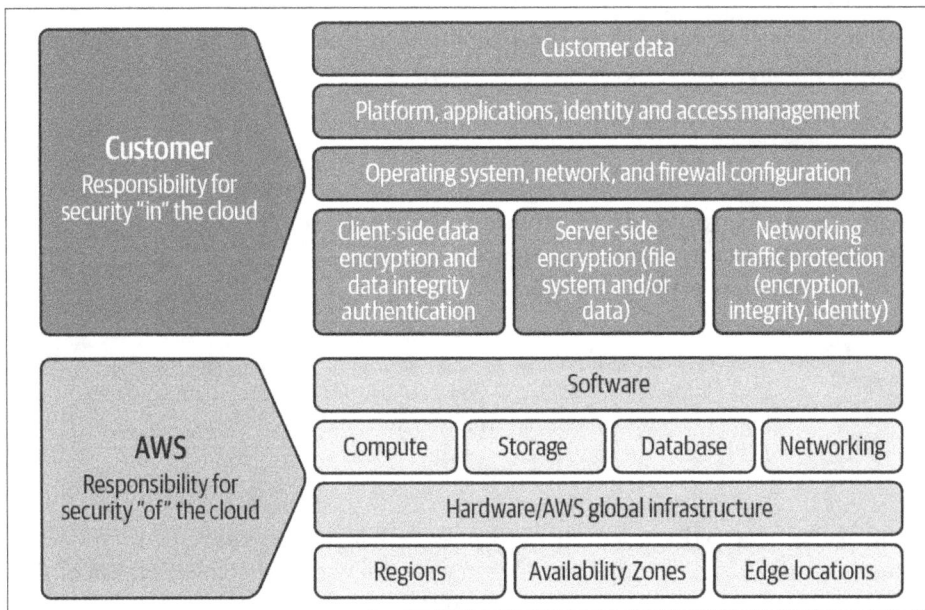

Figure 7-3. Shared responsibility model published by AWS

As you can see from Figure 7-3, there is a division of responsibilities between AWS and its customers. For example, the global hardware infrastructure and related software are managed by AWS, whereas the applications deployed on the infrastructure and the network as well as security configurations are managed by the customers. This scope changes for AWS-managed services as some of the network and security configurations are also managed by AWS.

With AWS-managed services you can achieve better operational efficiency as you do not need to put effort into configuring network or security controls to integrate your hardware infrastructure, which may reduce the chance of human errors. In addition, you will have better built-in scalability and better support from AWS. On the other hand, you will also have less flexibility with the configurations and may see the increased cost that comes with fully managed solutions.

VPC Endpoints Overview

Let's look at another example to understand this process better. Assume you have an EC2 instance within your VPC running an application that uploads images to Amazon S3. If you have not configured VPC endpoints for your VPC with S3 service, then the application running on the EC2 instance connects to S3 using the public internet. This approach is not secure and also not performant.

VPC endpoints are virtual devices that are highly available and scalable. Using VPC endpoints, you can enable a private connection to supported AWS services, so that you avoid routing through the public internet and stay within the AWS network to obtain better performance and security. There are two VPC endpoints: interface endpoints and gateway endpoints. Figure 7-4 provides a great explanation of how AWS VPC endpoints work.

> You can read more about VPC endpoints in the AWS documentation (*https://oreil.ly/Sf2m_*). You can also learn more about updating VPC endpoint policies from the documentation (*https://oreil.ly/JK4Pi*).

A few of the managed services in AWS provide native integration with VPC endpoints as managed VPC endpoints. Let's review a few of the analytics services that provide default integration with VPC endpoints.

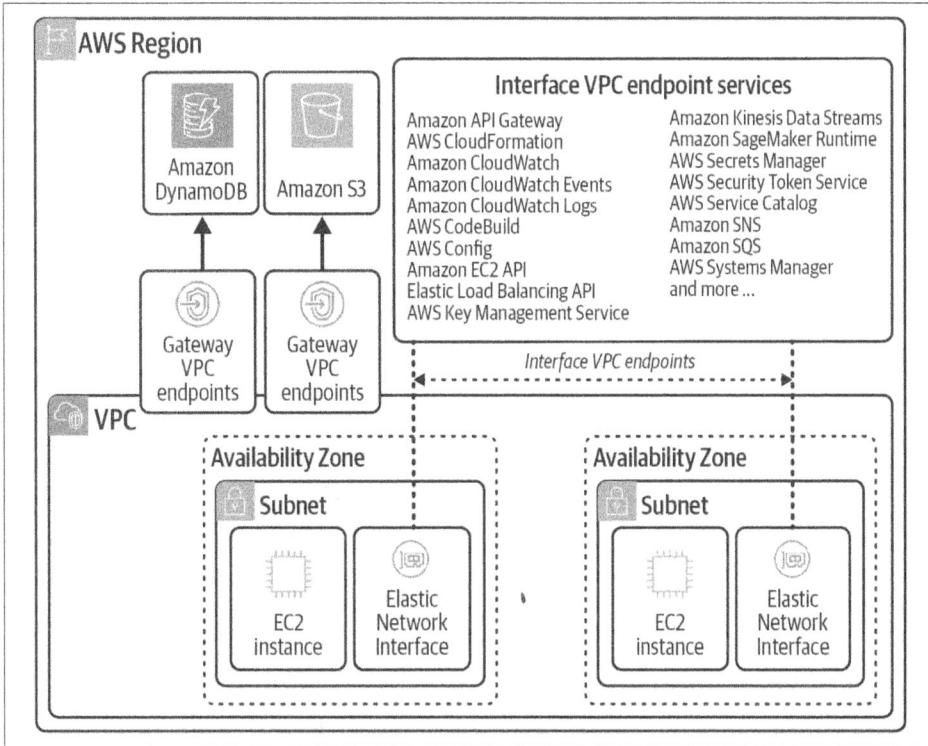

Figure 7-4. VPC endpoint integration in an AWS Region

Redshift-managed VPC endpoints

If you have client tools running in a VPC and would like to enable connection to a Redshift cluster or workgroup that is in a different VPC, then you can take advantage of Redshift-managed VPC endpoints to set up a private connection between them. This also works if you have a second VPC in a different AWS account with the additional step of using a Redshift cluster account (granter) to provide access to the connecting account (grantee). Redshift-managed VPC endpoints also work with Redshift Serverless workgroups.

You need to add the IAM policies `ec2:CreateVpcEndpoint` or `ec2:ModifyVpcEnd point` to your role to create or modify managed VPC endpoints in Redshift. Note that Redshift-managed VPC endpoints are not accessible from the internet.

There are a few considerations you need to be aware of while integrating Redshift-managed VPC endpoints:

- If you are configuring a Redshift provisioned cluster, then it should have the RA3 node type and a subnet group. In addition, make sure you have enabled cluster relocation (*https://oreil.ly/efJOB*) or multi-AZ (*https://oreil.ly/FiqFW*).
- The default port for accessing the Redshift cluster through the security group is 5439. You need to make sure to define valid port ranges of 5431–5455 and 8191–8215 for security group access for the VPC endpoints to work.
- If an Availability Zone is down, Redshift does not create an Elastic Network Interface for another AZ. You may have to create a new VPC endpoint.

Please read the Redshift documentation (*https://oreil.ly/EyK4t*) to learn more.

OpenSearch Service–managed VPC endpoints

Similar to Amazon Redshift–managed VPC Endpoints, if client applications running in your VPC need to access an OpenSearch domain then you can leverage Open-Search Service–managed VPC endpoints. This will enable a private connection as if the OpenSearch Service is available within your VPC. You can configure OpenSearch Service VPC endpoints if your VPC is in another AWS account as well.

Figure 7-5 represents the Amazon OpenSearch Service and AWS PrivateLink within the same VPC sharing a private connection. AWS PrivateLink is a service that enables private connectivity between resources within AWS VPCs with other services, including other AWS services, services hosted in other AWS accounts, and AWS Marketplace services. It routes traffic through the Amazon network, ensuring data stays private and secure without exposing it to the public internet.

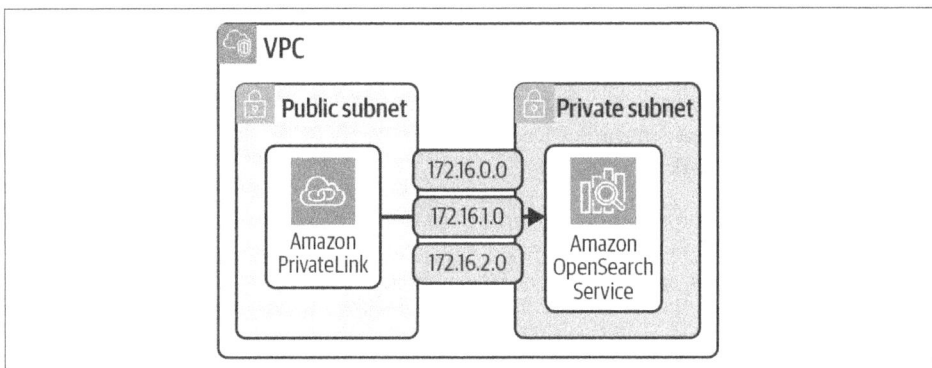

Figure 7-5. Amazon OpenSearch Service–managed VPC endpoints

The following are a few considerations to take note of when integrating OpenSearch Service–managed VPC endpoints:

- OpenSearch domains marked for public access cannot be accessed using interface VPC endpoints; they integrate only with domains launched within a VPC.
- You can connect only to OpenSearch domains available within the same Region.
- The HTTP protocol is not supported, so make sure to leverage HTTPS only.
- You cannot create an interface VPC endpoint with AWS CloudFormation, so the only options are creating one through the OpenSearch Service console or APIs.

For a complete list of considerations and limitations, please refer to AWS documentation (*https://oreil.ly/6eJMZ*). Next, let's understand how you can integrate authentication and authorization with the help of AWS IAM service.

User Authentication and Authorization

AWS Identity and Access Management (*https://oreil.ly/BFm0X*) (IAM) is a global service in AWS that enables authentication to AWS and provides flexibility to configure authorization through IAM groups (*https://oreil.ly/lkqlt*), roles (*https://oreil.ly/6ej3M*), and policies (*https://oreil.ly/JNWRP*). Let's dive deep into the different authentication and authorization mechanisms you can integrate with AWS IAM.

Authenticating Users with IAM Credentials

The simplest way to get started is by creating an IAM user with security credentials (access key and secret key) that you can use to log in to the AWS Console. You can configure IAM policies for the user to provide access to specific AWS service actions. Optionally you can add multiple users to IAM groups and attach permissions to the IAM group too.

Integrating AWS IAM user security credentials directly into your application or server is not a recommended approach, as there is a chance the security credentials might be misused; it is also not operationally efficient. This authentication method is ideal if there are non-AWS tools or applications hosted outside of AWS that plan to interact with AWS APIs.

IAM Role-Based Authentication and Authorization

IAM role-based authentication and authorization is the most common and recommended mechanism in AWS. The IAM role will have some set of permissions attached to it and IAM users or AWS services assume that role to perform the actions authorized to the IAM role.

Read more from AWS documentation on how you can create (*https://oreil.ly/nw7F4*) and use (*https://oreil.ly/gW88c*) an IAM role. Please make sure to follow the least-privilege principle, which means instead of providing full access to any service, you assign the exact actions you need for the service and also restrict access to the specific Amazon Resource Name (ARN) of the resource.

Service-Linked Roles

A service-linked role (*https://oreil.ly/R2vZC*) is a role that is linked to an AWS service directly and includes all the permissions that service needs to call other AWS services on your behalf. Service-linked roles will have inline policies that are related to that service and you cannot add managed policies to them.

Please note that a service role and service-linked roles are different: a service role is an IAM role that a service assumes to perform actions on your behalf, whereas service-linked roles are owned by the service and you cannot modify them.

Managed Versus Self-Managed Policies

For authorization, you need to assign policies to IAM roles or users; the policies can be managed policies, inline policies, or custom policies. Managed policies are provided by AWS and cannot be edited. You can create IAM roles and attach predefined managed policies such as read-only access or full access to a service. Managed policies help reduce operational overhead as all required permissions are already packaged and new permissions are automatically updated by AWS. Inline policies are directly embedded into the role and are not available for reuse or attachment to multiple roles. This is not the recommended approach, unless it's highly specific to that role itself.

Custom policies are new policies where you can include the exact specific actions you need on a service and the specific ARN on which you need the permission. This is the recommended method that follows the least-privilege principle, as managed policies may include a broader set of permissions that you may not need. Custom policies can be reused, which means once created, you can attach the same policy to multiple roles as applicable.

Enable Single Sign-on with AWS IAM Identity Center

AWS IAM Identity Center (*https://oreil.ly/roMOb*) is built on top of AWS IAM to centralize and simplify access to multiple AWS accounts and SAML-enabled cloud applications (e.g., Salesforce, Microsoft 365, Box), and to help integrate with Active Directory or other directory services for single sign-on (SSO). It eliminates the administrative complexity and operational overhead of managing permissions for each AWS account separately and boosts employee productivity. Let's understand how AWS IAM Identity Center integrates with a few of the AWS analytics services.

IAM Identity Center integration with AWS Lake Formation

AWS Lake Formation works with IAM Identity Center, which means you can integrate Identity Center with your organization's directory service to authenticate users to AWS with SSO and then data lake administration can configure fine-grained access on the data lake for the same users with Lake Formation permissions. Figure 7-6 provides a screenshot of the AWS Lake Formation console where you can grant permission to users or groups authenticated through IAM Identity Center.

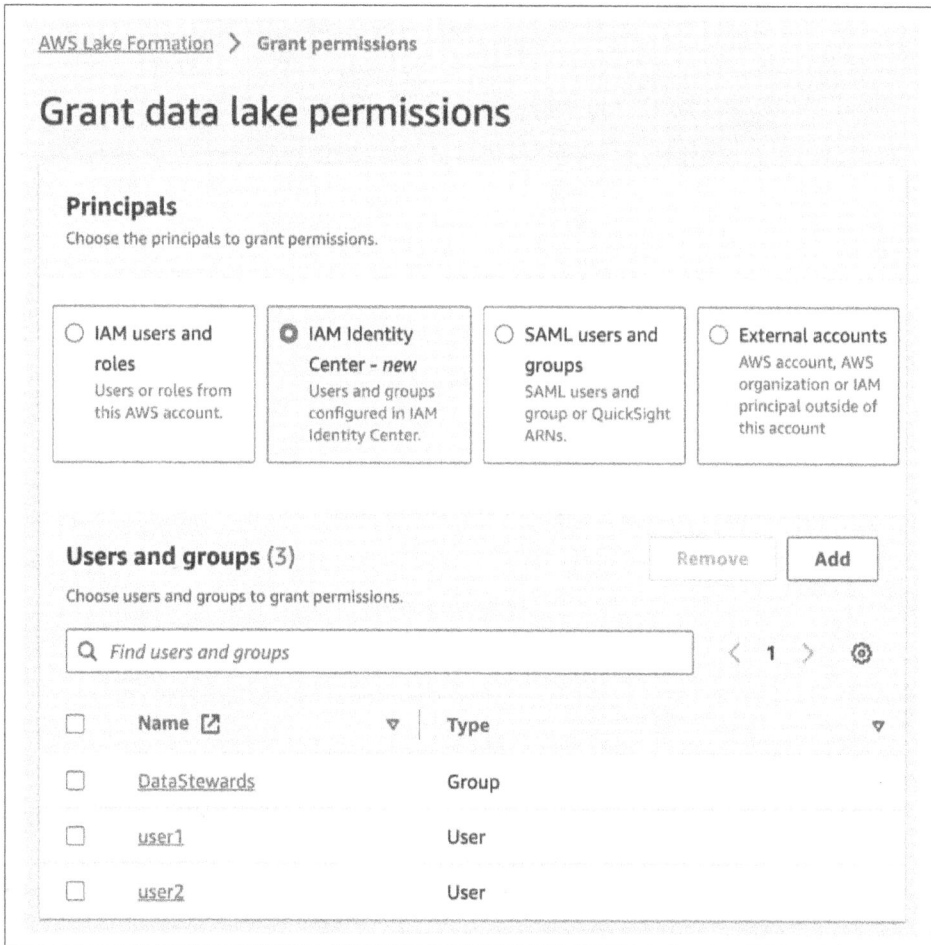

Figure 7-6. Lake Formation grant for IAM Identity Center principals

Lake Formation provides credential vending for temporary access to S3 data. Please note when leveraging AWS IAM Identity Center authenticated users in Lake Formation, by default CloudTrail includes the IAM role only as part of its audit logs to interact with the analytics services.

If you have used a user-defined role to register the Amazon S3 data location with Lake Formation, you can opt in to include the IAM Identity Center user's context in the CloudTrail events and then track the users that access your resources. To include object-level Amazon S3 API requests in CloudTrail, you need to enable Cloud-Trail event logging for Amazon S3 buckets and objects. Please read the AWS documentation (*https://oreil.ly/3GDRJ*) to learn how to enable this.

IAM Identity Center integration with Amazon DataZone

As you learned in Chapter 3, Amazon DataZone enables an organization to create a data lake, data warehouse, or machine learning environment, and helps integrate data access control, data analytics, data sharing, and data lineage across AWS accounts within an organization.

If you have configured IAM Identity Center, then you can enable SSO users or groups to log in to the DataZone domain data portal. To enable Identity Center integration in DataZone, you can edit the DataZone domain configurations and select the "Enable users in IAM Identity Center" checkbox where you can choose from the following two assignment modes:

Implicit user assignment
    With this option, all the users added to the IAM Identity Center directory can access the specified DataZone domain.

Explicit user assignment
    With this option, you can choose specific users or groups of the IAM Identity Center directory who will have access to the specified DataZone domain.

> Please note, once your domain is updated, you cannot change it later.

Next, let's understand what other mechanisms you can follow to secure your datasets in addition to AWS IAM.

Data Security and Privacy

Apart from IAM role-based authorization, there are several other data security factors that need to be addressed. Let's review what other data security approaches you should consider as a way to avoid unauthorized access to your datasets. The following are a few of the approaches you can consider to secure your data.

Secure Data in Amazon S3

You can avoid unauthorized access to Amazon S3 buckets or prefixes by specifying which IAM role, group, or user can access the S3 prefix. Optionally, you can also specify bucket policies to control cross-account access or provide access to external customers.

You can also consider integrating resource-based policies (*https://oreil.ly/JgLdd*) with which you can configure who has access to the resource (e.g., Amazon S3) and what actions they can perform on it. To identify which AWS services support resource-based policies, please check the AWS documentation (*https://oreil.ly/gY9vy*). For all S3 buckets, it is recommended to disable public access unless it contains website media assets that need to be publicly available.

Apart from the data in object stores, you may have data in databases hosted in AWS. Let's see how you can secure the database credentials to avoid unauthorized access.

Manage Database Credentials

It is not recommended to hardcode database credentials in applications or pass them through environment variables, as that creates a security risk of unauthorized users misusing them. In AWS, integrating AWS Secrets Manager (*https://oreil.ly/YUU7X*) is recommended, where you can store your database credentials, control access to secrets using IAM roles, and let your application code refer to Secrets Manager keys to get the credentials.

AWS Secrets Manager is a fully managed service that enables secured storage of database or other credentials and API keys; it also enables auto-rotation and retrieval of sensitive information. Figure 7-7 presents a high-level architecture showing how AWS Secrets Manager can be integrated to secure your database credentials. AWS Secrets Manager provides end-to-end encryption and integration with Amazon CloudWatch and AWS CloudTrail for logging and auditing of the key usage.

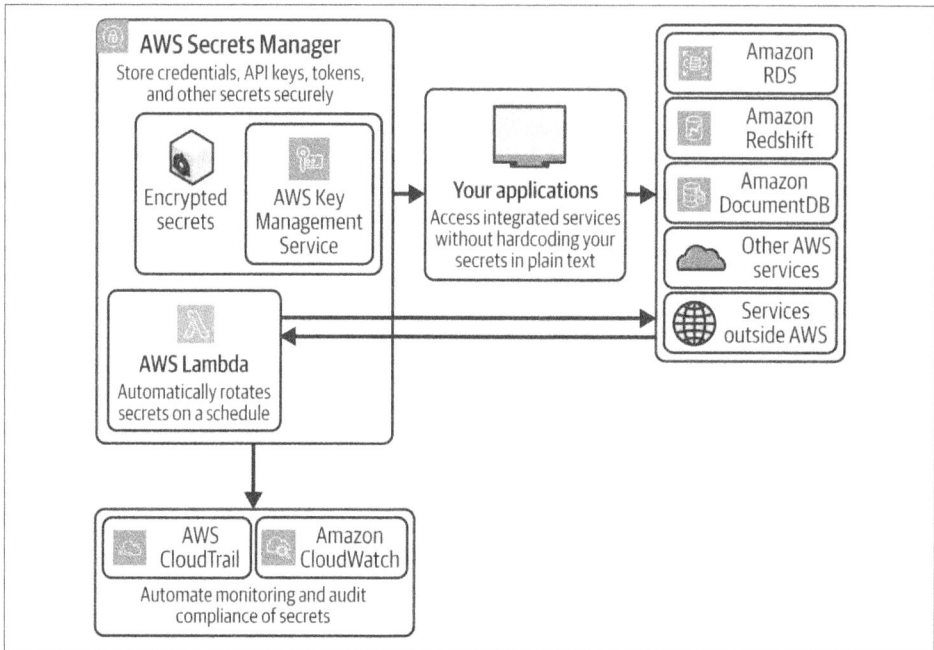

Figure 7-7. AWS Secrets Manager for database credentials management

Data Encryption and Decryption and Managing the Encryption Keys

Even if we have integrated user authentication and the right level of authorization with AWS IAM, we still need to make sure the data is encrypted with cryptographic keys and that only the authorized user can decrypt it for consumption. We need to make sure the data is encrypted both at rest and in transit.

There are two ways you can enable encryption at rest for your datasets. One is where the encryption and decryption happens on the server side, typical within the server infrastructure. The second one is client side, which means you encrypt the data first with your own key and then send or upload it to the server for storage. You can follow either server-side or client-side encryption based on your use case.

For encryption in transit, you should integrate SSL/TLS certificates that can encrypt data while it is getting transferred or moved to or from AWS services. All the AWS services that move data—such as AWS Data Migration Service (DMS), DataSync, AWS Backup, and AWS VPN—support encryption in transit by default.

Next, let's learn about AWS KMS and how it enables easier and safer management of encryption keys.

Managing Encryption Keys with AWS KMS

AWS Key Management Service (KMS) is a managed service that makes it easier to create and manage cryptographic keys in AWS. It natively integrates with several other AWS services to enable a centralized way to manage keys. You can look at the AWS documentation (*https://oreil.ly/JreX7*) to find all the services that integrate with AWS KMS.

You can benefit from certain advanced features of AWS KMS such as multiregion KMS keys (replica of KMS keys in each region), creating KMS keys in an external key store (protecting AWS resources using cryptographic keys outside of AWS), and connecting to KMS keys using private VPC endpoints.

Figure 7-8 is a high-level architecture taken from the AWS documentation (*https://oreil.ly/e8eLz*) that represents how you can integrate AWS KMS with other AWS services and how you can leverage Amazon CloudWatch for logging and AWS CloudTrail for auditing user or API actions related to KMS.

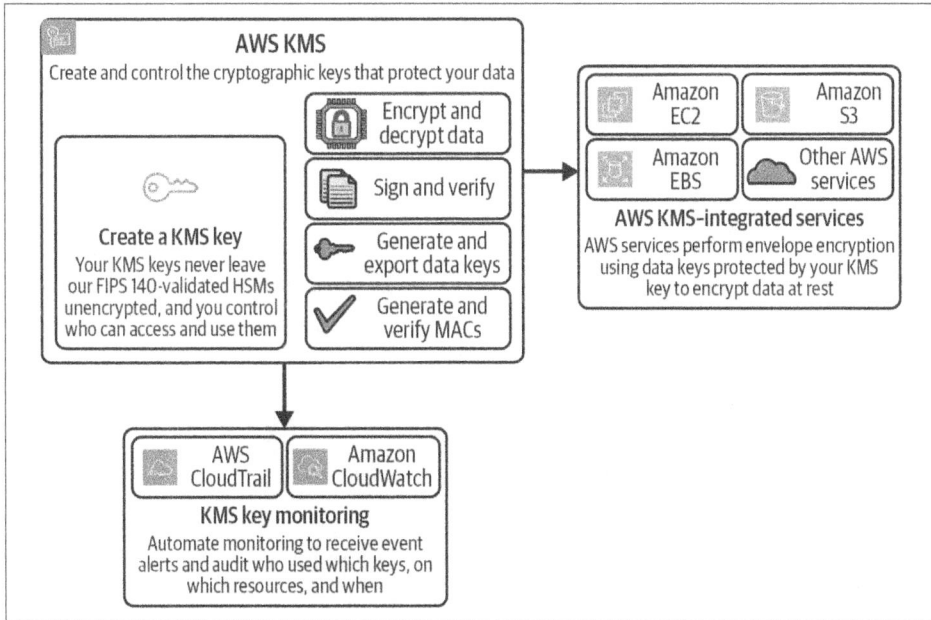

Figure 7-8. AWS KMS integration with some AWS services

Next, let's look at the different ways you can enable encryption in AWS services, which are either natively supported by the service or integrated with AWS KMS.

Enabling encryption and managing keys in AWS

Some AWS services such as Amazon S3 support encryption at rest natively (SSE-S3), whereas a few other services integrate keys from AWS KMS. Let's dive deep into the encryption options available in Amazon S3 to better understand the features:

- Server-wide encryption:
  - *SSE-S3*: Server-wide encryption (SSE) with Amazon S3 is the default encryption applied to all buckets in S3; the key is managed by Amazon S3. If you need to apply different encryption, then you can specify this while uploading objects to the bucket through the PUT request.
  - *SSE-KMS*: Server-side encryption with AWS KMS enables you to manage your own keys (e.g., create, edit, view, disable, enable, delete, rotate, monitor) with AWS KMS, which Amazon S3 will leverage to encrypt objects.
  - *DSSE-KMS*: Dual-layer server-side encryption (DSSE) with AWS KMS enables you to apply dual-layer encryption and can help organizations meet compliance standards that require multilayer encryption when objects are uploaded to Amazon S3.
  - *SSE-C*: This option enables you to provide a custom key that will be used by Amazon S3 to encrypt your objects.
- Client-side encryption:
  - With this option, when you upload objects to Amazon S3, it encrypts objects with the key provided by you with AES-256 encryption and then removes the key from memory. You need to provide the same encryption key while decrypting the objects.

Please note that when you integrate keys managed by AWS KMS, both the data and the KMS key should be in the same region.

Best practices for managing keys with AWS KMS

The following are some of the best practices you can follow while integrating AWS KMS:

Cross-account key sharing
> If you plan to share data with a consumer in another AWS account, then instead of creating separate KMS keys in each AWS account, you should plan to share the KMS key with the other account. Please refer to the AWS documentation (*https://oreil.ly/QacQq*) to learn how you can share KMS keys.

Enable multifactor authentication (MFA)
> For additional security, enable MFA for specific KMS actions such as `PutKeyPolicy` and `ScheduleKeyDeletion`.

Leverage key aliases
> With the help of key aliases, you can abstract away the key ARN or key ID from the end users and they can just refer to the key alias for integration. This also helps if you have a multiregion application, where instead of a region-specific ID, you can refer to the same key alias across regions.

Enable KMS key rotation
> AWS KMS supports automatic key rotation every year by default. In addition, you have the flexibility to define your key rotation frequency from 90 days to 7 years. This improves security as the application refers to key aliases and the encryption keys are rotated automatically based on the frequency you defined. In addition, for customer-managed keys, you have the flexibility to invoke key rotation.

> In addition, please refer to the AWS documentation (*https://oreil.ly/d0wxI*) for additional security best practices related to AWS KMS. Similar to Amazon S3, if you need to understand how other AWS services integrate with AWS KMS, then please refer to the AWS documentation (*https://oreil.ly/q622z*).

Enabling Encryption in AWS Analytics Services

Most AWS services support mechanisms to encrypt data at rest and in transit. Let's try to understand the encryption options available in a few of the popular AWS services.

AWS Glue

In AWS Glue, you can enable encryption for Glue Data Catalog and for Glue ETL jobs. When you enable encryption, you can configure the KMS key you would like to use for the encryption and decryption process. Figure 7-9 represents the two settings you can enable to encrypt metadata and connection credentials.

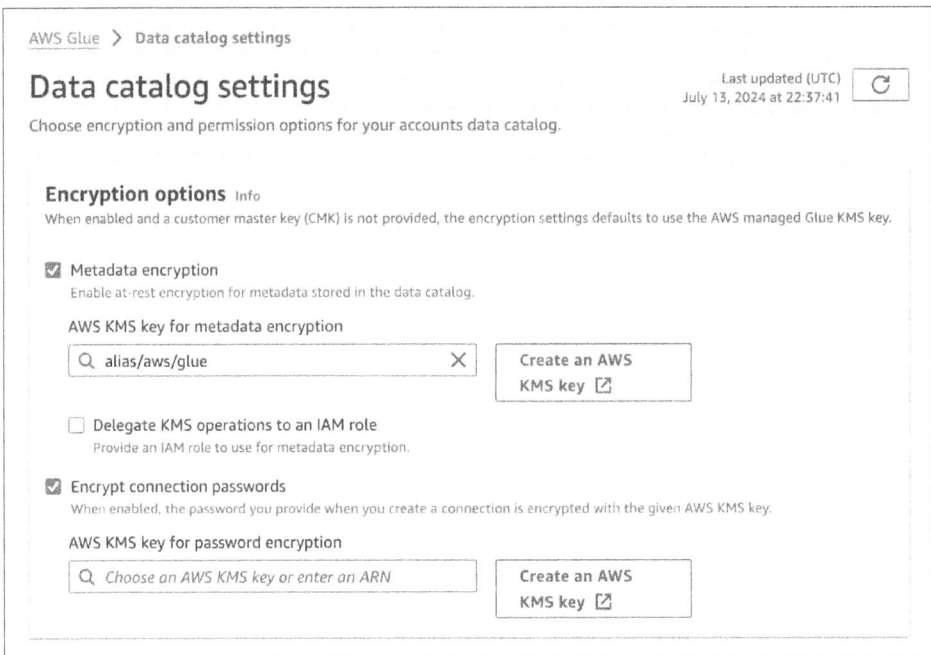

Figure 7-9. AWS Glue Data Catalog settings for encrypting metadata and connection credentials

Figure 7-10 represents Glue ETL job encryption settings, where you can encrypt data in Amazon S3 with SSE-S3 or SSE-KMS keys, encrypt logs in CloudWatch with the KMS key of your choice, and also enable encryption for the metadata stored by the Glue Job Bookmarks feature.

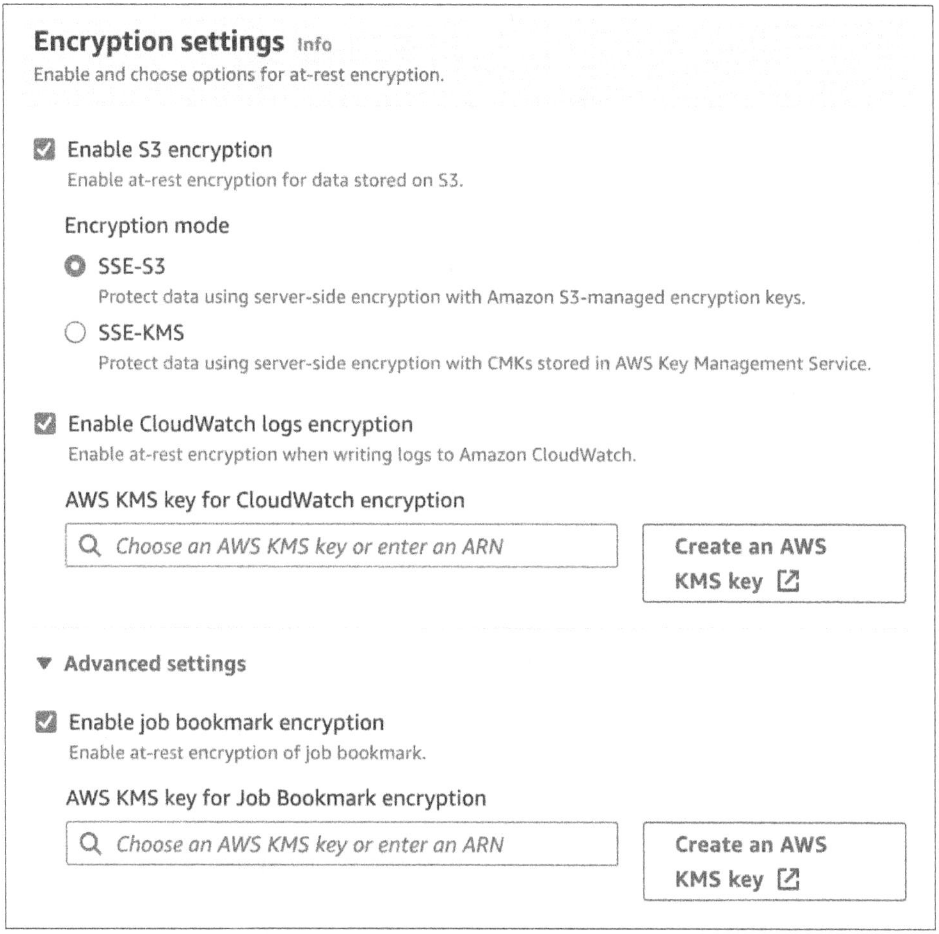

Figure 7-10. AWS Glue ETL job settings to enable encryption

Amazon EMR

Amazon EMR provides integration with AWS KMS for encryption at rest and in transit. In addition to that, it also provides other encryption options to support open source applications. Figure 7-11 represents the encryption options EMR supports, including:

- Encryption for data stored in Amazon S3 with SSE-S3, SSE-KMS, and data getting transferred over EMRFS with TLS.

- Encryption at rest for data stored in the write-ahead log (WAL) with SSE-EMR-WAL or SSE-KMS-WAL.

- Enable encryption for the data available in HDFS using AES-256 encryption.
- Default NVMe encryption for the EC2 instance store volume and default encryption options available for EBS volumes (*https://oreil.ly/oZ2Fc*).
- Encryption in transit depends on the support available for the open source applications as listed in the documentation (*https://oreil.ly/rQlQd*).

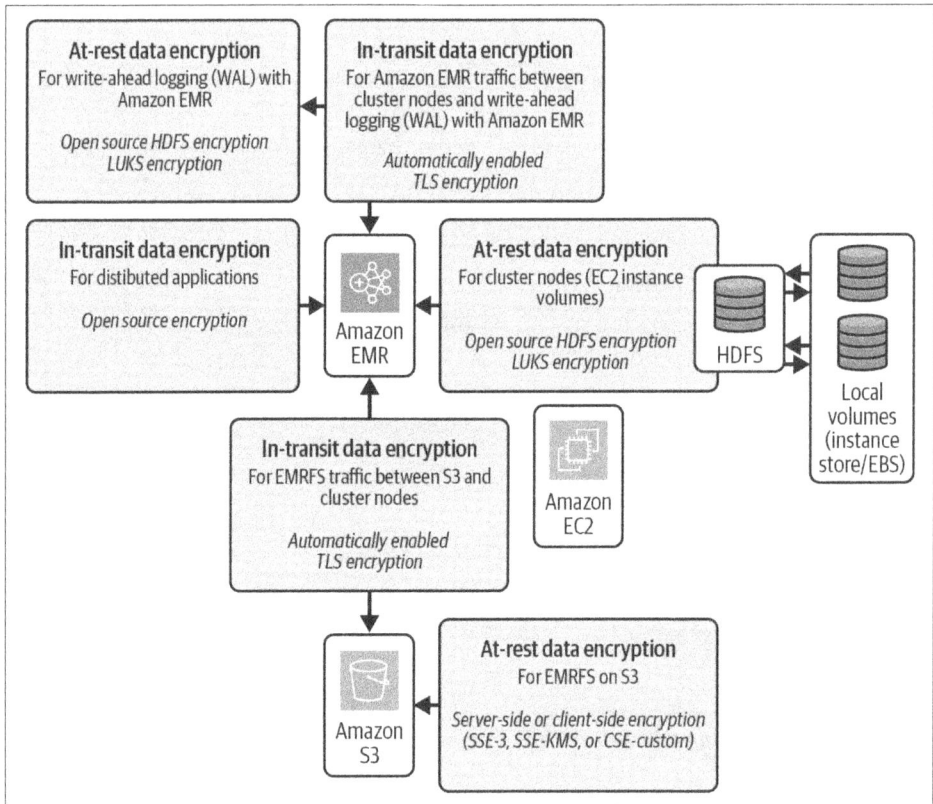

Figure 7-11. Encryption options available in Amazon EMR

Read the AWS documentation (*https://oreil.ly/z16Uc*) to learn more about the encryption options available in Amazon EMR.

Amazon Redshift

Amazon Redshift supports both encryption at rest and in transit. For encryption at rest, you can configure both server-side and client-side encryption.

Amazon Redshift uses a hierarchy of encryption keys to encrypt the cluster database. You can enable encryption either with AWS KMS or a hardware security module (HSM) depending on how you would like to manage your keys. Amazon Redshift provides easy integration with AWS KMS as represented in Figure 7-12.

Figure 7-12. Encryption options available in Amazon Redshift

But if you plan to integrate HSM for encryption, then you must use client- and server-side certificates to provide a trusted connection between the HSM and the Redshift cluster. Please note that if you enable encryption for an existing cluster by modifying its configurations, then Redshift automatically migrates your existing data to the new encrypted cluster. You can also enable encryption for the database password that you use for authentication using AWS KMS.

Amazon Redshift provides an HTTPS endpoint for encryption in transit. Redshift creates and installs AWS Certificate Manager (ACM)–issued certificates (*https://oreil.ly/HHHKM*) in each cluster. It leverages the SSL certificates to interact with other AWS services such as Amazon S3 and Amazon DynamoDB for data load and unload operations.

> Read more about encryption options available in Amazon Redshift from the AWS documentation (*https://oreil.ly/QRyMm*). To explain how we enable encryption, we provided three services as examples; please refer to the documentation for the other AWS services to learn how you can enable encryption for them.

Next, let's understand how to secure sensitive data within your datasets, if applicable.

Sensitive Data Detection and Redaction

As you process or ingest data into your data lake or data warehouse, privacy regulations may require you to detect PII (personally identifiable information) elements in your datasets and redact (remove or mask) them for consumption within the organization. Depending on the use case, you may have a requirement to keep the PII data in the raw layer and redact it in the final consumption layer or redact it in the raw layer itself.

When you consider redacting the PII elements in your data, it is necessary to consider both data at rest and in transit. Let's review what AWS service features we can integrate to detect and redact PII elements both at rest and in transit.

Integrating Amazon Macie for data at rest

Let's assume you have a lot of historical data available in Amazon S3 that needs to be scanned for PII. Then you can take action to redact it or notify respective stakeholders to review it manually.

Amazon Macie leverages machine learning and pattern matching to automatically detect sensitive data (e.g., names, address, phone number, credit card numbers, and more) from Amazon S3 in a cost-effective way. Figure 7-13 represents the workflow Amazon Macie follows for sensitive data detection.

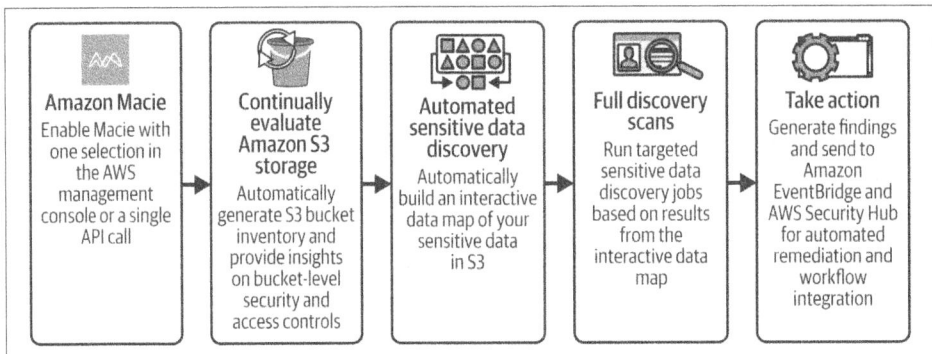

Amazon Macie
Enable Macie with one selection in the AWS management console or a single API call

Continually evaluate Amazon S3 storage
Automatically generate S3 bucket inventory and provide insights on bucket-level security and access controls

Automated sensitive data discovery
Automatically build an interactive data map of your sensitive data in S3

Full discovery scans
Run targeted sensitive data discovery jobs based on results from the interactive data map

Take action
Generate findings and send to Amazon EventBridge and AWS Security Hub for automated remediation and workflow integration

Figure 7-13. Amazon Macie on top of Amazon S3 to detect sensitive data

You can configure Amazon Macie to publish events to Amazon EventBridge and integrate notification mechanisms using Amazon SNS to alert respective stakeholders. Figure 7-14 explains how you can build that workflow.

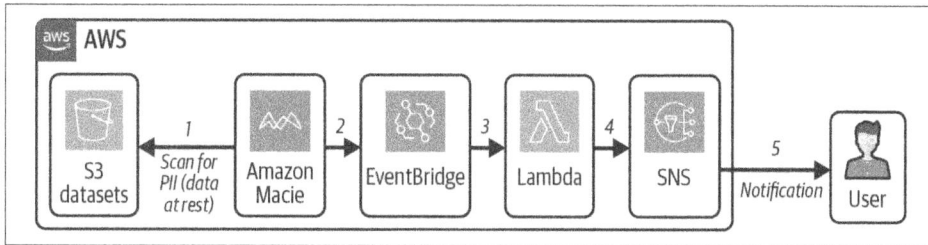

Figure 7-14. Reference architecture for Amazon Macie with S3 that sends notifications

Next, let's see how we can integrate the AWS Glue sensitive data detection feature that also enables us to process data to mask or redact elements.

Integrating AWS Glue sensitive data detection

AWS Glue allows you to define rules to detect sensitive data in your datasets and also can apply redaction rules such as remove a column, mask it, or store the masked data in a new column. While configuring, you can also specify if you would like to scan the complete dataset or a sample set of data to validate if sensitive data is present.

This feature supports a broad list of categories to detect sensitive data such as universal PII elements (e.g., email, credit card), HIPAA compliance standard fields (e.g., US driver's license, HCPCS code), networking elements (e.g., IP address, MAC address), and country-specific PII standard elements.

> You can review the complete list of supported elements in the AWS documentation (*https://oreil.ly/8e91a*).

Alternatively, you can also integrate a custom detection mechanism with a regular expression pattern. Figures 7-15 and 7-16 are from the AWS Glue Console and highlight how you can configure sensitive data detection parameters.

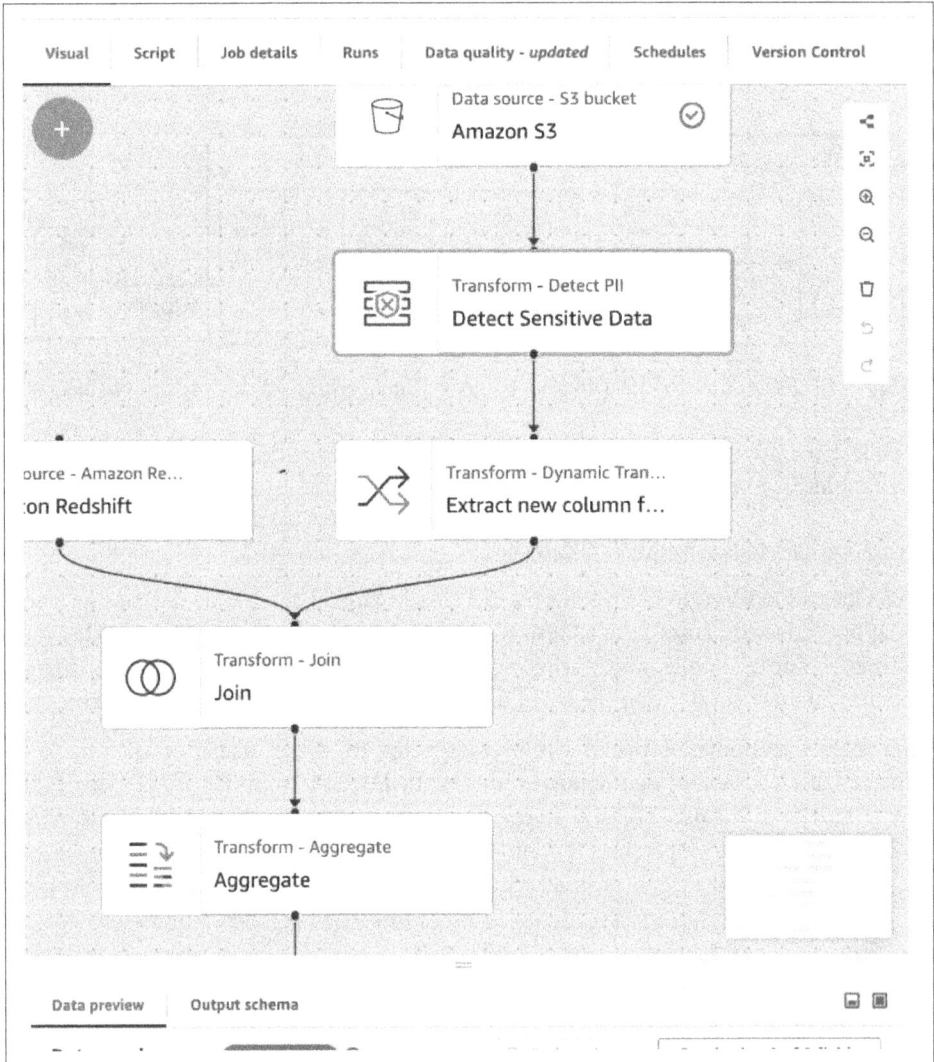

Figure 7-15. AWS Glue Studio screenshot showing the ETL pipeline

You can integrate Glue sensitive data detection for both data at rest (by reading from a Glue Data Catalog table) and in transit (by integrating it in Glue ETL jobs). Next, let's look at how you can integrate fine-grained access control on your data with AWS Lake Formation.

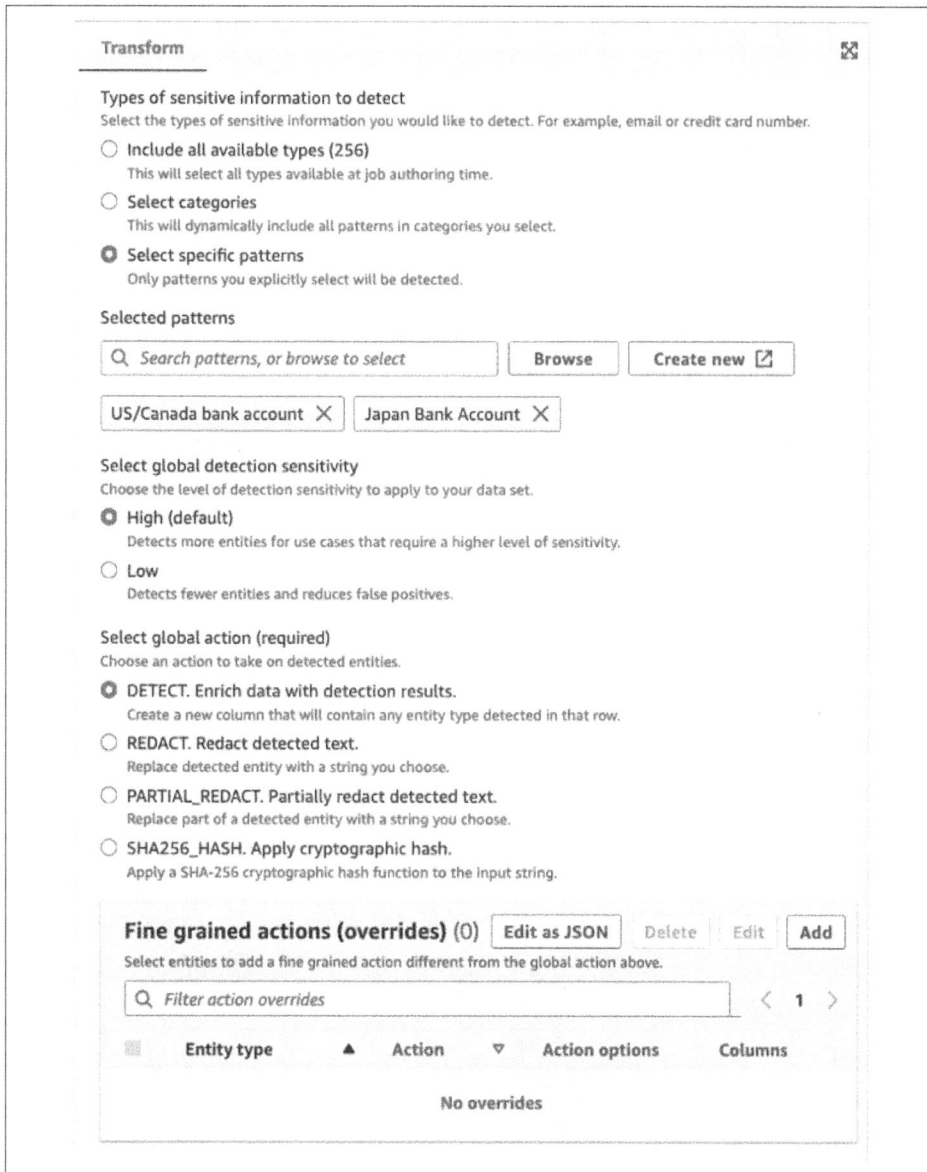

Figure 7-16. AWS Glue Studio screenshot showing options for sensitive data detection

Fine-Grained Access Control with AWS Lake Formation

To follow compliance standards and industry regulations, you need to have tighter security controls on your data and implement mechanisms that allow fine-grained access controls. You need the capability to define who can ingest data to your data stores and also who can access your data, not only databases and tables but also who can access which columns and rows.

In the AWS Cloud, the AWS Lake Formation service enables you to integrate fine-grained access control on your data lake and data warehouse. It integrates with several AWS analytics services such as AWS Glue, Amazon EMR, Amazon Athena, Amazon QuickSight, Amazon SageMaker, and Amazon Redshift and a few third-party apps such as Collibra, Privacera, Dremio, and Starburst.

Figure 7-17 shows a high-level architecture that illustrates how AWS Lake Formation integrates with data sources and analytics tools to provide fine-grained access control.

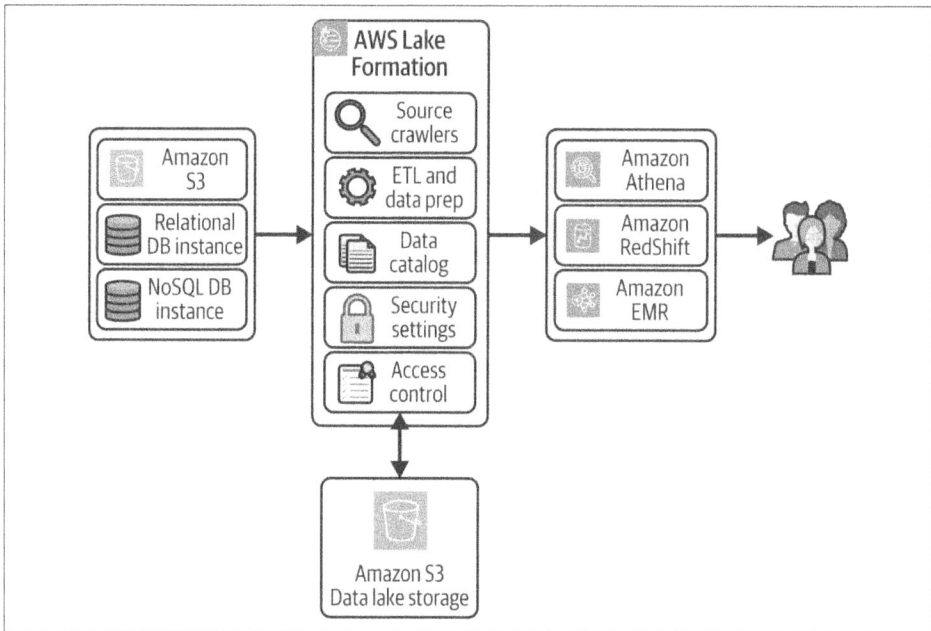

Figure 7-17. AWS Lake Formation architecture for data pipeline integration

To integrate AWS Lake Formation, you need to register your Amazon S3 prefix as the data lake location, define permissions for Glue Catalog databases, tables, columns, and rows and enable your end users to follow the defined permissions while consuming the data. AWS Lake Formation facilitates defining permissions based on attributes (attribute-based access control [ABAC]) and also based on tags (tag-based access control [TBAC]). TBAC is useful when you have a larger number of databases and tables and it's not operationally efficient to define access control for each table separately. It also helps when you have data from different domains or business units and you need to control access by teams by defining respective tags for tables or columns. Let's dive deep into the different levels of access control you can configure with Lake Formation.

Register the data lake location

As a first step, you need to register a data lake location in the Lake Formation console that points to an Amazon S3 path available in the same AWS account or a different AWS account. Figure 7-18 provides a screenshot of the Lake Formation console where you can register your S3 path as the data lake location.

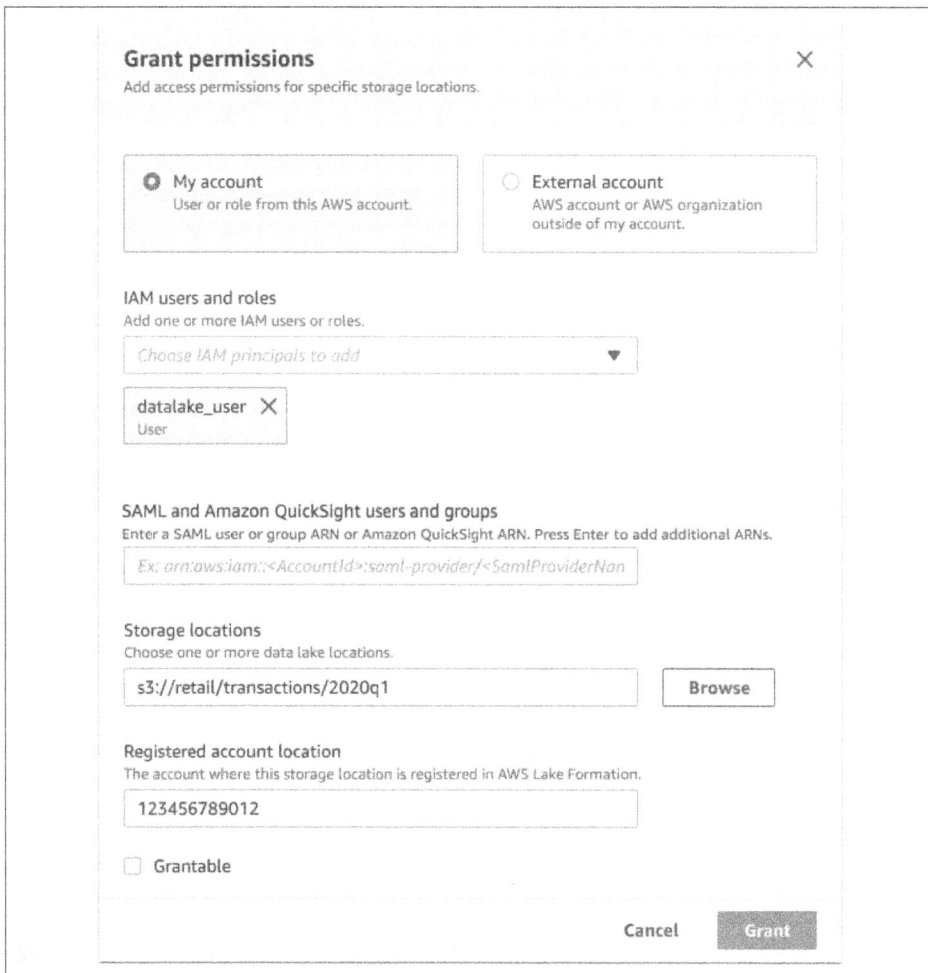

Figure 7-18. AWS Lake Formation: register data lake location

Granting permission to Glue Data Catalog databases, tables, and views

IAM principals who are not data lake administrators and would like to grant or revoke permissions would need additional IAM permissions such as `lake formation:<action>`, `glue:<action>`, and `iam:<action>`. Please read the Lake Formation documentation (*https://oreil.ly/PZxY6*) for a complete list of IAM permissions needed.

Name-based access control

You can manage permission for Glue Data Catalog databases, tables, and views using the AWS Console, AWS APIs, and Cloud Formation. Figure 7-19 represents a Lake Formation console screenshot that shows how you can select a database first and then all tables or specific tables under it to define access.

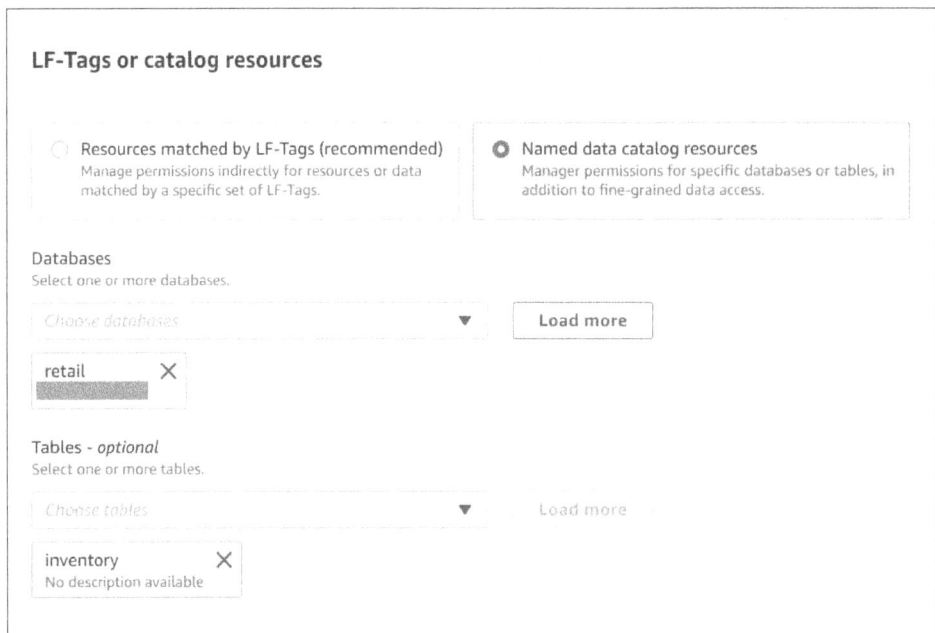

Figure 7-19. AWS Lake Formation: access control for Glue Data Catalog tables

Tag-based access control

As explained earlier, you can define Lake Formation tags (LF-Tags) for Glue Data Catalog resources and then assign permission on the tags to IAM principals. Lake Formation validates access to a resource when the IAM principal tag value matches the resource tag values. Lake Formation TBAC (LF-TBAC) is more scalable and reduces operational overhead as you have less grants to manage, so it is a great option when you have a large amount of resources for fine-grained access control.

Please note that you need to have tight control over who can create LF-Tags and who can assign LF-Tags through IAM policies, so that you can avoid duplicate redundant tags that may defeat the operational advantage you were expecting with LF-TBAC. Refer to the AWS documentation (*https://oreil.ly/pMGL6*) to understand which IAM permissions you should assign for managing metadata related to LF-Tags.

Row- and column-based data filtering

Apart from the database, tables, and views, Lake Formation also enables access control at the column and row level. Let's see how you can define row- and column-based data filters for permission management:

Access control based on column names (column-level security)
Let's assume you have a table with 10 columns, with 3 columns that include sensitive data that you do not want to expose to a specific set of users or groups. In this scenario, you can define column-level security in Lake Formation to define which columns IAM principals can access and which columns should be excluded.

Access control based on data in rows (row-level security)
Let's assume you have a common data lake table that includes the data of multiple business units with a column that captures the business unit name. You would like to define permissions so that the respective business unit users can see only the records belonging to them. In this scenario, Lake Formation row-based access control is helpful as you can define a row-based filter such as business_unit=BU1 and assign that to the respective business unit users for access. Please read more from the Lake Formation documentation (*https://oreil.ly/IM4k-*) on what PartiQL filter expressions you can integrate while defining row-level filtering.

Control access with both row- and column-based permissions (cell-level security)
Let's assume you have a requirement to define permissions for both rows and columns. If you combine the use case of column-level security and row-level security we, you might be able to meet a requirement that says the business units can see only the records belonging to them and instead of all the columns of the table, only the non-PII columns. There are a few additional IAM permissions needed to define cell-level security in Lake Formation; please refer to the Lake Formation documentation (*https://oreil.ly/eKOT9*).

Figure 7-20 provides a screenshot of the Lake Formation console that shows how you can define row- and column-based filtering.

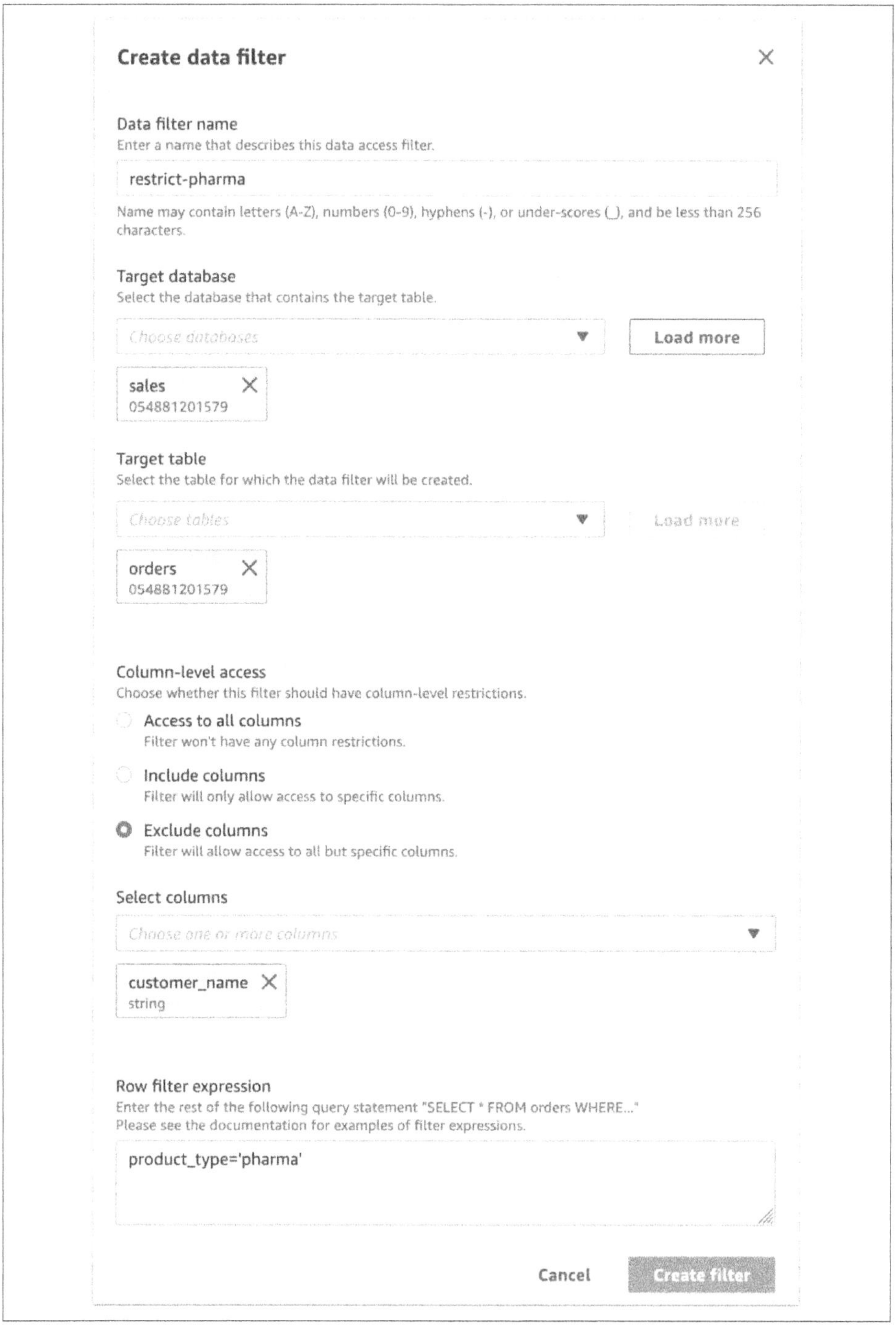

Create data filter　　　　　　　　　　　　　　　　　　　　✕

Data filter name
Enter a name that describes this data access filter.

```
restrict-pharma
```

Name may contain letters (A-Z), numbers (0-9), hyphens (-), or under-scores (_), and be less than 256 characters.

Target database
Select the database that contains the target table.

```
Choose databases                          ▼    Load more
```

```
sales          ✕
054881201579
```

Target table
Select the table for which the data filter will be created.

```
Choose tables                             ▼    Load more
```

```
orders         ✕
054881201579
```

Column-level access
Choose whether this filter should have column-level restrictions.

○ **Access to all columns**
　Filter won't have any column restrictions.

○ **Include columns**
　Filter will only allow access to specific columns.

◉ **Exclude columns**
　Filter will allow access to all but specific columns.

Select columns

```
Choose one or more columns                              ▼
```

```
customer_name  ✕
string
```

Row filter expression
Enter the rest of the following query statement "SELECT * FROM orders WHERE..."
Please see the documentation for examples of filter expressions.

```
product_type='pharma'
```

　　　　　　　　　　　　　　　　　Cancel　　　**Create filter**

Figure 7-20. Row- and column-based data filter in AWS Lake Formation

Next, let's review some of the best practices you can follow while integrating Lake Formation permissions.

Best practices to integrate AWS Lake Formation

Here are some of the best practices you should follow while implementing AWS Lake Formation:

Avoid bucket policies for Amazon S3 buckets registered as a data lake location.
When you register an Amazon S3 prefix as your data lake location, AWS Lake Formation manages access to its data through the Lake Formation authentication and authorization mechanism. So avoid additional bucket policies for these specific S3 buckets to have a consistent way to manage permissions.

Avoid using the AWS root admin user as the data lake admin user.
When you are setting up AWS Lake Formation for the first time, you are expected to create or declare a data lake admin, who will act as a Lake Formation administrator. Often to follow an easier route, customers use the root AWS IAM user as the data lake admin user, but to follow the least-privilege principle, you should create a separate IAM user to designate as the data lake admin for Lake Formation.

Avoid using the Lake Formation service-linked role in production.
As explained earlier, a service-linked role (SLR) is a specific type of IAM role that includes all the permissions needed by the service to call other AWS services. In general, it is not recommended to use service-linked roles in production, as they may create security risks and do not follow the least-privilege principle.

Please note there are a few limitations that you need to be aware of such as that Amazon EMR on EC2 does not support SLR-registered locations for data access, encrypted catalogs do not support SLR for cross-account sharing, and a large number of S3 locations registered for data access may cause failures because of IAM policy limits. Creating a separate IAM role is recommended for registering data locations with Lake Formation.

Best practices for cross-account sharing

Lake Formation leverages AWS Resource Access Manager for cross-account grants. The following are a few things to consider when integrating Lake Formation for cross-account data sharing:

- Leverage AWS Organizations to organize your AWS accounts, so that it's easier to grant permissions.

- Instead of granting permissions to many individual tables, look for an opportunity to combine them as a single database and use `All Tables` permissions for that database, which results in one grant.
- Instead of creating a resource link for each table that is shared, the data lake administrator should create a placeholder database and grant `CREATE_TABLE` permission to the `ALLIAMPrincipal` group. Then, all IAM principals in the recipient account can create resource links in the placeholder database and start querying the shared tables.

Best practices for tag-based access control

The following are some of the best practices you can follow while implementing TBAC in AWS Lake Formation:

- Before assigning LF-Tags to Glue Data Catalog resources, make sure to define them. As a best practice, you can designate a person or team who is responsible for defining tags and control that access through IAM permissions. Also plan to define tags in lowercase, as tag keys and values are converted to all lowercase when they are stored.
- Wildcards are not supported when you assign LF-Tags. If you would like to assign the same LF-Tag to all the tables of a single database, then assign it to the database, as all the tables within the database inherit the same tag. The inheritance of tags works for table to column too.
- Make sure to assign full table access for Glue ETL jobs, as that is a requirement for the ETL jobs without which the jobs will fail.
- Keep the tagging ontology as simple as possible. Having too many LF-Tags can make it difficult to manage and track permissions. Document the tagging ontology and share it with the data stewards so that they are very clear when/how to use the LF-Tags.

> There are a few additional considerations and limitations that you should be aware of, which are included in the AWS documentation (*https://oreil.ly/GfI1M*).

Next, let's learn how you can manage permissions in Amazon Redshift.

Database Security in Amazon Redshift

Amazon Redshift provides the following features for managing database security.

Manage permissions with GRANT and REVOKE

Similar to relational databases, you can create users or groups within Redshift and define what level of access they will have using the GRANT (*https://oreil.ly/olz5m*) or REVOKE (*https://oreil.ly/W0PZL*) command. Redshift supports SELECT, INSERT, UPDATE, DELETE, REFERENCES, CREATE, TEMPORARY, and USAGE permissions. By default, the superuser or the owner of the database object can query, modify, or grant permissions on the object. Objects owners get implicit GRANT, REVOKE, and DROP access on their objects that cannot be revoked.

Role-based access control

Role-based access control (RBAC) (*https://oreil.ly/pg4Et*) enables you to control access at both broader and finer levels. For granular control you can create roles, assign users to roles, and define permissions for the role. RBAC helps implement the least-privilege principle, and for any permission change instead of making changes at the object level, you can make changes at the role level that will impact all the users associated with the role.

RBAC also supports nesting roles, which means you can assign a role to a user or to another role. If you assign role 1 to role 2, then users assuming role 2 will have the permissions of both role 1 and role 2. To create roles the database user needs to have the CREATE ROLE permission, or the superuser can GRANT the CREATE ROLE permission to the user.

Row-level security

Row-level security (RLS) in Redshift enables granular access control on sensitive data where you can define which rows of a schema or a table can be accessed by which user or role. You can combine row-level security and column-based filters to implement fine-grained access control.

When RLS is enforced and users run a query, the returned result gets filtered based on the row- and column-level permission assigned to the user running the query. There are a few best practices you can follow while defining RLS policies such as avoiding complex statements in policies and not using excessive table joins in the policy definition.

Dynamic data masking

Dynamic data masking (DDM) (*https://oreil.ly/PPxD3*) in Redshift enables you to protect or mask sensitive data in table columns during query time. You can configure masking policies that apply custom obfuscation rules for specific users or roles. You can also integrate conditional dynamic data masking (*https://oreil.ly/GWdeA*) to apply masking at the cell level by writing conditions that may check the value of any columns in that row.

Next, let's learn how you can integrate fine-grained access control in Amazon Quick-Sight.

Fine-Grained Access Control in Amazon QuickSight

There are two ways you can enable fine-grained access control in Amazon Quick-Sight. One is with IAM policies and the other is with AWS Lake Formation.

Access control with IAM policies

Using IAM policies you can control which IAM user or role can take which action on QuickSight resources. For example, you can control which IAM user or role can create QuickSight dashboards or datasets and which users can access which visualization. In addition to QuickSight resources, you also need to provide access to underlying data sources such as the Amazon S3 prefix that the IAM user will need while accessing the dataset.

Access control with Lake Formation

Amazon QuickSight supports querying datasets managed by Lake Formation. This means if your QuickSight dataset is created through Athena on a dataset available in S3, then the queries will follow the column-, row-, and tag-based permissions defined in Lake Formation for the IAM user.

Next, let's review the different pillars of data governance and what AWS service features you can integrate to address them.

Data Governance

Apart from data security and privacy, the following are a few other pillars of data governance that need to be addressed for end-to-end data governance:

- Data Catalog for metadata management
- Data sharing
- Data quality
- Data profiling
- Data lifecycle management
- Data lineage
- Logging and auditing

Let's try to understand each of these pillars and what AWS services or features can help address them.

Metadata Management and Technical Catalog

Centralized metadata management is the key to integrating end-to-end governance. You might have multiple data sources including databases, data lakes, and data warehousing systems and for all these data stores you need to have a common metadata layer, on top of which you can integrate access controls, auditing, and reporting.

In the AWS Cloud, the AWS Glue Data Catalog serves as the centralized technical catalog and also provides Glue crawlers for schema detection. Let's try to understand both of these components.

AWS Glue Data Catalog

AWS Glue Data Catalog is a managed service that acts as a centralized technical catalog in AWS, where you can define virtual table schema on top of datasets in Amazon S3, as well as tables in relational databases, Amazon Redshift, DynamoDB, and many more other data stores through Glue connections.

AWS Glue Data Catalog is a highly available, scalable, and Hive Metastore–compatible catalog. It is serverless and integrates with AWS IAM for security controls and provides logging and auditing with Amazon CloudWatch and AWS CloudTrail. Figure 7-21 represents the high-level features of AWS Glue Data Catalog.

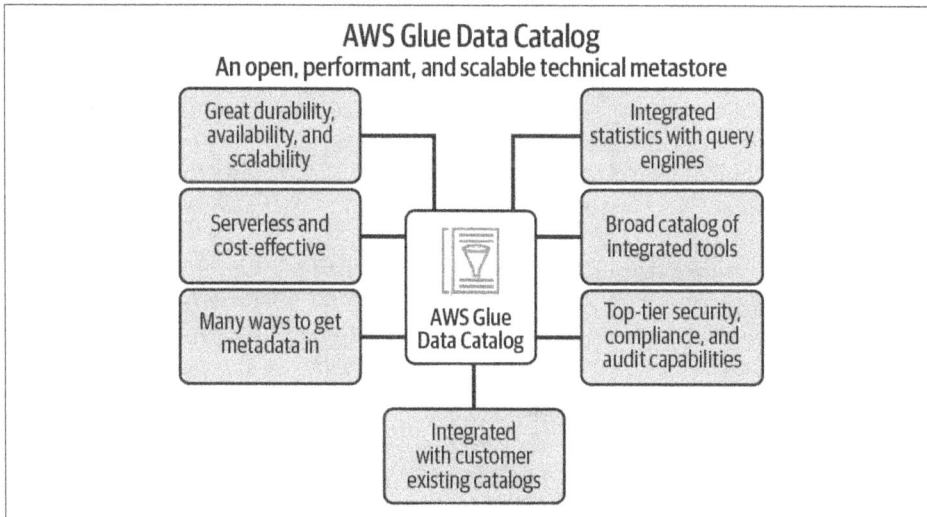

Figure 7-21. AWS Glue Data Catalog features

Other AWS services such as Amazon Athena, Amazon Redshift Spectrum, Amazon EMR or AWS Glue ETL jobs, AWS Lake Formation, Amazon DataZone, and Amazon QuickSight integrate with AWS Glue Data Catalog to fetch metadata and query data from the source tables.

AWS Glue crawler

AWS Glue crawler helps auto-detect the schema by scanning a subset of data from the data lake and creating metadata tables in Glue Data Catalog. There are scenarios where source systems send new datasets and to automate metadata discovery you can integrate Glue crawlers to create metadata tables and then trigger ETL jobs for transformations. You can integrate built-in classifiers or custom classifiers in Glue crawlers to parse the schema of the dataset in the data lake.

Amazon DataZone business glossary

Glue Data Catalog acts as a technical catalog in AWS, but business users generally struggle to discover metadata from technical catalogs as they are unfamiliar with the technical terms. In such situations bringing in a business catalog adds a lot of value, where you can map business glossary terminologies to technical attributes, so that business users can search the catalog through business terms.

Amazon DataZone (*https://oreil.ly/vBEWM*) solves this requirement by enabling you to define a business glossary, terms, and metadata forms with which business users can define metadata and enable users to search the metadata catalog. Amazon Data-Zone provides additional capabilities that enable you to share data through publisher and subscriber models. Let's learn about it in the next section.

Data Sharing

When you think of data sharing, there are several use cases that come to mind such as sharing data with your team members, with other teams, with other business units of the organization, or with external entities. For each use case, you need to have a secured mechanism and the architecture to share datasets.

We discussed AWS Lake Formation earlier, which enables you to implement fine-grained access control. It is one of the key components for sharing data, as you need to have control over what subset of data you are going to share and with whom. We can define data sharing within the broader categories represented in Figure 7-22. Let's review each one of them in detail.

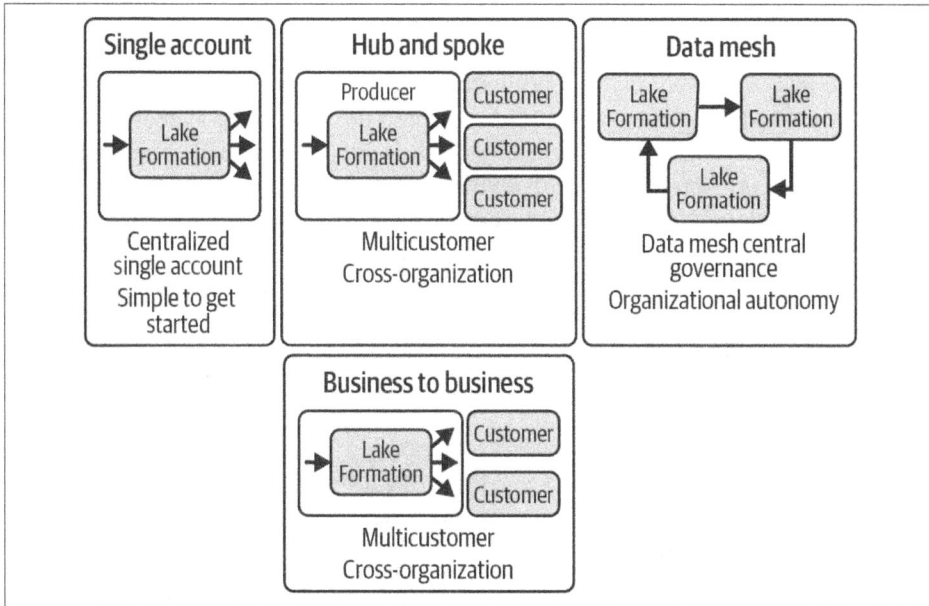

Figure 7-22. Different data sharing mechanisms

Share within a single AWS account

If you are planning to share data with your team members or with other teams within a single AWS account, then you can leverage AWS Lake Formation's fine-grained access control to define permissions for individual IAM users, roles, or groups. In this scenario, the assumption is you have a single data lake or data warehouse and the producers and consumers are within the same account.

Multiaccount, hub-and-spoke model for data sharing

Assume your organization is split into multiple business units and each business unit has its own AWS account. You have a centralized data lake or data warehouse and other AWS accounts act as consumers to query data from it. In that case, you can integrate AWS Lake Formation's cross-account data sharing capability (*https://oreil.ly/ 8Ln8L*) to control access to databases or tables from centralized data lake accounts for users of the consumer accounts.

Amazon Redshift provides a data sharing feature (*https://oreil.ly/F4rv8*), using which you can share live data of your cluster across Redshift clusters, workgroups, other AWS accounts, or AWS Regions. With this feature you can avoid copying data to other clusters and can serve live, up-to-date data to the consumers as soon as the data is committed in the source cluster. Producer Redshift clusters can create read-only *data share* objects referred to as *outbound shares*, and consumer clusters can receive these objects, referred to as *inbound shares*. Please note that you can integrate the Redshift *data shares* with AWS Data Exchange and AWS Lake Formation. Figure 7-23 provides a high-level architecture diagram that represents how Redshift data share can be integrated for multiple use cases.

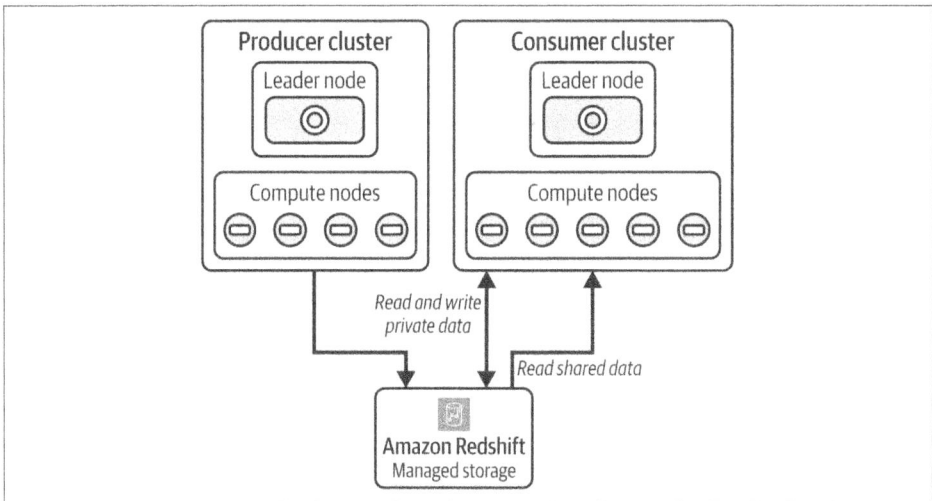

Figure 7-23. Amazon Redshift data share with producer and consumer clusters

In the hub-and-spoke model, there is no centralized governance and each producer is responsible for controlling access to its own consumers. Next, let's learn how you can implement centralized governance with a data mesh.

Data mesh with centralized governance

A data mesh is well suited to a multiaccount scenario, where your organization has multiple data lakes or data warehouses managed by respective business units or AWS accounts and you need to bring in centralized governance control to share data between them. Each of the AWS accounts will have AWS Lake Formation integrated to define fine-grained access control and you can integrate Amazon DataZone to set up the publisher-subscriber workflow. Learn more about data meshes from the AWS documentation (*https://oreil.ly/YMsUY*).

Figure 7-24 provides a high-level architecture of a data mesh on AWS, where producer and consumer accounts collaborate for data sharing with Amazon DataZone in the middle for centralized governance. This helps meet the four core principles of a data mesh: "domain-driven ownership," "data as a product," "federated governance," and "self-serve data platform."

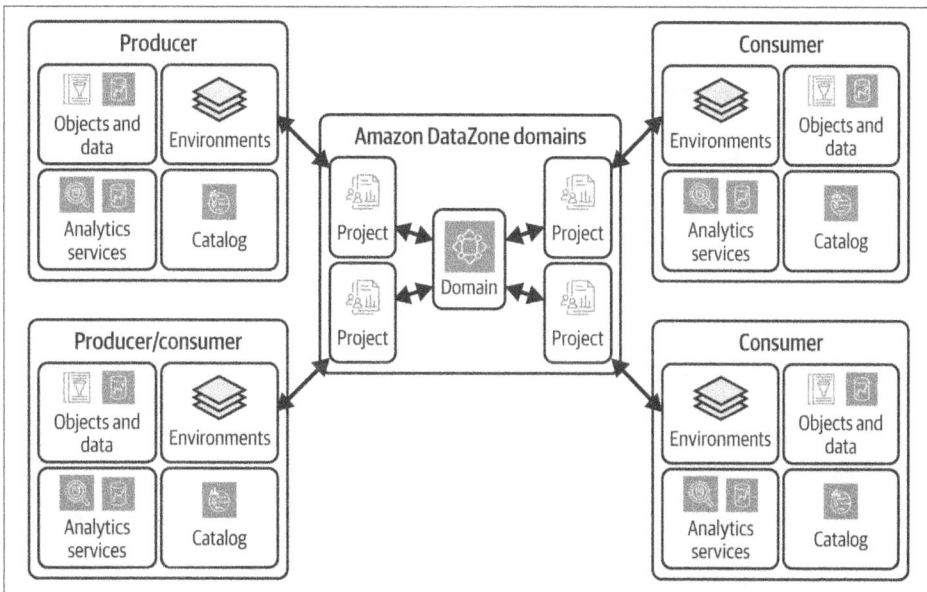

Figure 7-24. Data mesh reference architecture with Amazon DataZone

Figure 7-25 represents a technical flow of how a producer account shares a subset of data lake and data warehousing data to a consumer account using DataZone (Domain → Projects), enables fine-grained access control with Lake Formation, and enables querying using Athena or Redshift.

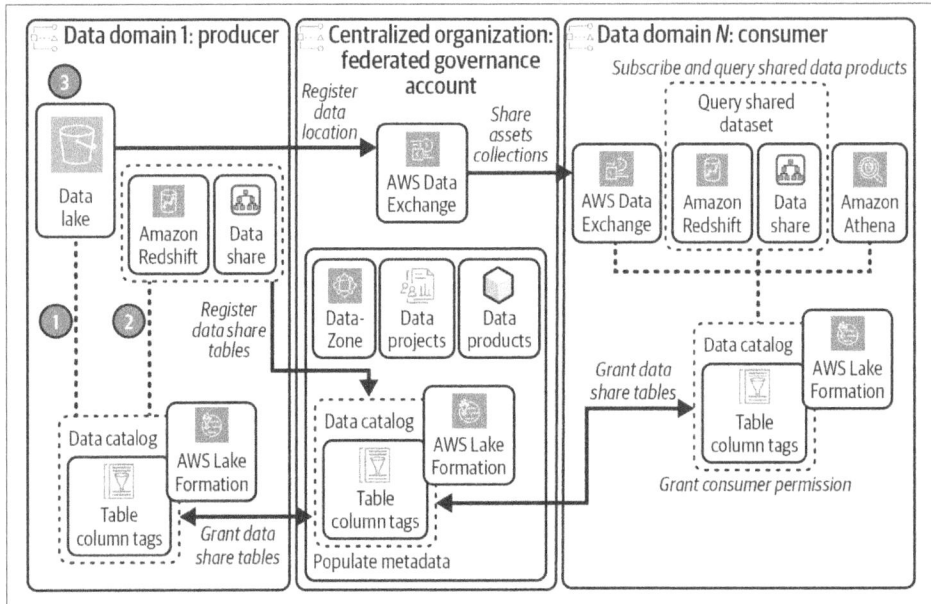

Figure 7-25. Reference architecture of data sharing in AWS

Next, let's review what options you have if you need to share data with external entities.

Cross-organization or business-to-business data sharing

There are instances when your organization needs to collaborate with other organizations for sharing data and deriving insights for business decisions. These are B2B (business-to-business) data sharing, where you can integrate AWS Clean Rooms (*https://oreil.ly/c8-uU*) on top of your data lake to share a subset of your data with your partners to aggregate datasets and derive cross-organization insights. Figure 7-26 provides a high-level architecture diagram that explains how AWS Clean Rooms integration works.

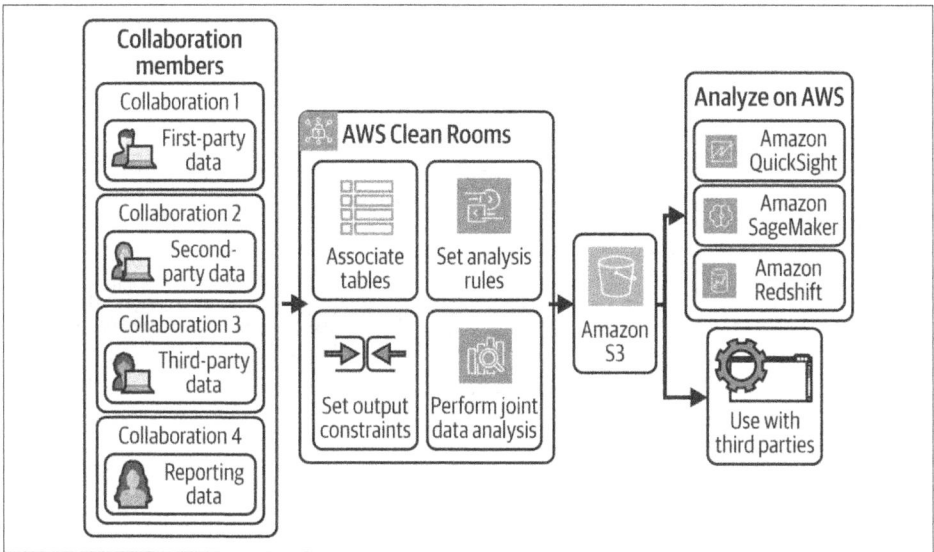

Figure 7-26. AWS Clean Rooms collaboration in AWS

Exposing data as a product in a data marketplace

Your organization might have a business model where the aggregated data you produce is represented as a product and needs to be available in a public data marketplace, from which end consumers can pay to subscribe to the datasets. In the AWS Cloud, AWS Data Exchange (*https://oreil.ly/9da3h*) enables building a data marketplace to which you can publish datasets or subscribe to third-party datasets available for free or with payment. AWS Data Exchange integrates with Amazon Redshift, Amazon S3, and AWS Lake Formation.

Figure 7-27 explains how you can make Amazon Redshift data available in the AWS Marketplace using AWS Data Exchange and let your consumers subscribe to it and query it using their Redshift cluster.

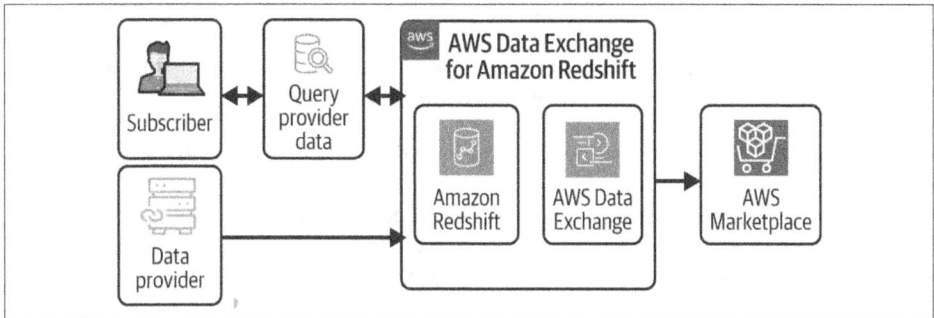

Figure 7-27. Amazon Redshift integration with AWS Data Exchange

Figure 7-28 represents how you can take advantage of AWS Lake Formation integration with AWS Data Exchange to share a subset of data lake data through the marketplace and let data subscribers consume it using AWS Glue, Amazon Redshift Spectrum, or Amazon Athena.

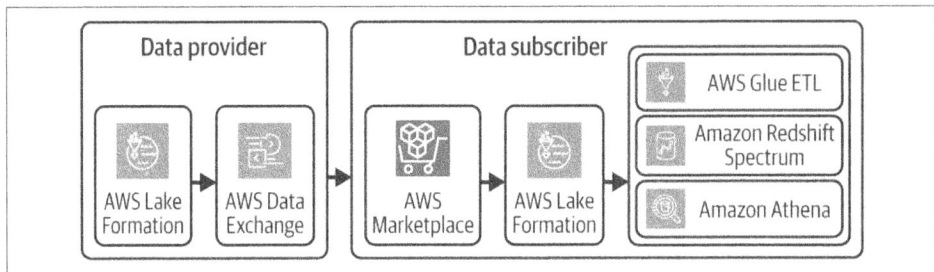

Figure 7-28. AWS Lake Formation integration with AWS Marketplace

Next, let's learn about the data quality pillar of governance and how you can integrate AWS Glue's capability for it.

Data Quality

As data gets ingested into the data lake or data warehousing systems, validating the quality of the incoming data becomes key before making it available for consumption. Low-quality data may lead to incorrect business decisions that you need to prevent.

If the data is structured or available in a tabular format (columns and rows), then you can apply standard validation rules, such as if the data follows predefined schema, if it has a minimum number of rows you expect, if the columns are populated with correct values, and if the values in a column fall within a defined range. You may also need to apply custom rules as applicable to your business.

For structured datasets, you can leverage AWS Glue Data Quality (*https://oreil.ly/juxpU*), which is serverless, cost-effective, and provides petabyte-scale processing capability. You can integrate the Glue Data Quality capability into the data available at rest (by defining a Glue Data Catalog table on top of existing data) or into the data in transit (by integrating the rules in Glue ETL jobs).

Figure 7-29 explains how you can integrate the Glue Data Quality feature. The feature recommends rules after analyzing the data, and as a data steward you can refine those rules and create a final ruleset. Then Glue evaluates those rules against the dataset to produce Data Quality check results. Data quality rule examples include validating the number of records, checking the data type of a column, or validating the completeness of the dataset.

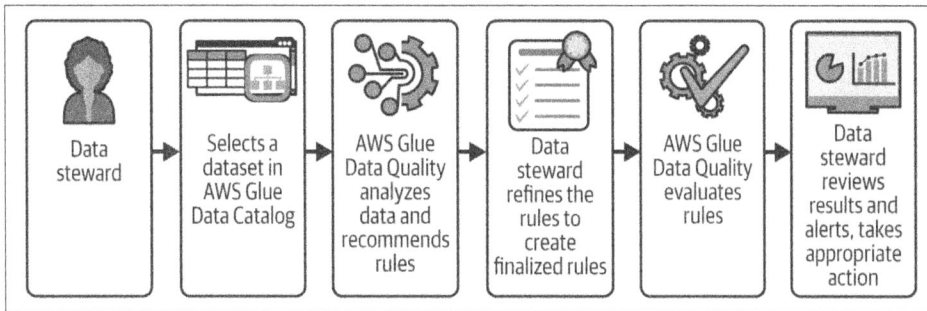

Figure 7-29. AWS Glue Data Quality workflow

If your data includes unstructured datasets or media files, then you can integrate AWS Artificial Intelligence (AI) services such as Amazon Rekognition, Amazon Comprehend, Amazon Textract or custom models deployed in Amazon Bedrock or Amazon SageMaker to extract metadata from the media files and then integrate data quality rules on the extracted metadata to validate the quality of the datasets.

Next, let's learn how you can profile your data for reporting or notify about anomalies.

Data Profiling

Profiling data is one of the ways to make sure the data you have received from the source systems or processed through the ingestion pipeline meets the expectation defined for those datasets. What you want to profile in the dataset differs based on source systems and the business rules defined by your organization. Some of the common ways you can profile your data may include:

- Number of rows received or processed for a specific dataset
- Number of columns expected in a data source
- Type of data (number or string or date) expected in a specific field
- Values of a column fall in the defined range; for example, a country code field has valid values or a month column has values between 1 to 12
- A numeric field value that follows the mean or median of all values in that field

In the AWS Cloud, you can leverage the following features or tools to implement your data profiling requirements:

Glue Data Quality rules
As explained in the previous section, you can leverage the Glue Data Quality Definition Language (DQDL) rules and integrate custom logic to profile your data.

AWS Glue Deequ framework (https://oreil.ly/pXx07)
> The AWS Glue Data Quality feature was developed from the open source Deequ framework, which you can customize as per your requirements. The framework also provides a lot of flexibility with which you can integrate your data profiling needs.

AWS Glue DataBrew recipes
> You can also integrate DataBrew recipes to scan values in columns or count the rows to profile your data. DataBrew provides predefined functions that you can integrate without writing any custom code.

AWS Samples Data Profiler utility (https://oreil.ly/k4CBy)
> This Data Profiler utility available in AWS Samples provides an option to profile the tables available in Glue Data Catalog using AWS Glue or Amazon EMR.

Third-party free or paid tools
> Apart from the preceding options, you can always look for third-party non-AWS tools that can help profile your datasets, provide periodic reports, and trigger alerts for anomalies.

Next, let's learn how you can maintain your data and control cost with data lifecycle management.

Data Lifecycle Management

Every dataset your organization uses or maintains has its own life span. Certain use cases may require the previous few years of data to be immediately available for analytics, whereas other use cases may need to access a subset of data infrequently, and older datasets may need to be archived or deleted. Apart from business needs, organizations also follow industry guidelines where they need to keep older data for a certain duration or delete specific customer data when the customer leaves the platform.

In Chapter 5, we explained in detail how you can leverage S3 storage classes (*https://oreil.ly/RYdki*) and S3 lifecycle configurations (*https://oreil.ly/7CBqZ*) to move data to different S3 storage tiers, how you can leverage export features in databases, and how you can leverage the expire snapshot features of open table formats.

As an alternative to native export features of databases, you can also write a batch script, which can export older data from the database to an object store or file storage layer and delete the same data from the database to save cost.

Next, let's learn about data lineage and how you can integrate it in AWS.

Data Lineage

Data lineage involves tracking and visualizing the journey of data from its source through various systems and transformations until it reaches its final destination. This process provides a detailed map of data flows, transformations, and storage locations, ensuring complete transparency and traceability throughout the data lifecycle.

Managing data lineage requires collecting various types of metadata to document the flow and transformation of data across an organization. The key types of metadata include:

Technical metadata
Captures details about data sources, schemas, transformations, and consumers.

Business metadata
Provides context by detailing data ownership, business definitions, and classifications to ensure appropriate data usage.

Operational metadata
Includes transformation schedules, execution timestamps, and data flow information, offering insights into data movement through different systems and processes.

Quality metrics
Assesses the data's accuracy, completeness, and job status to maintain high data quality.

Data lineage offers distinct benefits tailored to different personas within an organization:

- For data engineers, it enhances data quality by pinpointing where errors occur, allowing for efficient root cause analysis and timely rectification. Changes in data pipelines are easier to apply and validate because engineers can identify a job's upstream dependencies and downstream usage to properly evaluate service impacts.

- Data platform administrators benefit from data lineage by gaining comprehensive insights into data integration processes. This understanding helps them manage data from various sources accurately, ensuring seamless aggregation without data duplication or entity mismatch. Additionally, data lineage aids in regulatory compliance by providing clear audit trails, helping administrators meet compliance requirements like GDPR and CCPA.

- For data analysts and data scientists, the ability to view and track data flow as it moves from source to destination helps them better understand the meaning and context of a dataset or a particular metric.

- Business data consumers benefit from the improved data integration and quality, leading to more accurate and trustworthy data for decision making. They can rely on the data's integrity, knowing that any issues can be traced and addressed promptly, ensuring that insights derived from the data are valid and actionable.

AWS provides several services to help implement data lineage effectively.

Amazon DataZone

Amazon DataZone offers a comprehensive, API-driven data lineage feature (*https://oreil.ly/L_ziH*) compatible with OpenLineage, providing an end-to-end view of data movement over time. Users can visualize and understand data provenance, trace changes, and conduct root cause analysis when data errors occur. This service captures transformations of data assets and columns, offering a detailed view of data movement from source to consumption. The graphical interface for navigating data relationships enhances productivity and decision making. The lineage data includes activities inside the DataZone business catalog, catalog assets, subscribers who consumed those assets, and any additional activities captured using APIs.

Building lineage solutions with AWS Glue, Amazon Neptune, and Spline

This approach uses AWS Glue as the ETL engine to ingest, transform, and load data. The Spline agent captures runtime lineage information from Spark jobs in AWS Glue, recording the data's journey through various transformations. This data is then stored and modeled in Amazon Neptune, a graph database optimized for querying highly connected data. The captured lineage data is visualized using Neptune notebooks, providing interactive analysis capabilities for managing complex data relationships effectively. You can refer to the AWS blog (*https://oreil.ly/kQvyc*) for more details.

Amazon SageMaker ML Lineage Tracking

For machine learning workflows, Amazon SageMaker ML Lineage Tracking offers a robust solution to capture and visualize the lineage of machine learning models. This feature tracks and stores information about each step of the ML workflow, from data preparation to model deployment. SageMaker ML Lineage integrates with SageMaker Pipelines to provide detailed lineage information, ensuring reproducibility and governance of ML models. This capability is essential for establishing model governance, auditing model performance, and ensuring compliance with regulatory requirements. By capturing the complete lineage of ML workflows, SageMaker enables data scientists and engineers to understand the impact of data changes on model outcomes and maintain high standards of data quality and integrity throughout the model's lifecycle.

Apart from the above AWS service features, you also have the flexibility to configure other open source products such as DataHub (*https://oreil.ly/4nD6e*), Collibra (*https://oreil.ly/xENyI*), and Amundsen (*https://www.amundsen.io*). Next, let's learn how we should make sure logging and auditing is in place for your data platform to help meet governance and compliance needs.

Logging and Auditing

Logging and auditing is one of the key pillars of data governance, which enables you to analyze log data and also audit user actions for security and compliance needs. Let's understand which AWS services can be integrated for logging and auditing and how you can query these logs for deriving insights.

There are multiple options you can consider while looking for an AWS service that can store logs. Let's understand each of those options.

Amazon CloudWatch

Amazon CloudWatch is a managed logging service in AWS that not only enables you to store logs but also analyze logs, integrate alarms for anomalies, and create visualizations on log data for reporting. It natively integrates with all AWS services, which means without custom coding effort, AWS services can push logs to CloudWatch. Figure 7-30 provides a high-level architecture diagram that explains how Amazon CloudWatch works.

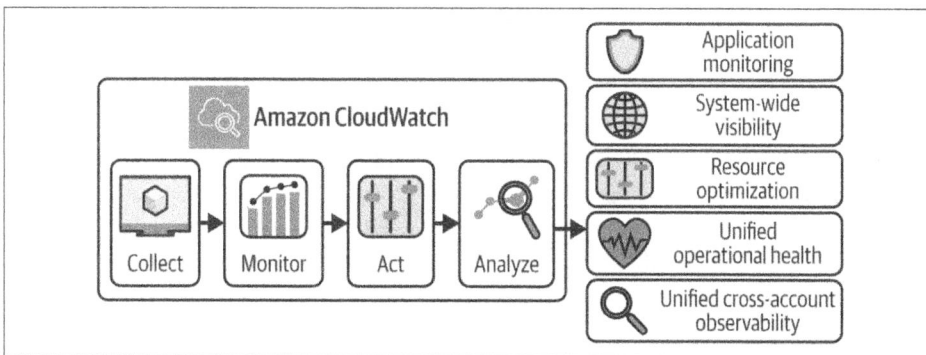

Figure 7-30. Amazon CloudWatch integration for logging and monitoring

Amazon OpenSearch Service

Amazon OpenSearch Service, previously known as Amazon Elasticsearch Service, is a managed service built for storing and analyzing logs. It is a distributed search and analytics engine built on Apache Lucene. It solves a wide range of use cases such as log analytics, security intelligence, operational analytics, and full-text search.

To ingest log data to the OpenSearch cluster, you can leverage open source tools such as Logstash or leverage its APIs for transactional insert, or you can load data through bulk loader APIs. You can integrate Amazon OpenSearch Dashboard (previously known as Kibana Dashboards) to build visualizations on log data.

Amazon OpenSearch Service can be a great logging solution if you would like to design your own indexes and manage the log schema for faster search. With OpenSearch, you can choose to have a fixed node provisioned cluster or can go with Amazon OpenSearch Serverless. You can also integrate Amazon CloudWatch alarms to monitor OpenSearch cluster health and configure alerts for cluster issues.

Amazon S3

You might have a use case where you may plan to just keep the log data in file storage and not invest in integrating a managed solution like Amazon CloudWatch. In that case, Amazon S3 can help you store the log data and you can integrate Amazon Athena to query the logs or Amazon EMR to process the logs for analytics.

Let's review an example of one of the analytics services such as Amazon Redshift and understand how you can enable logging for the cluster.

Logging and auditing in Amazon Redshift

Amazon Redshift natively integrates with Amazon CloudWatch and CloudTrail. It publishes several metrics to Amazon CloudWatch, which you can leverage to monitor cluster health, memory utilization, CPU utilization, read or write IOPS, user activity logs, and more. You can refer to the AWS documentation (*https://oreil.ly/w0ac3*) for a complete list of metrics Redshift publishes to Amazon CloudWatch. Alternatively, you can also consider pushing the logs to a specific Amazon S3 bucket.

Redshift publishes connection logs, user logs, and user activity logs. You can filter logs in CloudWatch by filtering the new log group created for the Redshift cluster that follows the */aws/redshift/cluster/<cluster_name>/<log_type>* path. For connection logs, the log group path will be */aws/redshift/cluster/<cluster_name>/connectionlog*.

Redshift also publishes audit logs to CloudTrail, where you can identify who made the request, from which IP it was made, what time it was, and additional request details. Refer to the AWS documentation (*https://oreil.ly/zDyvC*) to understand how you can enable audit logging for the cluster.

> Please note audit logging for a Redshift cluster is not enabled by default and you need to explicitly enable it by specifying a log export to CloudWatch or to an S3 prefix.

Amazon Managed Service for Prometheus and Grafana

Apart from logs, you may look for a dedicated solution to store application-level metrics for monitoring and build alerting and visualization on top of it. For such use cases you can integrate Prometheus (*https://prometheus.io*) for storing metrics and Grafana (*https://grafana.com*) to build visualizations. Both of these open source solutions are widely adopted in the industry for metrics monitoring or observability.

AWS also offers managed services for both of these open source tools (Amazon Managed Service for Prometheus (*https://oreil.ly/_zLg4*) and Amazon Managed Grafana (*https://oreil.ly/GIdQl*)) that you can integrate if you would like to reduce operational overhead or manage the open source versions and the related infrastructure hardware.

AWS CloudTrail to audit actions or API invocations

AWS CloudTrail (*https://oreil.ly/nNyu7*) is a managed logging solution to keep track of user activities or AWS API actions. You can also integrate it in a hybrid or multi-cloud environment. These logs are stored immutably to enable compliance audits of user actions and can aggregate multiple events to derive insights.

Analyzing CloudTrail logs using CloudTrail Lake

To analyze CloudTrail logs with ease, AWS offers CloudTrail Lake (*https://oreil.ly/GNMPa*) as a managed data lake service that you can use to aggregate, visualize, or query user activity data that includes AWS and non-AWS actions.

CloudTrail Lake enables you to write SQL queries to analyze the data and also offers visualization capability with CloudTrail Lake Dashboards. It also makes writing SQL queries easier by enabling SQL query generation with natural language prompts. Alternatively, you can integrate Amazon Athena to query from CloudTrail Lake or can integrate Amazon QuickSight or Grafana for visualizations.

Analyzing Logs Using AWS Services

Analyzing logs helps troubleshoot issues or aggregate user actions to derive insights that can help make business decisions. After understanding the AWS services that enable you to store logs, let's review how you can analyze these logs.

Amazon Athena

As documented in the AWS documentation (*https://oreil.ly/CfJfc*), you can integrate Amazon Athena to query logs of several AWS services such as CloudTrail, VPC logs, Application Load Balancer, Network Load Balancer, Route53, and more. You can also query Amazon S3 access logs (*https://oreil.ly/yzJYN*) and web server logs (*https://oreil.ly/ZGNzW*).

You can define an external table that points to an Amazon S3 prefix and specifies the input file format with the respective SerDes to query the data using SQL. SerDes represents the serialization and deserialization process that converts data from one format to another. Serialization primarily converts data from a readable format to a compressed/encrypted storage format (e.g., text to binary), whereas deserialization represents converting compressed/encrypted storage format back to readable format (e.g., binary to text).

Amazon CloudWatch Log Insights

Using CloudWatch Log Insights (*https://oreil.ly/Jh_MS*), you can interactively query different logs available in CloudWatch and identify operational issues in your source application or AWS services. It provides query generation using natural language and can auto-detect fields available in logs. You can visualize the insights data using graphs and save the query and the query result for future reference.

AWS CloudTrail Insights

AWS CloudTrail Insights continuously analyzes management events and baselines the API call volumes and error rates. It generates insights in case of anomalies such as the API call volume or error rates being more than the baseline pattern. CloudTrail Insights analyzes management events that occur in a single AWS region.

Amazon OpenSearch Dashboards

Amazon OpenSearch Dashboards is an open source visualization tool designed to work with an Amazon OpenSearch cluster. OpenSearch Service enables installation of OpenSearch Dashboards with every domain you create and works only with the hot data you have on the cluster.

Processing logs with Amazon EMR or AWS Glue

You have learned about several AWS services that natively support capabilities to analyze log data, but there might be scenarios where you receive custom log formats or log data that is not well structured for querying. In such cases, you might need a data processing framework where you can integrate custom logic to parse the input log data and write the standardized output for easier querying.

AWS Glue or Amazon EMR service with Apache Spark framework are great options for such use cases that can help process terabyte-scale log data using their distributed processing capability. After transforming the log data, you can write to Amazon S3 for querying using Amazon Athena.

Auditing AWS configuration changes with AWS Config

AWS Config is a managed service that continuously assesses the configurations of AWS services and helps in auditing configuration changes over time. It is a great tool for implementing change management, as AWS Config keeps history of all changes, provides a dashboard for monitoring, and also delivers change history to Amazon S3 for compliance auditing. You can also leverage AWS Config to record configurations for third-party resources, on-premises servers, software-as-a-service (SaaS) tools, and many other resources.

Conclusion

In this chapter, we have dived deep into different data security, privacy, and governance controls, including securing networks with VPC and security groups, authentication and authorization with AWS IAM, securing data with encryption and AWS Lake Formation fine-grained access control, and handling several other data governance pillars with AWS services.

Next, let's try to validate our knowledge with a few practice questions that may help you prepare for the AWS Certified Data Engineer Associate exam.

Practice Questions

These practice questions may help you understand what kind of questions to expect on the exam so you can prepare accordingly. The answers are listed in the Appendix.

1. Assume your five-member team is spread across the globe and your application's RDS database is hosted in the AWS us-east-1 region. You have already got the IP address of your individual team members and would like to restrict access only to those IPs.

    What is the best way to configure this access restriction with the least-privilege access principle?

    A. Include the IP addresses in the Route 53 service, where the database fully qualified domain name is configured to restrict the access.

    B. Include the IP addresses in the security group of the database to specify inbound access is allowed only from those IPs.

    C. Include the IP addresses in the NACL of the VPC, so that the restriction is at the subnet level for least-privilege access.

    D. Include the IP addresses in the security group of the database to specify inbound access is allowed from those IPs only on the database port for connection.

2. Assume you are building a three-tier web application that has a React JS–based web interface that invokes a REST API configured using Amazon API Gateway. The API invokes an AWS Lambda function that writes to or reads from the RDS database. The database instance is deployed in a private VPC and you need to configure the Lambda function in a way that it can connect to the database.

Please note this three-tier application will have several REST APIs, which means you will have multiple Lambda functions that need to interact with the database. What is the most operationally efficient way you can configure access for the Lambda functions to connect to the database?

A. Configure the Lambda function and the RDS instance within the same VPC. Include the Lambda function and the database within a single subnet and configure NACL so that they can interact with each other seamlessly.

B. Deploy the Lambda function in the same VPC as the RDS instance, then add the Lambda function's security group in the RDS instance security group as inbound access.

C. Create an IAM role for the Lambda function and add a policy to access the RDS instance.

D. Configure a VPC endpoint for the Lambda function so that it can access the RDS instance natively.

3. Assume you have data stored in one AWS account (Account 1), which is encrypted using AWS KMS keys. You have received a request from users of another AWS account (Account 2) to access your account's (Account 1) datasets. What is the most efficient way to make sure that they can access the encrypted data?

A. Configure separate AWS KMS keys that belong to each account and encrypt the data in Account 1 with the KMS keys of Account 2, so that users of Account 2 can access it.

B. Share the KMS key of Account 1 with Account 2.

C. Instead of using AWS KMS, integrate SSE-S3 encryption, so that AWS takes care of the encryption/decryption internally.

D. Create a KMS key alias in Account 1 and share the key alias with Account 2 to access the data.

4. Your organization has a centralized data lake that holds the data of multiple business units such as Finance, Marketing, and Human Resources. You are supposed to implement tighter security control so that employees can access only the data belonging to their business unit. What is the best way to implement security for this?

A. Integrate IAM groups for each business unit and configure IAM roles so that users can access only their business unit data.

B. Make sure each database table has `business_unit` as an attribute and integrate AWS Lake Formation with a row filter for the `business_unit` attribute.

C. Configure S3 bucket policies with IAM users to make sure users can access the data available in a specific S3 prefix.

D. Set up separate data lakes for each business unit and integrate Lake Formation for fine-grained access control.

5. Your organization is planning to integrate a centralized metadata catalog across data lakes and data warehousing systems. They would like to reduce operational overhead and look for a managed solution. Which option in AWS is better suited to this scenario?

A. Integrate Hive Metastore with Apache Ranger to build the centralized catalog in AWS.

B. Set up Hive Metastore with AWS-managed databases such as Aurora to reduce operational overhead.

C. Integrate AWS Glue Data Catalog as the centralized catalog that integrates with most of the analytics services.

D. Build a custom catalog on top of AWS-managed databases so that you have the flexibility to manage the metadata.

6. You have enabled CloudTrail in your AWS account and for compliance audits you would like to query and analyze the logs with less operational overhead. What is the easiest way to implement this?

A. CloudTrail logs are stored in S3, so you can use S3 `SELECT` feature to directly query from S3 without any additional service.

B. Integrate Amazon Athena on top of CloudTrail logs in S3 to allow querying using SQL.

C. Leverage CloudTrail Lake, which natively supports analyzing CloudTrail logs.

D. CloudTrail logs are nested in format and also have a larger data size. So integrating Amazon EMR to process and analyze the logs is the best possible way.

7. Your organization has four business units and each business unit has its own data warehousing system built on Amazon Redshift. Each of the business units got their own AWS account where the Redshift cluster is set up. You need to enable data sharing between business units, where one business unit can share a few tables with another business unit directly. What is the operationally efficient way to achieve this requirement?

A. Leverage Redshift data share to share one cluster's data with another cluster that belongs to the consumer business unit.

B. As Redshift data share does not support cross-account data sharing, you can expose the data to AWS Data Exchange and leverage fine-grained access control with AWS Lake Formation.

C. Export the data that needs to be shared to Amazon S3 and integrate Lake Formation fine-grained access control to share with the consumer business unit to query using Athena.

D. The easiest way is to set up AWS Clean Rooms collaboration by bringing in the four business units as collaborators and enabling data sharing and querying using Clean Rooms.

8. Your company has multiple business units and each business unit has its own AWS account. To structure the AWS accounts better, you have already integrated AWS Organizations. As part of your data backup strategy, you have defined a few AWS Regions where the backup data should be stored. To avoid human error, you would like to put restrictions so that no team can push backup data to an AWS Region that is not approved. What is the best way to achieve this requirement?

A. Create CloudFormation templates that configure backup policies to write backups only to approved AWS Regions. Let your team use only the Cloud Formation templates for configuring backups.

B. Define service control policies to restrict writing backups to unapproved Regions.

C. Configure AWS Backup in a central AWS account to trigger backup in other accounts and make sure the central account has a configuration to write to the approved Regions.

D. Create a custom utility that is managed by your organization's security team and is configured to write backups to approved Regions only. Define guidelines for all teams to use the common utility for backups.

9. Your mobile application has a backend relational database built on Amazon Aurora Serverless V2 with PostgreSQL as the database engine. You have batch analytics queries that run on the database every month for end-of-the-month reporting. Over the years, the data in the database has grown significantly and you have started seeing performance issues in the database queries. To improve the performance and also enable a few additional use cases, you have decided to move older data from the database to Amazon S3 for analytics. What is the operationally efficient way to implement this requirement?

A. Integrate stored procedures within the Aurora database that query older data and write to Amazon S3.

B. Write a custom AWS Glue ETL job that is scheduled to run every night and that queries older data from S3 and writes the output to Amazon S3.

C. Leverage the Export to S3 feature of Aurora PostgreSQL to automate the older data export requirement.

D. Create monthly database snapshots and copy them to Amazon S3 for analytics.

10. Your application is built using Amazon API Gateway for REST APIs, AWS Lambda for serverless compute, and Amazon Aurora as the backend database. Your security team identified that your Lambda function's Python code has hardcoded database credentials that are checked in to the Github repositories. To avoid the security risk, you are assigned to come up with the best way to configure the database credentials in AWS. Which of the following approaches would you suggest as the most secure solution?

A. Remove the database credentials from the Lambda function's Python code and configure them as environmental variables of the Lambda function.

B. Create a configuration database that has encryption at rest and stores all the database credentials. Let the Lambda function query the database in real time to query the latest credentials and then connect to it for querying.

C. Integrate AWS Secrets Manager to store the database credentials and the Lambda function to refer to the secrets in its code.

D. Create a database configuration file that is stored in an Amazon S3 bucket, which is only accessible to the Lambda function. Let the Lambda function read the credentials from the configuration file from S3 when it needs to query the database.

Additional Resources

The following are a few additional resources that will help you dive deeper and gain more knowledge on data security and governance in AWS:

- Organization and network security:
  - "Controlling Access with Security Groups" (*https://oreil.ly/71V39*)
  - "Scenarios for Accessing a DB Cluster in a VPC" (*https://oreil.ly/nGKBM*)
  - "Control Network Traffic with Security Groups for Your Amazon EMR Cluster" (*https://oreil.ly/ZiGiE*)
  - "Identity Providers and Federation" (*https://oreil.ly/i4r8m*)
  - "Amazon Security Lake and AWS Organizations" (*https://oreil.ly/g4j7U*)
- Data security:
  - "Data Protection in Amazon S3" (*https://oreil.ly/_jXz1*)

- Monitoring data security with AWS Managed Security Services (*https://oreil.ly/MMEKC*)

- "Security Best Practices for Amazon S3" (*https://oreil.ly/yZOXu*)

- Managing Redshift database security (*https://oreil.ly/NVJpv*)

- Security best practices for AWS KMS (*https://oreil.ly/d0wxI*)

- Data governance:

  - "Data Governance with AWS" (*https://oreil.ly/rmdcs*)

  - AWS Cloud Adoption Framework and data governance (*https://oreil.ly/LEMwH*)

  - Enterprise Data Governance Catalog (*https://oreil.ly/-nOVH*)

  - "AWS Offerings for Data Mesh" (*https://oreil.ly/ulZvn*)

  - "Monitoring and Optimizing the Data Lake Environment" (*https://oreil.ly/of0gM*)

## CHAPTER 8

Implementing Batch and Streaming Pipelines

In previous chapters, we provided an overview of AWS data analytics services and explained how to design a data ingestion pipeline, apply transformations, manage data stores, implement security and governance, and achieve operational efficiency for your analytics workloads.

In this chapter, we will provide a hands-on implementation guide of popular use cases for batch and streaming pipelines. Before getting started, please make sure you have created an AWS account and configured IAM permissions as described in Chapter 2.

Data Processing Pipeline

A data processing pipeline is a sequence of steps to refine and transform the data and make it available in a format that can be consumed by end users for analytics. The use cases for which data needs to be transformed may include the following:

- Cleansing data and improving data quality
- Transforming data by aggregating with internal datasets and applying specific business rules
- Formatting it for time series analysis or preparing data for machine learning model development
- Creating a specific data model for faster data analysis or BI reporting
- Making data available in a specific format to share with downstream systems

Figure 8-1 represents a high-level architecture for a data pipeline that includes data sources, data ingestion, data processing, and data consumption layers.

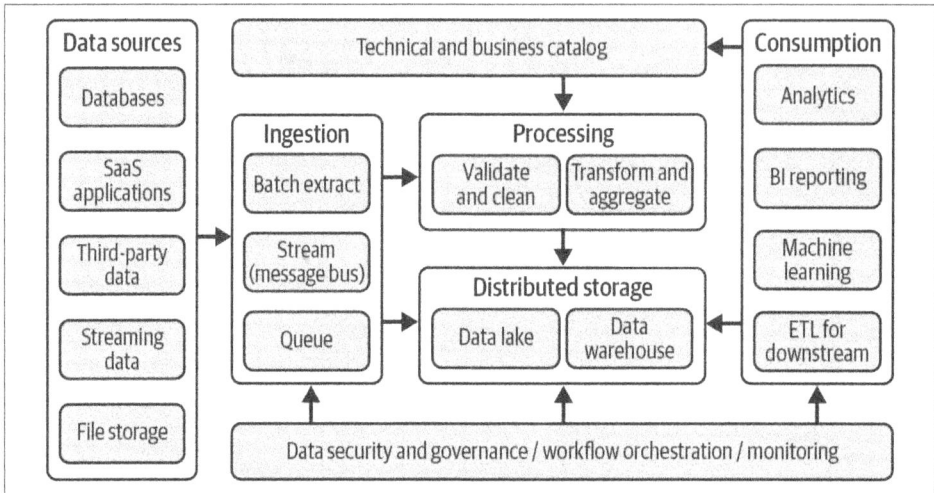

Figure 8-1. High-level architecture for data processing pipeline

Next, let's take publicly available sample datasets and implement a batch and streaming pipeline with detailed hands-on steps in AWS.

Implementing a Batch Processing Pipeline

Batch processing means combining multiple records or files to be processed at once. The processing frequency can be scheduled or executed on demand. Let's take an example use case and follow a step-by-step implementation guide to execute a data processing job as a batch.

> Please note that implementing the end-to-end solution will have some cost implications based on AWS public pricing for each service. Except for the AWS Glue PySpark job, the rest of the services might be eligible for the Free Tier so please check the AWS Free Tier documentation (*https://oreil.ly/8lGC-*).

Use Case and Architecture Overview

Figure 8-2 represents a high-level architecture that includes the following steps:

Step 1.1
   Input datasets are uploaded to the Amazon S3 Raw input bucket.

Steps 1.21 and 1.22

AWS Glue PySpark is triggered through an Amazon EventBridge scheduler.

Step 1.3

The Glue PySpark job loads the transformed data into an Amazon Redshift table.

Steps 2.1 and 2.2

A data analyst builds an Amazon QuickSight visualization that summarizes the data of the Redshift table.

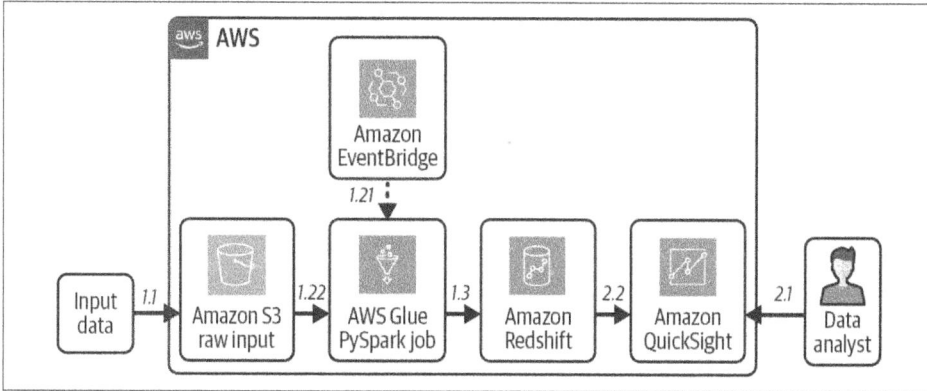

Figure 8-2. High-level architecture for batch data processing pipeline

Overview of Input Dataset

To explain the use case, we will refer to the publicly available sales dataset (*https://oreil.ly/YWGJZ*), which contains a list of over 20,000 sales opportunity records for a fictitious business. Each record has fields that specify the following:

- A date, potentially when an opportunity was identified
- The salesperson's name
- A market segment to which the opportunity belongs
- Forecasted monthly revenue

For this use case, let's assume these sales CSV files are maintained by your organization's Sales team and that they upload the input files to Amazon S3 input bucket at the end of every month. The aggregated output data is created through a series of data preparation steps, and the business team uses the output data to create business intelligence (BI) reports.

Step-by-Step Implementation Guide

Before beginning these steps, make sure you have the required permissions to create the resources required as part of the solution. Please note that we have used the us-east-1 region to deploy the solution but you can choose your preferred region before getting started.

> Please note the implementation steps in this chapter mention the Amazon S3 bucket name "ch8-ex1-input-data." Amazon S3 names should be globally unique within a partition (AWS partitions as specified in the AWS documentation (*https://oreil.ly/ME_l7*): aws [commercial regions], aws-cn [China regions], and aws-us-gov [AWS GovCloud (US) regions]). While implementing in your AWS account, please make sure to add a few random characters at the end of the bucket name so that it is unique.

Create Amazon S3 buckets

Refer to the following steps to create the Amazon S3 input bucket or prefix and upload the sales data CSV into it:

1. Navigate to the Amazon S3 console (*https://oreil.ly/DRHfd*).
2. Choose "Create bucket."
3. Specify the bucket name as ch8-ex1-input-data and leave the remaining fields as default as represented in Figure 8-3.

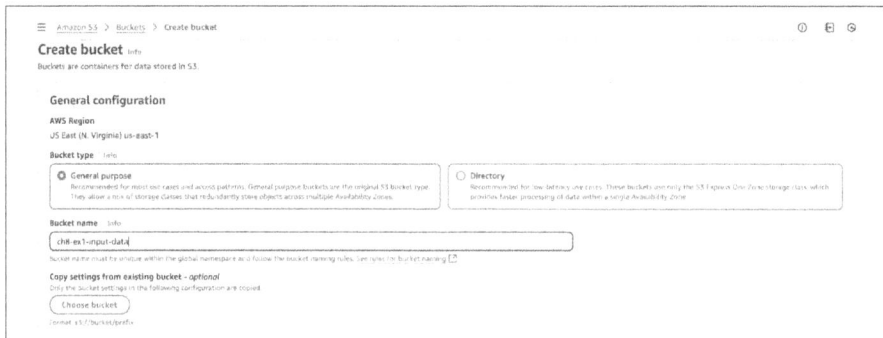

Figure 8-3. Create Amazon S3 bucket using AWS console

4. Choose "Create bucket."
5. On the bucket detail page, choose Upload.

6. Then choose "Add files" and upload the sales dataset (*https://oreil.ly/YWGJZ*) into it. Figure 8-4 represents the sales dataset file successfully uploaded to the defined S3 bucket.

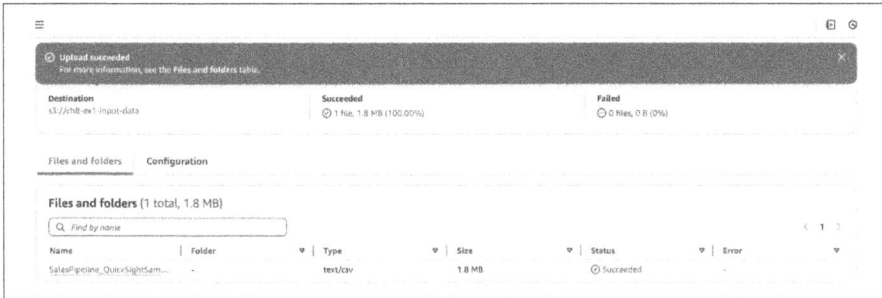

Figure 8-4. Amazon S3 console (object upload successful screen)

Create Amazon Redshift cluster

Refer to the following steps to create a Redshift Serverless cluster:

1. Navigate to the Amazon Redshift Serverless console (*https://oreil.ly/-wkF4*).

2. Choose "Create workgroup."

3. As represented in Figure 8-5, specify the Workgroup name as "ch8-ex1-redshift-serverless" and the Base capacity as 8, which is the default minimum. Then click Next.

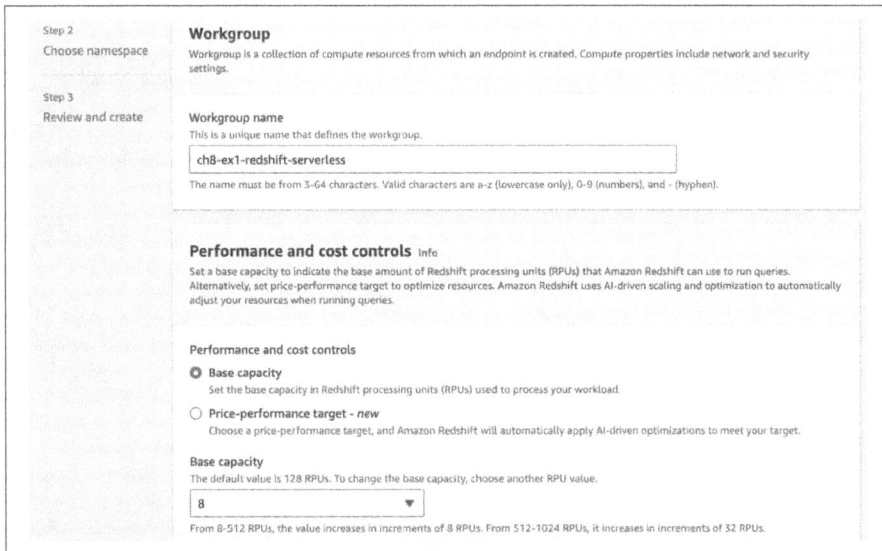

Figure 8-5. Amazon Redshift: create cluster using AWS Console

4. As represented in Figure 8-6, specify "salesdata" in the Namespace field with the "Create a new namespace" option. In addition, choose "Customize admin user credentials" and specify a password for your database.

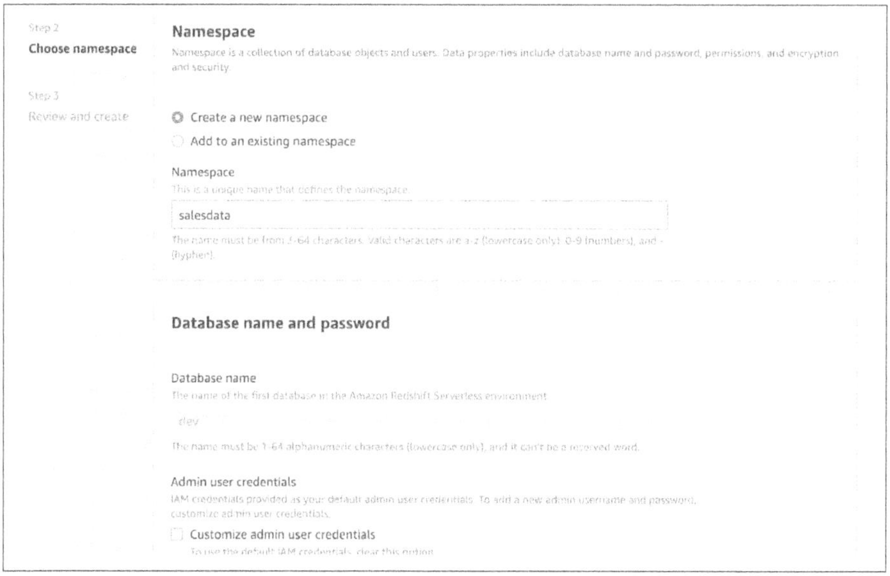

Figure 8-6. Amazon Redshift: create a namespace using the AWS Console

5. Under Permissions, select "Create IAM role" and select the "Any S3 bucket" option to create the IAM role. After creating, you should see the output in Figure 8-7. Please note, we have selected the "Any S3 bucket" option for this use case implementation but you can follow the least privilege principle and make the permission more restrictive to specific S3 buckets.

6. Leave the other values as default and Choose Next.

7. In the review screen, review the configurations and choose Create.

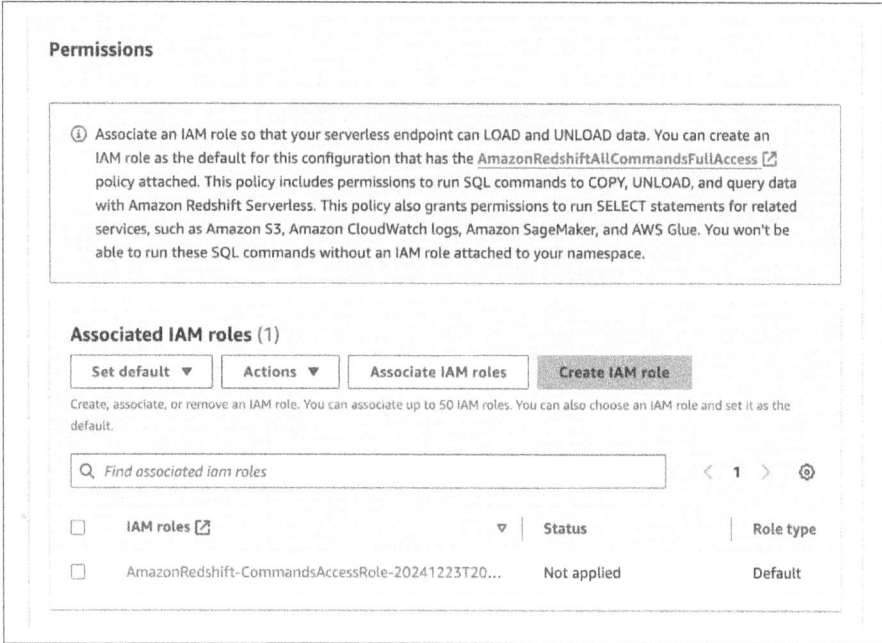

Figure 8-7. Amazon Redshift: associate IAM role to the cluster

In a few minutes, you should see that the "ch8-ex1-redshift-serverless" workgroup has been created and attached to the salesdata namespace.

You need to make sure that the security group attached to the Redshift cluster's workgroup has allowed inbound access on the "8182" port and also has allowed inbound access from the same security group as shown in Figure 8-8. You can select the same security group for the Glue job so it can connect to the Redshift cluster.

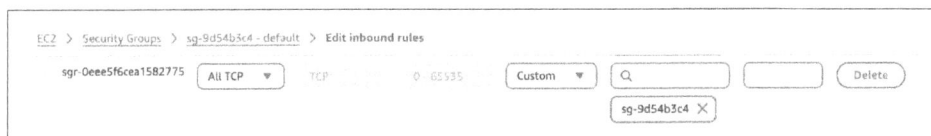

Figure 8-8. Amazon Redshift: attach inbound rule to the security group

Next, let's create a data connection in AWS Glue so that the Glue ETL job can leverage the connection to write to the Redshift cluster.

Create Glue data connection for the Redshift cluster

Before creating a Glue job, let's first create a data connection for the new Redshift namespace:

1. To create the connection, you will need the Redshift cluster's connection details. To get those details, navigate to the Redshift cluster workgroup page, then collect the JDBC URL from the General information section as shown in Figure 8-9.

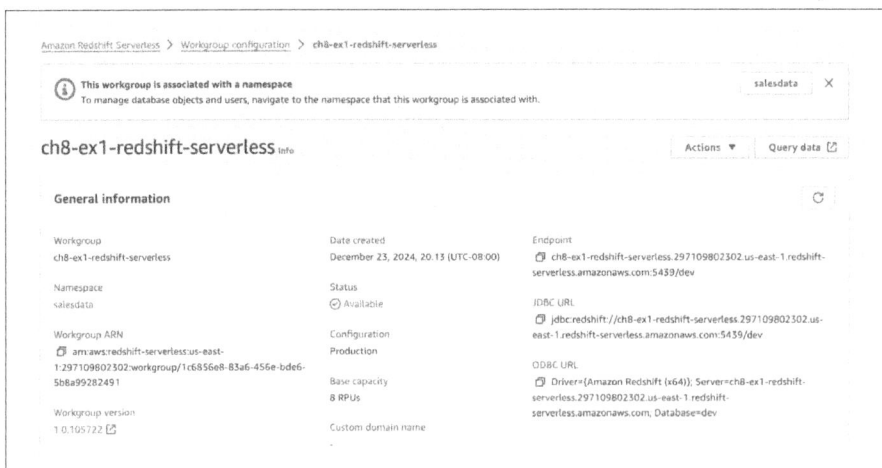

Figure 8-9. Amazon Redshift: cluster workgroup detail page

2. Also collect the VPC, subnet, and security group details from the Data access tab as shown in Figure 8-10.

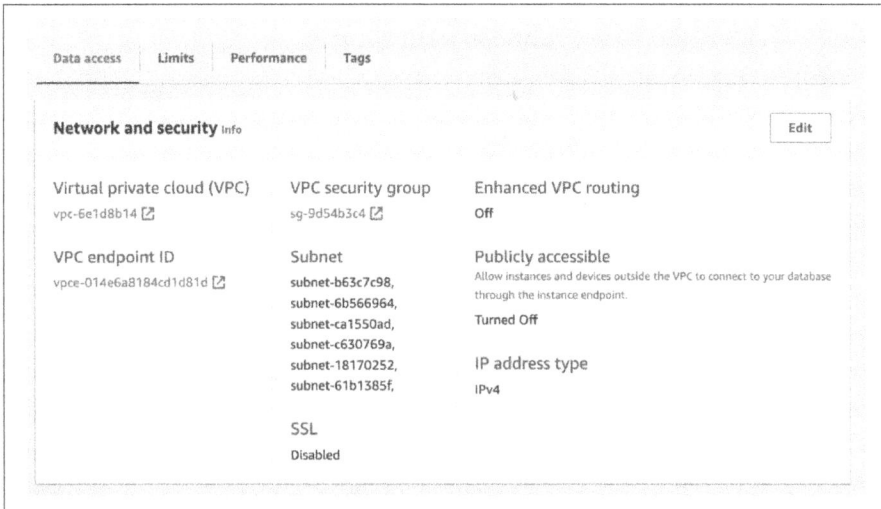

Figure 8-10. Amazon Redshift Cluster: Network connectivity and access security details

Save these details in a notepad, as they will be needed while creating the Glue connection.

3. Next, navigate to AWS Glue's data connection console (*https://oreil.ly/59LaV*).

4. Under Connections, choose "Create connection."

5. In Data sources, search for JDBC, select the JDBC connection option as shown in Figure 8-11, and choose Next.

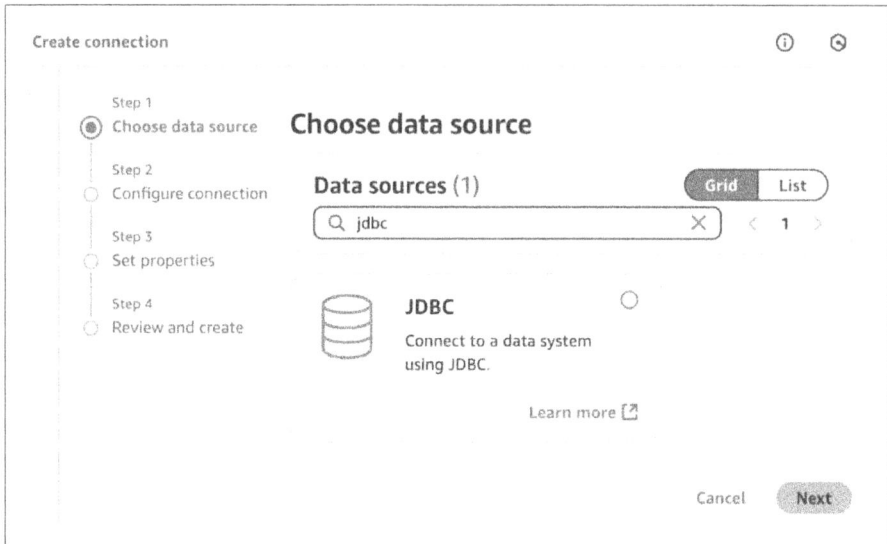

Figure 8-11. AWS Glue: create a data connection

6. As shown in Figure 8-12, specify the Redshift cluster JDBC URL and provide the Username and Password for authentication.

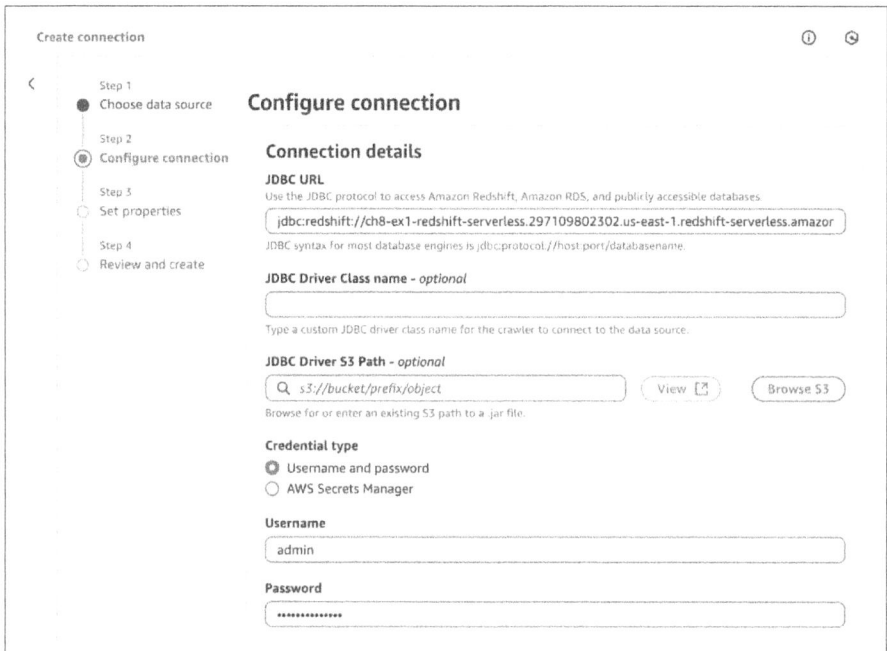

Figure 8-12. AWS Glue: configure data connection

7. As illustrated in Figure 8-13, expand the Network options section to specify the VPC, subnet (select one of the subnets that your Redshift cluster is assigned to), and security group. Then choose Next.

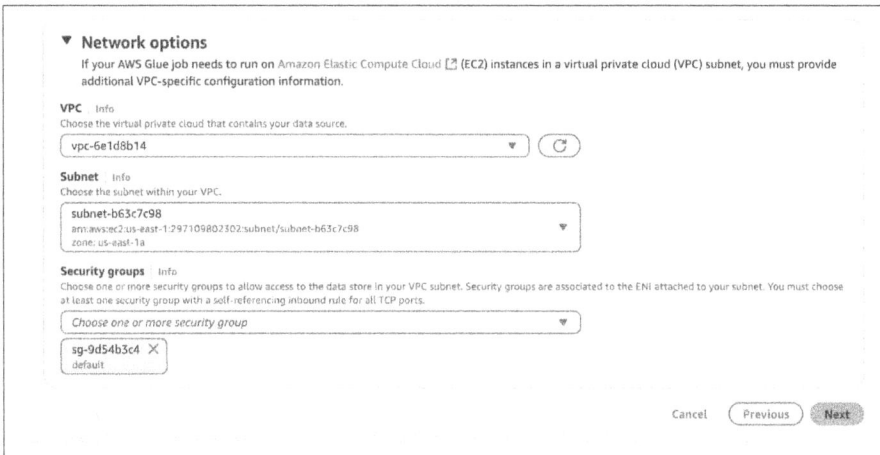

Figure 8-13. AWS Glue data connection: configure network

8. In the next screen specify the connection Name as "ch8-ex1-redshift-connection" as represented in Figure 8-14 and choose Next.

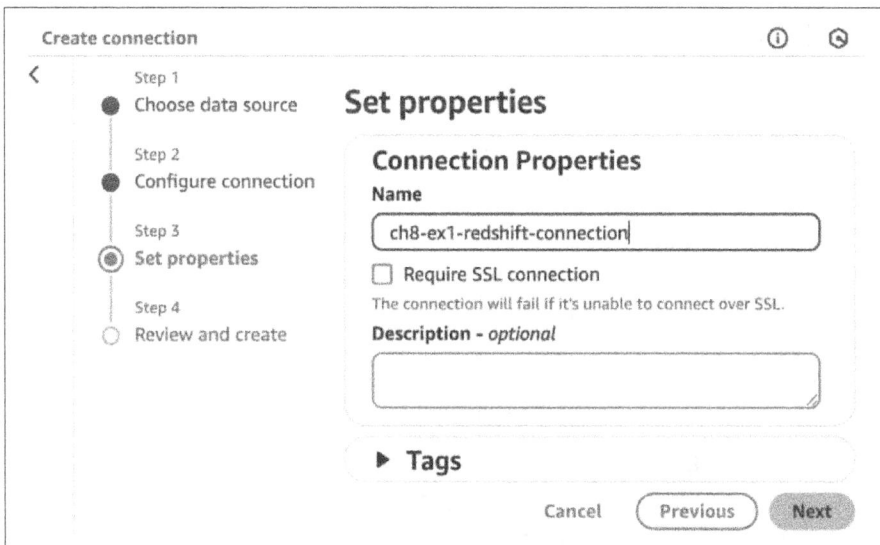

Figure 8-14. AWS Glue data connection: set properties

9. As represented in Figure 8-15, review the details in the final screen and choose "Create connection." This should take you to the connection detail page with a success message.

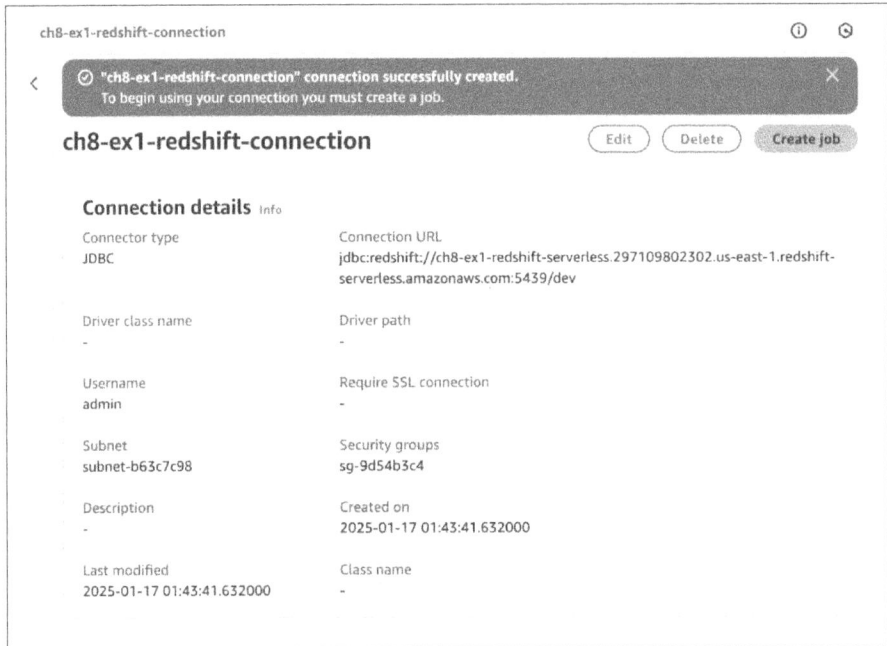

Figure 8-15. AWS Glue data connection detail

After we create the connection, we will create a Glue PySpark ETL job, which will ingest the raw data available in the Amazon S3 path to the Redshift Serverless cluster.

Create AWS Glue PySpark ETL job

Refer to the following steps to create a Glue ETL job through the Glue Studio interface:

1. Navigate to the Glue Studio console (*https://oreil.ly/1pzVQ*).

2. Choose Visual ETL, which will take you to the Studio editor.

3. From the Visual tab, add Amazon S3 as the source, configure its properties to point to the input S3 bucket where we uploaded the sales data CSV file, and specify the type as CSV as represented in Figure 8-16.

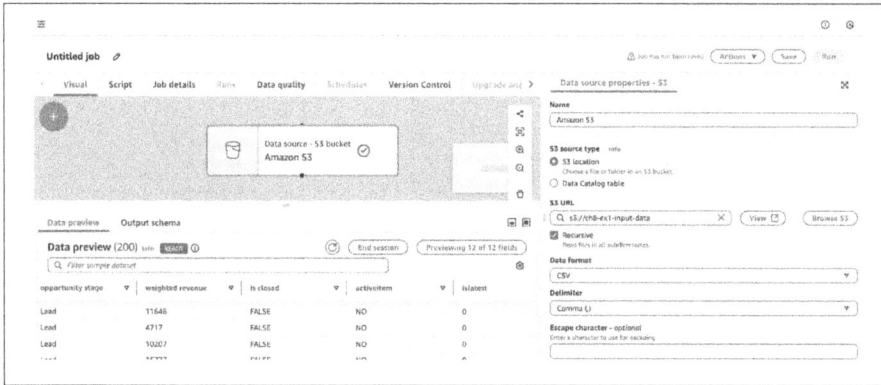

Figure 8-16. AWS Glue Studio: design ETL pipeline

4. As you make progress in the visual studio, it's better to save the job, which you can do by specifying a name for the Glue job (e.g., "ch8-glue-spark-etl-job") and choosing Save.

5. Please note that the CSV header has column names with empty space and before writing the data to Redshift, we need to rename the columns by replacing empty spaces with an underscore (_). To rename the columns, you can integrate the Change Schema transformation.

6. Choose the + icon in the visual editor and search "Change Schema," then choose that. As shown in Figure 8-17, choose Amazon S3 under Node parents, and rename the columns (e.g., "opportunity stage" to "opportunity_stage," "weighted revenue" to "weighted_revenue") to replace the empty space with an underscore.

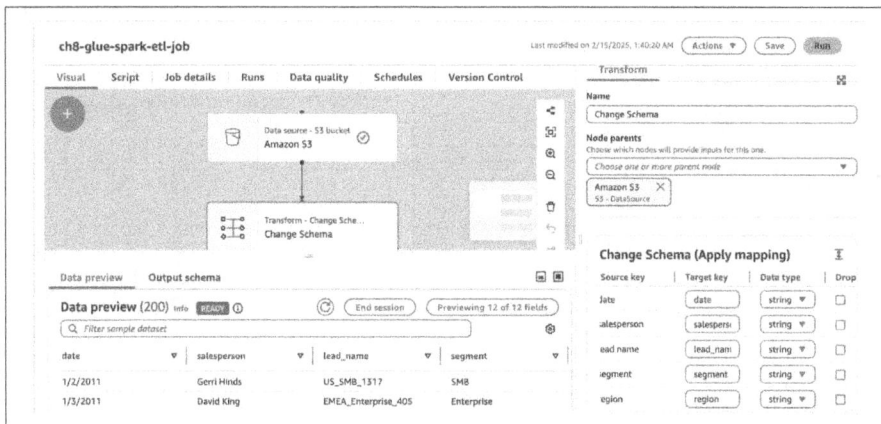

Figure 8-17. AWS Glue Studio: design ETL pipeline: change schema

7. Next choose the + icon in the visual editor and add "Redshift" as the target node. As represented in Figure 8-18, configure the Redshift connection properties by

specifying the Parent node as "Change Schema," the Data Connection name as "ch8-ex1-redshift-connection," the Schema as "public," and the Table as "sales."

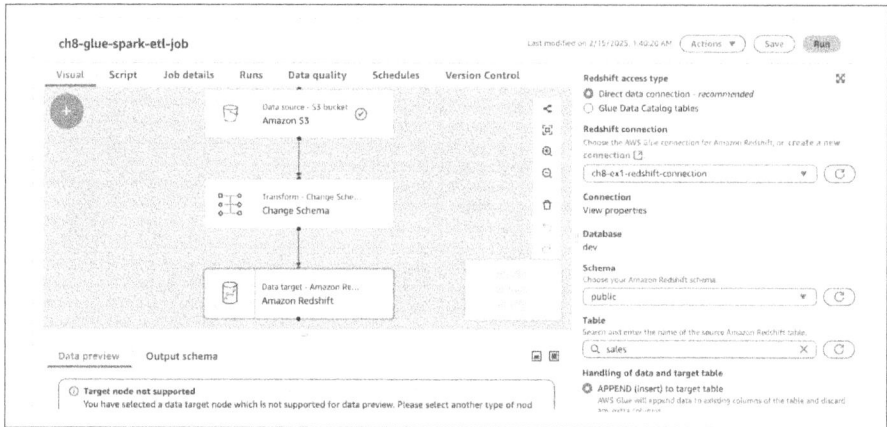

Figure 8-18. AWS Glue Studio: design ETL Pipeline—Redshift target

8. Make sure to configure the IAM role in the Job details tab so that it has permission to read the input S3 bucket, execute the Glue job, and write to the Amazon Redshift cluster.

9. Finally choose Run, which will trigger an execution, and you can see the status of the job in the Runs tab. As shown in Figure 8-19, the initial status of the run will be "Waiting," as it waits for the compute resources to get assigned.

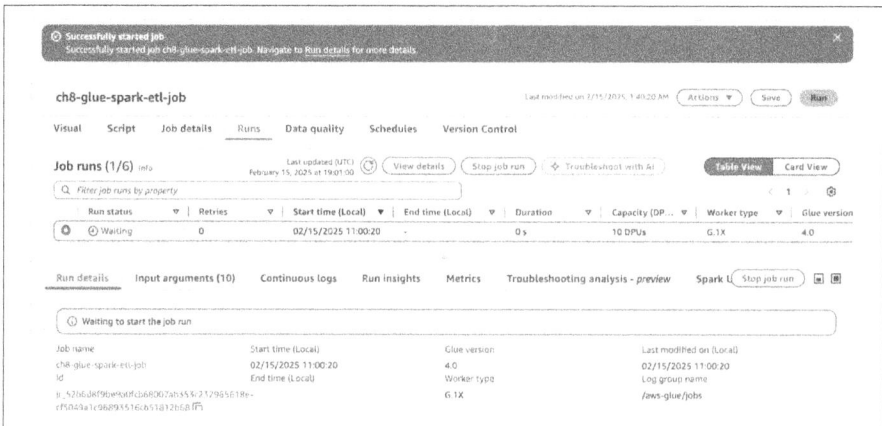

Figure 8-19. AWS Glue: ETL job run

10. Then you will notice the status transitions to "Running," and then "Succeeded" as represented in Figure 8-20.

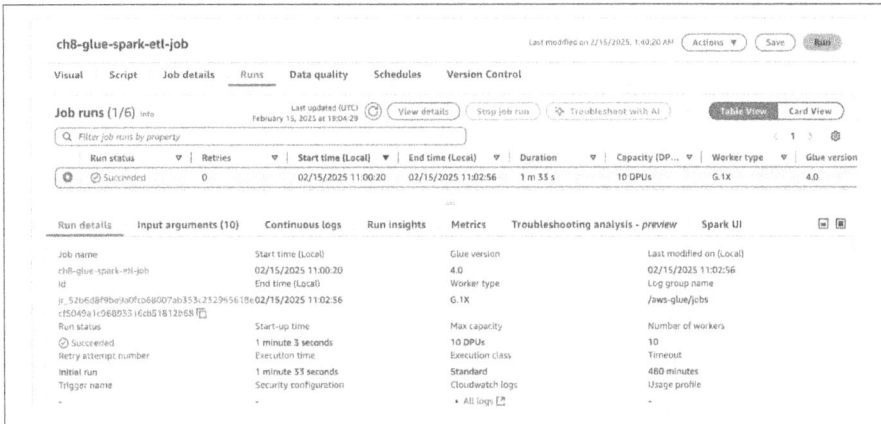

Figure 8-20. AWS Glue: ETL job run succeeded

11. After the job is successfully completed, navigate to the Redshift cluster (*https://oreil.ly/-wkF4*), choose the "salesdata" namespace and then choose "Query data," which will load the Redshift Query Editor v2.

12. Within the Query Editor, choose the "ch8-ex1-redshift-serverless" cluster, and navigate to native databases → dev → public → Tables, then execute a SELECT query on the "sales" table. You should see the output illustrated in Figure 8-21, which validates the Glue job ingested data to the Redshift cluster successfully.

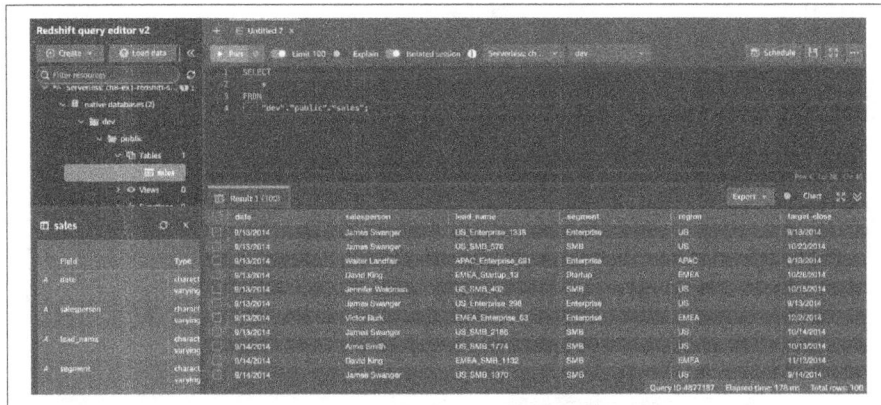

Figure 8-21. Amazon Redshift Query Editor v2 in the AWS Console

Next, let's create a visualization using Amazon QuickSight on top of the data ingested into the Redshift cluster.

Create Amazon QuickSight execution role using AWS IAM

Before creating the visualization, you will need to create an AWS IAM role that will act as QuickSight's execution role. For the execution role, you'll need to create or select an IAM role with the necessary permissions for QuickSight to interact with your VPC and Redshift cluster. Here are the permissions the role should have:

- VPC access:
  - ec2:CreateNetworkInterface
  - ec2:DescribeNetworkInterfaces
  - ec2:DeleteNetworkInterface
  - ec2:DescribeSubnets
  - ec2:DescribeSecurityGroups
  - ec2:DescribeVpcs
- Redshift access:
  - redshift:DescribeClusters
  - redshift:DescribeClusterSubnetGroups
  - redshift:DescribeClusterSecurityGroups
- If you're using Redshift Serverless:
  - redshift-serverless:GetWorkgroup
  - redshift-serverless:ListWorkgroups

Here's a sample IAM policy that includes these permissions:

```
{
    "Version": "2012-10-17",
    "Statement": [
        {
            "Effect": "Allow",
            "Action": [
                "ec2:CreateNetworkInterface",
                "ec2:DescribeNetworkInterfaces",
                "ec2:DeleteNetworkInterface",
                "ec2:DescribeSubnets",
                "ec2:DescribeSecurityGroups",
                "ec2:DescribeVpcs",
                "redshift:DescribeClusters",
                "redshift:DescribeClusterSubnetGroups",
```

```
                "redshift:DescribeClusterSecurityGroups",
                "redshift-serverless:GetWorkgroup",
                "redshift-serverless:ListWorkgroups"
            ],
            "Resource": "*"
        }
    ]
}
```

To create this role:

1. Go to the AWS IAM console.
2. Click on "Roles" in the left sidebar.
3. Click "Create role."
4. For "Trusted entity type," choose "AWS service."
5. For "Use case," choose EC2.
6. Click Next.
7. Attach the preceding policy (you can create a new policy with the JSON provided).
8. Give the role a name (e.g., "quicksight-redshift-vpc-access").
9. Create the role.

Once you create the role, attach a few additional permissions to this role as specified in the "Prerequisites" section of the AWS documentation (*https://oreil.ly/PMlNr*).

Remember, it's a best practice to follow the principle of least privilege. If you know exactly which VPCs, subnets, and Redshift clusters you'll be accessing, you can further restrict the "Resource" section of the policy to those specific ARNs for added security.

Sign up for and manage Amazon QuickSight

In the AWS Console's search box, search for "QuickSight" and choose that, which will load the screen shown in Figure 8-22 if you have not signed up for QuickSight yet.

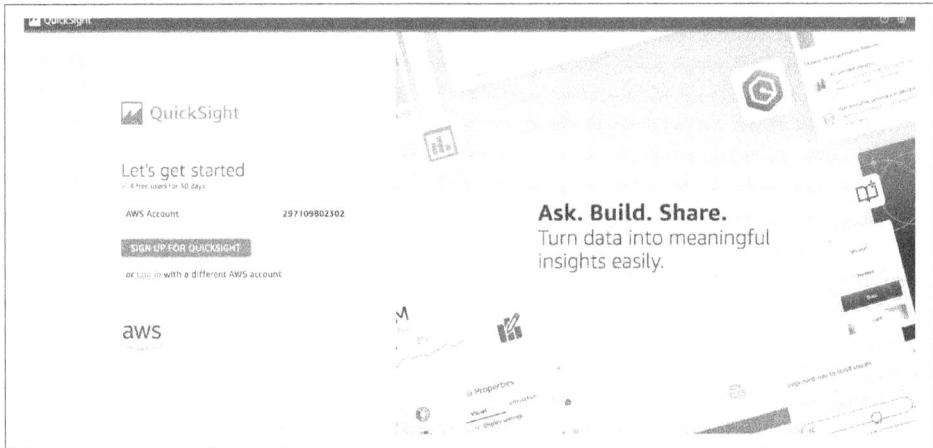

Figure 8-22. Amazon QuickSight: sign up screen

Choose "SIGN UP FOR QUICKSIGHT," which will load to the page in Figure 8-23. For the "Authentication method," choose "Use IAM federated identities & QuickSight-managed users," choose the AWS region where your Redshift Serverless cluster is created, and provide a QuickSight account name.

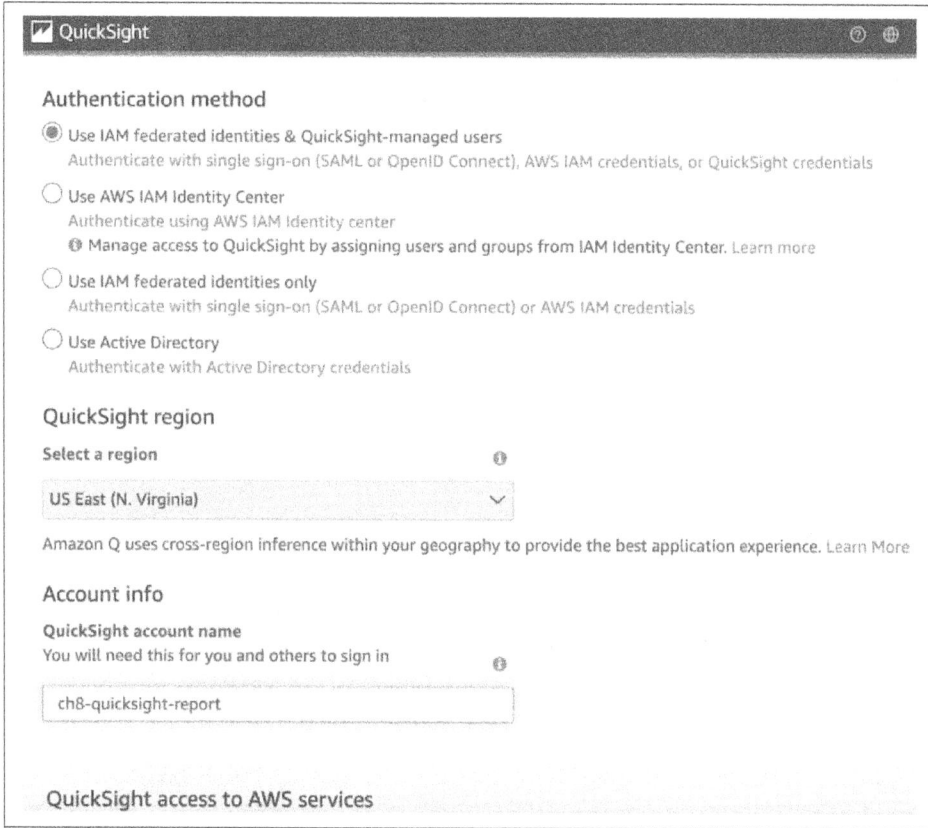

Figure 8-23. Amazon QuickSight: sign up properties

Once you submit, you should see something similar to Figure 8-24, which shows that the account was created successfully.

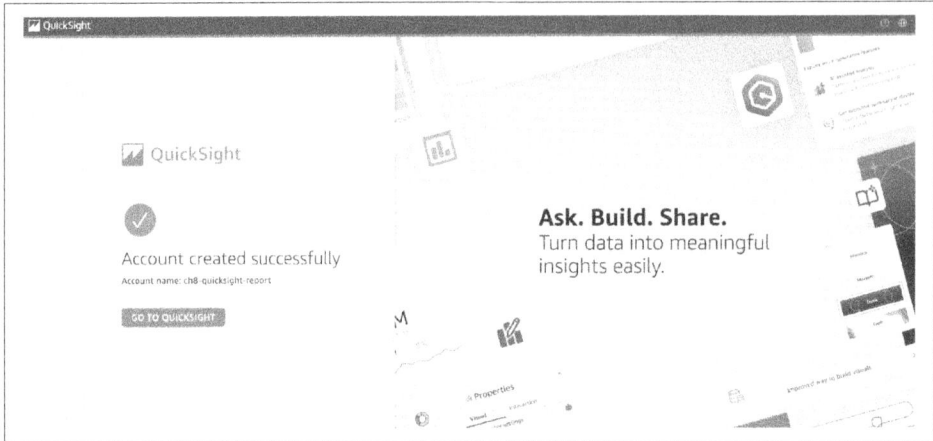

Figure 8-24. Amazon QuickSight: account created successfully

Next, let's add the VPC connection, so that QuickSight can connect to the Redshift cluster. Choose the profile icon on the top right corner and choose Manage QuickSight, which will take you to all the settings you can manage for QuickSight (Figure 8-25).

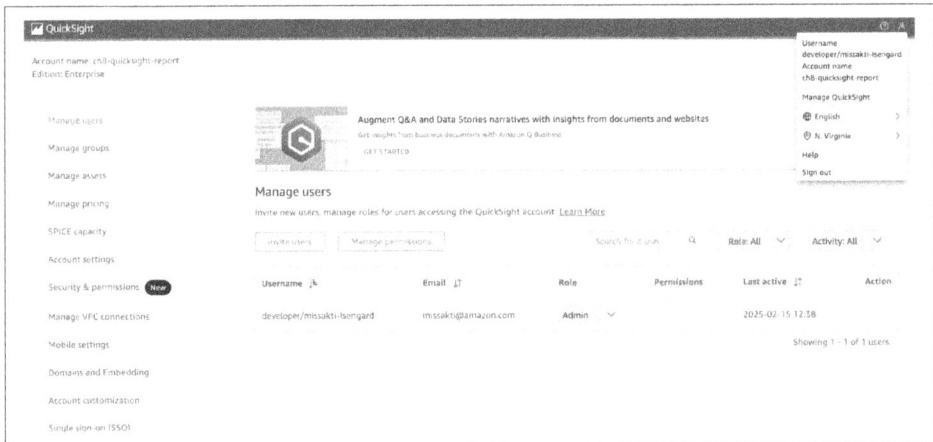

Figure 8-25. Amazon QuickSight: option to manage QuickSight

Then from the left navigation choose Manage VPC Connections and then Add VPC Connection, which will take you to a page similar to Figure 8-26:

1. Specify a name for the connection.

2. Specify the VPC ID (same as the Redshift cluster).

3. Select "quicksight-redshift-vpc-access" for the Execution role.

4. Select the subnet IDs for all the Availability Zones.

5. Select the same Redshift cluster security group for the Security Group IDs.

6. Choose Add.

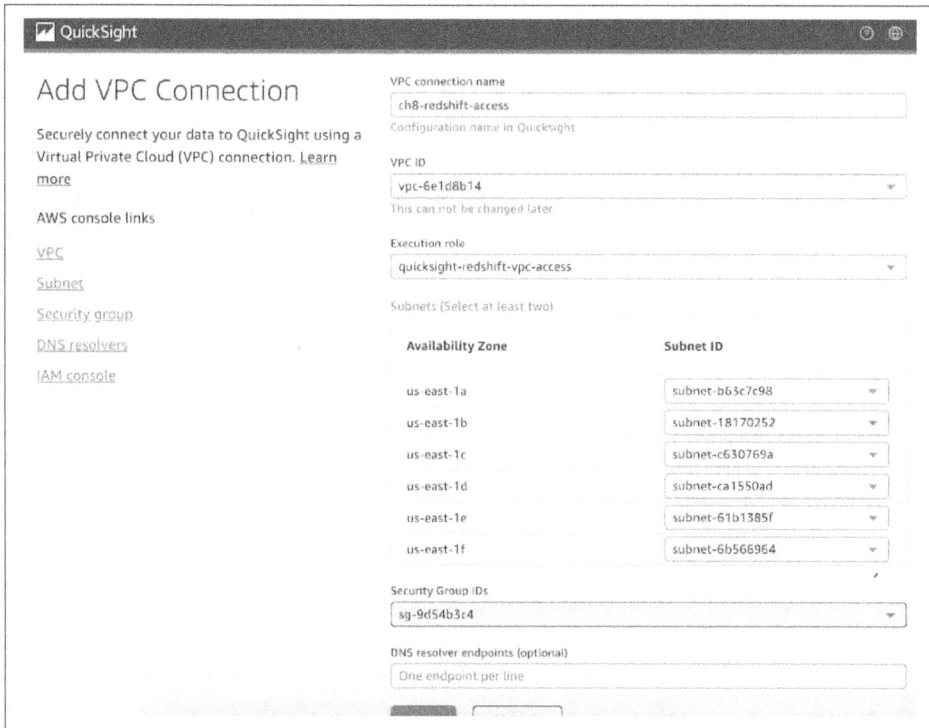

Figure 8-26. Amazon QuickSight: add VPC connection

You should see the VPC connection's initial status as UNAVAILABLE (Figure 8-27) and after a few minutes, the status should change to AVAILABLE, as shown in Figure 8-28.

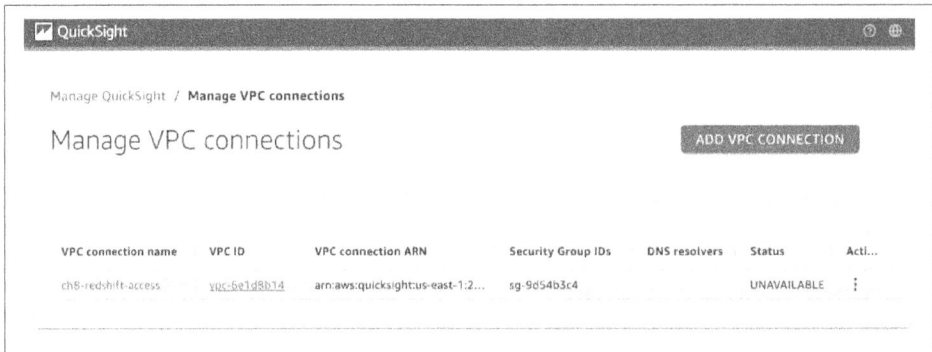

Figure 8-27. Amazon QuickSight: manage VPC connection in UNAVAILABLE status

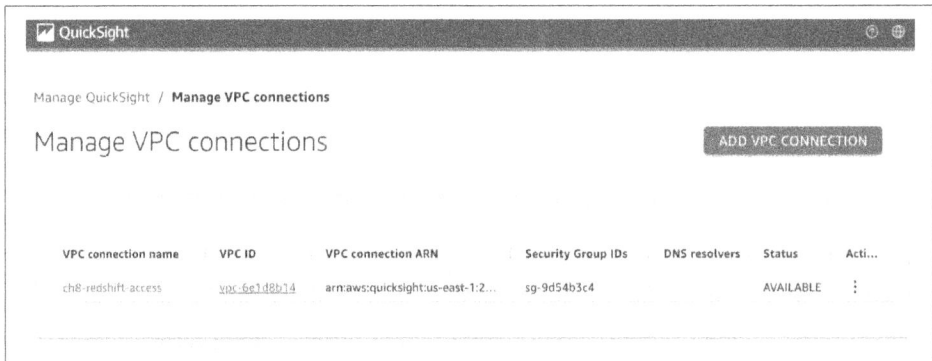

Figure 8-28. Amazon QuickSight: VPC connection now available

Next, choose "Security & permissions" from the left navigation of the Manage Quick-Sight page, and choose Manage for the "IAM role in use." In the next screen, choose "Use an existing role" option and select the "quicksight-redshift-vpc-access" role you created in the previous step. Then choose Save, as shown in Figure 8-29.

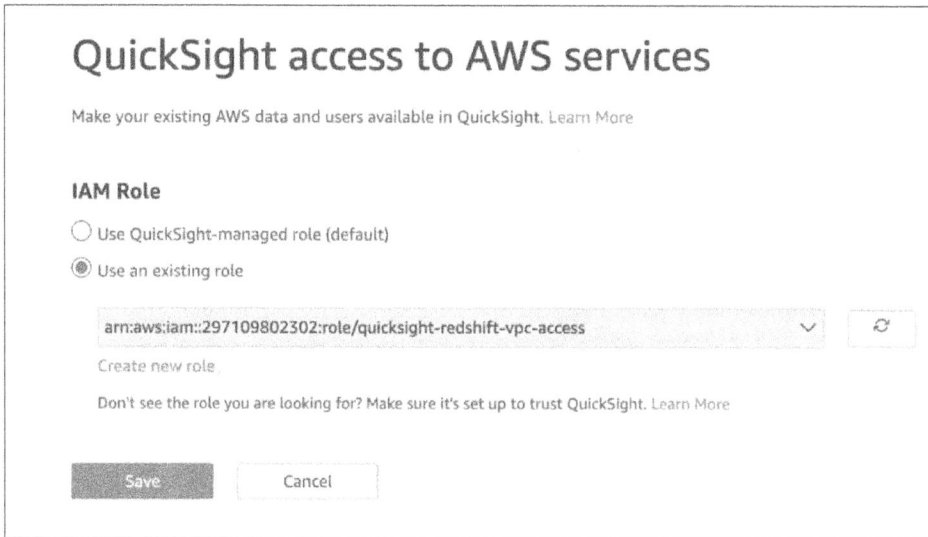

QuickSight access to AWS services

Make your existing AWS data and users available in QuickSight. Learn More

IAM Role

○ Use QuickSight-managed role (default)

◉ Use an existing role

arn:aws:iam::297109802302:role/quicksight-redshift-vpc-access ⌄ | ⟳

Create new role

Don't see the role you are looking for? Make sure it's set up to trust QuickSight. Learn More

[Save] [Cancel]

Figure 8-29. Amazon QuickSight: attach an existing role

These steps mark completion of the QuickSight setup. This should make you ready to create datasets and visualizations.

Create Amazon QuickSight visualization

Navigate back to the QuickSight home screen by clicking the QuickSight logo available in the top left corner and choose Datasets from the left navigation. Then choose "Create a Dataset," which will load a page similar to Figure 8-30, and choose the "Redshift - Manual connect" option.

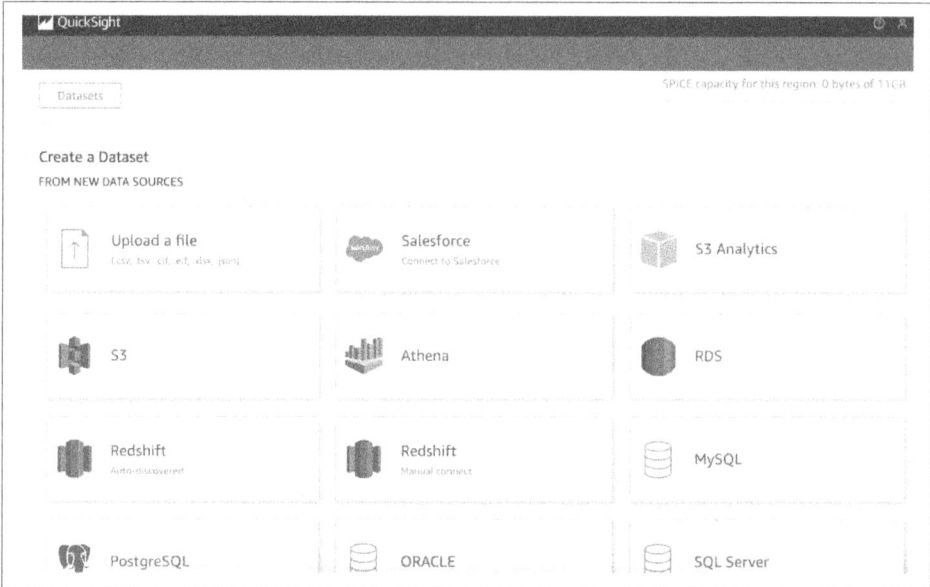

Figure 8-30. Amazon QuickSight: create a dataset

Populate the Redshift connection details in the New Redshift data source overlay with the same details you used while creating the Glue data connection (Figure 8-31). Choose Validate to confirm the connection is successful and then choose "Create data source."

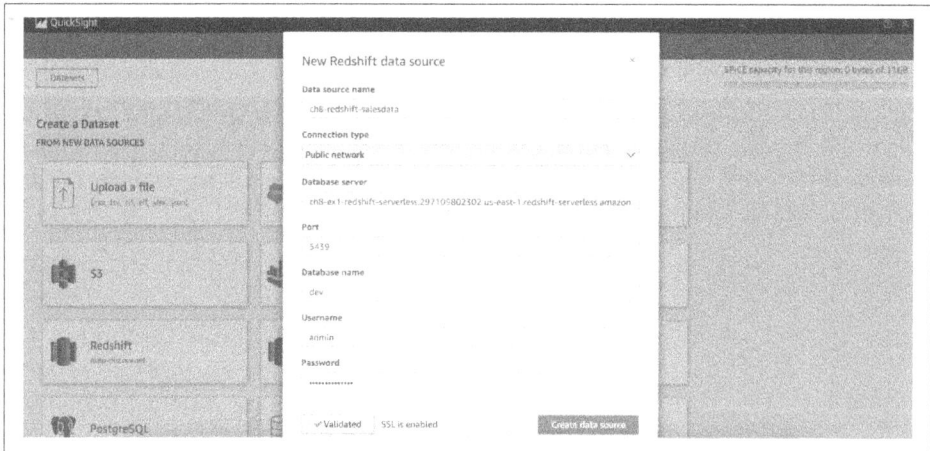

Figure 8-31. Amazon QuickSight: configure Redshift data source

In the next screen, choose "public" for Schema and "sales" for Tables and then choose Select (Figure 8-32).

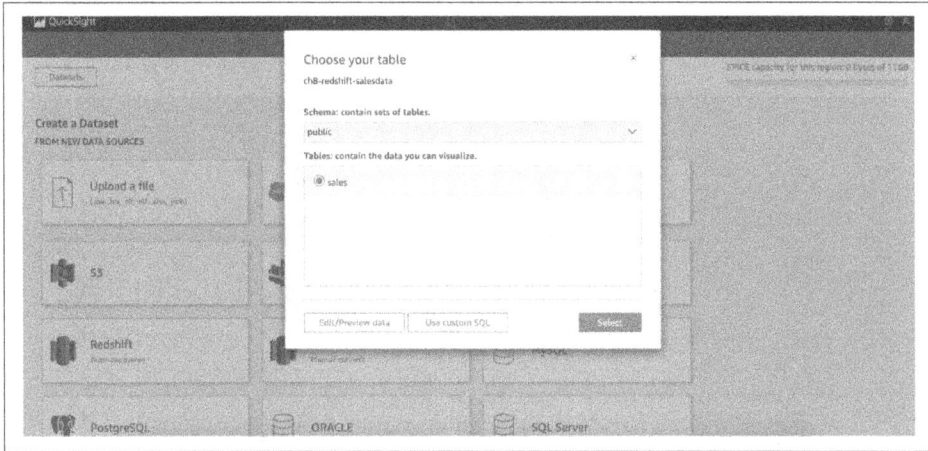

Figure 8-32. Amazon QuickSight: select Redshift table

In the following "Finish dataset creation" screen, choose "Import to SPICE for quicker analytics" and choose Visualize (Figure 8-33).

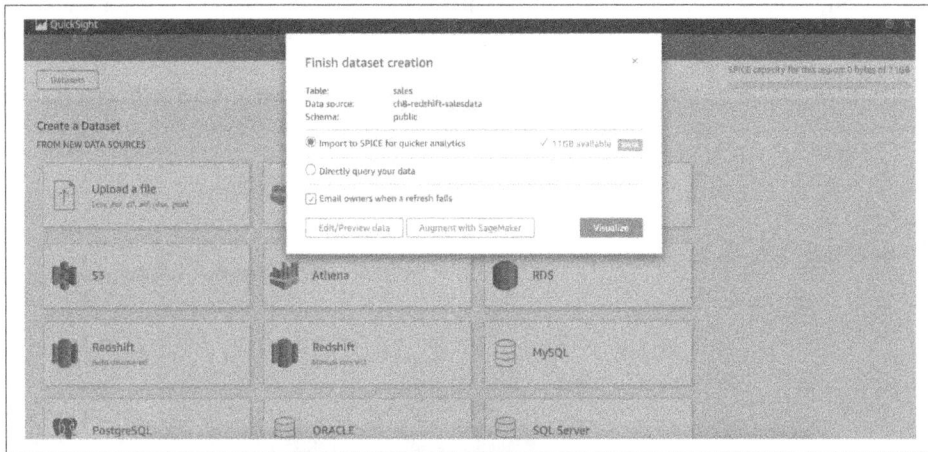

Figure 8-33. Amazon QuickSight: finish dataset creation

As shown in Figure 8-34, keep everything default and choose CREATE.

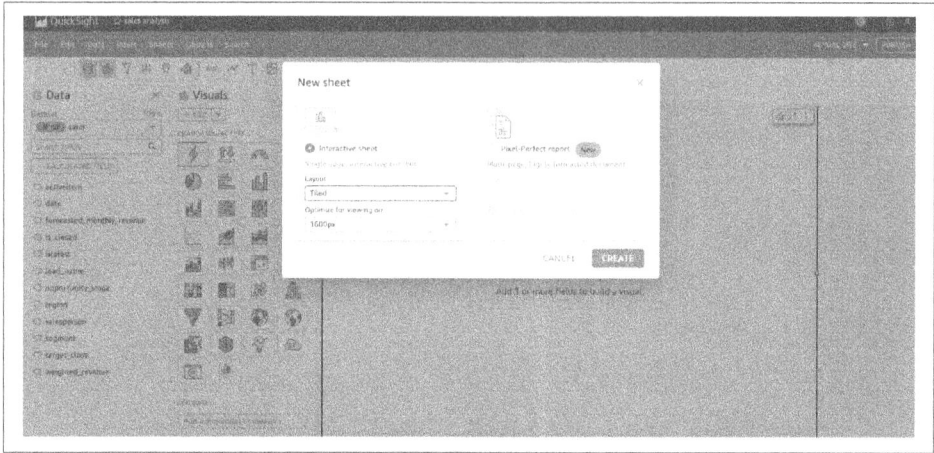

Figure 8-34. Amazon QuickSight: create sheet

This should open a blank canvas to design a visualization. Choose "Area line chart" for Visuals and then drag the "region" field for X AXIS and the "forecasted_monthly_revenue" field for VALUE and use the "segment" attribute for the COLOR.

This should load the visualization represented in Figure 8-35, which shows a graph to represent the count of "forecasted_monthly_revenue" by Region and Segment.

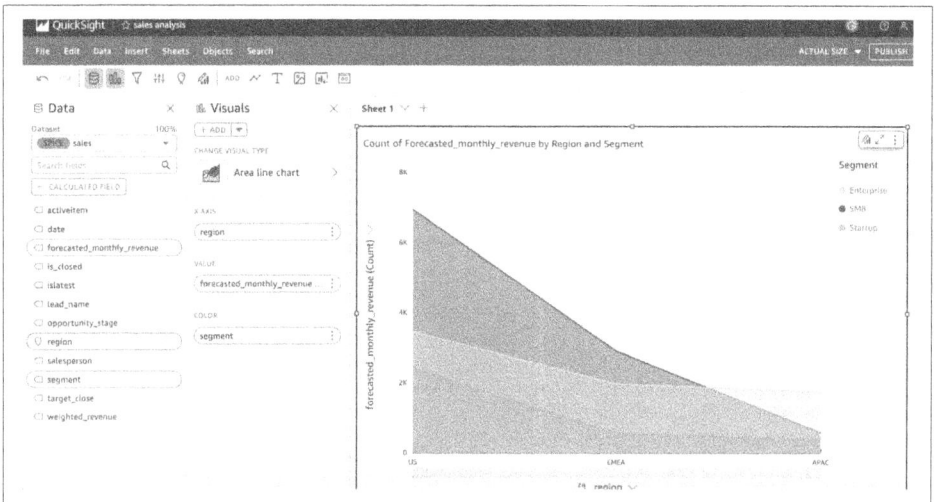

Figure 8-35. Amazon QuickSight: design visualization

Next, choose the PUBLISH option from the top right corner of the screen and specify "sales-data-forecast" as shown in Figure 8-36. Choose "Publish dashboard."

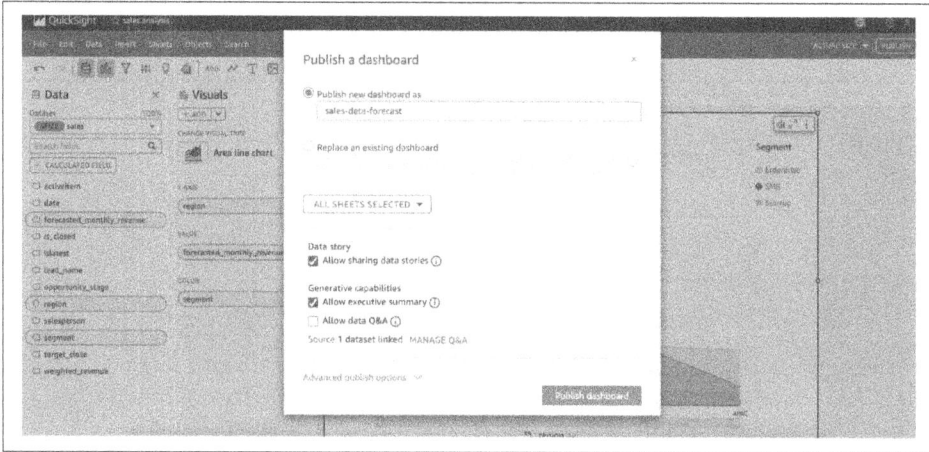

Figure 8-36. Amazon QuickSight: publish sheet to a dashboard

You should see a visualization like that in Figure 8-37 in your QuickSight dashboard, and hovering your mouse on the graph should show you the forecasted revenue break up for different segments in a region.

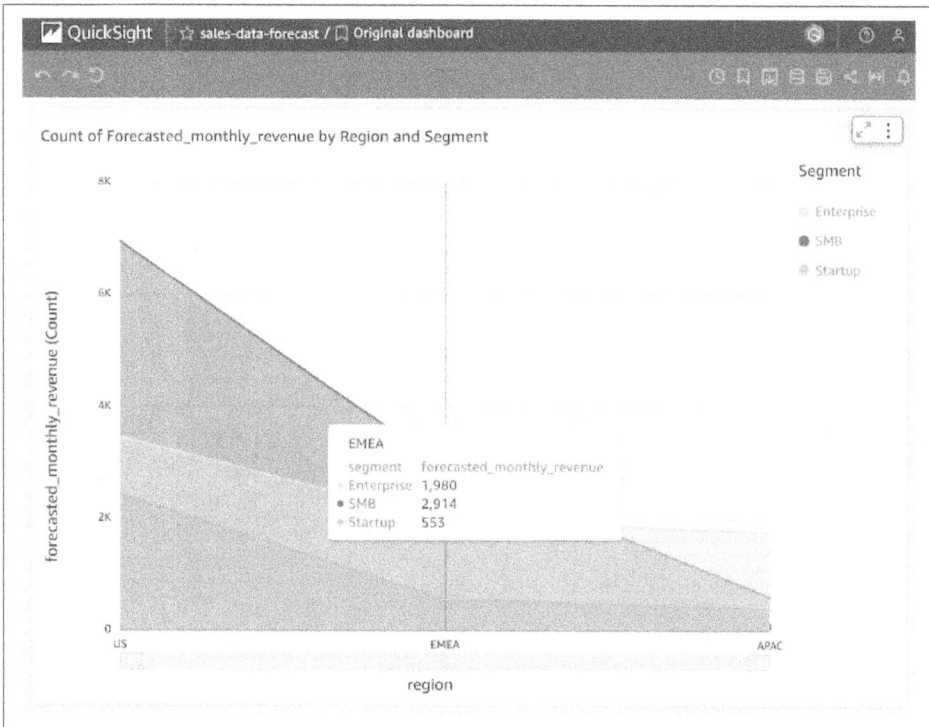

Figure 8-37. Amazon QuickSight: dashboard

Congratulations, you have successfully implemented the solution.

Best Practices and Optimization Techniques

There are certain best practices you can follow while implementing this architecture:

- Security:
  - Integrate AWS Secrets Manager to manage Redshift cluster credentials and avoid managing the user ID and password manually.
  - Restrict the security groups of the resources to the specific clusters.
  - Restrict IAM policies to the specific AWS resources instead of allowing permissions to the entire service to follow the least-privilege principle.
- Performance:
  - For Amazon S3 input datasets, implement partitioning for better structure and query performance.
  - For Amazon QuickSight, leverage SPICE for caching the datasets, which may help improve performance of the visualizations.
- Cost:
  - Enable autoscaling in the Glue job to avoid overprovisioning.
  - Define the base and max Redshift Processing Units (RPUs) for the Redshift serverless cluster to control the cost.

Next, let's learn how to implement a real-time streaming pipeline.

Implementing a Real-Time Streaming Pipeline

To get started, we need a data producer that generates streaming data, a message bus or buffering layer that can store the streaming data, and a consumer that can process the data in real time.

For the message bus or buffering the streaming data, AWS offers Kinesis Data Streams and AWS Managed Streaming for Apache Kafka (MSK). As a streaming consumer you have multiple options such as AWS Lambda, Spark Structured Streaming in AWS Glue or Amazon EMR, and Managed Service for Flink (MSF).

Let's get an overview of the use case and architecture that you will be implementing.

Use Case and Architecture Overview

Figure 8-38 provides a high-level architecture of the use case that integrates the following:

- Kinesis Data Generator (KDG) to generate sample streaming data
- Kinesis Data Streams (KDS) for storing the streaming data
- EMR Serverless with Spark Structured Streaming as a streaming consumer
- Amazon S3 as a data lake with Apache Iceberg as the open table format
- Amazon Athena as a query engine for data analysis

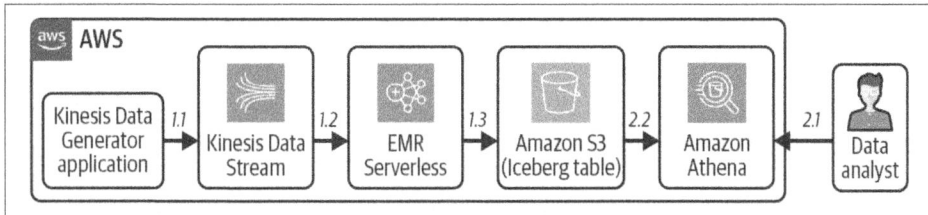

Figure 8-38. High-level architecture for streaming data processing pipeline

Step-by-Step Implementation Guide

As highlighted in the previous use case, before beginning these steps, make sure you have the required permissions to create the resources needed as part of the solution. Please note we have used the us-east-1 region to deploy the solution; you can choose your preferred region before getting started.

Creating a Kinesis data stream

You can refer to the following steps to create a Kinesis data stream, which will store the streaming messages that the streaming consumer applications will process:

1. Navigate to the KDS console (*https://oreil.ly/w0l9H*) and click the "Create data stream" button.
2. In the create page, specify the "Data stream name" as "ch8-kinesis-stream."
3. Keep everything else as the default value and choose "Create data stream."

Figure 8-39 shows the Kinesis Data Streams console for creating the stream.

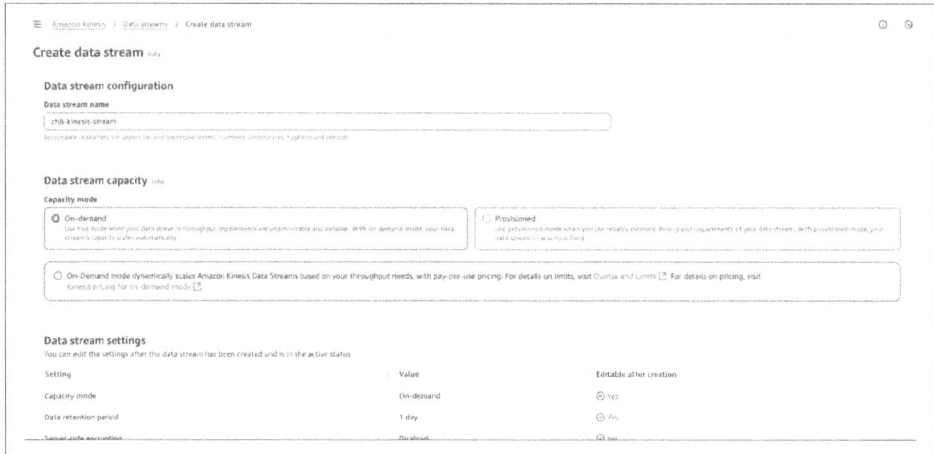

Figure 8-39. Kinesis Data Streams console: creating a new data stream

It will take a few minutes to create the stream and then you should see a success message: "Data stream 'ch8-kinesis-stream' successfully created." The status of the stream will be Active.

Setting up Amazon Kinesis Data Generator

Amazon Kinesis Data Generator (KDG) (*https://oreil.ly/wKeze*) is an open source tool that will enable us to generate sample data and publish messages to Amazon KDS. The tool provides a user-friendly web interface (Figure 8-40), where you can do the following:

- Create templates that represent the schema of the records for your use cases.
- Populate the templates with fixed data or random data.
- Save the templates for future use.
- Configure the tool to send thousands of records per second continuously to KDS.

The KDG tool requires you to create an Amazon Cognito user, which you will use to log in to the KDG portal. The KDG tool offers an AWS CloudFormation template that you can deploy to configure the Amazon Cognito user credentials. Please refer to the following steps to deploy the solution:

1. Refer to the KDG tool's help page (*https://oreil.ly/GI8Ac*) and click the "Create a Cognito User with CloudFormation" button to configure the Cognito user credentials.

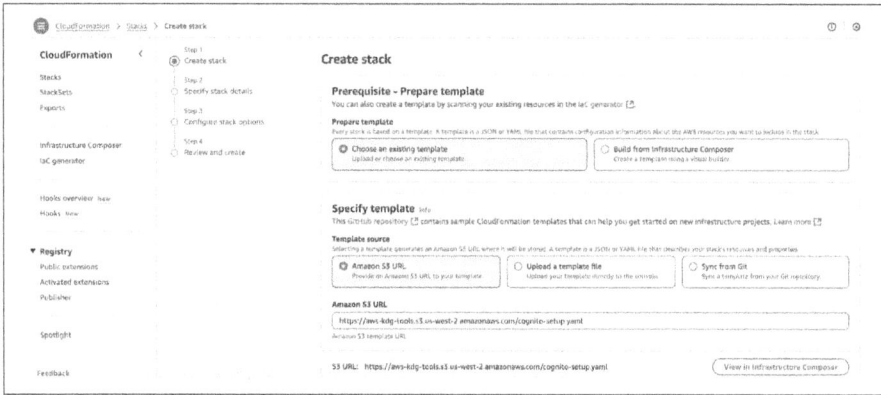

Figure 8-40. Creating a CloudFormation stack in the AWS Console

2. Specify the username and password you plan to configure (Figure 8-41).

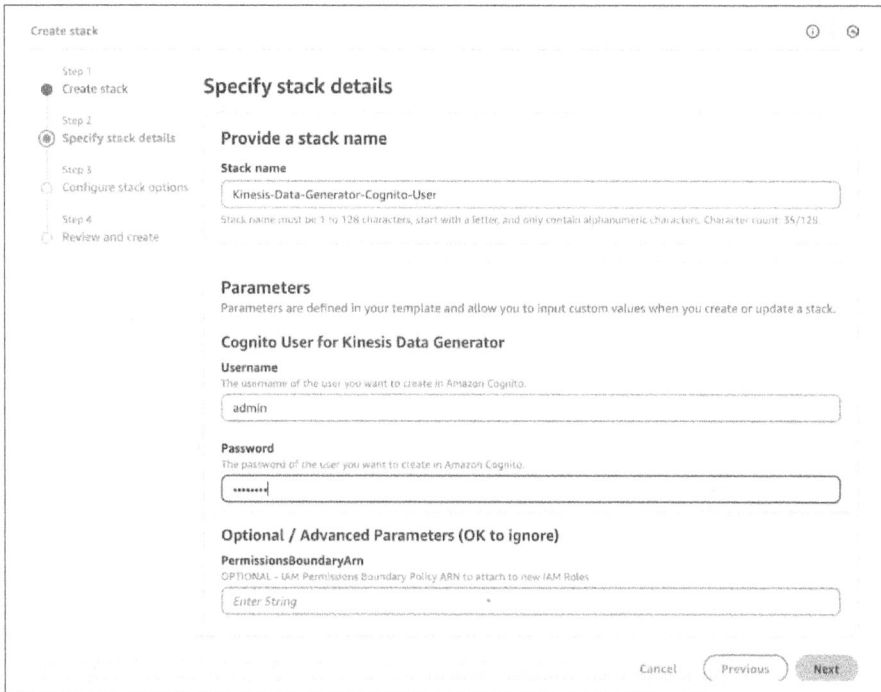

Figure 8-41. CloudFormation stack screenshot: specify stack name and credentials

3. Review the configurations and click Create.

4. It will take a few minutes to create the required resources and then you should see the status CREATE_COMPLETE.

5. Then navigate to the Outputs tab as shown in Figure 8-42 and click the URL value specified for the KinesisDataGeneratorUrl key.

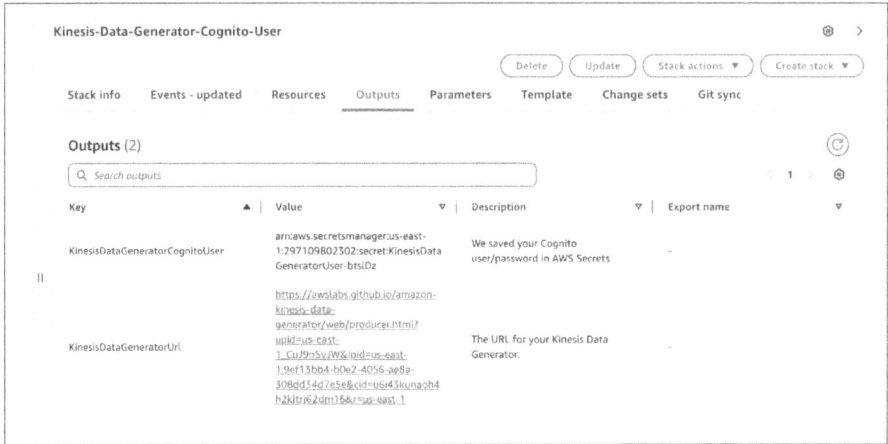

Figure 8-42. CloudFormation stack screenshot: Output tab

6. The Kinesis Data Generator URL will open a new page, where you need to provide the username and password you specified while deploying the Cloud-Formation stack.

7. Once the login is successful, you should see a screen similar to Figure 8-43, where after selecting your specific AWS Region, the delivery stream name will be available in the drop-down list to choose.

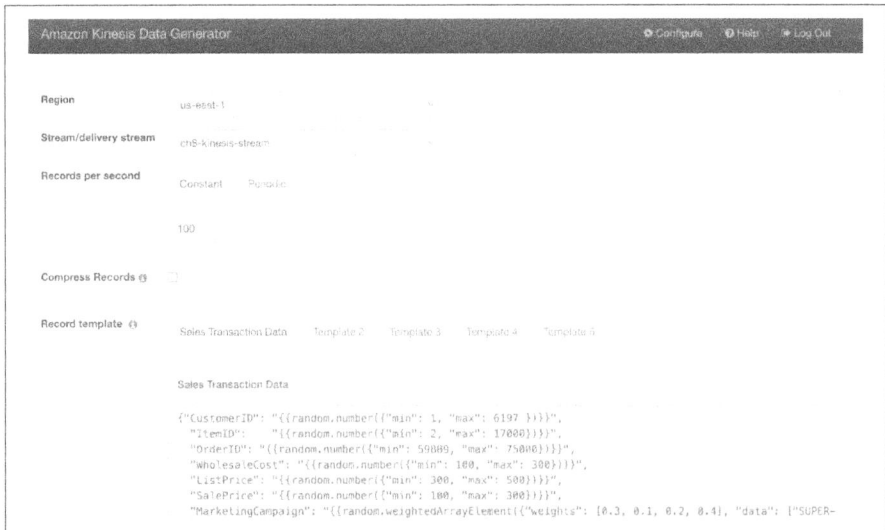

Figure 8-43. Kinesis Data Generator: configure screen

8. In the Record template, rename "Sales Transaction Data" to "Product Inventory Data" and paste the following JSON template inside the text area:

```
{"ProductID": "{{random.number({"min": 1, "max": 10000 })}}",
"ProductName": "{{random.weightedArrayElement({"weights":
[0.2, 0.2, 0.2, 0.2], "data": ["FRIDGE", "COOKWARE", "SHOES",
"PAINTING"]})}}",
  "ApplicableCountry": "{{random.weightedArrayElement({"weights":
  [0.5, 0.3, 0.1], "data": ["US", "UK", "GB"]})}}"
  "ListPrice": "{{random.number({"min": 300, "max": 500})}}",
  "DiscountedPrice": "{{random.number({"min": 100, "max": 300})}}",
  "MarketingCampaign": "{{random.weightedArrayElement({"weights":
  [0.3, 0.1, 0.2, 0.4], "data": ["SUPER-SAVER-WEEKEND", "THANKS-GIVING",
  "PRE-CHRISTMAS", "None"]})}}",
  "ShippingType": "{{random.weightedArrayElement({"weights":
  [0.1, 0.2, 0.2, 0.5], "data": ["EXPRESS", "NEXT DAY",
  "OVERNIGHT", "REGULAR"]})}}",
  "ShippingMode": "{{random.weightedArrayElement({"weights":
  [0.4, 0.5, 0.1], "data": ["AIR", "SEA", "BIKE"]})}}",
  "ShippingCarrier": "{{random.weightedArrayElement({"weights":
  [0.3, 0.1, 0.2, 0.4], "data": ["AIRBORNE", "ALLIANCE", "BARIAN",
  "DHL", "GERMA", "FEDEX", "TBS", "UPS"]})}}",
  "LastUpdatedDate": "{{date.now("DD/MMM/YYYY")}}",
  "LastUpdatedTime": "{{date.now("HH:mm:ss")}}"
}
```

9. Review the format by choosing the "Test template" button (Figure 8-44).

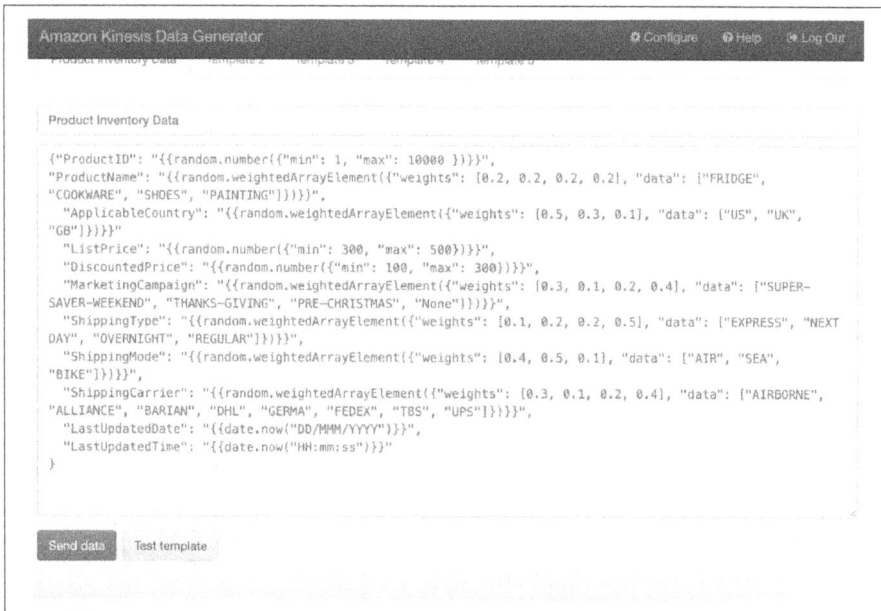

Figure 8-44. Kinesis Data Generator: testing the template

10. Finally, click the "Send data" button to send sample records to the Kinesis data stream named "ch8-kinesis-stream" (Figure 8-45).

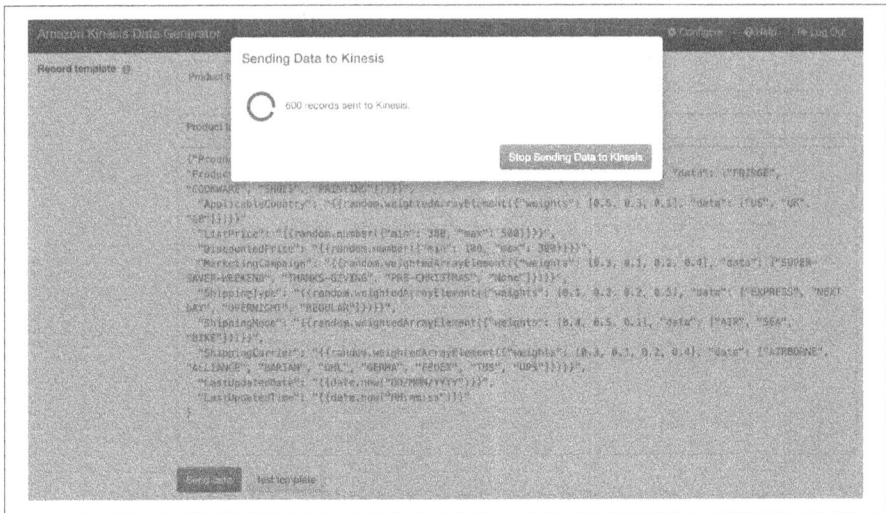

Figure 8-45. Kinesis Data Generator: sending sample data

11. Then, navigate to the "ch8-kinesis-stream" KDS stream within the AWS Console and select the Monitoring tab to validate the stream is receiving input records, as illustrated in Figure 8-46.

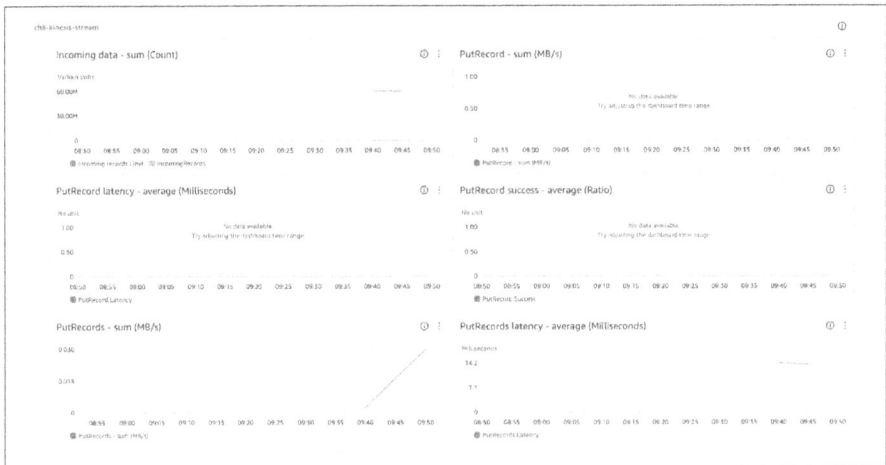

Figure 8-46. Kinesis Data Generator: monitoring the Kinesis data stream

At this step, you have incoming product inventory data available in the KDS and the next step is to create a stream consumer application.

Create Amazon S3 buckets for an Iceberg data lake and a streaming checkpoint

Refer to the steps from the previous batch processing pipeline solution to create the following Amazon S3 buckets:

s3://ch8-ex2-streaming-checkpoint
> To hold the streaming consumer application's checkpoint information. This will help when the application fails and needs to track to what point of the Kinesis data stream it has processed, and from which record it should resume processing.

s3://ch8-ex2-iceberg-data-lake
> To store the final processed data in Iceberg format.

s3://ch8-ex2-scripts
> To store the Spark Structured Streaming Python script.

Next, let's create the PySpark streaming application that will read from the Kinesis data stream and write to Amazon S3.

Creating an EMR Studio and EMR Serverless application

Use the following steps to create an EMR Serverless application and submit a Spark Structured Streaming job:

1. Navigate to EMR Studio (*https://oreil.ly/yOITj*), as you need a Studio to manage the EMR Serverless applications.

2. Choose Create Studio.

3. Choose "custom" from the "Setup options," specify a "name" for the studio (e.g., "ch8-ex2-emr-studio"), and select the "IAM role" that has the required permissions. Leave the other fields as default and choose "Create Studio and launch Workspace."

4. Once you have successfully created the Studio, navigate to the EMR Serverless console (*https://oreil.ly/htih2*), choose the Studio under "Manage applications," and click the "Manage applications" button as shown in Figure 8-47.

5. The action from the previous step should take you to the application list screen of the Studio. Here you need to choose "Create application."

6. Specify a name for the application (e.g., "ch8-ex2-spark-streaming-app") and set the Type as "Spark" and the Release version as "emr-7.1.0." Keep the Architecture as the default "x86_64" and for Application setup options choose "Use custom settings" (Figure 8-48).

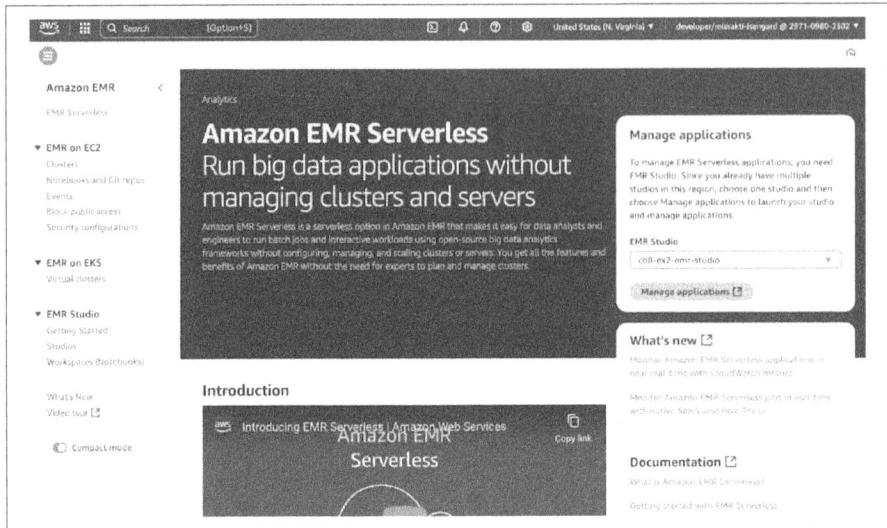

Figure 8-47. EMR Serverless console

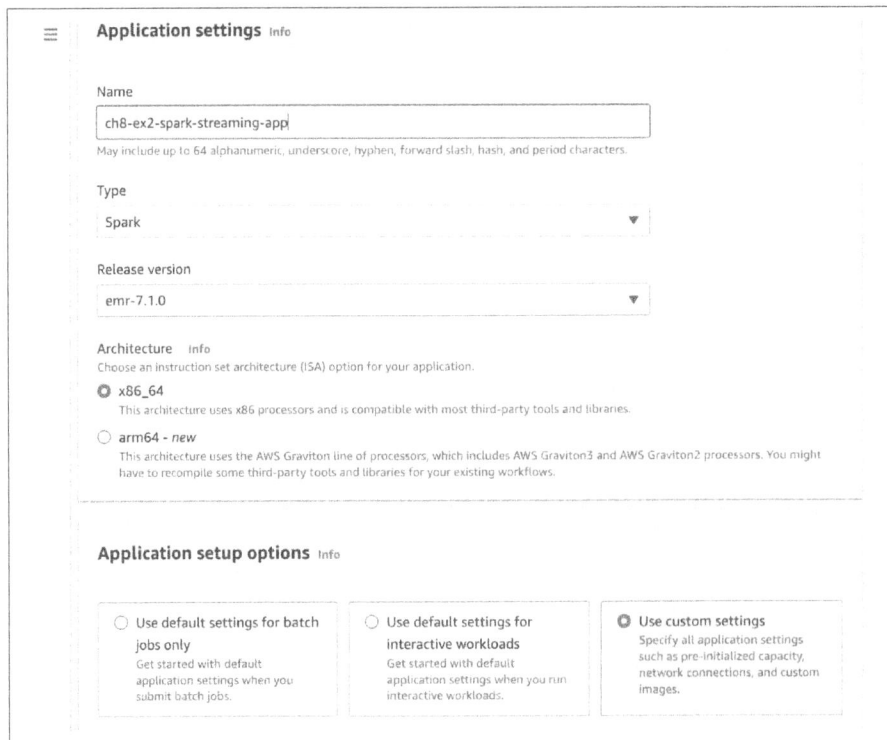

Figure 8-48. EMR Serverless console: configuring the application

7. Expand the "Network connections" section, specify the VPC where you plan to deploy the application, and choose all the applicable Subnets and Security groups. For this solution we have selected the default VPC, the related subnets, and the default security group (Figure 8-49).

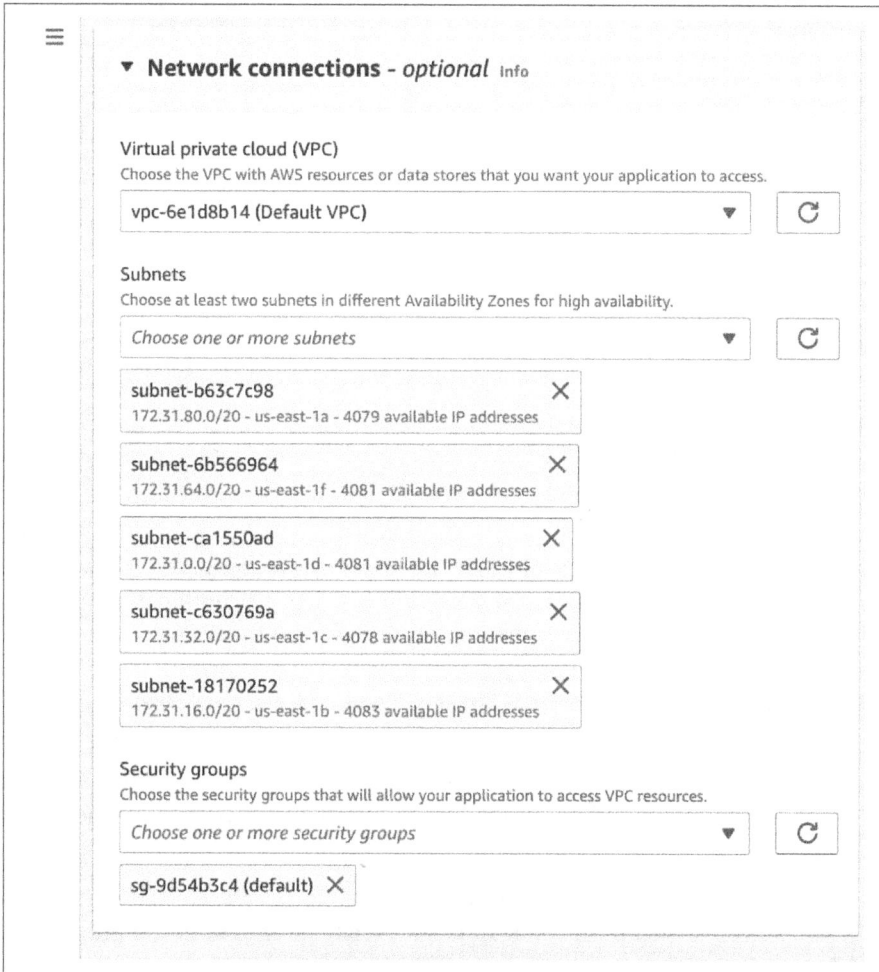

Figure 8-49. EMR Serverless console: configuring the network for the application

8. Leave the other field values as default and choose "Create and start application." This should take you to the application list page, where you will see the application status transitions from "Creating" to "Started" (Figure 8-50). Please copy the Application ID and save it on your local system, as it will be needed while submitting the Spark Streaming job using the AWS CLI.

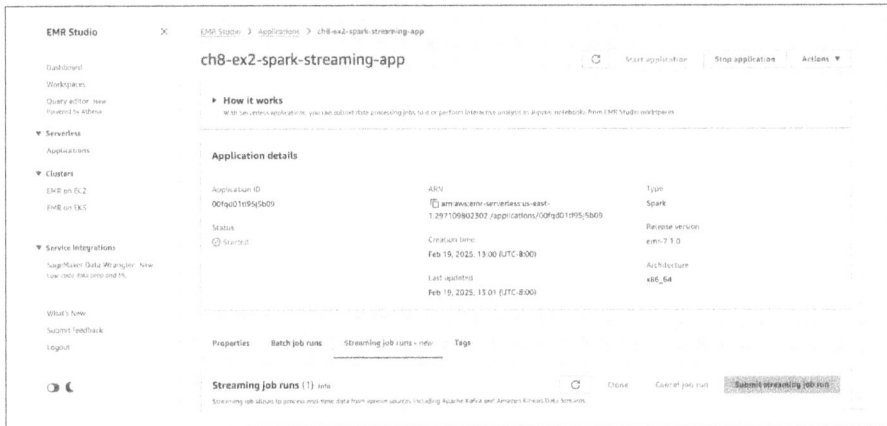

Figure 8-50. EMR Serverless console: application detail

Please note that while creating an EMR Serverless application, even if the VPC selection under the "Network connections" section is marked as optional, for a streaming application it is mandatory to deploy the application within a VPC.

Creating VPC endpoints for Kinesis Data Streams, Amazon S3, and EMR Serverless

When the streaming application is deployed within a VPC that will read from Kinesis Data Streams and write to Amazon S3, you need to create VPC endpoints for KDS, S3, and EMR Serverless, so that the application can connect to the respective resources.

To create VPC endpoints, navigate to VPC Service (*https://oreil.ly/Hstmx*), choose Endpoints from the left navigation, and choose "Create endpoint." Let's first create the EMR Serverless endpoint:

1. To create an endpoint for EMR Serverless, choose AWS services as the Type and choose "com.amazonaws.us-east-1.emr-serverless" as the service (Figure 8-51).

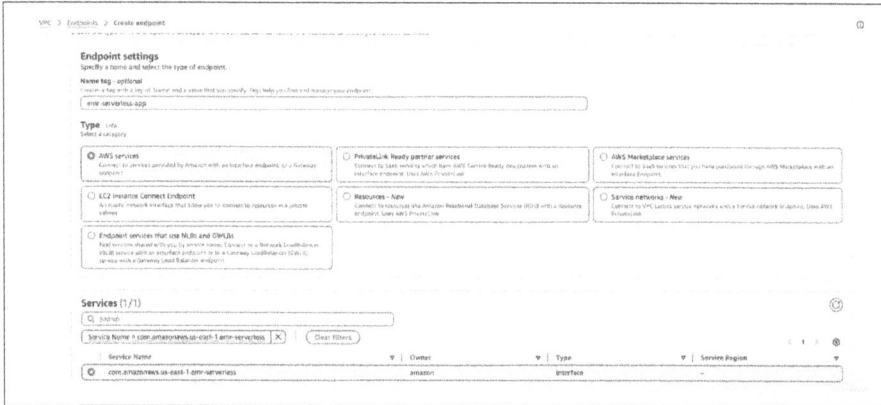

Figure 8-51. AWS VPC console: configuring the VPC endpoint for EMR Serverless

2. From the Network settings, choose the specific VPC where you deployed the EMR Serverless application and choose all the applicable Subnets with their Subnet ID (Figure 8-52).

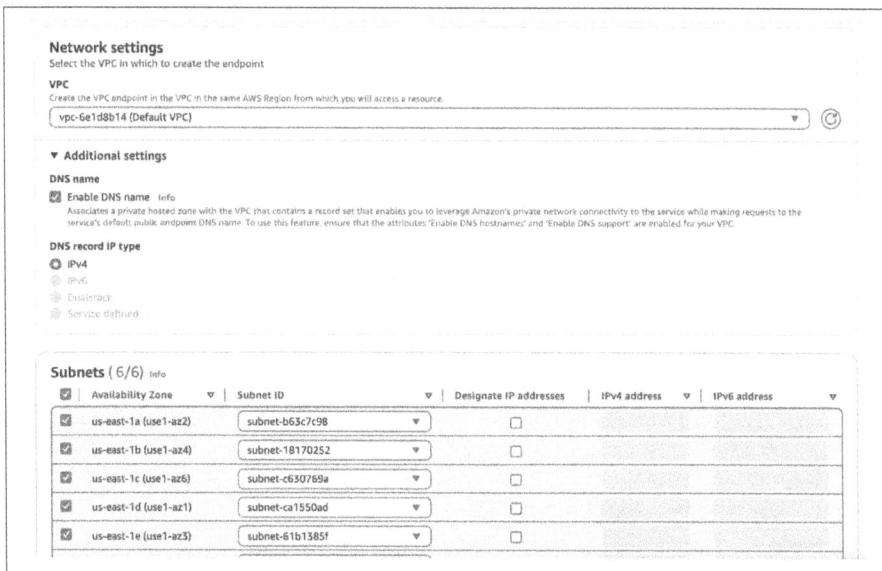

Figure 8-52. AWS VPC console: specifying the VPC for the VPC endpoint

3. Select the applicable Security groups, leave all other fields as default, and choose "Create endpoint."

Next, you can create the Kinesis Data Streams endpoint. Follow similar steps as you did for the EMR Serverless endpoint and choose the "com.amazonaws.us-east1.kinesis-streams" AWS service, as specified in Figure 8-53.

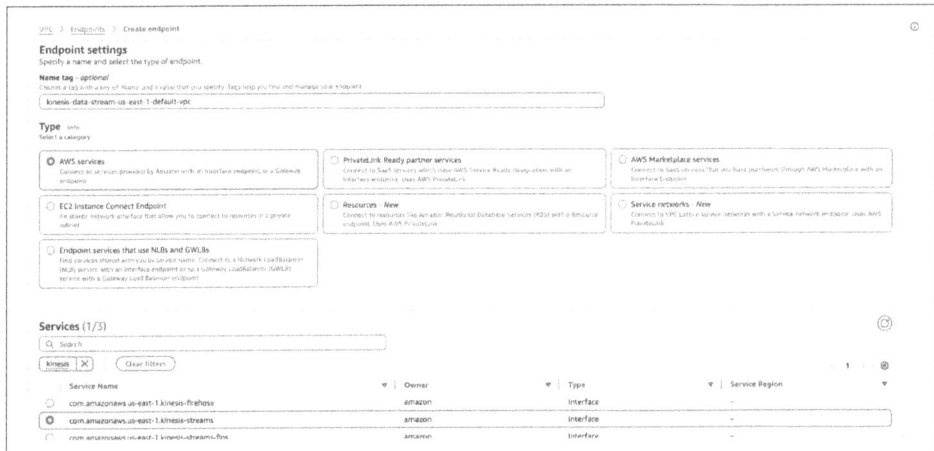

Figure 8-53. AWS VPC console: configuring the VPC endpoint for Kinesis Data Streams

Follow similar steps to create the Amazon S3 endpoint by selecting the service "com.amazonaws.us-east-1.s3" and choosing interface endpoints (Figure 8-54). Read "Choosing Your VPC Endpoint Strategy for Amazon S3" (*https://oreil.ly/OaNzi*) in the AWS documentation to learn when to use S3 gateway endpoints versus S3 interface endpoints.

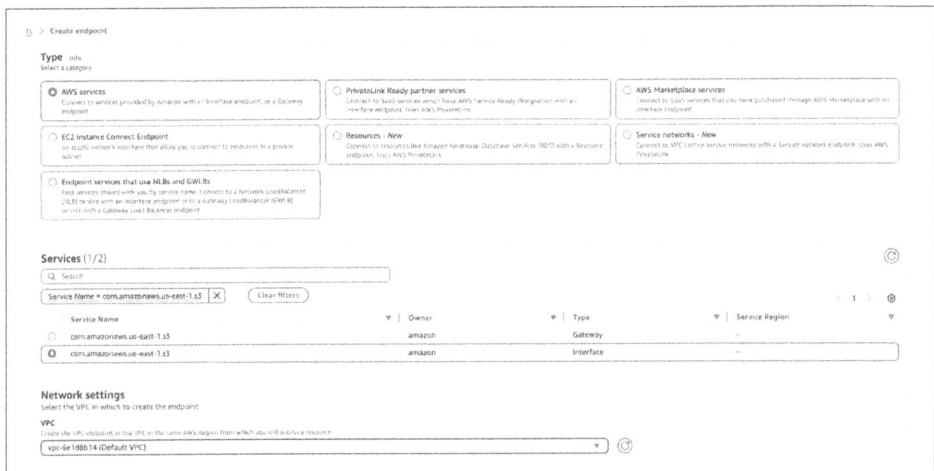

Figure 8-54. AWS VPC console: specifying the VPC endpoint for Amazon S3

Once all three endpoints are created, you are ready to submit the Spark Streaming job.

Submitting the Spark Streaming job to the EMR Serverless application

The Spark Structured Streaming job will read the JSON data from Kinesis Data Streams and write the output to Amazon S3 in Apache Iceberg format. Before triggering the job, let's first create the target Iceberg table using the Amazon Athena console:

1. Navigate to the Amazon Athena console (*https://oreil.ly/3f5AB*).

2. Execute the following SQL script that creates the "icebergdb" database first and then creates the "productcatalog" table that has the same attributes as the JSON data available in Kinesis Data Streams (Figure 8-55):

```
CREATE DATABASE icebergdb;
CREATE TABLE icebergdb.productcatalog (
    ProductID STRING,
    ProductName STRING,
    ApplicableCountry STRING,
    ListPrice DOUBLE,
    DiscountedPrice DOUBLE,
    MarketingCampaign STRING,
    ShippingType STRING,
    ShippingMode STRING,
    ShippingCarrier STRING,
    LastUpdatedDate TIMESTAMP,
    LastUpdatedTime STRING
)
LOCATION 's3://ch8-ex2-iceberg-data-lake/icebergdb/productcatalog/'
TBLPROPERTIES (
    'table_type' = 'ICEBERG',
    'format' = 'parquet',
    'write_compression' = 'snappy'
);
```

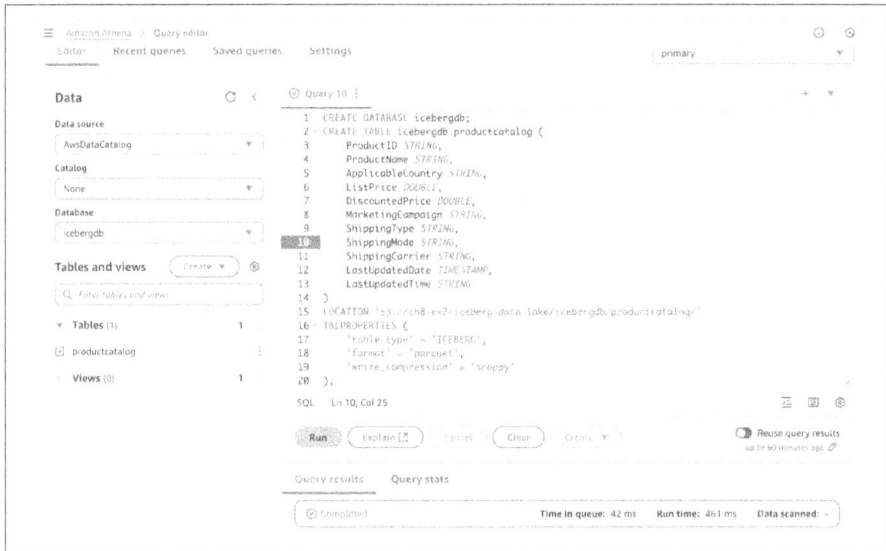

Figure 8-55. Amazon Athena console: query editor

Next, create a script in your local system text editor with the following code and save it as *stream-processor.py*. Make sure to modify the S3 data lake and checkpoint prefixes and the Kinesis stream name as highlighted in the script before finally saving it. Then upload *stream-processor.py* to an Amazon S3 path (e.g., *s3://ch8-ex2-scripts/*):

```python
from pyspark.sql import SparkSession
from pyspark.sql.streaming import DataStreamReader
from pyspark.sql.functions import *
from pyspark.sql.types import *
import base64
import time
# Initialize Spark session
spark = SparkSession.builder \
    .appName("KinesisToIcebergStreaming") \
    .config(
        "spark.sql.extensions",
        "org.apache.iceberg.spark.extensions.IcebergSparkSessionExtensions"
    ) \
    .config(
        "spark.sql.catalog.glue_catalog",
        "org.apache.iceberg.spark.SparkCatalog"
    ) \
    .config(
        "spark.sql.catalog.glue_catalog.catalog-impl",
        "org.apache.iceberg.aws.glue.GlueCatalog"
    ) \
    .config(
        "spark.sql.catalog.glue_catalog.warehouse",
```

```
        "s3://ch8-ex2-iceberg-data-lake/"
    ) \
    .config("spark.sql.defaultCatalog", "glue_catalog") \
    .config("spark.sql.parquet.compression.codec", "snappy") \
    .config("spark.sql.streaming.kafka.useDeprecatedOffsetFetching", "false") \
    .getOrCreate()

# Define the schema of your Kinesis data
schema = StructType() \
.add("ProductID", StringType()) \
.add("ProductName", StringType()) \
.add("ApplicableCountry", StringType()) \
.add("ListPrice", FloatType()) \
.add("DiscountedPrice", FloatType()) \
.add("MarketingCampaign", StringType()) \
.add("ShippingType", StringType()) \
.add("ShippingMode", StringType()) \
.add("ShippingCarrier", StringType()) \
.add("LastUpdatedDate", TimestampType()) \
.add("LastUpdatedTime", StringType())

# Read from Kinesis Data Streams
kinesis_stream = spark.readStream.format("aws-kinesis") \
    .option("kinesis.region", "us-east-1") \
    .option("kinesis.streamName", "ch8-kinesis-stream") \
    .option("kinesis.consumerType", "GetRecords") \
    .option("kinesis.endpointUrl", "https://kinesis.us-east-1.amazonaws.com") \
    .option("kinesis.startingposition", "LATEST") \
    .load()

# Parse the Kinesis data
parsed_stream = kinesis_stream \
    .select(from_json(col("data").cast("string"), schema).alias("parsed_data")) \
    .select("parsed_data.*")

# Write to S3 in Iceberg format
query = parsed_stream.writeStream \
    .format("iceberg") \
    .outputMode("append") \
    .option("path", "glue_catalog.icebergdb.productcatalog") \
    .option(
        "checkpointLocation",
        "s3://ch8-ex2-streaming-checkpoint/kinesis-to-iceberg/"
    ) \
    .start()

query.awaitTermination()
```

Next, open the Cloud Shell console by clicking the icon in the console header and submit the following AWS CLI command. Make sure to modify `<emr-serverless-application-id>`, `<iam-role-arn>`, and the `stream-processor.py` script path before submitting the command:

```
aws emr-serverless start-job-run \
--application-id <emr-serverless-application-id> \
--execution-role-arn <iam-role-arn> \
--mode STREAMING \
--retry-policy '{
    "maxFailedAttemptsPerHour": 5
 }' \
--job-driver '{
    "sparkSubmit": {
      "entryPoint": "s3://ch8-ex2-scripts/stream-processor.py",
      "entryPointArguments": [
        "s3://ch8-ex2-iceberg-data-lake/output"
      ],
      "sparkSubmitParameters": "--conf spark.executor.cores=4 \
--conf spark.executor.memory=16g \
--conf spark.driver.cores=4 \
--conf spark.driver.memory=16g \
--conf spark.executor.instances=3 \
--jars /usr/share/aws/kinesis/spark-sql-kinesis/lib/\
spark-streaming-sql-kinesis-connector.jar"
    }
}'
```

Figure 8-56 shows the execution of the command.

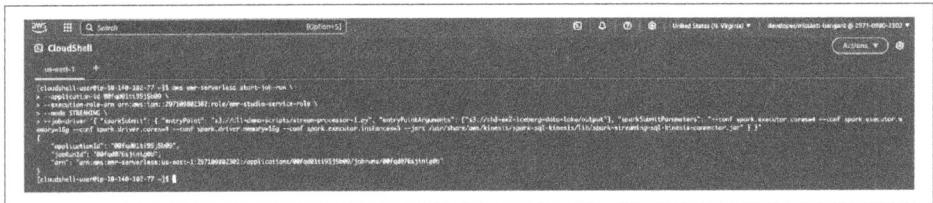

Figure 8-56. AWS Cloud Shell: AWS CLI command execution

Next, navigate to the EMR Serverless application detail page and choose the "Streaming job runs" tab, which should show the job status as "Running" as represented in Figure 8-57.

Figure 8-57. EMR Serverless Application: streaming job runs

You can choose the "Live spark UI" link, which will open the Spark History Server in a new tab (as represented in Figure 8-58). This will show the successful execution of the Spark job executors.

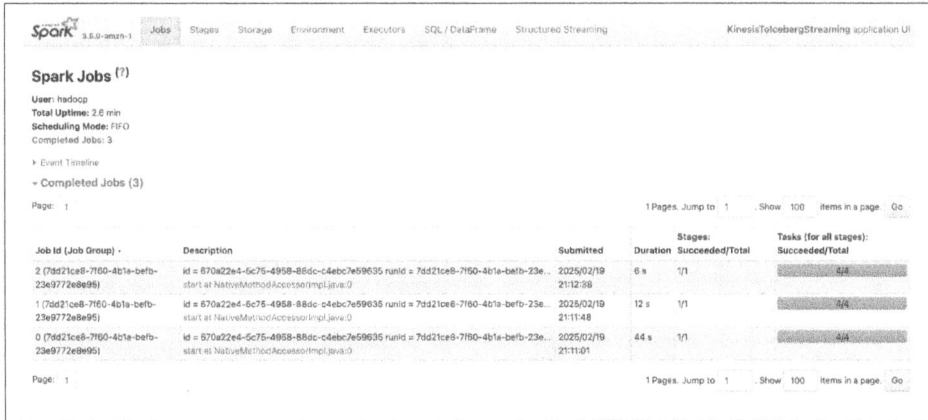

Figure 8-58. EMR Serverless application: job run's Spark History Server

To validate that the streaming output is getting written to the S3 data lake, you can navigate to the S3 data lake path (e.g., *s3://ch8-ex2-iceberg-data-lake/icebergdb/productcatalog/*), where you will notice two folders: *data* (to store the actual data in Parquet format) and *metadata* (to store Iceberg metadata in JSON format) (Figure 8-59).

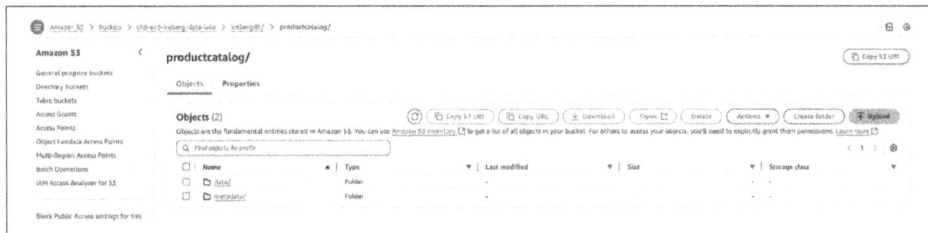

Figure 8-59. EMR Serverless Application: streaming output in an Amazon S3 bucket

Figure 8-60 shows the metadata in JSON format.

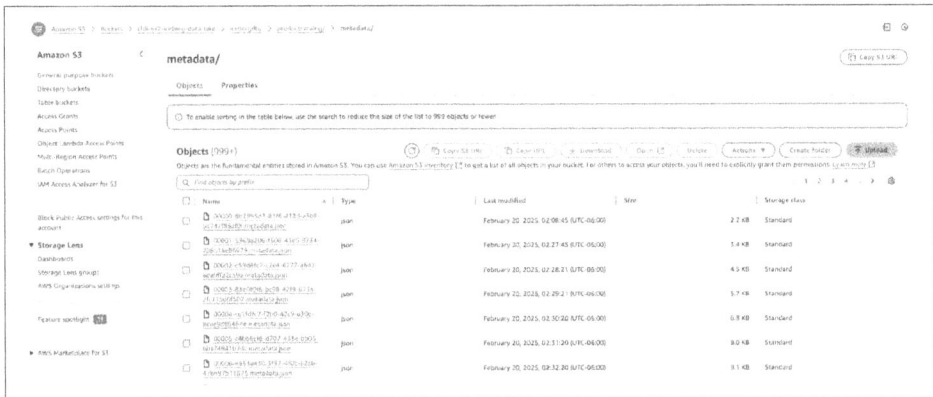

Figure 8-60. EMR Serverless application: Iceberg metadata in an Amazon S3 bucket

Figure 8-61 shows the data being written in Parquet format.

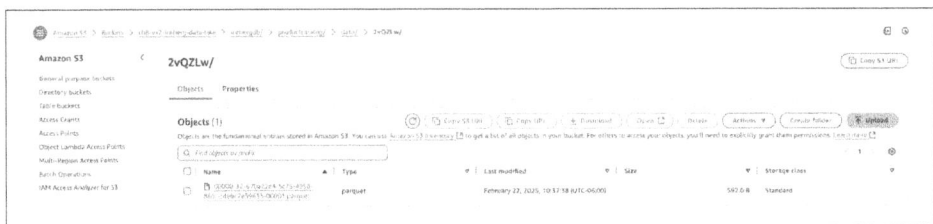

Figure 8-61. EMR Serverless application: Iceberg data in an Amazon S3 bucket

As a final step, you can navigate to the Amazon Athena console and query the `icebergdb.productcatalog` table to see the data in tabular format (Figure 8-62).

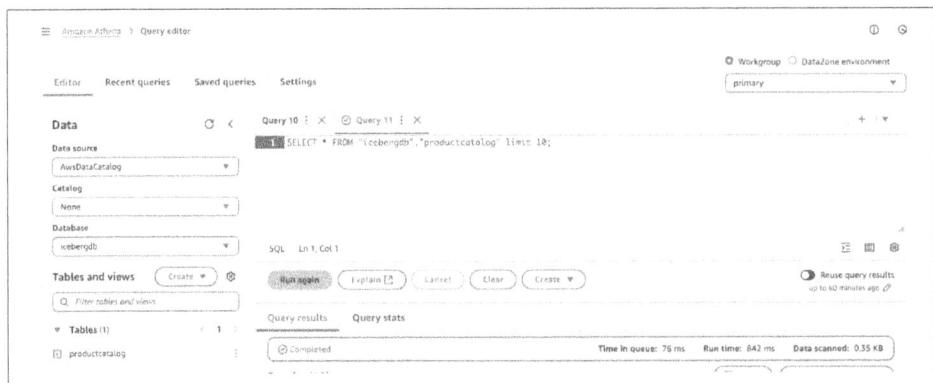

Figure 8-62. Amazon Athena console: query editor

Conclusion

In this chapter, we explained how you can implement a batch data processing pipeline with an AWS Glue PySpark job, and a real-time streaming job using KDS and Spark Streaming in EMR Serverless.

These are the two most popular use cases, but you can learn step-by-step implementations for other use cases from the AWS blogs included in the "Resources" section.

Resources

The following are a few additional resources that will help you dive deeper and gain more knowledge related to implementing data processing pipelines:

- "Implement a CDC-based UPSERT in a Data Lake Using Apache Iceberg and AWS Glue" (*https://oreil.ly/Wov64*)
- "Enforce Fine-Grained Access Control on Data Lake Tables Using AWS Glue 5.0 Integrated with AWS Lake Formation" (*https://oreil.ly/scohq*)
- "Stream, Transform, and Analyze XML Data in Real Time with Amazon Kinesis, AWS Lambda, and Amazon Redshift" (*https://oreil.ly/hvxWc*)
- "Build a Modern Data Architecture and Data Mesh Pattern at Scale Using AWS Lake Formation Tag-Based Access Control" (*https://oreil.ly/UjJkQ*)
- "Unlocking Data Governance for Multiple Accounts with Amazon DataZone" (*https://oreil.ly/6ND2s*)
- "Enhance Data Governance with Enforced Metadata Rules in Amazon Data-Zone" (*https://oreil.ly/Obd6b*)
- "Introducing End-to-End Data Lineage (Preview) Visualization in Amazon DataZone (*https://oreil.ly/yPv6U*)"

## CHAPTER 9

Practice Exam

This chapter is designed to help you assess your readiness and simulate the real certification experience. The following questions cover a wide range of topics and practical scenarios you can expect to encounter on the actual exam. We highly recommend you attempt each question before reviewing the detailed solutions and rationales provided. This will not only test your knowledge but also deepen your understanding of the core concepts and help you think critically about how to apply AWS data and analytics services effectively. The answers are listed in the Appendix. Good luck!

1. A company aims to construct an open source–based change data capture (CDC) pipeline to extract changes from an Amazon Aurora MySQL database and load the change streams into an Amazon S3–based data lake.

    As a Solutions Architect, which steps should you take to configure this pipeline? (Select three.)

    A. Enable binary logging on the Aurora MySQL database to allow change data capture.

    B. Deploy the Debezium MySQL connector directly on the Aurora MySQL instance to capture data changes.

    C. Deploy MSK Connect with the Debezium MySQL source connector to stream changes from Aurora MySQL to MSK topics.

    D. Deploy an Amazon MSK cluster to serve as the streaming platform for the change data.

    E. Set up AWS Database Migration Service (DMS) to replicate data from Aurora MySQL to Amazon S3.

F. Use Amazon Kinesis Data Streams to natively read the binary log from the Aurora MySQL database.

2. An ecommerce company collects customer activity events such as clicks, searches, and purchases in real time. These events are streamed to an Amazon Kinesis data stream. The company wants to ingest this streaming data into an Amazon Redshift table for further analyses.

Which solution will meet the requirement with the least operational overhead?

A. Set up an Amazon Managed Service for Apache Flink application to process the stream and write the results to Amazon Redshift.

B. Use an AWS Glue streaming job to read data from the Kinesis data stream and write it directly to Amazon Redshift using the Redshift Data API.

C. Use the streaming ingestion feature of Amazon Redshift to consume data directly from the Kinesis data stream.

D. Use Amazon Data Firehose to deliver the streaming data to an Amazon S3 bucket. Use the `COPY` command in Amazon Redshift to load the data from S3 at regular intervals.

3. A customer relationship management (CRM) solution company stores all its customer data in Amazon Aurora PostgreSQL to handle online transaction processing (OLTP) workloads. As the business grows, the company is experiencing scaling challenges when running analytical queries directly on the Aurora database, impacting the performance of its frontend applications.

To address this, the company wants a solution that enables scalable data analysis while offloading analytics from Aurora. The solution must ensure up-to-date data availability in the analytics environment and must be designed with the least operational overhead.

Which solution should you implement?

A. Set up AWS Glue jobs to extract data from Aurora PostgreSQL, load it into an Amazon S3 bucket, and then use the `COPY` command in Amazon Redshift to load the data into a Redshift table for analysis.

B. Use Amazon Database Migration Service (DMS) to replicate data from Aurora PostgreSQL to Amazon Redshift in near real time.

C. Enable Amazon Aurora zero-ETL integration to continuously and automatically replicate data from Aurora MySQL to Amazon Redshift for analysis.

D. Configure an Amazon Aurora read replica to export data to an Amazon S3 bucket using SQL queries, and use Amazon Redshift Spectrum to query the data directly from S3.

4. A data engineer is working on a project that involves AWS analytics services. The project's code is stored in a Git repository. The data engineer recently completed work on a feature branch named `optimize-glue-jobs` and now needs to integrate those changes into the main branch (`main`). They have already switched to the main branch locally.

Which Git command should the consultant use to bring the changes from `optimize-glue-jobs` into `main`?

A. `git pull optimize-glue-jobs`

B. `git merge optimize-glue-jobs`

C. `git rebase main`

D. `git checkout optimize-glue-jobs`

5. A media streaming startup is building an analytics platform on AWS to track user engagement across its mobile and web applications. The architecture includes Amazon Kinesis Data Streams, AWS Lambda, Amazon S3, and Amazon Redshift. The team wants to define this infrastructure using code that supports object-oriented programming constructs, can be reused across staging and production environments, and allows the use of Python for consistency with the rest of their stack.

Which approach best aligns with the team's goals?

A. Use AWS Cloud Development Kit (CDK) to define infrastructure as reusable constructs and deploy consistently across multiple environments.

B. Use the AWS Management Console to provision resources and export Cloud-Formation templates for reuse across environments.

C. Use AWS CLI scripts to sequentially create each service and pass configuration parameters for each environment.

D. Use AWS CloudFormation templates to define the infrastructure and replicate the templates for each environment.

6. A company runs large-scale Apache Spark–based ETL jobs regularly to process and transform massive data. The jobs are not time-sensitive and can tolerate interruptions. The company wants to minimize costs while leveraging a scalable solution for these recurring ETL workloads.

Which solution should the company choose?

A. Use Amazon EMR with exclusively On-Demand Instances to ensure job stability and predictable performance.

B. Use Amazon EMR with a mix of EC2 Spot Instances and On-Demand Instances, leveraging Spot Instance fleets for cost savings and On-Demand Instances for job stability.

C. Use AWS Glue as a fully managed serverless solution to run Spark ETL jobs without needing to manage EC2 instances.

D. Set up a self-managed Apache Spark cluster on EC2 Spot Instances to reduce costs and scale as needed.

7. A healthcare analytics company collects patient data from various sources and stores it in Amazon S3. The data is uploaded as CSV files, and each file must undergo schema validation and be converted to Apache Parquet format for optimized analytics and storage. The company requires a real-time, file-level processing solution that triggers transformations as soon as the files arrive in the S3 bucket. Source CSV files are around 10–100 MB. The solution must operate with the least operational overhead to ensure simplicity and scalability.

Which solution should the data engineer implement?

A. Configure Amazon S3 Event Notifications to trigger an AWS Lambda function. Use the Lambda function to validate the schema and convert the CSV file to Parquet format, storing the output back in Amazon S3.

B. Use AWS Glue crawlers to detect newly uploaded CSV files in Amazon S3. When new files are discovered, trigger an AWS Glue job to perform schema validation and convert the files to Parquet format.

C. Use Amazon S3 Event Notifications to trigger an AWS Step Functions workflow. Design the workflow to include schema validation and format conversion tasks using AWS Glue jobs.

D. Configure Amazon S3 Batch Operations to process files on a schedule. Use an AWS Glue job to validate file schemas and convert files to Parquet format.

8. A fintech company processes real-time transaction data to detect fraudulent activities. The company requires a stateful streaming data processing solution to monitor transaction patterns, maintain session state, and identify anomalies in near real time. They need a fully managed service to run and scale their stream processing applications with minimal operational overhead.

Which solution should the company choose?

A. Set up a self-managed Apache Flink cluster on EC2 instances to process the streaming data and maintain state for fraud detection.

B. Use AWS Lambda with Amazon Kinesis Data Streams to process the transaction data, storing state in an Amazon DynamoDB table for anomaly detection.

C. Use Amazon Managed Service for Apache Flink to build and run stateful stream processing applications.

D. Use Amazon EMR to run an Apache Flink cluster and process streaming data, managing state with an external database.

9. A media analytics company processes large datasets on Amazon EMR to analyze user engagement patterns and optimize content recommendations. The company wants to host the source code for its data processing jobs in a code repository to efficiently track code changes, collaborate across teams, and promote code reuse. They need a solution to seamlessly integrate the repository with their EMR Notebooks to streamline development and testing workflows.

Which solution should the company use?

A. Enable version control by storing EMR Notebook source code in an Amazon S3 bucket and manually tracking changes outside of EMR.

B. Use Amazon EMR Notebooks to directly associate a Git-based repository, such as AWS CodeCommit or GitHub.

C. Create a local copy of the Git-based repository on an EC2 instance and manually upload the job scripts to EMR Notebooks for processing.

D. Use AWS Glue Studio to manage and track the ETL scripts in the Git-based repository, then export them to EMR Notebooks when needed.

10. A retail company manages a large-scale data platform to analyze customer purchase behavior and enhance product recommendations. The company's data pipeline involves multiple stages, including stream-based data ingestion into an Amazon S3 data lake and data transformation using Amazon EMR and Amazon Managed Service for Apache Flink.

The pipeline must be highly scalable, available, and secure, while minimizing the operational overhead of managing the orchestration engine. The company also requires detailed monitoring and logging of each transformation job for debugging and optimization purposes.

Which solution should the company choose to orchestrate the data pipeline?

A. Set up a self-managed Apache Airflow cluster on Amazon EC2 instances to orchestrate the pipeline, ensuring complete control over the infrastructure.

B. Use AWS Glue workflows to manage the entire pipeline, configuring it to handle ingestion, transformation, and loading steps.

C. Deploy a custom Python-based orchestration engine on Amazon ECS, scaling the service as needed to manage pipeline execution.

D. Use Amazon Managed Workflows for Apache Airflow (MWAA) to orchestrate the pipeline, leveraging its fully managed environment for scalability, availability, and security.

11. A media streaming company operates a data pipeline that processes user activity logs in near real time to generate personalized recommendations. The pipeline uses multiple AWS Lambda functions for tasks like data parsing, transformation, and enrichment. Each Lambda function relies on the same set of third-party Python libraries for processing. To simplify library management and ensure consistency across functions, the company needs a solution to centralize and reuse these dependencies while minimizing operational overhead.

    Which solution should the company implement?

    A. Package the required libraries with each Lambda function's deployment package to ensure each function has all necessary dependencies.

    B. Use AWS Lambda layers to package the common libraries separately and apply the layer across all Lambda functions.

    C. Store the libraries in an Amazon S3 bucket and download them at runtime within each Lambda function to minimize deployment size.

    D. Configure an Amazon EFS filesystem to host the Python libraries, then mount this filesystem into each Lambda function to centrally manage dependencies.

12. A financial services company needs to incorporate third-party datasets, such as historical market data, economic indicators, and consumer spending trends, into its analytics platform hosted on AWS. The company wants a solution that allows it to easily discover, subscribe to, and use third-party data in the cloud.

    Which solution should the company implement?

    A. Use AWS Data Exchange to find and subscribe to third-party datasets.

    B. Use AWS DataSync to find and subscribe to third-party datasets.

    C. Use Redshift Data Marketplace to find and subscribe to third-party datasets.

    D. Use Redshift Data Sharing to find and subscribe to third-party datasets.

13. An ecommerce company uses Amazon Redshift to analyze customer feedback stored in a feedback table. The table contains a comments column with customer remarks. The company wants to identify feedback that includes case-insensitive keywords like "refund," "cancel," or "complaint" to track negative sentiment patterns. They need to write a SQL query using pattern-matching conditions to efficiently retrieve the relevant records.

    Which SQL query should the company use to achieve this?

    A. SELECT * FROM feedback WHERE comments = 'refund' OR comments = 'cancel' OR comments = 'complaint';

    B. SELECT * FROM feedback WHERE comments ~* '(refund|cancel|complaint)';

C. `SELECT * FROM feedback WHERE comments IN ('%refund%', '%cancel%', '%complaint%');`

D. `SELECT * FROM feedback WHERE comments ~ '%(refund|cancel|complaint)%';`

14. A healthcare company processes patient data daily to generate summary reports for compliance and operational insights. The ETL pipeline consists of multiple AWS Glue jobs, each handling tasks like data extraction, transformation, and loading into an Amazon S3 data lake. The pipeline must be orchestrated and triggered every day at a specific time. While the completion time for the entire pipeline is not critical, the company wants to prioritize cost-efficiency while ensuring reliable execution of all the jobs.

    Which solution should the company implement?

    A. Use AWS Lambda to trigger each AWS Glue job at the specified time and configure the jobs to use the default worker type for faster completion.

    B. Configure an AWS Glue workflow to orchestrate the multiple Glue jobs and set up a time-based trigger using a `cron` expression to schedule the workflow. Use the default worker type to minimize costs.

    C. Schedule each AWS Glue job directly using Amazon CloudWatch Events, configuring the jobs to use AWS Glue FLEX for cost savings.

    D. Configure an AWS Glue workflow to orchestrate the multiple Glue jobs and set up a time-based trigger using a `cron` expression to schedule the workflow. Use AWS Glue FLEX for the jobs to minimize costs.

15. A marketing analytics firm receives hundreds of *.csv* files from its clients on a daily basis, containing sales and customer transaction data. These files are uploaded to an Amazon S3 bucket. The firm needs to catalog this data in an AWS Glue Data Catalog to enable data querying and reporting. A data engineer is tasked to make the previous day's data accessible by 7:00 a.m. every day.

    Which solution should the data engineer implement to meet the requirement?

    A. Create an IAM role with the `AmazonS3FullAccess` policy and the `AWSGlue ServiceRole` managed policy. Attach it to the crawler. Specify the S3 bucket path of the source data as the crawler's data store. Set up the AWS Glue crawler to run on-demand and specify a database name for the output.

    B. Create an IAM role with the `AWSGlueServiceRole` managed policy and add an inline policy granting the crawler read permission on the specific Amazon S3 bucket containing the CSV data. Attach it to the crawler. Specify the S3 bucket path of the source data as the crawler's data store. Set up the AWS Glue crawler to run on-demand and specify a database name for the output.

C. Create an IAM role with the `AmazonS3ReadOnlyAccess` policy and the `AWS GlueServiceRole` managed policy. Attach it to the crawler. Specify the S3 bucket path of the source data as the crawler's data store. Create a daily schedule to run the crawler and specify a database name for the output.

D. Create an IAM role with the `AWSGlueServiceRole` managed policy and add an inline policy granting the crawler read permission on the specific Amazon S3 bucket containing the CSV data. Attach it to the crawler. Specify the S3 bucket path of the source data as the crawler's data store. Create a daily schedule to run the crawler and specify a database name for the output.

16. An ecommerce company uses various AWS services to collect, process, and store user activity data for tracking customer behavior and transaction trends. The data engineering team is tasked with designing a cost-effective solution that leverages Amazon S3, Amazon DynamoDB, and Amazon QuickSight to meet business reporting and archival requirements while minimizing costs:

- The most recent three months of data must be fetched from the DynamoDB table and displayed on a custom QuickSight dashboard for recent trend analysis.

- Older user activity data must be archived in a data lake for five years and remain accessible for occasional queries using Amazon Athena with reasonable performance.

- Data older than five years must be purged to comply with data retention policies.

Which solution should the data engineer implement to meet these requirements? (Select three.)

A. Use the Time to Live feature to automatically delete items older than 90 days from the DynamoDB table.

B. Store all user activity data indefinitely in the DynamoDB table. Configure the table to use the DynamoDB Standard-Infrequent Access (DynamoDB Standard-IA) table class to reduce cost.

C. Build an AWS Glue job to export user activity data from the DynamoDB table to Amazon S3.

D. Configure an Amazon S3 Lifecycle policy to transition user activity data older than 90 days to the S3 Infrequent Access (S3-IA) storage class and then permanently delete it after five years.

E. Configure an Amazon S3 Lifecycle policy to transition user activity data older than 90 days to the Amazon S3 Glacier Deep Archive storage class and then permanently delete it after five years.

17. A company has a single Amazon Redshift cluster shared by two teams: the Analytics Team and the Reporting Team. The Analytics Team performs data transformation and analysis to derive critical business insights, while the Reporting Team generates reports for business users.

Each morning, as business users access reports, the shared Redshift cluster becomes unstable due to the simultaneous demand for data transformation and reporting workloads. This issue causes delays in report generation and impacts overall system performance.

The company needs a solution to separate the workloads of the two teams while ensuring that the Reporting Team can access the transformed data without delay for publishing reports on an Amazon QuickSight dashboard.

Which solution will best meet these requirements with minimal impact on the workflow?

A. Separate the workloads into two Redshift clusters. Configure Amazon Redshift Data Sharing with the Analytics Team's cluster as the producer and the Reporting Team's cluster as the consumer.

B. Configure AWS Database Migration Service to replicate data from the Analytics Team's cluster to a separate cluster for the Reporting Team.

C. Separate the workloads into two Amazon Redshift clusters. Configure zero-ETL jobs to synchronize the required tables between the Analytics Team's cluster and the Reporting Team's cluster.

D. Separate the workloads into two Amazon Redshift clusters. Unload required tables from the Analytics Team's cluster into an Amazon S3 bucket. Create an Amazon Redshift Spectrum table in the Reporting Team's cluster to access the data.

18. An ecommerce company collects customer transaction data daily in an Amazon S3 bucket. The data is stored in uncompressed CSV format and is queried frequently by the analytics team using Amazon Athena to analyze purchase trends and customer behavior. The majority of their queries are analytical, focusing on transactions from a specific region or a specific period of time.

To optimize query performance in Athena and reduce costs, which combination of techniques should they use? (Select two.)

A. Convert the data from CSV to JSON format and compress the files using Snappy compression.

B. Bucket the data by region, year, and month.

C. Convert the data from CSV to Apache Parquet format and compress the files using Snappy compression.

D. Partition the data by region, year, and month.

19. A retail company uses an Amazon DynamoDB table in provisioned capacity mode to manage its inventory data. The application workload follows a predictable pattern: every Monday morning, there is a significant increase in activity as stores across the country sync their inventory data. During weekends, the workload drops to minimal levels as most stores operate in offline mode. The company needs to ensure that the application maintains consistent performance throughout the week.

Which solution will meet these requirements in the most cost-effective way?

A. Change the capacity mode to on-demand. DynamoDB will automatically scale to handle increased throughput requirements.

B. Increase the provisioned capacity to accommodate peak throughput levels.

C. Use AWS Application Auto Scaling to schedule higher capacity during Monday mornings when the workload spikes and reduce capacity during weekends to minimize costs.

D. Create a separate DynamoDB table for peak usage and switch the application to use this table on Mondays.

20. A data engineer is tasked with improving the performance of ad-hoc queries run on data stored in Amazon S3 using Amazon Athena. The dataset is partitioned by date, and over time, the number of partitions has grown significantly, causing a noticeable degradation in query planning performance.

Which solution will improve the query performance with the least operational overhead?

A. Create partition indexes in AWS Glue and enable partition projection for the specific table.

B. Merge old partitions periodically into larger ones to reduce the number of partitions.

C. Consolidate smaller files into larger ones periodically to reduce the number of files.

D. Restructure the data layout using a bucketing strategy.

21. A retail company stores its data across multiple sources: customer transaction data is saved in Parquet format on Amazon S3, inventory data resides in an Amazon Aurora MySQL database, and order history is stored in Amazon DynamoDB tables. The company's data engineering team needs to provide a solution that allows data scientists to seamlessly query all these data sources using SQL or SQL-like syntax. The solution should require the least operational overhead.

Which combination of solutions meets these requirements? (Select three.)

A. Use AWS Glue crawlers to crawl all data sources and store metadata in the AWS Glue Data Catalog.

B. Use Amazon Athena to query the Amazon S3–based data lake.

C. Migrate all data to a single Amazon Redshift data warehouse and use Redshift Spectrum to query the Parquet data on Amazon S3.

D. Use AWS Glue jobs to transform the data from all data sources to Apache Parquet files on Amazon S3.

E. Leverage Amazon Athena's federated query capability to access the Amazon Aurora MySQL database and the Amazon DynamoDB tables.

22. A company utilizes Amazon OpenSearch Service for log analytics. The current instance types struggle to meet performance demands with increasing indexing throughput, leading to delays and increased costs. The company seeks a cost-effective solution to enhance indexing performance without compromising data durability.

Which solution will meet the requirement?

A. Switch to UltraWarm storage for better performance in indexing-heavy workloads.

B. Migrate to OR1 instances.

C. Upgrade to larger general-purpose instances with increased CPU and memory resources.

D. Use Index State Management (ISM) to schedule the deletion of older data.

23. A data engineer is tasked with improving the usability and reliability of a data lake that stores large volumes of data in Amazon S3. The current system faces challenges with schema evolution, where changes to the schema disrupt workflows, and concurrent writes, which often result in inconsistent or corrupted data. The engineer must implement a solution that addresses these issues while ensuring compatibility with existing analytics tools.

Which solution will best address these challenges?

A. Partition the data by key attributes and implement a locking mechanism to manage concurrent writes.

B. Store the data using the Apache Parquet format and enforce schema validation during data ingestion.

C. Migrate the data lake to use the Apache Iceberg table format.

D. Use Amazon EMR to create custom scripts for handling schema changes and retrying failed writes.

24. A media streaming company needs to implement real-time analytics capabilities to monitor viewer engagement and streaming performance. The company processes large volumes of streaming data and plans to use Amazon Managed Streaming for Apache Kafka (Amazon MSK) and Amazon Redshift for its data pipeline. The objective is to derive near-real-time insights while minimizing operational overhead, leveraging existing business intelligence (BI) and analytics tools.

    Which solution will meet these requirements with the least operational overhead?

    A. Use a Kafka sink to stage data in Amazon S3. Use the COPY command to load data from Amazon S3 into Amazon Redshift to make the data available for near-real-time analysis.

    B. Connect Amazon MSK to Amazon Kinesis Data Firehose. Use Kinesis Data Firehose to stage the data in Amazon S3. Use the COPY command to load data from Amazon S3 into Amazon Redshift.

    C. Connect Amazon MSK directly to Amazon Redshift using the streaming ingestion feature. Define materialized views in Amazon Redshift to consume data from Amazon MSK topics.

    D. Use AWS Glue Spark Streaming jobs to read data from Amazon MSK, transform it as needed, and load the transformed data into Amazon Redshift.

25. An ecommerce company manages a data lake in Amazon S3 to store transaction and activity events. The data lake tables are updated once every 24 hours through an ETL pipeline. The company's BI layer queries the data via Amazon Athena every hour to refresh dashboards.

    The team needs a solution that ensures dashboard refresh while reducing query costs. Which solution will meet this requirement with the least operational overhead?

    A. Use Athena's --result-reuse-configuration API parameter to enable query result reuse, specifying the maximum age for cached results to ensure they are refreshed after the ETL updates the tables.

    B. Use a Lambda function to execute the queries hourly and store the results in an Amazon S3 bucket. Configure the BI layer to pull data from the S3 bucket.

    C. Partition the data lake tables by hour and adjust the BI queries to target the latest partition. Refresh dashboards hourly.

    D. Configure the BI layer to cache query results and manually clear the cache after the ETL process completes every 24 hours.

26. A large multinational retail company uses Amazon Athena to query a centralized data lake stored in Amazon S3. The company has multiple regional teams (e.g., North America, Europe, and Asia) that access the data lake during their respective working hours. As the company grows, data engineers notice increasing query queuing and performance degradation in Athena, particularly during peak hours for each region. The traffic patterns are predictable, with each region querying the data lake during specific time windows. The company wants to improve query performance while minimizing operational overhead.

Which solution would best address this issue with the least operational overhead?

A. Configure Amazon Athena Provisioned Capacity for each region, allocating dedicated query processing resources based on their peak usage hours.

B. Use Amazon Redshift instead of Athena to handle the increasing query workload and improve performance.

C. Create separate S3 buckets and Athena workgroups for each region to isolate query traffic.

D. Implement a query scheduling system to distribute query execution evenly throughout the day, reducing peak-time congestion.

27. A data infrastructure team has observed a steady increase in AWS Glue usage over the past six months. To optimize resource utilization and reduce costs, they aim to scale their AWS Glue jobs dynamically based on the need. Which approach should the team take to achieve this goal with minimal operational overhead?

A. Manually reduce the number of DPUs for all Glue jobs by 50% and monitor for any performance degradation.

B. Use AWS Glue autoscaling to dynamically adjust the number of DPUs based on workload demands, while monitoring metrics such as `workerUtilization` to validate performance.

C. Migrate all AWS Glue jobs to AWS Lambda to reduce costs and eliminate the need for DPU management.

D. Implement custom scripts to analyze job performance logs and dynamically modify DPU allocations before each job run.

28. A financial services company is building a data lake on Amazon S3 to store customer records, loan applications, and supporting documents. To comply with regulatory requirements such as PCI-DSS, the company needs to automatically identify and classify personally identifiable information (PII) such as names, addresses, and credit card numbers. Additionally, they want to detect custom data types, such as internal customer reference IDs and application form codes, which follow specific patterns.

Which of the following approaches best meet these requirements? (Select two.)

A. Enable Macie's managed data identifiers to detect common PII types like email addresses, credit card numbers, and national ID numbers.

B. Use AWS Lake Formation to detect and tag PII in S3 data using Macie integration.

C. Define custom data identifiers in Macie to detect sensitive information that matches specific patterns unique to the organization.

D. Use Amazon GuardDuty to scan S3 buckets and classify sensitive information based on anomaly detection.

E. Configure Amazon EMR with custom regex rules in Spark jobs to scan and classify S3 data containing internal reference data patterns.

29. A financial services company ingests transaction data from multiple sources into an Amazon S3–based data lake. Before processing the data with AWS Glue ETL jobs, the data analytics team needs to ensure the quality of the ingested data, checking for missing values, format inconsistencies, and duplicate records.

Which solution would best address this issue with the least operational overhead?

A. Use AWS Lambda to trigger a custom Python script that validates the data in S3 before AWS Glue processing begins.

B. Use AWS Glue Data Quality to define and run data quality rules on the source data in S3, and configure Amazon CloudWatch Alarms to notify the team of any quality issues.

C. Configure an Amazon Athena query that runs daily to check for anomalies in the ingested data and alerts the data team.

D. Use Amazon EMR with Apache Spark to run data quality checks on the ingested data before AWS Glue processes it.

30. A media analytics company is developing a serverless data pipeline using Amazon EMR Serverless to process streaming video engagement data. The pipeline includes multiple ETL jobs that require orchestration with job dependencies and automatic retries for failed jobs to ensure reliable execution. The company aims to minimize operational overhead.

Which combination of steps should the team take to address this requirement? (Select two.)

A. Deploy a self-managed Apache Airflow cluster on Amazon EC2 to orchestrate the workflow, providing full customization and control over job dependencies and failure handling.

B. Use AWS Step Functions to define a state machine that orchestrates Amazon EMR Serverless jobs.

C. Configure Amazon EventBridge to trigger Amazon EMR Serverless jobs based on predefined schedules, ensuring automated execution without additional orchestration logic.

D. Define IAM policies and roles that grant AWS Step Functions the necessary permissions to invoke Amazon EMR Serverless jobs.

E. Define IAM policies and roles for the self-managed Apache Airflow cluster on Amazon EC2 to securely interact with Amazon EMR Serverless Application.

31. A retail company uses Amazon Redshift to analyze customer purchase patterns and website traffic. The analytics team frequently runs complex aggregate queries on large datasets to generate real-time sales reports and personalized product recommendations. However, these queries are repetitive and resource-intensive, leading to high query execution times and increased compute costs.

Which approach would best optimize query performance while minimizing operational overhead?

A. Manually create Materialized Views (MVs) in Amazon Redshift and schedule periodic refresh jobs using AWS Lambda to ensure query performance improvements.

B. Manually create materialized views (MVs) in Amazon Redshift and use Query Editor v2 in Amazon Redshift to schedule refreshes of the materialized views.

C. Enable Automated Materialized Views (AutoMVs) in Amazon Redshift to automatically detect and maintain materialized views for frequently executed queries, improving performance without manual intervention.

D. Implement Result Caching in Amazon Redshift to store query results for repeated executions, reducing processing time for identical queries.

32. A financial services company currently uses Apache Airflow to orchestrate its on-premises data pipelines for ETL processing and reporting workflows. The company plans to migrate these workflows to AWS while minimizing code changes and operational overhead.

Which solution would best address this issue?

A. Deploy a self-managed Apache Airflow cluster on Amazon EC2, giving the team full control over the environment.

B. Convert the pipelines to AWS Step Functions workflows, leveraging the serverless AWS Step Functions workflow engine to reduce operational overhead.

C. Migrate the existing Apache Airflow workflows to Amazon Managed Workflows for Apache Airflow (Amazon MWAA).

D. Rebuild the workflows using AWS Glue workflows, which provide serverless orchestration and eliminate the need for Apache Airflow.

33. A large enterprise has multiple business units sharing a single Amazon Redshift cluster as their central data warehouse. The company wants to implement cost attribution metrics to track resource consumption by each business unit based on data scanned and CPU time used. To achieve this, they need to extract query execution details from Redshift system tables.

Which Amazon Redshift system table should the company use to obtain query-level metrics such as data scanned and CPU time for cost attribution?

A. SVL_QUERY_METRICS_SUMMARY

B. STL_SCAN

C. SVL_QUERY_REPORT

D. STL_WLM_QUERY

34. A company uses an AWS Glue job to process data in a specific database within the AWS Glue Data Catalog. The current IAM policy for the Glue job execution role is as follows:

```
{
  "Version": "2012-10-17",
  "Statement": [
    {
      "Effect": "Allow",
      "Action": [
        "glue:Get*",
        "glue:Create*",
        "glue:Update*",
        "glue:Delete*"
      ],
      "Resource": "*"
    }
```

```
        ]
    }
```

This policy grants excessive permissions and violates the least-privilege principle. As a data engineer, you are tasked with revising the IAM policy to ensure the Glue job has read-only permission to all the tables in database "db1." Which of the following changes would best meet this requirement?

A. Replace the Action field with `"Action": ["glue:GetDatabase", "glue:Get Tables", "glue:GetTable"]` and the Resource field with `"Resource": ["arn:aws:glue:us-west-2:123456789012:catalog", "arn:aws:glue:us-west-2:123456789012:database/db1"]`.

B. Add `"Action": [glue:GetDatabase", "glue:GetTables", "glue:GetTa ble"]` to the Action field. Replace the Resource field with `"Resource": ["arn:aws:glue:us-west-2:123456789012:database/db1"]`.

C. Replace the Action field with `"Action": ["glue:GetDatabase", "glue:Get Tables", "glue:GetTable"]` and the Resource field with `"Resource": ["arn:aws:glue:us-west-2:123456789012:catalog"]`.

D. Replace the Action field with `"Action": ["glue:Get*"]` and the Resource field with `"Resource": ["arn:aws:glue:us-west-2:123456789012:cata log", "arn:aws:glue:us-west-2:123456789012:database/db1"]`.

35. A data engineer is tasked with preprocessing raw CSV files containing sensitive customer information for an ML model training pipeline. The upstream data producer team uploads raw data files to an Amazon S3 bucket without a defined schedule. The data engineer must ensure that personally identifiable information (PII) is detected, anonymized, and partially redacted while still enabling transaction verification.

What steps should the data engineer take to achieve this? (Select three.)

A. Set up an AWS Glue workflow that listens to S3 `PutObject` data events.

B. Use an AWS Step Functions state machine to orchestrate a data pipeline with a time-based schedule.

C. Use the Detect PII transform in AWS Glue Studio to identify the PII fields in the dataset.

D. Create a rule in AWS Glue Data Quality to obfuscate the PII.

E. Permanently delete all PII data from the dataset to eliminate privacy concerns.

F. Partially redact detected PII text.

36. A company is building a centralized data lake on Amazon S3 and wants to enforce fine-grained access control on its data lake tables. The data lake will be accessed by multiple teams using various compute engines, such as Amazon Athena, AWS Glue, and Amazon Redshift Spectrum.

    To meet the requirements, the company needs a scalable solution to manage fine-grained access control across these compute engines. Which steps should you take to configure this environment? (Select three.)

    A. Enable Lake Formation permissions on the data lake by registering the Amazon S3 data lake location with AWS Lake Formation.

    B. Grant data permissions in Lake Formation to specific IAM users, roles, or groups to control access.

    C. Use AWS Identity and Access Management (IAM) policies to define access control for individual tables and columns in the data lake.

    D. Configure Lake Formation tags (LF-Tags) and assign them to tables and columns to enable scalable tag-based access control.

    E. Enable encryption on the Amazon S3 buckets and manage key-based access control using AWS KMS to enforce fine-grained table access.

    F. Add specific compute engines, such as Athena, Glue, and Redshift Spectrum, as principals in Lake Formation and grant them necessary permissions.

37. A healthcare organization manages a data lake on Amazon S3 storing sensitive patient information. To comply with strict healthcare regulations, the organization must apply two layers of encryption to all files uploaded to the S3 bucket.

    Which solution will meet this requirement with the least operational overhead?

    A. Use client-side encryption to encrypt data before uploading it to Amazon S3. Configure server-side encryption (SSE) for the S3 bucket to encrypt the data stored on S3.

    B. Use dual-layer server-side encryption with keys stored in AWS Key Management Service (DSSE-KMS).

    C. Use server-side encryption with AWS Key Management Service (AWS KMS) keys (SSE-KMS).

    D. Use both server-side encryption with AWS KMS keys (SSE-KMS) and Amazon S3–managed keys (SSE-S3).

38. A company is using AWS Glue to extract data from a MongoDB database and perform transformations before storing the results in an Amazon S3 data lake. During a security review, the team discovered that the database credentials were hardcoded directly into the Glue job script. The company needs to remediate this security vulnerability and ensure that the credentials are stored and accessed securely.

Which of the following solutions will meet this requirement?

A. Store the credentials in AWS Secrets Manager. Create a Glue connection to your MongoDB instance referring to the secret.

B. Store the credentials in the AWS Glue job parameters.

C. Utilize the AWS IAM Identity Center to authenticate to the MongoDB instance.

D. Store the credentials in a configuration file in an Amazon S3 bucket. Grant the AWS Glue job IAM access to the configuration file.

39. A global company is using Amazon QuickSight to build dashboards for their analysts. Each regional analyst group should be able to view data specific to only their respective geographic region, as determined by the region field in the dataset.

You have been tasked with configuring QuickSight to ensure this data segregation. Which steps should you take to configure the QuickSight environment to meet these requirements? (Select two.)

A. Create user groups in Amazon QuickSight for each analyst group and assign users to their respective groups.

B. Enable the "Filter by Region" option in the QuickSight dataset configuration panel and assign each group to their corresponding region filter.

C. Use Amazon QuickSight's row-level security (RLS) by creating a permissions dataset that maps analyst groups to the specific regions they are allowed to access.

D. Configure IAM policies to restrict access to specific rows of the dataset based on analyst groups.

E. Modify the source dataset by creating separate datasets for each region and assign them to the respective groups in QuickSight.

40. A company is setting up a multitenant Amazon MSK cluster to host event streams for multiple lines of business (LOBs). Each LOB has its own set of microservices that produce and consume messages to and from Kafka topics. The company requires that microservices of each LOB have permission to access only the Kafka topics associated with their LOB.

As a Solutions Architect, which steps should you take to configure IAM access control to enforce these requirements? (Select three.)

A. Enable IAM access control on the Amazon MSK cluster by updating the cluster's settings to use IAM as the authentication mechanism.

B. Create an IAM policy for each LOB, specifying permissions to allow access only to their respective Kafka topics using the `kafka-cluster:Topic` resource.

C. Configure IAM role-based access control (RBAC) within Kafka to assign permissions for each LOB's microservices to their respective topics.

D. Attach the appropriate IAM policies to the IAM roles assumed by each LOB's microservices.

E. Use Kafka ACLs (access control lists) to restrict access to topics for each LOB's microservices.

F. Use VPC security groups to isolate network traffic for each LOB, ensuring that microservices cannot access topics of other LOBs.

41. A healthcare analytics provider is building a data pipeline to process patient records and generate insights for hospitals. The pipeline ingests data from Amazon S3, processes it using Amazon EMR on EC2, and loads transformed data into Amazon Redshift for analysis.

Due to the sensitive nature of the data, the architecture must prevent public exposure of any data. The company also wants centralized management of sensitive parameters such as database usernames and API keys used within EMR jobs.

Which of the following should the company implement to meet these requirements? (Select two.)

A. Store all credentials in an encrypted S3 bucket, grant access via IAM roles with S3 read permissions.

B. Store sensitive credentials such as API keys and database passwords in AWS Systems Manager Parameter Store.

C. Configure an Amazon S3 Gateway VPC endpoint to ensure private access to S3 from the EMR cluster.

D. Inject all credentials and API keys into EMR cluster instances through environment variables at bootstrap.

E. Use EC2 instance user data scripts to hardcode database credentials in each node at launch time.

F. Mount the S3 bucket to the EMR cluster using S3FS and configure the route through a NAT Gateway.

42. A digital advertising company is building a real-time event streaming platform using Amazon Managed Streaming for Apache Kafka (Amazon MSK) to collect and process clickstream data. The Amazon MSK cluster is deployed in private subnets within a VPC. Kafka producers and consumers are deployed in separate Amazon Elastic Kubernetes Service (Amazon EKS) clusters, each running in different private subnets and in separate VPCs within the same AWS Region. The team must ensure only authorized workloads can access the Kafka brokers.

Which of the following configurations will help meet these requirements?

A. Associate the MSK brokers with a security group that allows inbound traffic on Kafka broker ports only from the security groups of the EKS worker nodes in both VPCs and establish VPC peering or AWS Transit Gateway connectivity between the clusters.

B. Associate the MSK brokers with a security group that allows inbound traffic on all ports from the entire VPC CIDR blocks of both EKS clusters to ensure connectivity.

C. Deploy a public-facing Network Load Balancer in front of the MSK brokers and use IP whitelisting to restrict access from each EKS cluster.

D. Enable internet access on the MSK cluster using a NAT Gateway and configure IAM authentication to control Kafka access from producer and consumer pods.

## CHAPTER 10

What's New in AWS for Data Engineers

Chapters 1 to 9 provided details on established AWS services and concepts that have been widely available since late 2024. AWS has since introduced several new features, with some currently in the preview phase and others having recently achieved general availability status.

This chapter aims to provide a high-level overview of some of these new features, which will help you get familiar with the new capabilities and answer questions related to these features should they appear in the certification exam.

The following are the new announcements that change how developers integrate AWS data analytics services:

- Amazon SageMaker Unified Studio
- Amazon SageMaker Catalog
- Amazon SageMaker Lakehouse
- Improving the developer experience with generative AI
- Amazon S3 Tables and S3 Metadata

Let's get an overview of each of these capabilities.

Amazon SageMaker Unified Studio

As explained in previous chapters, Amazon Web Services offer a wide range of data analytics services (e.g., Amazon EMR, AWS Glue, Amazon Athena, Amazon Redshift, and more) that customers can integrate to build an end-to-end data pipeline. These services help address analytical needs, but they require effort to assemble or require in-depth knowledge to integrate with each other through their respective service interfaces. To address the ease-of-use concern, during re:Invent 2024, AWS announced Amazon SageMaker Unified Studio (*https://oreil.ly/tc0Pb*).

Amazon SageMaker Unified Studio provides an integrated developer experience to use all your data and tools for analytics and AI. You can use Amazon SageMaker Unified Studio to discover your existing data and put it to work with familiar AWS analytics and machine learning services for model development, generative AI application development, big data processing, and SQL-based analytics assisted by Amazon Q Developer.

Figure 10-1 represents the high-level components of SageMaker Unified Studio, which also provides access to SageMaker Lakehouse and enables you to integrate governance capabilities with SageMaker Catalog (both are discussed in upcoming sections). While writing this chapter, streaming (Amazon MSK, Amazon Kinesis), business intelligence (Amazon QuickSight), and search (Amazon OpenSearch Service) services are not yet available through SageMaker Unified Studio but are planned as part of a future update.

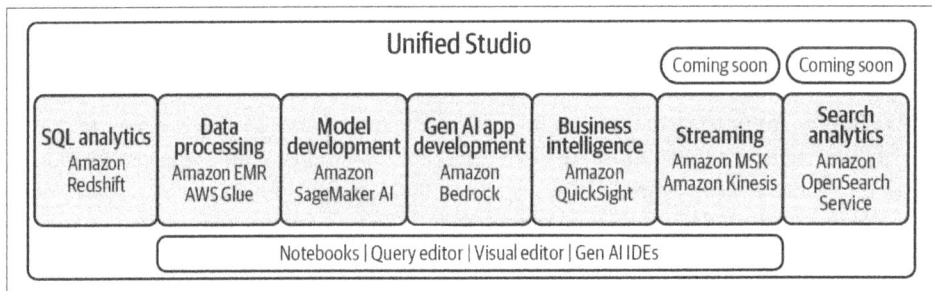

Figure 10-1. High-level components of SageMaker Unified Studio

The next generation of Amazon SageMaker is a platform that brings together all your favorite services and tools into a unified experience through the Unified Studio, with unified data access through the lakehouse, and end-to-end governance built-in for your data and AI.

Next, let's learn about SageMaker Catalog, which enables metadata management and governance.

Amazon SageMaker Catalog

Amazon SageMaker Catalog (*https://oreil.ly/b8-KX*) accelerates data discovery and collaboration. It enhances data discovery (*https://oreil.ly/z3PEH*) with generative AI that automatically adds business context to table attributes, making it easy for all users to find and understand data. Users can search data by business glossary terms or by technical attributes. It supports both centralized and decentralized governance models with seamless data sharing through publishing and subscribing workflows.

SageMaker Catalog also integrates AWS Lake Formation and Amazon DataZone capabilities to enforce security and fine-grained access controls (*https://oreil.ly/ bHmxV*) to ensure that only authorized users can access the right data and AI models for approved purposes.

In addition, SageMaker Catalog lets you gain visibility into data and machine learning model workflows with automated data quality reporting, and track lineage (*https://oreil.ly/yPv6U*) to understand asset transformations and usage across workflows.

Each catalog maps to one of the following storage types, which are represented in Figure 10-2:

- Create a managed catalog for Redshift Managed Storage
- Bring existing data stores into a federated catalog. Mount data from:
  - Amazon Redshift
  - Amazon S3 table buckets
  - External sources like Snowflake, MySQL

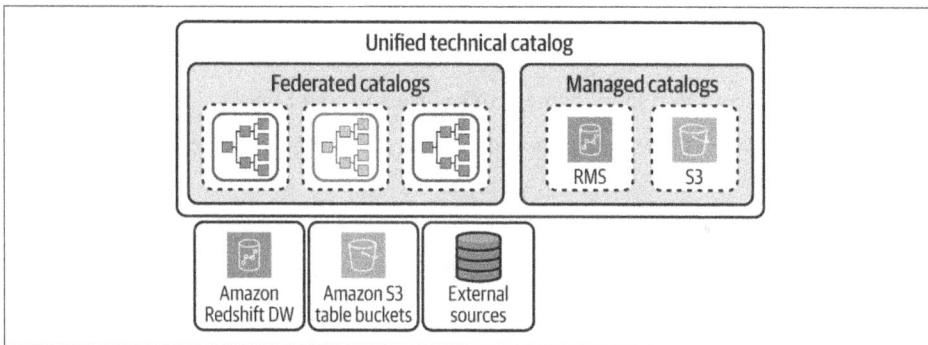

Figure 10-2. High-level components of SageMaker Catalog

The unified catalog simplifies building data products by enabling data producers and consumers to collaborate and bring in governance controls.

Amazon SageMaker Lakehouse

Organizations are building data-driven applications to guide business decisions, improve agility, and drive innovation. Many of these applications are complex to build because they require collaboration across teams and the integration of data, tools, and services.

Building advanced data-driven applications poses several challenges, such as:

- It is time consuming for users to learn multiple services' development experiences.
- Since data, code, and other development artifacts (e.g., ML models) are stored in different services, it is cumbersome for users to understand how they interact with each other and to make changes.
- Configuring and governing access to appropriate users for data, code, development artifacts, and compute resources (e.g., clusters, serverless endpoints) across services is a manual process.

To help customers address these challenges, AWS announced Amazon SageMaker Lakehouse (*https://oreil.ly/bBa4I*), which combines the capability of a data lake and data warehouse within a single interface. It brings in a single copy of data including structured, semi-structured, and unstructured data with a Unified Data Catalog.

As highlighted in Figure 10-3, the following are the high-level components of Sage-Maker Lakehouse:

- Flexible storage for diverse workloads
- Unified technical catalog that manages all data
- Integrated permission management to secure and share data
- Apache Iceberg APIs to access data from AWS Analytics services and open source engines

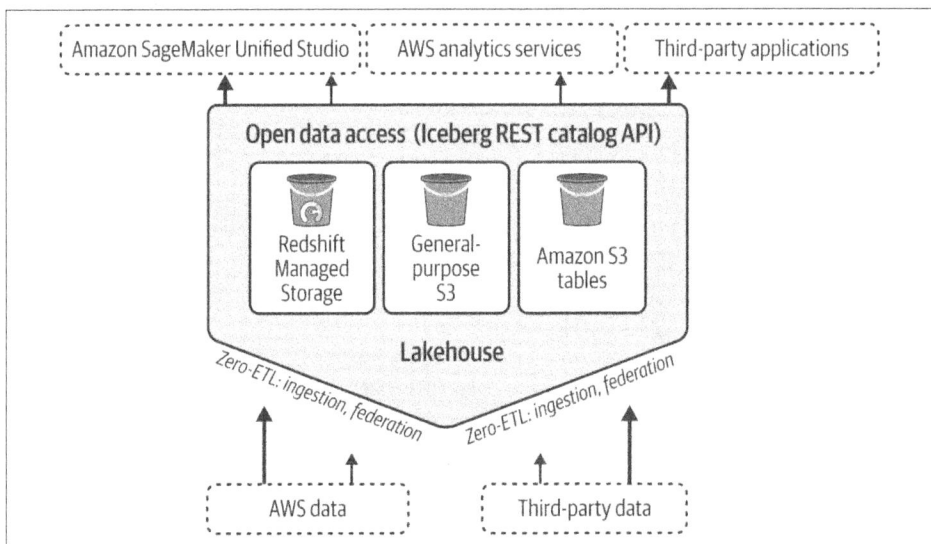

Figure 10-3. High-level components of SageMaker Lakehouse

Amazon SageMaker Lakehouse helps in unifying all the data available across multiple sources for your analytics and AI initiatives with a single copy of data, regardless of how and where the data is stored. SageMaker Lakehouse brings together your existing data across Amazon S3 data lakes and Amazon Redshift data warehouses. In addition, you can zero-ETL data from operational databases and enterprise applications to the lakehouse in near real time. You can also use hundreds of AWS Glue connectors to integrate across different data sources. Furthermore, you can access and query data in-place with federated query capabilities across third-party data sources.

The Iceberg-compatible API interface in SageMaker Lakehouse enables you to access and query all your data in-place with all Apache Iceberg–compatible tools and engines. This provides you with the flexibility to use the analytic tools and engines of your choice, such as your preferred SQL, Spark, BI, and AI/ML tools, and collaborate with data stored across Amazon S3 data lakes or Amazon Redshift data warehouses.

In addition, SageMaker Lakehouse provides a single place for integrated, fine-grained access controls that are consistently enforced across all your data in all analytic tools and engines. This enables you to define permissions once and securely share data across your organization.

Amazon SageMaker AI

With the announcement of a new generation of SageMaker including SageMaker Unified Studio and Lakehouse, AWS renamed the existing SageMaker service to SageMaker AI. As shown in Figure 10-4, SageMaker AI helps in model training, fine-tuning, and deployment, and provides approaches for optimization with model monitoring and MLOps governance.

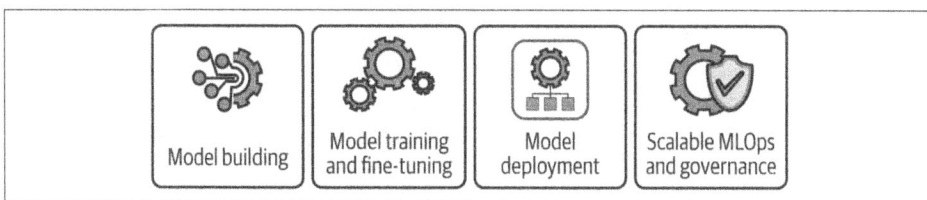

Figure 10-4. High-level components of SageMaker AI

As a refresher, the following are the unique capabilities of SageMaker AI:

- Amazon SageMaker AI provides access to high-performance, cost-effective, scalable, and fully managed infrastructure and tools for each step of the ML lifecycle. Using Amazon SageMaker tools, you can easily train, test, troubleshoot, deploy, and manage foundation models (FMs) at scale and boost productivity of developers while maintaining model performance in production.

- You can explore Amazon SageMaker JumpStart, which is an ML hub offering models, algorithms, and prebuilt ML solutions. SageMaker JumpStart offers hundreds of ready-to-use FMs from various model providers.

- Amazon SageMaker machine learning operations (MLOps) capabilities help you create repeatable workflows across the ML lifecycle to experiment, train, deploy, and govern ML models at scale while maintaining model performance in production.

- Amazon SageMaker provides purpose-built governance tools to help you implement ML responsibly. Amazon SageMaker Model Cards makes it easier to capture, retrieve, and share essential model information. Once the models are deployed, SageMaker Model Dashboard gives you unified monitoring across all your models by providing notice of deviations from expected behavior, automated alerts, and troubleshooting to improve model performance. Amazon SageMaker Clarify detects and measures potential bias using a variety of metrics to help you address potential bias and explain model predictions.

- With Amazon SageMaker Ground Truth, you can use human feedback to customize models on company- or domain-specific data for your unique use case to improve model output and task performance.

Amazon SageMaker AI continues to be the choice for customers who plan to develop custom models or fine-tune existing models, deploy models for batch/real-time inference, and leverage SageMaker AI's end-to-end ML development and MLOps capabilities.

Amazon S3 Tables

Over recent years, we have seen an increase in adoption of the Apache Iceberg table format for data lake use cases. To achieve optimal performance, Apache Iceberg tables need to be maintained by expiring older snapshots, optimizing files with compaction, and cleaning up unreferenced files. To reduce operational overhead, AWS announced Amazon S3 Tables (*https://oreil.ly/L_W2l*) as an S3 bucket type built for tabular data, which acts as a managed Iceberg table.

It supports the advanced capabilities of Apache Iceberg tables such as row-level transactions (UPSERT/MERGE), schema evolution, and queryable snapshots. Compared to an open source Iceberg table, it provides the following benefits:

- Optimized for analytics with up to 3x faster query throughput and 10x higher transactions per second
- Seamless integration with Query Engines
- Scales effortlessly as your data lake evolves

- Automates table maintenance:
  — Continually optimizes query efficiency and storage costs
  — Automates tasks like compaction, snapshot management, and unreferenced file cleanup

Amazon S3 Metadata

Amazon S3 Metadata (*https://oreil.ly/rDBlL*) helps instantly discover and understand S3 data through automated metadata that is updated in near real time. This enables data identification, curation, and business analytics.

The metadata includes system-defined metadata such as size, object source, etc., and custom metadata such as tags for SKU, transaction ID, content rating, and more.

The metadata gets captured when the object is uploaded to Amazon S3, and in near real time (within minutes) you get a read-only view of the metadata to query. These metadata elements are stored in S3 Tables, which is optimized for tabular data and is Iceberg compatible.

Improving the Developer Experience with Generative AI

There are several generative AI (GenAI) capabilities integrated into AWS's data analytics services that improve developer experience and productivity. The following presents a summary of the capabilities.

Generative AI–Powered Code Generation with Amazon Q Developer

Code generation is one of the most valuable implementations of generative AI, improving developer productivity. The Amazon Q Developer (*https://oreil.ly/pWbda*) code generation capability is integrated into multiple AWS services such as AWS Glue ETL jobs and interactive sessions, SageMaker Unified Studio notebooks, and Amazon Redshift Query Editor v2 for SQL code generation.

In AWS Glue, Amazon Q Developer supports both Python and Scala, the two languages used for coding ETL scripts for Spark jobs. Currently, code generation works only with the PySpark kernel.

The integration offers context-awareness capability, which carries the context from the previous user query only, within the same conversation. It does not retain context beyond the immediately preceding query. Currently, context awareness supports only a subset of required configurations for various nodes. Context awareness and DataFrame support are available in Q Developer Chat and SageMaker Unified Studio notebooks but not yet available in AWS Glue Studio notebooks.

Automated Script Upgrade in AWS Glue

AWS Glue added a new capability that enables developers to upgrade their Glue 2.0 (Spark 2.4.3, Python 3.7) projects to Glue 4.0 (Spark 3.3.0, Python 3.10). Upgrading Spark application code is complex as it involves the following challenges:

- A mix of imperative and declarative programming style code
- Spark configurations and default values that might have changed between different Spark versions, which needs to be tested while upgrading

This automatic Spark job upgrade leverages AI to automate both the identification (analyzes both the code and Spark configuration) and validation of required changes in your AWS Glue Spark applications.

The AI-driven upgrade plan generation looks at the following four areas for the upgrade and then runs automated validation jobs in your environment after the upgrade:

- Spark SQL API methods and functions
- Spark DataFrame API methods and operations
- Python language updates (including module deprecations and syntax changes)
- Spark SQL and Core configuration settings

Please note, the current implementation has the following limitations:

- Only limited to PySpark jobs that do not have additional dependencies
- Maximum 10 concurrent jobs per account

GenAI-Powered Troubleshooting for Spark in AWS Glue

Root cause analysis for job failures is one of the most time-consuming tasks as Spark jobs involve the following:

- Extensive connectivity and configuration options.
- Spark's in-memory processing and distributed partitioning makes it difficult to debug issues.
- Lazy evaluation of Spark transformations makes it difficult to accurately identify the actual reason for the failures.

The new GenAI-powered troubleshooting provides automated root cause analysis for failed Spark applications by analyzing job metadata and metrics/logs associated with the error signature; it also provides actionable recommendations with remediation steps. The capability is accessible from the Glue job list, job details, and monitoring page of the Glue console.

Figure 10-5 provides a screenshot of the Glue console that highlights the reason for the job failure and recommendations for resolving the issue.

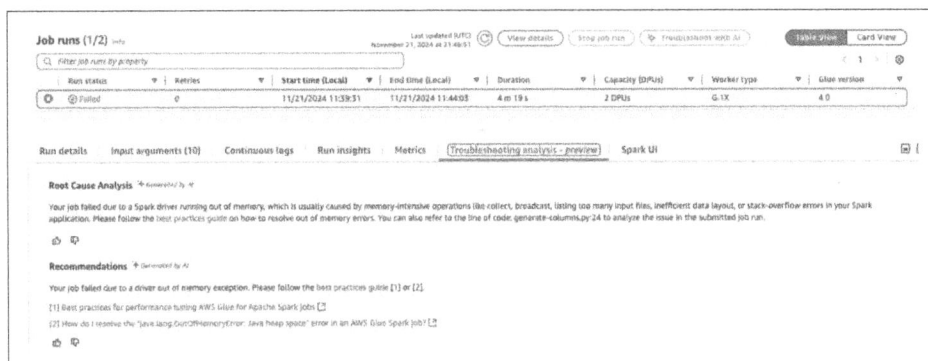

Figure 10-5. Spark application failure troubleshooting in AWS Glue

As a best practice, before implementing any suggested changes in your production environment, review the suggested changes thoroughly.

Conclusion

This chapter explained a few of the top features announced during re:Invent 2024 that change the way customers interact with AWS data analytics services. You can stay up to date with new feature announcements by reviewing the "What's New with AWS" page (*https://oreil.ly/B51K4*).

Resources

The following are additional resources that may help you learn more about these new capabilities:

- "An Integrated Experience for All Your Data and AI with Amazon SageMaker Unified Studio" (*https://oreil.ly/JcZNE*)
- "Foundational Blocks of Amazon SageMaker Unified Studio: An Admin's Guide to Implement Unified Access to All Your Data, Analytics, and AI" (*https://oreil.ly/kw2p6*)
- "Catalog and Govern Amazon Athena Federated Queries with Amazon SageMaker Lakehouse" (*https://oreil.ly/ValYY*)
- "Discover, Govern, and Collaborate on Data and AI Securely with Amazon SageMaker Data and AI Governance" (*https://oreil.ly/RPkXI*)

- "Access Your Existing Data and Resources Through Amazon SageMaker Unified Studio, Part 1: AWS Glue Data Catalog and Amazon Redshift" (*https://oreil.ly/w4htU*)

- "Access Your Existing Data and Resources Through Amazon SageMaker Unified Studio, Part 2: Amazon S3, Amazon RDS, Amazon DynamoDB, and Amazon EMR" (*https://oreil.ly/kvGEJ*)

- "Amazon Q Data Integration Adds DataFrame Support and In-Prompt Context-Aware Job Creation" (*https://oreil.ly/hceGG*)

Solutions to the Practice Questions

This appendix lists the solutions to the practice questions appearing at the end of Chapters 4–7 and the practice exam in Chapter 9.

Chapter 4

1. C: The zero-ETL integration between Salesforce and Redshift that AWS Glue provides is the most seamless, optimal-cost, and low-overhead solution for integrating Salesforce data into Amazon Redshift. AWS takes care of the heavy lifting of identifying new data from the source and continuously replicating it to the target Redshift. Where zero-ETL integrations are available, they are almost always the right solution.

2. C: Creating an S3 event notification that triggers the Lambda function directly when an S3 `ObjectCreated` event occurs, with a filter rule for *.txt* files, provides the most straightforward and least operationally complex solution for this requirement.

3. C: AWS Glue DataBrew offers a visual, low-code interface for designing data preparation workflows, making it ideal for handling the described data quality issues and transformations with minimal coding and operational overhead.

4. B: Amazon Data Firehose provides the most streamlined solution for consolidating real-time data from multiple AWS services and delivering it to Datadog with minimal operational overhead, offering built-in integrations and automatic scaling.

5. A: `UNNEST_STRUCT` is the function that solves the requirement here.

6. B: AWS DataSync is purpose-built for efficient, automated data transfer from on-premises to AWS, with change detection capabilities to minimize transfer times and built-in monitoring features, making it the ideal choice for this scenario.

7. B: Amazon Managed Workflows for Apache Airflow (MWAA) provides a fully managed, scalable orchestration service that can handle complex data processing pipelines with external dependencies, offering robust monitoring and management capabilities.

8. A: The `FindMatches` transformation in AWS Glue DataBrew provides a managed, ML-powered solution for identifying and merging duplicate records, offering the least operational overhead for deduplicating customer data at scale.

9. B: The Amazon Redshift Serverless streaming ingestion feature allows direct consumption of data from Kinesis Data Streams, providing the most streamlined and low-overhead solution for real-time data ingestion and analytics.

10. A, C: Monitoring shard-level metrics in CloudWatch helps identify performance issues, while modifying the partition key can improve data distribution across shards, addressing the root causes of the observed throughput and latency problems.

Chapter 5

1. A: Amazon S3 is a scalable, cost-effective storage service that integrates natively with Spark on Amazon EMR, making it ideal for big data processing workloads migrated from HDFS.

2. A: ISM policies in OpenSearch Service automate tiered storage transitions—Hot to UltraWarm to Cold—minimizing operational overhead while optimizing cost and performance for time-based access patterns.

3. C: Redshift Spectrum allows Amazon Redshift to directly query data stored in Amazon S3 without data movement, enabling seamless access to historical datasets.

4. B: S3 Lifecycle policies help with automatically deleting noncurrent object versions after a defined period, which directly addresses the storage cost increase caused by versioning.

5. A: AWS Glue crawlers automatically detect schema changes in S3 data and update the Glue Data Catalog with minimal manual effort, offering the least operational overhead.

6. A, B: Glue crawlers provide a low-overhead, automated way to catalog data from Amazon S3, RDS, and Snowflake into the Glue Data Catalog, enabling unified access without custom scripting or manual exports.

7. A, D: Partitioning prunes the data by allowing Athena to scan only the specific subfolders relevant to your query's filters, drastically reducing query time and cost. Using compressed file formats reduces the amount of data Athena needs to read from S3, which directly improves query speed and lowers data scan costs.

8. A: This design is the most efficient because using `UserID` as the partition key allows for a direct query to retrieve all orders for a specific user, while using `PurchaseTimestamp` as the sort key automatically organizes those orders chronologically, fulfilling both access patterns with a single, highly performant query operation.

9. B: Applying the `ALL` distribution style to small dimension tables is a key Redshift optimization strategy, as it places a full copy of the table on every node, which completely eliminates data redistribution costs during joins with large fact tables, significantly boosting query performance with minimal storage impact.

10. C: S3 Standard provides immediate access during the first year. Glacier Deep Archive is the lowest-cost option that still meets the 48-hour retrieval SLA (as it supports restores within 12–48 hours), making it the most cost-effective choice for long-term compliance storage.

Chapter 6

1. A, B: Implementing AWS Glue partition indexing and configuring Athena partition projection are the most effective solutions for improving query planning performance with partitioned data. Partition indexing creates a searchable index of partition locations, while partition projection eliminates the need to read partition metadata from the Glue Data Catalog.

2. B: `STL_LOAD_ERRORS` is the correct system table for viewing detailed information about `COPY` command load failures in Redshift. It contains specific error messages, row numbers, and other details crucial for troubleshooting.

3. A, B: Checking IAM configurations and examining network settings are the most effective approaches because Step Functions failures during Lambda invocation typically stem from permission issues or network connectivity problems.

4. A, C: Choosing multi-AZ deployment and implementing cross-region snapshot copy provide the highest availability with minimal operational overhead. Multi-AZ automatically handles failover, while cross-region snapshots provide disaster recovery capabilities.

5. C: Using the scheduler in Query Editor v2 is the most straightforward and cost-effective solution for scheduling long-running stored procedures in Redshift.

6. C: The AWS Glue workflow is the most efficient solution for orchestrating Glue components, offering native integration and minimal overhead.

7. A: Implementing Athena workgroups with query result caching is the most cost-effective solution while meeting the four-hour freshness requirement.

8. A: Using Amazon Q with natural language prompts provides the easiest way for non-expert users to create visualizations.

9. D: Publishing flow logs to S3 in Parquet format and using Athena for analysis provides the most cost-effective solution with minimal operational overhead.

10. A: Using AWS Glue Data Quality rules is the most efficient way to implement data validation requirements, offering a declarative approach with built-in functionality.

Chapter 7

1. D: In AWS security groups you can configure specific IP addresses to provide access to the RDS database. Option A also mentions the same but option D is the best answer as it follows the least-privilege principle and suggests configuring IP address access only for the database port for enhanced security.

2. B: Deploying the AWS Lambda function in the same VPC as RDS will enable network connectivity. Then adding the Lambda function security group into RDS inbound access will open up the firewall for access.

3. B: AWS KMS enables you to share the KMS key with another AWS account (*https://oreil.ly/QacQq*); that's the efficient way to provide access to the dataset.

4. B: AWS Lake Formation enables you to implement fine-grained access control on your data by integrating row-based, column-based, and tag-based filters.

5. C: AWS Glue Data Catalog is a managed service that reduces operational overhead as you do not need to manage any infrastructure and it scales with the number of metadata objects and number of requests.

6. C: AWS CloudTrail Lake is a managed service for aggregating, storing, and analyzing user and API activities across AWS environments. It allows for querying activity logs using SQL-based queries. It is the best answer as you can directly use it without any custom integration.

7. A: Amazon Redshift supports cross-account data sharing and you can enable the primary cluster to share with other Redshift clusters, which reduces operational overhead.

8. C: AWS Backup provides the capability to trigger backup from a central account and also define to which region data should be written. That's the best way to achieve the requirement.

9. C: Aurora PostgreSQL's export to S3 feature (*https://oreil.ly/z6drq*) makes the implementation simple and reduces operational overhead.

10. C: AWS Secrets Manager stores credentials in a secured way and the Lambda functions refer only to the Secrets Manager key, so anyone having access to the Lambda function code will still not be able to get the database login credentials.

Chapter 9

1. *Correct Answers*: A, C, D

   This scenario requires building an open source–based CDC pipeline from Aurora MySQL to Amazon S3, which strongly aligns with using Debezium and Apache Kafka.

   - Option A (Enable binary logging) – Correct: Debezium relies on MySQL binary logs for capturing database changes, making this step mandatory.
   - Option B (Deploy Debezium directly on Aurora MySQL) – Incorrect: Aurora MySQL is a managed database service and doesn't support direct installation of third-party software like Debezium connectors.
   - Option C (Deploy MSK Connect with Debezium) – Correct: Amazon MSK Connect runs Kafka connectors (like Debezium) natively, effectively capturing database changes from Aurora MySQL into Kafka topics.
   - Option D (Deploy an Amazon MSK cluster) – Correct: MSK provides a managed Kafka environment necessary for Debezium connectors to stream CDC events.
   - Option E (Set up AWS DMS) – Incorrect: AWS DMS is a proprietary service and does not meet the open source requirement stated in the scenario.
   - Option F (Use Kinesis Data Streams) – Incorrect: Amazon Kinesis does not natively support CDC directly from Aurora MySQL binary logs without additional tooling or integrations.

   References:

   - "Build an End-to-End CDC Pipeline with Amazon MSK Connect" (*https://oreil.ly/68sB9*)

2. *Correct Answer*: C

   This scenario requires ingesting real-time streaming data from an Amazon Kinesis data stream directly into Amazon Redshift with minimal operational overhead. The emphasis is on simplicity, minimal management, and AWS-native integrations.

   - Option A (Amazon Managed Service for Apache Flink) – Incorrect: Although technically feasible, using Apache Flink introduces additional operational complexity, including managing application code and MSF applications, making it less optimal for minimal operational overhead.

- Option B (AWS Glue Streaming with Redshift Data API) – Incorrect: AWS Glue streaming jobs combined with Redshift's Data API provide a valid streaming solution, but require more operational management, monitoring, and troubleshooting than direct ingestion approaches.

- Option C (Redshift streaming ingestion) – Correct: Amazon Redshift's native streaming ingestion directly consumes data from Kinesis Data Streams without intermediate storage or complex setup. This approach provides the lowest operational overhead.

- Option D (Kinesis Data Firehose + S3 + Redshift COPY command) – Incorrect: Although commonly used, this method involves additional steps such as managing intermediate S3 storage and scheduling COPY commands, resulting in increased operational overhead compared to direct streaming ingestion.

References:

- Amazon Redshift streaming ingestion (*https://oreil.ly/wIXBG*)

3. *Correct Answer*: C

This scenario requires offloading analytical queries from Aurora PostgreSQL to Amazon Redshift, with an emphasis on (1) minimal operational overhead and (2) near-real-time data synchronization.

- Option A (AWS Glue ETL + S3 + Redshift COPY command) – Incorrect: Although commonly used and technically feasible, this is a batch-oriented method that requires scheduled ETL jobs, additional data management, and introduces latency.

- Option B (AWS DMS replication to Redshift) – Incorrect: While AWS DMS is a valid replication approach and offers near-real-time replication, it still involves managing replication tasks, monitoring, and occasional troubleshooting, adding operational complexity compared to a fully automated zero-ETL feature.

- Option C (Aurora zero-ETL integration) – Correct: Aurora zero-ETL integration automatically replicates data from Aurora PostgreSQL into Amazon Redshift continuously without manual ETL management or intermediate storage. This AWS-managed solution provides real-time data synchronization with the least operational overhead.

- Option D (Aurora read replica + export to S3 + Redshift Spectrum) – Incorrect: Exporting data directly from an Aurora PostgreSQL read replica to Amazon S3 is not supported, as Aurora permits only data export operations (SELECT INTO S3) from a writer instance. Thus, this solution is technically infeasible.

References:

- "Aurora Zero-ETL Integration with Amazon Redshift" (*https://oreil.ly/OkmKq*)

4. *Correct Answer*: B

This scenario describes integrating changes from a feature branch (optimize-glue-jobs) into the main branch after switching to the main branch locally. The correct Git operation needs to merge feature changes into the current active branch (main).

- Option A (git pull optimize-glue-jobs) – Incorrect: git pull fetches and merges changes from a remote repository, not from a feature branch to a main branch.

- Option B (git merge optimize-glue-jobs) – Correct: git merge optimize-glue-jobs integrates changes from the specified local feature branch directly into the currently checked-out branch (main). This is exactly what's required.

- Option C (git rebase main) – Incorrect: git rebase main reapplies commits onto the main branch. You need to switch to the optimize-glue-jobs branch first to make this command work.

- Option D (git checkout optimize-glue-jobs) – Incorrect: git checkout optimize-glue-jobs switches to the feature branch rather than merging its changes into main.

5. *Correct Answer*: A

This scenario requires defining AWS infrastructure as code (IaC) using (1) object-oriented programming constructs, (2) reusable across environments, and (3) with explicit support for Python.

- Option A (AWS Cloud Development Kit) – Correct: AWS CDK supports defining infrastructure using familiar object-oriented programming languages such as Python and TypeScript. It allows developers to build reusable constructs, greatly simplifying consistency across staging and production environments.

- Option B (Manual provision + export to CloudFormation templates) – Incorrect: Using the AWS Management Console to provision resources and exporting CloudFormation templates lacks object-oriented capabilities and introduces manual overhead, making it less scalable and reusable.

- Option C (AWS CLI scripts) – Incorrect: CLI scripts are procedural focused and not designed for IaC usage.

- Option D (AWS CloudFormation templates) – Incorrect: While AWS CloudFormation offers infrastructure as code, it doesn't natively support object-oriented constructs or programming languages like Python. Thus, it doesn't align fully with the team's stated preferences.

6. *Correct Answer*: B

This scenario involves large-scale Apache Spark–based ETL workloads that are recurring, not time-sensitive, and can tolerate interruptions. The primary objective is minimizing costs while maintaining scalability and stability.

- Option A (EMR On-Demand Instances only) – Incorrect: Using exclusively On-Demand Instances ensures stability but is more expensive compared to the mixed Spot and On-Demand solution described in Option B. This doesn't align with the goal of cost minimization.

- Option B (EMR with Spot and On-Demand Instances) – Correct: Combining Spot and On-Demand Instances in Amazon EMR provides significant cost savings by leveraging lower-priced Spot Instances, while maintaining job stability through the use of some On-Demand Instances to mitigate interruptions.

- Option C (AWS Glue serverless solution) – Incorrect: While AWS Glue offers a fully managed, serverless Spark environment, it typically incurs higher costs for continuous, large-scale Spark workloads compared to optimized EMR setups with Spot Instances.

- Option D (Self-managed Spark on EC2 Spot Instances) – Incorrect: A fully self-managed cluster on Spot Instances could reduce costs but would significantly increase operational complexity and risks of job failures without any built-in fallback or stability guarantees provided by managed services such as Amazon EMR or AWS Glue.

7. *Correct Answer*: A

This scenario requires real-time, file-level processing triggered immediately upon file upload to Amazon S3, including schema validation and CSV-to-Parquet format conversion. The ideal solution must emphasize simplicity, scalability, and minimal operational overhead.

- Option A (S3 Event Notification + AWS Lambda) – Correct: Using Amazon S3 Event Notifications to trigger AWS Lambda functions provides immediate processing upon file arrival, effectively handling schema validation and conversion tasks for the given file size (10–100 MB). This solution offers simplicity, scalability, and minimal management overhead.

- Option B (AWS Glue crawlers + Glue jobs) – Incorrect: AWS Glue crawlers run periodically rather than reactively upon file arrival, thus not fulfilling the real-time requirement. It introduces latency and additional operational overhead.

- Option C (S3 Event Notification + AWS Step Functions + Glue jobs) – Incorrect: While technically possible, AWS Glue jobs are overkill for lightweight, individual file-based processing.

- Option D (Amazon S3 Batch Operations + Glue jobs) – Incorrect: Batch Operations are schedule-based rather than event-driven, failing the real-time processing requirement and causing processing delays. Additionally, Amazon S3 Batch Operations does not natively support integration with AWS Glue.

References:

- "Get Started with Amazon S3 Event-Driven Design Patterns" (*https://oreil.ly/iazpg*)

8. *Correct Answer*: C

This scenario requires stateful, near-real-time stream processing, strongly aligning with Apache Flink as an optimal technology. Additionally, the solution must be fully managed to ensure scalability and minimal operational overhead.

- Option A (Self-managed Apache Flink on EC2) – Incorrect: Deploying and managing a self-hosted Flink cluster significantly increases operational complexity and management overhead, conflicting with the fully managed requirement.

- Option B (AWS Lambda + DynamoDB) – Incorrect: While feasible for simple state handling, using DynamoDB as external state storage can increase latency and complexity. Lambda also has inherent limitations for complex, stateful stream processing scenarios at scale.

- Option C (Amazon Managed Service for Apache Flink) – Correct: Amazon Managed Service for Apache Flink (MSF) is specifically designed for stateful streaming analytics. It offers fully managed infrastructure, automatic scaling, and built-in state management, perfectly aligning with the minimal operational overhead and real-time fraud detection requirements.

- Option D (EMR-managed Apache Flink) – Incorrect: Although EMR simplifies cluster management compared to a self-managed setup, it still requires managing cluster lifecycle, configuration, and scaling, resulting in higher operational overhead compared to MSF.

9. *Correct Answer*: B

This scenario requires integrating Amazon EMR Notebooks seamlessly with a Git-based source code repository to effectively track changes, enhance team collaboration, and promote code reuse within EMR-based workflows. A solution must directly support version control without operational overhead.

- Option A (Store notebook code in Amazon S3) – Incorrect: Using Amazon S3 for storing notebook code lacks built-in version control capabilities, requiring manual effort for tracking changes and introducing unnecessary operational complexity.

- Option B (EMR Notebooks with Git repository integration) – Correct: Amazon EMR Notebooks natively integrate with Git-based repositories like AWS CodeCommit and GitHub. This enables users to pull, push, and manage notebook code changes directly within the notebook interface, meeting the seamless integration and collaboration goals.

- Option C (Local Git repository on EC2) – Incorrect: This manual method significantly increases operational overhead, complicates synchronization, and undermines real-time collaboration by requiring manual uploads of job scripts to EMR Notebooks.

- Option D (AWS Glue Studio to EMR Notebooks) – Incorrect: AWS Glue Studio primarily targets Glue-based workflows and doesn't directly support EMR Notebooks integration, introducing unnecessary complexity and operational overhead.

10. *Correct Answer*: D

    This scenario involves orchestrating a large-scale, multistage data pipeline across multiple analytics services, making Apache Airflow an ideal technology due to its flexibility and wide integration support. Additionally, the solution must be fully managed to minimize operational overhead, ensure scalability, availability, and security, and provide detailed logging and monitoring capabilities.

    - Option A (Self-managed Apache Airflow on EC2) – Incorrect: Deploying Apache Airflow manually on EC2 requires significant operational overhead for setup, maintenance, scaling, and security management, conflicting with the minimal overhead goal.

    - Option B (AWS Glue workflows) – Incorrect: AWS Glue workflows primarily orchestrate Glue-specific ETL jobs and lack native integration and flexibility for orchestrating comprehensive EMR and Flink-based pipelines.

    - Option C (Custom Python-based engine on ECS) – Incorrect: Building a custom orchestration solution introduces extensive complexity in development, deployment, maintenance, and scaling, resulting in higher operational overhead.

    - Option D (Amazon Managed Workflows for Apache Airflow - MWAA) – Correct: Amazon MWAA provides a fully managed, secure, and scalable orchestration service leveraging Apache Airflow. It supports comprehensive orchestration across various AWS analytics services (S3, EMR, Flink) with built-in detailed logging, monitoring, and minimal operational overhead.

11. *Correct Answer*: B

This scenario involves managing multiple AWS Lambda functions with shared third-party Python libraries. The company requires a solution that centralizes dependency management and ensures consistency.

- Option A (Package libraries with each Lambda) – Incorrect: Bundling libraries individually with each function increases duplication, deployment complexity, and maintenance overhead.

- Option B (AWS Lambda Layers) – Correct: AWS Lambda Layers allow common libraries to be packaged separately and centrally managed. This approach simplifies updates, ensures consistent dependencies across multiple Lambda functions, and significantly reduces operational overhead.

- Option C (Libraries stored in S3, downloaded at runtime) – Incorrect: Downloading libraries at runtime from S3 increases complexity due to managing runtime errors, library versions, and network dependencies.

- Option D (EFS filesystem mounted into Lambda) – Incorrect: Although technically feasible, using Amazon EFS introduces additional complexity in setup and management compared to Lambda Layers. It is also typically reserved for larger files or persistent storage needs rather than lightweight library management.

References:

- Managing Python dependencies with Lambda Layers (*https://oreil.ly/H8L5j*)

12. *Correct Answer*: A

This scenario involves easily discovering, subscribing to, and incorporating third-party datasets into an AWS-based analytics platform. The company requires a solution specifically designed for accessing and integrating external data in the cloud.

- Option A (AWS Data Exchange) – Correct: AWS Data Exchange is specifically designed to help customers find, subscribe to, and seamlessly integrate third-party datasets into their AWS environment, fully aligning with the scenario's requirements.

- Option B (AWS DataSync) – Incorrect: AWS DataSync is primarily for migrating data between on-premises and AWS or across AWS storage services. It does not offer capabilities to discover or subscribe to third-party datasets.

- Option C (Redshift Data Marketplace) – Incorrect: "Redshift Data Marketplace" does not exist as an independent AWS service.

- Option D (Redshift Data Sharing) – Incorrect: Redshift Data Sharing allows sharing data across Amazon Redshift clusters but does not enable discovery or subscription to external third-party datasets.

13. *Correct Answer*: B

This scenario involves querying a text column in an Amazon Redshift table to find records containing case-insensitive keywords ("refund," "cancel," or "complaint"). The SQL query needs efficient pattern-matching capabilities to detect these keywords within the comments text.

- Option A (Exact match with =) – Incorrect: Using the = operator performs an exact match against the entire column value and won't match partial strings or phrases within comments.

- Option B (Case-insensitive regex with ~*) – Correct: The ~* operator in Redshift performs case-insensitive regular expression matching, efficiently retrieving records containing the specified keywords anywhere within the text.

- Option C (IN operator with wildcards) – Incorrect: The IN operator does not support wildcard patterns; it only checks for exact matches within a defined list of values.

- Option D (Case-sensitive regex with ~) – Incorrect: The ~ operator in Redshift performs case-sensitive regex matching.

References:

- Pattern-matching conditions in Amazon Redshift (*https://oreil.ly/0uOSN*)
- Regular expression functions in Amazon Redshift (*https://oreil.ly/OHReQ*)

14. *Correct Answer*: D

This scenario requires orchestrating multiple AWS Glue jobs in a daily ETL pipeline with an emphasis on cost efficiency and reliable, scheduled execution. The solution should leverage AWS Glue's orchestration capabilities and cost-effective configurations.

- Option A (AWS Lambda to trigger Glue jobs with default worker) – Incorrect: Using AWS Lambda individually to trigger each Glue job adds complexity in orchestration and job dependency management. Additionally, the default worker type is typically more expensive than Glue FLEX.

- Option B (Glue workflow with default worker type) – Incorrect: While AWS Glue workflows provide reliable orchestration and scheduling, using the default worker type prioritizes speed over cost efficiency, increasing overall costs.

- Option C (Individual Glue jobs via CloudWatch Events with FLEX) – Incorrect: Scheduling each Glue job individually via CloudWatch Events is possible but complicates orchestration and increases operational complexity compared to a Glue workflow.

- Option D (Glue workflow with Glue FLEX) – Correct: AWS Glue workflows orchestrate and schedule multiple Glue jobs seamlessly, while Glue FLEX workers provide cost-effective execution suitable for non-time-critical work-loads, fully aligning with the company's requirement for reliability and cost-efficiency.

15. *Correct Answer*: D

This scenario involves cataloging CSV data from Amazon S3 into the AWS Glue Data Catalog, ensuring that the previous day's data is automatically accessible each day by 7:00 a.m. The ideal solution must automate catalog updating on a daily basis with appropriate permissions.

- Option A (On-demand crawler with `AmazonS3FullAccess`) – Incorrect: Using on-demand crawlers requires manual triggering, and the policy (`AmazonS3Full Access`) provides unnecessarily broad permissions, not aligning with security best practices.

- Option B (On-demand crawler with inline bucket-specific read-only policy) – Incorrect: While the permissions setup is secure, running the crawler on-demand does not automate daily batch processing, failing to meet the daily requirement.

- Option C (Scheduled crawler with `AmazonS3ReadOnlyAccess`) – Incorrect: Though scheduling meets the automation requirement, `AmazonS3ReadOnlyAc cess` provides overly broad access to all S3 buckets, not adhering to the principle of least privilege.

- Option D (Scheduled crawler with inline bucket-specific read-only policy) – Correct: This approach securely combines precise, bucket-specific permissions with automated daily scheduling, fully meeting the requirement to update the catalog automatically on a batch daily basis.

16. *Correct Answers*: A, C, D

This scenario requires designing a cost-effective data pipeline that integrates Amazon DynamoDB, Amazon S3, and Amazon QuickSight. The company requires recent data (last three months) to be quickly available via DynamoDB for QuickSight dashboards, while older data (three months to five years) must be archived affordably yet remain accessible through Amazon Athena queries with reasonable performance. Data older than five years must be automatically deleted.

- Option A (DynamoDB TTL to auto-delete data older than 90 days) – Correct: Using DynamoDB TTL ensures automatic deletion of data older than 90 days from DynamoDB, meeting the recent data requirement for QuickSight dashboards and reducing costs.

- Option B (Store data indefinitely in DynamoDB Standard-IA) – Incorrect: Keeping data indefinitely in DynamoDB Standard-IA class is costly and does not meet archival and cost-efficiency requirements for long-term data retention.

- Option C (AWS Glue job to export DynamoDB data to S3) – Correct: An AWS Glue job effectively moves data from DynamoDB to Amazon S3, enabling cost-efficient long-term storage in a data lake accessible via Amazon Athena.

- Option D (S3 Lifecycle transition to S3-IA, delete after five years) – Correct: The S3 Infrequent Access (S3-IA) storage class provides lower-cost storage with reasonable retrieval performance suitable for occasional Athena queries. The lifecycle policy ensures automatic deletion after five years.

- Option E (S3 Lifecycle transition to Glacier Deep Archive, delete after five years) – Incorrect: While Glacier Deep Archive is extremely cost-effective, it involves lengthy restoration delays (several hours) before data can be queried, failing the "reasonable performance" requirement.

17. *Correct Answer*: A

This scenario involves isolating workloads for Analytics and Reporting teams to address contention issues on a shared Amazon Redshift cluster. The optimal solution must effectively separate workloads, enable instant data availability for the Reporting Team, and minimize impact on the existing workflow.

- Option A (Separate clusters with Amazon Redshift Data Sharing) – Correct: Amazon Redshift Data Sharing allows the Reporting Team (consumer cluster) to immediately query transformed data from the Analytics Team's cluster (producer cluster) without data movement. This solution seamlessly isolates workloads and preserves current workflows.

- Option B (Use AWS DMS for replication) – Incorrect: AWS DMS introduces complexity and latency because replication tasks have to be managed separately, and data synchronization is not immediate, potentially causing delays in report availability.

- Option C (Separate clusters with zero-ETL jobs) – Incorrect: Zero-ETL integrations are primarily designed between transactional databases (like Aurora) and Redshift, not between two Redshift clusters. Thus, it's not a suitable approach for this scenario.

- Option D (Separate clusters with S3 unload and Spectrum tables) – Incorrect: This method introduces overhead and latency due to data unloading and reliance on external S3 storage. It impacts data freshness and increases operational complexity.

18. *Correct Answers*: C, D

This scenario requires optimizing Amazon Athena query performance and reducing query costs when analyzing transaction data frequently filtered by specific regions or time periods. The solution should include efficient storage formats and appropriate data organization techniques.

- Option A (Convert to JSON and compress with Snappy) – Incorrect: While JSON is flexible, it is not optimized for analytical queries in Athena. JSON typically leads to larger file sizes and slower performance compared to columnar formats like Parquet.

- Option B (Bucket data by region, year, and month) – Incorrect: Bucketing is most effective when applied to high-cardinality columns (e.g., user IDs). In contrast, region, year, and month are low-cardinality attributes better suited to partitioning.

- Option C (Convert CSV to Parquet with Snappy compression) – Correct: Converting CSV to Apache Parquet, a columnar format, significantly enhances query performance by allowing Athena to efficiently scan only relevant columns. Snappy compression further reduces storage size and cost, aligning with AWS best practices.

- Option D (Partition data by region, year, and month) – Correct: Partitioning by region, year, and month enables Athena queries to scan only the necessary partitions, greatly reducing data volume processed, speeding up queries, and lowering overall costs.

References:

- "Top 10 Performance Tuning Tips for Amazon Athena" (*https://oreil.ly/7reqL*)

19. *Correct Answer*: C

This scenario describes a predictable weekly pattern in DynamoDB workload—significant usage spikes every Monday morning followed by minimal weekend activity. The ideal solution must maintain consistent performance while optimizing costs through targeted capacity adjustments.

- Option A (Switch to on-demand mode) – Incorrect: Although on-demand automatically adjusts to workload changes, it's typically more costly for predictable traffic patterns compared to scheduled capacity adjustments with provisioned capacity.

- Option B (Increase provisioned capacity to peak traffic) – Incorrect: Adjust provisioning capacity to peak levels significantly increases costs, especially during weekends and off-peak periods when usage is minimal.

- Option C (Scheduled Auto Scaling) – Correct: Using AWS Application Auto Scaling to schedule higher capacity during predictable peak periods (Monday mornings) and lower capacity during off-peak periods (weekends) provides cost optimization and consistent performance aligned precisely with the workload patterns.

- Option D (Separate table for peak usage) – Incorrect: Managing multiple tables for different usage periods unnecessarily complicates application logic, increases operational overhead, and doesn't efficiently optimize costs compared to scheduled scaling.

References:

- Managing DynamoDB provisioned capacity with autoscaling (*https://oreil.ly/iBAB1*)

20. *Correct Answer*: A

This scenario describes performance degradation in Amazon Athena query planning due to a growing number of partitions in an Amazon S3 dataset. The solution should enhance Athena's query performance by optimizing partition handling with minimal operational overhead.

- Option A (Glue partition indexes and partition projection) – Correct: Creating partition indexes in AWS Glue and enabling partition projection in Athena significantly improves query planning speed by eliminating the need to retrieve partition metadata from Glue each time. This approach directly addresses the described issue and requires minimal operational management.

- Option B (Merge partitions periodically) – Incorrect: Merging partitions reduces the partition count but introduces complexity in managing periodic merging processes and can disrupt the existing partitioning strategy used by queries.

- Option C (Consolidate smaller files) – Incorrect: While consolidating files improves query execution performance, it doesn't specifically solve the partition metadata retrieval bottleneck causing query planning slowdowns.

- Option D (Restructure data using bucketing) – Incorrect: Restructuring data using bucketing could reduce the number of subfolders. However, this introduces complexity during the data restructure process and can disrupt the existing data processing pipeline.

21. *Correct Answers*: A, B, E

This scenario requires providing data scientists with seamless SQL-based querying capabilities across diverse data sources: Parquet files on Amazon S3, Aurora MySQL, and DynamoDB, while ensuring minimal operational overhead.

- Option A (AWS Glue crawlers for metadata) – Correct: AWS Glue crawlers efficiently crawl multiple data sources, automatically extracting schemas and maintaining metadata in the Glue Data Catalog. This simplifies schema management and data discovery.

- Option B (Amazon Athena for S3 querying) – Correct: Amazon Athena provides serverless SQL querying capability directly against Parquet files on S3, requiring no infrastructure management and ensuring minimal operational overhead.

- Option C (Migrate all data to Redshift) – Incorrect: Migrating all data into Amazon Redshift introduces significant operational overhead and complexity and isn't necessary since federated querying can directly access multiple data sources without moving data.

- Option D (AWS Glue jobs to transform all data to Parquet) – Incorrect: Transforming and replicating data from Aurora and DynamoDB to S3 using Glue jobs introduces additional ETL overhead, operational complexity, and latency that can be avoided with federated queries.

- Option E (Athena federated queries for Aurora and DynamoDB) – Correct: Amazon Athena's federated query capability enables direct SQL-based querying of Aurora MySQL and DynamoDB tables, eliminating the need for data movement and significantly reducing operational overhead.

22. *Correct Answer*: B

This scenario describes performance issues related to indexing throughput in Amazon OpenSearch Service. The company requires a cost-effective solution that specifically enhances indexing performance without compromising data durability.

- Option A (Switch to UltraWarm storage) – Incorrect: UltraWarm storage is optimized for cost-effective querying and long-term storage, not indexing-heavy workloads. It would not effectively improve indexing throughput.

- Option B (Migrate to OR1 instances) – Correct: OR1 instances are specifically designed for indexing-heavy workloads, offering up to 30% improved price-performance compared to other instance types. They leverage Amazon S3-backed storage, providing superior durability and operational simplicity, directly meeting the scenario's requirements.

- Option C (Upgrade to larger general-purpose instances) – Incorrect: Upgrading general-purpose instances can provide incremental performance improvements but lacks the indexing-specific optimizations and cost benefits offered by OR1 instances.

- Option D (Use Index State Management to delete older data) – Incorrect: ISM helps optimize storage by deleting older data but doesn't directly address indexing throughput performance issues.

23. *Correct Answer*: C

This scenario involves addressing two critical challenges in an Amazon S3 data lake: schema evolution disrupting existing workflows and inconsistent or corrupted data resulting from concurrent writes. The optimal solution should robustly handle schema changes, manage concurrent writes safely, and integrate smoothly with existing analytics tools.

- Option A (Partitioning and locking) – Incorrect: Manual partitioning and implementing custom locking mechanisms adds complexity, increases operational overhead, and does not inherently address the schema evolution issue.

- Option B (Apache Parquet format with schema validation) – Incorrect: While Apache Parquet is efficient for analytics workloads, it does not inherently support schema evolution. Enforcing strict schema validation at ingestion is rigid and can hinder flexibility.

- Option C (Migrate to Apache Iceberg) – Correct: Apache Iceberg provides native support for schema evolution, allowing schema changes without workflow disruptions. It also manages concurrent writes safely through snapshot isolation and atomic transactions. Iceberg seamlessly integrates with common AWS analytics services (Athena, EMR, Glue), meeting all the scenario requirements effectively.

- Option D (EMR custom scripts) – Incorrect: Writing custom scripts increases operational complexity and maintenance burden. It also lacks standardized, robust solutions for schema evolution and concurrent write management.

24. *Correct Answer*: C

This scenario involves building a near-real-time analytics pipeline to process streaming data from Amazon MSK to Amazon Redshift. The solution must minimize operational overhead, provide near-real-time insights, and seamlessly integrate with existing BI tools.

- Option A (Kafka sink → S3 → Redshift COPY) – Incorrect: While feasible, staging data in Amazon S3 and then loading it via COPY introduces latency and operational complexity, hindering true near-real-time analytics.

- Option B (MSK → Kinesis Data Firehose → S3 → Redshift COPY) – Incorrect: This approach involves multiple intermediate steps, causing additional latency and operational overhead, making it less suitable for near-real-time analysis.

- Option C (Native integration with Redshift streaming ingestion) – Correct: Amazon Redshift's streaming ingestion feature directly integrates with Amazon MSK, allowing near-real-time data availability without intermediate storage layers. Materialized views further optimize query performance for BI tools, resulting in the least operational overhead and meeting all scenario requirements.

- Option D (Glue Spark Streaming jobs → Redshift) – Incorrect: Using AWS Glue Spark Streaming jobs adds additional infrastructure complexity, requires operational maintenance, and involves higher cost compared to direct MSK-to-Redshift streaming ingestion.

25. *Correct Answer*: A

    This scenario involves optimizing Amazon Athena queries for a BI dashboard that refreshes hourly, with underlying data updated by ETL once every 24 hours. The chosen solution should reduce query costs while ensuring dashboards refresh efficiently with minimal operational overhead.

    - Option A (Athena query result reuse) – Correct: Athena's query result reuse efficiently caches query results, significantly reducing costs by avoiding redundant query processing. By setting the cache maximum age aligned with the ETL schedule (24 hours), dashboards remain accurate and timely, offering the least operational overhead.

    - Option B (Lambda-based query trigger with S3 caching layer) – Incorrect: Using AWS Lambda functions to execute queries hourly and storing results separately introduces additional management overhead and cost compared to Athena's built-in caching capability.

    - Option C (Partition tables hourly) – Incorrect: Partitioning data by hour does not align with the existing ETL schedule, which refreshes data only every 24 hours.

    - Option D (BI layer caching with manual cache clearance) – Incorrect: Manually managing cache invalidation introduces unnecessary operational overhead and potential human error, making it less efficient than Athena's automated caching mechanism.

26. *Correct Answer*: A

    This scenario involves addressing repeated performance degradation and query queuing in Amazon Athena due to teams querying a centralized data lake during specific peak hours. The solution must enhance query performance effectively, while requiring minimal operational overhead.

    - Option A (Athena Provisioned Capacity per region) – Correct: Amazon Athena Provisioned Capacity allows dedicated query-processing resources to be allocated during predictable peak usage windows. This solution directly improves query performance and reduces queuing without extensive operational management.

    - Option B (Use Amazon Redshift) – Incorrect: Migrating the workload to Amazon Redshift would introduce significant operational complexity, additional ETL overhead, and management costs, making it less suitable compared to Athena Provisioned Capacity.

- Option C (Separate S3 buckets and Athena workgroups) – Incorrect: Creating separate buckets and workgroups increases complexity and does not directly alleviate resource contention or improve query performance during peak hours.

- Option D (Implement query scheduling) – Incorrect: Implementing a query scheduling mechanism introduces substantial operational overhead and reduces flexibility, negatively impacting the regional teams' capability to perform ad-hoc analytics.

27. *Correct Answer*: B

    This scenario involves dynamically scaling AWS Glue jobs to optimize utilization and cost efficiency. The solution should require minimal operational overhead and automatically adjust resources according to workload demand.

    - Option A (Manual reduction of DPUs) – Incorrect: Manually reducing DPUs by a fixed percentage doesn't dynamically adapt to changing workloads, potentially causing performance degradation and requiring continuous monitoring and adjustments.

    - Option B (AWS Glue autoscaling) – Correct: AWS Glue autoscaling dynamically adjusts the number of DPUs based on real-time job demands. Monitoring metrics like `workerUtilization` validates job performance automatically, providing a balance between cost savings and minimal operational overhead.

    - Option C (Migrate jobs to AWS Lambda) – Incorrect: Migrating Glue ETL workloads to AWS Lambda is not practical because Lambda has significant execution time limits (15 minutes), resource limits, and is not optimized for the long-running ETL workloads typical of AWS Glue.

    - Option D (Custom scripts for dynamic scaling) – Incorrect: Using custom scripts introduces significant operational complexity, ongoing maintenance overhead, and potential for errors. AWS Glue's native autoscaling capabilities provide a more streamlined and efficient alternative.

28. *Correct Answers*: A, C

    This scenario requires automatically identifying and classifying personally identifiable information (PII) and detecting custom data types that match specific patterns in an Amazon S3 data lake. The solution must meet regulatory compliance (e.g., PCI-DSS) requirements efficiently and accurately.

    - Option A (Macie managed data identifiers) – Correct: Amazon Macie's built-in managed data identifiers automatically detect common PII types (such as email addresses, credit card numbers, and national IDs) out-of-the-box, providing comprehensive regulatory compliance coverage.

- Option B (Lake Formation with Macie integration) – Incorrect: AWS Lake Formation manages data lake permissions and data governance but does not provide native integration for detecting or tagging PII directly through Macie.

- Option C (Custom data identifiers in Macie) – Correct: Amazon Macie allows the creation of custom data identifiers using regular expressions to detect sensitive data matching unique, organization-specific patterns, addressing the requirement to identify internal customer reference IDs and custom form codes.

- Option D (GuardDuty anomaly detection) – Incorrect: Amazon GuardDuty is a security threat detection service focused on identifying security anomalies and malicious activities, not classifying or detecting structured sensitive data like PII.

- Option E (EMR custom regex in Spark jobs) – Incorrect: While technically feasible, using Amazon EMR with custom Spark jobs introduces significant complexity, operational overhead, and ongoing maintenance compared to Macie's automated and managed detection capabilities.

References:

- Amazon Macie managed data identifiers (*https://oreil.ly/2BklJ*)

- Creating custom data identifiers in Amazon Macie (*https://oreil.ly/cTV7o*)

29. *Correct Answer*: B

This scenario requires validating the quality of transaction data stored in an Amazon S3–based data lake before processing with AWS Glue ETL jobs. The solution must efficiently detect missing values, format inconsistencies, and duplicate records with minimal operational overhead.

- Option A (AWS Lambda with custom Python scripts) – Incorrect: Although Lambda can execute data quality scripts, managing custom scripts introduces significant development effort and ongoing maintenance, and lacks built-in data quality frameworks.

- Option B (AWS Glue Data Quality with CloudWatch Alarms) – Correct: AWS Glue Data Quality provides built-in rule-based validations to detect missing values, duplicates, and format inconsistencies on data stored in Amazon S3. Integrating with Amazon CloudWatch Alarms enables automated alerts, delivering a fully managed solution.

- Option C (Daily Athena anomaly queries) – Incorrect: Using Athena for daily data quality checks adds latency and complexity. It also lacks the structured, proactive data validation framework provided by AWS Glue Data Quality.

- Option D (EMR with Apache Spark for data quality checks) – Incorrect: Running data quality checks via Amazon EMR adds substantial operational complexity, additional cluster management overhead, and script development effort compared to AWS Glue's built-in data quality capabilities.

30. *Correct Answers*: B, D

    This scenario involves orchestrating Amazon EMR Serverless ETL jobs for streaming video engagement data processing. The solution must reliably handle job dependencies and automatic retries with minimal operational overhead.

    - Option A (Self-managed Airflow on EC2) – Incorrect: Deploying a self-managed Apache Airflow environment increases operational overhead significantly, requiring manual patching, maintenance, and scaling.

    - Option B (AWS Step Functions orchestration) – Correct: AWS Step Functions provides a fully managed, serverless orchestration capability, enabling robust definition of job dependencies, state transitions, and automatic retries for EMR Serverless jobs, aligning well with the requirements.

    - Option C (EventBridge schedule triggers) – Incorrect: Amazon EventBridge scheduling provides basic triggering capabilities but lacks advanced orchestration features like automatic retries, job dependency handling, or failure management.

    - Option D (Define IAM policies for Step Functions and EMR Serverless) – Correct: Defining IAM policies and roles ensures AWS Step Functions has appropriate permissions to securely invoke Amazon EMR Serverless jobs.

    - Option E (Define IAM policies for self-managed Airflow) – Incorrect: Since Option A (self-managed Airflow) is not suitable due to its higher operational overhead, setting IAM permissions for it is also not necessary.

31. *Correct Answer*: C

    This scenario describes repetitive, complex aggregate queries in Amazon Redshift causing high execution times and increased compute costs. The solution should optimize query performance with minimal manual effort.

    - Option A (Manual materialized views with AWS Lambda refresh) – Incorrect: Using AWS Lambda to manually schedule materialized view refreshes introduces additional complexity, operational overhead, and ongoing maintenance.

    - Option B (Manual materialized views scheduled via Redshift Query Editor v2) – Incorrect: While Redshift Query Editor v2 simplifies query scheduling, the materialized view generation process still involves development effort, configuration overhead, and manual intervention.

    - Option C (Automated materialized views [AutoMVs]) – Correct: Amazon Redshift's AutoMVs feature automatically identifies frequently executed queries and dynamically creates and maintains materialized views without manual scheduling or maintenance, significantly optimizing query performance with minimal operational overhead.

- Option D (Result caching) – Incorrect: Result caching helps reduce execution time for identical repeated queries but doesn't efficiently handle varying parameters or improve general aggregation query performance like AutoMVs.

32. *Correct Answer*: C

This scenario involves migrating existing Apache Airflow workflows used for orchestrating ETL and reporting pipelines to AWS. The company aims to minimize both code changes and operational overhead during this migration.

- Option A (Self-managed Apache Airflow on EC2) – Incorrect: Deploying Apache Airflow manually on EC2 introduces additional operational overhead, requiring ongoing infrastructure maintenance, management, and monitoring.

- Option B (Convert pipelines to AWS Step Functions) – Incorrect: While AWS Step Functions provide serverless orchestration, migrating existing Airflow DAGs to Step Functions would require extensive code rework, contradicting the goal to minimize code changes.

- Option C (Migrate to Amazon MWAA) – Correct: Amazon Managed Workflows for Apache Airflow (MWAA) provides a fully managed Apache Airflow environment on AWS. This approach minimizes both code changes (existing DAGs can be migrated directly) and operational overhead, as AWS manages infrastructure scaling, patching, and availability.

- Option D (Rebuild workflows with AWS Glue workflows) – Incorrect: Rebuilding existing workflows in AWS Glue workflows would require significant refactoring effort and code changes, increasing both migration complexity and operational overhead.

33. *Correct Answer*: A

This scenario requires extracting query-level metrics—specifically data scanned and CPU time—from Amazon Redshift system tables to enable accurate cost attribution across different business units.

- Option A (SVL_QUERY_METRICS_SUMMARY) – Correct: The SVL_QUERY _METRICS_SUMMARY system view provides comprehensive query-level performance metrics, including data scanned, CPU time, and I/O metrics. This makes it the ideal choice for accurate and detailed cost attribution.

- Option B (STL_SCAN) – Incorrect: STL_SCAN provides information specifically about table scans but lacks aggregated CPU usage data, making it insufficient for comprehensive cost attribution.

- Option C (`SVL_QUERY_REPORT`) – Incorrect: `SVL_QUERY_REPORT` contains summary statistics and basic metrics for queries but does not include the detailed CPU time or granular data scanned information needed.

- Option D (`STL_WLM_QUERY`) – Incorrect: `STL_WLM_QUERY` is focused on workload management metrics and concurrency information and does not provide detailed query-level data scan or CPU usage metrics.

34. *Correct Answer*: A

    This scenario requires modifying an overly permissive IAM policy to grant only read-only permissions to all tables in a specific AWS Glue Data Catalog database (db1). The solution must adhere to the principle of least privilege.

    - Option A – Correct: This option correctly specifies the minimum set of Glue actions needed for read-only access (`glue:GetDatabase`, `glue:GetTables`, and `glue:GetTable`). It includes resources explicitly at the catalog and database levels, precisely meeting the requirement for accessing all tables within the specified database.

    - Option B – Incorrect: While it specifies correct actions, it adds the actions to the existing list, which does not adhere to the least-privilege principle.

    - Option C – Incorrect: This option lacks the database-specific resource reference (`database/db1`).

    - Option D – Incorrect: Using `glue:Get*` is overly broad, allowing access to potentially unnecessary Glue resources beyond databases and tables. It does not strictly adhere to the least-privilege principle.

    References:

    - Managing access control with AWS Glue resources (*https://oreil.ly/UshmW*)

35. *Correct Answers*: A, C, F

    This scenario requires detecting, anonymizing, and partially redacting personally identifiable information (PII) from CSV files uploaded to Amazon S3 reactively. The solution must support partial redaction to retain sufficient data for transaction verification.

    - Option A (AWS Glue workflow triggered by S3 events) – Correct: AWS Glue workflows triggered by Amazon S3 event notifications (such as `PutObject`) provide immediate, automated processing whenever raw data files arrive, effectively handling uploads without a defined schedule.

    - Option B (AWS Step Functions with a time-based schedule) – Incorrect: AWS Step Functions with a time-based schedule does not fit the scenario's unpredictable upload pattern, potentially causing processing delays or missed files.

- Option C (Detect PII transform in AWS Glue Studio) – Correct: AWS Glue Studio's built-in "Detect PII" transform automatically identifies PII fields within datasets, streamlining data anonymization processes.

- Option D (AWS Glue Data Quality rule for PII obfuscation) – Incorrect: AWS Glue Data Quality rules focus primarily on validating data quality (format, completeness, duplicates) but do not directly provide functionality for obfuscation or anonymization.

- Option E (Permanently delete all PII data) – Incorrect: Completely removing all PII data prevents transaction verification, conflicting with the requirement for partial redaction that preserves data usability.

- Option F (Partially redact detected PII text) – Correct: Partial redaction maintains data integrity necessary for transaction verification while effectively protecting sensitive customer information, directly meeting compliance and usability requirements.

References:

- "Detect and Process Sensitive Data Using AWS Glue Studio" (*https://oreil.ly/7GMrj*)

36. *Correct Answers*: A, B, D

This scenario requires implementing scalable, fine-grained access control on Amazon S3 data lake tables accessed by multiple compute engines (Athena, Glue, Redshift Spectrum). AWS Lake Formation is ideal for centrally managing these permissions in a scalable way.

- Option A (Register S3 data lake location with Lake Formation) – Correct: Registering the Amazon S3 data lake location with AWS Lake Formation is essential to enable centralized governance and fine-grained permissions management across the entire data lake.

- Option B (Grant Lake Formation data permissions) – Correct: AWS Lake Formation allows you to grant table- and column-level permissions directly to IAM users, roles, and groups. This centralized permission model ensures consistent and fine-grained access control across all supported compute engines.

- Option C (Use IAM policies for access control) – Incorrect: IAM policies alone do not support fine-grained, column-level permissions directly. Additionally, IAM policies become cumbersome to manage as scale increases, making Lake Formation permissions preferable for fine-grained governance.

- Option D (Configure Lake Formation tags) – Correct: Lake Formation tags provide scalable, attribute-based access control. Assigning these tags to tables and columns simplifies permission management significantly, enabling easier administration across multiple teams and compute services.

- Option E (Enable encryption with AWS KMS) – Incorrect: AWS KMS provides encryption at rest but does not provide fine-grained access controls at the table or column level within data lake objects. It focuses primarily on securing data, rather than managing granular permissions.

- Option F (Add compute engines as principals) – Incorrect: Compute engines such as Athena, Glue, and Redshift Spectrum are integrated with Lake Formation but could not be explicitly added as principals. Permissions should be granted to IAM users, roles, or groups rather than the compute engines themselves.

37. *Correct Answer*: B

This scenario requires applying two layers of encryption on sensitive healthcare data stored in Amazon S3 to comply with strict regulations, while also minimizing operational overhead.

- Option A (Client-side encryption + server-side encryption [SSE]) – Incorrect: While technically providing two encryption layers, client-side encryption adds significant operational overhead, requiring management of encryption keys and client-side encryption logic.

- Option B (Dual-layer server-side encryption with KMS [DSSE-KMS]) – Correct: Amazon S3's DSSE-KMS automatically applies two separate encryption layers using AWS KMS-managed keys. It provides strong compliance assurance with minimal operational overhead, as AWS manages key storage, rotation, and encryption operations.

- Option C (Single-layer server-side encryption with KMS [SSE-KMS]) – Incorrect: SSE-KMS alone provides only a single encryption layer, insufficient to meet the stated requirement for dual-layer encryption.

- Option D (Combine SSE-KMS and SSE-S3) – Incorrect: Amazon S3 does not support applying two different types of server-side encryption simultaneously to the same object (e.g., SSE-KMS and SSE-S3). Therefore, this approach is not feasible.

References:

- Amazon S3 dual-layer server-side encryption with AWS KMS (DSSE-KMS) (*https://oreil.ly/tTYsp*)

38. *Correct Answer*: A

This scenario requires securely storing and accessing MongoDB credentials used by an AWS Glue job, eliminating the security risk from hardcoded credentials within the job script.

- Option A (AWS Secrets Manager with Glue connections) – Correct: AWS Secrets Manager securely stores database credentials, enabling AWS Glue connections to retrieve these credentials securely and dynamically at runtime. This approach eliminates hardcoded credentials, enhances security, and simplifies credential rotation.

- Option B (AWS Glue job parameters) – Incorrect: Using Glue job parameters for credentials is insecure, as parameters may inadvertently be logged or exposed in configurations, thus not fully addressing the security concern.

- Option C (AWS IAM Identity Center authentication) – Incorrect: AWS IAM Identity Center (formerly AWS SSO) doesn't directly support authentication to external databases like MongoDB. It manages user access to AWS services and resources, but is not suitable for this specific use case.

- Option D (Credentials in S3 configuration file) – Incorrect: Storing credentials in plaintext or even encrypted files on S3 introduces complexity and potential exposure risks. It requires additional custom logic to securely manage credential retrieval and rotation, unlike Secrets Manager's built-in secure access mechanism.

39. *Correct Answers*: A, C

This scenario involves configuring Amazon QuickSight dashboards to restrict data visibility so each regional analyst group can access data relevant to only their geographic region. The solution must efficiently enforce data segregation based on a field in the dataset, which points to row-level access control.

- Option A (Create QuickSight user groups) – Correct: Creating user groups in Amazon QuickSight simplifies user management, allowing easy assignment and consistent permission application across regional analyst groups.

- Option B (Enable "Filter by Region" in dataset configuration) – Incorrect: QuickSight does not have a built-in "Filter by Region" dataset option. Filtering based on user attributes is handled through row-level security (RLS).

- Option C (Implement QuickSight row-level security) – Correct: Amazon QuickSight's RLS provides granular, secure control over dataset rows, ensuring each analyst group sees data corresponding to only their assigned region.

- Option D (Configure IAM policies for row-level access) – Incorrect: IAM policies manage service-level or resource-level permissions, but they do not control row-level access within QuickSight datasets. Row-level security is handled internally by QuickSight.

- Option E (Create separate regional datasets) – Incorrect: Creating separate datasets for each region introduces unnecessary duplication, complexity, and maintenance overhead compared to using QuickSight's native row-level security capability.

References:

- Row-level security in Amazon QuickSight (*https://oreil.ly/_vQBX*)

40. *Correct Answers*: A, B, D

This scenario involves setting up a multitenant Amazon MSK cluster with microservices from multiple lines of business (LOBs). Each LOB must have restricted access only to its own Kafka topics. The optimal solution uses IAM-based authentication and authorization to ensure secure, granular access control.

- Option A (Enable IAM access control on MSK) – Correct: Enabling IAM authentication for the MSK cluster allows granular, identity-based control using AWS IAM, simplifying secure access management.

- Option B (Create IAM policies for each LOB using `kafka-cluster:Topic`) – Correct: Defining IAM policies with resource-level permissions (e.g., `kafka-cluster:Topic`) allows each LOB to have specific and restricted access to only their respective Kafka topics.

- Option C (Configure IAM RBAC within Kafka) – Incorrect: IAM-based RBAC within Kafka is not currently supported directly in Amazon MSK. IAM authorization is managed externally through IAM policies, not internally within Kafka RBAC.

- Option D (Attach IAM policies to IAM roles assumed by microservices) – Correct: Attaching the defined IAM policies to the roles used by each LOB's microservices ensures that each microservice inherits correct permissions, providing secure and seamless access control.

- Option E (Kafka ACLs) – Incorrect: Kafka ACLs are Kafka-native authorization mechanisms. Since IAM-based authentication and authorization are in use, IAM policies provide a simpler and more centralized approach compared to Kafka ACLs.

- Option F (VPC security groups for isolation) – Incorrect: VPC security groups manage network-level access control but do not provide topic-level granular control required by this scenario.

41. *Correct Answers*: B, C

This scenario involves building a secure data pipeline using Amazon EMR on EC2, Amazon S3, and Amazon Redshift to handle sensitive healthcare data. The solution must ensure data remains private and provide centralized, secure management of sensitive parameters like credentials.

- Option A (Encrypted credentials in S3 bucket) – Incorrect: Storing credentials in Amazon S3—even encrypted—introduces complexity and security risks in credential management, as S3 isn't optimized for secure key-value storage of parameters.

- Option B (AWS Systems Manager Parameter Store) – Correct: AWS Systems Manager Parameter Store securely stores sensitive credentials such as database usernames, passwords, and API keys. It provides centralized parameter management with granular access control and encryption, effectively addressing the secure credential management requirement.

- Option C (S3 Gateway VPC endpoint) – Correct: A Gateway VPC endpoint for Amazon S3 ensures that EMR clusters access data stored in S3 privately within the AWS backbone, without traversing the public internet, preventing data exposure.

- Option D (Inject credentials via environment variables at bootstrap) – Incorrect: Injecting sensitive credentials directly into environment variables on EMR instances can pose security risks due to potential exposure through logs or instance metadata.

- Option E (EC2 user data scripts to hardcode credentials) – Incorrect: Hardcoding credentials into EC2 user data scripts is insecure, exposing sensitive information and making credential rotation and management challenging.

- Option F (Mount S3 bucket via S3FS and NAT Gateway) – Incorrect: Using S3FS mounts with a NAT Gateway unnecessarily routes traffic via the public internet, increasing complexity, latency, and potential exposure risk.

42. *Correct Answer*: A

This scenario involves securely connecting Amazon MSK deployed in private subnets with Kafka producers and consumers hosted on Amazon EKS clusters in separate VPCs. The solution must restrict access exclusively to authorized workloads.

- Option A (Security groups + VPC peering or Transit Gateway) – Correct: Configuring MSK brokers with security groups that explicitly allow Kafka traffic only from security groups associated with authorized EKS worker nodes provides least-privilege access control. Establishing network connectivity between VPCs through VPC peering or AWS Transit Gateway enables secure and private communication without exposing traffic to the internet.

- Option B (Allow inbound traffic from entire VPC CIDRs) – Incorrect: Allowing traffic from entire VPC CIDR blocks excessively broadens access, weakening the security posture by granting unintended access to other workloads within these VPCs.

- Option C (Public-facing NLB + IP Whitelisting) – Incorrect: Deploying a public-facing load balancer unnecessarily exposes internal Kafka brokers to internet-based threats and complicates security management. IP whitelisting alone is less flexible than using private connectivity and security groups.

- Option D (NAT Gateway + IAM authentication) – Incorrect: Enabling internet access via NAT Gateway is inappropriate for internal Kafka communication and introduces unnecessary complexity and potential security risks. Kafka access control via IAM does not eliminate network-level security risks associated with public internet exposure.

Index

AWS PrivateLink, 72
AWS Resource Access Manager, 301
AWS SageMaker ML Lineage, 316
AWS Samples Data Profiler utility, 314
AWS Schema Conversion Tool (SCT), 70, 94
AWS SDK, data ingestion customization, 82
AWS Secrets Manager, 73, 283
AWS Serverless Application Model (SAM), 66,
    257
AWS Service Catalog AppRegistry, 76
AWS Shield, 73
AWS Skill Builder Labs, 11
AWS Snow Family, 71
AWS Snowball, 71
AWS Snowcone, 71
AWS Spark jobs, 110
AWS Step Functions, 65, 133, 252
AWS Systems Manager, 74
AWS Transfer Family, 71
AWS Trusted Advisor, 76
AWS Well-Architected Framework (WAF), 73

B

backup service (AWS Backup), 69
backup-restore resilience architectures, 259,
    261
bar charts, QuickSight, 211
batch data processing, 25
    and Amazon EMR, 55
    data transformation, 107, 127
    with Glue bookmarks, 109
    ingesting data, 80
    pipeline implementation, 328-354
        Amazon S3 buckets, creating, 330
        best practices, 354
        Glue data connection for Redshift clus-
            ter, 334-338
        Glue PySpark ETL job, creating, 338-341
        input dataset, 329
        QuickSight sign-up and management,
            344-349
        QuickSight visualization, creating,
            349-354
        Redshift Serverless cluster, 331-334
        use case and architecture, 328
        visualization, 342-343
Bedrock, 70
BI (see business intelligence)
big data, 16-18

AWS-supported services, 209
    and EMR, 54, 55, 115
    and Redshift, 57
block storage (EBS), 68, 152, 167
bookmarks, Glue, 109
box plots, QuickSight, 215
brokers, MSK clusters, 99, 101
bucketing of data
    creating buckets in Amazon S3, 330, 361
    data lake access control, 301
    S3 Data Lake, 200
Budgets, 76, 265
buffering hints, optimizing with Data Firehose,
    104
business intelligence (BI), 1
    (see also Amazon QuickSight)
    Athena use case, 53
    Glue DataBrew use case, 51
    metadata for, 161
    and Redshift, 57
business-to-business data sharing, 310-312

C

capacity mode, choosing data stream, 97
capacity reservations, Athena, 225
case modifications, formatting functions (Data-
    Brew), 130
Cassandra, 68
CDC (change data capture), 46, 80, 91-95
cdcMaxBatchInterval attribute, 93
cdcMinFileSize attribute, 93
CDK (Cloud Development Kit), 75, 257
CDN (content delivery network), 72
cell-level access control, Lake Formation, 299
Certificate Manager, 291
certification essentials, 1-11
    applying problem-solving process to ques-
        tions, 8-10
    exam format, 4
    exam topics, 3
    exam-style questions, 5
    focus for the data engineering persona, 10
    real-world problem-solving framework,
        5-10
    registering for exam, 5
    study plan, 10
change data capture (CDC), 46, 80, 91-95
CI/CD (continuous integration/continuous
    deployment), 30, 254

Glue Data Catalog, 164
near real-time data ingestion, 80
nesting functions, data structures (Glue Data-Brew), 130, 131
network security, 271-279
no-code data transformation, Glue DataBrew, 51
normalization of data, and schema design patterns, 188
NoSQL databases, 15, 67, 192-198
notebook-based development, Glue Studio, 112
notebooks, analyzing data using, 237-239

O
object storage, 152, 167, 179
on-demand mode, data stream capacity, 97
on-premises applications and data sources, ingesting into cloud, 95
online analytical processing (OLAP), 16, 188
online transaction processing (OLTP), 16
open table formats
    Athena support for, 52
    expiring snapshots from, 181
    with S3 Data Lake, 201
OpenSearch Service (see Amazon OpenSearch Service)
operators, DAG, 135
optimizing data lifecycle, 173-185
    Amazon S3 Lifecycle configuration tool, 178-179
    archiving data from DynamoDB and S3, 182-183
    expiring snapshots from open table formats, 181
    monitoring and management, 179-181
    S3 Intelligent-Tiering, 176-177
    storage classes, 173-176
    versioning for data resiliency and compliance, 183-185
ORC (optimized row columnar), file format, 156
ORC data format, 85, 201
orchestrating data pipelines, 133-143
    choosing best service, 142-143
    data ingestion, 133-143
    data transformation, 133-143
    ECS, 66
    EventBridge, 65, 139-141, 245
    Glue workflows, 137-138

MWAA, 134-136
    Redshift Query Editor v2, 138
    Step Functions, 133
    workflow orchestration, 28, 133
ownership, data classification by, 166

P
PaaS (platform as a service), 32
parallelism, 17
    enhanced fan-out consumers mode, KDS, 99
    MPP architecture, 55, 230
    Presto, 22
Parquet data format, 85, 93, 156, 201
partition indexes, 165
partition keys
    Athena, 229
    DynamoDB, 194
    MSK, 99, 101
    S3 Data Lake, 200
    shards in KDS, 98
partition projection, 229
partition skewing, 101
partitioning data, 113, 200
performance
    batch processing pipeline implementation, 354
    data pipeline tuning, 252-254
    database migrations, 104-105
    Glue Data Catalog for optimizing, 165
    KPIs (QuickSight), 217
    OpenSearch Service, 60
    SPICE in-memory cache for query, 210-211
permissions
    data classification's role in, 166
    Lake Formation management of, 63
    Redshift GRANT and REVOKE, 303
    setting user IAM, 36, 37
personalized data portal, DataZone, 62
personally identifiable information (PII), 131-132, 292
physical data modeling, 186, 189-191
pie and donut charts, QuickSight, 214
pivot tables, QuickSight, 217
PL/pgSQL, 122
PL/SQL (Procedural Language for SQL), 15
platform as a service (PaaS), 32
PostgreSQL database software, 231

Iceberg, 52, 156, 226, 401
tag-based access control (TBAC), 296, 298, 302
targets, EventBridge, 139
TaskManagers, Flink, 21
tasks, DAG, 135
TCL (Transaction Control Language), 15
technical metadata, 160
third normal form (3NF) schema, 188
third-party datasets, ingesting data from, 95
throttling errors, 254
tiered storage, 45, 169-170, 264
Transaction Control Language (TCL), 15
Transfer Family, 71
transformations, Spark, 19
transforming data (see data transformation)
treemaps, QuickSight, 215
triggers, in Glue workflows, 137
Trino (formerly PrestoSQL), 22
Trino SQL, 223
Trusted Advisor, 76

U

ultraWarm storage of data, 169
Union data transformation, Glue DataBrew, 130
UNLOAD command, Redshift SQL, 172
unstructured data, 17, 313
user authentication and authorization, 36, 72, 279-282
user-defined functions (UDFs), 227, 237

V

value aspect of big data, 17
variety aspect of big data, 17
velocity of big data, 17
veracity (reliability) of big data, 17

version control and collaboration, 183-185, 255
virtual network isolation, 71
virtual servers, cloud environment, 66
visualizations, 211-221
  AutoGraph feature, 218
  AWS IAM, 342-343
  bar charts, 211
  box plots, 215
  GenAI to build, 219-221
  Glue interactive sessions, 238
  histograms, 215
  KPIs, 217
  line charts, 211-214
  pie and donut charts, 214
  pivot tables, 217
  presentation formats, 218
  QuickSight, 342-343
  scatter plots, 214
  treemaps, 215
volume aspect of big data, 17

W

Well-Architected Framework (WAF), 76
Well-Architected Lenses, 76
worker nodes, Spark, 19
worker types, Glue, 109
workflow orchestration, 28, 133
workgroups, Athena, 224

X

x86-based instances, EMR, 116

Z

zero-ETL integrations, 89, 170, 401
zstd (Zstandard) format, data compression, 200

About the Authors

Sakti Mishra is an engineer, architect, author, and technology leader with more than 18 years of working experience in the IT product and service industry. He is currently working as a principal data and AI solutions architect at Amazon Web Services, where he helps customers solve complex data- and AI-related problems with cloud native architecture patterns.

Sakti is passionate about technologies and is always curious to learn about the latest innovations happening in the technology domain. During his career he has gained expertise in multiple industry domains and technologies such as big data, analytics, machine learning, artificial intelligence, generative AI, relational/NoSQL/graph databases, web/mobile application development, and cloud technologies such as Amazon Web Services and Google Cloud Platform.

Dylan Qu is a technology leader, architect, engineer, and public speaker with eight years of experience in the IT industry. He currently works at Amazon Web Services as a principal solutions architect, where he helps customers architect highly scalable, performant, and secure data solutions on AWS. Dylan has authored various blogs and whitepapers across a diverse range of technologies, such as big data, serverless, IoT, and machine learning. He is passionate about new technologies and adept at turning technical innovations into production workloads at scale.

Anusha Challa brings over 14 years of comprehensive experience to the analytics and data warehousing field. She has worked with hundreds of diverse clients and developed scalable data architectures to meet specific organizational needs. With a master's degree in computer science specializing in machine learning from Georgia Tech, Anusha has authored informative blogs and whitepapers covering topics such as data warehousing, data security, machine learning, and artificial intelligence. Anusha's expertise extends to public speaking engagements, where she's delivered presentations at major events including AWS re:Invent and the AWS Summit in New York, sharing her insights on data analytics and cloud computing. Passionate about her work, Anusha remains dedicated to exploring emerging technologies and industry trends in data analytics.

Colophon

The animal on the cover of *AWS Certified Data Engineer Associate Study Guide* is the mandrill (*Mandrillus sphinx*)—an iconic, vividly colored Old World monkey species native to west Central Africa.

Mandrills live in dense tropical forests, where they travel in large, loosely organized groups. These gatherings—called "troops"—can sometimes include over one hundred individuals. Males are significantly larger than females and display the most vibrant coloring, thanks to blood vessels close to the skin (responsible for the red) and light-reflecting collagen fibers (which create the blue).

Mandrills spend much of their time foraging along the forest floor, feeding primarily on fruits, seeds, leaves, and insects. They store food in large cheek pouches as they move, a handy adaptation in competitive environments. With their expressive faces, complex social hierarchies, and impressive appearance, mandrills stand out as one of the more distinctive primates of the African rainforest.

The mandrill is classified as vulnerable on the IUCN Red List. Many of the animals on O'Reilly covers are endangered; all of them are important to the world.

The cover illustration is by José Marzan, Jr., based on an antique line engraving from Lydekker's *Royal Natural History*. The series design is by Edie Freedman, Ellie Volckhausen, and Karen Montgomery. The cover fonts are Gilroy Semibold and Guardian Sans. The text font is Adobe Minion Pro; the heading font is Adobe Myriad Condensed; and the code font is Dalton Maag's Ubuntu Mono.

O'REILLY®

Learn from experts.
Become one yourself.

60,000+ titles | Live events with experts | Role-based courses
Interactive learning | Certification preparation

Try the O'Reilly learning platform free for 10 days.

www.ingramcontent.com/pod-product-compliance
Lightning Source LLC
Chambersburg PA
CBHW080128220326
41598CB00032B/4992